# Child
# Development

## PEARSON

At Pearson, we have a simple mission: to help people make more of their lives through learning.

We combine innovative learning technology with trusted content and educational expertise to provide engaging and effective learning experiences that serve people wherever and whenever they are learning.

From classroom to boardroom, our curriculum materials, digital learning tools and testing programmes help to educate millions of people worldwide – more than any other private enterprise.

Every day our work helps learning flourish, and wherever learning flourishes, so do people.

To learn more please visit us at **www.pearson.com/uk**

# Child Development

## Theory and Practice 0–11

### Second Edition

Jonathan Doherty & Malcolm Hughes

PEARSON

Harlow, England • London • New York • Boston • San Francisco • Toronto • Sydney • Auckland • Singapore • Hong Kong
Tokyo • Seoul • Taipei • New Delhi • Cape Town • São Paulo • Mexico City • Madrid • Amsterdam • Munich • Paris • Milan

**PEARSON EDUCATION LIMITED**
Edinburgh Gate
Harlow CM20 2JE
United Kingdom
Tel: +44 (0)1279 623623
Web: www.pearson.com/uk

_____

First published 2009 (print)
**Second edition published** 2014 (print and electronic)

ISBN: 978-1-292-00101-2 (print)
       978-1-292-00351-1 (ebook)
       978-1-292-01433-3 (eText)

**British Library Cataloguing-in-Publication Data**
A catalogue record for the print edition is available from the British Library

**Library of Congress Cataloging-in-Publication Data**
A catalog record for the print edition is available from the Library of Congress

Doherty, Jonathan, 1961-
   Child development : theory and practice 0-11 / Jonathan Doherty and Malcolm Hughes.
-- 2nd edition
      pages cm
   ISBN 978-1-292-00101-2
   1.  Child development.    2.  Early childhood education.    I.  Title.
   LB1115.D858 2013
   372.21--dc23
                                                                    2013033751

10 9 8 7 6 5 4 3 2 1
16  15  14  13

Print edition typeset in 9.5/12pt Giovanni Book by 35
Print edition printed and bound by L.E.G.O. S.p.A., Italy.

NOTE THAT ANY PAGE CROSS REFERENCES REFER TO THE PRINT EDITION

# Brief contents

# Contents

# Part 2 Early and Physical Development

## 8  Sensory and Perceptual Development

## Part 3  Cognitive and Social Development

# List of figures and tables

## Figures

# Tables

# Guided tour

## Introduction

In this book you will learn more about children and their development from conception to the end of childhood at age 11 – which is the end of primary or elementary schooling in many countries and the beginning of adolescence. You will learn about the vast range of capabilities that very young children quickly acquire and how, in the course of just a few years, this impressive range of skills, knowledge and understanding is extended even further. Your understanding of children and their development will depend on getting a grasp of the most important issues in child development.

In this chapter we set out what we think are the most important issues to explore about children and their development. We begin by considering the nature of child development and how childhood is generally understood. We also offer reasons why the study of child development is essential for practitioners working with children in daycare, playgroups, nurseries, schools, families and other settings.

Many **Chapter Introductions** begin with mini case studies to illustrate a concept or theme that is built upon within the chapter.

**Chapter Objectives** enable you to focus on what you should have learned by the end of the chapter.

## Chapter Objectives

By the time you have completed this chapter you should be able to answer the following questions:

- What is a theory?
- Why is theory necessary and valuable in the study of child development?
- What are the most important and influential developmental theories?
- How can we evaluate the usefulness of theories?
- How can we interpret developmental theories in relevant contexts?

## Focus on Theory

### Nutrition and the prenatal period

The prenatal period is the period of most rapid growth in one's entire life and a diet that supplies correct nutrients is needed for brain and body development. The developing foetus requires proper nutrients for growth at all of the stages and is totally reliant upon the mother to provide this. When this is denied, there is irrefutable evidence of the damage it causes to the child pre- and postnatal. Defects include low intelligence and serious learning problems in school (Lawlor *et al.*, 2006). Research findings link malnutrition to low birth weight, prematurity and cognitive deficiencies (e.g. Zhang *et al.*, 2005). Earlier research by Shonkoff and Phillips (2000) evidenced the impact of malnutrition on brain development, showing deficits in intelligence and attention capacity. In the prenatal period, the brain grows rapidly and a balanced diet is needed to supply correct nutrients.

Further deficiencies arising from mal- or undernutrition have also been reported in the research literature, some of which we call on now. In the first germinal stages of pregnancy,

**Focus on Theory** discusses key academic and professional research and theory, providing a secure and informed base for understanding.

## Controversy

### Is outdoor play devalued in primary educational practice?

Four years ago I visited Blackawton Primary School in Devon. All children (and staff) bring a change of clothes to school so that they can go outside whatever the weather, and the children (though not the staff) are encouraged to climb the tall trees that form one of the boundaries of the school. When Dave Strudwick, the head teacher, pointed the trees out to me, I was astonished and excited that challenging physical outdoor play was so encouraged.

In the United Kingdom, however, changes to educational practice in the past 25 years have seen a steady decline in the emphasis placed upon outdoor learning and physical play. Factors include a strong shift towards a focus on children's literacy and numeracy development, a narrowed view of the purposes of education, the adoption of a top–down model that valued classroom learning whereas the outdoors was denigrated as a place to 'let off steam' with little academic contribution (Lindon, 2005). This was despite a strong tradition of early childhood pioneers such as Friedrich Froebel, Margaret McMillan and Susan Isaacs

**Controversy** engages you in current issues and encourages debate.

**Policy, Research and Praxis** discusses developments in childcare practices and changes to UK Government policies.

## Policy, Research and Praxis

### Closing the gender gap in boys' reading

The issue of boys underachieving in reading is a long-established trend in this country and internationally. A study involving 31 European countries into the impact on the acquisition of reading skills for 3–15-year-olds found that boys were one of the groups at risk of low achievement (EURYDICE, 2011). In schools in England, girls outperform boys on all National Curriculum reading tests. By age 7, the gap between boys and girls is already well established and continues to widen through to GCSE (Clark with Burke, 2012).

Data shows that the gender gap in reading enjoyment and reading frequency is also widening. Three out of four (76 per cent) UK schools are concerned about boys' underachievement in reading. There is still no government strategy to address the issue. In 2011 an estimated 60,000 boys failed to reach the expected level in reading at age 11 (Boys Reading Commission, 2012). The Commission report highlights that the 'reading gender gap' is widening and calls for action to be taken in homes, schools and communities.

Research has found that 1 young person in 3 does not have books of their own (32.2 per cent)

---

**Ossification**
The process through which cartilage becomes bone.

**Skeletal age**
A way of estimating physical maturity based on the development of the bones in the body.

**Growth plates**
The area of growing tissue near the ends of the long bones in children and adolescents, also known as epiphyseal plates or physis.

**Fontanelles**
Gaps in the skull that allow the head of the baby to pass through the birth canal.

Alongside height and weight changes, internal changes take place in muscles and bones which are important for movement skills – the motor functions. Newborns have more bones in their extremities than older children and it takes until the end of the childhood period and into adolescence for all bones to be fully mature. Ossification, the process through which cartilage thickens to become bone, occurs rapidly in early childhood, beginning during the first 6 weeks *in utero* in the jaw and collarbone. Skeletal age is a measure of physical maturity and can be determined by X-ray to discover bone development. Different skeletal parts develop at different ages as do the growth plates – the growing tissue near the ends of the long bones. Females have a more developed skeletal system than males. Even at birth, girls are more advanced than boys, typically by between 4 and 6 weeks. Measuring head size is frequently used by doctors in early development because the rate of growth of the skull is more consistent to accommodate a growing brain within (see Figure 7.4). Gaps in the skull called fontanelles present before birth to allow a baby's head to squeeze through mother's dilated cervix, gradually close in the first 2 years.

Muscle tissue undergoes huge increases after birth. Two types of muscle fibre develop: *slow twitch*, which is associated with endurance, and *fast twitch*, associated with explosive power. By the end of the first year, these fibres are 30 per cent of adult size – and their size is believed to be mostly inherited. Although muscle fibres are present at birth, their constitution changes throughout the childhood period – gaining in length and thickness. Males

**Key Terms** are highlighted and defined in the text when they first appear. These terms are also included in the Glossary at the end of the book.

---

The previous section and the *Focus on Theory* feature discuss how play contexts provide children with many opportunities to foster social development. Now it is time to explore how children think about their own motives and those of other people. This is what is known as 'social cognition' (mentioned in Chapter 11 in the context of emotional development) and it bridges both social and cognitive development. What are the defining aspects of social cognition?

**Reflect** asks you to pause and engage in an activity and helps you become a reflective practitioner. They provide an opportunity to engage with and reflect on theories and issues raised throughout the text.

**The Twenty Statements Test (Humphries & Jobson, 2012).**

How would you describe yourself? Write down your 20 answers to the question, 'Who am I?' Afterwards, reflect on your answers. What do they say about your personality, temperament, behaviour, interests and values? Is this really who you think you are? Perhaps you might like to show the list to somebody else and see whether your idea of who you are is the person they think you are.

to relieve the distress. By 12 months when many infants are more mobile, they can app
or withdraw from unpleasant situations but the role of the parent/carer remains to
excessive distress for the child. Research has shown that if children become too stresse
often, it is more difficult for carers to pacify them, for children to learn to soothe them
and increases the chances of an anxious temperament (Macedo *et al.*, 2011).

### Connect and Extend

We all want children to become self-motivated and feel responsible for their own actions. How can carers and practitioners contribute to making this happen for all children? Read: Szente, J. (2007). Empowering young children for success in school and in life. *Early Childhood Education Journal*, 34, 449-453.

By the third and fourth years, children can verbalise their emotions, 'bad doggie' or
monster'. Although children are now at a stage to control their feelings actively more
tively, this is also a time to develop more long-standing fears. Parents often have to dea
their child's nightmares or help them come to terms with the dark – possibly when char
they know from books and television haunt their already vivid imaginations. It's no
fiction. Real situations affect children's emotions early in their lives. Television news rep
a tsunami disaster, the September 11th attacks in the United States and many other na
and local events can provoke fear in children. Parents can contribute very positively to he
their children regulate their fear about disasters by talking such events through with then
attaching messages of sympathy and reassurance to these conversations.

Children of school age have to make rapid gains in emotional self-regulation. Thi
time of new anxieties: pressures of daily 'tests' in physical and academic achievement

**Connect and Extend** gives suggestions of further texts, including journal papers which will deepen your knowledge and challenge you to place your study in the context of applied scientific method and research.

---

Before moving on, let's summarise what we have learned in the middle section of this chapter:

- Intelligence is the capacity for cognition and for cognitive development.
- Alfred Binet developed the first standardised intelligence test which was a scale systematically measuring higher-order thinking skills, memory, language and problem-solving abilities, unique to each individual.
- Contemporary theories favour explaining intelligence in terms of the cognitive processes involved when we engage in intellectual activities. Central to this point of view is the notion that mental competence changes over time.
- Howard Gardner's original theory of multiple intelligences included seven 'intelligences' (linguistic, logical-mathematical, spatial, bodily-kinaesthetic, musical, intrapersonal and interpersonal) and an eighth, that of naturalist intelligence, was added in 1999. Today, Gardner has added a ninth, existential intelligence, which is concerned with our spirituality.

**Summary 2**

At three points in each chapter, a short Summary of the preceding section will help consolidate your learning.

---

## Summary Table
### Prenatal Development

**Conditions for development** (pp 122-128)

**Growth in the womb** (pp 122-124)

Prenatal development is divided into three phases: germinal (0–2 weeks); embryonic (3–8 weeks); and foetal (9–38 weeks). The single fertilised cell – the zygote – divides into two, four and so on until a ball of cells (a blastocyst) is formed. The blastocyst attaches itself to the wall of the uterus. As cells continue to divide they develop characteristics to form different parts of the body, and the rate of development is so fast that by the time the embryo is renamed a foetus at 9 weeks it has already become a recognisable, if tiny human being. Between 22 and 26 weeks a point is reached

**Threats to development** (pp 128-138)

**Maternal diseases** (pp 128-130)

Rubella (commonly called German measles) is a very infectious viral illness passed on through droplets in the air. The virus is most dangerous to a baby if a woman is infected during the first 16 weeks of pregnancy. Rubella can cause miscarriage, stillbirth or birth defects in unborn babies, such as deafness, brain damage, heart defects or cataracts depending on which week of foetal development the virus is 'caught'. Other 'diseases' which can affect the unborn child are herpes and HIV.

**Drugs** (pp 130-132)

At the end of each chapter a Summary Table brings together the key concepts of the chapter to assist with review and revision.

---

## Going further

Arnett, J. and Hughes, M. (2012) *Adolescence and emerging adulthood: A cultural approach*. Longman. Where next for your study and scholarship? What happens after childhood? This book takes up where *Child Development 0–11* finishes and is co-written by Mal Hughes, one of the authors of this text. It covers the period from 12 to 25 years and offers a cultural and cross-cultural dimension on the study of developmental psychology. Harlow: Pearson Education.

Rose, C. (2011) *Self awareness and personal development: Resources for psychotherapists and counsellors*. Basingstoke: Palgrave Macmillan. Resources and support for qualified therapists and trainees as well as for other professionals who are engaged in the process of becoming more self-aware as part of their pro-

Benson, J., Benson, J. B. & Haith, M. M. (2009) *Social and emotional development in infancy and early childhood*. Oxford: Academic Press. Provides a resource for researchers and clinicians interested in social psychology and personality covering such areas as adoption, attachment, birth order, effects of day care, discipline and compliance, divorce, emotion regulation, family influences, preschool, routines, separation anxiety, shyness, socialisation, and the effects of television.

O'Moore, M. (2010) *Understanding school bullying: A guide for parents and teachers*. Dublin: Veritas Publications. This book explains the serious consequences of bullying for the victims, the bullies and society. The author places a strong emphasis on prevention and intervention at primary,

At the end of each chapter, further readings and relevant websites are suggested in the Going further section.

# Preface

Preparing this 2nd edition of *Child Development: Theory and Practice 0–11* has given us an opportunity to revisit the research that underpinned the first edition; to strengthen the connections between theory and professional practice; and to refresh the guidance on extending the reader's experience. We were very grateful for the way in which the first edition was received and adopted as a core text on many child development, child-care and education courses in the UK and further afield. We also received from students and tutors really helpful advice on how to improve the text and the features that had proved particularly helpful. One suggestion was to include an additional section in each chapter to demonstrate and discuss the connection between academic research, government policy and professional practice. This has become an important new feature: *Policy, Research and Praxis*.

We have also read with growing excitement the work of those researchers using brain scanning techniques – notably fMRI – to further reveal how our amazing brains first grow, develop throughout childhood and adapt to new challenges. You will find that many themes within the text are further explored using the results of brain scanning. These are results that have both illuminated and challenged the ideas which emerged from the first century of developmental science.

A temptation in many new editions is to keep adding new material for each chapter. We are grateful for the advice of the review panel and our editors who asked to look again at some sections. We believe we have produced a leaner and much improved edition without losing our aim of producing an accessible and comprehensive core text.

Despite these changes and additions, this text remains a journey through children's development that begins before birth and continues until the end of middle childhood at around 11 years. It brings together key ideas and theories in child development and applies them to the home and a variety of educational and care settings. It is written with four categories of audience in mind. Firstly, for all engaged in what has recently become known as the children's workforce in the health service, and in social and welfare services. Secondly, for trainees on initial teacher training courses in early childhood and primary education and those undertaking childhood or education studies. Thirdly, for teachers and learning assistants, managers and practitioners in schools, playgroups, crèches and other settings who are undertaking professional development. Lastly, this is a book written by parents for parents, who are the first and most powerful influence on the development of their children.

An understanding of children's development is of enormous benefit to parents and professional practitioners to help them recognise and meet the intellectual, linguistic, physical, social and emotional needs of children more effectively. The more informed we are of how children develop and the processes through which children learn, the more effectively we can optimise children's all-round development and learning. Of course, parents have a pivotal role to play in laying important foundations for children's development and early learning too. Parents and families provide the most influential context for children to flourish and play their part in fostering important continuity in care between home, early years settings and school. *Child Development: Theory and Practice* acknowledges the strong partnership that exists between parents, child-care professionals and educators, and this relationship, emphasised from the outset, continues to feature throughout the text. In writing and reading this text we are together studying childhood development from the moment of conception. It is our collective responsibility to get it right for our children: the right start to life for them to become all that they can.

The need to be informed on how children develop and how they learn is not disputed in terms of the content of many professional training courses and is a move well supported by policy and professional literature. For example, revised Professional Standards for Qualified Teacher Status, implemented from September 2007 also reflects a change away from a curriculum of subjects and requires future teachers to have understanding of the needs of the whole child. Standard Q5 states that teachers in training should:

> **recognise and respect the contribution that colleagues, parents and carers can make to the development and well-being of children and young people and to raising their levels of attainment**

and standard Q18 states that trainee teachers should:

> **understand how children develop and that the progress and well-being of learners are affected by a range of developmental, social, religious, ethnic, cultural and linguistic influences**

(TDA, 2007).

The framework for study and professional development provided by *Child Development: Theory and Practice 0–11* provides a key text to demonstrate addressing and meeting these standards and for wider use across all aspects of professional learning.

Since the nineteenth century, our understanding of childhood has undergone many changes, and developmental psychology has made a significant contribution. We now accept there are many different global 'childhoods' and we need to incorporate knowledge from sociology, feminist research, genetics and cultural studies to further inform us. The study of how children develop is complex and should not be conveniently packaged into one format – even into just one text, no matter how learned or comprehensive! And not everything new is necessarily of value. While neuroscience – the science revealed in part by fMRI scanning – has contributed much to our knowledge of the learning brain (Blakemore and Frith, 2005) particularly in mathematical and language learning, and learning disabilities, there is scepticism that some techniques flowing from new knowledge about the connection between brain activity and body movement – e.g. Brain Gym (Dennison, 2010) – lack a strong empirical base. The term 'neuromyths' (e.g. Pasquinelli, 2012) has been used to suggest that some claims are overgeneralised and simplified. Rather than being wholly dismissive, our view is that we should avoid any 'quick fix' or 'fix all' answers to developmental problems and that a theory remains just a theory until shown to apply in practice.

Application of theory into practice is a central feature of this text. We introduce you to a number of ideas, concepts and theories and then go on to explain or apply these to care, school and/or home contexts. To further assist with the application and exemplification of theory, we present practical situations spanning childhood in short stories or vignettes from the classroom, home and care settings, and these feature throughout the text. Chapter introductions have clear learning objectives, and many begin with a mini case study to illustrate a concept or theme that is built upon within the chapter. Chapters also include *Focus on Theory* features which present key academic and professional research findings, designed to provide a secure and informed base for understanding. The *Controversy* features engage the reader in current issues and the applications of theoretical knowledge to care and educational settings. Important and possibly unfamiliar terms are highlighted in bold and explained in nearby margin notes, and the text is punctuated by a number of *Reflect* features that ask you to pause and engage in an activity that strengthens the notion of child professionals as reflective practitioners.

At three points in each chapter, you can read a short summary of the preceding section. These summaries are restructured into a *Summary Table* at the end of the chapter to assist with review and revision.

Page margins also include an important innovation, the *Connect and Extend* features. You are encouraged to find these resources, texts, journal papers or articles by using an online electronic resource provided by your university, college or local library or by regularly visiting your library to immerse yourself in the texts available there. Feedback on this feature from the first edition has been very positive, with a number of tutors suggesting that students who habitually followed the study opportunities presented in the *Connect and Extend* features were particularly well prepared for assessment tasks. Some of the articles referenced are from the professional literature and will expand and deepen your knowledge. Other references are to scientific and theoretical papers from on-line journals and are selected to challenge you to place your study in the context of applied scientific method and research. At the end of each chapter, further reading and relevant websites are suggested in the *Going further* and *Useful websites* features.

*Child Development: Theory and Practice 0–11* is structured into three parts for maximum accessibility. We draw on broad areas of developmental psychology and relate these to 'cutting-edge' issues in education. We also argue for a holistic view of how children develop, and stress that development and indeed learning are very much a combination of motor, cognitive, intellectual and social functioning: a fundamental principle to the text's 'whole child' approach. Ecological development (for example, the influences of family, school, peers, television) is woven into and throughout the text, rather than have this as a discrete and concluding part of the text, and is a topic-based format adopted in contrast to a chronological age approach allowing for more integrated exploration of key themes.

The division of the text into three parts allows topics to be grouped together in a more coherent way and emphasises the connected themes of the text. *Part 1: Introducing Child Development* deals with the theoretical field of child development, its methods of study and key theories. The organising framework in the text separates the areas of child development for the purposes of analysis but readers are encouraged to view development as an integrated and holistic concept. The 'journey' of human development begins in Chapter 1 *Issues in Child Development* where we introduce newborns Kirsty and Niamh and describe some of their marvellous accomplishments and potentials. References are made to both historical and cultural traditions by introducing the fundamental questions that are at the very heart of the study of children. You are encouraged to take a broad view of the themes and debates integral to them, but also to view these as directly relevant to your interactions with children as a teacher, parent or carer. Chapter 2 is titled *Theories of Child Development*. Five broad theoretical frameworks are examined: learning theories; cognitive theories; psychodynamic theories; ecological theories; and biological theories. We suggest that an understanding of the scope of these theories and how these are interpreted practically are important for those engaged in academic and professional study of childhood or for practitioners already working with children.

Chapter 3 *Research Methods* introduces you to the different techniques used to capture how children grow, think and form relationships with others in classroom and care settings. We explain the methods used to gather data on children's abilities, thoughts and feelings, and that research findings will of course depend on the methods adopted. In the final part of the chapter, the relative merits of each of these methods is discussed in the context of schools, daycare and families. Chapter 4 *Nature and Nurture* begins by describing important genetic foundations and shows how, although we are all individuals, we share commonalities in our appearance and behaviours. Each of us is born with a particular set of instructions for development, and as unique individuals. Our genetic code acts as the instruction manual that we take with us on our journey through life. The chapter unravels some of the complexities in prenatal development by looking at the influence of heredity on development and at environmental factors that influence it.

*Part 2: Early and Physical Development* addresses the 'building blocks' of development and early learning. In Chapter 5 *Prenatal Development* the nine months of pregnancy are traced through its three phases of germinal, embryonic and foetal periods. Pregnancy is portrayed as a time of great joy and anticipation for parents and also the time in which the genetic patterning of the child takes place. Factors in the external environment known as teratogens that can negatively influence the health and future capacity of the unborn child are discussed. You will see how development of the central nervous system and growth of the brain are linked and shown to be crucial to behaviours and learning of the foetus in the womb. This theme is picked up in Chapter 6 *Neonatal Behaviour and Learning* which discusses a newborn baby's capabilities and shows clearly how early learning takes place through the integration of sensory, motor and perceptual development.

Chapter 7 *The Body and Physical Growth* begins by presenting information about general physical development and depicts the differential that exists in this area in children of the same chronological age. Highly topical is the issue of childhood obesity and the chapter explores the physical and psychological consequences of this ill-health. In Chapter 8 *Sensory and Perceptual Development* we meet Asifa, who at 1 year old is sitting up in her high chair, content, looking around and taking in people and things going on around her but finding the act of co-ordinating a spoon, food and her mouth difficult. Young children acquire motor skills from information they receive from their perceptual faculties, and perception is integral to almost every task that a child performs. Many activities that children engage in at school and at play require reasonable levels of perceptual-motor development and the chapter explores ways for parents, carers and teachers to promote this development.

*Part 3: Cognitive and Social Development* describes how children's minds and voices develop. Chapter 9 *Cognitive Development* places cognition at the centre of all other aspects of human development. We begin by discussing three different perspectives on thinking: Piaget's cognitive-developmental theory, Vygotsky's sociocultural theory and the more recent information-processing theories. We stress that no single approach can account solely for the complexity of how we think but that each set of theories has contributed to our understanding. The implications of theories for classroom practice are discussed before presenting a discussion on the nature of what constitutes intelligence: a topic that has received widespread attention in psychology and more recently in education. In Chapter 10 *Language Development* we argue that language is one of a child's most significant developmental milestones. The Latin word *infans* means incapable of speech, suggesting that this is not a facility children are born with and yet in just a few years almost all children become competent communicators and capable readers with a good command of the written word. We discuss the four components of language – phonology, how meaningful sounds are produced; semantics, referring to words and their meanings; grammar or the structure of language necessary for constructing meaningful sentences; and pragmatics which are the rules of language. Together these components provide a framework to help us understand the scope of human language. We analyse the main theoretical approaches and join in the debate as to whether language is acquired innately or whether it is learned. The chapter concludes with a discussion on bilingualism and the effects upon children of multi-language learning with particular reference to writing.

Chapter 11 *Emotions and Personality* shows how emotions, an often neglected aspect of the study of development, constitute an area that dominates our early lives. We argue how emotions are a vital foundation, on which are built all other mental skills. Interactions with others close to us, well before language is acquired, foster confidence and security, and enable children to achieve verbal, cognitive and motor milestones. We 'meet' Dani Coates, a 3-year-old in his first day at nursery, to introduce the topic of attachment, draw on recent research findings, and conclude with a discussion on the effects of child-care on early relationships. Chapter 12 *The Social and Moral World of the Child* asserts that being social is a feature of being human. Moving through changing social environments, children learn about the practices and values of the society in which they live. Experiences in childhood in a variety of social groups play an important part in making children who they are and who they become. The important role of children's play in their social experiences is discussed before moving on to children's understanding of their own feelings and those of other people, known as social cognition. This bridges both social and cognitive development and we illustrate how children come to understand who they are by discussing self-concept and self-esteem, through the topics of theory of mind and social identity. The three major socialisation influences on children are explored: the family (and parents in particular); peers; and schools and the media (for example, how children's viewing of television and their use of the Internet and interactive and/or video games affect their socialisation skills). The moral aspect of children's development is considered and illustrated with familiar examples of prosocial behaviour in educational contexts (citizenship education) and antisocial behaviour.

## About the authors

Dr Jonathan Doherty was formerly Principal Lecturer and Head of Early Childhood Education at Leeds Metropolitan University. Since April 2008 he worked as a Regional Adviser for National Strategies for Early Years and more recently as Head of Early Childhood Education at Manchester Metropolitan University.

Malcolm Hughes was PGCE Programme Leader and Senior Research Fellow in Educational Psychology at the University of the West of England, Bristol, UK. He is now Associate Director of UWE Global, the umbrella arm of the University responsible for the development of collaborative transnational education.

# Acknowledgements

We commend you to the study of children, childhood and child development. It has been an exciting time for us in preparing the second edition of this text, drawing on many years as school teachers, teacher trainers and as parents. We have been wonderfully privileged to share in the lives of so many young people as they have set off on their 'journey of life' and it is to those thousands of schoolchildren and our own inspirational children – Richard, Stephen, Rebecca, Stephanie, Christopher, Michael, Emily and Tom – that we dedicate this book.

We also wish to thank Catherine Yates, Jennifer Seth, Dawn Phillips, Kelly Miller, Lucy Chantler, Jonathan Price and Andrew Müller for their professionalism, advice, guidance, support and expertise, and to their team of academic reviewers for keeping to impossible deadlines and working so hard on the detail of the text. It is an amazing team at Pearson Education and again it has been a pleasure to work with them all. We would also like to thank the following reviewers for their valuable time, guidance and critique:

Dr. Norman Gabriel, Plymouth University
Anita L. Hansen, Universitetet i Bergen, Norway
Dr. Catherine Meehan, Canterbury Christ Church University
Yasmin Stefanov-King, University of Hull
Dr. Rebecca Westrup, University of East Anglia

Jonathan Doherty would like to express his appreciation for the support and encouragement given to him by his wife Katherine during the book's writing journey. Malcolm Hughes would like to signal his appreciation for his wife Sue, whose attention to detail and speed of work has contributed to the completion of this second edition. Thank you Sue for all you have done.

Jonathan Doherty
& Malcolm Hughes

# Publisher's acknowledgements

We are grateful to the following for permission to reproduce copyright material:

## Figures

Figure 1.3: Berk, L. E. (2006). *Child development* (7th ed.). Boston: Allyn & Bacon. Copyright © 2006 Pearson Education, Inc. Reproduced with permission; Figure 1.4: Based on Baltes, P. B., Reese, H. W., & Lipsitt, L. P. (1980). Life-span developmental psychology. In L. R. Goldberg, M. R. Rosenzweig, & L. W. Porter (Series Eds.), *Annual review of psychology* (Vol 31, pp 65–110). Palo Alto, CA: Annual Reviews. Reproduced with permission; Figure 3.2: From the Child Growth Foundation website (www.childgrowthfoundation.org/ghd.htm). © Child Growth Foundation, reproduced with permission. Further information go to www.healthforallchildren.co.uk; Figure 6.1: From Longe, J. L. (Ed.) (2006). *Gale encyclopedia of medicine*, 3rd ed. Farming Hills, MI: Gale, a part of Cengage Learning, Inc. Reproduced by permission; Figure 7.1: World Health Organization (2006). WHO child growth standards: methods and development. Geneva: WHO. www.who.int/childgrowth/standards/en/. Reproduced with permission; Figure 7.5: The International Association for the Study of Obesity [Chart: Prevalence of overweight and obesity in schoolchildren aged 10–16 years, as defined by body mass index 2001–2] (www.iaso.org); Figure 7.6: Doherty, J., & Brennan, P. (2007). *Physical education and development 3–11. A guide for teachers*. Abingdon, Oxon: Routledge. Reproduced with permission from Taylor & Francis; Figure 9.2: Praget, J. & Inhelder, B. (1967). *The Child's conception of space* (pp 211–222). Andover, Routledge. Reprodued with permission; Figure 12.2: Catalano, R. F., & Hawkins, J. D. (1996). The social development model: A theory of antisocial behavior. In J. D. Hawkins (Ed.) *Delinquency and crime: Current theories* (pp 149–197). New York: Cambridge University Press. Reproduced with permission.

## Tables

Table 3.2: Willan, J., Parker-Rees, R., & Savage, J. (Eds.) (2004). *Early childhood studies:an introduction to the study of children's worlds and children's lives* (p. 93). Exeter: Learning Matters. Reproduced with permission; Table 4.1: L. D. Thomas, Blinn College – Brenham. Table 6.1: Taylor, M., Houghton, S., & Chapman, E. (2004). Primitive reflexes and attention-deficit / hyperactivity disorder: Developmental origins of classroom dysfunction. International *Journal of Special Education*, 19, 1, 23–37 (table on p. 26); Table 7.2: Doherty, J., & Brennan, P. (2007). *Physical education and development 3–11. A guide for teachers*. Abingdon, Oxon: Routledge. Reproduced with permission from Taylor & Francis; Table 11.3: Based on Ainsworth, M. D. S., Blehar, M., Waters, E. & Wall, S. (1978) *Patterns of attachment: A psychological study of the strange situation*. Hillsdale, NJ: Erlbaum. Reproduced with permission; Table 11.6: Adapted from Tennant, M. (1997). *Psychology and adult learning*, 2nd ed. London: Routledge. Reproduced with permission; Table 12.3: After Kohlberg, L. (1984), *Essays on moral development* (Vol 2) Harper & Row, New York. Reproduced with permission.

## Text

Pages 89, 91: Two text extracts from Bryson. B, (2003). *A short history of nearly everything*. London: Doubleday. Reproduced with permission from Random House Ltd.

## Photographs

The publisher would like to thank the following for their kind permission to reproduce their photographs:

(Key: b-bottom; c-centre; l-left; r-right; t-top)

xxvi   Publisher's acknowledgements

Prelims- iii Pearson Education Ltd / Jules Selmes; Prelims xxviii Studio 8; Pages 2 Pearson Education Ltd / Jules Selmes; 4 Edward and Ella Hogan; 7 Alamy Images: MBI (5); DK Images: Vanessa Davies (2); Edward and Ella Hogan: (1); Pearson Education Ltd: Jules Selmes (3); Shutterstock.com: Russian Kudrin (4); 10 Bridgeman Art Library Ltd: (c) Glasgow University Library; 19 Pearson Education Ltd; 22 Pearson Education Ltd: Jules Selmes; 25 Pearson Education Ltd: Jules Selmes; 26 Pearson Education Ltd: Jules Selmes; 30 Studio 8; 37 Science Photo Library Ltd: Sam Falk; 39 Science Photo Library Ltd: Bill Anderson; 40 TopFoto: RIA Novosti; 41 Getty Images: Ted Streshinsky / Time & Life Pictures; 45 Pearson Education Ltd: Jules Selmes; 46 Getty Images: Nina Leen / Time & Life Pictures (br); Pearson Education Ltd: Tudor Photography (tl); 52 Getty Images: Popperfoto; 60 Pearson Education Ltd / Jules Selmes; 70 Edward and Ella Hogan; 75 Pearson Education Ltd: Jules Selmes; 76 Alamy Images: Deco; 80 Malcolm Hughes; 88 Pearson Education Ltd / Jules Selmes; 97 Pearson Education Ltd: Jules Selmes; 100 Science Photo Library Ltd: Paul D Stewart; 104 Pearson Education Ltd: Gareth Boden (b); Debbie Rowe (t); 108 Getty Images: Digital Vision / Rob van Petten; 118 Pearson Education Ltd: Jules Selmes; 120 DK Images: Howard Shooter; 123 Edward and Ella Hogan; 124 Edward and Ella Hogan: (t); (b); 148 DK Images: Vanessa Davies; 153 Pearson Education Ltd / Jules Selmes; Science Photo Library Ltd: RIA Novosti (t); 154 Pearson Education Ltd: Jules Selmes; 155 Lee and Lynsey Matthews: (b); Pearson Education Ltd: Jules Selmes (t); 157 Pearson Education Ltd: Tudor Photography (t); Tudor Photography (b); 158 Pearson Education Ltd: Tudor Photography (tl); Tudor Photography (b); Jules Selmes (tr); Jules Selmes (br); 174 Malcolm Hughes: (tl); (cl); (c); Pearson Education Ltd: Jules Selmes (b); 180 Pearson Education Ltd: Lisa Payne Photography; 181 Alamy Images: Jeff Morgan; 198 Malcolm Hughes; 204 Pearson Education Ltd: Tudor Photography (tl); Jules Selmes (l); Jules Selmes (cl); Jules Selmes (c); Jules Selmes (bl); 205 Pearson Education Ltd: Jules Selmes (tc); Jules Selmes (l); Jules Selmes (c); Clark Wiseman / Studio 8 (cl); Shutterstock.com: Anetta (tl); 206 Pearson Education Ltd: Tudor Photography (l); Jules Selmes (r); 207 Pearson Education Ltd: Jules Selmes (t); Jules Selmes (b); 218 Pearson Education Ltd / Jules Selmes; 223 Photo Edit Inc: Mark Richards; 228 Stephanie Breen: (tl); (t); (cl); (bl); 229 Richard Stagg: (tl); (t); (cl); (b); 230 Richard Stagg: (tl); (l); (cl); Stephanie Breen: (b); 231 Getty Images: Nina Leen / Time & Life Pictures (b); Pearson Education Ltd: Jules Selmes; 234 Pearson Education Ltd: Jules Selmes; 240 Pearson Education Ltd: Ian Wedgewood; 241 Pearson Education Ltd: Jules Selmes; 248 Pearson Education Ltd: Lord and Leverett / Pearson Education Ltd; 255 Pearson Education Ltd: Jules Selmes (tr); Jules Selmes (cr); Jules Selmes (bc); 256 Pearson Education Ltd: Jules Selmes; 257 Pearson Education Ltd: Jules Selmes; 258 Photo Edit Inc: Laura Dwight; 261 Pearson Education Ltd: Jules Selmes; 264 Pearson Education Ltd: Ian Wedgewood; 267 Photo Edit Inc: Michael Newman; 278 Pearson Education Ltd: Ian Wedgewood; 286 Pearson Education Ltd: Jules Selmes; 292 Image 100; 306 Shutterstock.com: Oksana Kuzmina; Angela Luchisniuc (b); 310 Bananastock: (5); DK Images: Steve Gorton (2); Dave King (4); Pearson Education Ltd: Lisa Payne Photography (3); Jules Selmes (1); 317 Pearson Education Ltd: Jules Selmes; 318 Pearson Education Ltd: Jules Selmes (t); Ian Wedgewood (b); 326 Brand X Pictures; 330 Stephanie Breen; 335 Edward and Ella Hogan; 340 Alamy Images: Ashley Whitworth; Pearson Education Ltd: Tudor Photography (b); 344 Corbis; 348 Alamy Images: Marmaduke St John; 351 Pearson Education Ltd: Jules Selmes; 364 Pearson Education Ltd / Jules Selmes; 367 Pearson Education Ltd: Jules Selmes; 368 Pearson Education Ltd: Jules Selmes; 370 Richard Stagg; 380 Catherine Yates; 389 Pearson Education Ltd: Jules Selmes; 391 Pearson Education Ltd: Tudor Photography / Pearson Education Ltd;. 405 Edward and Ella Hogan.

Cover images: *Front:* Corbis

All other images © Pearson Education

Every effort has been made to trace the copyright holders and we apologise in advance for any unintentional omissions. We would be pleased to insert the appropriate acknowledgement in any subsequent edition of this publication.

# Part 1
## Introducing Child Development

# Chapter 1
## Issues in Child Development

## Overview

# Introduction

In this book you will learn more about children and their development from conception to the end of childhood at age 11 – which is the end of primary or elementary schooling in many countries and the beginning of adolescence. You will learn about the vast range of capabilities that very young children quickly acquire and how, in the course of just a few years, this impressive range of skills, knowledge and understanding is extended even further. Your understanding of children and their development will depend on getting a grasp of the most important issues in child development.

In this chapter we set out what we think are the most important issues to explore about children and their development. We begin by considering the nature of child development and how childhood is generally understood. We also offer reasons why the study of child development is essential for practitioners working with children in daycare, playgroups, nurseries, schools, families and other settings.

By the time you have completed this chapter you should be able to answer the following questions:

- What is the study of child development?
- What are the fundamental issues and key terms?
- Why is knowledge of child development important?
- What are the key questions and fundamental issues of child development, and how do they relate to parenting, care situations and education?

**Chapter Objectives**

# Defining child development

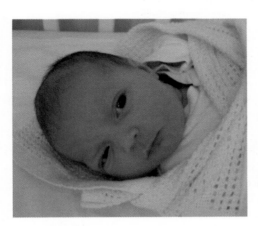

This is Niamh. She is just a few hours old.
*Source*: Edward and Ella Hogan.

To help you start refining your understanding of child development, let's consider two different views of a newborn child. The first is expressed by a friend, Edd Hogan, a 'first-time' father holding his new daughter Niamh (pronounced Neeve), who is just a few minutes old.

. . . I felt a rush of emotion: happiness, joy, awe, and relief. She was all there: two arms, two legs, and she was beautiful. In those first few hours a great deal goes through your mind – what will she become? Will she like what we like? How will she get on in school? What will her voice sound like? The feelings of love towards her were, and are, remarkable. We want her to grow up to know what it is to be loved. We want the best for our baby and we will support her in making her own choices as she grows up. Of course, we want to steer her to do certain things, like playing a musical instrument. Most of all, we want her to have a carefree childhood surrounded by a loving family.

**Reflect**

Niamh was born to Ella and Edd Hogan on 5 November 2007. Can you think back to your own feelings on seeing a new baby – perhaps your own baby, or a brother or sister – for the first time? Edd and Ella wished, most of all, that Niamh would have a 'carefree childhood surrounded by a loving family'. This, sadly – tragically in some cases – is not the birthright for all babies. Is there such a thing as a birthright?

Compare Edd Hogan's very personal account with that of Professor Robert Winston's introduction to the BBC television series *The Human Body*. Lord Winston is one of Britain's most respected medical academics and researcher of the human reproductive system. He said:

I want you to meet Kirsty who was born just over two hours ago. Mix together some protein, a little sugar, quite a lot of fat and about 75 per cent water with a selection of chemicals that you would find in any pharmacy and there we have it! Simple really and yet this tiny being is the most sophisticated and complicated living being on the planet. In the course of her lifetime (650,000 hours on average) she will achieve things that are amazing, fantastic and every bit miraculous.

(*Source*: Robert Winston, *The Human Body*, 20 May 1998, BBC Television)

Both Professor Winston and Edd Hogan see and understand the enormous potential for growth, change and development in the two newborns Kirsty and Niamh. Robert and Edd may have contrasting ways of expressing their sense of awe and wonder but both are already looking forward to the almost incredible changes that will happen in the lives of these two young children. In identifying and making sense of these changes, you will begin to construct your own understanding of child development.

## What is child development?

**Human development**
The pattern of change that all individuals undergo from conception through the span of life.

The study of any kind of **human development** is mostly about the study of change (Herrero *et al.*, 2012; Kagitcibasi, 2012; Côté *et al.*, 2002) and in order to understand it, we need to study the changes that children undergo beginning in the womb, through the post-natal period and continuing throughout childhood. The study of change can and should be a scientific enterprise. You may all remember doing science experiments at school by applying processes to a current physical condition and then observing the effects – the changes that happen. For example, gently heating iron sulphide with a strong acid and using the resulting malodorous gas (hydrogen sulphide – smelling of rotten eggs) to make stink bombs. The schoolboy experimenter changes the physical state of iron sulphide and acid using heat. By observing the change that takes place, the schoolboy knows more about the nature of the sulphide, the acid, the chemical effects of heat and the resulting chemical compound. He or she is engaged in a scientific – if somewhat mischievous – enterprise. So what does that tell us about changes we observe in children? Some research methods used in the study of child development are experimental and you can look ahead to Chapter 3 *Research Methods* to read examples of how experimental methods are used. That is not the whole picture, though, as experimental methods are not always relevant or practical. Indeed, practitioners working with young children tend to be more familiar with observing children directly, as a method to understand them and the progress they are making (more of this in Chapter 3).

Parents and teachers are not experimenters with children. The science that developmentalists – those who study human development – bring to the observation of changes in children tends to be naturalistic rather than experimental. However, natural scientific observation is more than the plain act of looking at people. Scientific observers must 'perceive' in order to add to their own knowledge. They do this by incorporating new perceptions into a framework of previous knowledge and ideas (Piaget, 1957). This idea needs a little explanation at this stage. Understanding something new does not grow out of nothing. We all have an idea – a schema the French psychologist Jean Piaget (see Chapter 2) would call it – of, say what a dog is, based on our observations and experiences of 'dog'. So the first time we see a fox we might perceive it to be a dog, in line with our current schema of 'dog'. Our new experience of seeing a fox, shared perhaps with somebody else who already has the language and understanding of 'fox' will lead us to adapt our understanding of 'dog' and to include in our range of knowledge a new schema of 'fox'. Adapting and including new ideas (the term we use is 'assimilating') is an important process in the development of understanding.

While we are talking about the scientific and personal process of assimilating new observations and understandings, do not go any further until you have followed the nearby *Connect and Extend* feature about Victor, the 'Wild Boy of Aveyron'. It is a fascinating story, one which marks the beginning point for the science of child development as this study was among the very first to attempt a scientific approach to understanding how children grow and flourish. By assimilating ideas from an enquiry into Victor, the 'Wild Boy of Aveyron', you can really develop your understanding of child development.

Reading Chapter 3 of this book will help you to understand how to best observe and study children's behaviour and development. You will be introduced to recognised expert observers of child development (for example, Piaget, Bruner and Vygotsky in cognitive development and Freud, Erikson and Bowlby in emotional and social development). These scientists did not apply particular 'treatments' to generate the changes they wish to observe (unlike a mischievous schoolboy making hydrogen sulphide or Jean-Marc Itard in the nearby *Connect and Extend*). Rather, by perceiving, identifying and making sense of the changes in children as they grow and develop, the expert theorists like those mentioned above help parents, nurses and teachers to check that all is well and 'going to plan'.

Until now, we seem to have been using the terms 'change' and 'development' as if they are freely exchangeable without taking account of any differences. Below we begin to sort out some of the common terms used when talking about children's development and see how the two concepts of change and development are linked.

**Naturalistic**
Observations of behaviour in natural contexts (e.g. homes, classrooms) rather than structured observations in laboratories.

**Schema**
A set of ideas about the common features of a particular object, being or concept.

● ● ● ● ● ● ● ● ● ● ● ● ●
**Connect and Extend**
Search online for the story of Victor, the 'Wild Boy of Aveyron', and into the work of Jean-Marc Itard, who tried to transform the 'wild boy' into a civilised Frenchman. There is also a reference in the *Going Further* feature at the end of Chapter 1.
● ● ● ● ● ● ● ● ● ● ● ● ●

● ● ● ● ● ● ● ● ● ● ● ● ●
**Connect and Extend**
How do we find out about children's development? To compare different scientific methods in a European context, read: Hofstetter, R. (2012). The transformation of the child. The 'eurekas' of human development, from science and romanticism: a 'naturalism' of childhood. *Paedagogica Historica*, February, *48*(1), 31–50.
● ● ● ● ● ● ● ● ● ● ● ● ●

## Terms of development

Teachers, early years practitioners and all professionals who work with children should be aware of complex processes and factors at work that influence the ways in which children such

**Human growth**
The gradual but not necessarily steady increase in size of the body.

**Maturation**
The process of following the 'biological developmental plan' contained in our genes.

**Genes**
Units of heredity composed of DNA, forming part of the chromosomes that make up the nucleus of the human cell.

**Learning**
The process through which a person's experiences of their environment result in relatively permanent changes to how people feel, think and behave.

• • • • • • • • • • • • • • • • •
**Connect and Extend**
For an excellent example of an enquiry into learning through experience, read: McGuigan, N. & Doherty, M. (2006). Head and shoulders, knees and toes: Which parts of the body are necessary to be seen? *British Journal of Developmental Psychology,* 24, 727–732.
• • • • • • • • • • • • • • • • •

as Kirsty and Niamh (who we 'met' earlier) grow, think, learn new skills, acquire knowledge and interact with others. Remember from earlier that human development is the pattern of change that all individuals undergo from conception through the span of life. The abundance and complexity of these changes is apparent even during the first few days of life. For example, think back to the photograph of Niamh at the beginning of the chapter. When that photograph was taken, any smile that newborn Niamh made was probably a reflex to a sensation – perhaps indigestion, yet just a few weeks later Niamh smiled in recognition and pleasure. Changes such as learning to smile enable very young children to display different aspects of personality, to tackle increasingly complicated tasks and to interact with their world and other people they encounter.

Development includes changes in **human growth** which are readily observable and measurable. These changes are fast-moving and enable children to, for example, support their own body weight, move around in a variety of ways, manipulate, and to build and destroy. Development is also about the process of **maturation**, or the biological developmental plan contained in our **genes**. This is the hereditary material that passes from parent to child that partly determines the physical 'milestones' that children achieve, such as learning to walk, and the psychological changes that allow them to think and interact with others. In addition, you should appreciate how growth and maturation differ from **learning**. Learning is the process through which a person's experiences of their environment result in relatively permanent changes to how people feel, think and behave (Schaffer, 2006; Georghiades, 2004). It is generally accepted that developmental changes occur as a result of both maturation and learning and this duality is an important idea.

Child Development includes physical growth, yet, as illustrated in Figure 1.1, is defined by the interdependence of learning, cognitive development – the emergence of the ability to think and understand – and maturation. The issue that remains is: to what extent are developmental changes, both physical and cognitive, due to heredity? For example, a person's height once fully grown is largely a matter of heredity, but during the maturation process both the pace of growth and the final outcome is affected by diet. In the same way, the capacity for cognitive development is determined by growth due to maturation and (as shown in Figure 1.1) cognitive ability is determined by the outcomes of learning through experience. Next we consider the extent to which the typical pattern of developmental change that occurs over time can be considered as stages linked to chronological age.

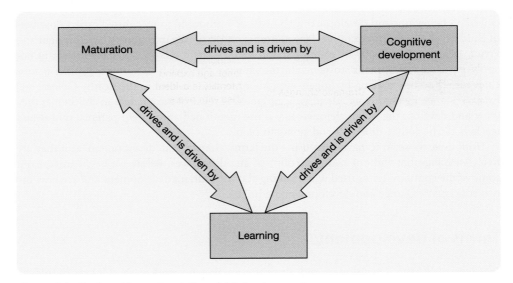

**Figure 1.1** The key drivers that define child development

# Stages of development

Child development is concerned with understanding the various processes that determine both the physical and psychological make-up of children. Our earlier definition of development emphasises the constant nature of change (growth and decline) throughout people's lives, and our study of change during a lifetime is informed by lifespan perspectives in psychology (e.g. Mayo, 2001). Development has been neatly summarised as 'the systematic and scientific study of changes in human behaviours and mental activities over time' (Bukatko & Daehler, 2001, p 4) and as a developmental framework, you will find it commonly presented in terms of periods of time. This tends to give an impression of discrete (distinctly separate) stages closely linked to chronological age and providing a very precise ordering of change. However, we encourage you to see development as more of a flow of constant change with notions of different stages serving only to provide a structure for observation and analysis. With this 'health warning' in mind, now study Figure 1.2, which shows commonly identified periods of development up to the emergence of adulthood.

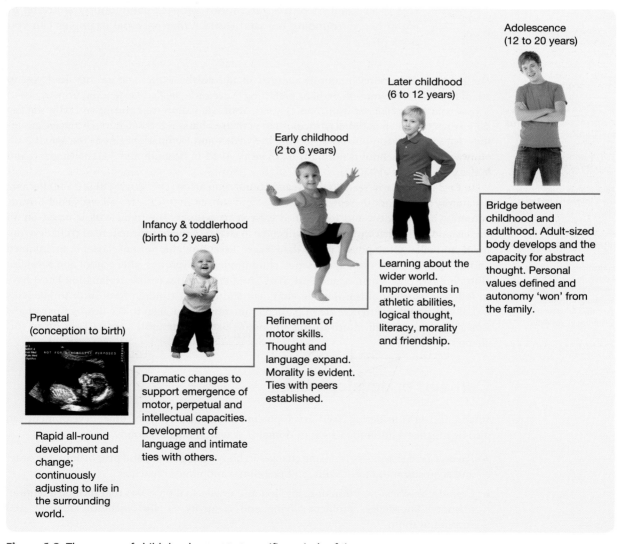

**Figure 1.2**  The course of child development at specific periods of time

*Sources* (photos): From left to right: Edward and Ella Hogan; © DK Images / Vanessa Davies; © Pearson Education Ltd / Jules Selmes; © Shutterstock.com / Russian Kudrin; © Alamy Images / MBI.

Too strict an adherence to any conceptual framework of child development structured by age can be problematical because development does not necessarily proceed in an orderly way. However, such structures as shown in Figure 1.2 can also be very helpful when commenting upon a child's development, for example, to refer to certain age-related stages of development, such as in the following comments: 'I remember when Toby was just learning to walk, at about 14 months . . .' (parent). Similarly, there are advantages in commenting upon observed changes in children as they progress through school: 'I've really noticed a big difference in Ellie's language skills from when she was 6. Her stories have got much longer with much more involved plots' (teaching assistant).

**Reflect**

Look at the developmental stages shown in Figure 1.2. Can you recall and record any observations you have made for each of these stages. For example, when Malcolm's wife was expecting their first child he used to sing to his yet-unborn daughter. Baby Rebecca moved around in a very excited way. Perhaps she was dancing or trying to get away from the horrible noise! This is an example of the yet-unborn Rebecca continuously adjusting to life in her surrounding prenatal world. What personal examples can you think of?

The memory of personal examples recalled in the nearby *Reflect* feature may lead you to adapt Figure 1.2 for yourself, perhaps preferring to see *early childhood* extending from ages 3 to 6 years and *later childhood* from 7 to 11 years. Your adaptation may correspond with the key stages prescribed in a national curriculum or with age phases represented in school-age groupings. For example, compulsory schooling in Sweden and Denmark begins at the age of 7. In Norway 'primary' school is normally 6–13 years, 6–12 in Belgium and 5–11 in England and Wales (Woolfolk *et al.*, 2012).

In England an Early Years (0 to 5 years) Foundation Stage (DfE, 2012; DfES, 2006) became a statutory framework in September 2008 – and revised in 2012 – for all registered private, voluntary, independent and maintained early years settings. The framework is based on an understanding (which we hope you will come to share) of the holistic nature of child development, and talks about phases rather than stages. Reception and nursery classes in maintained and independent schools, day nurseries, childminders, playgroups, after school and breakfast clubs, holiday play schemes, and Sure Start Children's Centres (more explanation later) have to follow a structure of learning, development and care for children from birth to five years old. If early years experiences are of particular interest to you, refer to the nearby *Connect and Extend* feature. We will return to this important national statutory context later on in this chapter.

**Connect and Extend**

Familiarise yourself with the national framework for the Early Years Foundation Stage (EYFS) in England using links from **www. education.gov.uk/**. Research the frameworks that exist elsewhere in Europe. For some background and starting points for your research, try: Stephen, C. (2006) *Early Years Education: Perspectives from a Review of the International Literature*. Edinburgh: Scottish Executive Education Department, available online.

## Domains of development

In addition to considering child development in specific periods of time, development can also be organised into broad areas or domains. A typical organisation is:

- *Physical development* – comprising changes in body size (growth) and proportions, the order and acquisition of motor skills, and perceptual and motor capacities.

- *Cognitive development* – thinking, intellect and intellectual processes that include attention, memory, knowledge, problem-solving and creativity. It also includes language and communication.

- *Social and emotional development* – the former includes understanding of 'self', relationships with others and sociability; the latter includes emotional expression, attachment, personality and temperament.

The later chapters of this book consider the domains of child development separately as some 'deconstruction' of development enables a better analysis of each of the domains. Nevertheless, you are encouraged to retain the idea of holistic development by looking for the many connections between the characteristics of each of the domains, and to transfer the holistic notion to their everyday interactions with children. Remember the scientific approach taken by Jean-Marc Itard to transforming Victor, the 'Wild Boy of Aveyron'? This was a holistic enquiry and the history of child development contains many such examples where scientists have developed their theories and ideas by closely observing the whole development of children. It is to the history of child development that we now turn.

---

Before moving on, let's summarise what we have learned so far:

- Child development is the study of changes in children over the timespan of childhood from conception to adulthood.
- It is a scientific study – usually naturalistic rather than experimental. Observations of children's changing abilities and characteristics take place in natural settings such as homes and schools.
- Expert observers are systematic and precise, and build their perceptions into theories.
- Knowledge of these theories helps all who nurture children to check that all is well and 'going to plan'.
- Child development is the study of changes due to both maturation (following the genetic plan) and learning (change due to experience).
- Such changes can be represented either in age-related phases or by referring to domains of development – physical, cognitive or social/emotional, all of which are strongly interconnected. In this book we stress a holistic interpretation of child development for the practical application of the ideas described.

**Summary 1**

---

# A history of child development

## The beginnings of child development

The study of child development has a comparatively short history, beginning 150 years ago or so. Despite its late acceptance as scientific enquiry (due, as we shall see, to a comparatively later interest in childhood as a distinct part of the human lifespan), the amount of study and scholarship has grown at pace for two reasons. Firstly, increase in scientific scholarship is in response to practitioners wishing to work in more enlightened ways with preschool and primary age children. Secondly, the depth of study acknowledges that parents, carers and childminders wish to bring a more informed approach to their parenting or child-caring practices. One reason for this comparatively recent interest has been the change in societal attitudes to the concept of childhood (Davis, 2011; Taylor, A., 2011). A brief trawl through the history of childhood reveals very different earlier views of children from contemporary beliefs about childhood. How did we get to where we are today? What and where were the origins of this aspect of developmental psychology that we call child development?

To answer these questions we should return to medieval Europe where, some writers assert, no concept of childhood (as we perceive it) was known before 1600. Philippe Aries in his influential and landmark book *Centuries of Childhood* (1962) writes that the lack of precision

Some historians believe that children in medieval Europe dressed and behaved as small adults.

*Source*: © Glasgow University Library, Scotland / The Bridgeman Art Library.

**Epoch**
A period of history marked by notable events relevant to the issues being discussed.

• • • • • • • • • • • • • • • •

**Connect and Extend**
For a full account of the changing experiences and perceptions of childhood, read: Heywood, C. (2001). *A history of childhood: Children and childhood in the West from medieval to modern times.* London: Blackwell. Heywood examines the different ways in which people have thought about childhood as a stage of life.

• • • • • • • • • • • • • • • •

in medieval society in counting such things as years of age accounted for childhood being ill-defined, with no references to stages of development whatsoever. Children very much 'belonged to adult society' (p 125) and were encouraged to resemble 'mini adults' in their clothing and demeanour. Far from having the toys that characterise the pastimes and experiences of many children's lives nowadays, children of 6 or 7 years old would have been engaged in the adult world of work and adult pastimes. This view does not go unchallenged by other historians. For example, Linda Pollock in her book *Forgotten Children: Parent–Child Relations from 1500 to 1900* (1983) rejects the kind of stereotype Aries offers – that the concept of childhood was almost absent, and that children were cruelly treated. Instead Pollock provides a much more humane picture of childhood in the medieval period and what came after.

The 'Age of Enlightenment' was an eighteenth-century movement in European philosophy which advocated reasoning and logic as the primary basis of intellectual authority rather than irrationality and superstition. The 1700s saw a shift away from these medieval values and attitudes and began an epoch where strong social influences, fuelled by the writings of philosophers, began to place a different emphasis upon children and child-rearing practices. Two such philosophers, John Locke and Jean-Jacques Rousseau, held strikingly contrasting ideas but both nevertheless have had a lasting effect on shaping contemporary thinking about the development of children.

In *An Essay Concerning Human Understanding* (1690), John Locke proposed that no knowledge is innate and the mind of a child on entry into this world is as a *tabula rasa* or blank slate upon which experience writes. Locke proposed that environmental experiences mould the child and, furthermore, he stressed the importance of early experience. He was not an advocate of harsh discipline, but believed that children's behaviour should be properly managed by parents, who could be strict with their children when necessary. These beliefs are reflected in the behaviourist approaches of later psychologists.

In contrast, Jean-Jacques Rousseau stressed childhood as a time of innocence. He believed that children are born with a sense of right and wrong, and as active beings in possession of their own personalities and intellect. Rousseau encouraged educators to capitalise on the natural curiosity of the child but through exploration of the environment (reflected in the later writings of Piaget in the twentieth century). Rousseau's views on child-rearing are set out in his famous novel *Emile* (1762) where he clearly expounds that the role of adults is to guide and respond to the natural instincts of children. Rousseau and Locke were both philosophers rather than scientists – using naturalistic methods of observation as described earlier. The observations of both Locke and Rousseau may appear to us now as unmethodical and disordered, and therefore distanced from the more scientific era in the history of childhood development which followed.

The origins of the scientific study of child development can be traced to the nineteenth century. Charles Darwin, keen to discover the roots of our existence as a species and stemming from his theory of evolution, began detailed records of his son's first years of life. In what became known as the 'baby biographies' (1877) Darwin published a paper based upon his 37 year-old recorded observations of the child's early reflexes, later learned or 'willed' voluntary movements, his language and emotions. The following is an excerpt from the paper 'A biographical sketch of an infant':

> During the first seven days various reflex actions, namely sneezing, hickuping, yawning, stretching, and of course sucking and screaming, were well performed by my infant.

On the seventh day, I touched the naked sole of his foot with a bit of paper, and he jerked it away, curling at the same time his toes, like a much older child when tickled. The perfection of these reflex movements shows that the extreme imperfection of the voluntary ones is not due to the state of the muscles or of the coordinating centres, but to that of the seat of the will. At this time, though so early, it seemed clear to me that a warm soft hand applied to his face excited a wish to suck. This must be considered as a reflex or an instinctive action, for it is impossible to believe that experience and association with the touch of his mother's breast could so soon have come into play.

(1877: pp 285–286)

Similar work undertaken on his own son by the German scientist Wilhelm Preyer provided further detailed information about sensory development, and the acquisition of language and motor skills, particularly the development of movement as an act of deliberate will rather than reflex. The accounts of Darwin and Preyer were amongst the earliest recorded systematic and scientific observations of children. This work provided the catalyst for further work in the United States, where one of the pioneers of American psychology, G. Stanley Hall, employed a questionnaire on preschool children and was able to collect data on the nature of children's thinking by comparing responses by gender and ethnic origin (Hall, 1891a).

Within ten years of the publication of Hall's study on 'The contents of children's minds on entering school', Frenchman and psychologist Alfred Binet had developed the first standardised intelligence test which was a scale systematically measuring higher-order thinking skills, memory, language and problem-solving abilities, unique to each individual. The technique of mental testing was born using a measurement scale that took account of individual's mental abilities. This was the first IQ test. It was used (and more sophisticated versions continue to be used) by psychologists and other professionals involved in testing children's rates of development in educational settings. So began the scientific method for the study of children.

**Scientific method**
The application of scientific principles in an orderly manner, and with the appropriate technique, to find an answer to a question.

## The scientific study of child development

In preparing to write this chapter, we have identified six factors that have influenced the scientific study of child development:

1. The more systematic study of human development by scientists such as Darwin, Preyer and Hall led to the twentieth-century theorists and their theories of child development (which will be discussed in Chapter 2).

2. The establishment of universal public education in Western Europe during the early decades of the twentieth century led to a demand for knowledge of how children develop and for information on the best teaching methods (Søreide, 2006; Cardak, 2004). The demand for knowledge is replicated in the developing nations of the world and includes perspectives of children's education as a political movement (Stasavage, 2005).

3. New knowledge from individuals and agencies with professional interests in children's health have contributed a greater understanding of physical growth patterns and nutrition and the effects on educational progress (Li, 2009; Pillay, 2006; Weisbrot et al., 2006; Knyazev et al., 2002).

4. Research into children's thinking abilities, fuelled in part by an emphasis on achievement (standards) and testing in schools (Russ, 2011; Pasnak et al., 2008; Topping & Trickey, 2007).

5. The emergence of an increased role for public care and social services has heightened interest in the development of social and emotional intelligence and the conditions that promote or adversely affect such development (D'Oosterlinck et al., 2006; Poulou, 2005; Lopes et al., 2004).

6. Lastly, a relatively new interest in parenting skills has arisen and can be readily seen in the plethora of books on this subject (for example, *Effective Parenting for the Hard-to-Manage Child: A Skills-based Book* by Georgia DeGangi and Anne Kendall, 2007) that now fill the shelves of popular booksellers and supermarkets (Secco *et al.*, 2006). This includes the child-care skills of parents with intellectual impairment (Remberk *et al.*, 2012).

Now, well into the second decade of a new century, two facts are apparent. Firstly, knowledge of children's growth and development has increased and is disseminated on a much wider scale than in previous decades. Secondly, the interdisciplinary nature of the subject is very evident in modern child development textbooks, and in school and university courses. The study of child development in the twenty-first century is approached from various branches of learning: law, anthropology, education, paediatrics, and cognitive, social and neural-psychology – and this diversity of approach is far from being static! As new information comes to light, new paths of enquiry are called for and are being followed (Johnson & Easterling, 2012; Masson, 2006). For example, a comparatively new path of enquiry is the cross-cultural contexts of childhood, particularly the effects of globalisation on social and moral development.

**Interdisciplinary**
Study or research that draws on more than one branch of learning.

• • • • • • • • • • • • • • • •

**Connect and Extend**
For a full account of an example of a new path of enquiry being followed, read: Masson, J. (2006). The Climbié Inquiry – context and critique. *Journal of Law and Society*, 33, 221–243.

• • • • • • • • • • • • • • • •

## Cross-cultural contexts of childhood

As well as reflecting on the historical and European perspectives on childhood there are many reasons why looking at other cultures can help further our understanding of child development. The point is well made by Barbara Rogoff, a Professor of Psychology and one-time editor of the journal *Human Development*, who writes:

> The process of looking across cultural traditions can help us become more aware of cultural regularities in our own as well as other people's lives, no matter which communities are most familiar to us. Cultural research can help us understand cultural aspects of our own lives that we take for granted as natural, as well as those that surprise us.
>
> (2003, pp 7–8)

Children's development is affected in complex and profound ways by the culture in which they grow up. Compare growing up in a fishing village in Sardinia with growing up in an industrialised city in the Netherlands. At first glance the experiences of children in Sardinia and in Rotterdam may seem totally unconnected, almost discrete. Of course, different experiences of childhood will have profound effects on the way that society organises children's services, including education. The following feature, *Policy, Research and Praxis*, explores the implications of one developing view of childhood on national policy.

## Policy, Research and Praxis

### Childhood in the UK today: Implications for public policy

Every generation wants to do its best for its children and young people. Growing up as a child in the twenty-first century is about living in changing and diverse societies that enrich through culture, language and faiths. Children nowadays live in a digital world with rapid advances in technology. They are influenced by the media and by their peers as to what to wear, what to eat, and what they must look like. There are increased demands on them to achieve academically at all phases of education but with the prospect of fewer employment opportunities at the end. It is important to know how children today experience childhood to inform and shape future policy. Knowing what makes children thrive as happy individuals is more than a measure of happiness, it is a mirror on the successful functioning of a society. In the UK, Government pledges and legislation seek to reduce child poverty and improve services, increase attainment, improve safeguarding procedures and provide early intervention to those children and families in most need.

The Good Childhood Report (2012) presented findings from seven annual surveys of more than 30,000 children aged between 8 and 16 between 2005 and 2011, focused particularly on England. The research behind this report sought to learn about children's lives and the issues that affect them: their relationships with others and the role of the family. It explored their views of poverty, of events and people that influence their lived experiences and subjective well-being. Since children represent over 1/5 of the total UK population, promoting good well-being is important for children's current childhoods but also for their lives as future adults. Whilst the majority of children are happy in their lives, around 4 per cent of eight-year-olds and 14 per cent of 15-year-olds are not happy and have low subjective well-being. The report found that choice and family were the biggest influences on being happy. The quality of relationships within a family was more important than family structure. Stability in the home environment had a positive impact on well-being. Low well-being was connected to feeling of unhappiness with family and friends, fears about safety, personal image and anxieties about the future. Unhappy children were more likely to be bullied and have eating disorders. The report identified six priorities for a happy childhood:

- having the conditions to learn and develop;
- having a positive self-image and an identity that is respected;
- being financially secure;
- having positive relationships with family and friends;
- having a safe and suitable home and local environment and
- opportunities to take part in positive activities to thrive.

These were the voices of children. In a time of significant political, economic and social change in this country, there are important messages for parents and policy makers to listen to in order to prevent the escalation of such issues and to provide proper support for children and young people in their childhoods.

What aspects of culture have the strongest influence on the development of children? How do different aspects of culture relate to each other? Who is more influential, teachers or peers? To answer these questions we can turn to a helpful theoretical model developed in 1989 by Urie Bronfenbrenner – a renowned psychologist and a co-founder of the Head Start programme for disadvantaged preschool children in the United States. Bronfenbrenner mapped the many interacting social contexts that affect development with his *bio-ecological model* of development (Bronfenbrenner & Evans, 2000; Bronfenbrenner, 1989). The *bio* aspect of the model recognises that people bring their biological selves to the developmental process. The *ecological* part recognises that the social contexts in which we develop are ecosystems because they are in constant interaction and influence each other. The model is illustrated in Figure 1.3.

By referring to Figure 1.3 you can see that every child develops within a **microsystem** of his or her immediate relationships and activities. For a child, it might be the close family, friends or teachers and the activities of play and school. This is the child's own 'little world'. Within it relationships are reciprocal – they flow in both directions. The child's behaviour affects the parent and the parent influences the child. Microsystems exist and interact within a **mesosystem**, which is slightly more distant from the child because they do not involve him or her directly

**Microsystem**
The child's own close family and friends.

**Mesosystem**
The extended family, friends, neighbours and teachers in school.

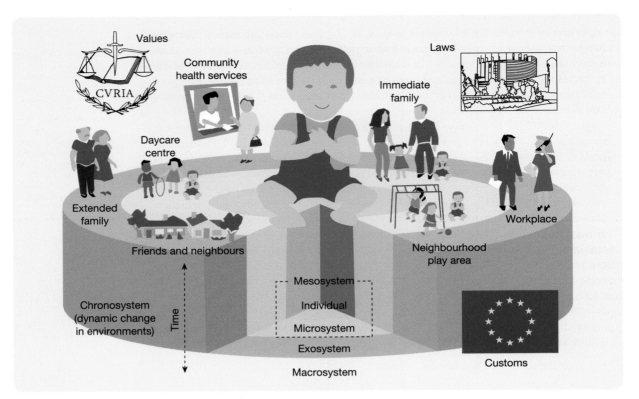

**Figure 1.3** Urie Bronfenbrenner's biological model of human development

*Source*: Berk, L. E. (2006). *Child development* (7th ed.). Boston: Allyn & Bacon. Copyright © 2006 Pearson Education, Inc. Reproduced with permission.

but nevertheless they influence his/her life. It is the set of interactions and relationships among all the elements of the micro-system – the family members interacting with each other or with the teacher. Again, all relationships are reciprocal – the teacher influences the parents and the parents affect the teacher, and these interactions affect the child.

The mesosystem of interacting microsystems also interact with the exosystem, another layer which includes all the social settings that affect the child, even though the child is not a direct member of the system. Examples are the teachers' relations with school managers; parents' jobs; the community's resources for health, employment, or recreation; or the family's religious affiliation. The macrosystem is the larger society – its values, laws, conventions and traditions all of which influence the conditions and experiences of the child's life. These systems help us to think about the many dynamic forces that interact to create the context for individual development. We asked earlier 'Who is more influential, teachers or friends?' Well, according to Bronfenbrenner's model, teachers are part of the child's mesosystem and friends are part of the microsystem. Therefore friends are closer to the child than teachers and certainly closer than local employers or national politicians. Perhaps one of the problems with Bronfenbrenner's model is that it takes little account of different ecologies (interactions of people within their environment) that impact at different times during a lifespan. However, put simply, the earlier in life, the more influential homes and families will be.

Let us now return to a comparison of how cultural aspects can and do affect children's development. Despite children from both Sardinia and Rotterdam sharing the same 'macrosystem'– in this case the European Union – their early life experiences of their microsystems – close families – are likely to be very different. Families as microsystems are the mini-societies for young children, and each society will contain its own rituals and have particular expectations about how children will behave, how they should dress.

**Exosystem**
The cultural system outside the family, e.g. church or parents' employment.

**Macrosystem**
The larger society in which the family exists.

● ● ● ● ● ● ● ● ● ● ● ● ● ● ● ● ●
**Connect and Extend**
For an excellent enquiry into understanding how children develop in a cultural sense, see: Chan, E. (2004). Narratives of experience: How culture matters to children's development. *Contemporary Issues in Early Childhood*, 5, 145–159.
● ● ● ● ● ● ● ● ● ● ● ● ● ● ● ● ●

Perhaps we may have an oversimplified idea of the romantic, pastoral idyll of a childhood on the shores of the Mediterranean compared with children's experience of a high-pressure, industrialised and technocratic world of a modern European city. On closer inspection, the cultural experiences of children from Sardinia and the Netherlands are likely to have a number of common features with regard to work, play, parenting and societal experiences.

**Reflect**

Consider how the various systems in Bronfenbrenner's model in Figure 1.3 will affect the development of children in different cultural settings. Does the example, given recently of a child growing up in Sardinia compared with a child in Rotterdam, provide too little contrast? What examples would bring out more distinctive comparisons and what are the reasons for such distinctions?

It would appear that both historical and cultural comparisons of childhood tell us much about adult views of children and childhood. Renowned psychologists, Jerome Bruner and Helen Haste wrote: 'it can never be the case that there is a "self" independent of one's cultural-historical existence' (1987, p 91). Furthermore, associating the role of culture with children and families helps us avoid **ethnocentrism** and stereotyping, and allow us to view child development as fluid and adaptive. The *Focus on Theory* which follows provides an introduction to an international enquiry of childhood behaviour, the findings of which support a theory that children's views of self and adults' perspectives of childhood are **cultural-centric**.

**Connect and Extend**

For a study of family structures, functioning, roles and values, fundamental in family therapist's activities for better understanding the psychological, cultural and social factors for different clients and interventions read: The family in Romania: Cultural and economic context and implications for treatment by Mihai, A. & Butiu, O. (2012) *International Review of Psychiatry*, April 24(2), 139–143.

**Ethnocentrism**
Evaluating other races and cultures using criteria specific to one's own.

**Cultural-centric**
Views, beliefs and practices are restricted to a particular set of cultural values.

## Focus on Theory

### The Six Cultures Project

An early, but nonetheless illuminating study which investigated childhood in different cultures was the *Six Cultures Project* (Whiting & Whiting, 1975). This historical study was the first systematic investigation of children's behaviours in a range of different cultures around the world and provided detailed information on children's social interaction, play and their relationships with adults. Taking place in six contrasting settings, the research team recorded behaviour of the Rajputh (India), Baco (Philippines), Mixtecans (Mexico), North Americans (USA), Gusii (Kenya) and the Hokan (Okinawa) cultures.

Findings of this study revealed that each culture had its own set of expectations and behaviour for its children. The Gusii of Nyasongo in Kenya, for example, emphasised early training for work in their agricultural society, with children of 7 assuming many adult responsibilities. In contrast, the Baco tribe in the Philippines believed that development was a slow process that cannot be hurried. In the Kahalapur district of India, the Rajputh viewed their children as passive beings in need of protection. Play was a major feature in the activities of children in all the cultures studied but the nature of play varied too. In Kenyan society at that time, children's play was found to resemble adult activities. Children hunted and built huts, and play was seen to be a rehearsal for the later adult way of life. The North American children in the study also played and although this play also imitated adult activities, it was centred around the work of adults in the home and playing with toys.

A later study of the same cultures (Whiting & Edwards, 1988) revealed how the interactions of adults and children differed according to societal expectations and that these expectations varied according to the stages of development. Kahalapur mothers hand-fed children of 5 and bathed those as old as 11 years. In the extended family culture of Kenya, children were taught to respect their elders and were discouraged from initiating interactions with adults. Childhood was a period for instructing children in skills appropriate for adult life but again this varied according to culture. In predominately agricultural societies, many important skills were taught by adults to children. In societies with more complex economies, being literate was seen as an important skill to be mastered early in life.

Mothers of children in the Orchard Town district in the United States, and who were at home all day with their children, provided early instruction in self-feeding, encouraged self-reliance by encouraging children to play. Mothers also postponed instruction to daughters in the skills of motherhood. This is in contrast to societies with less developed industry or technology where children are skilled in caring for younger siblings from an early age.

These two studies showed that there are goals for childhood that are universal, but that there are also stark cultural differences which relate to a society's economy, social organisation and value systems. Data from both studies also showed that adults across all the cultures consciously changed their behaviour according to the age and gender of the children and many believed that age affected children's capabilities to learn and perform skills in that society.

## Summary 2

Before moving on, let's summarise what we have learned in the middle section of this chapter:

- In a brief history of child development we considered childhood as a distinct phase of development within the course of a lifespan development perspective.
- We explored the philosophical differences between considering the child as a *tabula rasa* (Locke) and as an active being already in possession of personality and intellect (Rousseau).
- The scientific study of child development can be traced back to Darwin (English evolutionary scientist), Preyer (German developmental scientist) and Hall (pioneer of American psychology).
- Six factors influence the scientific study of child development: the development of
  - systematic study;
  - universal public education;
  - new childhood agencies;
  - research into children's thinking;
  - public care services;
  - parenting skills.
- Children's development is affected in complex and profound ways by the culture in which they grow up and the factors can be represented in Urie Bronfenbrenner's bio-ecological model of development (1989).
- The findings of international enquiries of childhood behaviour support a theory that children's views of self and adults' perspectives of childhood are cultural-centric.

We have been concerned with trying to understand factors influencing the study of child development. Much of the argument has, by necessity, been theoretical in nature. Now we need to see these theoretical perspectives in the practical context of how professionals work with children. In the final section of this chapter we will look at how to best work with children, how to achieve developmentally appropriate teaching and how to develop a framework for study by considering key questions, controversies and themes.

# Principles of child development

## Why is the study of child development important?

Many texts on child development articulate reasons why the study of child development is important. Some suggest that study enables us to know more about children, to glean information about human nature, to learn more about the origins of certain developmental problems (e.g. Down's syndrome, dyslexia, attention-deficit hyperactivity disorder) or to gain further insight into adult behaviour. We understand these reasons to be important and relevant but we add one other important one: to appreciate that children develop holistically. Practitioners and educators need to work with children in ways that appreciate uniqueness. There are different rates and patterns of development but – and this is a very big 'but' – the study of child development tells us how to best work with children now, and is not an accurate predictor of individual future achievement.

In furthering our understanding of children and their development, it is wise to remember that children function as complete human beings. In school and at home, children bring all their complexities and experiences to each situation. Although it is often convenient to subdivide children's development into various sections either by domain or by age stage, the holistic nature of child development means there is an equal need to emphasise the continuity of development, since it is the accumulation of experiences from every aspect of development that creates what the child is today (Poddiakov, 2011). Aspects or domains of development addressed separately (such as physical, intellectual, linguistic, social and emotional functioning) need to be treated and interpreted as making the expansive and interdisciplinary field of development more accessible to the reader. These aspects should not be considered discrete because each domain influences and is influenced by the others (Berk, 2006). By taking an holistic approach to studying child development, you can gain a more informed approach to optimising children's development and learning, an important idea to which we now turn.

**Connect and Extend**
For a good example of difficulties with predicting future literacy achievement, read: Simpson, J. & Everatt, J. (2005). Reception class predictors of literacy skills. *British Journal of Educational Psychology*, 75, 171–188.

## Optimising children's development and learning

In any group of children there are apparent differences between children of the same chronological age, for example, in their height, build, skills, energy and disposition to learning. Practitioners have to work with both the apparent differences and the antecedents of difference among the pupils. For example, practitioners have to plan for learning, to teach and assess effectively, to respond sensitively to individual needs and to teach in inclusive ways.

**Antecedents**
Earlier events and circumstances; what happened, or what was before, to bring about the present situation.

**Reflect** | Visualise the face of the most effective teacher you had at school. What was his or her name? What were the characteristics of your most effective teacher? What skills and knowledge did they bring to teaching? What set this effective teacher apart from other teachers you remember?

Effective teaching is predicated on an understanding of how a child's physical, cognitive, linguistic, social and emotional development affects his or her learning. Good practitioners, as well as having other attributes and skills, are experts in child development. Knowledge gained by reading this book will enable you to recognise this important link between development and learning, and how practitioners plan and implement learning episodes that are developmentally appropriate to the needs of the young people they work with. Here are some specific ways (Hughes, 2011) in which developmentally appropriate teaching is achieved.

Effective practitioners:

- have a greater understanding of general patterns of development in children from pre-school to the end of primary school;
- recognise the extent and importance of development in the years preceding formal schooling (0–5);
- understand that early learning occurs through the integration of sensory, motor, perceptual and cognitive mechanisms;
- know that early learning is high speed, enduring and critical;
- can identify milestones in both fine and gross motor development;
- appreciate how learning is linked to perceptual development as a cognitive activity;
- relate processes of thinking, learning and problem-solving to intellectual development;
- understand that language organises, represents and expresses knowledge – language acquisition and cognitive development are profoundly linked;
- recognise how children's feelings about themselves and towards their peers can affect their learning and achievement;
- know that adults' responses affect children's emotional development.

By recognising important connections, this deep understanding about child development can become integral in planning learning experiences, in making use of strategies for grouping children, differentiating work to more closely match ability, and setting appropriate individual targets in all areas of learning.

## Adopting a framework to develop personal principles

To become expert in child development and to develop personal principles is to know, to understand and be able to apply what you have learned in your work with children. To help you focus on these learning objectives, we suggest you consider a historic and much referenced framework for studying child development (Baltes *et al.*, 1980). The framework 'constructed' by Paul Baltes, Professor of Psychology at the Free University of Berlin, and his colleagues identifies three major goals: to describe, to explain, and to optimise development. Since the audience for this book is all those working with children, whether in schools, in the home, extended families, or care and play settings, an understanding of how to apply knowledge of children's development in practice is very relevant and permeates the narrative throughout this text.

You should think of description ('to describe', the first of Baltes' three major goals) as specifying how individuals change over time by tracing the characteristics of development from *in utero* (before birth) through to the end of the primary school years – not forgetting to see child development as part of the full lifespan. Explanations will be offered in the forthcoming chapters as to why children grow and behave as they do by making reference to each of the domains of development outlined earlier (physical, cognitive, social and emotional), and we will include examples of development from life settings. Finally, we will help you to apply your new knowledge and understanding by considering a range of strategies to optimise the conditions that promote children's development. Look at Figure 1.4 to see how the framework suggested by Paul Baltes and his colleagues can be applied to developing principles of child development.

## Applying principles of child development

Since the beginnings of education and other children's services, policy makers and professional practitioners have attempted to apply new knowledge and understandings – perhaps created using appropriate frameworks as in Figure 1.4. However, applying principles of child development in political and state structures is not without controversy because the interpretation of

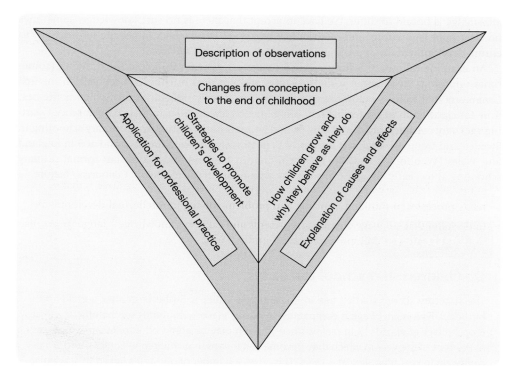

**Figure 1.4** A framework for becoming expert in child development

The outer framework describes major goals for any study in applied sciences and the inner framework is specific to child development.

*Source*: Based on Baltes, P. B., Reese, H. W. & Lipsitt, L. P. (1980). Life-span developmental psychology. In L. R. Goldberg, M. R. Rosenzweig, & L. W. Porter (Series Eds) *Annual Review of Psychology* (Vol. 31, 65–110). Palo Alto, CA: Annual Reviews. Reproduced with permission.

Too young for school? Children in England and Wales start school at 5 years old, younger than in many other European countries.

*Source*: © Pearson Education Ltd.

**Connect and Extend**

To look for developmentally appropriate issues in children's services, read: Swanson, M., Wall, S., Kisker, E. & Peterson, C. (2011). Health disparities in low-income families with infants and toddlers: Needs and challenges related to disability. *Journal of Child Health Care*, March, *15*(1), 25–38.

**Connect and Extend**

For another view of developmentally appropriate structures in children's services, read: Wilkinson, T. (2002). Developments in child and adolescent mental health services in the Netherlands. *Journal of Psychiatric & Mental Health Nursing*, *9*, 379–380.

knowledge is bound to differ. We have to accept that there is no sure knowledge, sometimes no clear right and wrong, and often only a best guess at how we can use the information to ensure developmentally appropriate structures in children's services.

An example follows in a feature called *Controversy* where we look at the differing (sometimes opposing) views about some structures and practices in children's services. In the first *Controversy* that follows below we examine the potentially difficult area of when is the best time for children to begin formal schooling. As described earlier in this chapter, school starting ages vary considerably across Europe and as a reminder, compulsory primary schooling in Sweden and Denmark begins at the age of 7, in Norway and Belgium at 6, and at 5 in England and Wales (Woolfolk *et al.*, 2012). Do children in England and Wales start formal primary schooling at too early an age? Consider the arguments in the following *Controversy* feature.

## Controversy

### Do children start school too early?

The statutory school starting age in England and Wales is 5 (the term after a child's fifth birthday). Five years of age is comparatively young as many countries set the official age at 6 or 7 (Black *et al.*, 2011). In reality, since children may be admitted into Reception classes at the start of the year in which they become 5, it means that children in England and Wales can begin formal schooling at 4 years. This raises a number of questions linked to academic achievement and developmental readiness, and the obvious question as to whether the starting age for English and Welsh children needs to be raised to be in line with that of other countries.

In a celebrated paper (1989), Martin Woodhead – the then Professor of Childhood Studies at the Open University, UK – explains the origins of early school starting age in England and Wales. He concludes that the 1870 Education Act was intended to protect children from domestic exploitation and to establish a school-leaving age that provided employers with a suitable age for children to enter the workforce. In the twenty-first century these same pressures no longer remain, but are replaced by the increasing practice of children starting school at the beginning of the year in which they become 5. Woodhead also believes that falling birth rates and the drive to give 'summer-borns' – those born between April and August – the same amount of time in schools as their older peers have been influential in schools now favouring annual admission policies.

In 2007 Sue Rogers and Janet Rose looked at the advantages and disadvantages of early entry to school. Their findings show that an early start to education does appear to be beneficial for young children, but the age at which they start may have potentially negative consequences if they are placed in an environment that is not suited to their developmental needs. This study by Rogers and Rose drew on studies over the last twenty years. For example, in 1998, Caroline Sharp – principal research officer for the British National Foundation for Education Research – cited two studies (Tymms *et al.*, 1997; Sharp & Hutchinson, 1997) that present clear findings to support a case for pupils in England and Wales starting formal schooling later. Professor Peter Tymms and colleagues at Durham University (1997) examined progress in mathematics and reading assessments in a sample of over 1000 children and found that children who were older in the year group performed better in both. In another study of over 114 schools, Caroline Sharp and Dougal Hutchinson (1997) found that attainment was related to age and season of birth. Older children (autumn born) who completed a full year performed best and younger children (summer born) who also completed a full year did not perform as well as class mates with one or two terms fewer in school. The authors suggest that the match between the developmental needs of younger 4-year-olds and the quality of provision in Reception classes is an important factor in the academic attainment of summer-born children.

In 1998 Mills and Mills investigated teaching in Hungary, Switzerland and Belgium for Channel 4 UK Television, and found strong similarities in curriculum content and teaching approaches. Although emphasis is placed on oral language and numeracy (alongside listening, attention, motor and memory skills), reading, writing and written maths are not part of the preschool curriculum. It is believed that some preschool children are not developmentally ready for such tasks. At age 6 on formal entry to primary school, reading, writing and numeracy skills develop rapidly. Mills and Mills suggest that the British practice of neglecting oral language and the introduction of abstract tasks – existing in thought alone – too early, are contributing to underachievement. In another earlier international study on reading literacy Elley (1992) found that the ten countries who began teaching reading at a mean average age of 6.3 years scored high in measures of pupil attainment, with Finland, Sweden, Norway and Iceland the highest. All these four countries began reading instruction at age 7. (These findings have been borne out in recent studies where different European school systems have been revisited to check out the currency of the original findings, e.g. Altwicker-Hámori & Köllö, 2012.)

Such a weight of evidence must surely fuel the debate for delaying the age children begin school and providing a curriculum that is developmentally appropriate for their needs. Do children in England and Wales begin formal primary school education too early?

# Key questions and themes in child development

Identifying the best age for beginning formal primary education is a key idea in child development, but it is not the only one. For over 150 years, those undertaking any kind of research into children's development have been confronted with a number of key questions that continue to exercise the minds of researchers and practitioners. What are those fundamental questions that are at the very heart of the study of children? These might stem directly from your own interest in picking up this book. Perhaps you are a professional working with or wishing to work with children, a trainee-teacher or an interested parent?

 **Reflect** — **From your own professional learning perspective, list some key questions that you expect to be addressed in this text. What for you are the big issues and themes?**

Perhaps some of your questions are similar to those below:

- What is the first memory we have?
- What does the world look like to a newborn baby?
- What makes us similar . . . but then so different in other ways?
- How can children in the same family appear to be different?
- Who is really responsible for the care and upbringing of our children?
- How does where we live influence our development?

- How do we learn language? How is it that some young children can speak several languages fluently but have never been formally taught any?

- How does growing up in the twenty-first century differ from growing up 100 years ago? What place do the new technologies have in the lives of children?

- Is one form of education superior to another and what of those children who are schooled at home?

These questions are typical of the puzzles of child development. Developmental psychologists combine many of these key questions, these recurring puzzles into themes that provide a connected context for the detail of their research. For the purposes of clarity and structure, we have identified five key themes of child development.

## Is development a continuous process or one of stages?

•  •  •  •  •  •  •  •  •  •  •  •  •
**Connect and Extend**

Take your thinking to a new level. Formal thought processes such as abstract thinking are fascinating and the presence of formal thought disorder (FTD) in childhood is sometimes viewed as a possible precursor of psychotic symptoms. Read: Bruin, E. I., de; Verheij, F., Wiegman, T. & Ferdinand, R. F. (2007). Assessment of formal thought disorder: The relation between the Kiddie Formal Thought Disorder Rating Scale and clinical judgment. *Psychiatry Research*, January, *149*(1–3), 239–246.
•  •  •  •  •  •  •  •  •  •  •  •  •

Here we consider if development is smooth and progressive, or rather a series of discrete stages like a plateaux of development with little changing during each stage, but with new behaviours marking a change of stage. The issue is whether development mirrors slow and steady changes over time, like a flower unfolding, or the defined stages of being that a caterpillar goes through to become a butterfly. In the next chapter you will read about theorists such as Albert Bandura whose social learning theory (1977) views development as a continuous process and Jean Piaget who advocates a discontinuous perspective and who proposes the existence of stages. In Piaget's theory (1952b), children's thinking between the ages of 7 and 11 years is deemed to be 'concrete' since they can understand that an object such as a lump of Plasticine remains the same mass even when moulded into a different shape. In adolescence, teenagers will be much more able to think in abstract ways, for example, about 'objects' not in the real and tangible world, such as in advanced mathematical or scientific problems.

Changes over time may appear very definitely stage-like in appearance, particularly when comparing the thinking and behaviour of a 3-year-old to that of a 9-year-old. However, observing changes on a much smaller scale, perhaps weekly, would show a picture of development that is more continuous. Consider the following story.

Marco (aged 8 months) peered into the large basket of toys his grandparents had put together for him. Carefully he reached into the basket and grasped a small rattle. After looking at this for a few seconds, this was dropped. Marco got hold of the basket with one hand and tipped it forward. With his other hand he reached back into the basket and fumbled around before selecting a bright blue plastic frog. 'Marco!', exclaimed his mother, 'I've not seen you do that before!' In a matter of a few weeks, Marco's reaching and grasping, control over movement and understanding of location has enabled this to take place. Is this development that is steadily increasing or a complete new stage?

When answering this question, most psychologists take the view that development has both elements of continuity (gradual and unbroken) and discontinuity (separate stages marked by major changes). Indeed, influential psychologists Robert Sternberg and Lynn Okagaki (1989) suggested that the attempt to characterise development as uniformly continuous or discontinuous is based on the false presupposition of an 'either–or' debate. They considered attempts at any such debate to be misleading and that the real question for developmental psychologists is to find out how these continuous and more discrete aspects arise in the course of development.

We consider this analysis to be accurate. Development should be considered as being largely continuous but having certain stages characterised by 'milestone' changes, due to developmental processes. For example one 'milestone' – starting to walk – requires a biological

*Source*: © Pearson Education Ltd / Jules Selmes.

maturity of around 9–14 months where this new skill is clearly different from the child's abilities in previous months. See the *Reflect* below for a personal example. In the months that follow, the walking skill slowly and steadily improves during the toddler stage. Findings on qualitative changes in children's thinking and problem-solving abilities in mathematics (Rittle-Johnson & Siegler, 1998) support this combined viewpoint of milestone changes that characterise identifiable stages and steady improvement and development during each stage.

**Reflect**

Consider these two examples from the authors' parenting experiences. Jonathan recalls that his two boys began to walk at quite different times. In contrast, Mal's three children all walked for the first time within a few days of each of their first birthday and he remembers being amazed that nature's clock was keeping such accurate time! Was there an inbuilt programme that decided the day of those first few steps, or did he and his wife happen to provide the right encouragement and circumstances? Was it heredity or environment?

## What roles do heredity and training play?

Above all other themes in child development, the issue of 'nature versus nurture' has caused most debate! Nature, our genetic inheritance, refers to what is biologically bequeathed from our parents at the moment of conception. Nurture refers to training and education that influence our physical and psychological state after birth. These factors include and are evident in parenting, child-care practices and choices as to what type of schooling is best for children. Nurture is the powerful experiences of interacting with others who teach us skills, knowledge and help us to form understandings. For example, the question of whether children acquire language from being pre-programmed to do so (the brain being 'hard-wired' for language acquisition), or as a result of learning it from parents, siblings and teachers, fits into this theme of heredity versus environment. Think back to the earlier story of Victor, the Wild Boy of Aveyron (p 5). What is the significance of the observation that Victor managed to learn only a very basic vocabulary and found it very hard to associate normally with other people? Now consider the following story about Maria and Helena.

Maria, 9-years-old, and her sister Helena, who is 7, live in an apartment in the outskirts of Madrid. Their parents have tried to give both children similar experiences and share their time equally between them both. Friends of the family and teachers have commented that it is difficult to see both girls as sisters. Maria is average height for her age, if a little underweight. She enjoys playing with her friends and has a keen interest in swimming and ballet. Helena is tall for her age with dark hair, compared with Maria's light auburn. She prefers to spend her time reading at home. She feels awkward in the company of adults and has few close friends of her own.

How do you account for the differences between Maria and Helena? Have Maria and Helena made life choices (reading or ballet) that are a result of genetic differences between them, or were there subtle differences in their environment that pushed them in one direction or another? The influence of the environment on development has been described by the influential environmental psychologist Joachim Wohlwill using four different metaphors (1973). Even after 40 or so years his descriptions remain relevant and helpful. Firstly, he compares the influence of environment on development as an amusement park where you choose your ride but once on this there is no getting off, just as we have some choice over what we want to experience in life, but have no control over its effect on us. Secondly, he compares the influence of environment to a hospital bed, where, as patients, we have no control over the environment and wait for factors and events outside our control to dictate what happens to us. Thirdly, he compares the influence of the environment to swimming in a race where the starting gun (your genetic makeup) signals the start of the race and the pool is the environment that supports your behaviour. Finally, he compares the influence of the environment to a tennis match with its obvious interaction between players and constant change in circumstances.

The metaphor of the amusement park seems particularly useful as it more closely reflects the developing ability of children to make decisions based on their growing knowledge of themselves and of their formative experiences. For example, choosing the 'Waltzers' as a ride and not the 'Helter-Skelter' can have an important impact on a child's physical as well as emotional well-being, even if only temporarily. Similarly, choosing one group of friends or one set of activities over another can have a significant effect on what children achieve and become. So which is more influential, our family history (nature) or how we are brought up and the decisions we make (nurture)?

**Epigenesis**
The interaction between forces of environment (nurture) and factors of heredity (nature).

Historically, theorists have taken opposing stances on this question of **epigenesis** – the interaction of nature and nurture. Those advocating the importance of heredity, such as developmental psychologist Arnold Gesell (1928), believed that genetic processes led naturally to the changes in growth through maturation. In contrast, behaviourists such as John Broadus Watson – once called the father or founder of behaviourism (Plaud, 1991) – held that the training and appropriate education shaped the course of a child's development regardless of genetic makeup. Rather like the argument between seeing development as stages or as continuous, the current view – an interactionist stance (Perovic & Radenovic, 2011) – is one that accepts neither nature nor nurture as more or less influential on development. It is more common nowadays to talk of how nature and nurture interact, rather than to see one or the other as being more influential.

## How important are individual differences and situational factors?

**Sociocultural context**
The knowledge and cultural tools that a child acquires from other members of the community.

Because children grow up in such diverse environments, the social settings in which they live will clearly have effects upon some aspects of their development. The home, playgroup, nursery, school and local neighbourhood together form a child's **sociocultural context**. The issue in this theme is to what extent children's sociocultural context determines who they are and the type of people they will become.

This theme is similar to the second theme, 'nature versus nurture', particularly with regard to the influence of hereditary factors, but perhaps the subtle difference is that it is the influence of social factors that is in question in this the third key theme of child development, rather than the nature of care, education and encouragement a child receives. Do traits of personality, for example, remain unaltered in every social situation or change according to the situation? Can we really expect the shy child who is normally reserved in class and who appears to be reluctant to answer aloud, to exhibit similar traits in the company of peers? In the story below, personality characteristics normally associated with aggression find an outlet in a martial arts class.

Ben is 10 years old and the only child of loving parents who live with him. From an early age, his parents found Ben difficult to cope with. He seemed to have boundless energy and was constantly striving to challenge himself physically. He found relationships with his peers difficult, feeling a need to compete against them and show off his physical prowess. In the last three to four years, this has become worse and at school he was labelled as 'aggressive' owing to his playground behaviour. He now wants to join a new karate class set up in the town but his parents believe this would not be right for him and would lead to increases in his aggressive behaviour. Is this the right decision? What would you advise?

Recall environmental psychologist Joachim Wohlwill's first metaphor of the amusement park. We suggested that choosing a particular ride (e.g. the Waltzers) can have a big impact on the chooser. Choosing certain friends and pastimes, such as Ben's karate for example, either for the child when younger or allowing choice by the child when older, can have a substantial impact, particularly on emotional and social development. Sociocultural factors can affect children's feelings about themselves and how they express themselves emotionally. Once again, any controversy can be resolved by accepting that social contexts and individual characteristics are both influencing factors in development (Makagon, 2012).

## Do children play active or passive roles in their own development?

The previous themes have illustrated the controversies surrounding them and the often contrasting views taken by writers and theorists. This theme of activity and passivity is not one that has the same dichotomy of views in the present day. As we have seen earlier in this chapter, some theorists (check back to remind yourself who we are talking about) viewed the child as a passive being who was shaped by the environment and by the influence of parents and other significant adults. Contemporary thinking on this issue (heavily influenced by Jean Piaget) views children as active seekers of information, shaping and eager to direct the course of their own development (Bugental & Goodnow, 1998). In this view, the child is perceived as an agent who is responsible for his or her own behaviour, has some degree of freedom of choice regarding actions and is capable of giving reasons for those choices. In the context of education and care, this view is illustrated in the story below.

Mr and Mrs Patel are taking their child for the first time to a local nursery for children aged 3–4 years. As they enter the building they are met by an atmosphere of calmness and activity. Children are busily engaged in drawing and mask-making, some pouring water into different sized containers, and three children are using small spades and trowels in a sand trough. At one table the children are sitting with jigsaws and others are building with large construction blocks on a carpeted area of the room. Adult helpers facilitate and support this but do not lead or direct. Children are actively engaged in their work and play. They are choosing their activities, making their own decisions.

*Source:* © Pearson Education Ltd / Jules Selmes.

This story shows that children are clearly not *tabula rasa* – blank slates upon which experience writes – like John Locke believed. (You might refer back to our brief history of child development earlier in the chapter, pp 9–11.) Instead of being passive recipients of their environment, children actively engage in their environments. They already possess character traits of curiosity and persistence from their biological inheritance; they also construct meaning about the world from their interactions with it. Inherited character traits encourage one child to be shy of others, while another is more extrovert; or to show a particular talent for music, sport or language or mathematics. Experience sustains or suppresses traits, characteristics and interests, usually as the experience of 'success' feeds the motivation to strive for more and the experience of failure can destroy confidence.

## What is the relationship between the different areas of development?

As previously argued, separating the domains of development is for the convenience of study only. The holistic nature of development is a truer picture and strongly emphasised in this book. Development does not proceed in one area and pause while another area 'takes over'. There is no stage-like development taking place in one area at a time. As we have already emphasised, individual differences due to biological inheritance and the effects of environment are mighty influences on a child's development. Continuous and continuing development occurs for every child albeit at difference paces in all domains, rather than happening in isolation.

Misunderstanding of this important point can lead to variance in the expectations of adults. For example, a tall 11-year-old whose physical appearance suggests certain advancement in physical maturity, may well display social, language or intellectual development that is much less advanced. Similarly, the physically smaller child of the same age may be much more advanced in other domains. It is important that the whole picture is taken into account as well as an awareness of individual differences. In understanding the interrelated nature of development, it is important to appreciate how the areas of development do overlap. This **synergy** can be seen in the practical example of Monique.

**Synergy**
The combined effect or action of two or more (areas of development) that exceeds the sum of the individual (area).

Monique is 9-months-old. Over the past few months, her mother and father have helped to feed her and encouraged her to hold the plastic cup on her high chair and guide it to Monique's lips. The cup sits in front of her as usual but one morning while waiting, she looks at it intently [perception] and moves a hand towards it. At first she knocks the cup but then grasps it firmly and raises it off the plastic tray [physical]. 'Oooh', she gurgles [language] as her mother rushes over smiling and saying, 'What a clever girl. Well done Monique!' Monique beams back at her [social] and gurgles again.

9-month-old Monique.

*Source*: © Pearson Education Ltd / Jules Selmes.

Can you see how the different areas of development are linked in the example of Monique? Balance is the key to understanding the themes presented. You may have definite views on a particular theme and may take one side's view while dismissing the other, or indeed you may choose to keep an open mind. As understanding of human development increases, contemporary views on these themes have tended to take a less radical stance. For example, as mentioned earlier, the sometimes over-rehearsed 'nature versus nurture' debate is now replaced by the debate of how nature and nurture work together (Stables, 2012).

We now summarise what you have learned in the final section of this chapter:

- The study of child development tells us how to best work with children now, and should not be considered as an accurate predictor of individual future achievement.
- Effective practice with children begins with an understanding of how a child's physical, cognitive, linguistic, social and emotional development affects his or her learning. Some specific ways were suggested by which developmentally appropriate practice is achieved.
- A framework for the study of child development was suggested, formed around controversies, key questions and themes.
- One example of a controversy was explored. 'Do children start school too early?' 'What is the best age to begin formal schooling?'
- Key questions were posed and included 'How do we learn language? How do we explain that some children learn language much more quickly than others?'
- Five major themes of child development building on the the historical 'nature versus nurture' argument were explored:
  - development as continuous or in stages;
  - the roles of heredity and training;
  - individual differences and situational factors;
  - children as active or passive in their own development; and
  - the relationship between different areas of development.

**Summary 3**

## Conclusion

In this opening chapter, you have been encouraged to appreciate the various domains of children's development but also to adopt a holistic view, the sort exemplified by the *Every Child Matters* agenda. All those who work with children in England have to 'take on board' *Every Child Matters*, a national initiative that continues to ask profound questions of the children's workforce; have we truly taken on the lessons learned during 150 years of study of child development?

In 2003, the UK Government published a green paper called *Every Child Matters* (DfES, 2003b). This was published alongside the formal response to the report into the death of Victoria Climbié, a young girl who was horrifically abused and tortured, and eventually killed by her great-aunt and the man with whom they lived. In response to these tragic events, the UK Government published *Every Child Matters: The Next Steps*, and passed the Children Act 2004.

*Every Child Matters: Change for Children* (2004) was a new approach in England to the well-being of children and young people from birth to age 19. Its main implication is to see all members of the children's workforce as members of a professional team working in and through extended school provision. An excellent child worker is one who can work well as a member of a team of teachers, social workers, police officers and health workers, and who can lead a team of counsellors, advanced skills teachers and learning support staff, to ensure the well-being of children. *Every Child Matters* defines the outcomes for children and therefore the rights of children to: be healthy; stay safe; enjoy and achieve; make a positive contribution; and achieve economic well-being. Together these outcomes for children define the end result of a 'childhood journey' successfully made. At the time of writing this 2nd edition of *Child Development* it is not clear that the current Coalition Government is willing to press ahead with the original aspirations of the *Every Child Matters* agenda despite the tragic story of Baby P.

• • • • • • • • • • • • • • • • •
**Connect and Extend**
For details of what happened to Victoria Climbié, read: Rustin, M. (2004). Learning from the Victoria Climbié Inquiry. *Journal of Social Work Practice, 18*, 9–18. An Internet search of the relevant government websites will provide information about the current standing of the *Every Child Matters* agenda.
• • • • • • • • • • • • • • • • •

Peter Connelly (also known as 'Baby P' and 'Baby Peter') was a 17-month old British boy who died in London after suffering multiple injuries over an eight-month period, during which he was repeatedly seen by NHS health professionals and Haringey Children's services and professionals. The case caused shock and disgust among the public and in Parliament, partly because of the horrific nature of Peter's injuries, and also because Peter had lived in the area of North London, under the same child-care authorities that had already failed ten years earlier in the case of Victoria Climbié.

We haven't yet discussed the outcomes of *Every Child Matters* with Edd and Ella Hogan. However, we are sure the five rights and outcomes are what they would hope for their daughter Niamh, who we met for the first time at the beginning of this chapter. During the course of a childhood journey children are supported, encouraged, taught and cared for by parents such as Edd and Ella, and practitioners who must know about how best to ensure the rights of the children for whom they are responsible. The study of child development provides an excellent beginning to understanding those rights and ensuring the outcomes required by *Every Child Matters: Change for Children* and *The Good Childhood Report 2012* which we discussed in the *Policy Research and Praxis* feature earlier in the chapter.

So far, key questions have been raised that encourage you to take a broad view of the themes and theories of child development, and to view these same themes and theories as highly relevant to what you do as a parent, carer or teacher. Remember from the beginning of this chapter that both Professor Winston and Edd Hogan saw and understood the enormous potential for growth, change and development in the two newborns, Kirsty and Niamh. In the next chapter we will begin to make sense of the almost incredible changes that will happen in the lives of these two young children. We will identify important theoretical approaches in child development and start to interpret theories of childhood in relevant contexts. In identifying and making sense of theoretical approaches, and by exploring some of the controversial issues they raise, you will begin to construct your own understanding of child development.

## Summary Table
### Issues in Child Development

## Defining child development (pp 4–9)

### What is child development? (pp 4–5)

Child development is the study of changes in children over the timespan of childhood from conception to adulthood. It is the study of changes due to both maturation and learning, and these changes can be represented either in age-related phases or by referring to domains of development – physical, cognitive or social/emotional.

### Terms of development (pp 5–6)

It is a scientific study – but not experimental as observations of children's changing abilities and characteristics take place in natural settings such as homes and schools. Such observations are made by expert observers who are systematic and precise, and build their perceptions into theories. Knowledge of these theories helps those who nurture children to check that all is well and 'going to plan'.

### Stages of development (pp 7–8)

Child development is the study of changes due to both maturation (following the genetic plan) and learning (change due to experience). Such changes can be represented either in age-related phases or by referring to domains of development – physical, cognitive or social/emotional.

## A history of child development (pp 9–16)

### The beginnings of child development (pp 9–11)

During the 'Age of Enlightenment' a philosophical dichotomy developed between views of a child as a *tabula rasa* – a clean slate (Locke) – and children as active beings, already in possession of personality and intellect (Rousseau).

### The scientific study of child development (pp 11–12)

Factors influencing the scientific study of child development (traced back to Darwin, Preyer and Hall) were identified as new interests in: scientific methods of enquiry; teaching methods and standards of education in newly established universal public education systems; children's health including social and emotional development; and parenting. These factors were related to the growing demand for authentic information from those responsible for the nurture of children.

### Cross-cultural contexts of childhood (pp 12–16)

Children's development is affected in complex and profound ways by the culture in which they grow up and cultural influences can be represented in models of development such as that of Urie Bronfenbrenner (1989). The findings of international enquiries of childhood behaviour support a conclusion that children's views of self and adults' views of childhood are cultural-centric.

## Principles of child development (pp 17–21)

### Why is the study of child development important? (p 17)

A study of child development tells us how to best work with children now, but should not be considered as an accurate predictor of individual future achievement.

### Optimising children's development and learning (pp 17–18)

Developmentally appropriate teaching begins with an understanding of how a child's physical, cognitive, linguistic, social and emotional development affects his or her learning.

### Adopting a framework to develop personal principles (p 18)

A framework for the study of child development was suggested formed around controversies, for example, 'Do children start school too early?' and key questions including 'How do we explain that some children learn language much more quickly than others?'

## Key questions and themes in child development (pp 21–27)

Some major and contrasting themes of child development to be explored are: continuous development versus stages of development; the influence of heredity – the 'nature versus nurture' argument, training and the sociocultural context; contrasting views of children as active and passive learners; and the potential synergy of these key themes.

## Going further

Newton, M. (2003) *Savage girls and wild boys: a history of feral children.* **Faber and Faber, new edition.**
A collection of six individual histories including The Wild Boy of Aveyron, caught running naked in woods in provincial France in 1800 which formed the basis for a memorable film by Truffaut. Another film by the German director Werner Herzog dramatises the appearance of Kaspar Hauser in the streets of early nineteenth-century Nuremberg, after a mysterious 16-year imprisonment in a dark and tiny cellar. (Try an Internet search for excerpts from the films.)

Stearns P. N. (2010) *Childhood in world history (Themes in world history).* **Routledge; 2nd edition.**
The book is organised chronologically, moving from agricultural and classical civilisations to 'modern' childhood in

the twentieth century. It includes a fascinating chapter on the history of children's happiness.

Rousseau, J.-J. (2004) *Emile: Or, on education.* **Public Domain Books.**
Rousseau explores the ideas of a natural education and upbringing, and questions the very foundations of society.

Hughes, D. (2009) *Principles of attachment-focused parenting: Effective strategies to care for children.* **Norton Professional Books.**
Attachment theory is an important idea in your study of child development. Look ahead to Chapter 11 (Emotions and Personality). Daniel Hughes' book attempts to equip caregivers with practical parenting techniques rooted in attachment theory and research.

# Chapter 2
## Theories of Child Development

### Overview

# Introduction

In the opening chapter, we discussed the various stages and themes of child development, and we encouraged you to view the ideas you met as highly relevant to what you do or plan to do as a professional practitioner, therapist, teacher or parent. In this chapter we will identify important theoretical approaches in child development and start to interpret those theories in relevant contexts. We want to give you a flavour of the range of theories that have been developed and to provide a 'helicopter view' of the main theoretical perspectives – the developmental legacy of the last hundred years or so. This is important and exciting reading because theories are like foundation stones upon which we build our practice. Without theory it would be impossible to make sense of the complex world of children, and if we cannot make sense of their world, how best can we encourage and support children's development?

First, a story. A group of adults are sitting around the long table in the middle of the school library. The meeting hasn't started yet and there is a general shuffling of papers and murmered conversation. The headteacher clears her throat and looks around the table. 'Can I call the meeting to order please. Welcome everybody. I would like to start by asking Mrs Britten – Dale's class teacher – to remind us where we are with Dale.'

Mrs Britten looks around the table a little apprehensively. Gathered around are a paediatric nurse, a family counsellor, a social worker, the educational psychologist and the school Special Needs Co-ordinator. This is the 'Team around the Child' formed by the Local Authority to co-ordinate the work of the practitioners supporting Dale and his family. Mrs Britten glances at her notes and begins.

'Dale is a non-identical 7 year-old twin brother. Both boys, Dale and Robert were taken into care not long after they were born as their mother was a drug addict. The boys lived with foster parents until they were $2\frac{1}{2}$. They now live with their maternal grandmother who they call "Mum".

The boys are fiercely competitive and argue most of the time. They are very physical with each other and Dale has been known to self-harm. The boys have got persistently worse at home so Grandmother is struggling more and more.

Last September the boys were placed in my class which lasted $2\frac{1}{2}$ weeks before they had to be separated. They were physically and mentally abusive to each other and Dale would be the same with other children in the class. At first the class was a very tense and scared group of people, adults and children alike, as the boys could fly off the handle at a moment's notice.

Recently Mr Jones (a visiting behaviour therapist) observed Dale for an hour and claimed that he was "angelic", that the school was doing a fantastic job and that there was nothing he need do. I am afraid to say that his visit was no use at all.'

The headteacher cleared her throat again and Mrs Britten fell silent. 'Thank you. I am sure we have benefitted from the guidance of Mr Jones and the reassurance that we are making progress.' 'But we aren't, and neither is Dale.' Mrs Britten looked a little tearful. 'I try to do everything you all suggest, but it makes no practical difference. What you say is all very well in theory, but. . . .'

Interpreted from case notes made and used in Hughes, M. W. H. 'Developmental psychology and education', in Gillibrand, R., Lam, V. & O'Donnell, V. (2012) *Developmental psychology*. Harlow: Pearson Education.

**Chapter Objectives**

By the time you have completed this chapter you should be able to answer the following questions:

- What is a theory?
- Why is theory necessary and valuable in the study of child development?
- What are the most important and influential developmental theories?
- How can we evaluate the usefulness of theories?
- How can we interpret developmental theories in relevant contexts?

# The purpose of theory

## What is theory?

As in other forms of scientific research, child development is based upon the observation of the phenomena – the happenings – of childhood. Systematic observations are organised into patterns of behaviour that have antecedents and consequences. You can think of this as the ABC of theory generation: the way in which we make sense of what we observe is to construct meanings from the Antecedents, Behaviour and Consequences of particular phenomena. If these observations are conducted in reliable and valid ways (the **scientific method**) then the meanings we construct are more likely to apply to more children than just the individuals or groups the scientist observes (see Figure 2.1). Scientific observations are real and factual, yet facts alone do not make a science. What is needed is a way of combining and interpreting facts, and theories are the way that science makes sense of what scientists observe and record.

**Scientific method**
The application of scientific principles in an orderly manner and with the appropriate technique, to find an answer to a question.

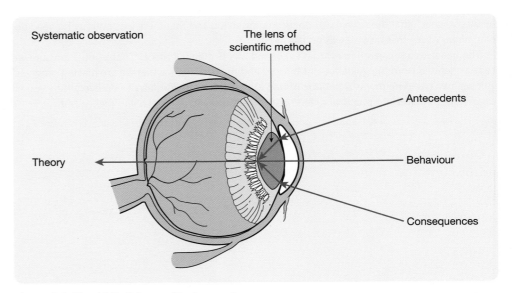

**Figure 2.1**  The ABC of theory development

Figure 2.1 depicts systematic observation of behaviour, its antecedents and consequences. A theory is formed (in the context of child development) by the systematic observation of how children behave, in what context (the antecedents) and the consequences of the behaviour for the child and for others around the child. The scientific method acts like a lens, to focus these observations and organise them in order to create a theory about the behaviour being observed. In Chapter 3 there is a personal account of one of the authors sitting on the landing at 2 a.m. and studying the miracle that was – and is – his first daughter Rebecca, as she played with her toys. You will be able to judge to what extent observations of Becca exploring her world were systematic or just the normal behaviour of a doting father. Whether systematic or not, such observations are by itself not enough to support the development of theory. We also need explanations of the changes of behaviour by considering earlier observations, contextual or environmental factors and physical changes, for example growth. These are the antecedents of the behaviour we are observing. At the same time we should also consider the consequences of the observed changes in behaviour for future development. These three sets of observations are concurrent and inter-dependent, and for most of us the meanings we derive – the sense we make – of our observations are intuitive and thoroughly naturalistic. Together, and over time, systematic observations can be used to create theories about how and why we think children develop as they do.

What do we mean by a theory? Here goes – a theory is a system of concepts that connect to form a framework of ideas that promote understanding. Burrhus Skinner (usually known as B. F. Skinner), a highly influential American psychologist, author and inventor, provides a more precise definition of the development of theory using scientific methods:

> **It is an attempt to discover order, to show that certain events stand in lawful relations to other events. The methods of science are designed to clarify these uniformities and make them explicit.**

(Skinner, 1953, p 35)

As a means of combining diverse ideas into a coherent framework, theories are either formal, and take the form of laws or axioms, or informal – which might be likened to being one stage on from our intuitive feelings about the world. Before going further, we need to understand the origin of scientific theory in order to appreciate the importance of using scientific methods to make sense of laws and axioms, and of the theories of child development. To find the origin of these theories we need to take a trip back in history to the time of Ancient Greek philosopher and scientist, Aristotle.

**Reflect**

**What theories do you know? Take no more than five minutes to note down all the scientific theories and laws you can remember. For example, you may remember the name of Einstein's General Theory of Relativity and the detail of Newton's Third Law of Motion: 'For every action there is an equal and opposite reaction'. Write lists under two headings: *Theories* and *Laws*. Once finished – what do you think turns a theory into a law? Do all laws start out as theories?**

Refer back to Figure 2.1. The observations of behaviour, its antecedents and consequences are 'focused' by application of scientific method to 'show that certain events stand in lawful relation to other events' as Skinner argued. The use of scientific methods to create theory has a long and exciting history, perhaps beginning with the Ancient Greek philosopher and scientist, Aristotle (384–322 BC), who founded the science we know as logic. The Greek word *logos* translates as 'reason'. Aristotle was the most prominent pupil at the Academy created by the Greek philosopher Plato (427–347 BC) who, in turn, was the first great thinker to use the term 'philosophy', derived from two Greek words: *philos* meaning loving and *sophia*, wisdom. Plato's philosophy did not accept that scientific experiment could establish any facts, because he considered the mind as the primary source of wisdom. However, Aristotle became critical of Plato, arguing that all things are subject to change and therefore observation of change was

**Theory**
A framework of concepts that assist in organising and explaining observations.

**Laws**
Statements describing an unchanging relationship between observations made for all cases in the same context: e.g. the law of gravity (because the apple always falls given the same conditions of temperature and pressure anywhere on the Earth's surface).

**Axioms**
Self-evident principles or ones that are accepted as true without proof. For example: any two points can be joined with a straight line.

the key to wisdom. This chimes well with the arguments presented in Chapter 1 about considering the study of child development as the observation of change. There has been enormous historical change in our understanding of the world and we can trace our understanding of psychology and child development as part of that historical journey.

Many would argue that theories can work in practice, to improve, enable, inform, provide for and explain. We will spend a good deal of the rest of this book tracing the connection between theory and practice and the research that helps to create theory. However, there is a danger of 'theory overload' as too many disorganised theories can create a very confusing picture. The history of child development has thrown up a myriad of theories, so how best can we make sense of them all? Almost all theories of child development can be organised into five theoretical approaches, as we show below. These theoretical approaches are: learning theories; cognitive theories; psychodynamic theories; ecological theories; and biological theories. As we begin to consider each of these theoretical approaches we should also begin to evaluate the usefulness of each of these approaches in practice. How can these theories apply in the context of working with children? What use are these theories anyway?

## The evaluation of theories

Good theories are grounded in the valid and reliable application of appropriate scientific method. We have all heard people say – rather like Mrs Britten in the story above – 'That's all very well in theory, but . . .', as if theory is a long way from the reality of practice. Well, Kurt Lewin (1890–1947), a social psychologist, once coined the phrase that 'there is nothing as practical as a good theory' (quoted in Marrow, 1969). We agree and would argue that the value of having theories is that they allow us:

- to explain phenomena, for example, in an educational context, explaining the processes children go through when learning to read;
- to predict, perhaps about the circumstances in which children as young as 3 years of age show stereotypical gender-based behaviour;
- to allow events and behaviours to be influenced by providing for a range of strategies to be used; and
- to understand the 'terrain' of development by acting as a guide or map to negotiate our way through what can seem complex science.

In summary, theories provide information that can help teachers influence children's learning by providing **developmentally appropriate practice (DAP)**, enable carers to optimise child-care environments, empower therapists to provide the most appropriate treatment, and support parents to identify and interpret their children's behaviours.

**Developmentally appropriate practice (DAP)**
Ways of working with children that are suited to their stage of development.

. . . . . . . . . . . . . . . . .

**Connect and Extend**
For an excellent example of using theory to plan for developmentally appropriate practice in mental health work, read: Newman, L. & Birleson, P. (2012) Mental health planning for children and youth: is it developmentally appropriate? *Australasian Psychiatry*, 2012, 20(2), 91–97.

. . . . . . . . . . . . . . . . .

**Summary 1**

Before moving on, let's summarise what we have learned so far:

- Systematic observations are organised into patterns of behaviour that have antecedents and consequences.
- Use of the scientific method allows scientists to construct universal theories.
- Theories help to make sense of what scientists observe and record.
- The universal rules for scientific method were established over many years and in many different contexts.
- The value of having theories is they allow us to explain, understand and to predict behaviour and to help teachers, carers, therapists and parents to be better at what they do.

# Theoretical approaches in child development

In our Preface and in Chapter 1 we explained that the stance adopted in this book is one that views development as a process of change. Based on this, you will understand why we think it appropriate for you to use and apply the criteria for evaluating theories that were proposed by psychologists Jonathan Gewirtz and Martha Peláez-Nogueras (1992) because these criteria are all directly concerned with change. They are:

- How well do the theories explain how children change as they develop? What empirical evidence is provided for their explanations?
- How do the theories account for the various factors, such as culture, that influence developmental change?
- How well do the theories account for individual differences that exist in children's growth and development?
- Finally, the brevity and simplicity of explanation are important attributes of a good theory.

Keep these criteria in mind as you read in the next section about the theories that make up each of the five theoretical approaches. The change criteria above will help you form a useful initial impression of the strengths and usefulness of each approach. You may also wonder what observations of behaviour, antecedents and consequences led to the formulation of these theoretical perspectives and how the application of scientific method led to the conclusions that characterise these theories.

In the section that follows we present and examine the five broad theoretical frameworks and the theorists who have had a significant impact on human development, and then relate their theories to the fundamental issues in child development discussed in the previous chapter. You will note that each of the five frameworks contains theories that are sometimes contradictory and that there is some repetition of ideas between the five frameworks. The five theoretical frameworks are:

- learning theories;
- cognitive theories;
- psychoanalytical theories;
- ecological theories; and
- biological theories.

This chapter is a short introduction to the theories of child development because the detail of these perspectives and their implications will be studied in depth in the chapters that follow. By including an overall framework of theoretical approaches here, we are emphasising the holistic and interdependent nature of aspects of development and providing you with a 'scheme' for organising your own existing knowledge and new knowledge of child development. In the latter part of the chapter we show just one or two applications of these theories to practical situations in home and educational settings to whet your appetite for what follows in the remainder of this book. But for now let's turn to the five theoretical approaches. Remember to apply the four criteria for evaluating theories when recording your own understanding of each of the theories presented:

1. Does the theory provide a complete explanation?
2. Is there evidence for the theory?
3. Does the theory account for cultural and individual differences?
4. Is the theory straightforward and appeals to common sense?

The first set of developmental theories are about learning.

# Learning theories

Theories of how children learn are among the oldest of all theoretical perspectives of child development and developed concurrently with early psychology in the nineteenth century. Learning theories are concerned with how learning affects change and development, how the environment influences a child's development and how a child understands the world through experiencing their environment. The legacy of relatively early behaviourist theories – a full explanation is coming up – is still visible in many of the professional practices in today's schools and other contexts. For example, much time is given in primary school class-rooms to the gaining of automatic and accurate recall of basic number facts such as number bonds to 10 and 20, and multiplication tables. Automatic and accurate recall is learned through regular practice, reward and repetition (Delogu *et al.*, 2012; McCabe *et al.*, 2011). It is a kind of training regime advocated by theorists such as John Watson.

Watson (1878–1958), an early leading advocate of the importance of learning in child development, boldly stated:

> **Give me a dozen healthy infants, well formed, and my own specified world to bring them up in and I'll guarantee to take any one at random and train him to become any type of specialist I might select – doctor, lawyer, artist, merchant, chief, and yes, even beggar-man and thief, regardless of his talents, penchants, tendencies, abilities, vocations, and race of his ancestors.**

(1924/1925, p 82)

Watson's view is typical of the emphasis early developmentalists placed on the environment shaping the development of children through a **behaviourist** perspective. This tradition argues that any theories about human behaviour should be based on what can be observed, rather than conjecture about cognitive processes that cannot be observed. Behaviourists (those who adopt a behaviourist perspective) consider development as a continuous process of change that the environment shapes and one that could be differed according to the individual. In Watson's view, children were passive recipients of experience and *tabula rasa* (a 'clean slate' – see Chapter 1) to be 'written on' by experience. There are clear messages also for parents. Watson (1928) wrote that parents hold total responsibility for the upbringing of their children and they should avoid any sentimentalism or mollycoddling, and treat children firmly, dispassionately and as young adults. You may remember from Chapter 1 that the historical view that children play passive roles in their development is one not generally accepted today by theorists or practitioners. As earlier stated, the influence of behaviourist approaches and theory can still be discerned, particularly how behaviour can be conditioned by our experiences.

 **Reflect**  John Watson (1928) wrote that parents should treat children firmly, dispassionately and as young adults. What are the 'pros and cons' of this argument?

Principles of **classical conditioning** were formed from work by Russian physiologist Ivan Pavlov (1849–1936), where a **neutral stimulus** elicits a response if paired with another stimulus that already elicits that response. In a famous study Pavlov observed a dog salivating repeatedly in response to the clinking sound of food trays because the dog associated the sound with the arrival of food. The smell and appearance of food make dogs salivate (and us, of course!) as saliva is required for chewing and swallowing – preparing the food for its journey to the stomach. The sound of the food trays became a stimulus for the dog to salivate as there was an association between the sound and the smell and appearance of food.

Pavlov then conducted experiments where he conditioned dogs to salivate to just the sound of a bell, which had been paired with the arrival of food. Follow-up work by Watson used

**Connect and Extend**

To find out more about the role of repetition in second language learning, read: Rydland, V. & Aukrust, V. G. (2005). Lexical repetition in second language learners' peer play interaction. *Language Learning*, 55, 229–274.

**Behaviourist**
A learning perspective which considers that everything we do – acting, thinking and feeling – can be regarded as behaviours which are conditioned by our experiences.

**Classical conditioning**
Learning that pairs a response with a stimulus that leads to the stimulus evoking the response.

**Neutral stimulus**
A stimulus that initially produces no specific response other than focusing attention (in the example on this page, focusing attention on the rat).

these same principles to explain behaviours exhibited by children. In an infamous study (Watson & Raynor, 1920), a 9-month-old baby (Little Albert B.) was trained to fear a rat (neutral stimulus) after pairing this stimulus with loud banging sounds. The child overcame initial tendencies to touch the rat without fear but through the associations exhibited fear of it and cried and turned away from the animal. Watson concluded that the environment was the key factor in explaining development and not innate emotions, tendencies or thinking capabilities.

In **operant conditioning** (Skinner, 1966), children 'operate' on the environment by engaging in certain observable behaviours because of the (usually) pleasurable effects of those behaviours. This type of learning involves the attachment of a new response to an old stimulus (in contrast to classical conditioning). The emphasis is on the consequences of behaviour and not on pairing certain stimuli together. According to Skinner, any stimulus that results in that behaviour being repeated reinforces it. Usually the stimulus involves food, reward, attention or social approval, such as might be heard when a child says to another, 'I liked playing with you today, would you like to come to my party?' Something pleasurable – going to a party – follows from a behaviour, which in this case is playing well together.

**Positive reinforcement** is anything that increases the likelihood of a desired behaviour being repeated in the same situation. Such reinforcement in the context of a home or classroom could be a smile, a word of praise or other rewards for 'good' behaviour. Such rewards increase the likelihood of that behaviour happening again. For example, we may want to encourage polite asking behaviour rather than demanding behaviour in a child. If there is some music playing that the child does not like and the child asks politely for a change of music, then by changing the music the parent is reinforcing the target behaviour, that of asking nicely. In contrast, **negative reinforcement**, although also leading to an increase in the future frequency of a desired behaviour, does so in a different way. Suppose somebody has a headache and takes two aspirin but the headache continues. Next they try two codeine and the headache goes away. The removal of the negative experience of having a headache reinforces the behaviour of taking codeine. Negative reinforcement is sometimes confused with punishment.

Punishment lessens the likelihood of unwanted behaviour because a negative condition is introduced or experienced as a consequence of the behaviour. The use of a frown, a rebuke or the withdrawal of privileges in response to unwanted behaviour decreases the likelihood of the behaviour being repeated.

**Operant conditioning**
Learning where the likelihood of behaviour recurring is increased by reinforcement and decreased by punishment.

**Positive reinforcement**
A reward. Anything that increases the likelihood of behaviour being repeated in the same situation.

**Negative reinforcement**
Similar to a reward. When something negative is removed from a person's experience as a way to increase the likelihood of a wanted behaviour happening again.

B. F. Skinner.

*Source*: Sam Falk / Science Photo Library.

• • • • • • • • • • • • • • • •
**Connect and Extend**
To find out more about
the role of reinforcement
in learning attitudes and
behaviour read: Scaglioni,
S., Arrizza, C., Vecchi, F.
& Tedeschi, S. (2011).
Determinants of children's
eating behaviour *The
American Journal of Clinical
Nutrition*, December, 94(6),
200–211.
• • • • • • • • • • • • • • • •

**Social learning theory**
Explains how children learn
by watching and imitating
others in social situations.

**Observational learning**
Where significant learning
takes place by watching
other people model
behaviour.

**Social cognitive theory**
The view that children learn
by classical and operant
conditioning (features of
behaviourism) and by
observing others.

Both classical and operant conditioning have proved enormously successful in behaviour modification and are integral to the techniques used by therapists, teachers and carers in addressing problems such as thumb-sucking, eating behaviours and temper tantrums. Critics of the approach believe it underplays the important role of the emotions and motivational factors in how children respond to stimulation. For example, some stimulations are pleasurable and are likely to reinforce the behaviour, while others are not and may be stoically borne by the subject without any positive or negative reinforcement taking place.

**Social learning theory** may be seen as a response to such criticism. Some theorists (notably Julian Rotter, Albert Bandura and Edwin Sutherland) subscribe to a viewpoint that while accepting the role of conditioning in learning, they propose that children also learn by watching and imitating others. Psychologist Albert Bandura (1977) proposed the concept of **observational learning** where significant learning takes place merely by watching other people who act as 'models'. In a series of classic experiments, nursery children watched an adult repeatedly punch and kick a Bobo doll, both live and on video. Soon afterwards the children were given the opportunity to play with the doll themselves and accurately replicated the destructive actions they had observed the adult performing earlier. Although there was no reinforcement of this behaviour (nobody praised the children for kicking and punching the doll), there was conclusive evidence that learning had taken place. Contemporary advocates of this approach regard modelling as a powerful tool for learning that has both negative (for example, the replication of aggressive behaviours seen on television) and positive (sharing, turn-taking, etc.) outcomes. The theory contributes to our knowledge of cognition and was refined as **social cognitive theory** (Bandura, 1989b) to place emphasis on four sets of cognitive processes within observational learning:

1. Attention – the child notices something in the environment.

2. Retention – the child remembers what was noticed.

3. Reproduction – the child produces an action that is a copy of what was noticed.

4. Motivation – the environment delivers a consequence that changes the probability the behaviour will be performed again (reinforcement and punishment).

In developmental terms, these processes become more sophisticated as children mature and develop more effective self-regulation of behaviours (Johnson *et al.*, 2012; Carpendale & Lewis, 2004). Social cognitive theory captures the influence of the environment on learning, particularly the modelling of behaviour by those in different social contexts of childhood (Bronfenbrenner, 1989) (see Chapter 1, Figure 1.3). Social Cognitive theory has been criticised (e.g. Horwitz, 2005) for not paying sufficient regard to wider contextual factors such as gender, educational background and socioeconomic status.

## Cognitive theories

Theorists taking this viewpoint assert that development of cognitive areas inside the brain influence the ways in which children understand the world. Psychologists sharing this view are interested in discovering the workings of the mind and how children think, reason and solve problems. A fuller consideration of these theories appears in Chapter 9 but it is important for you to now gain an overview of the main theories, starting with cognitive developmental theory.

## Cognitive developmental theory

**Cognitive
developmental theory**
Emphasises cognition
over other aspects of
development such as
personality.

Jean Piaget is undoubtedly the theorist who has had the single greatest impact on research in child development and therefore profoundly influenced many of today's working practices evident in early childhood settings and some primary schools. Piaget's **cognitive developmental theory** (1952a) focuses on the ways in which children adapt to their environments. This view

Jean Piaget's theory of stages of cognitive development has profoundly influenced working practices in schools.
*Source*: Bill Anderson/ Science Photo Library.

upholds adaption as a process in which the child actively seeks out ways to understand the environment and gradually attunes to the conditions that different types of environment impose. Piaget believed that all children pass through four similar periods in their cognitive development due to the fact that all children possess a very similar potential to learn. He proposed that the nature of the effect of children's environments on children's passage through the four periods does not differ significantly in any important respect. He proposed a series of four periods of cognitive development common to all children:

1. *Sensorimotor period*: from birth to age 2 years. Children experience the world through movement and senses and learn that objects permanently exist, even though they cannot always be seen or touched.

2. *Pre-operational period*: from ages 2 to 7, children acquire major (e.g. running) and minor (e.g. drawing) motor skills to travel through and manipulate the world around them.

3. *Concrete operational period*: from ages 7 to 11, children begin to think logically about events they experience and can order, evaluate and explain them.

4. *Formal operational period*: after age 11, children develop abstract reasoning – ideas that exist only in thought, e.g. 'loyalty'.

Piaget believed that children display qualitative differences in their thinking as they mature and move through each of the four stages. He also placed importance on active learning (as opposed to passive learning by observation) which seems to have left lasting impressions on many practitioners and educationalists. Although many of his ideas form the basis of practice in playgroups, nurseries and classrooms today, there has been increased criticism of his work in recent years. Critics such as Linda Siegal and Charles Brainerd – developmental

For Lev Vygotsky, children acquire the values and skills of society through their social interactions.

*Source:* Ria Novosti / TopFoto.

● ● ● ● ● ● ● ● ● ● ● ● ● ● ● ● ●
**Connect and Extend**
To understand the complementary nature of the work of Jean Piaget and Lev Vygotsky, read: Shayer, M. (2003). Not just Piaget; not just Vygotsky, and certainly not Vygotsky as alternative to Piaget. *Learning and Instruction, 13,* 465–485.
● ● ● ● ● ● ● ● ● ● ● ● ● ● ● ● ●

**Information-processing approaches**
These view cognitive development as a series of steps to process information from the environment.

psychologists – have questioned the samples used for his empirical work and his lack of attention to the social and cultural factors in learning and development.

## Sociocultural theory

In contrast to Piaget who concentrated on individual development, this set of theories (attributed to Lev Vygotsky, 1987, and Jerome Bruner, 1966) emphasise the child's social interactions with significant others, such as parents, teachers and peers. It is through these interactions that children are able to acquire the important values and skills of a society and it is through sociocultural context and interactions that children develop increasingly complex and higher-order thinking abilities. This theory stresses the role that adults play in progressing learning by pitching their teaching just beyond current understanding but within reach of that which a child will understand with assistance. The key to success was in the language, e.g. the vocabulary used by these more knowledgeable others (parents, practitioners or teachers) in framing tasks for child learners. We can observe sociocultural theory in action during activities involving children learning to read, write and performing computational activities in mathematics. Vygotsky's approach favoured 'leading activities', social interactions that produce major developmental accomplishments and prepare the child for the next period of development. These leading activities do mirror Piagetian stages because, as Vygotsky (1962) argues, society structures the social processes of child-rearing in similar ways to developmental stages. A second contrast to Piagetian theory is, as the name suggests, the emphasis placed upon culture, both in understanding cognitive development and in developing authentic assessments.

## Information-processing approaches

**Information-processing approaches** use an analogy of the 'mind as computer' (Siegler, 1998; Klahr & Wallace, 1976). When operating a computer we input information from the environment, such as words, numbers, images and sounds. The software encodes the information, and processes it before being translated back into an output onto the screen or through the speakers. The information-processing analogy says that some of the processes of the brain perform the same functions of accepting inputs, encoding, processing and outputting. This does not imply that the human mind operates like a computer, but that the model of mind as computer allows investigators more precisely to plot and predict actions and outcomes. Researchers in information-processing approaches are interested in the mental operations acting on the flow of information through the cognitive system that shed light on children's perceptual, memory, retrieval and decision-making capabilities at different ages. Over time, the strategies used by children to solve problems change as successful strategies are adopted (like solving a similar but less complex problem) and the less successful ones abandoned (such as trying every possible combination in a seemingly endless set of possibilities).

The approach views development as continuous, rather than stage-like and stresses that, like computers, the human mind has only a limited capacity to process information, but as development progresses, changes to our mental structures allow for more sophisticated strategies, evidenced in the thinking and outputs of older children. Similarly, a knowledge-based approach (Chi *et al.*, 1989) takes a similar focus on how the brain deals with information. This perspective views development as largely continuous, but acknowledges there will be differences for both individuals and cultures, based on learners' experiences of creating 'examples' of how things usually work out. Put another way, a knowledge-based approach explores the way in which individuals use knowledge of how things have worked in the past to solve problems in the present. These ideas will be further considered in Chapter 9.

## Psychoanalytic theories

So far, the perspectives on development have involved mental processes and those associated with learning. In psychoanalytic theories, a much greater emphasis is placed on the emotions and on personality (and these will be returned to in greater depth in Chapter 11). Almost all psychoanalytic theories are about relationships – for example, mothering and fatherhood – and have their roots in the work of Sigmund Freud, who is often hailed as one of the greatest thinkers of the twentieth century. His views on personality and motivation continue to invite controversy even today.

The theory of **psychosexual development** (Freud, 1962) states that behaviour is governed by unconscious (the brain working while your 'back is turned') as well as conscious processes (deliberate thinking about something). Freud argued that some processes are present at birth, while others emerge in later development. A second key idea is that many facets of our personality such as aggression and sexuality originate in early childhood drives, for example to hold on to waste products in the body until a time when it will give greater pleasure to release them. These early childhood drives sometimes conflict with external forces such as those exerted by parents, family or other significant others to adjust behaviour to social norms and expectations. For some children conflict between their drives and social expectations remain unresolved and so become internalised conflicts affecting thoughts and emotions, and directly affecting behaviour.

Freud's theories of development are characterised by instinctive drives of pleasure which are mitigated by the development of social conscience and moral judgement. However, the conflict between pleasure taking and socialisation is not always appropriately resolved. Any lack of opportunities to have needs appropriately met have negative consequences on personal feelings of self-worth and forming relationships (covered in Chapters 11 and 12). Despite Freud's valuing family influences and early childhood experiences in personality development, there are few strong advocates of Freud's theory today. Thomas Keenan (2002), senior lecturer in psychology at the University of Canterbury, New Zealand, summarises criticisms of Freud's theory: the theory is relevant to observations in one culture; that it relies on boys for study; and that many of Freud's claims have not been substantiated in more recent studies.

The last of our psychoanalytical theories is psychosocial theory (developed by Erik Erikson, 1963) which built upon many of Freud's ideas but placed greater emphasis on the social and cultural factors of development. For many practitioners, psychosocial theory can be more comfortably accepted than Freud's, as there is less emphasis on basic human needs and more on social adjustment in the environment. Erikson focused on emotions and personality traits, and considered children to have a more proactive and less reactive role in their own development. He proposed that social relationships were not formed as a result of the environment, but through a series of conscious acts that grew out of a child's emerging identity. Unlike Freud, Erikson believed that children are active in their own environment,

**Connect and Extend**
Have there been radical changes in fatherhood since Freud formulated his theories? Read: Mander, G. (2001). Fatherhood today: Variations on a theme. *Psychodynamic Practice*, 7, 141–158.

**Psychosexual development**
The view that behaviour is governed by unconscious as well as conscious processes.

Erik Erikson proposed that at every stage there are internal personal conflicts to resolve before a child can progress to the next stage.
*Source*: Ted Streshinsky/ Time & Life Pictures/ Getty Images.

eagerly seeking out new information and actively dealing with the everyday conflicts of life. Development has been widely and consistently conceptualised as stage-like and, in keeping with this, Erikson proposes a series of eight stages that extend from birth through to old age (*infancy, early childhood, play age, school age, adolescence, young adulthood, adulthood* and *mature age*). In each of these stages he identifies internal personal conflicts to resolve, such as that between trust and mistrust in early childhood. Erikson argues that conflicts in each stage must be successfully resolved before progressing to the next stage. For example, he elaborates many personal conflicts – the need for intimacy whilst faced with feelings of isolation – that people can and do identify with. Although Erikson's theory is criticised for failing to explain these conflicts and being vague about their causes (Payne, 2007), his theory has shaped, as we shall see, much of today's thinking on the impact of the family and social interaction on children's development.

**Reflect**

Erikson's 'young adulthood' stage – ages 18 to late 20s – is defined by an internal conflict of *intimacy vs isolation*. People explore relationships leading towards longer-term commitments. Successful conciliation of the conflict can lead to comfortable relationships and a sense of security and care within a relationship. Avoiding intimacy and fearing commitment can lead to isolation, loneliness and sometimes depression. Do you recognise this in yourselves or your friends? Perhaps you might have to think back some way to your own 20s!

# Ecological theories

In obvious contrast to some lack of attention to the role of the environment in the perspectives presented so far, ecological theories provide us with detailed accounts of the influence of the environment upon development. Those psychologists who develop ecological theories of development recognise that the different circumstances in which children live and how they are brought up are important influences on how children develop. In all cultures, important influences can be identified and described in, for example, immediate family arrangements: single parent families; parents who are divorced; children brought up by grandparents; and children in care. Size of family, economic stability and home location are all factors that may mean the experiences of children are very different. It is the effect of these experiences and those in wider contexts that ecologists seek to study. Therefore, an ecological perspective on development highlights the interaction of systems at different levels and places high significance on the environment with which a child interacts.

## Ecological systems theory

**Ecological systems theory**
A theory which emphasises the different social contexts or systems – e.g. the family – in which a child develops.

As previously described in Chapter 1, renowned psychologist Urie Bronfenbrenner's ecological systems theory (1989) is a systemic view that contributes to our understanding of development by incorporating broad sociocultural factors in children's lives. The bioecological model (Bronfenbrenner & Morris, 1998) fixes the child at its centre and acknowledges biological makeup, cognitive capacities and socio-emotional traits that influence and are influenced by the environment. Dismissive of much laboratory research, Bronfenbrenner believed that development should be studied in the home, schools and community where children live. He saw children as active participants in this process and that parents were important influences on development, rather than considering maturation or parenting practices separately. The world of children was 'a set of nested structures, each inside the next, like a set of Russian dolls' (1979, p 22) and it is this organisation that forms his view of development in four systems that was explained in Chapter 1 and will be returned to in Chapter 12.

Bronfenbrenner's theory contributes a much richer description of environmental influences. The four systems in his model (the microsystem, mesosystem, exosystem and the macrosystem) change over time, due to internal factors such as illness or external factors such as starting school. Thus a child's development is the result of a changing mixture of ecological systems. However, the theory has been criticised over the past twenty years (Tudge *et al.*, 2009; Shaffer, 1999; Sontag, 1996) for a lack of clarity on how children learn from their experiences in different environments and make use of the information they receive from their environmental experiences. Bronfenbrenner's theory places the child at the centre of the social contexts of systems (Figure 1.3). What about the rest of life? Which theories apply to development during adolescence and adulthood?

More recently, lifespan theories have concentrated on continuity throughout the entire lifetime (Wiley *et al.*, 2011) and on the order of significant developmental periods over time, for example, changes as children develop through infancy, childhood and adolescence. In the psychodynamic approach described earlier, Erik Erikson's 'stages of development' extend throughout the lifetime, including adulthood and old age. However, Erikson's theory is based on very different principles of internal conflicts to those of ecological systems we are considering here. In modern lifespan theory, it is not the social context that largely determines how we develop (Shepherd *et al.*, 2012): our social context influences how successful we are at adapting to the changes that take place, but does not change the common developmental events that we all experience during a lifespan. These events seem to fit a kind of plan that is common to all. Age-related experience orders the changes that children and adults go through at about the same periods in their lives and according to a common plan. Time also brings change from unplanned factors that can shape development in ways that are more unpredictable: family bereavements, moving house, serious illness, falling in love, divorce – all of which can happen at any time of life. The theory confirms the power of relationships that exist among the family, with peers and others we come into contact with, and elaborates Bronfenbrenner's bioecological model by promoting the social environment as the major influence on human development.

Dynamic system theory is – in a definition provided by psychologists Margaret Harris and George Butterworth – 'the study of the ways in which systems that are open to the effects of the environment, change over time' (2002, p 42). Advocates of this approach view development as a process of change to a system and the system as a set of connected parts, with the dynamic element coming from the relationship between parts in constant motion. These are quite complex ideas, so let's explore an example of what we mean. The most obvious example of dynamic system theory is a family – made up of different members and demonstrating behaviours that are the result of their individual past experiences but, importantly, also the external and internal influences that operate on each of them as a member of the family system.

As Figure 2.2 shows, different members of the family (viewed as components of the system) interact with each other and with other outside influences to a greater or lesser extent. It is typical for all members of the family to have a common heredity and/or history and to interact with each other. The dynamics of the family system, and the development of the individuals within the family is some function of the different impact on family members of other hereditary and historical factors.

A key feature of dynamic systems theory is that development is not controlled by one factor alone and not seen in the polarised terms of nature or nurture, but contributions from each part allow more complex behaviours to emerge. More than a decade ago, British nurse educator Doreen Crawford (2002) made a case for health professionals understanding the dynamic forces at work in the family in order to ensure a balanced provision of healthcare. Earlier, Esther Thelen and Linda Smith (1994), both developmental psychologists researching into cognition and word learning, referred to a continual reorganisation within the system (for example, a family) that accounts for its great strengths of adaptability and stability, and argue that new capabilities emerge out of the interplay between the different parts and different factors. Thelen and Smith use the metaphor of a mountain stream with its whirlpools and eddies.

● ● ● ● ● ● ● ● ● ● ● ● ● ● ● ● ●
**Connect and Extend**
For findings of research into how children, adolescents, teens and adults learn, which addresses shifts from sociocultural to technocultural theories of cognition and learning, read: Petrina, S., Feng, F. & Kim, J. (2007). Researching cognition and technology: How we learn across the lifespan. *International Journal of Technology and Design Education*, Preprint, 1–22.
● ● ● ● ● ● ● ● ● ● ● ● ● ● ● ● ●

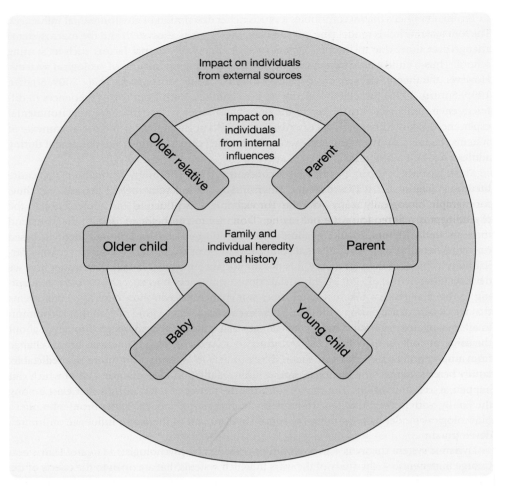

**Figure 2.2** The family as a system

Such irregularities cannot be explained by some master plan of the stream falling neatly and evenly from the top of the mountain. The master plan of gravity accounts for the fact that the stream falls but does not account for the different paths it takes and the different patterns on the surface of the water. Rather, the turbulence results from many factors operating together, such as variations in slope, the placement of boulders on the stream bed, differences in the density of the material that forms its banks and the depredations of sheep and human hill walkers. These factors determine the development of the stream system into its current state. The best examples of this theory relate to the development of early motor skills, a topic considered in more detail in Chapter 6.

## Biological theories

**Maturation theory**
Focuses on the unfolding of genetically determined sequences of development.

Theories in this perspective connect physical growth to social and psychological development by proposing that many aspects of development are rooted in biological processes, e.g. our knowledge of genetics, the nervous system, and electrical activity in the brain. The **maturation theory** focuses on the unfolding of 'genetically determined sequences of development' (Rathus, 2004, p 27) and asserts that these sequences unfold independently of external experiences. The maturational school founded by Arnold Gesell at the beginning of the last century expounded a nativistic view that development is governed by genetic processes which determine a sequence of development for all children. A more recent example (Schore, 2005) combines maturation theory and dynamic systems theory to understand the development of emotions. Maturation theory emphasises the role of 'nature' over that of 'nurture' in complete contrast to the behaviourist views of Pavlov and Skinner.

Is she 'biologically ready' to walk? Maturational theory proposes that nature, rather than nurture, determines when we achieve new skills.

*Source:* © Pearson Education Ltd / Jules Selmes.

The maturation theory has particular relevance for charting the progress of early motor skills (e.g. sitting, standing, reaching and walking) to later skills (e.g. running, jumping, throwing and catching). The theory emphasises the need for children to be biologically 'ready' to acquire behaviour patterns. Is the infant in the nearby photograph 'biologically ready' to walk? For example, this principle of readiness is referred to in the old saying: 'Don't try to run before you can walk'. Maturation theory proposes that children develop through a series of largely invariant stages marked by developmental milestones – such as sitting and standing – observed by Arnold Gesell a hundred years ago. Gesell's conclusions led to a general adoption of developmental milestones and to descriptive statements about the development and capabilities of children at given ages, which have provided useful benchmarks for many parents, carers and practitioners over the past 60 years. Although these milestones and descriptions provided parents and others outside the medical profession with detailed information about children's capabilities, it did assume a universal truth: that statements for children in Western contexts (mainly the United States and Europe) held true for children from different cultures. In the United Kingdom, charts of development produced by Sheridan (1975) to meet the needs of professional childhood practitioners also suffered from the same Eurocentric criticism. While few developmentalists today completely accept neither the nativist – everything occurs naturally – view of Gesell, nor the universal application of detailed charts of child development, the maturation theory did lead to interesting debates on the nature–nurture issue and to more informed monitoring of patterns of development by doctors, nurses and therapists. A greater emphasis on nature being responsible for the timing of developmental milestones is given in the theories of ethology (coming up next), rooted in Darwin's theories of evolution.

**Ethology** is the study of the evolutionary basis of behaviour and evolved responses (for example, symptoms, say, a blocked nose, as a reaction to a viral infection, which provide protection against a worse ailment) for the continuation of a species (Duff, 2010). It had its historical roots in Charles Darwin's proposal of 'survival of the fittest' in the nineteenth century. Darwin's theory of evolution was very much influenced by observations of inherited traits and adaptive behaviours that improved the rate of survival of a species in a process known as **natural selection**. Successful traits and behaviours which have survival advantages – standing upright, communication of danger – are passed on, while those with little or no advantage or some disadvantage to survival will eventually disappear. More modern interpretations still champion that development is a progressive adaptation of children to their environments and believe that, in order to fully understand the behaviour of any species, it is necessary to observe behaviours occurring in context. In order to understand how chimpanzees develop, one must observe them in their natural habitat as this provides insight into their social structures and organisation. With regard to children's development, this means placing the utmost importance on settings such as classrooms, playgrounds and in the home where behaviour can be observed naturally occurring.

In the 1930s, zoologists Konrad Lorenz and Nikolaas Tinbergen developed Darwin's earlier work by arguing that development is the result of a mutual interchange between the inherited

• • • • • • • • • • • • • • • •
**Connect and Extend**
This paper takes a fresh look at the nativism–empiricism debate, presenting and defending a nativist perspective on the mind. Margolis, E. & Laurence, S. (2012). In defense of nativism. *Philosophical Studies*, 2012, Preprints, 1–26, 26p; *10*, 3–17.
• • • • • • • • • • • • • • • •

**Ethology**
Both the science of animal behaviour and the science of character formation in human behaviour.

**Natural selection**
Physical or behavioural changes leading to a survival advantage are passed on through genes. If no advantage is gained, these are eventually not passed on.

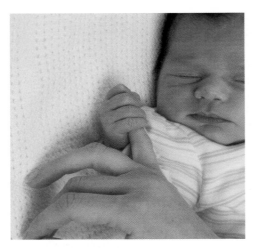

Ethologists believe infants are genetically equipped with behaviours such as grasping.

*Source*: © Pearson Education Ltd / Tudor Photography.

**Imprinting**
The development in a newly born of a pattern of behaviour, showing recognition and trust, usually for its own species.

**Critical periods**
Periods of time in the development of the brain during which its self-organising capability is at its most potent.

**Sensitive periods**
Brief periods of time when an individual is very responsive to influences in the environment.

• • • • • • • • • • • • • • • • •
**Connect and Extend**
A key issue in development of speech perception and production concerns the possible existence of an early sensitive period that facilitates language acquisition. Read: Welton, M. A. and Cohen, A. J. (2008). Is there a sensitive period for representation of phoneme sequences? *The Journal of the Acoustical Society of America*, May, 123(5), 3079–3089.
• • • • • • • • • • • • • • • • •

and biological basis of behaviour and the specific environment in which it takes place. The theory proposes that infants are genetically equipped with behaviours such as sucking, grasping and smiling that are 'species-specific', all essential to meet the child's needs. Modern ethologists believe that these (and other) behaviours are typical across all cultures, with findings supporting that the emotional expressions of joy, sadness and anger are common in many modern cultures (Bryant & Barrett, 2008).

First learning takes place in the context of a process called imprinting. Chicks, for example, become imprinted upon their mothers during their first day, but if another 'mother' such as a farmer handles and feeds the chicks, imprinting will still occur.

In a piece of classic historic work, Konrad Lorenz (1974) studied the behaviour of goslings following their mother goose. He concluded that the behaviour of following mother is not pre-programmed; rather what is pre-programmed is the tendency to follow and that who or what the goslings follow depends upon their environment (see the photograph of Lorenz and his gosling family).

Imprinting in animals occurs only during brief time slots known as critical periods, times when the animal is more biologically prepared to take on new behaviours (Bischof *et al.*, 2002). In humans, similar 'windows of opportunity' do exist in what have been referred to as sensitive periods (Sharma & Campbell, 2011). These are brief time slots in development when humans are very responsive to influences from the environment. Studies on language acquisition (e.g. Weerman, 2011) have shown that language is more easily acquired in the years up to the end of middle childhood but more difficult at and after adolescence (remember the language difficulties faced by Victor, the Wild Boy of Aveyron – Chapter 1).

These goslings follow Konrad Lorenz because they imprinted on him rather than their mother, during their 'critical period'.

*Source*: Nina Leen / Time & Life Pictures / Getty Images.

Ethology has also contributed to our understanding of social behaviours including aggression, co-operation and attachment. The work of John Bowlby in the late 1950s is particularly interesting and although explored more fully in Chapter 12 is worth a short introduction in this round-up of biological theories. Bowlby's attachment theory (1958) attempted to explain the bond that exists between mother and child from an ethological perspective. He argues that the emotional bond between the mother and child was not related to early sexuality as Freud's psychosexual theory proposed, but was a secure base from which the infant could make increasingly 'risky' moves to interact with the environment and then to return to safety. From an ethological stance, this bond provides the pattern for future relationships. Bowlby's argument is that security in early infancy paves the way for successful attachments in later life, which in the longer term contributes to the successful reproduction of the species.

More recent interpretations of the ethological viewpoint include **evolutionary developmental psychology**. Psychologists David Geary and David Bjorklund (2000) argue that development is a combination of inheritance and the effects of the environment upon behaviour, governed by an interactive process of nature *and* nurture (called epigenics – introduced in Chapter 1). These processes are responsible for determining our **phenotype**, observable behavioural characteristics resulting from hereditary characteristics and life experiences as opposed to our **genotype** – the full set of inherited instructions we carry, the 'effects' of which may or may not be observable. This genotype–phenotype distinction was first proposed by Danish botanist, plant physiologist and geneticist Wilhelm Johannsen in 1911, to make clear the difference between the differing effects of heredity and environment on the final appearance and behaviour of any organism. We discuss the theory underpinning the practice of genotyping – identifying the full set of inherited instructions – in the upcoming *Focus on Theory* feature. Genotyping and phenotyping have been more recently applied to human development in attempts to understand the relationship between social and non-social aspects of the world and how these are processed. Keenan (2002), citing the work of evolutionary psychologist David Buss (1995), gives two examples: children's relationships with parents and the effects of early environments on physical maturation. In summary the ethological perspective stresses our biological inheritance and innate capabilities but also proposes that the learning experiences we have influence our development.

**Evolutionary developmental psychology**
The study of genetic and environmental factors that govern human behaviour.

**Phenotype**
The observable characteristics of an individual, the way we develop, inherited from parents together with effects of physical and social environments.

**Genotype**
A person's complete collection of genetic instructions for creating and replacing cells.

## Focus on Theory

### Can genotyping accurately predict children's future behaviour?

Genotyping is the process of determining differences in the genetic make-up (genotype) of an individual by examining the individual's DNA sequence. If children were routinely genotyped at birth, would it be possible to predict their behaviour at home and school? Might this knowledge provoke early interventions to modify aggressive behaviour or treat conditions such as asthma?

Let's start with aggressive behaviour. Recent research (e.g. Bernet *et al.*, 2007) has started to clarify how a child's environment and genetic make-up interact (epigenics) to create a violent adolescent or adult. For example, in the Bernet research, males who were born with part of a particular gene (part of their genotype) and also were maltreated as children had a much greater likelihood of manifesting violent antisocial behaviour as adolescents and adults (phenotype). Also, individuals who were born with particular parts of the serotonin gene (part of their genotype) and also experienced multiple stressful life events were more likely to manifest serious depression and suicidal tendencies (phenotype). This research of William Bernet and his colleagues used convicted murderers as research subjects and this choice of subjects brought the epigenics of extreme violent behaviour into stark relief. What of less extreme forms of behaviour that we might meet in families, care contexts and schools? Let's look at two examples: autism and asthma.

Autism (also in Chapter 6) is a disorder of neural development which brings about difficulties with social interaction and communication, and exhibiting unusual and repetitive behaviour. The disorder is usually diagnosed before a child is 3 years old. What proportion of autism can be explained by genotype? Autism has a strong genetic basis: early studies of twins (e.g. Freitag, 2007) indicate that 90 per cent of the differences between autistic and non-autistic individuals is due to genetic effects.

Asthma is a complex disease with genetic and environmental causes (epigenics). It affects more than 6 per cent of children in the developed world (Fanta, 2009). Because of genetic complexity, genotyping has been been difficult to determine. However, in 2010, a study of 3377 children with asthma and 5579 healthy children was published (Sleiman *et al.*, 2010). The researchers examined genetic variations across entire genomes, and compared and contrasted the affected and unaffected groups. They discovered a region on one chromosome that together with a previously unassociated chromosome statistically correlated with susceptibility to childhood asthma. One of the chromosomes contained a gene that allowed the body to produce natural killer cells – a critical component of the immune system (Sleiman *et al.*, 2010).

This may be a key finding that promises a cure for childhood asthma and is an excellent example of theory in action. What other conditions could be researched in this way? Perhaps you could do some research online for other conditions or disorders such as epilepsy, diabetes or attention-deficit/hyperactivity disorder (ADHD).

**Reflect**

'I am now in my late fifties. After a shave in the morning I emerge from rinsing off the last of the soap and stare into the mirror above the sink. It seems more and more – and it is alarming – that it is my dad staring back at me. I am a very different person from my dad but the older I get the more I look like him. Although I do still have some hair left on my head!' Thinking about yourself or somebody else you know very well, what characteristics would you attribute to phenotype, and which (if observable) to genotype?

## Comparing the five theoretical approaches

In our discussion of the five theoretical approaches – learning, cognitive, psychoanalytical, ecological and biological you may have noticed that there are two sets of theories that take either a predominantly nature or nurture perspective. Therefore an important idea to grasp at the end of this section of the chapter is that each of the five approaches contain sets of theories that are both complementary and contrasting. Study Figure 2.3 for a representation of what we mean. You will notice that the two main influences on development are heredity and the environment, and where the two overlap – the dynamic relation between the two – is epigenics. The different sets of theories explaining development, such as biological or psychoanalytic theories, span across the continuum provided by the effects of heredity and the environment. The figure shows that the five main learning theories are woven throughout the two main influences on development, like the threads of a cloth. This will become even more apparent the further you read into *Child Development: Theory and Practice 0–11*. No matter what

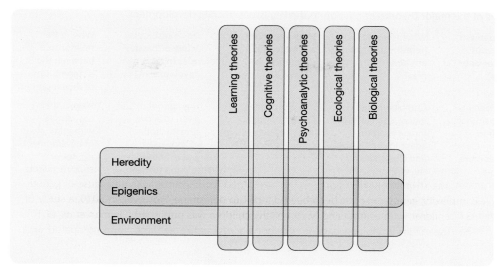

**Figure 2.3** Organising theories of child development

The five theoretical approaches contain theories that stress the influence of heredity, environment or the dynamic relation between heredity and environment – epigenics.

set of theories you are talking about, and no matter which domains or stages of child development you are studying, the bi-fold influences of heredity and environment will be constant throughout.

In the previous section you will have noticed obvious similarities among the major theoretical approaches, as well as many differences between them. These differences are due to three sets of factors. Firstly, the scientific thinking that prevailed at the time when each of the approaches were first proposed; secondly, the influence of other theorists working overtime on a particular approach; and lastly, variations in the methods the theorists used. There is an important warning to sound. No one theory is all-encompassing and no one theoretical approach provides definitive answers.

Of course, you may prefer one approach to another and that preference will inform your professional practice, or you may adopt a more eclectic approach that combines elements of several theories together. Each theoretical approach contributes to our understanding of child development to a greater or lesser extent, depending on which aspect of child development is being explored. Remember the five fundamental questions of child development that were identified and discussed in the previous chapter. They were:

1. Is development a continuous process or one of stages?
2. What roles do heredity and the environment play?
3. How important are individual differences and situational factors?
4. Do children play active or passive roles in their own development?
5. What is the relationship between the different areas of development?

How do these fundamental questions relate to the theoretical approaches we have been exploring in the preceding sections of this chapter? What kind of answers do the theories provide? Remember, for practitioners it is not enough just to know about theories and to apply them without any thought because the implications have to be worked out in practice (Love, 2012), but knowing about them is a start!

Table 2.1 is a meta-analysis of the theories discussed in this chapter and how these answer these same fundamental questions. Do you agree with the summary statements in each cell?

**Table 2.1**  A meta-analysis of the major theories in relation to the key issues in child development

|  | Is development a continuous process or one of stages? | What roles do heredity and the environment play? | How important are individual differences and situational factors? | Do children play active or passive roles in their own development? | What is the relationship between the different areas of development? |
|---|---|---|---|---|---|
| **Cognitive theories** | Clearly stage-like in Piagetian theory. Information processing theory views it as more continuous development. | Combination of nature and nurture. Innate need to adapt to stimulation and challenges in the environment (nature vs. nurture). | Not a prominent feature in Piaget. Vygotsky believed in cultural differences. | High priority is given to active construction of knowledge, and continual revision through experience. | Piaget's theory has associations with other areas of development, e.g. social constructivism. |
| **Learning theories** | Behaviourists saw it as continuous. Learned responses are acquired gradually. | Emphasis on nurture through conditioning and modelling. | Children's behaviour varies from child to child. Learning is highly situational. | Passive role for children as they are shaped by their environments. Bandura's view is more active. | Learning permeates all areas of development. |
| **Psychoanalytic theories** | Stage-like (Freud's psychosexual and Erikson's psychosocial). | Combination of nature and nurture. Impulses present at birth are acted upon by experiences. | Stages are universal. Children move through the stages differently. | Active. Instincts become mediated by society for socially acceptable behaviours. | Links are made by Erikson to social, emotional and cognitive development. |
| **Ecological theories** | Stage-like but change is on-going. Dynamic systems recognise constant reorganisation of components. | Interaction of both. Biological factors combine with others in the environment. | Inborn characteristics combine with environmental factors at multiple levels (Bronfenbrenner). | Both active and passive. Activity influences the contexts that then influence development. | Claims permeates all areas. |
| **Biological theories** | Discontinuous through stages (Gesell). Existence of sensitive periods (Bornstein). | Behaviour is biologically based but requires appropriate environments to adapt successfully. | One course of development for all members of the human species. Individual need to be biologically 'ready'. | Active. Organisms possess biologically pre-programmed behaviours to adapt to the environment. | Interrelationship among all areas of development. |

**Summary 2**

Before moving on, let's summarise what we have learned in the middle section of this chapter:

- Behaviourist theorists conclude that personal experience is the key factor in explaining development and not innate emotions, tendencies or thinking capabilities – social learning theorists believe that children also learn by watching and imitating others.
- Cognitive developmental theory focuses on the ways in which children adapt to their environments – whereas sociocultural theory emphasises the child's social interactions with significant others.
- The theory of psychosexual development states that behaviour is governed by unconscious as well as conscious processes – whereas psychosocial theory places greater emphasis on the social and cultural factors of psychological development.
- Ecological theories provide us with detailed accounts of the influence of the interaction of different social environments upon development – whereas dynamic system theory argues that the effects of environmental systems change over time.

- Theories in the biological perspective connect physical growth to social and psychological development. Ethology is the study of the evolutionary basis of behaviour, whereas evolutionary developmental psychology studies a combination of inheritance and the effects of the environment.

# Theory into practice

## Implications of theory for educators, carers and parents

As a practitioner working with children or as a student engaged in academic study of childhood, you will need to be aware of the full range of theories that we have presented, since awareness of only one or two theoretical approaches can lead to unhelpful assumptions and predictions. We argue that your understanding and appreciation of a full range of these theories is necessary to develop your professional practice to become **praxis** (Kemmis, 2010), that is to say practice that is informed by theory. Table 2.2 presents contexts for the theories and a brief interpretation of the events in each of the contexts. Our intention is to help you begin to apply theories to situations in practice.

**Praxis**
Professional practice informed by theory.

## Alternative 'new' perspectives

More recently, feminist theory has been linked to child development (Hedlund & Lindberg, 2012). Feminist theory provides a particular sociocultural approach promoting: women's rights of contract and ownership; rights to abortion, access to contraception and quality prenatal care; protection from domestic violence, sexual harassment and rape; and workplace rights, including equal pay and maternity leave. Links between feminist theory and child development include issues of social justice, gender stereotyping and the use of appropriate language. These form the basis of a feminist sociocultural theoretical approach we might term the **'feminist perspective'**.

One inspirational example of somebody who successfully linked feminist theory, child development and issues of social justice was Montessori. Maria Montessori (b.1870) was an

**Feminist perspective**
Links feminist theory and child development and includes issues of social justice, gender stereotyping and the use of appropriate language.

**Table 2.2** Interpretations of key theories of child development

| Context example | Theoretical perspective | Interpretation |
| --- | --- | --- |
| Home: Argument between parent and child resulting in the parent smacking the child. Later the child hits out at another in the playground. | Learning theories (Bandura) | Aggressive behaviour modelled by adults becomes learned by the child who sees hitting as acceptable behaviour. |
| School: Older children assist younger pupils with learning to read. | Cognitive theories (Vygotsky) | Peer tutoring. Development is a product of social interaction with others. The assistance provided by others promotes intellectual development and higher cognitive functions. |
| Care: Child in a nursery freely explores through trial and error. Staff do not criticise her mistakes. | Psychoanalytic theories (Erikson) | Increase in curiosity from language, motor and cognitive development leads to exploration and experimentation. Lack of criticism from others for mistakes leads to a confident and autonomous individual. |
| Community: A school fête attended by pupils, parents, neighbours and local small businesses. | Ecological theories (Bronfenbrenner) | Mesosystem. Interaction takes place between the child and other members of the local community. Family, peers and school are still central in this stage. |
| School: Some people have the view (*Controversy*, Chapter 1) that it is only in Reception class that children should begin to learn to read. | Biological theories (Gesell) | Readiness. Children's nervous systems need to be sufficiently mature for them to show certain behaviours or skills. This is an assumption of stage readiness. |

Maria Montessori's revolutionary method of education is used in many nursery schools and primary schools across the world.

*Source:* © Getty Images / Popperfoto.

Italian teacher, philosopher and physician best known for her method of education for children from birth to adolescence. Her early work centred on women's rights and social reform which helped to formulate a revolutionary method of education. The Montessori method is characterised by: individual teaching and individuality; children's self-directed activity; teachers matching children's learning environments to developmental level; and the role of physical activity in forming concepts and gaining mastery in practical skills. The method is in use today in many settings (mainly nursery and primary schools) and throughout the world. Maria Montessori died in the Netherlands in 1952, after a lifetime devoted to the study of child development. She remains one of the few great theorists who transformed her ideas into a way of organising classrooms, schools, curricula and pedagogy. There remains and continues to grow a rich and important seam of research into the applications, effects and outcomes of her methods.

Another link between feminist theory, child development and issues of social justice is presented in the upcoming feature *Policy, Research and Praxis*, which discusses developments in childcare practices and changes to UK Government policies. After the feature, we will return to the connections between the feminist theoretical perspectives and evolutionary theories.

**Curricula**
A set of courses, and their content, offered in a school or university.

**Pedagogy**
The ways or methods of teaching and learning – how something is taught in schools.

## Policy, Research and Praxis

### A child-care revolution? Plans to allow staff to look after more children

In Britain 27 per cent of family income is spent on childcare, the second highest in the world yet, despite this, the quality of care in the UK is believed to be behind many other European countries. There is strong evidence that childcare has a powerful influence on children's early development. High-quality care is crucial to the development of babies and young children and can have a positive long-term impact on later learning, predicting achievement in maths and literacy (Sylva *et al.*, 2008). The Effective Provision of Pre-School Education (EPPE) Project (2004) found that quality of early years provision is related to better intellectual and cognitive development and social and behavioural development in children at entry to and throughout primary school. Children made more progress in preschool settings where trained teachers are present. Better-qualified staff offer higher quality support for children aged 30 months to five years in developing communication, language, literacy, reasoning, thinking and mathematical skills (Mathers *et al.*, 2011).

The UK Government's vision for a dynamic childcare market was presented in the publication *More Great Childcare* (DfE, 2013). Plans to build a stronger and more professional early years workforce and to drive quality through everything are to be achieved through raising the status and quality of the workforce and giving parents more choice. This has run into trouble already and proposals to alter adult–child ratios have caused furore with parents, nursery and childminding organisations. Currently childminders and nursery staff can look after 3 children aged 1–5 per staff member, and one child under 1 year. When qualified staff are present, one staff member can look after 4 children aged 2 years. Proposals are for the figures to increase so that staff can look after 4 children aged 1–5 and 2 children under 1 year. When qualified staff are present, the ratio would be increased to allow 6 children to be looked after by one member of staff. Staffing regulations in the UK have existed largely unchanged since the 1970s and adult–child ratios are more restrictive than in many

European countries, where many do not set national mandatory ratios for children of any age. Countries such as Denmark, France and Germany where adult–child ratios are higher than the UK are also seen as providing high-quality care for preschool children. Early years minister Elizabeth Truss argues that relaxing the current restrictions on ratios will improve quality and make child-care more available. She wants fewer but better qualified staff looking after young children which will free providers to offer more places by allowing greater flexibility, so that providers will only be able to operate with more children per adult if they employ high quality staff. This will give providers extra income to pay staff more, and it will give more parents the choice of a great childcare place for their child.

Many Nursery staff and childminders are appalled by these plans, viewing them as flawed. Thousands have signed petitions to ignore the Government proposals. They see children's safety being compromised and quality sacrificed. Children in areas of disadvantage are likely to be first affected since care providers in these areas are unlikely to command the high fees in the more affluent areas. As a result, children from low income families are more likely to be cared for in settings looking after more children per staff member. This in itself could foster a two-tier system of care as higher income parents will demand care providers stay with generous ratios. Parents of low incomes do not have that choice. They also argue that increased revenue gained by cutting ratios will simply be diverted to increasing profit margins rather than enhancing quality of provision for children at this crucial stage of their development. More great childcare, but at whose expense?

This century, some feminists and sociologists have become suspicious of evolutionary theories particularly when such theories view sexual difference as being incapable of evolutionary change because of pre-existing cultural value judgements about human nature (Kember, 2001). It is to be welcomed that importance of social justice in feminist approaches has gained influence in recent years, becoming embedded in many courses on childhood and early childhood studies. A focus on social issues provided by feminist approaches questions the categorisations made in some theories (e.g. Piaget), the masculine perspectives taken of behaviour modelling (e.g. Bandura) and the lack of attention to the nature of parent–child relationships in different societies and cultures (e.g. Freud).

**Reflect**

Almost all the theorists we have mentioned to this point, and almost all that we will quote in this and future chapters, are men! Both the writers of this book are men. So is it true, as we asserted above, that 'feminist approaches have become embedded in many courses on childhood and early childhood studies'? Are new theorists more likely to be women than men? Why might feminist perspectives be particularly important at this time? In the remainder of the text we could focus, where possible, on perspectives from women writers. What are your thoughts on this intention?

A further example to that of the feminist perspective of a sociocultural theoretical framework has developed from the work of influential psychologist Lev Vygotsky in the 1920s and 1930s. Social constructivism proposes a more appropriate way of understanding learning where individuals have multiple identities matched to differing social context (family or school) and make active choices for themselves (Lindon, 2005). Social constructivism is now viewed as a set of interrelated theories that synthesise the theoretical perspectives that went before (and which we have discussed in this chapter) to create a paradigm.

The paradigm of social constructivism acknowledges the biological processes of growing up, but maintains that changes are structured and mediated by society and culture (Patterson, 2008). These sociological approaches begin with the idea that childhood is socially constructed – an idea formed through social interaction – created by the social attitudes prevalent

**Social constructivism**
An approach that draws upon sociology, cross-cultural studies and philosophy.

**Paradigm**
Philosophical or theoretical framework of any kind resulting from the application of scientific theory – simply a different way of viewing the world.

at a particular time and in particular contexts. The emphasis on interaction relates directly to the importance given in social constructivism to language development and learning through language. We will return to social constructivist theory in Chapters 10 and 12, but before finishing this chapter we will consider one further more recent theory of development, that of spiritual development.

## Theories of spiritual development

● ● ● ● ● ● ● ● ● ● ● ● ● ● ●
**Connect and Extend**

The French republican principles upon which public education is based include strict separation of religion from schooling. Read: Limage, L. (2000). Education and Muslim identity: The case of France. *Comparative Education*, 36, 73–94, and then compare with a study a decade later. Veinguer, A. A., L. F. Javier R. & Dietz, G. (2011) Under the shadow of Al-Andalus? Spanish teenagers' attitudes and experiences with religious diversity at school. *British Journal of Religious Education*, March, 33(2), 143–158.
● ● ● ● ● ● ● ● ● ● ● ● ● ● ●

In some European countries a clear and robust division is maintained between schooling and spiritual development through religious education. For example, the French Government insists that schools are not places for the teaching of religious doctrine and that no sign of religious allegiance should be worn in school. In the United Kingdom, church and state education are closely linked by law, by history and through the development of a multi-ethnic, multi-faith Britain. Of course there are tensions (e.g. single-faith schools, school uniform, the observance of celebrations and festivals in schools) but there is no widely held view in Britain that schooling and spiritual development should be separated. Attempts have been made to apply stage models of spiritual development based upon stages – a stage model – to how children develop ideas about God and about religion in general.

The most well-known, now historic, stage model of spiritual development is that of James Fowler, a developmental psychologist, in his *Stages of Faith* (1971). Fowler proposed a staged development of spiritual development across our lifespan, which is concerned with the people's relatedness to the ideas of the mystery of life and the universe. The framework of stages in spiritual development may not be religion specific, but in a multi-faith society each faith wants religious education and experience in schools to reflect the stories, tenets, scriptures and practices of their church. For some church leaders the delivery of a universal common curriculum in state schools, even one which is multi-faith in character, will not do.

The meanings of faith are socially constructed and, as we said in relation to the theory of social constructivism, our spiritual and religious experience gives meaning to our existence because of the profound nature of our interactions, particularly during the significant events of our lives. Again, the emphasis on interaction relates directly to the importance of language development and learning through language.

Language is the medium for understanding social meaning, which, in terms of children's development, is how they understand their experiences and express themselves in the socio-cultural group to which they belong. Theorists of social constructivism argue against adults over-directing children's early learning and recommend a facilitating role for practitioners in nursery and school provision. Support for this perspective is strong in early childhood pedagogy in the United Kingdom, the *Te Whariki* curriculum in New Zealand and the Reggio Emilia schools in Italy. The perceived over-direction of learning and the establishment of a single universal curriculum (particularly in relation to spiritual development and religious education) are reasons that lead some parents to educate their children at home. There are many other reasons why parents do decide to educate their children at home and it is not always a decision that goes unchallenged by the authorities (Blok, 2004). For example, read the stance taken by the Dutch Government in 2003:

● ● ● ● ● ● ● ● ● ● ● ● ● ● ●
**Connect and Extend**

To access an overview of European websites supporting home-schooling, find the 'education-otherwise' organisation website, currently at **www.education-otherwise.org/Links/HE_Europe.htm**
● ● ● ● ● ● ● ● ● ● ● ● ● ● ●

> In order for a family to homeschool in the Netherlands, the family must get an exemption from school registration for deeply held religious or philosophical reasons. This exemption is very difficult to achieve and is not available once a child begins attending public school. The Dutch Constitution states: 'all persons shall be free to provide education . . .' In spite of this 'freedom', the Dutch Minister of Education, Maria van der Hoeven, has stated that 'homeschooling is not a right of parents'. Accordingly, the Minister of Education is meeting with the Education Committee of the Second Chamber, the Dutch House of Representatives on October 30, 2003 in order to discuss the regulation of homeschoolers. The Minister would like to restrict homeschooling so

that parents will only be allowed this educational choice if they agree to supervision and inspection by educational authorities.

(*Source*: The Home School Legal Defence Association of the Netherlands, 2008)

Reasons why some parents continue to arrange to educate their children at home and the arguments about home-schooling are explored in the *Controversy* feature below.

## Does home schooling have an adverse effect on children's development and academic achievement?

In England and Wales it is estimated that 170,000 children are now being educated at home. In Russia, home schooling is the fastest growing form of education (Staroverova, 2011) and this mirrors a huge growth in home schooling over a decade ago in the United States (Ray, 2002). Claims from sceptics of home schooling argue that, 'The proper place to learn is in a school' or 'Teachers are trained to teach children, parents are not.' These arguments are countered by responses from advocates of home schooling such as, 'As a family we now have more quality time together' and 'My children just love to learn now!' So why do increasing numbers of parents choose home schooling for their children?

Home schooling was once viewed as a choice for the gifted few (Rivero, 2002), or for those with particular learning (Arora, 2006) or behavioural difficulties, for those being bullied (Francis & Mills, 2012) for whom schooling at home was necessary due to problems with regular attendance at school (Rothermel, 2003), or for some whose homes are so distant from school that home schooling and distance learning are the only viable options (Green, 2006). Now the situation has changed and the number of children receiving this form of alternative education is rising. There are many reasons offered for the attraction of home schooling. For example, it provides more time together for families, it offers a much broader curriculum and one that allows for individual attention. Many parents believe it provides more opportunities for religious and moral training than a school curriculum, and that home schooling is more successful because education provision can be more attuned to the individual interests and needs of the children.

The claim that home schooling is more successful does not go unchallenged (Lubienski, 2003; 2000), and just what effect does home schooling have on children's social development and on achievement? The National Home Education Research Institute (USA) reports a number of early studies that conclude children fare very well in terms of social and emotional development from home schooling. As early as 1986, the researcher J. W. Taylor found that home-educated children have significantly better self-esteem than their peers in public schools. Another early study by researcher Richard Medlin (1991) found that home educators address the needs of children in various areas (personal identity, values and moral development, relationships and social skills, etc.) and at the same time, Shyers (1992) found home-educated children had significantly less problem behaviour than peers in conventional school systems. Based on this early research, Henk Blok (2004) concluded that home-schooled children perform better on average in the cognitive domain (language, mathematics, natural sciences, social studies), but differ little from their peers at school in terms of socio-emotional development.

Much of the evidence about the comparative outcomes of home schooling and standard schooling is American, and so European studies tend to depend upon the finding of American researchers such as Brian Ray. This is understandable as home schooling is illegal in many European states (Spiegler, 2003; Petrie, 2001) despite being considered by many as a human right (Monk, 2003). There are two questions for you to consider. If home schooling is so successful, why don't people do it more? If home schooling is so successful, why is it prevented in the Netherlands?

**Connect and Extend**

For more research into home schooling, access David Galloway's (2003) editorial to a 'Special Issue on Home Education'. *Evaluation & Research in Education*, 17.

**Summary 3**

We now summarise what you have learned in the final section of this chapter:

- No one theory is all-encompassing and no one theoretical approach can provide definitive answers.
- However, theories of childhood can help us to answer the fundamental questions raised by any study of development, including questions of: continuity or stages; heredity or environment; difference or situation; active or passive; and the relative importance of different areas of development.
- Understanding and appreciation of theories is necessary to develop professional practice to become praxis, that is to say practice that is informed by theory.
- More recently developed approaches (e.g. the feminist perspective, theories of social constructivism and theories of spiritual development) have raised doubts about the over-direction of learning in schools and the appropriateness of one standard curriculum.
- A standard curriculum and the sometimes challenging social contexts of schooling leads some parents to educate their children at home.

## Final thoughts on theory in the study of child development

At the end of the first chapter we wrote about the tragic case of Victoria Climbié, killed by her great aunt and the man with whom they lived. You may remember that in response to these terrible events, the UK Government published *Every Child Matters: The Next Steps*, and passed the Children Act 2004. Also published as part of the *Every Child Matters* agenda was *The Common Core of Skills and Knowledge for the Children's Workforce* which sets out the basic skills and knowledge needed by people (including volunteers) whose work brings them into regular contact with children, young people and families.

The skills and knowledge of the Common Core were described under six main headings:

1. effective communication and engagement;
2. child and young person development;
3. safeguarding and promoting the welfare of the child;
4. supporting transitions;
5. multi-agency working;
6. sharing information.

**Connect and Extend**

For details of *The common core of skills and knowledge for the children's workforce*, access **www.every-child-matters.org.uk/Home** or use 'Common Core of Skills' in an Internet search engine.

Over time the UK Government continues to expect everyone working with children, young people and families to be able to demonstrate a basic level of competence in these six areas of the Common Core. The Core forms part of qualifications for working with children, young people and families and acts as a foundation for training and development programmes.

Four of the six headings are what we might term 'transferable skills' that might and probably should apply in any number of professional settings, but we think numbers 2 and 3 are very different. Number 3 speaks specifically of safeguarding and promoting the welfare of the child and addresses Section 11 of the Children Act 2004 which places a statutory duty on key people (you) to make arrangements to safeguard and promote the welfare of children in specific areas including:

- New systems for vetting and barring people whose jobs will bring them into contact with children and vulnerable adults.

- What to do if a practitioner is worried that a child is being abused: best practice guidance for those who work with children in order to safeguard their welfare.
- National minimum standards for private fostering.
- Support for looked-after children in light of a duty to promote their educational achievement as well as safeguarding and promoting their welfare.

Number 2 of the headings (Child and young person development) places a clear responsibility on all those who aspire to working with children to be expert in child development. As we said earlier in this chapter, deep understanding of the theories of child development allows us to do things: to explain phenomena; to predict what might happen given a particular way of doing things; to provide a range of strategies to be used; and to negotiate our own way through this complex science. We hope you now feel well on your way to understanding how knowledge of the theories of childhood will help you to become an expert in child development.

## Conclusion

We want to re-emphasise that theories give us information that can help teachers provide developmentally appropriate practice (Hughes, 2011), enable carers to optimise child-care environments (Watamura *et al.*, 2011), therapists to provide the most appropriate treatment (Reynolds *et al.*, 2012), and parents to identify and interpret their children's behaviour (Stephenson & Dowrick, 2005). So, you can think of theories as having the potential to underpin our strategies to safeguard and promote the welfare of children, and to ensure their cognitive, social and psychological development.

Earlier we touched on the scientific method developed over many hundreds of years by which theories in child development and other sciences have been developed. We explored the idea of scientific method as a focus for the observation of changes in children's behaviour, and the antecedents and consequences of those changes. Observations allow us to develop important ideas in pretty much the same way, as the theorists that used scientific observation and study of children were able to develop their ideas. What follows in the next chapter are the strategies, methods and research designs used by the famous theorists to study children's development.

## Summary Table
### Theories of Child Development

### The purpose of theory (pp 32–34)

#### What is theory? (pp 32–34)

A theory is a means of combining diverse ideas into a coherent framework. B. F. Skinner provides a more precise definition of the development of theory using scientific methods: 'It is an attempt to discover order, to show that certain events stand in lawful relations to other events' (1953, p 35). A theory is formed (in the context of child development) by the systematic observation of how children behave, and organised into patterns of behaviour that have antecedents and consequences. The way in which we make sense of what we observe is to construct meanings from the **A**ntecedents, **B**ehaviour and **C**onsequences of particular phenomena. If these observations are conducted in reliable and valid ways (the scientific method) then the meanings we construct are more likely to apply to more children than just the individuals or groups observed.

## The evaluation of theories (p 34)

Theories allow us to explain phenomena, to predict, to provide a range of strategies to be used, and to understand the complex science of child development. Theories provide information that can help teachers influence children's learning by providing developmentally appropriate practice, enable carers to optimise child-care environments, therapists to provide the most appropriate treatment, and parents to identify and interpret their children's behaviours.

Gewirtz and Peláez-Nogueras (1992) propose four criteria for evaluating theories.

1. How well do the theories explain how children change as they develop? What empirical support is provided for their explanations?
2. How do the theories account for the various factors, such as culture, that influence developmental change?
3. How well do the theories account for individual differences that exist in children's growth and development?
4. Finally, the brevity and simplicity of explanation are important attributes of a good theory.

## Theoretical approaches in child development (pp 35-50)

### Learning theories (pp 36-38)

Theories of how children learn are concerned with influence of the learning environment on a child's development rather than how a child understands the world through experiences. Theorists are John Watson, Ivan Pavlov, B. F. Skinner and Albert Bandura.

### Cognitive theories (pp 38-41)

Theorists taking this viewpoint assert that development of cognitive areas inside the brain influence the ways in which children understand the world and behave. Theorists are Jean Piaget and Lev Vygotsky.

### Psychoanalytic theories (pp 41-42)

In psychoanalytic theories, a much greater emphasis is placed on the social and cultural factors in the development of emotions, motivation and personality. Theorists are Sigmund Freud and Erik Erikson.

### Ecological theories (pp 42-44)

Ecological theories provide us with detailed accounts of the influence of the environment upon development and highlight the interaction of family and other social systems. Theorists are Urie Bronfenbrenner, Esther Thelen and Linda Smith.

### Biological theories (pp 44-48)

Theories in this perspective connect physical growth to social and psychological development by proposing that the roots of these aspects of development are rooted in biological processes, e.g. our knowledge of genetics, the nervous system, and electrical activity in the brain. Theorists are Arnold Gesell, Konrad Lorenz, John Bowlby, David Geary, David Bjorkland and David Buss.

### Comparing the five theoretical approaches (pp 48-50)

Differences in the five theoretical approaches are due to three sets of factors: prevailing thinking at the time when each of the approaches were first proposed; the influence of other theorists working overtime on a particular approach; and variations in the methods the theorists used. No single theory is all-encompassing and no one theoretical approach can provide definitive answers.

## Theory into practice (pp 51-57)

### Implications of theory for educators, carers and parents (p 51)

Understanding and appreciation of a full range of child development theories is necessary to develop professional practice to become praxis, practice that is informed by theory. For example, free play in a nursery includes being able to make mistakes. Lack of criticism from others for mistakes made as part of play leads to a confident and autonomous individual.

### Alternative 'new' perspectives (pp 51-54)

**A feminist perspective**. Links between feminist theory and child development include issues of social justice, gender stereotyping and the use of appropriate language. These form the basis of a feminist sociocultural theoretical approach we might term the 'feminist perspective'. One inspirational example of somebody who successfully linked feminist theory, child development and issues of social justice was Maria Montessori.

**Social constructivism**. The theory proposes that developmental changes are structured and mediated by society and culture. Childhood is socially constructed during the social events of our lives and founded on the importance of language development and learning through language.

### Theories of spiritual development (pp 54-56)

James Fowler (1971) proposed a staged development of spiritual development across our lifespan, and is concerned with the people's relatedness to the ideas of the mystery of life and the universe. The meanings of faith are socially constructed and there is an emphasis on the importance of learning through language.

**Final thoughts on theory in the study of child development** (pp 56–57)

Published as part of the *Every Child Matters* agenda was *The Common Core of Skills and Knowledge for the Children's Workforce* which sets out the basic skills and knowledge needed by people (including volunteers) whose work brings them into regular contact with children, young people and families. Number 2 of the main headings (Child and young person development) places a clear responsibility on all those who aspire to working with children to be expert in child development. To become an expert in child development, it is important to understand the implications of the theories of childhood.

## Going further

Robinson, L. (2007) *Cross-cultural child development for social workers: An introduction.* London: Palgrave Macmillan.
An exciting and innovative text which draws on literature from Britain and North America to explain child development from a cross-cultural, black and ecological perspective.

Barker, R. (2008) *Making sense of Every Child Matters: Multi-professional practice guidance.* Bristol: The Policy Press.
An edited book which provides child practitioners in public, private and voluntary settings with a valuable text to guide their practice.

Daly, M. & Taylor, W. (2006) *Understanding early years theory in practice: An accessible overview of major child development theories (Professional Development).* Oxford: Heinemann.
Packed with real-life examples and case studies to set theory in context. Covers all the major theorists and theories covered in childhood courses.

Slee, P. & Shute, R. (2003). *Child development: Thinking about theories.* London: Arnold.
A highly informative text in a style that students and researchers will find very engaging.

## Useful websites

http://www.learning-theories.com/

A 'Knowledge Base and Webliography' for:
- Behaviorist Theories (5)
- Cognitive Theories (6)
- Constructivist Theories (5)
- Descriptive Theories (3)
- Design Theories & Models (3)
- Humanist Theories (3)
- Identity Theories (3)
- Learning Theories & Models (11)
- Motivation Theories (3)
- Paradigms and Perspectives (5)
- Social Learning Theories (2)

http://every-child-matters.co.uk/
One site that provides up to date information about the latest developments for the Every Child Matters policy and professional practice agenda.

# Chapter 3
## Research Methods

### Overview

# Introduction

In the last chapter we explained that theories of child development are almost always generated from systematic observations of behaviour to 'show that certain events stand in lawful relation to other events' (Skinner, 1953, p 35). We looked at the history of scientific method as a context in which the five main theoretical perspectives were developed, and we began to trace the connections between theory and professional practice. We also argued that evaluation of the usefulness and application of theory often begins by considering to what extent there is any evidence for the theoretical conclusions drawn. In a 'nutshell': is research in child development valid and reliable? To answer this question we have to look at the methods used to capture information, the methods used to analyse the data and to generate the theories. Therefore, our task in this chapter is to form a better understanding *of* the research into child development by understanding *about* the research. Then, perhaps, we can make better sense of the fascinating world of children.

## Chapter Objectives

By the time you have completed this chapter you should be able to answer the following questions:

- Why is it important to know how to study children and child development?
- How are practice and research connected?
- What are the most common research methods used to study child development?
- Which methods are used in particular circumstances?
- What ethical considerations must we observe when studying children?

# Researching children

## Studying children in school, day-care and family settings

Our understanding of childhood grows from experience and study. Indeed, it is often our 'everyday' experiences that spark our interest and lead us to engage in more systematic study; to read and to research in order to deepen and enrich our understanding of what we experience. Two examples of a desire to find out more are personal anecdotes by the authors of this book.

> Jonathan Doherty remembers: *As a young primary school teacher in the 1980s, I remember being fascinated by the diverse and complex behaviours of children witnessed daily in my classroom. I wanted to find out exactly how to capture what I saw. Many of my observations were snapshots of children's lives, key moments that might never be repeated.*
>
> Malcolm Hughes recalls: *It was 2 o'clock in the morning and just like most '2 o'clocks', I was up with Rebecca – our 18-month-old. She was wonderful company, babbling and toddling around the landing, with the entire contents of her toy box strewn haphazardly outside our closed bedroom door. Mum was sleeping and this had become my precious time with Becca. We sang songs and played. She talked non-stop – not bad for a vocabulary of 40 words or so. I was entranced by her every move, her every experiment with each toy: does it make a noise; can I throw it; can I take it apart? She was great at taking things apart, simple wooden puzzles, shape sorters and lots of things that weren't meant to come apart. I wanted to capture those moments (moments that lasted hours!), watch and share in every second of her growing, her learning and her play. She's 29 today, a teacher and primary school manager, and I think she still likes taking things apart to see how they work.*

So what methods are best to try to capture how children grow, think and form relationships with others at home or in a classroom? The specific methods or strategies used to gather data on children's abilities, their thoughts and feelings will of course depend on what you start out to discover. In formal research (rather than the dimming memories of a doting father) what you set out to discover is often referred to as your research question, and the way you set about finding answers to this question is your research method.

**Reflect**

Recall some time spent with very young children. (If you haven't done this, plan now to spend some time with a very young child – perhaps less than 6 months old.) How do you communicate with a very young child? Think very carefully about the language you use, the tone of voice and the facial expressions you use. What makes very young children happy? How do you calm a baby who is distressed? What makes them giggle with delight?

At the start of Chapter 2 we explored the generation of theory through research and how research can inform practice. You may remember the phrase coined by social psychologist Kurt Lewin: 'there is nothing as practical as a good theory'. The relationship between theory and practical application is not always clear, and the same could be said for research and professional practice. Sometimes it is necessary to encourage colleagues to 'research into what we do, and do what we research' because at times it is difficult to see how some of the research in which we engage relates to the core business of teaching child development and childhood studies – making a contribution to the educational enterprise by which we enhance our way of life. We are not the only ones to signal that there may be too big a gap between research and practice, as you will read in the *Controversy* feature opposite.

## Controversy

### Is there a gap between research and practice?

Charles Desforges, expert classroom researcher, neatly summed up concerns about a gap between research and practice when he wrote, 'researchers have got lost in thought whilst practitioners have gone missing in action' (2004, p 15). Desforges is reflecting on the need for a relevant research base in education that is predicated on evidence, rather than simply 'tips for teachers' and asserts that a high-quality professional knowledge base will be an asset to generations of learners.

However, assembling a high-quality professional knowledge base is no easy task. Desforges warns of 'dragons in methodological mazes' (*ibidem*) that diverts our thinking and involvement in too many small-scale questions, when the drive should be towards empowering learners and promoting their autonomy. Tensions between research (or theory) and practice have existed for some time. David Hargreaves (1996) in the annual UK Teacher Training Agency lecture 'Teaching as a research-based profession: possibilities and prospects' asserted that: 'the gap between researchers and practitioners [is the] fatal flaw in educational research.' This assertion by Hargreaves raises the question: What form does this gap take? Here are some potential gap-formers:

- There is a professional requirement on developmental academics to *do* research, (whether or not the research is needed) that it is different from that being done elsewhere, is relevant to practitioners, or is cost-effective. To move from doing teaching to doing research is viewed as a promotion and a requirement for further promotion.

- Thousands of research papers are published each year in journals that are not read by practitioners. The findings are rarely tested in practice.

- Practitioners tend to engage in research only as part of a course of study leading to higher-level qualifications.

- Very little research is a shared enterprise between academic researchers and practitioners. Practitioners and their pupils are viewed as the subject of research, not as authors or co-authors.

More recent evidence (e.g. Sarita Davis and colleagues, 2013) suggests that little has changed in the last 16 years since Chris Woodhead, the then Chief Inspector of Schools in England, commissioned from James Tooley of Newcastle University a report (1998) on the quality of educational research. Tooley's conclusion was that the majority of research is partisan, conducted in a biased way or logically incoherent: 'The picture emerged of researchers doing their research largely in a vacuum, unnoticed and unheeded by anyone else.' In a foreword to the report, Woodhead says that much of the research being done is 'methodologically suspect' and 'intellectually second-rate' and 'at best no more than an irrelevance and a distraction'.

The report said that it is estimated that £70m a year is spent on educational research, about 90 per cent of it government money – enough to employ 2800 teachers or to equip 70 secondary schools with networked computers for every pupil. It suggests that a better alternative to 'the literally thousands of small-scale research projects' would be to use the money for a dozen or so carefully focused, better quality projects.

At around the same time David Shaffer (1999) observed that practitioners desire answers, while researchers rarely provide them. Practitioners see a lack of clarity in conclusions to research studies cloaked in language like, 'it is too early to draw conclusions . . .' and 'results may suggest . . .'. Researchers see such statements as necessary cautions in highly complex problems but practitioners view cautions as a degree of equivocation that makes the research pointless.

• • • • • • • • • • • • • • •
**Connect and Extend**
Is this an example of
bridging the gap between
research and practice?
'In an emergent field of
research, African scholars
are beginning to challenge
the prevailing (Western)
theories of citizenship and
democracy.' (Abstract
p 179) Read: Wainaina,
P., Arnot, M. & Chege, F.
(2011). Developing ethical
and democratic citizens
in a post-colonial context:
citizenship education
in Kenya. *Educational
Research*, 2011, 53(2),
179–192.
• • • • • • • • • • • • • • •

The research practice gap is not confined to child development or education. In 2003, Beth Seymour, Sue Kinn and Norrie Sutherland report a continuing failure to narrow the research practice gap in clinical practice. In 2004 Michael Burke, Fritz Drasgow and Jack Edwards noted a knowledge gap in the context of psychological research and human resource management. So how can the gap between researchers in child development and practitioners be resolved? A persuasive argument that the gap can be closed is provided by Donald McIntyre (2005). McIntyre proposes three strategies:

1. All research processes culminates in a critical trial by teachers in the context of their own practice.

2. Appropriate research strategies should be designed and adopted with closing the gap in mind.

3. The development of 'knowledge-creating schools' – schools where research is done.

*Source*: http://news.bbc.co.uk/1/hi/education/137001.stm (accessed 15 July 2012).

*Child Development, Theory and Practice 0–11* is, in part, an attempt to bridge the gap between research and practice by bringing important, relevant and recent research in child development to the critical attention of readers. During your study of child development you will want to test the application of research findings when working with children in professional settings. What research can you trust? What kinds of research are likely to produce results that are valid and reliable? Which research can be applied universally? To make these judgements you need to know about the research approaches used to produce the results, because any research is only as valid and reliable as the methods used to conduct it.

## Research approaches – paradigms

The brief description of a history of child development in Chapter 1 of this text reveals the contemporary picture to be one of systematic enquiry based on the scientific method – ideas that we met in Chapter 2. In summary, the scientific approach uses objective, measurable and repeatable techniques to gather information about children. The scientific approach requires a 'constant cycle of theorizing, empirical testing of the resulting hypotheses, and a revision (or even outright rejection) of theories as the new data comes in' (Bukatko & Daehler, 2001, p 41). Glenda MacNaughton and Sharne Rolfe, researchers into early childhood, make a useful analogy between researchers and detectives, in that both researchers and detectives search for clues about how and why certain things happen, and ask questions about something that puzzles or intrigues them (2004). MacNaughton and Rolfe go on to propose that, just like detectives, researchers have different ideas as to how to approach searching and questioning.

Some investigators like to pursue their research in a logical and step-by-step fashion, while others prefer a less defined and more fluid and intuitive approach – not tied to scientific processes and techniques. Neither the logical nor the intuitive approach is necessarily right or wrong since both offer insights in the area that reflect the particular way of looking at the world. More experienced readers will of course immediately realise that these two approaches correspond to two of the paradigms used in educational research (Cohen *et al.*, 2007). The first paradigm – involving the use of quantitative research methods and statistical analysis – stems from the views of eighteenth century empiricists such as Thomas Hobbes and John Locke (remember Locke from Chapter 1 – he believed the human mind to be a clean slate to write on; a *tabula rasa*) who viewed the world in absolute terms of truths and untruths. Quantitative research is associated with positivist research methods where theories are positively affirmed through strict scientific method. Positivist methods define the phenomena (the happenings)

**Quantitative research methods**
Analysis that involves counting observations of occurrence and change, and manipulating the totals using statistical methods.

**Empiricists**
People who reject sticking to out-of-date beliefs and opinions, preferring instead to rely on observation and experience.

**Positivist research methods**
Based on a belief that the only authentic knowledge is scientific knowledge, and that such knowledge can come only from positive affirmation of theories through strict scientific method.

we observe as quantifiable and suitable for objective investigation. Researchers who favour this approach when studying children set out to test hypotheses based on theory, collect data before they analyse, and draw conclusions from it. An example of this method is in the nearby *Connect and Extend* – the tip-of-the-tongue paradigm.

Alternatively, using the interpretivist or postmodern paradigms, a researcher avoids initial ideas about what might be happening, works from the data to the conclusion, may modify the enquiry as understandings develop, and usually employs qualitative research methods of observation in natural settings and interpretation. This type of research has special appeal to those in educational settings since classrooms lend themselves to observation and analysis in a more open-ended way and teachers are often keen to make observations that reflect classroom life (Chan, 2011; Child, 2004).

Whichever approach – positivist or interpretivist – is taken in the study of children's development, it must be remembered that both approaches are highly disciplined and systematic in their own ways. An approach is selected as being best suited to the values and experience of the researcher, the context of the research and the specific research aims, often framed as research questions, which are set at the outset of the research and then often refined in the light of initial findings. Setting research questions is often the most difficult initial step and it is a telling part of any critique of a piece of research to see how the research questions are framed and contextualised in the opening section of the report.

When researchers have decided what they want to know, they carefully frame research questions which address their line of enquiry, check the context in which they will be working to ensure the subject of study is relevant, topical and important, then design their methodology. Research methodology is the procedures adopted to collect, organise, analyse and interpret data to find answers to research questions. What research options are open to researchers? What research methods are most commonly used? What are the advantages and challenges of different kinds of research in child development? With these questions in mind, in the next section we will consider the range of strategies available to gather data about children.

**Interpretivist research methods**
Based on a belief that a researcher works from the data to the conclusion and employs qualitative research methods of observation in natural settings and interpretation.

**Qualitative research methods**
Analysis that highlights themes or patterns perceived through detailed observation of phenomena.

**Research questions**
The specific questions of a study for which the researcher is seeking answers.

**Connect and Extend**

Read a technical report of a study which used the tip-of-the-tongue experimental paradigm in a phonological retrieval task. Read: Buján, A., Galdo-Álvarez, S., Lindín, M. & Díaz, F. (2012). An event related potentials study of face naming: Evidence of phonological retrieval deficit in the tip-of-the-tongue state. *Psychophysiology*, 2012, *49*(7), 980–990. This could make you expert in tip-of-the-tongue research!

Before moving on, let's summarise what we have learned so far:

- Much of the research undertaken in recent years into childhood and learning is open to challenge that it is not closely related to the needs of childhood practitioners.

- The use of the scientific method should allow us to construct more universally applicable theories, strategies and treatments.

- Almost all research in child development can be situated in either the qualitative (interpretive approaches) paradigm or the quantitative (empirical approaches) paradigm.

- Researchers usually first try to describe their interest in the subject of the research and to identify research questions.

Summary 1

# Research methods

Some of the most commonly used research methods in child development are experimental methods, correlation methods, surveys, case studies, reports from narrative, observations in context and psychophysical methods. Before we discuss and explore each of these methods it is important to note that these research methods are not completely discrete – by which we mean being individually different and distinct rather than discreet (action to avoid social

**Triangulate**
To use more than one research method to further validate the findings of a study.

• • • • • • • • • • • • • • • •

**Connect and Extend**
For an example of 'triangulation', read: Warin, J., Solomon, Y. & Lewis, C. (2007). Swapping stories: Comparing plots: Triangulating individual narratives within families. *International Journal of Social Research Methodology*, 10, 121–134.

• • • • • • • • • • • • • • • •

**Independent variables**
Those aspects in the environment that the researcher is able to control.

**Dependent variables**
Those aspects of the situation which result from researchers manipulating independent variables.

embarrassment). It will become very clear during this chapter that researchers often adopt a multiple research design in which they engage in a mix of research methods to triangulate their results. This needs some explanation. In surveying, a position is fixed by triangulation (taking two different sightings of a point) and so the term 'triangulation' is used in research to indicate that two different methods are used to check out the data from each method adopted. For example, researchers may start with a questionnaire of a selected section of the target population (e.g. a thousand 10-year-olds) then follow this up with 10 case studies drawn from interesting responses to the questionnaire.

## Experimental methods

This method of research enables a cause-and-effect relationship between variables. If that sounds a bit baffling try thinking of this method as answering the question: what would happen if . . . ? Researchers assess the current condition or state of affairs before any action, sometimes termed an independent variable, is introduced. After an independent variable is introduced by the experimenter, the effect of that variable on the context is assessed. If this still sounds like nonsense, try thinking of this method as the 'bull in the china shop' method. We assess the china shop as being full of interesting and beautiful pieces of china and porcelain. If we introduce a bull into the shop and allow the bull to run around for a few minutes we can observe the effects of the bull on the shop – shattered china, total destruction. Independent variables – or perhaps we could say varia*bulls* (sic) – are controlled by the investigator (if the bull can be thought of as controllable) and dependent variables are the anticipated reaction or consequences of the introduction of the independent variable (the bull). The extent of the destruction in the china shop – how many plates are totally destroyed, partially damaged or just dislodged – is the dependent variable.

An example of experimental research is one study undertaken by Maria Legerstee and colleagues at the Center for Infancy at York University (US) to discover whether infants could distinguish faces of other babies from the face of a puppet (1998). The independent variables were the different images shown to them on video of different faces, and the dependent variables were different responses of looking, smiling and vocalising of the infants during the time they were engaged in these behaviours. If you would like to know what the researchers concluded then do look up the results in Legerstee, M., Anderson, D. & Schaffer, A. (1998). Five- and eight-month-old infants recognize their faces and voices as familiar and social stimuli. *Child Development*, 69, 37–50.

Some experiments create distress among young children. For example, babies are sometimes upset by the appearance of puppets as part of a project showing images of other babies and puppets. Is it OK to temporarily distress a child to pursue a scientific enquiry? We found some fascinating 'footage' at **www.youtube.com** by putting in the search term 'baby experiment'. View the experiments, bearing in mind Article 36 of the United Nations Convention on *Rights of the Child*: children have the right to protection from any kind of exploitation.

Experimental methods like the recognition study by Maria Legerstee and colleagues are usually undertaken in laboratories (such as the 'Center for Infancy' referred to above). The level of control exercised by a researcher in a laboratory allows for more confident assertions to be made about causes in developmental phenomena, and experimental methods have been viewed as particularly successful when experiments are replicated by others (Rogers & Ozonoff, 2005; Herwig *et al.*, 2001) and when the experiment is focused on an easily identified and isolated aspect of behaviour (Mondloch & Maurer, 2004). However, there are many aspects of children's behaviour, such as at family meals, which can only be viewed in the context where the behaviour occurs: the home, school or playgroup. Therefore the researcher has to leave their laboratory and travel 'into the field'.

Field experiments take place in natural settings such as at home or in school. They are seen as more realistic as development is affected by many variables, all of which might be important to those studying children. Field experiments have been used in studying aspects of child development and developmental psychology for some considerable time. For example, in their now classic study on the effects of media violence on Belgian delinquent boys, Professor Jacques-Phillipe Leyens (psychologist at the Catholic University of Louvrain, Belgium) and colleagues (1975) presented violent film images to the boys each evening for one week in the institution where the boys lived and recorded the instances of aggressive behaviours daily. Results that media violence does increase aggressive behaviour were consistent with those of Liebert and Baron (1972) carried out earlier under laboratory conditions.

When experimental research is conducted in the field, it is sometimes referred to as natural or quasi-experimental. So, for example, to provide additional evidence that a new treatment or teaching technique is having a different effect to more traditional methods, researchers in the field use two groups: an experimental group to which the treatment or technique is applied and a control group which in every other way are treated the same except for the new treatment or technique. When evaluating experimental research of all kinds, we look for evidence that the treatment of the two groups is the same and that other factors or variables do not contribute to perceived differences as a result of applying the independent variable. This can be challenging in natural settings, where conditions are not so readily controlled as in a laboratory.

More recently than Leyen's field experiments in the 1970s, C.-Y. Lai and C.-C. Wu (researchers in Taiwan) used a quasi-experimental research design 'in the field' to investigate the effects of using handheld computers to support co-operative learning activities (2006). Groups of pupils were provided with handheld computers and parallel groups worked without. They found that handheld computers enhanced both students' attitudes and performance in learning, and promoted better interactions among students and teachers. In another example (2004) Kenneth Drozd from the University of Aarhus in Denmark looked at the use of certain experimental designs when assessing children's language development. He found that children underperformed owing to the additional language demands associated with some experimental tasks.

In summary, experimental methods, whether in the laboratory or in the field, seek to find the connection between a course of action like a new treatment or a set of teaching techniques (see the nearby *Connect and Extend* feature) and the effect of applying that treatment or technique to a target group. Another way of finding connections and associations between observations of behaviour, causes and consequences is to use a correlation method, and that is where we turn next.

## Correlation methods

These methods provide information on the relationship between two variables. Investigators do not interfere with subjects' environments in any way. They do not apply any independent variables or withhold an independent variable from a control group. Researchers who use a correlation method make observations of two different variables and look to see whether there is a statistical connection between the occurrences of the two variables. Let's go back to our 'bull in the china shop' metaphor. Let's suppose a researcher introduces a bull into a china shop, measures the size of the bull and the number of smashed plates and vases. After many introductions of bulls into china shops, much careful measuring of different sized bulls and accurate counting of smashed plates and vases, the researcher may find a significant relationship between the size of the bull and the amount of destruction. Of course, there may be other

**Field experiments**
Those research studies carried out in real-world settings, such as in the home or in educational settings.

**Control group**
A 'parallel' group similar to an experimental group and treated in the same way, except that the experimental treatment is not applied.

• • • • • • • • • • • • • •
**Connect and Extend**
A control group does not appear to have been used in the research reported by Squires, G. (2001). Using cognitive behavioural psychology with groups of pupils to improve self-control of behaviour. *Educational Psychology in Practice*, 17, 317–335. How much more valid would the findings have been had one been included?
• • • • • • • • • • • • • •

• • • • • • • • • • • • • •
**Connect and Extend**
For an example of (arguably) quasi-experimental methods in a child developmental context, read: Dimitriadis, C. (2012). Provision for mathematically gifted children in primary schools: an investigation of four different methods of organisational provision. *Educational Review*, May, 64(2), 241–260.
• • • • • • • • • • • • • •

variables that come into play, such as the amount of time the bull is in the shop and the distance between the display stands. During the study, the researcher may find a more significant relation between the time the bull is in the shop and the amount of destruction – a better correlation.

Correlation studies have investigated the relationships between such variables as measures of intelligence and reading abilities, and between family influences and truancy rates. Remember that influential and important study from the 1970s into the effects of media violence on Belgian delinquent boys. That study suggested that children who watch a lot of television tend to imitate the actions of characters on screen. From this research an investigator may form a hypothesis that children who watch a lot of television are more inclined towards aggressive behaviour towards others. The researcher would collect data on how much 'violent television' was watched by a target group and how much violence was being displayed by members of the group.

Using an appropriate statistical procedure (there are a number available depending on the type of data and how it is structured) a researcher can calculate a correlation coefficient which is a number value of the strength and direction (positive or negative) of the two variables which ranges from −1.00 to +1.00. If the number value is calculated as zero, the two variables are unrelated. The sign of the coefficient shows its direction. Correlation methods reveal relationships between two variables – say examination results and amount of television watched: an increase or decrease at a similar or dissimilar rate would be a positive correlation (the more of one thing, the more of the other). In a negative correlation, as the values of one of the variables increase, the values of the second variable decrease (the more of one thing, the less of the other thing). For example, there is a negative correlation between television viewing and examination grades – pupils who spend more time watching television tend to have lower examination grades (Sigman, 2007). Correlations of ± (plus or minus) 0.70 or above indicate strong relationships and those of ±0.20 or less show weak relationships.

Results of studies on television violence (such as that of Professor Leyens and his team) show moderate positive correlations between violent behaviour towards others and the amount of violence viewed on television, but they show only that a relationship exists. The causes of the relationship are not indicated by the correlation coefficient. Although correlation designs do reveal relationships between variables we cannot infer that one thing causes another directly, only that frequencies in both variables increase or decrease at a similar or dissimilar rate.

So why can't we say that one variable causes another? It is simple really – correlation studies cannot tell you whether naturally violent children choose to watch more violent television, or whether watching more violent television makes you appear a more naturally violent child. Of course, there may be a whole host of other 'causes' of violent behaviour, such as social class or access to alcohol.

## Surveys

Survey methods (generally viewed as quantitative methods) involve asking a series of closed questions to access information about people's attitudes or personal perceptions. Surveys are effective in providing information on broad-based patterns of development. Often they are used in large-scale studies that gather data from other records kept about the target population, such as anonymised medical records. Another very common technique is to use printed or electronic questionnaires, or interview methods with a representative sample of the population – a group that resembles the larger population about which data are being collected. Members of the target population fill in information, react to statements on the printed questionnaire form using a scale of possible responses, or respond to questions from an interviewer who enters the information on a form.

Surveys provide statistical information that can be organised into tables, tested for statistical significance (techniques that check whether the same results could be produced randomly)

---

**Hypothesis**
A supposition which provides a starting point for further investigation.

**Correlation coefficient**
A statistical measure that summarises the strength and direction of the relationship between two variables.

**Representative sample**
A group that resembles the larger population about which data are being collected.

**Table 3.1** The ten countries with the most births

| | Country | Estimated births 2007 |
|---|---|---|
| 1 | India | 24 073 392 |
| 2 | China | 17 778 908 |
| 3 | Nigeria | 5 428 253 |
| 4 | Indonesia | 4 960 256 |
| 5 | Pakistan | 4 919 004 |
| 6 | Bangladesh | 4 417 163 |
| 7 | USA | 4 264 142 |
| 8 | Brazil | 3 097 174 |
| 9 | Ethiopia | 2 860 779 |
| 10 | Democratic Republic of Congo | 2 798 765 |
| | World | 131 698 130 |
| | UK | 648 482 |

*Source*: Ash, R. (2007). *The Top Ten of Everything* (p 54). London: Hamlyn. Hamlyn cite that this is data from US Census Bureau, International Data Base (IDB).

and analysed for patterns. Statistical patterns allow researchers and other childhood professionals to make predictions about individuals and other estimations. Many people are fascinated with statistics of every kind: the tallest, heaviest, most expensive, most popular of everything. *The top 10 of everything* is a Hamlyn book compiled by Russell Ash in which survey data provide information that allow estimates to be made. Table 3.1 is included in *The top 10 of everything*.

**Reflect**   As India's birth rate is consistently high and China's is subject to curbs, the population of India is set to overtake that of China by 2030. What other information would you need so that you could estimate which countries have the highest birth rate and population density? How might a similar table to Table 3.1 look in 20 years' time?

The above *Reflect* feature raises a number of important points. To begin with, the estimated birth was a 'head count' not expressed as a fraction of the current population, there was no information about the size of the country, and nothing about the death rates or gross national product. In other words there was insufficient information to chance any conclusions about how the table might look by 2030. Even though surveys are very useful ways of gathering large amounts of information (research data), they are always open to the critique that the information is partial, incomplete and could have been very different if researchers had asked a different thousand people to the thousand people they did ask, or had asked different questions. Even very large surveys can be suspect if they miss large portions of the target population.

For example, a national census in the United Kingdom takes place every ten years. This is by far the largest survey that takes place in this part of Europe. The UK Government aims for 100 per cent return of census forms providing information about every person residing in the United Kingdom on the census date. Results from the census in 1991 led officials to believe that 3.8 per cent of the population had been missed. Now there is no real problem in missing out just 3.8 per cent, if that is randomly scattered throughout the target population, but will be more problematic if it systematically misses out just one particular part of the population, e.g. the homeless. For the 2001 census a second study was undertaken – the One Number Census (ONC). The ONC's aim was to identify and adjust for the number of people and households not counted in the 2001 Census. The extent of this under-counting was identified

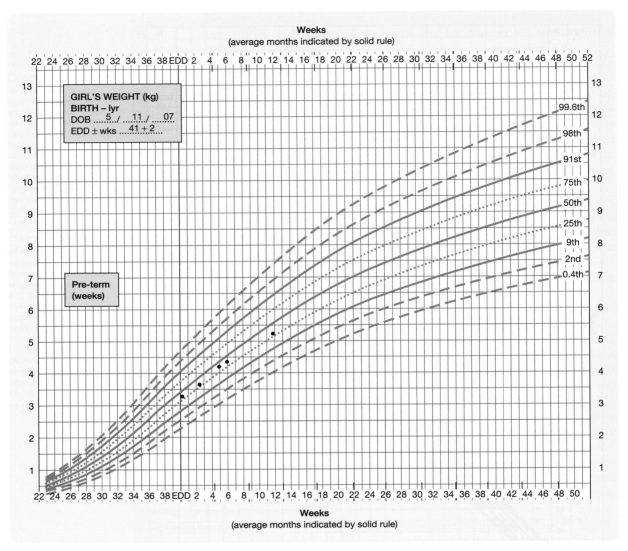

**Figure 3.2** Niamh's growth chart

*Source*: The Child Growth Foundation website (www.childgrowthfoundation.org/ghd.htm). Copyright © Child Growth Foundation, reproduced with permission.

they choose a special case or several special cases to observe, to document and to analyse. Descriptions and analysis related to observation of a very small sample of the target population are often presented as case studies and is the type of study that we now explain.

Matthias Kontny is a paediatrician and a friend who lives and practises in the village of St Oldberg, near Aachen, North Germany. We share an interest in music, particularly choral singing. When I last visited, Matthias complained that the growth tables he uses in his work with children are all American, and he wondered whether there would be any difference if he could access tables developed in his region of Germany. What do you think? Do you think there would be significant regional, national or ethnic differences in growth tables created from regional data? What might account for such differences? You may want to refer to Chapter 1 when we considered the relative importance of nature and nurture on the development of children.

# Case studies

An advantage of studies such as these is that they allow researchers to study individual children as well as groups such as families, classes, year groups and even communities. Researchers (e.g. Magos, 2012; Jurkowski et al., 2012; Bone 2010) tend to work with one of three types of case study:

- *Exploratory studies* – an example might involve a ward sister trying to find out the effect on the recovery rates of children, if any, of a newly created play area.

- *Descriptive studies* – an example in a home context might provide detailed information on how a foster child settles into an existing family over a period of time, and what lessons that might have for supporting foster families during the settling-in period.

- *Explanatory studies* – an example is an investigation of the effects on educational provision for all pupils of integrating comparatively large 'come-and-go' groups of travelling children into a small village primary school.

Case studies of all three types can provide valuable insights into development and are relevant to a wide variety of home, school and community settings. Possible drawbacks which can lead to findings being challenged include unsystematic collection of data, the researcher's own bias and subjectivity and often a lack of application to other similar 'cases' (generalisability). Therefore, as you may remember, it is often wise to use a combination of methods (such as interviews and questionnaires) in conjunction with case study methods to lessen such effects and to provide more validity and reliability. Remember that this process is called triangulation. Getting information from more than one source is often used when writing reports on individual target children.

# Reports from narrative

Next we will look at narrative accounts of children's development. It is generally accepted that the first scientific attempt to record development were the baby biographies or diaries of King Henry IV of France, who recorded early development and child-rearing of his son Louis the Dauphin in the seventeenth century. A century later, Charles Darwin used the same method to detail his son William Erasmus Darwin's development, to answer questions about human development that arose from his writings on the descent of man and the evolution of our species as mentioned earlier. Nowadays, reports about children are generally accepted to be of three main types. Firstly, self-narrative from children, which is normally in the form of a structured interview or questionnaire. Certainly children are good judges of their own histories and feelings and their truthfulness ratings – the extent to which children know and tell the truth about themselves – are equal to those of adults (Fitzgerald et al., 2002). However, there can be problems with children's lack of understanding of questions, slowness to respond and limited attention – problematic in both interviews and questionnaires.

A second source of reports is from close family, which have an advantage in that information is usually gleaned from observations over some considerable time and in a variety of situations (King Henry IV of France and Charles Darwin are examples – by self-testimony). Problems associated with reports from family members centre around misremembering details and time frames, aligning the truth of what happened too closely with the myths and evolving stories of family history, and underplaying aspects of development in children that closely mirror family members' own history. Methods to increase validity of parental reports on their children involve training parents to be more impartial observers, regular phone calls to gather information, encouraging the use of structured diaries and even bleeping devices which when activated require the recording of child behaviours or activities at that time (Strina et al., 2005).

**Generalisability**
The extent to which theories developed from the observation of a few cases can be said to be valid for other similar cases.

**Validity**
The property we would give to research which uses methods that accurately measure or describe the behaviour we are observing.

**Reliability**
The measure by which we judge that, if an experiment or observation is carried out at a different time or in a different place, very similar results would be forthcoming.

**Connect and Extend**
Read the report of a study which uses three methods of data gathering: questionnaires, e-mail conversations and face-to-face interviews: Nutbrown, C. & Clough, P. (2004). Inclusion and exclusion in the early years: Conversations with European educators. *European Journal of Special Needs Education*, 19, 301–315.

Finally, teachers and peers can provide important information. Teachers can report on a wide range of developmental factors including attentiveness, sociability and disruptiveness. Teachers are expert in reporting on cognitive and educational progress and increasingly (as noted at the end of Chapter 2) are expected to be experts in child development. Although less common in practice, friends and peers can also provide a rich account of the target child's social status in the classroom. Narrative of teachers and peers, family members and the target subject or subjects themselves can provide very rich and exciting data, but many researchers prefer to observe the target subject when trying to understand the developmental implications of the behaviour they are studying. What are the principles, challenges and strengths of research by direct observation? We will explore these now.

## Observations in context

**Naturalistic observation**
Observations made in real-life settings.

Many researchers and practitioners favour observing the behaviours of children in their every-day environments of home, playground, day-care settings and classrooms and using methods of **naturalistic observation**. Practitioners working with children use checklists, time and event sampling, record sheets and profiles for assessment purposes.

These tools and the skills to use them are similar to those required when observing children in laboratory conditions, and there is an abundance of literature on observational techniques (some of which is listed at the end of this chapter). Observations can, of course, be undertaken in laboratories in **structured observation** where the researcher sets up a situation to provoke behaviour so that it can be studied and recorded systematically. This technique does yield important data but suffers from a major disadvantage that children do not necessarily behave in the artificial conditions of a laboratory as they do under more normal conditions in the settings just described.

**Structured observation**
Observations that a researcher records in situations specifically constructed for that purpose. Frequently occurring under laboratory conditions.

There are many scenes of childhood that careful observation in natural settings can reveal, and the list provided by researcher Jenny Willan and colleagues in Table 3.2 identifies many aspects of development. The original title of the table was *What to look at*. A potential difficulty with naturalistic observations is the effect that an observer (or team of observers) may have upon the observed behaviour of a child or children. This potential difficulty needs to be addressed in the early stages of any research study. Concerns about effects of observers in the natural setting has resulted in hidden video cameras in classrooms or researchers being required to spend large amounts of time becoming part of the setting so that such observer

**Table 3.2** Aspects of development to study through observation

| | |
|---|---|
| Physical development | Inside and outside play (use of space, boys and girls, preferences) |
| Communication skill | Activities (educational, play, imitative) |
| Emotional well-being | Gendered play |
| Intellectual abilities | Learning |
| Moral and spiritual development | Behaviour in different situations |
| Social relationships | Interaction in peer groups |
| Critical incidents (birth of a new baby, starting school, separating from a parent) | Interaction with parents Interaction with different adults |
| Comparisons of ages and stages | Special needs |
| Types of play (free play, directed play, solitary play, interactive play) | Special settings (hospital, sickroom, dentist, first day at nursery) |
| Patterns of play (play with materials, role play, imaginative play) | Special situations (tests, unfamiliar settings) |

*Source*: Willan, J., Parker-Rees, R. & Savage, J. (Eds) (2004). *Early childhood studies: An introduction to the study of children's worlds and children's lives* (p. 115). Exeter: Learning Matters. Reproduced with permission.

presence is minimised. Ethical and practical concerns related to the observation of teachers' and pupils' behaviour is further discussed in the *Focus on Theory* feature later in this chapter.

Observation's greatest advantage as a strategy for collecting data about children is in illustrating how people behave in everyday life (Quar *et al.*, 2012). Classic and influential research in Australia by Rolfe and Crossley (1991) on the effects of play environments on the social behaviour of pre-school children used direct observation in indoor and outdoor play to categorise peer interactions. They concluded from their observations that children's outside play was significantly more social than indoor play. In this study the approach adopted was a 'business as usual' one where the researchers did not interfere with normal life but became an accepted part of the setting, observing and recording events as they naturally happened. They become part of the setting but not members of the community. The photograph here shows a typical scene of a child at play in a nursery. What can you say about such a snapshot observation? The photographer is capturing an observation and has become part of the scene but is not part of the community he or she is observing.

At other times researchers become more than part of the setting. They adopt an **ethnographic approach** in trying to understand meanings in children's behaviours of a culture or distinct social group, rather than a single individual (Kangas *et al.*, 2012). This is achieved by researchers becoming part of the community to be studied over several months or years, keeping journals of field notes to record the social processes or values of a particular community and becoming very much part of that community's way of life. Ethnographic studies help us to understand the challenges faced by minority ethnic groups in multicultural societies (Alexander, 2006); academic achievement of pupils who are first or second generation immigrants compared with their parents (Areepattamannil, 2012) and school achievement as a factor of parent's education and income account (Kao, 2000). The next set of research methods involve new approaches to behaviour and cognitive activity – psychophysical methods.

Some researchers believe it is best to observe children in a natural and unobtrusive way.
*Source*: © Pearson Education Ltd / Jules Selmes.

**Ethnographic approach**
A research method in which a researcher tries to understand a culture or society by living or being within it.

## Psychophysical methods

Psychophysical methods have become increasingly popular in recent years and utilise techniques that measure relationships between behaviour and physiological responses. The use of measures of physical reactions is predicated on the assumption that measurable changes in our brains and central nervous systems are linked with changes in observable behaviour. Research techniques rely on specialist equipment and knowledge, of which some examples (Keenan, 2002) are:

- electroencephalographs (EEG) to measure electrical activity in the brain;
- functional magnetic resonance imaging (fMRI) to identify areas of the brain involved in a range of tasks;
- heart variability monitors – heart rate increases when we become more excited or stressed;
- galvanic skin response – change in electrical resistance of the skin due to fear, anger, startle response and sexual feelings; and
- changes in cortisol – an important hormone in the body, sometimes called the stress hormone.

The use of psychophysical methods has a long and exciting history (Robson, 1999; Fechner, 1860/1966) and there can be no doubting the contribution of psychophysical methods to

**Connect and Extend**

For an excellent introduction to the potential of functional magnetic resonance imaging (fMRI), read: Huettel, Scott A. Event-related fMRI in cognition (2012). *NeuroImage*, August, *62*(2), 1152–1156.

knowledge of behaviour–physiology relationships in child development. However, bear in mind that these are research methods for the laboratory rather than in the more natural settings of home, school and playgroup. What effect might this have on the reliability and generalisability of the results? Look at the nearby *Connect and Extend* feature for an example of research using psychophysical methods in a variety of settings rather than just the laboratory and make a judgement as to how successful laboratory methods can be.

We have looked at some of the most common research methods used in studies of child development: experimental methods, correlation methods, surveys, case studies, observations in context, reports from narrative and psychophysical methods. We now summarise where we have got to and then look ahead to how researchers select, combine and interpret these research methods when constructing research designs. We will start with a diagram which shows how what we have learned about research methods, and what we are going to learn about research designs, fit together.

**Connect and Extend**

Functional magnetic resonance imaging was carried out in 12 children with ADHD and in 12 healthy control children. Read Siniatchkin, M., Glatthaar, N., Müller, G., Prehn-Kristensen, A., Wolff, S., Knöchel, S., Steinmann, E., Sotnikova, A., Stephani, U., Petermann, F. & Gerber, W.-D. (2012). Behavioural treatment increases activity in the cognitive neuronal networks in children with Attention Deficit/ Hyperactivity Disorder. *Brain Topography*, July, 25(3), 332–344.

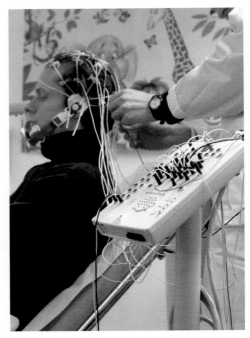

Psychophysical methods measure relationships between behaviour and physiological responses. This man is undergoing an EEG to measure the electrical activity in his brain.

*Source*: © Deco / Alamy Images.

## Summary 2

Before moving on, let's summarise what we have learned in the middle section of this chapter:

- Researchers often adopt a multiple research design in which they engage in a mix of research methods to triangulate their results.
- Experimental methods introduce something different (an independent variable) into a context and see what happens – the 'bull in the china shop'.
- Correlation methods may reveal that relationships between variables increase or decrease at a similar or dissimilar rate. The increase or decrease can be inverse for a negative correlation.
- Survey methods involve asking a series of questions to access information about a target population, people's attitudes or personal perceptions.
- Case study methods allow researchers to study individual children, families, classes, year groups and communities. Used by themselves case studies are open to the charge that results are unlikely to be universally applicable or valid for more than the target subjects.
- The narratives of teachers and peers, family members and the target subject or subjects themselves can provide very rich and exciting data about individuals.
- The greatest advantage of research by observation is that systematic observation allows the researcher to describe and illustrate how people behave in everyday life. This is sometimes done by the observer becoming part of the context of the subject: the ethnographic approach.
- Psychophysical methods measure relationships between a subject's behaviour and their physiological responses.

# Doing ethical research

Figure 3.3 is split into two main sections. The light blue area on the left indicates a way of looking at research from a quantitative and empirical standpoint – counting and measuring observations in the real world. The light green area on the right represents a much more interpretative paradigm where highly detailed personal data are explored. The green area in the middle represents the overlap between the two paradigms and shows that there is a continuum between qualitative and quantitative approaches. Research methods are indicated by the orange arrows which are placed along the quantitative–qualitative continuum. The remainder of this chapter is going to identify and explain the four main research designs and the way that cross-cultural studies and ethical issues span and remain important factors in the full range of research in child development. Figure 3.3 shows our understanding of how all these elements of research – paradigms, methods and research designs – fit together. At the end of the chapter, try to redesign Figure 3.3 to illustrate your understanding of the interrelationships between different research methods in child development – a good test of your understanding.

## Research designs

Investigators are interested in combining research methods to achieve the most valid, reliable and generalisable results, and there are four research designs commonly used to investigate aspects of child development. **Longitudinal designs** allow researchers to follow progress of an individual or a group of children over time to measure patterns of change and stability. A major advantage of this design is that it allows individual differences in functioning over time to be observed and analysed (Bowes *et al.*, 2004) – an important idea when dealing with child

**Longitudinal designs**
Those studies involving the same subjects over a considerable period of time.

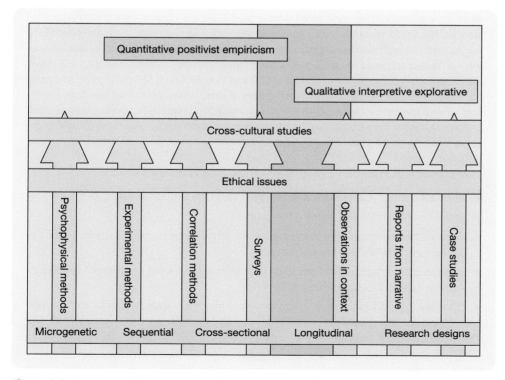

**Figure 3.3** How research paradigms, methods and designs fit together

development, which of course occurs 'over time'. The timescales for these studies vary from several months to several years! For example, Michael Guralnick and colleagues at the University of Washington (2006) studied the peer relationships of young children with mild developmental (cognitive) delays recruited at 4–6 years of age in a longitudinal study across a two-year period. Another example of a longitudinal study is presented in the upcoming feature *Policy, Research and Praxis*, which uses a mixed research methods approach to follow the progress of 3000 children aged 3 to 16 years. After the feature, we will turn to the next research method – cross-sectional designs.

## Policy, Research and Praxis

### Researching with children. Performing against the odds: developmental trajectories of children in the EPPSE 3–16 study

In this book we share research on child development and the ways in which that research is carried out to help readers understand the methods of conducting research with children. One landmark study into children's developmental trajectories from early childhood to adolescence is the Effective Provision of Pre-School, Primary and Secondary Education (EPPSE 3–16) project (Siraj-Blatchford, 2011). The project is also published as a Research Report (DfE-RR128) and is included to show how research of this status influences national policy and practice.

The research was a large-scale longitudinal study that followed the progress of over 3000 children aged 3–16 from 1997. The research investigated how the child, the family and the pre-school and school interact with each other to influence children's development up to early secondary age. It explored *why* and *when* some children 'succeed against the odds' while others who can be considered privileged, fall behind despite their positive circumstances. The EPPSE research used a variety of methods to collect data. An initial pilot study was carried out with disadvantaged children (Siraj-Blatchford, 2010). Cognitive assessments were collected and used to create individual learning trajectories. Four interest groups (two with low socio-economic status children (SES) and two with high SES children) created the frameworks for the child and family case studies. A review of international literature identified general themes for the in-depth interviews which took place with parents, teachers and children. Other analyses including questionnaires created specific questions for the interviews and provided a visual timeline of children's family, history and learning up to the end of primary school.

Improvements in academic progress which can counter disadvantage are:

- stimulated in homes which nurture children's cognitive and social skills
- evident early in children's learning life-courses
- nurtured through good or excellent quality pre-school settings, particularly for boys from families with low socio-economic status
- stimulated by teaching strategies that result in children feeling encouraged to work to achieve beyond their predicted attainment
- stimulated when schools help children to deal effectively with difficulties and through emotionally and practically supportive relationships with parents, peers/friends and networks in the wider community
- dependent upon effort and active engagement from children themselves and others.

There are important implications for practice from this research for teachers and for policy makers. The home is a powerful context for learning and the implications for parenting initiatives are substantial. Parents who are actively engaged with their children provide valuable emotional support and establish positive attitudes to learning such as being consistent and persevering from an early age. The research has implications for teachers in supporting vulnerable children and developing school 'communities of learning'. It also has implications for recruiting teachers into schools with disadvantaged communities and working successfully with vulnerable children.

The study is important in showing that children with successful development trajectories are helped by those around them to develop resilience and able to learn and achieve. In contrast, those who have are less successful, from both high and low SES families have little protection against the risks they encounter.

•••••••••••••••••
**Connect and Extend**
Another interesting example of a longitudinal study is: Lerkkanen, M.-K., Rasku-Puttonen, H., Aunola, K. & Nurmi, J.-E. (2004). Predicting reading performance during the first and the second year of primary school. *British Educational Research Journal*, 30, 67–92.
•••••••••••••••••

Take time to look at the 2005 article by Nordhagen *et al.*: 'Parental reported bullying among Nordic children' in the nearby *Connect and Extend* feature. It is an excellent example of a cross-sectional design research method. **Cross-sectional designs** examine children of different ages at the same point in time and make comparisons between their abilities or performances. For example, in 2005, Zeena Harakeh and colleagues, from the Universities of Nijmegen and Maastricht, used a cross-sectional study including 428 Dutch two-parent families with at least two adolescent children (aged 13–17 years). They examined the association between parental rules and communication (also referred to as anti-smoking socialisation) and adolescents' smoking.

Another example is a classic study on children's independence. Researchers in child development Harriet Rheingold and Carol Eckerman (1970) used this design with children of different ages between 12 and 60 months to measure how adventurous these children were when their mothers were placed at one end of a lawn. By observing where and how far the children travelled, the researchers were able to gather data from a large group of children in a short time, rather than having to record their observations over an extended time as in a longitudinal study.

•••••••••••••••••
**Connect and Extend**
For a fascinating cross-sectional comparative study focusing on prevalence of bullying, from questionnaires filled in by parents, read: Nordhagen, R., Nielsen, A., Stigum, H. & Köhler, L. (2005). Parental reported bullying among Nordic children: A population-based study. *Child-Care Health & Development*, 31, 693–701.
•••••••••••••••••

**Cross-sectional designs**
Those where individuals of different ages are studied at the same point in time.

**Reflect**

Some research that you read may seem very out of date. The above example of Harriet Rheingold and Carol Eckerman's 1970 research (on how adventurous infants are at different ages during their first 5 years) might well be timeless – we don't really know as any replication of their research has not been published. What kinds of research are timeless and how would you know if research is out of date? What makes for good and timeless research?

Often considered as combining the best of both designs, **sequential designs** involve examining groups that represent a cross-section of age groups over a period of time. For example, a teacher might be interested in changes to children's reading abilities over time. The teacher's research design might involve a small group of 6-year-olds and a similar sized group of 9-year-olds. This forms the cross-sectional component. The study would measure the reading abilities of each child in each group initially and then retest regularly, for instance at the end of each term for 3 years. Comparisons could then be made between the changes (progress in reading ability) of each child over this time. An illuminating example of a sequential design is that by Aaron Wichman (research psychologist at Ohio State University) and colleagues when taking a fresh look at the relationship between intelligence and birth order position in the family (e.g. eldest of three) (Wichman *et al.*, 2006).

**Sequential designs**
The study of groups of children of different ages over long periods of time.

## Focus on Theory

### How do infants learn to deal with feeling afraid? A sequential analysis

Do children learn to be afraid, to feel distressed about new experiences or of meeting new people? Is this an innate reaction – something you are born with – or learned from experiences where new things or people prove to cause discomforting or dangerous? Whether innate or learned, how do children learn to cope with new, potentially upsetting experiences? Let us consider a recent example. Last week we visited some young friends Lee and Helen Card. We were the first of their friends to be invited around to meet their very new baby, Lucas. He slept for much of the time we were there and of course we had plenty of cuddles of the new little chap. Even when he awoke he was perfectly at ease and looked at us quite unconcerned.

Nevertheless, Lucas will learn to be wary of us, rather like Niamh Hogan did (who we re-met earlier in this chapter) when she got a little older than Lucas. (See Chapter 11 on social referencing for an account of how Niamh learned to cope with assessing potential dangers when meeting somebody 'new' – or re-meeting somebody who has become unfamiliar.) Lucas will learn to be wary of us unless we have plenty of contact with him as he explores his new world. Novelty in all forms can be distressing to young children.

My theory then is that it is an innate behaviour at certain stages of development to be afraid of novelty. However, children learn to cope with that fear of new things and new people using a variety of learned strategies. Further consideration of the case studies of Niamh and Lucas will not test my theory but we do have examples of where researchers have used sequential analysis methods to test the ideas that we have about how infants learn.

Lee and Helen Card and their new baby, Lucas.

Lucas is just 4 days old.

*Source*: Malcolm Hughes.

In 2004, researchers Susan Crockenburg and Esther Leerkes used sequential research methods with 87 low-risk infants and their mothers, observed at 6 months after birth. (Low-risk is a judgement that the kind of other behaviours shown by the infants were typical of children of this age and that they were unlikely to be adversely affected by the experience.) The researchers showed the infants novel toys – something, as the word 'novel' suggested, they had not been exposed to before.

Three issues were investigated: (a) the effects of mothers' behaviours when attempting to control or mitigate infant distress to seeing the new toys; (b) stability of infants' attempts to avoid distress by looking away from the toy – ignore it and it will go away (c) the dynamics between infants' attempts to avoid distress and mothers' behaviours to mitigate the distress.

By 6 months, some infants reduce their own distress to novelty by looking away from the novel toy or by self-soothing (perhaps by head shaking or hand-clasping). Similarly, maternal support has comparable effects. The children were less upset. Where mother and baby worked together and infant and maternal behaviours co-occurred, the infants showed less distress than comparable infants whose mothers did not. These findings implicate both infants and mothers in the development of learning behaviours during the infant's first year.

Therefore my theory is that Lucas Card will be naturally afraid of novelty, new things and 'new' or unfamiliar people. My theory is that he will learn behaviours like looking away and self-soothing and that the effect of these behaviours will be enhanced by the reaction and behaviour of first-time mum Helen (and Lee, of course).

*Source*: Crockenberg, S. C. & Leerkes, E. M. (2004) Infant and maternal behaviors regulate infant reactivity to novelty at 6 months. *Developmental Psychology*, Vol 40(6), Nov, 2004, 1123–1132.

**Microgenetic designs**
These designs study changes in development that occur quickly and over short periods of time.

**Connect and Extend**
For an example of a microgenetic study of how simple division strategies develop over a short period of time, read: Robinson, K. M. & Dubé, A. K. (2008). A microgenetic study of simple division. *Canadian Journal of Experimental Psychology/Revue canadienne de psychologie expérimentale*, September, 62(3), 156–162.

In **microgenetic designs** the same children are studied repeatedly over a short period of time and this provides an in-depth analysis of children's behaviour while it is changing. Akin to the longitudinal study, these designs involve repeated observations to inform the researcher of even the smallest changes over a short period of time which may last from several days to several weeks. This type of design has proved particularly useful when investigating the strategies children use to acquire new knowledge and skills in language acquisition and solve problems in maths and science (Garcia-Mila *et al.*, 2011).

Longitudinal, cross-sectional, sequential and microgenetic designs are used extensively in studies in child development and each has strengths and weaknesses in gathering information about change in development. Some of the strengths and weaknesses are summarised in Table 3.3.

**Table 3.3** Advantages and disadvantages of developmental research designs

| Design | Descriptor | Advantages | Disadvantages |
| --- | --- | --- | --- |
| Longitudinal | Studies an individual or group repeatedly over time. | Provides good information about development at different ages. Cost is usually low because there is no need for continuous data collection. | Problems over continuity. Effects of research practice may interfere with data. Time consuming. |
| Cross-sectional | Studies groups of different ages at the same point in time. | Quick to administer. Illuminates group differences. Shows age-related changes efficiently. | Unable to address individual children. Cohort effect (a particular group at a particular time) may distort age differences. |
| Sequential | Observes different cohorts repeatedly over time. | Allows both longitudinal and cross-sectional comparisons. | Can be costly and time consuming. Results may not be generalisable beyond the groups studied because of the use of different cohorts. |
| Microgenetic | Investigates mastery of (usually) a new task in short, closely matched sessions. | Permits a detailed analysis of change. Offers a more complete picture of short-term development. | Requires intensive study time. Research practice may distort data because of the intensity of the observation schedule. |

# Cross-cultural research

While these designs discussed above provide information on developmental changes in families, school and day-care settings in one context, researchers are also keen to know how their findings compare with similar groups or individuals in other cultures. Remember Matthias Kontny (mentioned in one of the earlier *Reflect* features), a paediatrician in St Oldberg, Germany, who questioned the use of growth tables from the United States. Comparisons of research findings with other cultures address the challenges of creating 'universal truths' – true for all cultures – in child development. Cross-cultural studies involve children from different cultures in comparing one or more aspect of development. Are there developmental differences between a child growing up in Bangladesh and one from Jamaica?

In the context of multicultural classrooms and children's centres where children from many ethnic backgrounds come together, knowledge of similarities and differences will be valuable to any teacher or carer. This type of research (e.g. VanderLaan *et al.*, 2011) draws conclusions about children from different ethnic or socioeconomic groups (e.g. white middle-class with low family income) from the same society, and also reveal how changes in a society, including increases in divorce, child-care practices, parenting and whole school achievement influence children's development.

Divorce, parenting and child-care are not value free. Cross-cultural studies, like all research, need to take account of the emotions and attitudes of those being researched. As we said earlier, children are not here to be experimented on, should not be the subject of intrusive and potentially damaging attention and observation and must be considered as more than members of a convenient sample of the target population. What we have to think about are the ethical considerations of research.

**Cross-cultural studies**
Such studies compare children in different cultural contexts.

• • • • • • • • • • • • • • •

**Connect and Extend**

For a cross-cultural perspective on cross-cultural research, read: Mattingly, C. & Lawlor, M. (2000). Learning from stories: Narrative interviewing in cross-cultural research. *Scandinavian Journal of Occupational Therapy,* 7, 4–14.

• • • • • • • • • • • • • • •

# Ethical considerations when studying children

When undertaking any study involving children, all researchers need to understand the ethical issues associated with such investigations. The complex nature of the scientific investigation of children's development makes children immediately vulnerable to psychological and even physical harm. In an historic and much quoted study of childhood fears, Watson (1919) introduced a small dog into the pram of a 6-month-old infant and the child, not unexpectedly, became frightened. Watson concluded that the child had a fear reaction to dogs and moving toy animals! Watson's experiment would not be allowed to take place today and professional organisations in both Britain and America now publish ethical guidelines to protect children as subjects and adults as researchers and ensure that research adheres to strict ethical codes. The area is complex, and incorporates issues that range from those are more obvious and easily avoided, such as denying children food for long periods, isolating them, or physically restraining them, to much more subtle issues. Several examples for you to consider are given below.

- Is it ethical to conduct observations on a class or group of children without informing them of what is going on?

- If I test children, is it ethical to inform them that they performed badly on the test(s) because of the effect this would have on their performance in later tests?

- Can requests to a mother be justified to leave her infant of 12 months alone for an extended period of time to study the effect on separation?

The ultimate responsibility is with the investigator but guidance produced by the British Psychological Society (BPS) in 2006 and the Society for Research in Child Development (2007) provides researchers with clear directions in conducting any form of study involving children, the main points of which appear in the *Focus on Theory* feature that follows.

## Focus on Theory

### Ethical guidelines for researching children

Those participating in psychological research with children should have confidence in the investigators. Good research is only possible if there is mutual respect between investigators and participants.

- **Protection from harm**. Foreseeable threats to the participant's well-being, health, values or dignity should be eliminated. Investigators may not do physical or psychological harm to participants.

- **Informed consent** of parents or others who act on the child's behalf should be obtained, preferably in writing. This requires that the parent or other legally responsible adult be told the purposes of and all features of the research that may affect his or her willingness to allow the child to participate.

- **Withdrawal**. Children and their parents may withdraw at any time from the study and for any reason.

- **Confidentiality**. Participants have a right to expect that information provided will be treated confidentially and if published will not be identifiable.

- **Debriefing**. Children and their parents should be offered information about the findings of the study in language they understand. If concealment or deception is thought essential to the conduct of the research, the investigator(s) must satisfy a committee of peers that this judgement is correct.

Investigators share responsibility for the ethical treatment of research participants with their collaborators, assistants, students and employees.

## The case for informed practice

In the *Controversy* feature near the beginning of this chapter we discussed whether or not there was a gap between research and practice, which raised some real concerns that a Chief Inspector of Schools and others (including the authors of this text) had, and have, about the value and impact of much of the current research into children's development and learning. The UK Government Department for Children, Schools and Families (DCSF) is aware of those kinds of concern and also appears to hold a view that practice can and should be informed by high-quality, recent and relevant evidence.

On the Department for Education (England) Standards website (accessed 15 April 2013) are pages reserved for The Research Informed Practice Site (TRIPS) which attempts to offer easy access to essential research findings for teachers, governors, parents and all those who support them in the development of school-age students. The aim is to help make sure that new theories of child development are informed by good and up-to-date evidence. Grouped under themes such as assessment and gender, the site aims to provide accessible digests of research.

Themes covered include behaviour, early years, motivation, speaking and listening, thinking skills and special needs. Selecting the Early Years theme brings a list of fascinating digests of research. The following are a selection of digests from the complete list. What research methods would you expect each of the studies to use? What research design is likely to have been adopted (the title of number 9 contains a big clue)? Are cross-cultural aspects likely to be covered? Would Thomas Hobbes or John Locke approve of the paradigm chosen?

1. Can instructional and emotional support in the Key Stage 1 classroom make a difference for children at risk of school failure?

2. Observational learning during shared book reading: the effects on preschoolers' attention to print and letter knowledge.

3. The impact of preschool on young children's cognitive attainments at entry to Reception.

4. A classroom investigation of the growth of metacognitive awareness in kindergarten children through the writing process.

5. Inequality in the early cognitive development of British children in the 1970 cohort.

6. The impact of teacher-directed and child-directed pretend play on cognitive competence in kindergarten children.

7. The long-term contribution of early childhood education to children's performance – evidence from New Zealand.

8. Learning from their mistakes: glimpses of symbolic functioning in $2\frac{1}{2}$- to 3-year-old children.

9. Parental involvement in the development of children's reading skill: a 5-year longitudinal study.

10. 'I didn't expect that I would get tons of friends . . . More each day': children's experiences of friendship during the transition to school.

Before finishing this chapter, access one or more of the research digests listed above at **www.education.gov.uk/**. Remember that all websites sometimes change the content of web pages and it is certainly true that some of the digests will appear under more than one theme. Check to see whether you were able to predict what kinds of research methods, research designs, cross-cultural and ethical aspects were used or included. If you predict correctly, then you are well on the way to knowing how practice and research are connected, to know what are the most common research methods used to study child development and to explain which methods are used in particular circumstances. You are becoming more expert in research into child development.

## Summary 3

We now summarise what you have learned in the final section of this chapter:

- Research designs combine research methods to achieve the most valid, reliable and generalisable results.

- Longitudinal designs allow researchers to follow an individual or a group of children over time to measure patterns of change.

- Cross-sectional designs examine children of different ages at the same point in time and make comparisons between their abilities or performances.

- Sequential designs involve examining groups that represent a cross-section of age groups over a period of time.

- Microgenetic designs involve repeated observations to inform the researcher of even the smallest changes over a short period of time.

- Cross-cultural studies involve children from different cultures in comparing one or more aspect of development.

- Researchers are now expected to observe ethical guidelines to protect children as subjects and ensure that their research adheres to strict ethical codes.

# Conclusion

Chapter 3 *Research Methods* has provided an overview of qualitative and quantitative methods of gathering information about children's development and you are encouraged to consult some of the other texts (as shown in the *Going further* section) for more information. Although all the research paradigms, methods and designs we have talked about are relevant to child development studies, the use of observation in natural settings is perhaps the most common, tried and tested method. You should find Table 3.2 particularly helpful – the table showing aspects of development that may be studied using observation. In my research, rather than straightforward observational methods, I favour correlation methods in cross-sectional research designs. That may be because I am more comfortable working in an empirical positivist paradigm using quantitative research methods and statistical analysis.

Confused? If the last sentence doesn't mean much to you (it's a kind of 'acid test' of understanding this chapter because understanding suggests you can 'talk the talk' as well as wanting to 'walk the walk'), then we suggest you re-read the chapter, playing close attention to the methods adopted by researchers who we headline in the *Connect and Extend* features. Now would also be a very good time to check out your own learning by attempting to redesign Figure 3.3, *How research paradigms, methods and designs fit together*.

What next? In Chapter 4 *Nature and Nurture* you will study the foundations of child development, what we know of prenatal development and how very early development and learning are integrated. To begin, you will study the genetic factors that shape our individuality, and how heredity and environment act together in the process of creating each unique individual. So it is to the fascinating study of genetics that we now turn.

# Summary Table
## Research Methods

## Researching children (pp 62–65)

### Studying children in school, day-care and family settings (pp 62–64)

Much of the research undertaken in recent years into childhood and learning is open to the challenge that it is not closely related to the needs of childhood practitioners. This challenge is strenuously denied by the research community and there are many examples of up-to-date robust studies that have high levels of validity, reliability and generalisability. The use of the scientific method in many of the studies used in the *Connect and Extend* features allow researchers to construct more universally applicable theories, strategies and treatments.

### Research approaches – paradigms (pp 64–65)

Almost all research in child development can be situated in either the qualitative (interpretive approaches) paradigm or the quantitative (empirical approaches) paradigm. Even beginning or student researchers strive to describe their interest in the subject of the research, to identify research questions and to position their study within one of the research paradigms.

## Research methods (pp 65–76)

Researchers often adopt a multiple research design in which they engage in a mix of research methods to 'triangulate' their results – they use more than one method of data collection to maximise validity and reliability.

### Experimental methods (pp 66–67)

Experimental methods introduce something different (an independent variable) into a context and see what happens – the 'bull in the china shop'. Researchers observe the dependent variables, the behaviours or conditions that can change with the introduction of the independent variable. Most experimental methods are used in laboratory conditions but some experiments are conducted 'in the field' – a school, care setting or home.

## Correlation methods (pp 67–68)

Correlation methods reveal relationships between two variables – say, examination grades and amount of television watched – the instance of which increase or decrease at a similar or dissimilar rate; this would be a positive correlation. In a negative correlation, as the values of one of the variables increase, the values of the second variable decrease – like an 'inverse' correlation. The word 'negative' is a label that shows the direction of the correlation. For example, there is a negative correlation between TV viewing and examination grades – pupils who spend more time watching TV tend to have lower examination grades.

## Surveys (pp 68–72)

Survey methods involve asking a series of questions to access information about the demographics of a target population, people's attitudes or personal perceptions. Large-scale surveys provide national and international census information and the weighing and measuring of many thousands of babies and young children enable researchers to create growth tables used by paediatricians and other healthcare workers.

## Case studies (p 73)

Case study methods allow researchers to intensely and deeply study individual children, families, classes, year groups and communities. Used by themselves, results from case studies are unlikely to be universally applicable or valid for more than the target subjects.

## Reports from narrative (pp 73–74)

Narratives (spoken or written accounts of events and histories) of teachers and peers, family members and the target subject or subjects themselves can provide very rich and exciting data about individuals. There may be high levels of validity and reliability in terms of the subject of the research but it is unlikely that researchers would claim high levels of generalisability.

## Observations in context (pp 74–75)

An advantage of research by observation is that systematic observation allows the researcher to describe and illustrate how people behave in everyday life. This is sometimes done by the observer becoming part of the context of the subject: the ethnographic approach. Some examples of observation research are physical development, communication skills, emotional well-being, gendered play, and interaction with parents and teachers.

## Psychophysical methods (pp 75–76)

Psychophysical methods associate relationships between a subject's behaviour and their physiological responses meas-ured using electroencephalographs, functional magnetic resonance imaging, heart variability monitors, changes in the acidity levels of the skin and the release of cortisol – the stress hormone.

## Doing ethical research (pp 77–84)

Figure 3.3 is a key illustration of how research methods and designs are positioned within the main research paradigms of child development. It also depicts the way in which the four main research designs, cross-cultural studies and ethical issues span the full range of research in child development.

## Research designs (pp 77–81)

Longitudinal designs allow researchers to follow an individual or a group of children over time to measure patterns of change, whereas cross-sectional designs examine children of different ages at the same point in time and make comparisons between their abilities or performances. Sequential designs combine the advantages of longitudinal and cross-sectional studies by examining groups that represent a cross-section of age groups over a longer period of time, in contrast to microgenetic designs which involve rapidly repeated observations to inform the researcher of even the smallest changes over a short period of time.

## Cross-cultural research (p 82)

Cross-cultural studies involve children from different cultures in comparing one or more aspect of development as researchers are keen to know how their findings compare with similar groups or individuals in other cultures. Studies often reveal how changes in a society, including increases in divorce, child-care practices, parenting and whole school achievement influence children's development irrespective of other cultural differences.

## Ethical considerations when studying children (pp 82–83)

Researchers are now expected to observe ethical guidelines to protect children as subjects and ensure that their research adheres to the strict ethical codes provided by the British Psychological Society (BPS) in 2006 and the Society for Research in Child Development (2007).

## The case for informed practice (pp 83–84)

The UK Government Department for Children, Schools and Families Standards website includes pages reserved for The Research Informed Practice Site (TRIPS) which offers easy access to essential research findings for those engaged in working with children. The aim is to help make sure that practice in schools and play settings is informed by good and up-to-date evidence.

# Going further

Dell Clark, C. (2010) *In a younger voice: Doing child-centered qualitative research* (Child Development in Cultural Context Series). Oxford: OUP.
Adults were once children, yet a generational gap can present itself when grown-ups seek, in the course of their research, to know children's lives. *In a younger voice* discloses how qualitative research, tailored to be child-centred, can shrink the gap of generational misunderstanding.

Boyden, J. & Bourdillon, M. (2011) *Childhood poverty: Multidisciplinary approach*. Basingstoke: Palgrave Macmillan.
An investigation using innovative research methodologies of the changing situation of poor children over time in four developing countries.

Greene, S. & Hogan, D. (Eds) (2005) *Researching children's experience: Approaches and methods*. London: Sage.
Comprehensive interdisciplinary guide that is excellent on the theoretical perspectives underpinning research methods.

MacNaughton, G. M., Rolfe, S. & Siraj-Blatchford, I. (2004) *Doing early childhood research: International perspectives on theory and practice*. Maidenhead: Open University Press.
Provides a much deeper and expansive coverage of undertaking research with young children within an inter-cultural framework.

# Useful websites

http://oro.open.ac.uk/view/faculty_dept/fels-ccdl.html (accessed 16 July 2012)
The Open University (UK) open research online database of research papers on Childhood, Development and Learning (674 papers when accessed).

www.srcd.org/
The website of the Society for Research in Child Development. The Society has produced excellent guidelines on ethical considerations when studying any aspect of development in children.

http://www.fmrib.ox.ac.uk/
The website of the Oxford University Centre for Functional MRI of the Brain. There is so much work going on at the moment around the world using fMRI technologies. Here is one 'cutting edge' research centre that will give you a good overview of the current areas of research in development.

# Chapter 4
## Nature and Nurture

### Overview

# Introduction

In Chapter 3 we explored the connection between research in child development and professional practice in schools and nurseries, healthcare and social services. We looked at the most common qualitative and quantitative methods of gathering information about children's development, in what circumstances they are used and the ethical considerations that must be observed. Now we need to build on our study of how the scientific method is used for observing change in children as they grow, to learn where development begins. We can use the historical arguments and controversies of child development and what constitutes scientific study, to focus on the foundations of human development. Now we turn to beginnings of life itself, our own unique lives and the magical way in which each of us begins.

Consider this. If your parents had not bonded exactly when they did (possibly even down to the precise millisecond), you as a reader would not be here at all. I would not be here either if the experience was not the same for my parents. If our parents' parents had not had that experience too, then our parents would never have existed.

> If we go back five generations – about 150 years or so – our ancestral line would be 32 people, if ten generations then each of us has 1024 ancestors that we could trace as a 'bloodline'. If you go back in time for twenty generations, the ancestral line has raised the number of people procreating on your behalf to 1,048,576. By thirty generations, the figure exceeds one billion and if you were to go right back sixty-four generations to the time when *The Roman Empire* ruled much of the Mediterranean, Northern Europe and Britain, the number of people in your direct line is about one million trillion. In other words, many times more than the total number of people that has ever lived. Staggering.
>
> Is something not right with these calculations? How can you have more direct ancestors than the number of people who have ever lived? In fact it is not that the calculations are wrong. We are overlooking one important fact: our ancestral line is not pure. Sorry, but there will have been times when someone on one side of the family will have procreated with someone not too distantly related. Incestuous? Yes, but mostly at a discrete distance from immediate family. Most of the people we see around us in our everyday lives are probably quite closely related to us. In a most literal sense, we are all family. If you compare your genes with anyone else's, they will be 99.9 per cent the same and it is that degree of sameness that makes us all human.

(Adapted from Bryson, 2003, with permission)

This chapter sets out to unravel some of the complexities in prenatal development by looking at the influence of heredity on development and at environmental factors that influence it. We begin by describing important genetic foundations and show how, although we are all individuals, we also share common things in our appearance and behaviours. Having established this common ground, the chapter then goes on to describe some of the external influences that are present in the environment since these too are integral to shaping who we are and who we will ultimately become. The chapter then cements the association of nature and nurture by looking at how both inherited and environmental foundations interact with each other.

**Chapter Objectives**

By the time you have completed this chapter you should be able to answer the following questions:

- How does each human life begin?
- What is a genetic code?
- How might understanding the human genome help us to prevent and cure diseases and other human conditions?
- How do dominant and recessive genes define our genotype?
- What is behaviour genetics?
- To what extent do we inherit our personality, behaviours, weaknesses and strengths?
- What does research into children with Down's Syndrome tell us about how to support their development?
- How do factors of heredity and differences in environment interact to define development?

# Genetic foundations

## Our unique beginnings

Let's begin at the very beginning with conception. Stories of 'where we come from' go back to the earliest of times and are strangely interwoven with folk tales about babies being found under gooseberry bushes or being brought by a passing stork! The truth is less bizarre and far more exciting. Sperm produced in the male testes are ejaculated in seminal fluid at the climax of the sexual act. These then enter the woman's vagina and swim through the uterus into her Fallopian tubes. Fertilisation takes place when one male sperm and a woman's **ovum** unite and create a single cell called a **zygote**. The time that the ovum spends in the Fallopian tube is crucial as not all sperm will survive the hazardous journey between vagina and Fallopian tube: only 300–500 sperm will reach the ovum. One 'champion sperm' burrows into the ovum. This is the process of conception. Fertilisation is complete and the ovum now attaches itself onto the wall of the uterus and starts the three periods of prenatal development that are described later in the chapter. If the ovum is not fertilised, it moves along the Fallopian tube to the uterus and is expelled as part of normal menstruation. In order to understand our genetic beginnings it is necessary to understand *what* we inherit at conception, and, once this is established, we can then examine *how* this influences the people we are through our appearance and the behavioural characteristics that we show. To do this it is necessary to know about the genetic code.

**Ovum**
The gamete produced by the female which, if fertilised, forms the new being.

**Zygote**
A fertilised egg.

## The genetic code

We are each made up of billions of tiny units called **cells** – skin cells, brain cells, blood cells. Each cell carries the whole genetic code for each one of us and acts as our own 'construction and instruction manual' – more of this later. Cells are such amazing things that our human brains can barely comprehend their extraordinary capabilities. Author Bill Bryson certainly trumpets their value in acclaiming:

**Cells**
The smallest unit of an organism that is classified as living. They contain an individual's genetic code.

There isn't a thing they don't do for you. They let you feel pleasure and form thoughts. They enable you to stand and stretch and caper. When you eat, they extract the nutrients, distribute the energy, and carry off the wastes – all those things you learned about in school biology – but they also remember to make you hungry in the first place and reward you with a feeling of well-being afterwards so that you won't forget to eat again. They keep your hair growing, your ears waxed, your brain quietly purring. They manage every corner of your being. They will jump to your defence the instant you are threatened. They will unhesitatingly die for you – billions of them do so daily. And not once in all your years have you thanked even one of them.

(Bryson, 2003, p 451, with permission)

Each cell has a nucleus (or centre) and inside the nucleus are rod-like structures called chromosomes which store and transmit genetic information. Chromosomes are matched pairs (with the exception of the XY pair in males – to be discussed shortly): one chromosome in each pair is inherited from the mother and one from the father: each ovum contains half the chromosomes and the successful sperm contains the other half needed to complete the zygote – the fertilised egg. Numbers of chromosomes vary according to species – fruit flies have 4 pairs, chimpanzees have 24 pairs and we humans have 23 pairs of chromosomes.

**Nucleus**
The centre of the cell body.

**Chromosomes**
Rod-shaped structures in each cell body that contain DNA, store and send genetic information and in humans are arranged in 23 pairs.

## Chromosomes and genes

Each chromosome is like a long coiled thread consisting of a chain of genes – sections of chromosome – like links on a bracelet. The length of each gene varies – and it has been estimated that there are between 30 000 to 40 000 genes lying along each human chromosome (International Human Genome Sequencing Consortium, 2001). Chromosomes are made up of a chemical called deoxyribonucleic acid (DNA), a long double-helix-shaped molecule similar to ladder rungs with each base pair of chemical units that make up the DNA being deliberately and specifically located across the rungs. The base chemicals that make up DNA are adenine, thymine, cytosine and guanine: chemicals from which cells are duplicated. A good representation of how genes are formed on the chromosome is given in Figure 4.1.

Our cells need to duplicate for all of us to grow and to develop, to replace those cells which die or are damaged. Think about overdoing it when sunbathing. The skin can be burned by

**DNA**
Deoxyribonucleic acid: molecules of DNA make up the chromosome.

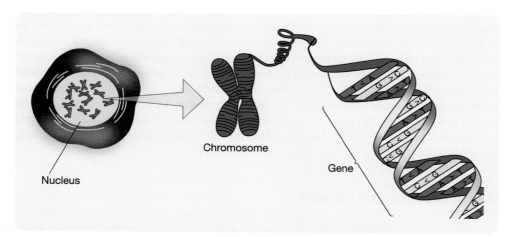

**Figure 4.1** Genes, chromosomes and the nucleus of a human cell
In each human cell there are 23 pairs of chromosomes and each chromosome can be 'unwound' to show many thousands of genes – each gene a unique combination of base chemicals: adenine, thymine, cytosine and guanine.

**Mitosis**
The process of cell
duplication.

● ● ● ● ● ● ● ● ● ● ● ● ● ●
**Connect and Extend**
You might like to remind
yourself of some of the
basic biology of inheritance
and human variation. The
BBC have some excellent
interactive materials at:
**www.bbc.co.uk/schools/
gcsebitesize/biology/**
(accessed 20 July 2012).

● ● ● ● ● ● ● ● ● ● ● ● ● ●

**Genetic code**
The specific sequence of
base chemicals in our
DNA that determines our
inherited characteristics.

**Genetics**
The study of how genes
transmit biological traits
over generations.

**Human genome**
The sequence that specifies
the order of all hereditary
information encoded in the
DNA for all humans.

the ultraviolet rays and our skin cells are killed – the skin turns red and painful. Cells below the skin's surface cells must duplicate quickly to replace the dead ones above. DNA allows our cells to duplicate through a process of mitosis. Enzymes move up the DNA spiral, splitting the spiral apart, then each base chemical pair of adenine/thymine and cytosine/guanine bonds with a new chemical pair from the area surrounding the cell to recreate two identical copies of the original DNA spiral. At this stage the cell splits to form two identical cells and the chromosome copies itself exactly, as each new cell contains the same number of chromosomes and has identical chemical pairings.

DNA is the basis of our inheritance because it contains everything passed from parents to children. The special sequence of our DNA's four chemical units: adenine, thymine, cytosine and guanine (A, T, C, G) makes up our genetic code and it is this code that determines all our inherited characteristics.

The order in which each person's genes are arranged in the complete collection of chromosomes is a person's genotype – all the instructions needed for creating replacement and new cells, for growth, maintenance and for development. The study of how genes transmit biological traits over generations is called genetics – and understanding genetics is one of the keys to understanding child development.

The entire sequence of genetic code – the whole hereditary information encoded in the DNA for all humans – makes up what is known as the human genome. The genome is our personal construction and instruction manual where chromosomes are the chapters and genes are the individual instructions contained in the text of these chapters. You might like to think of the construction of the human genome in another way. Genes are like the keys of a piano. Each key plays one note. Monotonous perhaps, but when combined with other genes they create chords and melodies of any number of possibilities. Chromosomes are like other instruments in the orchestra. Put together all the genes and chromosomes, the notes with all the instruments of the orchestra, and you have the 'great symphony of existence known as the human genome' (Bryson, 2003, p 493).

**Reflect**    What kind of research, what paradigm (think back to Chapter 3), would be involved in finding out that there are at least 20 000 genes lying along each human chromosome and 23 chromosome pairs (International Human Genome Sequencing Consortium, 2001)?

Recent investigations such as the Human Genome Project – an international scientific investigation to determine all the genes in the human genome – has increased our knowledge of which genes are responsible for specific human traits and conditions. The value of such research lies in providing much needed information about the prevention and cure of many modern diseases and conditions including Alzheimer's, autism, asthma, depression, diabetes and cancer. Since the year 2000, there have been many accounts of the Human Genome Project and its potential for enormous universal benefit that a complete knowledge of the human genome might bring (e.g. Garay & Grey, 2012; Sulston and Ferry, 2002). A working draft of the complete human genome was released in 2000 and a complete one in 2003, with further analysis still being published (e.g. Xia *et al.*, 2012).

## Using the human genome

**Cloning**
A procedure for producing
multiple copies of
genetically identical
organisms.

Some observers believe scientists are going too far and are at risk of drawing ever closer to the baby-bottling (growing and 'conditioning' babies outside of the human womb) and Bokansky processing (cloning one fertilised egg from one embryo by retarding development) so graphically described in Huxley's *Brave New World* – see the nearby *Connect and Extend*. Research into genetic testing and gene therapy will, without doubt, transform scientific knowledge but it is as yet uncertain whether the potential benefits to our species outweigh possible risks and ethical dilemmas of experimenting with human life.

Experiments involving cloning are not that fantastic, and certainly not new. Cloning is a procedure for producing multiple copies of genetically identical organisms. In essence this means producing an artificial identical twin. Cells are removed from an embryo and replaced with DNA from a donor parent. What is produced is a new clone with the same appearance and genetic make-up as the original: but with one significant departure. The personality of the new clone may be completely different even though appearance and capacity are identical. The process cannot take into account learning or experience of the new clone. Although investigations with plants and animal embryos date back to the 1970s, recent advances have enabled scientists to clone animals, undoubtedly the most famous of which took place in 1995 in the Roslin Institute in Scotland with the cloning of 'Dolly', a sheep. Dolly may have opened the door of opportunities for science across the world but such research raises many political, ethical, moral and social questions. Consider the evidence in the following *Controversy* feature and remember that the 'success' of Dolly makes attempts at human cloning inevitable.

**Connect and Extend**
There are many online editions of Aldhous Huxley's futuristic novel *Brave New World* – **www. huxley.net/bnw/index.html**. Just reading Chapter 1 will give you a really good idea about the concerns that many people have about genetic experimentation.

## Controversy

### Is human cloning a 'miracle' of science or a road to disaster?

Scientific advances are frequently surrounded by controversy. Sceptics probably poured scorn on humankind's early exploitation of fire, wind and water; and breakthroughs such as the invention of the wheel, the steam engine and space travel have had their share of critics. The Human Genome Project begun in the 1990s enquired into areas of human existence that for many ought not to be investigated at all. Although met with fear and suspicion from some people, others have heralded gene research as a worthwhile advancement in human learning and capability. Currently, the debate into human cloning is likely to divide people into one of two 'camps'. Consider the evidence on both sides.

Pro-cloning activists argue that genetic research offers unlimited benefits to our species. Early deaths from cancer, and diseases such as Alzheimer's and Parkinson's, could be vastly reduced or even eliminated. At present patients suffering from chronic and degenerative kidney diseases receive organ transplants but there is a tragic shortage of suitable and compatible donor organs. What if we could grow new kidneys using the patient's own healthy cells? Currently the treatment of leukaemia can include transfer of a donor's bone marrow to the sufferer, a traumatic experience for donor and recipient, and not always successful, although success rates are improving. Genetic research offers the chance of cloning new healthy bone marrow in the body using the body's wonderful ability to quickly replace damaged and dead cells. Genetic research could mean the end of chemotherapy, and the potential for doctors to grow replacement organs and glands outside of the body for subsequent sophisticated 'spare part' surgery.

Advocates view cloning as making possible the renewal of brain, blood, heart and lung cells. They argue that cloning can save millions of lives and offer the potential for a much better quality of life for many people. Cloning can provide hope for infertile couples. Current fertility technology is painful, heartbreaking and often ineffective and cloning could offer something better. It could end many of the problems with cosmetic surgery where skin grafting operations have gone wrong. Finally, it would allow parents to ensure that genetic problems such as heart abnormalities and sickle cell disease are not passed onto their children.

On the other hand, critics of cloning argue that it raises fundamental questions about human nature and identity. Does cloning destroy our human uniqueness and strike at the very heart of family and society? By touching on human creation itself, are we playing God – is this knowledge (like the fruit of the tree of knowledge of good and evil – Genesis Chapter 3) we were not meant to have? Graphic warnings are given by the most strident critics about gene mutation – speculation about the potential of cloning techniques to create monsters with awful abnormalities. Some critics are less radical and although they argue against human cloning on ethical reasons – that it is plain wrong and unnatural – they foresee that a safe technology might be developed in the future. Others worry that this technology might end up in the wrong hands. Albert Einstein's work on atoms was intended to benefit humankind by explaining the most complex yet fundamental workings of our existence. Who would have suspected that his theory could result in the building of an atomic bomb with the threat of destroying the human race? Some critics see cloning as having the same potentially lethal consequences for our species. The balance of ethical argument since 2000 rejects cloning (e.g. Strong, 2008; Fasouliotis & Schenker, 2000). What do you think? Should research into cloning be encouraged with effective safeguards and proper supervision, or rejected as immoral and dangerous?

## Summary 1

Before moving on, let's summarise what we have learned so far:

- Fertilisation takes place when male sperm and a woman's ovum unite and create a single cell called a zygote.
- We are each made up of billions of tiny cells. Each cell carries the whole genetic code for each one of us.
- Each cell has a nucleus and inside the nucleus are rod-like structures called chromosomes which store and transmit genetic information.
- Chromosomes are made up of a chemical called deoxyribonucleic acid (DNA) which is a chain of genes.
- Our cells need to duplicate for all of us to grow and to develop. Cells duplicate by genes matching the pattern of base chemicals through a process of mitosis – cells splitting to create identical sets of genes in each new cell.
- The order in which each person's genes are arranged in the complete collection of chromosomes is a person's genotype.
- The study of how genes transmit biological traits over generations is called genetics.
- The entire sequence of genetic code for all humans makes up what is known as the human genome.
- Cloning is a procedure for producing multiple copies of genetically identical organisms.

## Heredity

We are not clones of our parents because we get half of our genetic information from our mother's ovum and half from our father's sperm. Our gene mix is unique. Nevertheless, our parents do, between them, contribute all of our genetic code. They define our complete genotype – our personal human genome. The transmission of individual characteristics and traits from one generation to the next – what might be loosely termed our 'human nature' – is based on heredity. What we inherit from our parents provides the potential for us to do certain things but also provides limits on our capabilities. Rules of heredity are responsible for many physical characteristics such as eye and hair colour and our physical size (as we shall see shortly). It is a factor in how intelligent we are, how social, how happy or sad we appear, and even for what interests us. Now we explore this exciting idea in a very common context for the study of the laws of heredity – the family.

**Reflect**

Consider your own family. In what ways do you resemble your parents? How are you different from them? Can you notice similarities and differences between parents and children of other families you know? Perhaps you can see more of one parent in a child than in another in the family? Family photographs are a good place to observe such similarities. A painting *My Parents and I* by Frida Kahlo (1936), depicts a family tree showing three generations together and even the untrained eye should be able to detect similarities in the appearance of the family members. It would be easier still if all the images of the generations were of individuals at about the same age.

## Genotypes and phenotypes

The physical, visible expression of the genotype that you can observe in an individual is called his or her phenotype. Phenotypes are made up of a unique collection of inherited genetic instructions in the genes (genotype), influences in the environment, and the interaction between genotype and the environment. Genotype and phenotype provide a good framework for exploring how genes and the environment interact because it is these factors together that determine who we are and influence our individual characteristics. Put another way, it is the reason why no two people can ever be *exactly* alike.

For example, if a child inherits a particular mix of genes that signal a temperament inclined to excessive boisterous behaviour, but the parents raise the child in a quiet and calm environment, and teach the child coping strategies for this behaviour, the interaction of the inherited genes with the environment may allow the child to be able to control this behaviour and act appropriately. We will consider the interaction of heredity and environment later in this chapter but for now let us consider how genes determine our individuality.

## Dominant and recessive genes

If we only had a few genes, then combinations of genes – such as those that determine height, skin and eye colour – would be limited in number and people would appear quite alike. But this is not the case. Humans have many thousands of gene pairs capable of producing billions of possible combinations, each combination arising from the union of one sperm and one ovum! The union of sperm and ovum sets off a process of cell division (which includes an exchange of genetic material called crossing over) that makes the possibilities for creating unique hereditary combinations almost limitless (Qin *et al.*, 2009; Friedberg *et al.*, 2005) and that is why, despite being very similar, we are all so different.

Earlier we said that all chromosomes are in matching pairs (except for the XY chromosome in males). Two forms of each chromosome are present in the zygote, one inherited from the father and the other from the mother. The relationship between genes making up these chromosome pairs is interesting. Genes are also found in pairs (except in the sex chromosomes)

**Connect and Extend**

What particular problems and opportunities arise when researching families? Read: Perles, A. & Lindsay, J. (2003). Methodological triangulation in researching families: Making sense of dissonant data. *International Journal of Social Research Methodology*, 6, 25–40.

**Crossing over**
The exchange of material between chromosomes from both parents, during the first division of cells, resulting in new combinations of genes.

**Connect and Extend**

There are some wonderful interactive animations of cell division and 'crossing over' on the Internet. Try **www.cellsalive.com/meiosis.htm** (accessed 20 July 2012) or web search for an alternative site.

**Dominant gene**
A gene that if present in a gene pair will be expressed as a characteristic, e.g. brown hair.

**Recessive gene**
A gene that by itself in a gene pair will not be expressed as a characteristic, but will be expressed if two recessive genes are present e.g. red hair.

**Allele**
A version of the gene pair.

**Dominant–recessive inheritance**
The combination of one powerful allele that affects our characteristics and a recessive allele which, though at odds with its dominant partner, remains dormant.

and the genes making up each gene pair are either a dominant gene or a recessive gene. Each form of a gene pair is called an allele, and each allele is made up of a gene pair that, with a combination of dominant or recessive genes can affect a child's characteristics and so become a dominant gene pair. Another gene which, when paired with a dominant gene does not affect a child's characteristics, becomes redundant and is called recessive. This dominant–recessive inheritance allows for a dominant allele to be the one to be expressed. It is the recessive gene that remains in the cell, unexpressed but capable of being passed on to future generations.

This part of genetics is not that easy to understand on first reading so let's see if we can use an illustration to explain what we mean. Consider Figure 4.2. In this figure both mother and father have a dominant gene for dark hair (D) and recessive gene for red hair (R). Red hair appears in people with two copies of a recessive gene on chromosome 16 which causes a change (a mutation during the crossing-over process) in the MC1R protein. It is associated with fair skin colour, freckles and sensitivity to ultraviolet light as the mutated MC1R protein is found in the skin and eyes instead of the darker melanin (the protein which is produced in the skin after exposure to sunshine and gives some of us a suntan). As you can see, only one allele will result in a child with red hair and one allele will see the disappearance of the red hair gene altogether. In the other two alleles, the dark hair dominant gene will ensure the child has dark hair but the red hair recessive gene can be passed on to future generations.

One note of caution. Just because there is only one allele that would guarantee a red-headed child does not mean that, in any family with parents like those illustrated in Figure 4.2, only one child out of four will be redheaded. Both I and my wife had mothers who had red hair and fathers who had no red hair in the immediate family. This would suggest that both we both inherited a DR allele and, yet, two of our three children have beautiful red hair.

Now let's see what happens if just one of the parents contributes the recessive gene. Figure 4.3 shows that, although two combinations contains the recessive gene, all the children are dark-haired and two children carry the recessive gene for red hair for possible transfer to the next generation. Although the recessive gene in Figure 4.3 is possibly transferred to the next generation, it is becoming less likely for the recessive gene to be paired with another recessive gene and so result in a baby with red hair. However, lessening of numbers from one generation to another in a particular family should not be taken to mean that red-headedness is dying out. Remember that two out of my three children have red hair and it is perfectly possible that if I had fathered a dozen children, all of them could have been red-headed with a RR allele. This could have been the start of a red-headed teaching dynasty!

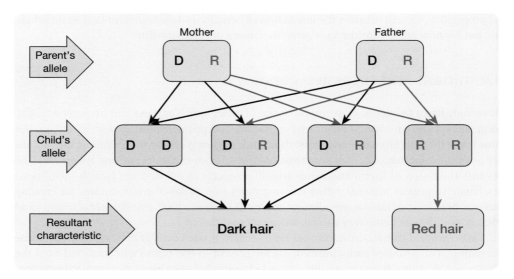

**Figure 4.2** Dominant and recessive genes in both parents

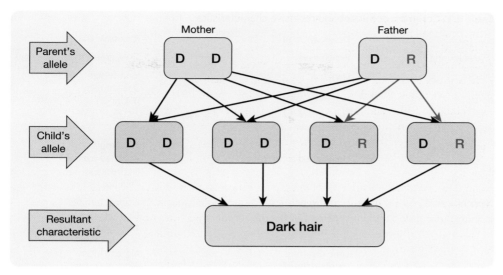

**Figure 4.3** Dominant and recessive genes in one parent

For another example, how well we see is determined by a dominant–recessive inheritance. The gene pair responsible for normal vision is a dominant allele whereas nearsightedness is a recessive one. Thus a child who inherits alleles from parents with at least one dominant gene will have good sight because the normal sight allele is dominant. In another situation, if both parents have normal vision, is it possible that the child is nearsighted? The answer is 'Yes', provided that each parent has inherited forms of the allele containing both the dominant gene (so both have normal vision) and if each is a carrier of the recessive gene for nearsightedness. What other characteristics are decided in this way? Table 4.1 shows some of the more common characteristics that are either dominant or recessive.

Some traits have no clear genetic base but are begun and are modified by experience and the environment. Take musical ability as an example and the case of Nathan, a friend of mine, aged 4 who has just started at the local nursery. It is very unlikely that he inherited a musical talent from one or both parents (no music gene has ever been identified) but he wants to copy his musical parents and take music lessons at an early age – perhaps learn to play an instrument. He has been exposed to music at home before he arrives at the nursery and will probably be encouraged to join a choir or musical group later in school. It might be that an interest by association in a particular type of music is taken up, such as listening to or playing classical music. If, however, opportunities or encouragement had not been forthcoming, then the penchant for (interest in or attraction to) music would not have been expressed.

Has this 2-year-old girl inherited musical talent from her parents?

*Source*: © Pearson Education Ltd / Jules Selmes.

This example sits at one end of a continuum of phenotypes where there is little evidence of any genetic contribution to a characteristic behaviour – in this case, the love of music – but perhaps a link to general intelligence, to which there is a genetic contribution. The other end of the phenotype continuum might well be engaging in sun worship for hours in the poolside sunshine of a summer holiday. If you never go brown, just very sore and red (because the expression of your genotype – red hair, fair skin, little or no melanin), it is very unlikely that you will learn to love sunbathing, even if encouraged from an early age and spoiled with

**Table 4.1**  Common dominant and recessive characteristics

|  | **Dominant trait** | **Recessive trait** |
|---|---|---|
| Eye colouring | Brown eyes | Grey, green, hazel, blue eyes |
| Hair | Dark hair<br>Non-red hair<br>Curly hair<br>Full head of hair<br>Widow's peak | Blonde, light, red hair<br>Straight hair<br>Baldness* |
| Facial features | Dimples<br>Unattached earlobes<br>Freckles<br>Broad lips | No dimples<br>Attached earlobes<br>No freckles<br>Thin lips |
| Appendages | Extra digits<br>Fused digits<br>Short digits<br>Fingers lack 1 joint<br>Limb dwarfing<br>Clubbed thumb<br>Double-jointedness | Normal number<br>Normal digits<br>Normal digits<br>Normal joints<br>Normal proportion<br>Normal thumb<br>Normal joints |
| Blood | Blood type A<br>Blood type B | Blood type O<br>Blood type O |
| Other | Normal vision<br>Good hearing<br>Immunity to poison ivy<br>Normal pigmented skin<br>Normal blood clotting<br>Normal hearing<br>Normal hearing and speaking<br>Normal – no PKU | Near-sightedness<br>Forms of deafness<br>Susceptibility to poison ivy<br>Albinism<br>Haemophilia*<br>Congenital deafness<br>Deaf mutism<br>Phenylketonuria (PKU) |

* Sex-linked characteristic.

*Source*: L. D. Thomas, Blinn Colege – Brenham.

Lecture notes available at **http://www.learningace.com/doc/4433709/fa6673194f2ef7f01db17580a62292a8/hampa** (accessed 1 July 2013)

**Connect and Extend**
If there is no music gene, then is love of music related to general intelligence? Read: Kanazawa, S. & Perina, K. (2012). Why more intelligent individuals like classical music. *Journal of Behavioral Decision Making*, July, *25*(3), 264–275.

**Multifactorial transmission**
The combination of genetics and the environment that produce complex characteristics.

plenty of foreign holidays in the sun. This does not mean that a child who inherits a particular gene or does not inherit a particular gene is unable to do anything to improve their lot. Many characteristics are in fact a combination of inherited and environmental factors through a blending process called **multifactorial transmission**. The exact blend determines where you are on the phenotype continuum.

## More about X and Y chromosomes

**Gametes**
Specialised sex cells. Each gamete has 23 single chromosomes, rather than the usual 23 pairs.

**Meiosis**
Cell division that forms gametes.

You already know that when sperm and ovum unite at conception, the cell that results is a zygote containing 23 pairs of chromosomes. **Gametes** (or sex cells) are created through a process of cell division called **meiosis**. This process halves the number of chromosomes that are normally present so that a gamete has only 23 single chromosomes or half the number found in conventional cells. This is important because the random shuffling of one chromosome from each pair into separate gametes means the chances of children being exactly the same is very small. Biologists James Gould and William Keeton (1996) estimated this at 1 in 700 trillion. That is why siblings in the same family sometimes look very different – because they are! It is even more important in evolutionary terms because this vastly increases the chances of members of the species being able to survive. By shuffling the genetic information that each person carries, the chance of that individual being able to adapt and survive in the environment increases. It is through meiosis that we are genetically unique.

Differences in the chromosomes are linked to increasing the survival chances of the species (that is why we have not been able to identify a music gene, because music, though very important and enjoyable, is not crucial to the survival of the species).

In every country, a greater number of males are conceived (about 120 on average) compared with 100 females. Now this might surprise you because from what we have learned so far it would be quite natural to assume that the ratios of girl to boy births is the same – but this is not so. Of the 23 pairs of chromosomes in each cell, the 23rd contains the sex chromosomes, which dictate the gender of the offspring. In females the pair are made up from XX chromosomes, in males from XY. Sex is determined by whether the sperm that fertilises the ovum is X-bearing or Y-bearing. Hence, it is the man who determines the sex of the children – a fact that could have changed British history if the Tudor King Henry VIII had understood that he had unconsciously passed on Y-bearing sperm to at least two of his six wives.

The sex chromosomes carry many other genes in addition to those that determine sex. This is where evolution has taken a hand to preserve the species. If a gene is defective on a female X chromosome, a healthy gene on the partner X chromosome compensates. If a male has a defective X chromosome, there may not be a healthy partner gene on the Y chromosome because Y chromosomes are smaller and carry fewer genes. So, the higher mortality rate that exists in males means that more of them need to be conceived to be born and survive. Boys are more vulnerable to prenatal problems (Evans, 2006) and congenital disorders (Judd, 2007). The same vulnerability stays with them throughout life. Males have shorter lives (Jones, 2007), more behaviour problems (Lee, 2007) and more learning difficulties (Farrell, 2006). Certainly, sex differences in behaviour seem to exist. So much so that a branch of genetics, behaviour genetics, is studied (e.g. Walker & Plomin, 2005) to account for the extraordinary differences and similarities between human behaviours – and not just differences between the sexes.

**Reflect** Do males have more learning and behavioural difficulties? What is the evidence? Apply the information above that boys have more behavioural difficulties and specific learning difficulties than girls to a setting that you know. What evidence can you find that confirms or contradicts the above?

## Behaviour genetics

Phenotype – the collection of characteristics you can observe in an individual – includes not just the physical characteristics but also behavioural traits such as intelligence and personality. It is more likely that shy parents will have shy children, high-achieving children at school will have one or more high-achieving parents (Matthews *et al.*, 2003), and alcoholics will beget alcoholics (Yalisove, 2004). What is apparent is that, despite links between personality, intelligence and heredity, genetic causes are more often explored for physical differences rather than cognition or social behaviours. Why might this be the case?

Well, there is no difficulty in seeing the link between the physical characteristics of a child and those of the parents passed to the child through the matching of genes in the chromosome pairings. As I said in an earlier chapter, each morning as I wash the shaving suds from my face and peer into the mirror through the steam and condensation, I see a likeness of my dear departed father staring back at me – I even think I'm starting to dance like my Dad. That's the key isn't it? It makes perfect sense for us to look like our parents, particularly as we get

● ● ● ● ● ● ● ● ● ● ● ● ● ●
**Connect and Extend**
For a scholarly discussion of the work of Francis Galton, read: Waller, J. (2004). Becoming a Darwinian: The micro-politics of Sir Francis Galton's scientific career 1859–65. *Annals of Science*, 61, 141–163.
● ● ● ● ● ● ● ● ● ● ● ● ● ●

Francis Galton established the study of behaviour genetics.

*Source*: © Science Photo Library/Paul D. Stewart.

older ourselves, but do we behave like them as well? Do I dance like my Dad because of a dominant dance gene – we think not! Or, do all well-rounded men in their late-50s dance in the same way? Before we get too bogged down in a discussion of dance genes, we think we had better get back to a consideration of the implications of behaviour genetics for understanding child development.

Behaviour genetics was established in the middle of the nineteenth century by Francis Galton – an English anthropologist, inventor and writer – who wrote about the inheritance of giftedness, using family as the context for his studies. Family giftedness was an unsurprising interest on the part of Galton, as he was considered a genius during his own lifetime (Bulmer, 2003). The development of behaviour genetics and its close association with the development of the science of psychology continued well into the twentieth century. Why? In part, because of the dominance of behaviourist theories (refer back to Chapter 2) in the first half of the twentieth century, and also the link that was developed between behaviour genetics and criminal psychology and psychopathology – the study of mental illness. The chief source of data for behaviour genetics are 'twin studies' (which we come to shortly in this chapter), because in twin studies we have the potential to identify variables in human development that owe more or less to nature than to nurture, one of the key issues of child development identified in Chapter 1.

## Heritability

**Psychopathology**
The study of mental illness.

**Heritability**
An estimate of the correlation $0 \leq 1$ between a behaviour or condition, and an identified gene.

**Pathology**
The science of bodily disease.

An important idea here is heritability – an estimate in the form of an index between 0 and 1, where 0 stands for behaviour or condition that has no correlation with an identified gene, and where 1 stands for a perfect correlation between a behaviour or condition and an identified gene. In the case of most diseases now identified as genetic, such as Huntington's disease, there is a better than 0.999 correlation between having the identified gene and the disease and a similar correlation for not having either. On the other hand, such traits as learning mother-tongue language are entirely environmentally determined – they have a heredity index of 0, as language experts have found that any child (if capable of learning a language) can learn any human language as mother tongue. Notice now and during the following discussion that examples with highest indexes are to do with pathology and psychopathology, and the lowest with learning – the latter is an important idea.

However, the contrast between learning and pathological traits is diminishing as heritability index estimates have become increasingly sophisticated. For example, early studies of intelligence (e.g. Binet, 1916), which mostly examined young children, found heritability measures of 0.4 to 0.5. Subsequent analyses have found that genetic contribution to measures of intelligence increases over a lifespan, reaching a heritability of 0.8 in adulthood (Plomin, 2004). Another example of increased sophistication is in the area of multivariant analysis where specific cognitive abilities (e.g. mental processing speed, memory, spatial reasoning) overlap greatly, such that the genes associated with any specific cognitive ability will affect all others (Goldberg & Weinberger, 2004). For highly heritable traits – generally pathological traits – it is now possible to search for individual genes that contribute to variation in that trait. For example, several research groups have identified genes and their location on the chromosome that contribute to schizophrenia (Harrison & Owen, 2003). You should again note – rather like the notion of a phenotype continuum, e.g. being more or less prone to schizophrenic behaviour – that extremes of a given behavioural disorder may also represent an extreme of genetic and/or environmental variation (Sesardic, 2005).

••••••••••••••••••

**Connect and Extend**

For a practical paper on identifying children's personalities read:
Shiner, R. & Caspi, A. (2003). Personality differences in childhood and adolescence: Measurement, development, and consequences. *Journal of Child Psychology and Psychiatry (formerly Journal of Child Psychology and Psychiatry and Allied Disciplines)*, 44, 2–32.
••••••••••••••••••

# Genetic and chromosome abnormalities

Genetic disorders arising from inheriting a pair of abnormal recessive alleles are one way in which chromosome abnormality can occur. One example of this is sickle-cell anaemia, a disorder in which the body's red blood cells become crescent-shaped from a lack of oxygen. The misshapen cells cause blocked blood vessels, swelling and reduced blood flow. Other genetically inherited disorders include cystic fibrosis, causing overproduction of mucus in the lungs and digestive tract; haemophilia, typified by excessive bleeding commonly in males; and spina bifida – cleft spine – causing spinal fluid build-up in the brain. The metabolic disorder phenylketonuria (PKU) and Tay–Sachs disease, a degenerative wasting of the nerve cells, are further examples of this type of inherited disorder.

A second way in which genes have a negative influence upon development occur in chromosome disorders which are not ordinarily present in a child's parents but are caused by chromosomes failing to separate or through part of the chromosome breaking off. Problems in meiosis in the union of sperm and egg can result in serious physical or mental disorders. Over twenty plus years ago it was estimated that 1 in every 156 children born in the Western world have some form of chromosome abnormality (Milunsky, 1992), and more recent studies have not shown any significant change in these ratios (e.g. BMJ, 2006). Let's take a look in Table 4.2 at the different chromosomal abnormalities or disorders, and note their likely causes. After that, we will take a closer look at the chromosomal disorder Trisomy 21 – named so because it is chromosome 21 that is abnormal. We also know the condition as Down's Syndrome.

**Connect and Extend**

Explore the website 'Gene Gateway – Exploring Genes and Genetic Disorders' at **www.ornl.gov/sci/ techresources/Human_ Genome/** (accessed 20 July 2012 – you may need to search for this website but as it is a government website it should be around for quite some time). On the website you can download a free wall poster of the Human Genome Landmarks and also explore the traits and disorders associated with each of the different human chromosomes.

# Down's Syndrome

One of the most common chromosomal abnormalities is Down's Syndrome (DS) a condition that affects 1 in 600 children (Conner *et al.*, 2012; Pennington *et al.*, 2003). In most cases, approximately 92 per cent of the time, Down's Syndrome is usually caused by the presence of an extra chromosome 21 in all cells of the individual. In these cases, the extra chromosome originates in the development of either the egg or the sperm. Consequently, when the egg and sperm unite to form the fertilised egg, three – rather than two – chromosomes 21 are present. As the embryo develops, the extra chromosome is repeated in every cell so that three copies of chromosome 21 are present in all cells of the individual. Trisomy 21 occurs more frequently in mothers under 21 or over 35 and the risk is increased with age. At 30, a woman has less than a 1 in 1000 chance of conceiving a child with DS but by age 35 this rises to 1 in 400 (Holding, 2002). Reasons for these differences are not known for certain, but is most probably linked to female hormonal imbalances at both ends of the reproductive age (Brill, 2007).

**Down's Syndrome**

A chromosome disorder in a child receiving three rather than the normal two chromosomes. Also known as Trisomy 21.

**Reflect**

The incidence of children born with Down's Syndrome is not evenly spread. For example, there was a cluster of children with DS born to mothers who had attended a school in Dundalk, Ireland. You can read about the cluster following the reference provided in the nearby *Connect and Extend* feature. Why do you think clustering might naturally happen? What reasons are suggested in the paper by Dean *et al.*, for this kind of clustering?

**Connect and Extend**

Read a turn-of-the-century investigation: Dean, G. *et al.* (2000). Investigation of a cluster of children with Down's Syndrome born to mothers who had attended a school in Dundalk, Ireland. *Occupational and Environmental Medicine*, 57, 793–804.

Children with Down's Syndrome have a distinctive physical appearance. They can suffer from congenital disorders such as heart problems and bowel abnormalities, are susceptible to eye problems such as cataracts, and to illnesses like leukaemia. There is a pronounced risk of Alzheimer's disease as they get older. The syndrome is characterised by irregularities in overall development.

**Table 4.2** Chromosomal disorders and abnormalities

| Disorder type | Description | Examples |
|---|---|---|
| Dominant gene disorders | In dominant gene disorders, there's a 50–50 chance a child will inherit the gene from the affected parent and have the disorder. | *Achondroplasia*, a rare abnormality of the skeleton that causes a form of dwarfism.<br>*Huntington disease*, a disease of the nervous system that causes a combination of mental deterioration and a movement disorder affecting people in their 30s and 40s. |
| Recessive gene disorders | Everyone carries some abnormal genes, but most people do not know this because a dominant normal gene overrules the abnormal recessive one. However, if a foetus has a pair of abnormal recessive genes (one from each parent), the child will have the disorder. | *Cystic fibrosis*, a disease most common among people of northern European descent that is life threatening and causes severe lung damage.<br>*Sickle-cell disease*, a disease most common among people of African descent in which red blood cells form a 'sickle' shape (rather than the typical doughnut shape), which can get caught in blood vessels and cause damage to organs and tissues.<br>*Tay–Sachs disease*, a disorder most common among people of European (Ashkenazi) Jewish descent that causes mental retardation, blindness, seizures and death.<br>*Beta thalassaemia*, a disorder, most common among people of Mediterranean descent, that causes anaemia. |
| X-linked disorders | These disorders are determined by genes on the X chromosome and are much more common in boys, because the pair of sex chromosomes in males contains only one X chromosome (the other is a Y chromosome). | *Haemophilia*, which prevents the blood from clotting properly. |
| Chromosomal disorders | Some chromosomal disorders are inherited but most are caused by a random error in the genetics of the egg or sperm. The chance of a child having these disorders increases with the age of the mother. | *Down's Syndrome.* |
| Multifactorial disorders | This includes disorders that are caused by a mix of genetic and environmental factors. Their frequency varies from country to country, and some can be detected during pregnancy.<br>Multifactorial disorders include *neural tube defects*, which occur when the tube enclosing the spinal cord does not form properly. | *Congenital heart defects.*<br>*Obesity.*<br>*Diabetes.*<br>*Cancer.*<br>*Spina bifida.* Also called 'open spine', this defect happens when the lower part of the neural tube does not close during embryo development, leaving the spinal cord and nerve bundles exposed.<br>*Anencephaly.* This defect occurs when the brain and head do not develop properly, and the top half of the brain is completely absent. |

There are also delays in cognitive development (Bates, 2004) and difficulties in visual, auditory and sensory processing. Milestones in language acquisition are also delayed (Galeote *et al.*, 2012), resulting in difficulties in speech and language expression and a limited vocabulary. Motor skills are slow to develop in such skills as holding the head steady and walking (Buckley & Sacks, 2001). Reactions are slower and it takes longer to process information than for most children without DS. Social development is greatly impaired and there can be delays in smiling, laughing and making eye contact with adults and peers. Children with DS can get frustrated easily and display unco-operative, even aggressive behaviours. On the plus side, children with DS are very often very social, loving and affectionate; benefit from excellent preschool experiences and early intervention programmes; respond well to encouragement in their surroundings (Kunagaratnam & Loh, 2010; Sanz & Menendez, 2010) and to a secure and loving family environment.

Before moving on, let's summarise what we have learned in the middle section of this chapter:

- The transmission of individual characteristics and traits from one generation to the next – our 'human nature' – is based on heredity.
- The process of cell division called meiosis includes an exchange of genetic material called 'crossing over'.
- The collection of characteristics you can observe in an individual is called his or her phenotype.
- Phenotypes are made up of inherited genetic instructions (genotype) and the interaction between genotype and the environment (multifactorial transmission).
- A dominant gene will be expressed as a characteristic, e.g. brown hair.
- A recessive gene from only one parent will not be expressed as a characteristic, e.g. red hair, but can be passed to future generations.
- A recessive gene from both parents will be expressed in the genotype.
- Behaviour genetics accounts for the differences and similarities between human traits and behaviours.
- Heritability is an estimate of a correlation of a behaviour to an identified gene.
- Genetic and chromosome abnormalities are due to (1) inheriting a pair of abnormal recessive alleles, e.g. sickle-cell disease, or (2) chromosomes failing to separate or through part of the chromosome breaking off.

**Summary 2**

# Environmental foundations

## A variety of contexts for development

We can think of genes as providing the blueprint for our development due to their role in the production of cell growth and in the development of the brain and the central nervous system. However, factors in the environment influence how the messages in our genes are put into action (Sigelman & Rider, 2006).

Ecological systems theory (Urie Bronfenbrenner's work outlined in Chapter 2) referred to a number of environments that influence children's development, and which change as they grow older. In the early years, parents and the home environment are the main influences on development. As children get older and their environments extend beyond the microsystem, friends, neighbours, school, sports and youth clubs become more important influences. However, it is the family that is and remains a major influence upon children's development. In his model, Bronfenbrenner describes a bidirectional influence existing in families whereby each member affects each other so that an interrelationship is apparent. The family environment is the first environment that young children come into contact with and it is here they explore their new world with its strange new people, toys and objects. Here they develop attachments, learn language and social skills and a developing understanding of themselves and their beliefs. Development is positively influenced in warm and secure family units, with advances in self-esteem, empathy and even higher IQ scores being reported (Burke, 2003). Environments with authoritative parenting that has consistent expectations and sets clear

The family environment is where children develop attachments, learn language and social skills and develop understanding of themselves and their beliefs.

*Source*: © Pearson Education Ltd / Debbie Rowe.

limits for behaviour produces socially mature behaviour, better self-confidence and higher academic achievement (Kay, 2006). In contrast, in families where there is divorce, poverty, or joblessness, it could be argued that such factors weaken the family structure and lead to health and psychological problems in family members.

The school has important contributions to make to the all-round development of children. Schools are complex social institutions and ones in which children spend considerable time.

*Source*: © Pearson Education Ltd / Gareth Boden.

The school is very often a focal point of a community and has important contributions to make to the all-round development of children. These in themselves are complex social institutions and ones in which children spend considerable time: daily, some 6 hours or more. In the same category could also be placed playgroups, nurseries, and day-care centres in terms of the social impact they have upon children's development. In the following feature, *Policy, Research and Praxis*, you can read how Bronfenbrenner's ecological model of development informed the revision of a national strategy in relation to early years provision.

## Policy, Research and Praxis

### Ecological systems and enabling contexts for development

Bronfenbrenner's ecological model of development provides a useful theoretical model in the study of child development and one commonly studied in courses in child development. It was this model that was used in *The Early Years Learning and Development Literature Review* (Evangelou *et al.*, 2009) which informed the revised Early Years Foundation Stage (EYFS), the curriculum in England for children from birth to age 5 begun in 2010 and which became statutory in September 2012. In the review, Bronfenbrenner's model was an appropriate one to discuss the best supporting contexts for children's early learning and development.

The approach taken by the writers was in line with the interactionist tradition, which conceived development as being located within a set of nested social contexts originally proposed by Bronfenbrenner (1979). His principles of the ecology of child development are highly appropriate for the review. These are: (i) at the centre of the model is the developing child; (ii) the child affects and is affected by the environments he/she experiences and development is determined by these; (iii) the family is the most important influence on the child; (iv) the number and the quality of connections between the people in these environments (e.g. teachers talking to parents) have implications for development.

Bronfenbrenner saw development taking place through processes of progressively more complex interactions between the child and the persons, objects, and symbols in its immediate environment (Bronfenbrenner, 1989). The review placed emphasis on the relations and interactions a child has with others and how these influence development. In relation to children under 5, this refers to those people immediately around the young child (the family), and over time includes a wider sphere of people (relatives, peers, neighbours, teachers, etc.).

It includes the physical environments and resources interacted with in the various settings of home, preschool and school, such as sand, water, bricks and mark-making materials, and the routines and events in the lives of children at home and in settings. These are influenced by wider policies and cultural characteristics that inform a child's values and belief systems.

The review goes on to discuss the supportive processes that shape development and highlighted the following factors as important contexts for development:

- Positive relationships with others. Development is influenced by rich, relational experiences that take place both at home and in learning settings or schools with parents and staff.
- Children's learning. Play, and the role of talk and narrative are recognised as important vehicles to enhance learning.
- Rich and appropriate environments and resources refer to the equipment and materials in both indoor and outdoor environments and the opportunities these offer to foster development.

> - Partnerships with parents and carers. Engaging parents in their child's learning has a direct influence on learning and achievement.
> - Taking culture into account. Vygotsky's socio-constructivist account of learning (1978) is repeated evidence of the influence of the social and cultural contexts in development.
>
> The *Early Years Learning and Development Literature Review* draws upon Bronfenbrenner's ecological systems theory, and the nested social contexts referred to underscore the impact of close family on development and the vital role of parents in supporting children's learning and development which is central to the revised EYFS framework.

**Connect and Extend**

For a paper putting ecological systems theory into action, read about the impact of imprisoned fathers on children's development in Dyer, W. J., Pleck, J. H. & McBride, B. A. (2012). Imprisoned fathers and their family relationships: A 40-year review from a multi-theory view. *Journal of Family Theory and Review*, March, 4(1), 20–47.

Other places where children live and play affect their development. The 'resources' that a community offers – safe places to play with like-minded peers – can foster social and language skills. The presence of parents, grandparents and neighbourhood amenities all impact on their sense of self and helps to develop citizenship. In communities with high crime and unemployment where there is often an absence of opportunities, the ties that link families together and families to other families become loose and the incidences of antisocial behaviour, truancy, and substance abuse among young people rise. Systems theory acts as a robust reminder of the variety of environmental contexts that children experience and the importance of these contexts in their development. With the blueprint already provided through genetic inheritance, these different environments act alongside this to shape all aspects of development. Environmental factors work in conjunction with genetics and it is this alliance that is considered now.

## Interaction of heredity with the environment

The interaction of heredity and the environment shapes children's growth and behaviour, and this means that genotype and phenotype provide a good framework for exploring how genes and the environment interact. Researchers commonly study this interaction either through adoption or twin studies. In the former, studies investigate similarities between adoptive children and their adopted parents on the assumption that biological parents have made no contribution to the social environment; or to similarities and differences between other siblings in the same household.

Studying twins has also been an effective tool in unravelling the issue of nature versus nurture. The effects of genes and the environment cannot be separated for individuals, but they can through twin studies. These studies produce heritability estimates which we explained earlier. For instance, attention deficit hyperactivity disorder (ADHD) among children has a heritability estimate of around 0.8 or 80 per cent (Nigg, 2006). We can infer from this that most differences in symptoms result from genetic differences. For loneliness in adulthood – these findings from a twin study in the Netherlands – the heritability estimate is around 50 per cent (Boomsma *et al.*, 2005). For childhood delinquency, the figure is between 20 per cent and 30 per cent (Hill & Maughan, 2001), which indicates both genetics and the environment account for differences in delinquency at an individual level. Although far from agreed upon, there is some evidence that Type 1 diabetes in children may be mainly genetic, although possibly triggered by a life event (Raine *et al.*, 2006).

Remember, the value of heritability – an estimate of the correlation $0 \leq 1$ between a behaviour or condition, and an identified gene – lies in explaining trait differences due to variations in genes or environment, but they are limited in not being able to do the same for traits in people from different environments. There is no clearer analogy to illustrate this point than the one offered by evolutionary geneticist Richard Lewontin (1976) which we slightly modify. Take a handful of garden seeds and plant these (mixed genes) into two gardens we shall call

A and B. Garden A is well cared for while Garden B is neglected. As the seeds grow, any differences among the new plants in Garden A can be attributed to genes since plants in this garden have the same environment for growing. Plants in Garden A should be expected to grow better than those in Garden B. Is this because of genes, the different environments offered by each garden or a combination of both? Clearly, because the range of genes is similar in both gardens, it must be the effect of the environment that caused the difference.

Both genes and environment contribute flexibly to development although there is variation according to the particular trait. Of course, this is a sociological argument, and, although many research projects (often fitting well with the garden metaphor above) have studied twins reared together and apart, and adopted and non-adopted siblings, some of the research is open to the challenge that truly scientific methods have not been adopted. Let's explain by taking an example. Suppose we were investigating success rates of helping people to stop smoking by administering drugs and/or receiving psychological therapy.

Almost all scientific experimental designs create four groups randomly from the target population – in this case of smokers who want to give up:

1. a group that receives both drugs and therapy;

2. a group that receives therapy alone;

3. a group that receives drugs alone; and

4. a fourth group that receives no treatment.

(A fifth group could receive a placebo drug.)

So instead, if we only had two groups – those that receive a combination treatment and those that do not – then all we could look at would be the combined effect and not a scientific comparison of the effects of drugs and psychological therapy. In child development studies we could only look at the combination of genes and environment if the genes are identical as in the case of identical twins or if the environment was so controlled (in laboratory conditions perhaps) that we could guarantee identical experiences for the subjects over a considerable period of time – perhaps even a lifespan. Also, recent evidence has shown that 'identical twins' are more genetically discordant than originally thought (Little, 2011). However, studies of identical twins still offer the possibility of saying something useful about the effects of environment, but the study of non-identical twins or siblings is open to the challenge of observations being the result of a mix of genes and environment, and therefore could be considered to be unscientific.

These concerns about twin studies are not new. Back in 1999, developmental psychologist Sidney Segalowitz concluded that many human twin studies which produced heritability estimates had serious methodological flaws. He considered that heritability is consistently overestimated because of confusion about the biological basis of twinning, the consistent and often gross underestimation of the environmental variance, and that heritability estimations are often added together to create hugely exaggerated heritability values, when it makes no sense so to do. He further concludes that, despite bad research design, behaviour geneticists continue to publish results implying that their heritability results are valid.

Why is this argument important? Well, much is claimed for the study of twins and siblings in family settings, and it is important that you can critically review such claims and make up your own mind about our concerns about scientific method. With these concerns in mind we now look at the contribution of the study of twins to our understanding of child development.

## Twins

A pregnancy with twins occurs when a zygote (the united cell made from the sperm and the ovum) in the cell duplication process following conception separates into two clusters of cells, and two life forms are created. These are identical (monozygotic) twins (MZ). Since mitosis

• • • • • • • • • • • • • • • •
**Connect and Extend**
Read more about concerns with twin research:
Little, C. M. (2011). Genetics and twins. *Newborn and Infant Nursing Reviews*, December, *11*(4), 185–189.
• • • • • • • • • • • • • • • •

**Identical (monozygotic) twins**
Children in the same pregnancy who have developed from the same fertilised ovum.

involves exact genetic replication, these babies will be identical. They are alike and of the same sex (identical triplets develop if the original zygote splits twice in a row, producing four identical cells of which one dies). If two or more eggs are released from the woman's ovary and are fertilised, two babies are produced. Twins here are fraternal (dizygotic) twins (DZ), that is, two girls, two boys or one of each. Their genetic materials are as potentially different as two siblings born at different times, in contrast to identical twins who develop from a fertilised egg splitting and forming two cells.

**Fraternal (dizygotic) twins**
Children in the same pregnancy who have developed from two separate fertilised ova.

Multiple ovulation can be triggered by fertility drugs as well as for genetic reasons, and the increased use of fertility treatments has seen an increase in multiple births (Bell, 2008; Blondel & Kaminski, 2002). Some fertility drugs overstimulate a woman's ovaries and result in pregnancies with twins, triplets or quadruplets. The probability of multiple births also increases with the increasing age of the mother (Martin *et al.*, 2003) and researchers have reported some cultural variances in the likelihood of multiple births within and between different populations (Blondel *et al.*, 2006; Katz *et al.*, 2001).

**Reflect**    Many parents dress their identical twins in identical clothes and give them very similar experiences, including making sure they are in the same classes at school, while other parents try to stress the differences between their twins. Which approach would you take and why?

## Twin studies

Twin studies offer a fascinating insight into the comparative effects of multifactorial transmission – the relative impact of nature and nurture and into gender differences.

*Source*: © Digital Vision / Rob van Patten / Getty Images.

Twin studies, of which there have been and continue to be many examples (see the *Focus on Theory* feature opposite) are useful for comparative studies of the development of MZ and DZ twins, and siblings (Anastasi, 2007). Behaviour geneticists and others interested in child development have studied twins reared together and apart, and adopted and non-adopted siblings. We will make much reference to this research during subsequent chapters, because twin studies offer a fascinating insight into the comparative effects of multifactorial transmission – the relative impact of nature and nurture and into gender differences. The importance of twin studies is that it is not just the physical characteristics that are shared: personality traits such as sociability, attachment or anxiety are also shared (McCrae *et al.*, 2000) and this was noted by early researchers into human behaviour.

The interest in studying twins scientifically extends across many cultures. Its origins lie in the late nineteenth century with the publication in 1883 of *Inquiries Into Human Faculty and Its Development* by Francis Galton (a name we met earlier), in which he proposed (later to be proved accurate), that identical twins come from a single egg while non-identical twins come from two separate eggs. Galton's work drew international interest and contributed to the publication in 1937 of *Twins: A study of heredity and environment* by biologist Horatio Newman, educationalist Frank Freeman and statistician Karl Holzinger, which was seen as a landmark in thinking on the nature versus nurture debate. Just prior to the outbreak of the Second World War, research into twins took a more sinister direction and became embroiled with the politics of race. The experiments of Josef Mengele in the Auschwitz concentration camp were marked by scientific rigour but also abject cruelty and inhumanity.

Nevertheless, medical research recognises the value of twin research which, combined with new technologies, is able to separate some of the genetic base for diseases such as cancer and diabetes, and reveal new ways of treating these maladies (Maecker *et al.*, 2003). What does research tell us about the similarities and differences between both types of twins? The *Focus on Theory* box below presents some findings from the past decade or so.

**Connect and Extend**
The nearby reference to the experiments of Josef Mengele is an important example of how we must never ignore the ethics of research into child development. Access information about this sordid and extreme example at a website such as **www.historylearningsite. co.uk/joseph_mengele.htm** (accessed 21 July 2012). What safeguards are necessary now and who should police them?

## Focus on Theory

### Twin studies

In this feature we will explore a number of twin studies in a variety of professional contexts. Each study is introduced with a research question (there is an explanation of research questions in Chapter 3). We encourage you to access each of the studies and so enrich your appreciation of how twin studies are able to inform practice in different professional contexts.

#### Is there a helpfulness gene?

In July 2004, Jane Scourfield, Bethan John, Neilson Martin and Peter McGuffin reported on their study into prosocial behaviour (behaviour on the part of an individual which is to the benefit of another or the group) using twin data from 682 families. Parent and teacher reports were used to examine the genetic and environmental influences on prosocial behaviour in 5–16-year-olds. There were no significant differences in the heritability estimates of genetic influence on male and female prosocial behaviour; however, increasing genetic influences were seen with age. This emerged as a trend in parent data and reached statistical significance in teacher data.

Scourfield, J., John, B., Martin, N. & McGuffin, P. (2004). The development of prosocial behaviour in children and adolescents: A twin study. *Journal of Child Psychology and Psychiatry (formerly Journal of Child Psychology and Psychiatry and Allied Disciplines)*, 45, 927–935.

#### Do infertility treatments create difficult babies and overanxious parents?

A study (2003) by Lucy Tully, Terrie Moffitt and Avshalom Caspi of King's College London, compared measures of parental adjustment, parenting and child behaviour in families with 5-year-old twins who were conceived after *in vitro* fertilisation (IVF) or ovulation induction (OI) with families whose twins were naturally conceived (NC). This study found no long-term effects of infertility and assisted reproductive technology (IVF/OI) on parenting and child behaviour in families with twins, using measures of parental adjustment, and parent and teacher ratings of the twins' behaviour. IVF/OI mothers and their partners agreed with each other about discipline more than NC couples, but otherwise no other differences in parenting were found. Overall, this study provides evidence that families who conceive twins following IVF/OI are functioning well and that the experience of fertility treatment does not lead to long-term difficulties for parents or children.

Tully, L. A., Moffitt, T. E. & Caspi, A. (2003). Maternal adjustment, parenting and child behaviour in families of school-aged twins conceived after IVF and ovulation induction. *Journal of Child Psychology and Psychiatry (formerly Journal of Child Psychology and Psychiatry and Allied Disciplines)*, 44, 316–325.

#### Are some babies born to be antisocial?

Also in 2003, Terrie Moffitt, Avshalom Caspi and colleagues investigated genetic influences on antisocial behaviour in a representative-plus-high-risk sample of 1116 pairs of 5-year-old twins using data from four independent sources: mothers, teachers, examiner-observers previously unacquainted with the children, and the children themselves. They aimed to find out whether or not early childhood antisocial behaviour is a strong prognostic indicator for poor adult mental health. Variation in antisocial behaviour was agreed upon by all informants; no bias was detected in mothers', teachers', examiners' or children's reports, and thus was pervasive across settings. It was found that antisocial behaviour was influenced by genetic factors (82 per cent) and experiences specific to each child (18 per cent). This study and four others of very young twins show that genetic risks contribute strongly to population variation in antisocial behaviour that emerges in early childhood.

Arseneault, L., Moffitt, T. E., Caspi, A., Taylor, A., Rijsdijk, F. V., Jaffee, S. R., Ablow, J. C. & Measelle, J. R. (2003). Strong genetic effects on cross-situational antisocial behaviour among 5-year-old children according to mothers, teachers, examiner-observers, and twins' self-reports. *Journal of Child Psychology and Psychiatry (formerly Journal of Child Psychology and Psychiatry and Allied Disciplines)*, 44, 832–848.

## Are some babies more likely to be hyperactive?

The main aim of this study, reported in 2001 was to confirm a high heredity estimate for hyperactivity using a sample of 268 twin pairs aged 7–11 years. Forty-six hyperactive twin pairs (pairs in which at least one twin was pervasively hyperactive) and 47 control twin pairs were assessed using psychological tests. Confirming findings from previous twin studies the researchers, Jonna Kuntsi and Jim Stevenson found a substantial proportion of hyperactivity was considered to be due to genetic effects (71 per cent parent ratings and 57 per cent teacher ratings) and there was significant evidence of genetic effects on extreme hyperactivity.

Kuntsi, J. & Stevenson, J. (2001). Psychological mechanisms in hyperactivity: II The role of genetic factors. *Journal of Child Psychology and Psychiatry (formerly Journal of Child Psychology and Psychiatry and Allied Disciplines)*, 42, 211–219.

## Why are some children more likely to suffer from depression?

In 2003, Frances Rice, Gordon Harold and Anita Thapar reported on a study of genetic factors in childhood depression. Were genetic factors more or less responsible for a depressive reaction to negative life events? The researchers sent questionnaires to the families of a sample of twins aged between 8 and 17 years. Responses were obtained from 1468 families and an analysis of negative life events, behaviour-dependent life events and depression symptoms was undertaken separately for children (aged 8 to 10 years) and adolescents (aged 11 to 17 years). Differences in genetic and environmental factors were tested. It was found that adolescence was associated with a greater number of behaviour-dependent life events. Genetic factors made a significant contribution to a depressive reaction to negative life events, and symptoms of depression were greater for adolescents than for children.

Rice, F., Harold, G. T. & Thapar, A. (2003). Negative life events as an account of age-related differences in the genetic aetiology of depression in childhood and adolescence. *Journal of Child Psychology and Psychiatry (formerly Journal of Child Psychology and Psychiatry and Allied Disciplines)*, 44, 977–987.

## Why are some adolescents more likely to start smoking?

In 2003, Victoria White and colleagues reported on an Australian study to assess the genetic and environmental factors contributing to smoking habits in adolescents and young adults. Twins initially aged between 13 and 18 years were surveyed three times between 1988 and 1996. A total of 414 pairs of identical and same-sex fraternal twin pairs participated in all three surveys (this was a longitudinal study). The twins answered a questionnaire on their own smoking status and reported on the use of tobacco by parents and friends. At all three surveys, current smokers were more likely to have parents who smoked and to have smokers among their peers. Genes and environmental factors, both common and unique, contributed to variation in smoking behaviours. Genes seem to have a direct influence on variations in the smoking behaviours of young adults but environmental factors play the greater role in determining variation in tobacco smoking among adolescents and young adults.

White, V. M., Hopper, J. L., Wearing, A. J. & Hill, D. J. (2003). The role of genes in tobacco smoking during adolescence and young adulthood: a multivariate behaviour genetic investigation. *Addiction*, 98, 1087–1100.

## What about smoking and drinking alcohol in China?

Using standard twin methodology, Christina N. Lessov-Schlaggar and colleagues reported on a 2006 study aimed to examine the relative contribution of genetic and environmental influences on cigarette smoking and alcohol drinking in a sample of adult Chinese twins. More than half of the male twins were smokers (58 per cent), and 32.5 per cent reported alcohol consumption. Nearly all female twins were non-smokers (99.2 per cent) and non-drinkers (98.7 per cent); therefore, genetic analysis was limited to male data. In contrast to the Australian study above, Chinese men's current smoking was significantly heritable (75.1 per cent), with no evidence for a significant contribution of shared environmental effects. Heavy smoking was more strongly influenced by genes (66.2 per cent) than shared environment (8.7 per cent). Similarly, current drinking was more strongly influenced by genetic effects (59.5 per cent) than by shared environmental effects (15.3 per cent).

Lessov-Schlaggar, C. N., Pang, Z., Swan, G. E., Guo, Q., Wang, S., Cao, W., Unger, J. B., Anderson Johnson, C. & Lee, L. (2006). Heritability of cigarette smoking and alcohol use in Chinese male twins: The Qingdao twin registry. *International Journal of Epidemiology*, 35, 1278–1285.

## Are some children more likely to understand what they read?

In 2006 Janice Keenan and colleagues reported behaviour genetic analyses of reading and listening comprehension. Although the twin sample was of limited size, they found substantial, and significant, genetic influences on individual differences in both reading and listening comprehension. In addition, word recognition and listening comprehension each accounted for significant independent genetic influences on reading comprehension. Together, they accounted for all the genetic influence on reading comprehension, indicating a largely genetic basis for individual differences in reading comprehension.

Keenan, J. M., Betjemann, R. S., Wadsworth, S. J., DeFries, J. C. & Olson, R. K. (2006). Genetic and environmental influences on reading and listening comprehension. *Journal of Research in Reading*, 29, 75–91.

## Is there a strong link between DNA and general cognitive ability?

In 2005 Nicole Harlaar and colleagues found five DNA markers were associated with general cognitive ability in a sample of 7414 7-year-old twins. These children have also been studied at 2, 3, 4 and 7 years of age on measures of cognitive and language development and behaviour problems; family environment was also assessed. The association was stronger with verbal than non-verbal ability and with reading more than mathematics performance. Stronger environmental correlations were found for pre-school measures of the family environment (chaos and discipline) rather than maternal education and father's occupational class.

Harlaar, N., Butcher, L. M., Meaburn, E., Sham, P., Craig, I. W. & Plomin, R. (2005). A behavioural genomic analysis of DNA markers associated with general cognitive ability in 7-year-olds. *Journal of Child Psychology and Psychiatry (formerly Journal of Child Psychology and Psychiatry and Allied Disciplines)*, 46, 1097–1107.

## Is autism inherited?

Autism is considered the most heritable of neurodevelopmental disorders, mainly because of the large difference in concordance rates between monozygotic and dizygotic twins. In 2011, Hallmayer, Joachim and his team completed structured diagnostic assessments (Autism Diagnostic Interview–Revised and Autism Diagnostic Observation Schedule) on 192 twin pairs. Heritability rates for 'strict' autism for male *twins* varied from 58 per cent for 40 monozygotic pairs and 21 per cent for 31 dizygotic pairs. For female *twins*, the heritability rate was 60 per cent for 7 monozygotic pairs, and 27 per cent for 10 dizygotic pairs.

Hallmayer, J., Cleveland, S., Torres, A., Phillips, J., Cohen, B., Torigoe, T., Miller, J., Fedele, A., Collins, J., Smith, K., Lotspeich, L., Croen, L. A., Ozonoff, S., Lajonchere, C., Grether, J. K. & Risch, N. (2011) Genetic Heritability and Shared Environmental Factors Among Twin Pairs With Autism *Archives of General Psychiatry*, November 2011, 68(11), 1095–1102.

# The scope and types of interaction

As shown in the *Focus on Theory* feature, the interactions between genes and the environment are complex. The contemporary view is that the environment influences the expression of one's genes. This view is based on earlier research into range of reaction (Plomin, 1995) which suggests that, rather than viewing behaviour as fixed by our genes, a range of possible outcomes are established in response to environmental differences. We know that some of an individual's traits (such as eye colour) are genetically determined, but the range of reaction idea is associated with more complex behaviours. Limits are placed on abilities due to one's genotype but are modified according to the environment. We will illustrate this with an example. Hypothetically take two children, Maria and Karl, of the same age (9 years old) inheriting two different genotypes, one of poor and the other of good potential. We know that the genotype of each child imposes boundaries on their abilities. If Maria is brought up in an environment with little stimulation or one of impoverishment, her genotype sets a ceiling on how much she can achieve under these circumstances. Even in a 'better' environment, the advances are likely to be rather small. Karl has a different genotype. His achievements even under poorer conditions may be modest, but under stimulating circumstances may be quite advanced and his achievements accelerated. Both children show differences in their range of reaction. In the case of Maria, where the range of reaction is very narrow and pathways are restricted, this shows strong canalisation – cognitive or growth impairment and restriction (Cooke & Foulder-Hughes, 2003; term by Waddington, 1962). Strong interventions in the home and school environments are required to alter the course of development.

Gene expression is also influenced by the environment. The historic and influential analysis by psychologists Sandra Scarr and Kathleen McCartney (1983) of the interaction of genetics and environment is still relevant and used today. Scarr and McCartney described how interactions happen in three possible ways. In passive interactions, parents with particular genetic predispositions may create a home environment that suits the dispositions their children have inherited from them. They often seek a school environment that fosters this trait in their child. As we suggested earlier, parents who are musical and wish their child to develop this ability will seek to make music an integral part of home life. When the child enters formal education, the parents may try to develop musical abilities through encouragement to join choirs and school bands, and to take private lessons outside school. Sport and the performing arts in general are further avenues for passive interactions.

Evocative interactions are a second pathway where traits influence the environment through inherited tendencies to produce responses in other people. The smiling baby produces a positive response from adults: this reinforces smiling as a good thing to happen in the baby's repertoire of newly acquiring social skills, and stimulates adults to encourage this behaviour.

Finally, active interactions involve pathways in which the individual seeks out experiences that are in keeping with inherited tendencies. An example is niche picking (Stamps & Groothius, 2010), a term describing how individuals choose environments that are compatible with their inherited dispositions. Expression is given to their predispositions by selecting activities and friends that match their predilections. The child at 5 who gravitates to the construction corner in the classroom and enjoys building with cardboard boxes may well become an engineer in later life. So too the boisterous 7-year-old with limitless energy and a preference for rough-and-tumble play in the school playground is likely to be seen playing in the local rugby team as a teenager and adult. The expression in the genes for physical challenge is enhanced by the experiences the child selects throughout life.

**Range of reaction**
Possibilities for development arising from interaction with one's environment.

**Canalisation**
Heredity restrictions on development to a single or few outcomes.

**Passive interactions**
Structures and environments provided by parents to suit their child's genetic traits.

**Evocative interactions**
Traits in children that cause other people to behave toward them in certain ways.

**Active interactions**
Interactions sought out by individuals that are in keeping with their inherited tendencies.

**Niche picking**
A term for where individuals choose environments that are compatible with their inherited dispositions.

We now summarise what you have learned in the final section of this chapter:

- Factors in the environment influence how the messages in our genes are put into action.
- Ecological systems theory refers to a number of environments (e.g. homes and schools) that influence children's development.
- Researchers commonly study genetic and environmental interaction through adoption or twin studies.
- Heritability estimates are high for attention deficit and hyperactivity disorder whereas heritability estimates are low for childhood delinquency.
- Twins do not just share physical characteristics. Personality traits such as sociability, attachment or anxiety are also shared.
- Research suggests that behaviour is not fixed by our genes but does provide a range of possible outcomes – a 'range of reaction'.
- Interactions between genotype and the environment happen in passive, evocative and active ways.

**Summary 3**

# Conclusion

There is an old joke which goes something like this. How do you tell the sex of a chromosome? Answer: search in its genes (jeans)! Of course we now know that we would not search in any genes but would start with the sex chromosomes, chromosome 23, and check for the XY pairing. We might also look for other evidence in chromosomes that contain genetic material, particularly that displaying chromosomal disorders and abnormalities which are more likely to affect boys than girls. We already know a good deal about cells, chromosomes, DNA and genes, but the truth is that we are still discovering how characteristics, traits, appearance and behaviour are transferred from one generation to another and what genetic differences there are between girls and boys.

We also explored the effects of the environment on development and there are a number of very helpful sociological and ecological models that neatly capture the many environmental factors that can impact. The evidence presented in this chapter is quite clear: both genes and the environment are linked in complex and momentous ways, and both fashion a child's development. This chapter explained first of all the genetic foundations that shape who we are and then the environmental ones. The inextricable link between the two was presented in the final section and highlighted with evidence from different sources, including recent research findings from studies on twins. This chapter enables you to account in part for the similarities and the differences you observe in the development of children, to check that all is as expected or to identify that something unanticipated is happening – often the sign for special measures to be taken. Our genetic map is set down at the split second of time of our conception and, although some abnormalities can then occur, for the vast majority of us – even we weaker males – our cells then look after us in amazing ways for the remainder of our lives.

This concludes Part 1 of *Child Development: Theory and Practice 0–11*. In Part 1: *Introducing child development* we have explored the issues and theories of child development, and discussed the most commonly used research methods for looking at the foundation of development and the extent to which what we are and what we become is a function of both our genetic nature and our environmental nurture. In Part 2, we will focus on early and physical development, starting with the main milestones of prenatal development. In Chapter 5 we will explore what happens between conception, the all-important first few divisions of the zygote cell, and the birth of a human baby (with millions of cells) some 9 months later.

We will explore how factors in the external environment can negatively influence foetal health and capacity, and explore the link between early brain development, and the behaviour and learning of the foetus. For the time being, we can now all groan together when we hear that old joke: 'How do you tell the sex of a . . . ?'

# Summary Table
## Nature and Nurture

## Genetic foundations (pp 90–94)

### Our unique beginnings (p 90)

Sperms produced in the male testes are ejaculated in seminal fluid at the climax of the sexual act. These then enter the woman's vagina and swim through the uterus into her Fallopian tubes. Fertilisation takes place when male sperm and a woman's ovum unite and create a single cell called a zygote. One 'champion sperm' burrows into the ovum. This is the process of conception. Fertilisation is complete and the ovum now attaches itself to the wall of the uterus and starts the three periods of prenatal development.

### The genetic code (pp 90–91)

We are each made up of billions of tiny units called cells and each cell carries the whole genetic code for each one of us. Each cell has a nucleus and inside the nucleus are rod-like structures called chromosomes which store and transmit genetic information. Chromosomes are matched pairs – with the exception of the XY pair in males. One chromosome in each pair is inherited from the mother and one from the father. Each ovum contains half the chromosomes and the successful sperm contains the other half needed to complete the zygote – the fertilised egg. We humans have 23 pairs of chromosomes.

### Chromosomes and genes (pp 91–92)

Each chromosome is like a long, coiled thread, consisting of a chain of genes. Chromosomes are made up of a chemical called deoxyribonucleic acid (DNA), made up of four base chemicals from which cells are duplicated. Our cells need to duplicate for all of us to grow and to develop, and do so through a process of mitosis. Cells duplicate through replicating the DNA and splitting so each new cell contains the same number of chromosomes and has identical chemical pairings. The special sequence of our DNA's four chemical units makes up our genetic code and it is this code

that determines all our inherited characteristics. The order in which each person's genes are arranged in the complete collection of chromosomes is a person's genotype. The study of how genes transmit biological traits over generations is called genetics and the entire sequence encoded in the DNA for all humans makes up what is known as the human genome.

### Using the human genome (pp 92–94)

Cloning, an example of using the human genome, is a procedure for producing multiple copies of genetically identical organisms. Cells are removed from the embryo and replaced with DNA from a donor parent. What is produced is a new clone with the same appearance and genetic make-up as the original. Pro-cloning activists argue that cloning can save millions of lives and offer the potential for a much better quality of life for many people. Critics of cloning argue that it raises fundamental questions about human nature and identity, destroys our human uniqueness and creates speculation about the potential of cloning techniques to create monsters with awful abnormalities.

## Heredity (pp 94–103)

### Genotypes and phenotypes (p 95)

The collection of characteristics you can observe in an individual is called his or her phenotype. Phenotypes are made up of a unique collection of inherited genetic instructions in the genes (genotype), influences in the environment and the interaction between genotype and the environment. Genotype and phenotype together combine factors that determine who we are and influence our individual characteristics, the reason why no two people can ever be *exactly* alike.

### Dominant and recessive genes (pp 95–98)

Almost all chromosomes are in matching pairs, one inherited from the father and the other from the mother. Genes are also found in pairs (except in the sex chromosomes) and each form of a gene pair is called an allele, with a combination of dominant or recessive genes. A dominant gene is one that if present in a gene pair will be expressed as a characteristic, e.g. brown hair. Another gene which, when paired with a dominant gene does not affect a child's characteristics, becomes dormant and is called recessive, e.g. red hair. The recessive gene remains in the cell, unexpressed but capable of being passed on to future generations (red hair can miss one or many generations). Recessive genes will only be expressed when paired with another recessive gene.

## More about X and Y chromosomes (pp 98–99)

Evolution is the process by which the strongest characteristies of a species (over time) are preserved. If a gene is defective on a female X chromosome, a healthy gene on the partner X chromosome compensates. If a male has a defective X chromosome, there may not be a healthy partner gene on the Y chromosome because Y chromosomes are smaller and carry fewer genes. The higher mortality rate that exists in males means that more of them need to be conceived to be born and survive. Boys are more vulnerable to prenatal problems and congenital disorders. The same vulnerability stays with them throughout life. Males have shorter lives, more behaviour problems, and more learning difficulties.

## Behaviour genetics (pp 99–100)

Behaviour genetics was established in the middle of the nineteenth century by Francis Galton who wrote about the inheritance of giftedness, using his family as the context for his studies. The development of behaviour genetics and its close association with the development of the science of psychology continued well into the twentieth century because of the dominance of behaviourist theories in the first half of the twentieth century, and also the link with criminal psychology and psychopathology – the study of mental illness. The chief source of data for behaviour genetics are 'twin studies' because in twin studies we have the potential to identify variables in human development that owe more or less to nature than to nurture.

## Heritability (p 100)

Heritability is an estimate using an index between 0 and 1, where 0 stands for behaviour or condition that has no correlation with an identified gene, and where 1 stands for a perfect correlation. In the case of Huntington's disease, there is a better than 0.999 correlation between having the identified gene and the disease and a similar correlation for not having either. Learning mother-tongue language is entirely environmentally determined and has a heredity index of 0. Early studies of intelligence found heritability measures of 0.4 to 0.5, but subsequent analyses have found that the genetic contribution to measures of intelligence increases over a lifespan, reaching a heritability of 0.8 in adulthood.

## Genetic and chromosome abnormalities (p 101)

Genetic disorders can arise from inheriting a pair of abnormal recessive alleles. An example is sickle-cell anaemia, in which the body's red blood cells become misshapen, causing less uptake of oxygen. Other examples are cystic fibrosis, haemophilia and spina bifida. A second set of chromosome disorders are not ordinarily present in a child's parents but are caused by chromosomes failing to separate or through part of the chromosome breaking off. Problems in the union of sperm and egg can result in serious physical or mental disorders, including Down's Syndrome.

## Down's Syndrome (pp 101–102)

Down's Syndrome (DS), a condition also called Trisomy 21, affects 1 in 600 children and in most cases is caused by the presence of an extra chromosome 21 in all cells of the individual. It occurs more frequently in babies of mothers under 21 or over 35 and the risk increases with the mother's age. Children with Down's Syndrome can suffer from congenital disorders such as heart problems and bowel abnormalities, are susceptible to eye problems and to illnesses such as leukaemia and Alzheimer's disease as they get older. The syndrome is characterised by irregularities in overall development, delays in cognitive development, and difficulties in visual, auditory and sensory processing. Language acquisition is also delayed, resulting in difficulties in speech and language expression.

# Environmental foundations (pp 103–113)

## A variety of contexts for development (pp 103–106)

Children experience a number of environments that influence their development and which change as they grow older. In the early years, parents and the home environment are the main influences on development. As children get older their environments extend to friends, neighbours, school, sports and youth clubs; however, it is the family that remains a major influence upon their development. Environments with authoritative parenting produce socially mature behaviour, better self-confidence and higher academic achievement. In contrast, being in a family where there is divorce, poverty and joblessness may lead to health and psychological problems in family members.

## Interaction of heredity with the environment (pp 106–107)

Genotype and phenotype together provide a framework for exploring how genes and the environment interact. Both genes and environment contribute flexibly to development, although there is variation according to the particular trait. Researchers commonly study this interaction either through adoption or twin studies, but some of the research is open to the challenge that truly scientific methods have not been adopted.

### Twins (pp 107–108)

If a zygote separates into two clusters of cells, two life forms are created. These are identical (monozygotic) twins (MZ). Since mitosis involves exact genetic replication, these babies will be identical. They are alike and of the same sex. Fraternal (dizygotic) twins (DZ), i.e. two girls, two boys or one of each, are the result of two different eggs being fertilised at the same time and developing side by side in the womb. Their genetic materials are as potentially different as two siblings born at different times, in contrast to identical twins.

### Twin studies (pp 108–111)

Twin studies are comparative studies of the development of MZ and DZ twins, and siblings. Behaviour geneticists and others interested in child development have studied twins reared together and apart, and adopted and non-adopted siblings because twin studies offer a fascinating insight into the comparative effects of multifactorial transmission – the relative impact of nature and nurture and into gender differences. It is not just the physical characteristics: twins' personality traits such as sociability, attachment or anxiety are also shared.

### The scope and types of interaction (p 112)

Research into 'range of reaction' suggests that rather than viewing behaviour as fixed by our genes, a range of possible outcomes are established in response to environmental differences. Limits are placed on abilities due to one's genotype but are modified according to the environment. However, where the range of reaction is very narrow and pathways are restricted, this shows strong canalisation – cognitive or growth impairment and restriction. Interactions between genes and environment happen in three possible ways. In passive interactions, parents create a home environment that suits the dispositions their children (the passive receivers) have inherited from them. Evocative interactions are where genes influence the environment through using inherited tendencies to produce responses in other people, e.g. frequent smiling. Finally, active interactions are where the individual seeks out experiences that are in keeping with inherited tendencies.

## Going further

Bryson, B. (2004). *A short history of nearly everything.* London: Black Swan.
Although not intended as an academic text, this marvellous book contains a wealth of information and is certainly worth dipping into. Chapters 24 and 26 are relevant here.

Carey, N. (2012) *The epigenetics revolution: How modern biology is rewriting our understanding of genetics, disease and inheritance.* London: Faber & Faber, Icon Books Ltd.
Biologist Nessa Carey explains such diverse phenomena as how queen bees and ants control their colonies, why tortoiseshell cats are always female and why we age, develop disease and become addicted to drugs. Carey also reveals the amazing possibilities for humankind that epigenetics offers for us all – and in the surprisingly near future.

Weissmann, G. (2012) *Epigenetics in the age of Twitter: Pop culture and modern science.* New York: Bellevue Literary Press.
A hugely entertaining and instructive book that has a strong cultural flavour to the explanations of popular science.

## Useful websites

www.comparefutures.org
Nature or nurture? This site compares chances of a successful childhood and adolescence (defined by going to University and being in employment) by postcode. Is epigenetics part of a postcode lottery in the UK today?

www.dsrf.org
A website owned by the Down's Syndrome Research Foundation. There is much useful information on this condition.

www.ornl.gov/hgmis/resource/medicine.html
The official site of the Human Genome Project.

# Part 2
## Early and Physical Development

# Chapter 5
## Prenatal Development

### Overview

# Introduction

In Chapter 4 we explained that our genetic map is set down at the precise moment of our conception and continues with the multiple divisions of cells. We learned a good deal about cells, chromosomes, DNA and genes, and how characteristics, traits, appearance and behaviour are transferred from one generation to another, including genetic differences between girls and boys. The link between genetic and environmental factors was presented and highlighted with evidence from recent research studies on twins.

We now turn to what happens after conception. First there are the all-important first few divisions of the zygote cell, then the development of the human embryo into a viable foetus and finally into a fully formed unborn infant. Before getting too involved in the biology of this development, let us share in the reactions of two people, Jeevan and Sahana, who have just discovered that Sahana is expecting their first child. First of all they can hardly believe that it is happening to them. They check and check again the pregnancy test result. They even take photographs of the test result. This is so exciting for both of them and such good news that they can hardly wait to tell their families and friends.

Sahana had been experiencing some headaches, breast tenderness and backache, similar to those she usually experienced before her period. However, missing her period was a sign that something was different and so Sahana had rushed out to buy a pregnancy test kit. The test identified the hormone *human chorionic gonadotropin* (better known as hCG) which is produced during pregnancy. Traces of this hormone are found in Sahana's blood and urine and at the time of the test the presence of hCG was about the only sign that Sahana and Jeevan had of their new baby. (At 4 weeks, an embryo is still very small – about 1 mm long.) Nevertheless, Sahana and Jeevan decided to tell everybody straightaway.

Of course, family and friends were full of advice about Sahana's pregnancy; about being careful now about what Sahana ate and things she should avoid. She was warned about morning sickness and the headaches and tiredness but everyone agreed it would all be worth it. Her sister said, 'You wouldn't want to do anything to harm your baby or to interfere with development and when baby is born you'll be so glad of this.' Sahana listened to everyone's advice but decided to do what felt natural and right for her. Both she and Jeevan couldn't help wondering what was going on inside her. How was their baby growing? Was this growth as it should be? Could their baby taste what Sahana ate, and hear what she and Jeevan were saying? When would she feel the baby move? Would their baby be healthy?

This chapter will explore child development before babies are born – the period before childbirth. To answer some of Sahana and Jeevan's questions and many others about how babies develop in their mother's womb, we will focus on the three periods of pregnancy and the main milestones of prenatal development. Next, we will explore how factors in the external environment can negatively influence foetal health and capacity. Finally, we will explore the link between early brain development, and the behaviour and learning of the foetus.

By the time you have completed this chapter you should be able to answer the following questions:

- What are the three phases of pregnancy and what happens during each of them?
- What are teratogens?
- What are Wilson's six principles and why are they important?
- Which teratogens have (or had) the most effect upon embryonic and foetal development?
- Which processes characterise prenatal brain development?
- How do foetuses behave?
- What learning takes place in the womb?
- Does 'hot-housing' using music work?

# Conditions for development

## Growth in the womb

**Gestation**
The process of being carried in the womb between conception and birth.

**Prenatal development**
The progress of maturity of a baby prior to birth.

**Foetus**
An unborn human, more than 8 weeks after conception.

**Germinal period**
The first period of prenatal development, in the first 2 weeks after conception.

**Blastocyst**
A hollow ball formed by cells in the first 4–10 days after fertilisation.

**Embryo**
A human offspring in the first 8 weeks from conception.

The human **gestation** period lasts 38 weeks (265 days). Although these 9 months of pregnancy are a time of great joy and anticipation for the parents, they are also a vitally important time in the development of the new being, the time in which genetic patterning takes place and stages in our **prenatal development** unfold. Prenatal development is often divided into three phases (germinal, embryonic and foetal) and a brief summary of each phase is given below. In each description we refer to foetal weeks rather than weeks of pregnancy, because a woman is considered pregnant from the first day of her last menstrual period – a recordable physical event. This means that at conception, around the end of the second week of a cycle, a woman is considered to be 2 weeks pregnant. Her pregnancy lasts for 40 weeks; the gestation period of a **foetus** is 38 weeks.

This first phase or **germinal period** lasts for approximately 14 days. Within a few hours of conception, cell division starts by a process of mitosis described in Chapter 4. (Remember, this dividing process continues until the original single cell becomes the billions of cells that form the complete human.) The fertilised egg (called a zygote) divides into two cells which continue to divide and divide again. New cells do not float away but stick tightly together in a cluster forming the **blastocyst**, a ball-like structure of between 60 and 80 cells (Figure 5.1). Deep inside it is the **embryo**, supported on the outside by cells that protect and nourish.

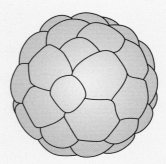

**Figure 5.1** The blastocyst is a ball-like structure of 60 to 80 cells

In the germinal period the blastocyst travels down the Fallopian tube towards the uterus. As it approaches the uterus or womb, the blastocyst produces a number of small tendrils which burrow into the uterine wall and implant themselves into the mother's blood supply. Roughly half of all fertilised eggs implant successfully. If implantation is successful, the outer layers of the blastocyst continue to protect and nourish the other cells inside a thin but tough membrane called the amnion, containing amniotic fluid. This fluid provides a protected environment and allows the embryo to move and grow. At this stage the blastocyst is only an 'embryo' in a very technical sense. It's just a ball of cells, with all the cells pretty much the same.

The second phase or embryonic period is from the third to the eighth week after implantation is complete. During this time three layers of cells form – the ectoderm, mesoderm and endoderm. These three layers will form the baby's organs and tissues. The ectoderm will become the nervous system (which includes the brain), and the skin, hair, nails, mammary glands, sweat glands and enamel for the teeth. The mesoderm will become the heart, circulatory system, skeleton, connective tissues, blood system, urinogenital system and the muscles. The endoderm will house the lungs and develops into the lining of the gastrointestinal tract, the liver, pancreas and thyroid. The placenta has also begun to form and is producing some important hormones, including hCG. Earlier we explained that it is during this period that pregnancy can be confirmed using a test that identifies the presence of this hormone in the blood or urine of the mother.

In the embryonic period the embryo takes on a more human appearance: limbs start to grow; skin and muscles form; sense receptors, nerve cells and internal organs develop. Facial features of a mouth, nose and ears can just be discerned using an ultrasound scan. The photograph below shows the ultrasound scan image of Niamh at foetal age 8 weeks (Edd and Ella's baby girl who we have 'met' several times in earlier chapters). Niamh's first scan shows her as a tiny foetus just a few millimetres in length. The womb (a sausage-shaped darker area) is small. Edd remembers seeing Niamh's tiny heart beating. For Edd and Ella, seeing their baby for the first time was an amazing moment. However, it was not possible to see whether they should be thinking about girls' or boys' names at 8 foetal weeks despite the embryonic period being a time of accelerated sexual development. In males, a gene on the Y chromosome triggers a chemical reaction resulting in the production of testes. In females, there is no such reaction and ovaries are produced. So although Niamh is already Niamh and not Nigel it is impossible to tell this from the ultrasound scan image.

The image of Niamh's first scan is very blurred and grainy. It is created by projecting very high frequency sound waves into Ella's tummy and forming images from the distortions of the sound waves that bounce back to the receiver. Despite their 'blurriness', trained operators can detect sufficient evidence that allows doctors to measure and assess the growth of the foetus, and to make a judgement that all seems well and Niamh is developing normally.

The foetal period (9–38 foetal weeks) or third phase takes place over the last 30 weeks of pregnancy. After 8 foetal weeks, the embryo is medically renamed a foetus and is a much more recognisable human being. Now begins a period of rapid growth and development. By the third month, co-ordination of nervous and muscular systems facilitates many movements; the foetus can stretch, kick and leap around the womb – well before the mother can feel any movement. The digestive and excretory systems are working to allow swallowing and urination. Development is so fast that by the end of the third month, the sex of the foetus can be detected by ultrasound. In the ultrasound image taken of Niamh at foetal age 12 weeks, her head, body and legs are visible (the head is on the left). The dark

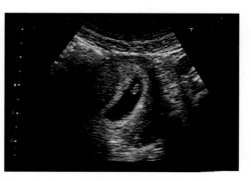

Niamh's first scan, at about 8 foetal weeks.
*Source*: Edward and Ella Hogan.

**Uterus**
Another name for the womb.

**Womb**
The organ in which a baby is carried between conception and birth.

**Uterine**
Of or belonging to the womb.

**Amnion**
The innermost membrane that encloses the embryo.

**Amniotic fluid**
Forms inside the amnion to protect the embryo.

**Embryonic period**
The second period of prenatal development, 3–8 weeks after conception.

**Ectoderm**
One of the three layers of cells in the embryo, which will develop into the nervous system, skin, hair, nails, mammary glands, sweat glands and tooth enamel.

**Mesoderm**
One of the three layers of cells in the embryo, which will develop into the heart, circulatory system, skeleton, connective tissues, urinogenital system and muscles.

**Endoderm**
One of the three layers of cells in the embryo, which will develop into the lungs, the lining of the gastrointestinal tract, liver, pancreas and thyroid.

• • • • • • • • • • • • • •
**Connect and Extend**
For information about embryonic stem cells development – an area of great interest and controversy – connect to **www.eurostemcell.org/** and a videoclip which explains where stem cells come from at **www.eurostemcell.org/ films/a-stem-cell-story/ English**
• • • • • • • • • • • • • •

**Foetal period**
The third and final period of prenatal development, taking place 9 weeks after conception and extending until the end of the pregnancy.

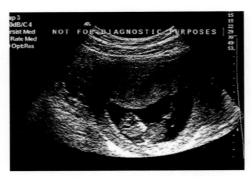

Niamh's second scan, at 12 foetal weeks.

*Source*: Edward and Ella Hogan.

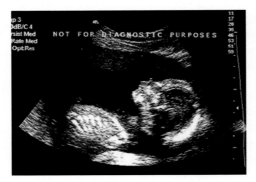

Niamh's third scan, at about 20 weeks.

*Source*: Edward and Ella Hogan.

half-moon area around Niamh is the womb. She is 9 cm long and weighs 45 grams (equivalent to 2 AA batteries). Her eyes are slowly 'moving' to the front of her face, her nose is more pronounced and her ears are fully developed.

At 20 foetal weeks Niamh has grown to 28 cm long and weighs over 450 grams (almost half a bag of sugar). Her weight gain has increased to around 70 grams a week – just think how many new cells that is. The lower photograph shows Niamh's developed facial profile, chest and the different densities of her rib cage. Her eyebrows and eyelids are fully developed and finger nails cover her finger tips. By now she is developing sleeping and waking patterns, and reacts to loud sounds and sudden movements by her mother, Ella.

In the last 3 months of pregnancy all the organs and nervous systems mature quickly and are capable of continuing to function if the foetus is born prematurely. In fact, between 22 and 26 foetal weeks, a point is reached where the foetus is capable of survival outside the womb. This is known as the age of viability. In the last 10 foetal weeks the heart rate is more predictable, there is an increase in activity (ask any expectant mother!) and clear sleeping and waking cycles. In the final month, much of the earlier activity diminishes. Sleep is increased and the baby curls up in the classic foetal position at the base of the uterus in preparation for birth. A summary of the major events throughout pregnancy appears in Table 5.1.

## The external environment

We may have given the impression that a foetus is always cocooned in a safe and protective environment inside mother, immune from the world outside. This is not quite the case. After the thalidomide disaster of the 1960s – see below for more details – it became apparent and more accepted that a developing embryo could be highly vulnerable to certain environmental agents that have negligible or non-toxic effects on adults. So, the safety and future health of the foetus that the mother's womb affords can be adversely affected by external influences known as teratogens (from Greek, meaning 'the making of monsters').

**Reflect**    Most estimates of the incidence of congenital abnormalities in Britain are around 2 per cent of live births but we have no idea of the true incidence of foetal abnormality. Why is this? If you are not sure at the moment, make a note to return to this question at the end of the chapter.

Teratogens are environmental factors or agents (something that produces an effect) capable of harming or malforming a developing embryo or foetus (Holmes, 2011). Typically these are drugs or diseases that cause a host of functional defects, congenital abnormalities and even death. Teratogal susceptibility is influenced by the quality of the uterine environment

**Table 5.1**  Milestones in prenatal development

| Periods of development | Aspects of development |
|---|---|
| **Germinal period (first 2 weeks)**<br>First 2 weeks | Cells divide, cluster and move towards the uterus<br>Blastocyst becomes implanted onto the uterine wall |
| **Embryonic period (3–8 weeks)**<br>3–4 weeks | Brain and central nervous system begin forming<br>Blood vessels formed<br>Heart beat established<br>Digestive and urinary systems appear<br>Head, eyes, ears and mouth form<br>Limbs appear as buds<br>Umbilical cord functioning |
| 5–8 weeks | Formation of thyroid, pituitary and adrenal glands<br>Blood cells produced in the liver<br>Limbs continue to grow<br>Elementary brain functions<br>Eyes open<br>Main body structures form<br>Hands and feet form webs |
| **Foetal period (9 weeks to birth)**<br>9–12 weeks | All major body organs now formed<br>Sex organs differentiated<br>Fingers and toes fully formed<br>Muscles that support limbs are formed |
| 13–16 weeks | Fingernails and toenails grow<br>Cerebrum area of brain expands<br>Skin forms as translucent layer<br>Sweat glands appear<br>Reflexes present |

**Table 5.1**  *Continued*

| Periods of development | Aspects of development |
|---|---|
| 17–20 weeks 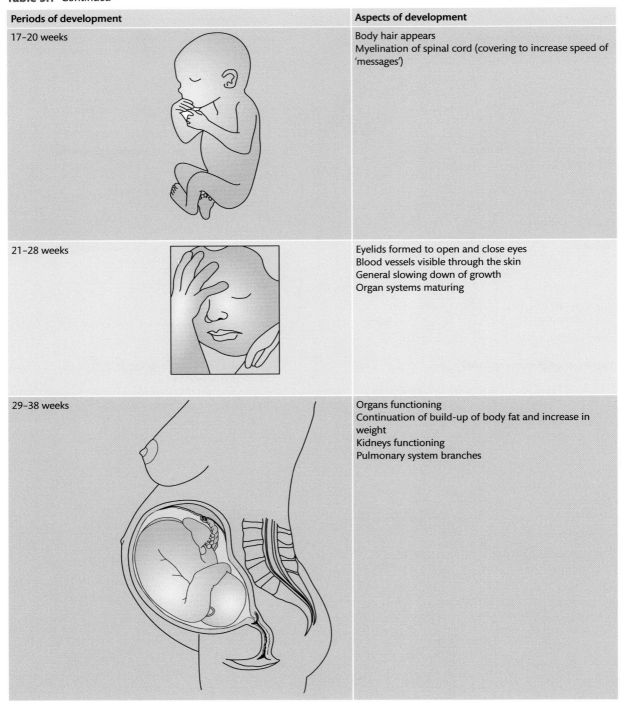 | Body hair appears<br>Myelination of spinal cord (covering to increase speed of 'messages') |
| 21–28 weeks | Eyelids formed to open and close eyes<br>Blood vessels visible through the skin<br>General slowing down of growth<br>Organ systems maturing |
| 29–38 weeks | Organs functioning<br>Continuation of build-up of body fat and increase in weight<br>Kidneys functioning<br>Pulmonary system branches |

(Garmendia & De Sanctis, 2012) and the genetic make-up of the mother (Ainsworth *et al.*, 2011). Effects are most traumatic during 'sensitive periods', when a particular part, organ or capacity of the child is developing, particularly the first 3–4 months of pregnancy when the major body organs are being formed, so much so that abnormalities can be accurately detected by the end of the first trimester (Becker & Wegner, 2006). However, the effects of these harmful influences – teratogens – on the developing brain of the unborn child may be less obvious to begin with. Slowness of the sensory, motor and language systems, sleep disorders and behavioural problems may become apparent only well after birth (Rowe & Siebner, 2012). What principles apply for how drugs and diseases can cause functional defects and congenital abnormalities in new-borns?

## Wilson's six principles

Worldwide, and for more than 50 years, research into drugs and diseases that cause functional defects and congenital abnormalities has been based upon the development and refinement of *the six principles of teratology*. These principles of teratology were established by anatomist Jim Wilson (1959) in his *Environment and Birth Defects*. These principles continue to guide the study and understanding of teratogens and their effects on a developing embryo or foetus. We have edited the original text for purposes of clarity:

1. Susceptibility to teratogens depends on the genotype (a person's complete collection of genetic instructions for creating and replacing cells) of the embryo or foetus and the manner in which this interacts with adverse environmental factors.

2. Susceptibility to teratogens varies with the developmental stage at the time of exposure to an adverse influence. There are critical periods of susceptibility to agents like drugs and for particular organ systems affected by these agents.

3. Teratogens act in specific ways on developing cells and tissues to begin sequences of abnormal development.

4. The access of adverse influences to developing tissues depends on the nature of the influence, degree of exposure to the mother, speed of transfer through the placenta and absorption by the embryo or foetus, and the maternal and embryonic/foetal genotypes.

5. There are four main outcomes of abnormal development (death, malformation, growth retardation and functional defect).

6. Outcomes of abnormal development increase in frequency and degree as the 'dosage' of teratogen increases from the '*no observable adverse effect level*' (NOAEL) to a dose which is 100 per cent lethal (100L).

Much has already been discovered about the effects of teratogens on embryos and foetuses. For convenience we have summarised what has been discovered under four headings: maternal diseases, drugs, environmental teratogens, and maternal characteristics. Under each heading we make reference to Wilson's six principles of teratology and nearby we also indicate some key modern research in the *Connect and Extend* features. Before discussing these teratogens in depth, check what you have learned so far in the *Summary 1* feature below.

**Trimester**
A 3-month period of the 9-month pregnancy.

**Connect and Extend**

Highly sensitive periods may have significant short-term and long-term effects on the newborn. Read more about the importance of sensitive periods in Nafee, T. M., Farrell, W. E., Carroll, W. D., Fryer, A. A. & Ismail, K. M. K. (2008). Epigenetic control of fetal gene expression. *BJOG: An International Journal of Obstetrics and Gynaecology*, 115, 158–168. When are the most sensitive periods?

Before moving on, let's summarise what we have learned so far:

- Prenatal development is divided into three phases: germinal (0–2 weeks); embryonic (3–8 weeks); and foetal (9–38 weeks).
- Growth is by the single fertilised cell – the zygote – dividing into two, four and so on until a ball of cells is formed: a blastocyst.
- The blastocyst attaches itself to the wall of the uterus. As cells continue to divide they develop characteristics to form different parts of the body.

Summary 1

- The rate of development is very fast so that by the time the embryo is renamed a foetus it has already become a recognisable, if tiny human being.
- Between 22 and 26 weeks a point is reached where the foetus is capable of survival outside of the womb – the age of viability.
- Throughout the period of gestation, normal growth and development follow a consistent pattern.
- A developing embryo can be highly vulnerable to certain environmental agents – external influences known as teratogens, many of which have negligible or non-toxic effects on adults.
- Effects are most traumatic during 'sensitive periods', when a particular part, organ or capacity of the child is developing, particularly the first 3–4 months of pregnancy when the major body organs are being formed.
- Jim Wilson developed the six principles of teratology which continue to inform and guide research into the effects of teratogens.
- Teratogens can be summarised under four headings: maternal diseases, drugs, environmental teratogens and maternal characteristics.

# Threats to development

## Maternal diseases

Material in this section has drawn on information from the UK National Health System website NHS Direct at **www.nhsdirect.nhs.uk**. This website provides detailed and up-to-date information and advice.

### Rubella

Rubella (commonly called German measles) is a very infectious viral illness. The virus is passed on through droplets in the air from the coughs and sneezes of infected people. Two of the main symptoms of the rubella virus are a red-brown coloured rash and a fever. Rubella during pregnancy can be serious because it can cause birth defects to develop in the unborn baby and is most dangerous to a baby if a woman is infected during the first 16 weeks of pregnancy (Wilson's 2nd principle). Rubella can cause miscarriage, stillbirth or birth defects in unborn babies, such as deafness, brain damage, heart defects and cataracts (Wilson's 5th principle). This is called congenital rubella syndrome (CRS) and it is transmitted to the baby through the placenta (Wilson's 4th principle). If a woman contracts rubella during the weeks 1–10 of the first trimester, there is a very high risk (up to 90 per cent) that a baby will be affected. After week 10 the risk to the baby is reduced; however, they may develop problems with their sight or hearing, which may not become apparent until they are older. After week 16 the risk to the baby is low.

In the United Kingdom, a rubella vaccine was introduced in 1970. Originally, it was only given to girls to protect them during pregnancy later in life but the vaccine is now offered to all children as part of national immunisation programmes. However, if the vaccine is administered to only selected infants as it was in Italy and Germany then this might not be sufficient to interrupt rubella transmission, and continued epidemics of CRS are more probable (Gabutti *et al.*, 2002). So, susceptibility to the virus is linked to take-up of the vaccine

(Elaziz *et al.*, 2010) rather than the genotype of the mother or foetus (Wilson's 1st principle). Susceptibility to other viral infections such as herpes, HIV/AIDS, chicken pox and influenza have also been linked to prenatal disorders (Rafiefard *et al.*, 2008). Let's look first at herpes.

## Herpes

There are two types of the herpes virus: simplex virus, type 1 (HSV-1) which is more likely to cause herpes on the face, such as cold sores around the mouth, and type 2 (HSV-2) which is more likely to cause herpes on the genitals, such as blisters on the penis or vulva (entrance to the vagina). Around 80 per cent of people with genital herpes never know that they are carrying the virus because there are often no symptoms (or very mild symptoms which are almost unnoticeable, such as a slight itchiness or red patch of skin in the genital area). This means that many cases of herpes go undiagnosed. However, even with no symptoms, it is possible to pass genital herpes on to a sexual partner.

In some instances, the herpes virus can pose problems during pregnancy. If a woman had genital herpes before becoming pregnant, the risk to the baby is very low. This is because during the last few months of pregnancy, babies develop antibodies to all the infections that the mother has had in the past. The antibodies then protect the baby during the birth, and for several months afterwards. However, if a woman catches genital herpes during the early or later stages of pregnancy, there is a chance that the baby could catch herpes when passing through the birth canal, and precautions need to be taken. If a woman develops herpes during the early stages, she may be advised to take antiviral medication to control the symptoms, and prevent a further infection later on. A vaginal birth is normally possible. Catching genital herpes during the last few months of pregnancy means that the baby does not have time to develop any antibodies, and the virus can be passed on just before or during the birth. The baby may then develop a severe infection. In such cases, a **Caesarean section** is usually recommended as there is a very rare chance a baby will develop a condition called neonatal herpes. This affects only one or two in a hundred thousand babies but can cause various complications including damage to the skin, eyes and brain (Wilson's 3rd principle), specifically the neural tube (Nørgård *et al.*, 2006). Other sexually transmitted viruses, for example, syphilis, can also cause similar complications.

## HIV and AIDS

The human immunodeficiency virus (HIV) is a sexually transmitted infection (STI) that attacks the body's immune system, which provides a natural defence system against disease and infection. HIV infects special cells, called CD4 cells, which are found in the blood, and are responsible for fighting infection. After becoming infected, the CD4 cells are destroyed by HIV. Although the body will attempt to produce more CD4 cells, their numbers will eventually decline and the immune system will stop working. This leaves a person who is infected with HIV with a high risk of developing a serious infection, or disease, such as cancer.

Acquired immune deficiency syndrome (AIDS) is a term that is used to describe the latter stages of HIV, when the immune system has stopped working and the person develops a life-threatening condition, such as pneumonia (infection of the lungs). The term 'AIDS' was first used by doctors when the exact nature of the HIV virus was not fully understood. However, the term is no longer widely used because it is too general to describe the many different conditions that can affect somebody with HIV. Specialists now prefer to use the terms 'advanced' or 'late stage' HIV infection.

If a woman has HIV, and becomes pregnant, she needs additional medicines. Without treatment, there is a one in four chance that the baby will develop HIV (Wilson's 3rd principle). With treatment, the risk drops to one in a hundred. Some 85 per cent of mothers who have the HIV virus have been observed to suffer from major depressive episodes and have significant suicidal thoughts (Kwalombota, 2002). Mothers are normally recommended to have a

• • • • • • • • • • • • • • • •
**Connect and Extend**
For further information about the timing of herpes infection during pregnancy, read: Bánhidy, F., Dudás, I. & Czeizel, A. (2011) Trimester dependent preterm births in pregnancy with genital herpes. *Central European Journal of Medicine*, August 2011, *6*(4), 449–455.
• • • • • • • • • • • • • • • •

**Caesarean section**
An operation for delivering a child by cutting through the wall of the mother's abdomen.

Caesarean section because this further reduces the risk of the virus being passed on to the baby. However, in some circumstances, a vaginal delivery may be possible. Postnatal mothers with the HIV virus should not breastfeed the baby because the virus can be transmitted through breast milk.

# Drugs

It is widely known that almost any kind of prescription or illegal drugs taken by the mother during pregnancy, particularly during the first trimester, can cause harm to children. Medical practitioners are very aware of the potential problems and it is common practice for careful questioning of women about the likelihood of their being pregnant before any drug is prescribed or dispensed. Firstly, we will consider the possible effects of mothers taking prescribed drugs, and then look at the research about the development of foetuses whose mothers drink alcohol, smoke tobacco or take illegal drugs.

## Thalidomide

**Connect and Extend**

The story of thalidomide is an important one. For a comprehensive description of what happened and why, visit **www.thalidomidesociety. co.uk**. What are the lessons for the scientific world to learn? Caution: some of the images are potentially upsetting.

**Connect and Extend**

For a more complete and contemporaneous study of thalidomide, read: Timmermans, S. & Leiter, V. (2000). The redemption of thalidomide: Standardizing the risk of birth defects. *Social Studies of Science*, 30, 41.

More than any other event, the thalidomide tragedy alerted the world to the teratogenic potential of drugs. Thalidomide was marketed in 1956 to combat morning sickness and as a sleeping tablet. Before its release, inadequate tests were performed to assess the drug's safety, with catastrophic results for the children of about 20 per cent of women who had taken thalidomide during their early pregnancies. If thalidomide was taken throughout the sensitive period, the consequence could be severe defects of ears, arms and legs and of internal malformations, which often led to early death. From 1956 to 1962, an estimated eight to twelve thousand infants were born with deformities caused by thalidomide, and of those only about five thousand survived beyond childhood (Silverman, 2002). Malformations and deformities were limited to tissues of mesodermal origin. Remember from earlier in this chapter that mesodermal cells are one of the three kinds of cells formed in the second phase of pregnancy, the embryonic stage. That is why thalidomide mainly affected the development of arms and legs, ears, the cardiovascular system and stomach muscles.

Abnormal development of long bones produced a variety of limb defects. Any of the bones could be shortened or, in severe cases, were totally absent. Legs could be similarly affected to arms, although less frequently and less severely. Cleft palate was a rare complication and the central nervous system was not adversely affected, as reflected by normal intelligence. The types of malformations could be related to the developmental stage of the embryo at the time of taking the drug (Wilson's 2nd principle) so a child being born with no ears and deafness was associated with the exposure to thalidomide on the 35th to 37th day and absence of arms with the 39th to 41st day within the sensitive period of 35 to 49 days after the last menstruation (Bwire *et al.*, 2011).

*Daily Telegraph* (29 February 2008): 'Mothers sue over epilepsy drug. A group of women who took epilepsy medication while pregnant are suing for damages, claiming the drug harmed their children. The mothers, some of whose children cannot walk or talk properly, say they were prescribed the drug Epilim to combat fits. Some of the women claim their children have foetal anti-convulsant syndrome, which can involve physical and learning difficulties. At least 20 cases are pending at the High Court.' If the mothers had a case, then who might have been responsible? (Remember that newspaper accounts are not 'tested' accounts in the same way that peer-reviewed academic journals are subjected to expert scrutiny.)

## Alcohol

Foetal alcohol syndrome is characterised by retarded prenatal growth which then commonly continues after birth. The brain does not grow to the expected size, there is developmental delay, and skull and face bone anomalies; cardiac anomalies may also occur (Toso *et al.*, 2007). Effects seen in a child depend on the duration of exposure (Wilson's 4th principle) to substantial maternal alcohol consumption during pregnancy. The full effects of this syndrome occur when the expectant mother has at least eight drinks per day (2 grams of alcohol per kilogram) but even a small amount of alcohol – different studies define *small* in different ways – can cause some retardation of prenatal and post-natal neurological development (Autti-Rämö *et al.*, 2002) and is associated with babies born prematurely (Avalos *et al.*, 2011). Such children when assessed later in their development have lower than average intelligence scores and are more disruptive, self-absorbed, anxious and antisocial (Morleo *et al.*, 2011; Steinhausen *et al.*, 2003).

**Connect and Extend**

For a fuller picture of the effects of alcohol on teenage expectant mothers in Sweden read: Otterblad Olausson, P., Haglund, B., Ringbäck Weitoft, G. & Cnattingius, S. (2004). Premature death among teenage mothers. *BJOG: An International Journal of Obstetrics and Gynaecology*, 111, 793–799.

## Nicotine

Studies over time have linked smoking tobacco with premature births, heart defects, cancer and infant death (e.g. Iñiguez, 2012; Franco *et al.*, 2000) and there is evidence for the lasting effects of smoking during pregnancy on the temperament, behaviour and academic performance of the child (e.g. Martin *et al.*, 2006). The risk of sudden infant death syndrome (SIDS) increases (Wilson's 5th principle) significantly when a mother smokes during her pregnancy and **post-partum** (Lavezzi *et al.*, 2007; Chang *et al.*, 2003; Horne *et al.*, 2002). The more cigarettes are smoked, the greater the harm (Adgent, 2006; Källén, 2001). Relatively recently, it was reported that one in eight women in the United Kingdom continues to smoke during pregnancy, one of the highest rates for smoking in pregnancy in Europe (No Smoking Day, 2008). The UK Government Department of Health has set a, some might argue, modest target of reducing smoking in pregnancy in England to 11 per cent or less by the end of 2015 (Department of Health, 2011a), a target already achieved by 2008 for the United Kingdom as a whole. It is not only mothers who carry risk, as fathers who smoke are more likely to produce abnormal sperms and increase the risk of childhood cancer in their children (Blackburn *et al.*, 2005).

**Post-partum**
Following childbirth.

## Caffeine

In the late 1990s there was a flurry of research activity (e.g. Alm *et al.*, 1999; Leviton, 1998; Cook *et al.*, 1996) which appeared to find that there was an association between drinking coffee and low birth weights, premature births and SIDS. For example, in 1998 Dr R. P. K. Ford and colleagues from the New Zealand Cot Death Study Group (Universities of Auckland and Otago) examined the association between maternal caffeine consumption during pregnancy and the risk of SIDS. They undertook a nationwide case-control study surveying parents of 393 SIDS victims and parents of 1592 control infants. Caffeine consumption in each of the first and third trimesters (Wilson's 2nd principle) was estimated by questionnaire. Heavy caffeine intake was defined as 400 mg/day or more (equivalent to four or more cups of coffee per day) and was associated with foetal harm. It was also found that infants whose mothers had heavy caffeine consumption throughout their pregnancy had a significantly increased risk for SIDS. We have discussed the most common 'everyday drugs' – what about illegal substances?

## Cocaine

Like caffeine, there was also a good deal of research published in the late 1990s about the use of cocaine by mothers during pregnancy (Schuler & Nair, 1999; Fischer *et al.*, 1999). Cocaine use during pregnancy has been associated with *abruptio placentae* (separation of the placenta from the uterus before the delivery of the foetus – a life-threatening condition for the foetus which occurs in about 1 in 500 deliveries), prematurity, foetal loss, foetal distress (Gingras *et al.*, 2005), decreased birth weight, limb defects, urinary tract malformations, and poorer brain development (Sharpe, 2001). However, the contribution of cocaine to the incidence of congenital malformations is difficult to assess because of problems with the research methodology. Cocaine abuse is often associated with taking many different kinds of drugs, with alcohol consumption, smoking, malnutrition and poor prenatal care, so it is difficult to separate out the peculiar effects of cocaine. Nevertheless researchers have found that mothers taking illegal drugs (e.g. cocaine, heroin) miscarry (Hulse *et al.*, 1998) or produce premature babies, and one, more recent, study found these babies to be 'less interested' in learning than their peers and generally less emotionally intelligent and engaged (Singer *et al.*, 2004). In the next section we will discuss teratogens that can be, or historically were, commonly found in the everyday surroundings of families in the developed world.

● ● ● ● ● ● ● ● ● ● ● ● ● ● ●
**Connect and Extend**
It's not just cocaine. Read Watson, S. M. R., Westby, C. E. & Gable, R. A. (2007). A framework for addressing the needs of students prenatally exposed to alcohol and other drugs. *Preventing School Failure*, 52, 25–32.
● ● ● ● ● ● ● ● ● ● ● ● ● ● ●

## Environmental teratogens

### Chemicals and metals

Pregnant women through their occupations and domestic lives may come into contact with chemical substances that can cause potential harm to their unborn babies or lower their chances of becoming pregnant in the first case (Wennborg *et al.*, 2001). Exposure to solvents, paints, herbicides and pesticides fall into this category and outcomes of abnormal development increase in frequency and degree as the 'dosage' of these teratogens increases (Wilson's 6th principle). For example, epidemiologist Linda Magnusson and colleagues at the University of Aarhus, Denmark produced an analysis of childhood conditions by maternal job titles in pregnancy (2006). They found a greater likelihood of different atopic conditions such as wheezing (early wheezing not diagnosed as asthma), asthma, hay fever and atopic eczema during childhood for occupational groups such as bakers, pastry cooks, and confectionary makers, dental assistants, electrical and electronic assemblers, sewers and embroiderers, and bookbinders and related workers. An excess risk ratio for hay fever was found following maternal gestational exposure to organic solvents (e.g., tetrachloroethylene used in dry cleaning). Furthermore, a greater incidence of asthma was observed in children of shift workers. Though the cause of this is difficult to pin down, it may be because shift work can disrupt the mother's body clock and so interfere with the production of hormones by her body. In 2007, Marja-Liisa Lindbohm and colleagues at Tampere University Hospital, Finland found an increased risk of miscarriage in pregnant mothers working in dentistry due to higher levels of exposure to mercury amalgam, some acrylate compounds, solvents and disinfectants. Mercury is not the only dangerous metal teratogen nor the most dangerous.

Atopic conditions
Allergic reactions which have genetic connections but are triggered by environmental teratogens.

Lead is especially dangerous and risk from lead exposure is still to be found in many occupations including construction workers, steel welders, bridge reconstruction workers, firing range instructors and cleaners, painters, foundry workers, scrap metal recyclers, auto repairers, and cable makers and splicers. Although these are primarily male occupations, they add to general level of lead in the atmosphere which can be concentrated in high-density industrial environments. Add the use of leaded fuels and lead piping and this creates a dangerous environment for expectant mothers.

However, fathers too who are exposed to some substances can pass problems on to the genotype of a foetus. Dutch male workers employed as painters at 3 months before pregnancy had a significantly increased risk of congenital malformations and functional developmental disorders in offspring compared to carpenters (Hooiveld *et al.*, 2006). The greater the exposure to organic solvents in the paint the more pronounced was the children's malformations (Wilson's 4th principle). There was some indication of an increased risk in offspring among painters with intermediate and high model predicted exposure. The risk for children of low birth weight seemed to be slightly increased among painters as well. How does lead get into the body?

Lead exposure occurs when lead dust or fumes are inhaled, or when lead is ingested via contaminated hands, food, water, cigarettes or clothing. Lead entering the respiratory and digestive systems is released to the blood and distributed throughout the body. However, more than 90 per cent of the total body burden of lead is accumulated in the bones, where it is stored. Lead in bones may be released into the blood, re-exposing organ systems long after the original exposure. During pregnancy, calcium in a mother's bones goes into the bloodstream, and when calcium leaves the pregnant mother's bones, so does lead. Lead poisoning of the foetus through the mother usually leads to miscarriage or still birth, and even a slightly elevated blood lead level can cause developmental problems, including damage to the organs and brain. Children may be born early, underweight or not fully developed. Calcium also comes from a new mother's bones to make breast milk. So breast milk may also contain lead. In this case, breast may not be best. Lead is generally present in very small amounts in our everyday lives and exposure to normal levels – the natural background presence – is not dangerous, but what about another background presence, that of radiation?

## Radiation

Background radiation is that which the general population is exposed to, including natural and artificial sources. Background radiation varies by location – e.g. higher levels by large granite outcrops, cosmic radiation at high altitudes, or raised levels near to nuclear waste outfall points but there is no evidence that normal natural background radiation has any major effect upon the body.

However, we would probably guess there to be a huge risk to unborn children if exposed through their mothers to high levels of radiation. The most obvious example of the release of high levels of 'man-made radiation' was an event that became known by just one word, Chernobyl.

In April 1986 there was a huge explosion and fire at the Chernobyl nuclear power plant in the Ukraine, which resulted in at least 5 per cent of the radioactive reactor core being released into the atmosphere and downwind. Twenty-eight people died within 4 months from radiation or thermal burns, 19 have subsequently died, and by 2004 there were 9 deaths from thyroid cancer, apparently due to the accident.

Researcher Melissa English of the International Studies centre at Nazareth College reports that following the accident 400,000 people were evacuated and resettled to another place following the disaster, but millions of others continued to live in contaminated areas. She continues 'The radioactive results were staggering. People exposed to the immediate radioactive clouds often died within a week from radiation poisoning. People living farther away from the incident suffered immediately from thyroid cancer. Since then, accident birth defects have gone up 22%; the live birth rate has decreased immensely' (Nuclear Energy Institute, 2005).

In terms of long-term and widespread congenital damage the evidence is less clear. For example, in 2005 a press release from the World Health Organization, the United Nations Development Programme and the International Atomic Energy Agency reported:

> This was a very serious accident . . . however, we have not found profound negative health impacts to the rest of the population in surrounding areas, nor have we found widespread contamination that would continue to pose a substantial threat to human health, with a few exceptional, restricted areas. . . . In an estimated five million people currently living in areas of Belarus, Russia and Ukraine that are contaminated with radionuclides [radioactive atoms] due to the accident . . . there has been 4,000 cases of thyroid cancer, mainly in children and adolescents . . . and survival rate among such cancer victims, judging from experience in Belarus, has been almost 99%.

(www.iaea.org/NewsCenter/Focus/Chernobyl/pdfs/pr.pdf)

•••••••••••••••••
**Connect and Extend**
So, has the Chernobyl accident caused childhood leukaemia? Read: Hoffmann, W. (2002). Has fallout from the Chernobyl accident caused childhood leukaemia in Europe? *The European Journal of Public Health, 12*, 72–75.
•••••••••••••••••

Chenobyl was a major accident that drew worldwide alarm at the possible consequences for those who lived near to the plant and for the unborn children of those affected, but what of more low-level risks? Are there every day 'manmade' sources of radiation that might pose a threat to the safe development of a foetus?

More low-level risk to unborn children from radiation may be present through mother's contact with microwave ovens, televisions and video-recorders, mobile phones and outside power lines. In the latter case a Norwegian study (Blaasaas *et al.*, 2004) evaluated selected birth outcomes for children with the following defects: central nervous system (CNS) defects, cardiac defects, respiratory system defects, oesophageal defects and clubfoot. The distances between maternal addresses, during pregnancy, and power lines were obtained from maps, and magnetic fields in the residences were estimated based on distance, current, voltage and configuration. The highest increased risks were seen for hydrocephalus – a build-up of fluid inside the skull, which can increase pressure and cause damage to the brain – and for cardiac defects but such increases were not considered significant.

There has been some research (e.g. Mckinney *et al.*, 2003) into whether childhood leukaemia and non-Hodgkin's lymphoma can be caused by fathers' exposure to ionising radiation (as part of their occupation) before the conception of the child, and, more generally, to investigate whether such radiation exposure of either parent is a cause of childhood cancer. It is also now typical for foetuses to be subject to diagnostic medical radiation. Magnetic resonance imaging (MRI), computed tomography (CT) and ultrasound scans also carry risks, although much of the evidence remains inconclusive (Menias *et al.*, 2007; Bradley *et al.*, 2006; Matthews, 2006; Osei & Kotre, 2001). Despite this research, there is a need for more studies to be carried out to determine the risk at different levels of exposure to radiation, particularly to the familiar and common parts of contemporary living, such as mobile phones and computer screens. In response to public concerns regularly expressed in the media, the UK Government has made available advice in published reports and on websites, and the *Policy, Research and Praxis* feature below provides an example to read before considering the third of the environmental teratogens, maternal characteristics.

## Policy, Research and Praxis

### Government support for healthy pregnancies

Policy directions geared to giving children the best start to life reflect a message that being healthy begins long before infancy and recognise the crucial importance of the pregnancy period for this to happen. Campaigns and government pledges in the UK are offering support for parents-to-be and advice on healthy pregnancies.

Start 4Life, for example, the UK Government's social marketing initiative began a new phase in 2012 with a wider remit that includes maternal health (Department of Health, 2012a). The new campaign encourages expectant mothers and families with young children under 5 to adopt behaviours that will give them the best start to their lives. Launched in May 2012 with accompanying cinema advertising and a Hollywood film, the campaign explores issues for parents and provides guidance on maintaining healthy lifestyles during pregnancy. There is also a toolkit for health professionals in their roles in supporting pregnant mothers. A new digital service, the NHS Information Service for Parents was also launched in 2012 giving new parents advice on staying healthy in pregnancy, how to prepare for birth and how to look after their baby. New parents can watch videos of midwives bathing babies and parents discussing issues that affected them in pregnancy and the ways in which they supported each other.

According to the Department of Health (2012b) website, in some areas of England 3 in 10 women continue to smoke when they are pregnant despite the significant increase to the risk of stillbirth, cot death and respiratory problems. Almost 1 in 10 drink more than the recommended lower-risk pregnancy guidelines, increasing the risk of miscarriage or still birth and stunting growth. One in six are obese despite the potential for a more difficult pregnancy, riskier birth and a less healthy baby. The government has pledged to improve maternity care by appointing an additional 4200 health visitors. Every woman is to have one-to-one midwife care during their labour and birth, and parents-to-be will be provided with information to help them make choices about where and how they give birth.

Most medical research in the past has concentrated on the health of early pre-term babies born before 32 weeks who are the highest risk of poor health outcomes, but less is known about the longer term health outcomes of moderate and later pre-terms (born between 32 and 36 weeks) compared with full-term babies (39–41 weeks). Joint research involving several Universities and the National Perinatal Epidemiology Unit (Boyle *et al.*, 2012) into gestational age and associated health problems found that babies born even a few weeks prematurely have a higher risk of health problems at 3 and 5 years of age. Such problems show themselves as low weight gains, asthma, wheeze and other illnesses or disabilities. These results challenge previous views that long-term health outcomes for moderate and later pre-term babies are similar to those of babies born at full term. Whilst the researchers recognise that further exploration of the factors that influence health outcomes is needed, these findings have implications for healthcare services in terms of informing future planning, planning provision for young children, and for obstetricians managing high-risk pregnancies.

# Maternal characteristics

## Emotional state

Maternal characteristics include the mother's emotional state and stress levels which can lead to problems in both pregnancy and in labour. Stress during the prenatal period has negative effects on pregnancy and birth outcome by altering the maternal immune function (Coussons-Read *et al.*, 2003). Furthermore, maternal stress is commonly cited as an important risk factor for spontaneous abortion – natural termination of the pregnancy by miscarriage. The majority of miscarriages occur within the first 3 weeks after conception (5 weeks after the last menstrual period). Studies focused on clinical pregnancy (greater than 6 weeks) miss the most critical period for pregnancy continuance. In 2006, epidemiologist Pablo Nepomnaschy and colleagues at the University of Michigan examined the association between miscarriage and levels of maternal urinary cortisol during the first 3 weeks after conception. Pregnancies characterised by increased maternal cortisol during this period were more likely to result in spontaneous abortion. This evidence links increased levels in this stress marker with a higher risk of early pregnancy loss in humans.

Stress during pregnancy appears to be one of the determinants of delay in motor and mental development in infants of 8 months of age and may be a risk factor for later developmental problems. High levels of stress in early pregnancy (Wilson's 2nd principle), of pregnancy-specific anxiety in mid-pregnancy and high early morning values of cortisol in late pregnancy predict lower mental and motor developmental scores in infants of 8 months (Huizink *et al.*, 2003). There are also some indications that maternal stress during pregnancy contributes to symptoms of attention deficit and hyperactivity disorder (ADHD) in children, particularly boys (Rodriguez & Bohlin, 2005).

**Cortisol**
Known as 'the stress hormone' because stress activates cortisol secretion which can be identified in urine and saliva.

• • • • • • • • • • • • • •
**Connect and Extend**
To study the increased risk of adverse outcomes in labour in obese women, read: Usha Kiran, T. S., Hemmadi, S., Bethel, J. & Evans, J. (2005). Outcome of pregnancy in a woman with an increased body mass index. *BJOG: An International Journal of Obstetrics and Gynaecology*, 112(6), 768–772.
• • • • • • • • • • • • • •

## Physical condition

**Pre-eclampsia**
A complication of pregnancy. Women with pre-eclampsia have high blood pressure, and high levels of protein in their urine. If left untreated, it can develop into eclampsia, the life-threatening occurrence of seizures during pregnancy.

**Thromboembolism**
The formation in a blood vessel of a clot (thrombus) that breaks loose and is carried by the bloodstream to plug another vessel.

**Perinatal mortality**
Still births plus early neonatal deaths (deaths at under 7 days of life).

**Macrosomia**
A newborn with an excessive birth weight.

A heritable predisposition (Wilson's 1st principle) to gain weight together with changing attitudes to body size have an independent role in the development of maternal body weight. Differences in each woman's heritable predisposition to gain weight and any changes in body image might explain why some women gain a dangerous amount of weight in association with pregnancy (Hernandez, 2012). Obesity causes major changes in many features of maternal metabolism. Insulin resistance appears to be central to these changes and may also be involved in increased energy accumulation by the foetus. Maternal obesity is associated with many risks to the pregnancy, with increased risk of miscarriage (three-fold) an increased risk of pre-eclampsia and thromboembolism. There are risks to the foetus, with increased perinatal mortality and macrosomia (Yu *et al.*, 2006). The blunt truth is that maternal obesity is associated with a more than doubled risk of stillbirth and neonatal death compared with women of 'normal weight' related to their height (Kristensen *et al.*, 2005).

 **Reflect**   Reducing smoking and drinking less alcohol in pregnancy are beneficial for the foetus; but if this increases maternal anxiety, could the foetus be worse off?

Poor or undernutrition for the expectant mother is directly linked to foetal health. The following *Focus on Theory* feature reviews some of the evidence on the importance of nutrition for mother and foetus.

## Focus on Theory

### Nutrition and the prenatal period

The prenatal period is the period of most rapid growth in one's entire life and a diet that supplies correct nutrients is needed for brain and body development. The developing foetus requires proper nutrients for growth at all of the stages and is totally reliant upon the mother to provide this. When this is denied, there is irrefutable evidence of the damage it causes to the child pre- and postnatal. Defects include low intelligence and serious learning problems in school (Lawlor *et al.*, 2006). Research findings link malnutrition to low birth weight, prematurity and cognitive deficiencies (e.g. Zhang *et al.*, 2005). Earlier research by Shonkoff and Phillips (2000) evidenced the impact of malnutrition on brain development, showing deficits in intelligence and attention capacity. In the prenatal period, the brain grows rapidly and a balanced diet is needed to supply correct nutrients.

Further deficiencies arising from mal- or undernutrition have also been reported in the research literature, some of which we call on now. In the first germinal stages of pregnancy, malnutrition result in problems in the central nervous system (CNS) (Zile, 2001). In the last stages of the foetal period, malnutrition problems result in low birth weight (Rao *et al.*, 2001) and babies born with small heads – a constraint to full cognitive development (Murcott, 2002; Barker *et al.*, 2001). Babies of malnourished mothers have more chance of developing heart disease in later life (Barker, 2012). There is also evidence that the prenatal environment is important in the aetiology (a study of the cause or causes) of childhood asthma, and babies born with low birth weight due to poor prenatal nutrition have a high risk of developing Type 2 diabetes later in their lives (Prentice & Moore, 2005). There is another interesting historical example of the effect of famine in the Netherlands during the Second World War showing effects on birth weight and development, not only of children born to the starved mothers, but also of their grandchildren (Lumey, 1992). For further elaboration of this study check the reference and access the paper online.

Obesity is now generally believed to begin in the womb (Yu *et al.*, 2006). Children are twice as likely to be obese if the mother was obese in pregnancy because poor nutrition in the womb may remodel the brain circuitry to dispose children to become obese in later life (Lamerz *et al.*, 2005). Deficiencies in nutrition cause cells in the baby's pancreas to be programmed abnormally and the negative effects of this can be seen either in the short term or appear later (Waterland & Garza, 2002). Furthermore, it has been established over the past 20 years that a foetus's cardiovascular functioning is programmed *in utero* by hormone factors and mother's nutrition (de Almeida *et al.*, 2006).

Educating expectant mothers to be serious about what they eat in pregnancy is essential. Regular vitamins and minerals are essential. Folate (folic acid – a water-soluble form of Vitamin B9) is important in preconception and in the first 3 months of pregnancy for reducing the risk of damage to the neural tube and spinal cord (Balluz *et al.*, 2000). Iron intake should increase by 50 per cent in pregnancy as this is vital for red blood cells and the production of tissues (Leary *et al.*, 2005). Although the argument swings in different directions, we now believe breast-feeding benefits both mother and baby. It strengthens the immune system, builds bone density, assists with absorption of iron and can help the mother regulate excessive weight gain (Akobeng *et al.*, 2006).

So, proper nutrients received by the mother and transmitted to the baby are essential. In short, you are what your mother and your grandmother ate.

## Maternal age

Not unconnected to physical state – being obese or malnourished – is the age of the mother-to-be. There is a good deal of discussion in the media about the ideal age to bear children and that the very young mothers and older mothers runs physical risks both to themselves and to the development of their babies. Historically in the UK and in many other cultures women used to have their first child not very long after they first ovulated and continued bearing children until the end of their reproductive life – a span of thirty years or so. In global traditional cultures this remains the case although the cultural norms are changing rapidly, particularly in newly developed countries, due to globalisation, particularly access to contraception, and to further and higher education.

Young teenage girls in all cultures do become pregnant and there is much concern about the risks associated with teenage pregnancy (e.g. Vinson, 2012). The risks are physical (both to mother and child) and emotional (Cox *et al.*, 2012; Deutscher *et al.*, 2006). The younger the mother, the greater the likelihood of premature birth (Bader *et al.*, 2010), subsequent low birth weight (Strang-Karlsson *et al.*, 2008) and associated developmental abnormalities (e.g. Jegelevičienė, 2012).

Although before the First World War it was typical for British women of all social and economic groups in the UK to have their first child before they were 20, this is no longer the case. What is the current age profile of first-time mothers and what effects can this have? The following account draws on figures from the UK Office of National Statistics (ONS, 2013). You can find the most up-to-date statistics on the same site.

The number of women who are leaving it later in life to have children has increased. In 2011, the average age of mothers for all births is 29.4 years, with the average age for first time mothers rising to 27.9 years. The number of women having children in their 30s and 40s has climbed steadily over the last 20 years at a time when the overall birth rate has been dropping.

Nearly half of all live births in 2011 were to mothers aged 30 and over. Later pregnancies occur particularly among the professional classes, where women pursue a career before starting a family. The drawback to later parenting is that as a woman gets older their fertility declines (Wallace & Kelsey, 2010), there is greater risk of miscarriage (Heffner, 2004) and of developmental abnormalities.

For example, a woman's risk of having a baby with chromosomal abnormalities increases with her age. Down's Syndrome (see Chapter 4 *Nature and Nurture*) is the most common chromosomal birth defect, and a woman's risk of having a baby with Down's syndrome is 1 in 1250 births at age 25, 1 in 1000 at age 30, 1 in a hundred at 40 and 1 in 10 at 49 (ASRM, 2003).

In this section we have discussed threats to development under four main headings: maternal diseases (e.g. rubella, herpes and HIV); drugs (e.g. thalidomide, alcohol, nicotine, caffeine, and cocaine); environmental teratogens (e.g. chemicals, metals and radiation); and maternal characteristics of the emotional state, physical condition and age. Before looking at the next section of the chapter on cognitive development, check your understanding of what you have read using the *Summary 2* feature.

## Summary 2

Before moving on, let's summarise what we have learned in the middle section of this chapter:

- Maternal diseases that can harm the developing foetus include rubella, herpes and HIV infection.
- Drugs taken by the mother that can harm the child include alcohol, nicotine, caffeine, cocaine and some prescribed drugs. The tragic example of thalidomide was quoted and explored.
- Mother's exposure to some environment agents such as some chemicals typically found in solvents, paints, herbicides and pesticides, and metals such as lead can cause harm to the baby pre-partum. Fathers too who are exposed to some substances can pass problems on to the genotype of a foetus.
- Certain types of radiation can also harm the foetus but the effects may not be seen until later childhood.
- Some maternal characteristics such as emotional state, stress levels, physical condition and maternal age can also impact on good birth outcomes.

# Early cognitive development

## Prenatal brain development

Because the human brain is such a complex organ it takes longer to mature than all the other organs of the body. It is this complexity and the wonderful things the human brain allows us to do that separate us from other species and which explain why development of the human central nervous system takes such a long time to mature.

But is it really such a long time? We suggest that this is all relative. The complex feats that we as a species are capable of are capacities not easily won and certainly not won all at once. Think of our ability to use language, to walk upright, to perform the most complicated mental calculations and to demonstrate such a range of emotions as we have. Certainly some species at birth do take less time to be independent from the mother; they move around quicker and

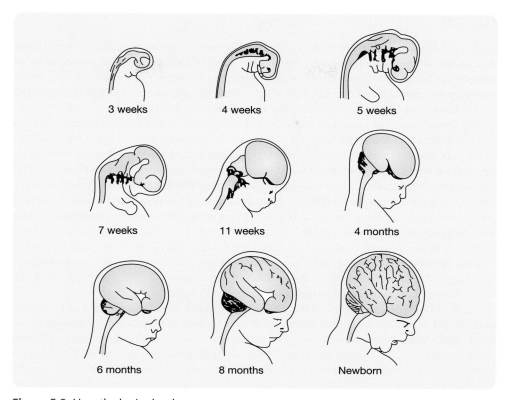

**Figure 5.2** How the brain develops

*Source*: From Chudler, E. H. (1996). Neuroscience for Kids website (from **http://faculty.washington.edu/chudler/dev.html**).

learn basic survival skills almost immediately. But they are not able to think, to act, to com-municate or show their emotions to the extent that we as humans can. As the next chapter discusses, all of these wonderful cognitive abilities take time. For the present, let's find out how a foetus's brain develops because this is the control centre for all our capabilities!

Three weeks after fertilisation, about a third of the fertilised egg forms the central nervous system (CNS). The CNS consists of the spinal cord and brain together. Three weeks after con-ception, part of the CNS folds to form a hollow tube which is the first stage of brain develop-ment. The tube contains the cells that will create the neurons and supporting tissue of the brain and CNS. The inside forms the spinal cord and at the top of the tube more cells grow to create the bulge we recognise as the brain. By the fifth week, the primitive brain divides into three sections: the forebrain, midbrain and hindbrain (Figure 5.2).

At about 5 weeks a series of visible bulges forms the brainstem which develops into the **medulla** (7–8 weeks), the **pons** (after 8 weeks) and lastly the forebrain regions. According to Slater and Bremner (2003), by 9 weeks the forebrain divides to form two cerebral hemispheres (i.e. the classic brain shape). The outer layer or cerebral cortex is the area associated with language, memory and thinking. The lack of development in this area before 10 weeks accounts for foetal behaviours being predominately reflexive and not yet controlled by this area of the brain.

After 15 foetal weeks, further reorganisation takes place establishing more sophistication in the higher brain centres. The texture of the brain up to this time is smooth, but by 26 weeks, folds appear to increase the surface area that allow for expansion taking place underneath. Brain development and growth remain steady and continuous and the foetus responds to the womb environment in ways that indicate a growing capacity to learn. In the next section we follow the responses of the foetus and show that learning does indeed begin in the womb.

**Medulla**
The continuation of the spinal cord within the skull, forming the lowest part of the brainstem.

**Pons**
Part of the brainstem that links the medulla and the thalamus (which are the two masses in the forebrain).

• • • • • • • • • • • • • • • •

**Connect and Extend**
Foetuses exhibit significantly more right-arm movements than left-arm movements at every gestational age. For an interesting example from Bulgaria of research into how we become right- or left-handed, read: Stoyanov, Z., Nikolova, P. & Pashalieva, I. (2011). Season of birth, Geschwind and Galaburda hypothesis, and handedness. *Laterality: Asymmetries of Body, Brain, and Cognition*. September, 16(5), 607–619.

• • • • • • • • • • • • • • • •

# Foetal behaviour and learning

In Chapter 4 it was established that an individual's genetic code acts as an instruction manual that we take with us on our journey through life. Each of us is born with a particular set of instructions for development. But how does a baby in the womb know what to do? What organises this unfolding of development which occurs for each one of us? How is it arranged so that the processes that need to take place do so and at the proper times?

The answer to these questions lies in the development of the foetus's brain and CNS and crucially in the capacity for learning. Until fairly recently there was not much known about in utero behaviour but due to advances in technology and ultrasonic scanning techniques, new and exciting insights are now revealed to us. With these insights comes confirmation that the prenatal stage is of the utmost importance. Scans signal that the normal journey of development is being followed or can identify problems along the way. Observations of *in utero* behaviour also serve to predict possible developmental trajectories in the future. As developmental scientists William Fifer and Charles Moon (2005) suggest, the 'roots of child development are being uncovered by investigating neuro-behavioural development during the foetal period' (cited in Slater & Bremner, 2003, p 96). What we are proposing is that a range of *in utero* behaviours blend genetic adaptations to life in the womb with preparation for life after birth. What the foetus does and the capacity for learning are central to this proposal.

Gains in brain development and the CNS allow for more organised patterns of behaviour in the foetal period. An important feature of the early period of gestation is movement of the foetus, and a variety of movement patterns have been recorded. Detailed observations of foetal activity using new three-dimensional and relatively traditional two-dimensional techniques (Campbell, 2004) show movements that include independent finger movement, thumb sucking, yawning, hand contact with the face, breathing patterns, and head rotation and flexion. Researchers such as Professor Stuart Campbell at London's Create Health Clinic – author of '*Watch Me Grow. A Unique, 3-Dimensional Week-by-Week Look at Your Baby's Behaviour and Development in the Womb*' (Campbell, 2004) – propose that some foetal movements are programmed to adapt to restrictions in the womb environment (e.g. stepping), while others (e.g. yawning and 'breathing') are in preparation for behaviours after birth. We have drawn upon evidence from Professor Campbell's work (2004, 2005) and the 2007 edition of *Your Pregnancy Bible* edited by Dr Anne Deans for the remainder of this section on foetal behaviour and learning, unless otherwise stated.

These movements reflect a change from spontaneous reflexive movement to distinct movement patterns. Reflexes such as the tonic neck reflex – a distinct and post-partum movement pattern in which the foetus (or post-partum the baby) adopts the pose of a fencer when the head is turned – have also been recorded as early as 7 foetal weeks and continue throughout the period of gestation and the first year post-natal (Campbell, 2004). Associated with the changes in movement patterns are increases in neuromuscular development which suggest that certain foetal movements and behaviour are regulated by systems in the spinal cord and lower brainstem (Harris & Butterworth, 2002). This is similar to the lull in activity recorded just before 6 months which coincides with newly created midbrain control of specific behaviours. After this time, movements appear to be more finely controlled, such as can be seen in facial expressions and finger movements. This strongly indicates that motor control is now being taken up by higher brain systems to produce more precise movement responses (Deans, 2007).

Linked to movement are fluctuations in the states of arousal of the foetus. These vary from periods of inactivity to periods of increased movement: specifically quiet sleep, active sleep, quiet awake and active awake – known as the four states (Kintraia *et al.*, 2006). Interesting earlier findings from reproductive health expert Janet DiPietro and her colleagues (1996) show that by 28 weeks, foetuses are awake 11 per cent of the time. This figure rises to 16 per cent just before birth. Foetuses seem to spend more time awake in the third trimester because their neurological organisation has improved and they are preparing themselves for birth.

**In utero**
Within the uterus.

Even prenatal, their growing brains seek stimulation and their growing bodies are exploring their immediate environment. This is no different from the approach adopted by children at play: the same drives are present and begin during their prenatal lives (Campbell, 2005).

The womb environment and the external environment as experienced by the foetus are ones of changing stimuli to which the foetus responds. This is achieved through their developing senses. The somatosensory system which governs tactile sensations is well developed *in utero*. Touch is the first sense to be developed (Cotterill, 2003) beginning at about 8 weeks. There is evidence of face touching at about 15 weeks and thumb sucking. As the foetus moves around in the womb, there are many opportunities to make contact with the uterine wall. There is much physical contact in, for example, multiple pregnancies but the question of whether a foetus feels pain directly is still the subject of debate mainly between pro-life groups (those who are opposed to abortion) and pro-choice groups (those who argue for the rights of women to choose whether or not to carry a foetus to full term). Current research seems to support the view that foetuses feel pain and use behaviours similar to crying to complain about it (Derbyshire, 2010; Gingras *et al.*, 2005).

Gustation, or the sense of taste, is also well developed in the foetus. By 8 weeks a foetus can distinguish sweet and non-sweet tastes. A foetus swallows amniotic fluid from 12 weeks, and foods and other substances in the mother's diet are experienced and responded to from this time. At 14 weeks nerves in the taste buds are connected to the cortex in the brain and send information about the salty taste of the amniotic fluid to the medulla at the base of the brainstem. The olfactory system, enabling the foetus to smell, functions from 6 to 7 months, allowing the foetus to both taste and smell the food the mother eats! Prior to this, a plug of tissue blocks the amniotic fluid from entering the upper nose. Fluid in the nose transmits odours, which allows the foetus to smell in the liquid environment of the womb: similar to the way we smell in air.

Vision is the least developed sense as it is the most complex sensory system. In spite of this, the human species is better equipped visually at birth than most other mammals, many of whom are born with their eyelids closed. Humans open their eyes at about 4 foetal months although development begins as early as 4 weeks. Although the least developed of all our sensory systems, there is good evidence of visual ability at 26 foetal weeks (Del Guidice, 2011). The delay in this sense is directly related to the complexity of the visual system. Vision begins with the eyes, channelling stimuli by way of the optic nerve and continuing to the brain to the occipital cortex (the brain's visual centre). As yet there is no immediate need to see in the dark environment of the womb but this sense will be very important as a neonate in making sense of a very new environment outside the womb.

The sound of the mother's heart makes the womb environment far from quiet. Sounds also from outside pass through the womb wall and the foetus reacts to these. Auditory stimuli are filtered through the amniotic fluid. If sounds are loud or sudden, a foetus reacts. By 28 weeks they blink in reaction to sounds. There is evidence that a foetus can hear the mother's voice and certain other sounds in the environment outside the womb.

Some of the most interesting research into foetal hearing could be viewed as historic but the principles have been re-established in more modern studies (Draganova *et al.*, 2005; Holst *et al.*, 2005). For example, in a study in Northern Ireland, developmental psychologist Peter Hepper (1996) found that neonates whose mothers watched the BBC television programme *Neighbours* during pregnancy responded to the same theme tune played again several days after birth. Babies whose mothers did not watch the programme did not show the same reaction. Hepper's results showed that in the latter stage of pregnancy, a foetus is capable of reacting to a repeated stimulus placed on the mother's stomach and responds again when the stimulus is altered. In another important earlier study by DeCasper and Spence (1986) infants listened to a recording of mother reading Dr Seuss's *The Cat in the Hat* or to rhyming stories. They had previously 'listened' to these stoies *in utero*. They sucked nipples hardest at the Seuss story which has been taken as an indicator of prenatal memory and learning. Both studies are good evidence of foetal learning through habituation where the child attends to a new stimulus and

**Somatosensory system**
A sensory system that detects experiences labelled as touch or pressure, temperature, pain, muscle movement and joint position including posture, movement, visceral (internal) senses and facial expression. Visceral senses have to do with sensory information from within the body, such as stomach aches.

**Connect and Extend**
In a study assessing the effects of exposure to tobacco, cocaine and vibroacoustic stimulation during pregnancy, foetal 'crying' was observed. Read more at Gingras, J. L., Mitchell, E. A. & Grattan, K. E. (2005). Fetal homologue of infant crying. *Archives of Disease in Childhood – Fetal and Neonatal Edition*, 90, F415–F418, available at **http://fn.bmj.com/cgi/content/abstract/90/5/F415**

**Neonate**
A newborn baby.

**Habituation**
Evidence of learning where a child 'makes a habit' of attending to a new stimulus and stops attending to sensations that become boring.

**Connect and Extend**

For an excellent summary of prenatal behaviour read: Hepper, P. (2005). Unravelling our beginnings. *The Psychologist*, *18*, 474–477, available at **www.thepsychologist.org.uk/archive/**

stops attending to other sounds that have become boring. As others have indicated and over a number of years, this suggests the foetus has a real capacity to acquire and remember information (DiPietro, 2005; Gingras *et al.*, 2005; Sirois & Mareschal, 2004).

 **Reflect**   The foetus exhibits REM (rapid eye movement during dreaming) – does a foetus dream? If so, what about?

Listening to music, particularly some kinds of classical music, is said to have psychological and physiological benefits to all of us, but researchers are far from agreeing on the extent of these benefits. Some researchers (examples are provided in the upcoming *Controversy* feature) have found improvements in intellectual, motor, social abilities and creativity. Others claim that listening to music *in utero* can lead to later better than typical progress in reading, mathematical reasoning and abstract thinking, even in creating more positive attitudes towards school. Used as therapeutic contexts, music has shown improvements in the communication of children with autism and these positive effects appear to transcend cultures (Schellenberg *et al.*, 2007). As part of **hot-housing** the development of unborn babies, many organisations and child experts advocate aiming specific kinds of music at the foetus. Others argue this is all nonsense and that normal development occurs through the absence of rather than presence of additional and unnecessary stimuli. So what effect, if any, does music have on the foetus and then on older children's IQ? This question is considered in the *Controversy* feature below.

**Hot-housing**
Intense exposure to stimuli or study in order to stimulate the child's mind.

## Controversy

### Can listening to music really improve children's IQ?

The foetus is a musical being! Auditory development begins early in the embryonic period. As a sense, audition is well developed by the time a baby comes to be born. Responses to music from the 'outside' is shown in body movement and heart rate changes. A foetus responds to sounds from 22 weeks and is influenced by sounds outside the environment, hence the positive effects to be gained by playing soothing music or talking to the baby in the womb. Studies agree that music can be learned *in utero* and remembered after birth. Peter Hepper's 1996 study (mentioned earlier) is a good example and is evidence of foetal learning through habituation where the child attends to a new stimulus and stops attending to sounds that become boring.

We know too that infants possess very good musical abilities, perhaps building on the early experiences in the womb. We are wired for language. Could it be the same for music? MRI techniques can now provide pictures that show what effect it has on the structure of the brain, either through direct measuring of the whole brain or in specific regions. Pantev and colleagues (1998) found the auditory cortex – the audio centre of the brain – is larger in musicians than in non-musicians. A study by Elbert and colleagues (1995) found that playing a string instrument at an early age produces some increase in that part of the cerebral cortex that receives sensory input from the fingers. Against strong evidence of the relationship between music and early learning, the so-called 'Mozart effect' has engendered great interest and some misconceptions. There is a widely held belief that exposure to Mozart's music increases intelligence. I recently observed a classroom of 6- and 7-year-olds where music by Bach, Mozart and Haydn was playing loudly and continuously except during whole class interactive teaching episodes. However, reports have become vastly oversimplified and point to an over-eagerness for quick-fix answers, although it would be fair to report that the presence of the music of Bach, Mozart and Haydn in the classroom I observed did contribute to a civilised environment (as did the soft furnishings, carpets and mood lighting).

Learning and practice of music increases one's musical ability – true. Casual listening to a piece of music from Mozart will cause improvement in cognitive ability – untrue. The original study (Rauscher *et al.*, 1993) assigned 36 college students to three groups: 10 minutes listening to Mozart's Sonata in D for two pianos, a tape of relaxing instructions or silence. The groups underwent a spatial test afterwards. Scores were higher for the Mozart group. So results seemed to suggest that listening to music increases the brain's ability in spatial reasoning. But two vital parts of the report were ignored by a public keen for such a sensational revelation (Bangerter & Heath, 2004). Firstly, the groups were tested on spatial ability only and not on general intelligence. Secondly, testing on the effect lasted just a few minutes. A follow-up experiment two years later by the same authors with a larger sample found the 'Mozart effect' present only on the first of 5 days' listening. More recent research remains at best inconclusive (Crncec *et al.*, 2006; Jackson & Tlauka, 2004; Ivanov & Geake, 2003) but mostly dismissive that any such effect exists (McKelvie & Low, 2002).

What does this mean? Well it may mean increased sales of Mozart's piano recordings but no confirmed evidence for the Mozart effect on IQ. What do you think? Does playing music by Mozart, Bach and Haydn improve development in unborn babies and IQ in children? Discuss this with some of your colleagues.

So, is playing classical music to unborns a good idea? Will it make any difference whatsoever to their development and to their life chances? These are the kinds of questions that many expectant couples often consider along with what to eat, whether to drink any alcohol at all, and what measures are necessary to protect their new tiny life during the time of pregnancy. Pregnancy is a revered state in all cultures. Becoming pregnant engenders many different emotions – excitement, pride, anxiety, uncertainty and perhaps profound relief if new parents have been trying to start a family for some time!

As a parent-in-waiting there are many decisions to make in advance of a child being born. Thinking about some of these questions in advance of the birth event may help to take some of the anxiety out of taking on this new role. There is no doubt that pregnancy is a stressful time (as well as a happy and exciting one!). Tessa Livingstone (2005) in her book *Child of Our Time*, records that in a survey of mothers-to-be, 94 per cent worried that their baby would not be healthy and 80 per cent reported fear of childbirth.

**Summary 3**

We now summarise what you have learned in the final section of this chapter:

- The brain begins to form in the first 3 foetal weeks.
- The brain and spinal cord form together as a hollow tube and develop into a recognisable brain shape by 9 foetal weeks.
- The foetal brain 'learns' to focus on relevant information received in the developing central nervous system and to ignore other stimuli – a process called inhibition.
- A range of *in utero* behaviours blend genetic adaptations to life in the womb with preparation for life after birth.
- Changes in movement patterns are increased in neuromuscular development which suggests that certain foetal movements and behaviour are regulated by systems in the spinal cord and lower brainstem.

- Distinct periods develop of inactivity and increased movement: specifically quiet sleep, active sleep, quiet awake and active awake – known as the four states.
- Prenatal brains seek stimulation as growing bodies explore the immediate environment – no different from the approach adopted by children at play.
- Touch is the first sense to be developed beginning at about 8 foetal weeks.
- Current research seems to support the profile case that foetuses feel pain and use behaviours similar to crying to complain about it.
- Some people believe you can enhance the development of the foetus by providing additional stimuli including classical music, while others argue that normal development occurs through the absence of unnecessary and intrusive stimuli.

# Conclusion

Here's an excerpt from a blog 'The Diary of a Goldfish' written in 2006 which we accessed when looking for people's views about what happens between conception and birth.

> Anyway, Rosemary is having an ultrasound scan on Thursday – in Hampshire [an English county] the first scan they offer is at twenty weeks apparently. So hopefully by the end of this week I will be subjecting you to a blurry photograph of the famous foetus. I know you can't wait. They might even be able to tell whether it is a he-tus or a she-tus, depending on its exhibitionist tendencies. This also means that Tinker [the blogger's name for the unborn child] is approximately half way between nothingness and somethingness.
>
> You know foetuses cry in the womb, but because there's no air, we can't hear them? When I read this I wondered, what on earth does a foetus have to cry about? It is safe and warm, has everything it needs in the way of food and drink and it doesn't see anything scary. What's more, it has always been there. They can hear things though, and apparently, the foetus will remember music and voices it hears at this stage later on when it is a person. Adrian proposes to play it nothing but Bach, but I know Rosie is secretly subjecting it to Songs from the Musicals. Hmm yes, I have now answered my own question about what foetuses might have to cry about.
>
> (Source: **http://blobolobolob.blogspot.com/2006/03/ i-danced-myself-right-out-womb.html**, accessed 12 October 2012)

This insight serves to highlight some important ideas that we have reviewed in this chapter. A foetus develops according to its genotype and some aspects of that development are fixed at the point of conception – for example, whether the foetus 'is a he-tus or a she-tus'. However, in so many other ways the development of an unborn child can be adversely affected by a profuse set of external influences known as teratogens. Research into prenatal development, some of which is quite recent, shows how a pregnant mother's emotions, diet and general health can affect foetal growth. These factors are of real importance and so too are new insights into brain development and how they shape the development of physical behaviour, capacities, emotions, thinking and learning of the unborn child. Despite the detailed images and observations of scientists such as Professor Stuart Campbell – a researcher using high definition images of foetuses at London's Create Health Clinic – the world of the unborn child remains something of a mystery in terms of how development can be enhanced by the experiences a mother can give her baby pre-partum.

You might conclude, and we would agree, that normal development appears to be the result of abstinence from and avoidance of teratogens and there is little evidence that any positive developmental gains can be made by applying certain experiences to the unborn child (such as the works of Bach or 'Songs from the Musicals'). Any reserve or restraint the scientific community might have about the positive impact of identified stimuli on foetal development is certainly not the case with newly born children and it is to what happens after birth that we now turn. In Chapter 6 we will consider the characteristics and capabilities of newborns, study how the neonate's brain is constructed to learn and discuss the importance of early stimulating experiences for integrated development and learning.

Finally, we were intrigued by our blogger's assertion that '. . . apparently, the foetus will remember music and voices it hears at this stage later on *when it is a person.*' Not the part about remembering music and voices – the jury is still out on much of the scientific research that has taken place in this context. No, we are interested in the notion that the foetus becomes 'a person', post-partum. Have you read anything in this chapter which would suggest that this is no more than a mistake and that we can recognise a foetus as a person at a much earlier stage than at birth? If so when does the ball of cells, the blastocyst – that many people would be unlikely to consider as a person – develop into a person and what are the characteristics or attributes of being a person? Check through the *Summary Table* to see if 19 foetal weeks can be considered 'half way between nothingness and somethingness'. It's a very interesting thought.

## Summary Table
### Prenatal Development

## Conditions for development (pp 122–128)

### Growth in the womb (pp 122–124)

Prenatal development is divided into three phases: germinal (0–2 weeks); embryonic (3–8 weeks); and foetal (9–38 weeks). The single fertilised cell – the zygote – divides into two, four and so on until a ball of cells (a blastocyst) is formed. The blastocyst attaches itself to the wall of the uterus. As cells continue to divide they develop characteristics to form different parts of the body, and the rate of development is so fast that by the time the embryo is renamed a foetus at 9 weeks it has already become a recognisable, if tiny human being. Between 22 and 26 weeks a point is reached where the foetus is capable of survival outside of the womb – the age of viability. Throughout the period of gestation, normal growth and development follow a consistent pattern.

### The external environment (pp 124–127)

The safety of the foetus that the mother's womb affords can be adversely affected by external influences known as teratogens, which are environmental factors or agents capable of harming or malforming a developing embryo or foetus.

## Threats to development (pp 128–138)

### Maternal diseases (pp 128–130)

Rubella (commonly called German measles) is a very infectious viral illness passed on through droplets in the air. The virus is most dangerous to a baby if a woman is infected during the first 16 weeks of pregnancy. Rubella can cause miscarriage, stillbirth or birth defects in unborn babies, such as deafness, brain damage, heart defects or cataracts depending on which week of foetal development the virus is 'caught'. Other 'diseases' which can affect the unborn child are herpes and HIV.

### Drugs (pp 130–132)

Drugs taken by the mother during pregnancy, particularly during the first trimester, can cause harm to children. Medical practitioners are very aware of the potential problems (highlighted by the prescription of the drug thalidomide in the 1950s) and it is common practice for careful questioning of women about the likelihood of their being pregnant before any drug is prescribed or dispensed. Expectant mothers should refrain from smoking, alcohol and caffeine as well as harmful illegal drugs such as cocaine and heroin.

### Environmental teratogens (pp 132–135)

Pregnant women through their occupations and domestic lives may come into contact with chemical substances that can cause potential harm to their unborn babies or lower their chances of becoming pregnant in the first case. Exposure to solvents, paints, herbicides and pesticides fall into this category, and outcomes of abnormal development increase in frequency and degree as the 'dosage' of these teratogens increases. Lead is especially dangerous and risk from lead exposure is still to be found in many occupations. There is also a huge risk to unborn children if exposed through their mothers to high levels of radiation.

### Maternal characteristics (pp 135–138)

The mother's emotional state and stress levels can lead to problems in both pregnancy and in labour by altering the maternal immune function and is commonly cited as an important risk factor for spontaneous abortion. Most estimates of the incidence of congenital abnormalities in Britain are around 2 per cent of live births, but we have no idea of the true incidence of foetal abnormality because the vast majority of miscarriages occur within the first 3 weeks after conception (5 weeks after the last menstrual period). Finally, poor or undernutrition for the expectant mother is directly linked to foetal health.

## Early cognitive development (pp 138–144)

### Prenatal brain development (pp 138–139)

The human brain takes longer to mature than all the other organs of the body. Three weeks after fertilisation, about a third of the fertilised egg forms the central nervous system (CNS) consisting of the spinal cord and brain together. By the fifth week, the primitive brain divides into three sections: the forebrain, midbrain and hindbrain, and by 9 weeks the forebrain divides to form two cerebral hemispheres – the classic brain shape. At about 10 foetal weeks, the cerebral cortex expands rapidly enabling more sophisticated messages to be sent to the muscles which allow for foetal movements to be altered through a process of inhibition. After 15 foetal weeks, further reorganisation takes place, establishing more sophistication in the higher brain centres. The texture of the brain up to this time is smooth, but by 26 weeks folds appear to increase the surface area that allow for expansion taking place underneath. This growth continues steadily up to and beyond birth.

### Foetal behaviour and learning (pp 140–143)

A range of *in utero* behaviours blend genetic adaptations to life in the womb with preparation for life after birth. These foetal movements and behaviour are regulated by systems in the spinal cord and lower brainstem. Distinct periods develop of inactivity and increased movement: specifically quiet sleep, active sleep, quiet awake and active awake – known as the four states. Touch is the first sense to be developed beginning at about 8 foetal weeks, and current research seems to support the case that foetuses feel pain and use behaviours similar to crying to complain about it. Some people believe you can enhance the development of the foetus by providing additional stimuli including classical music, while others argue that normal development occurs through the absence of unnecessary and intrusive stimuli.

## Going further

Nosarti, C., Murray, R. M. & Hack, M. (Eds) (2010) *Neurodevelopmental Outcomes of Preterm birth: From childhood to Adult Life*. Cambridge University Press.
The improved survival of very pre-term and very low birth weight infants in recent decades has been associated with an increase in the prevalence of physical and neurodevelopmental problems. Any aspiring paediatricians, neurologists, child psychiatrists and child psychologists will find this fascinating reading.

Bracewell, M. A., Hennessy, E. M., Wolke, D. and Marlow, N. (2007) The EPICure study: growth and blood pressure at 6 years of age following extremely preterm birth. *Archives of Disease in Childhood: Fetal and Neonatal Edition*, Vol 2), 108–114.
Pre-term children are at risk for reduced growth in early childhood, which may predispose them to later changes in blood pressure. EPICure 2 studied growth and blood pressure (BP) in extremely pre-term (EP) children at age 6 years. The project collected information on all babies born in England during 2006 between the gestational ages of 22 weeks and 26 weeks + 6 days.

Hetherington, E. M., Parke, R. D., Gauvain, M. & Locke, V. O. (2006). *Child psychology: A contemporary viewpoint*, 6th edn. London: McGraw-Hill.
Chapter 3 covers the entire prenatal period in depth. There is detailed coverage of the influence of teratogens.

Livingstone, T. (2005). *Child of our time*. London: Bantam Press.
Chapter 1 is very accessible indeed: an enjoyable read that also provides much factual information about early development. It also contains a number of mini surveys and activities that are useful for revision purposes.

Slater, A. & Lewis, M. (Eds) (2002). *Introduction to Infant Development*. Oxford: Oxford University Press.
Peter Hepper's chapter (3) is excellent and contains valuable information on foetal learning and behaviour.

# Useful websites

www.ob-ultrasound.net
Obstetric ultrasound is the use of ultrasound scans in pregnancy. Since its introduction in the late 1950s, ultrasonography has become a very useful diagnostic tool in obstetrics. This site explains the procedure and provides many wonderful images produced by scans.

www.visembryo.com/baby/index.html
The Visible Embryo is a visual guide through fetal development from fertilisation through pregnancy to birth.

http://www.psych.qub.ac.uk/Research/Centres/
FetalBehaviourResearchCentre/
Website of the Fetal Behaviour Research Centre.

The Fetal Behaviour Research Centre is home to research exploring the behaviour of the foetus.

The key aims of the research centre include: to gain a better understanding of all aspects of prenatal behavioural development and to investigate the behavioural, perceptual and learning abilities of the foetus.

http://www.who.int/nutrition/publications/
fetal_dev_report_EN.pdf
An excellent cross-cultural global report 'Promoting Optimal Fetal Development' from the website of the World Health Organization.

# Chapter 6
## Neonatal Behaviour and Learning

## Introduction

We concluded in Chapter 5 that there remains some mystery whether the development of the unborn child can be enhanced by the experiences from 'outside' the womb. Research into pre-natal development shows both how a pregnant mother's emotions, diet and general health can affect foetal growth, and how brain development shapes the physical development, behaviour, capacities, emotions, thinking and learning of the unborn child. You may remember that a foetus develops according to its genotype and some aspects of that development are fixed at the point of conception – for example, sex, whether the foetus 'is a he-tus or a she-tus'. However, in so many other ways the development of an unborn child can be adversely affected by a manifold set of adverse external influences.

Adverse external influences – teratogens – are much less likely to affect a baby during the first trimester – the first 3-month period of the 9-month pregnancy – than in the final two trimesters. During the final trimester a baby puts on weight and perfects patterns of behaviour needed imme-diately after birth – swallowing, sucking, yawning and grasping. A baby doubles in length and trebles in weight and this dramatic growth is mainly due to **hypertrophy** (cell fattening) rather than cell division (**hyperplasmia**) that characterised development in the first two trimesters. There is also intense brain development, with new cells and speedy connections between cells con-stantly forming. In the final weeks before birth a baby turns to become **cephalic** (head down) and doesn't move around as much, adopting a foetal position as there isn't much space left to move around in. However, a foetus still attempts stretching and flexing of the legs and arms which can be very uncomfortable for a mother. By 38 foetal weeks or perhaps a little earlier or later, every-thing is ready for the foetus to be born.

**Hypertrophy**
Growth by cell fattening.

**Hyperplasmia**
Growth by cell division.

**Cephalic**
Pertaining to the head.

By the time you have completed this chapter you should be able to answer the following questions:

- What is the association between obstetric experience and patterns of child development?
- What are the characteristics and capabilities of newborns?
- How are learning and development integrated?
- How is the neonate's brain constructed to learn?
- What is the importance of early stimulating experiences for development?
- What kinds of early stimulating experiences are appropriate for very young children?

**Chapter Objectives**

# Childbirth

Childbirth is a pivotal event marking the boundary between development *in utero* and development in the first few weeks and months *post-partum*, but it does not just mark a boundary. What happens during birth can affect the development of a baby in the first few weeks and months, and later on during childhood. One of the themes of this book is that normal experience allows for normal development and that we can explore 'normal' experience and development by looking at what can happen when things go wrong. You may remember that in Chapter 5 we spent some time investigating the effect of teratogens on the foetus in order to better understand what normal development should occur. The same idea applies now. However, before we consider the characteristics and capabilities of newborns and study how the neonate's brain is constructed, let's take a quick look at what some call the 'miracle of birth'.

Human childbirth is divided into three stages of 'labour' – an interesting word that indicates this process can be very hard work for both mother and baby! The first stage (see Figure 6.1) achieves the shortening and then the dilation of the cervix. Labour is considered to have started when the cervix is 3 cm dilated, and ends with full dilation. Contractions begin in the first stage of labour although they may be irregular at first. During this stage the mother is discouraged from 'pushing down' – contracting her abdominal muscles. The second stage, often called the 'pushing stage', starts when the cervix is fully dilated and ends with the ejection of the foetus. In the third stage, the placenta detaches from the uterine wall and is expelled through the birth canal.

This process can be quite short but often happens over an extended period of many hours during which both baby and mother can become very tired. Birth, though an entirely natural and normal event can also be a dangerous time for both baby and mother. According to the Office for National Statistics (ONS, 2010), the perinatal baby mortality rate in England and Wales (latest available) is 4.2 deaths per 1000 live births, and for mothers the maternal mortality ratio in developing countries is 2.4 per 1000 births versus 0.16 per 1000 in developed countries (World Health Organization, 2012).

Yet for the vast majority of new parents in the developed world, childbirth is one of the most exciting and life-affirming moments of their lives. Remember what Edd Hogan wrote for Chapter 1 to describe his feelings at the birth of his new baby daughter, Niamh:

> . . . I felt a rush of emotion: happiness, joy, awe, and relief. She was all there: two arms, two legs, and she was beautiful. In those first few hours a great deal goes through your mind – what will she become? . . . What will her voice sound like? The feelings of love towards her were, and are, remarkable. We want her to grow up to know what it is to be loved. . . .

This is a father's viewpoint. How does a mother feel during childbirth and about her new baby? One of the most awe-inspiring and affecting websites is the one helping parents to tell birth stories. From **www.birthstories.com** we have selected part of the birth story by Kelly Camden:

> I retreated to the deepest parts of my mind, reviewing scenes from my childhood like an old film. Every spoken word, whether or not it was directed to me, became a distraction. I wanted silence. I just sat there, letting my body do its work. I didn't want to move or be touched, just be still. Contractions came and went, and in between I would drift off, resting without sleeping. Soon the sunlight was shining softly into the room. My labour was changing. I felt the baby moving, like thunder rumbling through me, and I had to surrender. I pulled together every bit of strength I had left. Suddenly, I was re-energized as if I had slept through the night.
>
> Finally, at 9:03 on a Monday morning, my son was born. The midwife immediately put him in my arms. I was stunned, for the sight and sensation of holding your own child for the first time is not truly conceivable beforehand. He did not cry or breathe right away, and everything appeared to be in slow motion. I was speechless and

**Dilation**
Widening of the cervix caused by contractions in the uterus.

**Cervix**
The neck of the womb.

**Contractions**
The shortening of the uterine muscles during childbirth.

**Placenta**
A flattened circular organ in the uterus of pregnant mammals nourishing and maintaining the foetus through the umbilical cord and expelled after birth.

**Perinatal**
Of or relating to the time immediately before or after birth.

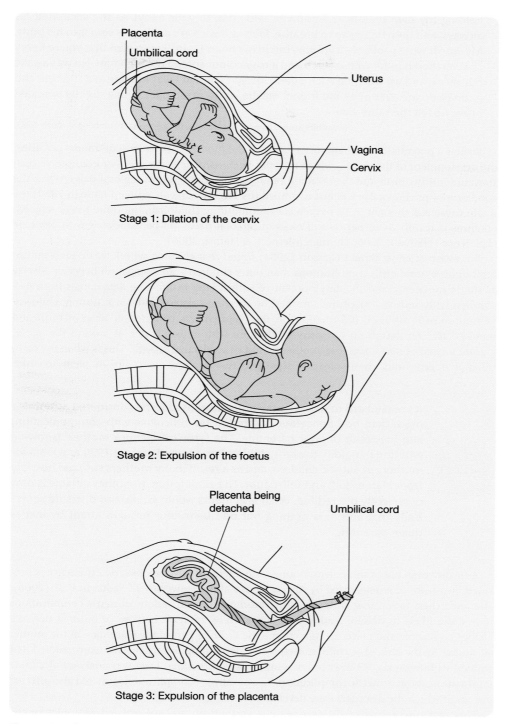

Stage 1: Dilation of the cervix

Stage 2: Expulsion of the foetus

Stage 3: Expulsion of the placenta

**Figure 6.1** The three stages of labour

*Source*: From Longe, J. L. (Ed.) (2006). *Gale encyclopedia of medicine*, 3rd ed. Farming Hills, MI: Gale, a part of Cengage Learning, Inc. Reproduced by permission.

holding my own breath. The midwife said, 'Talk to your baby!' as she suctioned his airways, and then he began to breathe. I felt as if we were calling his soul into his body. My words were probably a jumble, but in my heart I said, 'I'm so glad that you're here!'

I watched him fill with oxygen and a rosy colour spread through him. He was awake but silent, and we watched each other closely. I felt that I was looking at a stranger and gazing into the eyes of an old friend. Maybe, as he gazed back with a slightly wrinkled brow, he felt the same way.

(www.birthstories.com/stories/homebirth/like-thunder-rumbling-through-6283)

**Trauma**
A physical wound or injury, physical shock following injury or an emotional shock sometimes leading to long-term neurosis.

Birth is a potentially traumatic affair for baby and mother and the level of trauma can affect the development of the child – which may not be immediately obvious. For example, oxygen starvation during birth and the resultant brain damage can result in cerebral palsy. When the condition of cerebral palsy was first identified (by English surgeon William Little in 1860) the major cause was thought to be oxygen starvation during childbirth, but quite recent research confirms that only 5–10 per cent of cases of cerebral palsy can be associated with obstetric experience (Pharoah, 2006; Thorngren-Jerneck & Herbst, 2006).

**Autism**
A mental condition characterised by self-absorption and a reduced ability to respond to or communicate with the outside world.

**Obstetric**
Relating to childbirth and the branch of medicine and surgery related to midwifery.

Australian scientist Emma Glasson (2004) found that children who later develop autism tend to have more birth complications than other children – an association between adverse obstetric experience and the development of autism later in life. The data comes from 465 children with autism, 481 of their normal brothers and sisters, and 1313 'normal children' without autistic siblings. Information on the children was collected at time of birth and matched to later data from a registry of children with autism. Later, at around the age of 2 years, a child's brain undergoes another period of accelerated growth. This is when the combination of genes and adverse obstetric experience that we think causes autism, seems to strike.

**Reflect**

It's really hard to believe now but autism used to be considered as nothing more than odd behaviour (suggested by difficulties with communication) and the result of poor parenting. The term 'refrigerator mother' (showing emotional frigidity towards children) was coined around 1950 as a label for mothers of autistic children, and as a result many mothers suffered horribly from blame, guilt and self-doubt. The assumption of mother's blame is now completely discredited. What arguments would you use to dissuade somebody that autism is nothing but odd behaviour brought about by inadequate parenting?

A further example of the potential long-term effects of adverse obstetric experience is provided by a team of scientists led by Angela Favaro at the University of Padua in Italy (2006). The researchers found that children whose mothers suffered serious obstetric complications were more likely to develop eating disorders such as anorexia nervosa or bulimia nervosa. Diabetes, anaemia and placental infarction – the death of part of the placenta – in the mother all added to the risk of a child subsequently developing anorexia. The team studied 114 women with anorexia, 73 with bulimia and 554 with neither. Data was analysed alongside information about obstetric complication. The number of complications suffered also affected the age at which the disorders were developed.

**Connect and Extend**
For a description of psychological symptoms in 8–12-year-old children with cerebral palsy and their impact on the child and family, read: Parkes, J. *et al.* (2008). Psychological problems in children with cerebral palsy: A cross-sectional European study. *Journal of Child Psychology & Psychiatry*, 49, 405–413.

Although cerebral palsy, eating disorders and autism are not isolated examples of the developmental problems that have been associated with childbirth, fortunately the vast majority of babies come through the birth experience unscathed. They emerge into a brighter and noisier world, where needs and capabilities are linked in profound and complex ways which we need to understand. This chapter is organised around three main questions. What are newborns like? What can they do? How do they learn? Let us address the first of these and consider the characteristics and capabilities of newborn babies by listening to the imaginary words of a newborn – a neonate.

# The characteristics and capabilities of newborns

Hello. I've just arrived and I'm feeling a bit squashed. I'm OK though and have got used to the bright lights and all the noise. I weigh about 7$\frac{1}{2}$ pounds and I am about 50 cm long. I am a little shorter and not as heavy as a boy, but this varies a lot. You might have noticed that my head is quite big for the size of my body and a little out of shape. That's because when I was being born I had to squeeze through my mother's pelvis. Don't worry, it'll be OK in a short while as the bones of my skull sort themselves out. Apart from a large head (about a quarter the size of my whole body), my legs look short and are a bit bowed. My skin? Yes, it has a funny colour to it. That's because I am covered with an oily protective coat called the vernix caseosa. Oh yes, the hairs. At the moment they are all over my body. This is because my prenatal hair or lanugo is still present although it will disappear pretty soon. After three or four days my skin can turn a bit yellow and I might develop neonatal jaundice. Don't worry, this is a non-threatening condition that disappears shortly, particularly if I do a little sun-bathing. OK. Now that I'm here, what can I do? (And where's my mummy?)

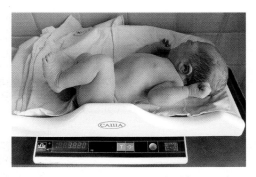

A newly born baby being checked for weight.

*Source*: Ria Novosti / Science Photo Library.

### Connect and Extend

It is currently thought that 60 per cent of full-term infants develop jaundice on the second or third day after birth, and that 80 per cent of premature babies develop it between the fifth and seventh day after delivery. Connect to **www.childliverdisease.org** for more information on this common neonatal condition.

In the (not too distant) past, neonates were thought of as helpless beings, totally ill-prepared for their journey ahead. Certainly little baby Sasha in the photograph looks pretty helpless. However, we now know this to be incorrect and that babies are well equipped for surviving, close to their mother in their new life outside the womb. They arrive with a range of reflexes, psychological and behavioural capabilities, and a voracious appetite to do and to know. These wonderful new beings are, in many ways, ready to meet the challenges ahead in the novel and very different surroundings. Let us look at how the newborn's sensory capabilities equip her to deal with the next stage of life.

**Vernix caseosa**
A cheese-like substance covering the foetus that prevents chaffing.

**Lanugo**
Soft hair covering the whole body of the foetus.

**Jaundice**
A yellowing of the skin or whites of eyes caused by slow functioning of the liver.

## Sensory capabilities

### Touch

The newborn's sense of touch is well developed at birth. Touch is an important way for a baby to communicate in the new surroundings. There are sensitive areas on the palms, soles of the feet and in the mouth that are linked to certain reflexes (these will be discussed in the next section). Sensations against the skin provide comfort and security. Holding a baby has a soothing effect upon the infant and when this is on the adult's left side the baby is soothed further by hearing the adult's heartbeat as well as allowing the baby's head to turn to look at the person holding her. Touch informs about temperature and the baby will cry in response to a cold

**Reflexes**
Automatic responses to stimulation. Many fade out in the first year after birth.

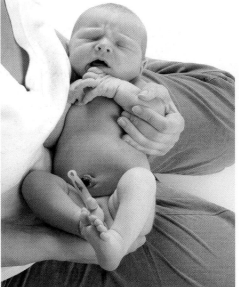

The soothing effect of being held.

*Source*: © Pearson Education Ltd / Jules Selmes.

temperature. Responses to pain are similar: crying, elevated heart rate, sweating and muscle tension. There is some evidence that babies feel pain more than adults, and poorly controlled pain in infants can result in lifelong adverse consequences such as a neuro-developmental problem, poor weight gain, learning disabilities, psychiatric disorders, adult chronic pain and alcoholism (Marcus, 2006; Jarvis, 2004). Babies are sensitive to texture and to change of position – see *Proprioception* below – have very sensitive skin, but may not respond to a very light touch.

## Smell

**Innate**
Born with or inborn due to naturally occurring experiences prior to birth or heritable dispositions.

**Bonding**
Becoming emotionally attached.

**Visual acuity**
Sharpness of vision.

**Visual accommodation**
The change in shape of the lens in the eye.

Some preferences for smell are thought to be innate and, of course, there is a strong connection between smell and the development of taste preferences (Mennella, 2007b). Babies can identify pleasant smells and turn away from unpleasant ones. Common foods such as bananas and chocolate invoke smiles and licking actions but babies turn away from nasty smells such as ammonia. There is a sensitivity towards the mother's milk which fulfils an important early bonding role as well as a survival one. Because neonates can recognise the smell of their mother's milk (Marmet *et al.*, 2000) even in the first days, they turn their heads towards the mother and are guided to the nipple for breast-feeding by this sense. This same sense allows the mother and child to recognise each other, again fulfilling a survival role. They are even discriminatory, being able to distinguish the smell of their mother's amniotic fluid to that of someone else (Varendi *et al.*, 1998) so, if breast-fed, babies can distinguish the smell of their mother's breasts from those of other women who are breast-feeding.

## Taste

Newborns have the capacity to experience the four taste sensations – salty, sour, bitter and sweet but show a preference for sweet taste by licking and smiling (Mennella, 2007a). This may be important for their early survival as they respond well to the sweetness present in the mother's milk. The sensation of the milk, plus the actual act of sucking serves as further soothing for the infant. Newborns show a dislike for sour taste and can be observed pursing their lips in disgust (Mennella & Jagnow, 2001). By 4 months they show some liking for salty tastes, a liking that might act as a preparation for solid foods to come and even of a tendency to high blood pressure in the future (Zinner *et al.*, 2002).

## Vision

Much of the classic research on the development of vision took place in the 1980s and 1990s possibly because until then the hardware was not available to measure the least mature of all the senses at birth. A newborn's vision is poor – approximately 20/400. This is equivalent to seeing only the big letter 'E' on an eye chart. Vision slowly improves to 20/20 by age 2 years – but this sense is able to fulfil its functions and early requirements adequately. Babies will turn their head towards a light and will stare at bright, shiny objects, open their eyes when held upright, close their eyes when a pencil light is shone directly into them, blink in response to movement and like looking at high-contrast patterns and shapes (Casey & Richards, 1988). Visual acuity, or the sharpness of vision is limited to objects up to about 20 cm away and remains so for about three months. Visual accommodation, which brings objects into focus is very poor,

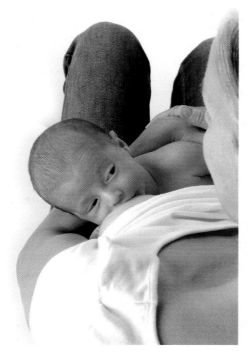

The distance a newborn can see is limited to about 20 cm – perfect for gazing at his mother's face while feeding!

*Source*: © Pearson Education Ltd / Jules Selmes.

but improves quickly over the first two months (Hainline & Abramov, 1992). That is not to say that newborns cannot see, but that their vision is blurred. The distance of 20 cm is important as it equates to the average distance the face of an adult cradling a baby is away from the baby's face. Here again nature has given a helpful hand by further assisting with mother–infant bonding. Neonates are fascinated by human faces and gaze attentively at their mother's face when being cuddled or fed. Vision holds important clues to the strange new environment the newborn has entered. Babies look around their new surroundings for things that interest them: the adoring face of a parent or relative suddenly pressed up close, or the bright pink rabbit that has just appeared! They prefer coloured rather than plain white but the ability to discriminate is limited: a facet that makes decorating the new nursery at home in bright colours rather meaningless at this stage! Newborns are soon able to track moving objects – preferring to look at moving objects rather than stationary ones (Hamer & Norcia, 1994; Kellman & von Hofsten, 1992). Vision is the most important sense for getting information about the new environment but it is naturally limited at this stage due to perceptual constraints and the immaturity of the developing brain (Valenza *et al.*, 2006).

Newborns are able to track moving objects and prefer them to still objects.

*Source*: © Pearson Education Ltd / Jules Selmes.

## Hearing

Systems associated with hearing function well at birth. As described in the previous chapter the foetus hears sounds through the mother's abdomen, and in the womb they respond to external sounds. Studies have shown that newborns can distinguish the mother's voice from that of others, which suggests a familiarity from time spent *in utero* (Barker & Newman, 2004). They prefer human female voices, largely because they have quite a high pitch. Have you noticed that when adults speak to babies they use a higher pitch – around 260 cycles or complete vibrations per second. This is the best pitch for adults to communicate with newborns. Speaking in high-pitched tones with expression and rising at the end of sentences are two other useful communication strategies. From birth they can distinguish between sound patterns, and are able to differentiate between different intonations in words, such as loud sounds or angry words. They respond quickly to sounds around them by turning their heads. The ability to locate sound improves quickly. Newborns appear to be pre-wired to respond positively to the mother's voice but not to that of the father (Figueiredo *et al.*, 2007). As you will have already seen, this is evidence of prenatal learning, being able to recognise the mother's voice having been exposed to it for months *in utero*. The ability to respond and differentiate sounds very early on helps enormously with later language acquisition.

• • • • • • • • • • • • • • • • •
**Connect and Extend**
Research from the University of Surrey Baby Lab has shown that babies can categorise colour at 4 months. Understanding how infants and toddlers can categorise things is important, as categorisation is a core part of development, and many other cognitive abilities, such as language acquisition, depend upon it. Connect to **http://www.surrey.ac.uk/psychology/research/babylab/**
• • • • • • • • • • • • • • • • •

## Proprioception

In addition to the normal five senses, neonates have a sixth sense: proprioception. Proprioception is the 'internal' sense the body has: that of position and balance, movement and posture, muscles, bones, joints and all of their interrelated combinations. Proprioception gives us an awareness of where our body is and what it is doing. Think of it like the internal gyroscope in navigation systems, telling us up from upside-down, making turns and going backwards. More than that, it acts as a system check that lets us know the position of our limbs, fingers and head and what our facial expression is, without having to consciously look to find out. It is due to this sense of proprioception

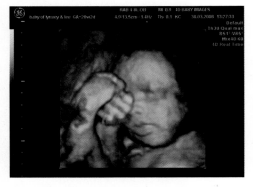

Proprioception develops in the womb, as you can see in this 3D scan of Max, who is rubbing his eyes and has moved his foot up to his face.

*Source*: Lee and Lynsey Matthews.

• • • • • • • • • • • • • • • • •
**Connect and Extend**
The other five senses are combined with proprioception to make sense (!) of and to react to the world around us. Who is better at this, males or females? Does it matter who is better? Read the results of a Norwegian study: Sigmundsson, H., Haga, M. & Hopkins, B. (2007). Sex differences in perception: Exploring the integration of sensory information with respect to vision and proprioception. *Sex Roles*, 57, 181–186.
• • • • • • • • • • • • • • • • •

that we are able to function so efficiently in space and to explore our world and the world of others.

In Chapter 5 we explored the importance of reflexive and deliberate movements of a foetus in the womb. The sixth sense of proprioception develops *in utero* in the same ways as the other senses and some would argue even more so. The foetus can run his hand constantly over his face, suck his fist, scratch and pat his cheek, bring his knees up, take hold of his umbilical cord and use it as a pillow (Campbell, 2004) – see the 3D scan of Max at 28 weeks. The unborn baby is exploring the environment, which includes himself. The vast majority of us develop this sense, use it and keep it but there are a few unfortunate individuals who have been known to lose proprioception in part, leading to problems in the development of some specific cognitive capacities; the ability to attribute mental states to oneself and others, and to understand that others have beliefs, desires and intentions that are different from one's own (Chasiotis *et al.*, 2006).

**Reflect**

Some people act with surprise when we start talking about a sixth sense – proprioception. It's also probably true that most people would not recognise the term, having been taught from a young age that there are five senses (often matched to the fingers of one hand). Why do you think this is? Some answers are given in an article in *New Scientist* by Bruce Durie which argues that we have 21 senses; 'Doors of perception', *New Scientist*, 29 January 2005, Issue 2484, p 34. Now you should be able to answer the question 'Is proprioception a real sense?'

**Summary 1**

Before moving on, let's summarise what we have learned so far:

- Human childbirth is divided into three stages of labour: dilation of the cervix brought about by contractions of the uterus; 'the pushing stage' – ejection of the infant; and ejection of the placenta.

- Birth is a potentially traumatic affair for baby and mother, and the level of trauma can affect the development of the child.

- Oxygen starvation during birth and the resultant brain damage can result in cerebral palsy. Some 5–10 per cent of cases of cerebral palsy can be associated with obstetric experience.

- Babies are well equipped for surviving, close to their mother in their new life outside the womb. They arrive with a range of reflexes, psychological and behavioural capabilities, and a voracious appetite to do and to know.

- Newborns can experience the four taste sensations (salty, sour, bitter and sweet) and show a preference for sweet.

- A newborn's vision is poor; accommodation is limited to objects about 20 cm away.

- Newborns can distinguish the mother's voice from that of others which suggests a familiarity from the time spent *in utero*.

- The sixth sense of proprioception gives us an awareness of where our body is and what it is doing.

# Primitive reflexes

Have you ever had someone wave their hands really close to your eyes or strike you just below the bent knee with a hard object? Your natural reaction in the first case is to blink and jerk your head back and in the second for your lower leg to suddenly shoot forward. These are reflex actions or reflexes. According to psychologist Helen Bee, reflexes are 'physical responses triggered involuntarily by specific stimuli' (2000b, p 83). It should be remembered that they are automatic responses to stimulation, with no conscious thinking and are in no way learned. Reflexes do not involve higher brain functioning because at this stage in neonatal development, the brain has a capacity for low-level functioning only. As the cerebral cortex in the brain develops, this area takes responsibility for voluntary control of many actions. Reflexes serve several important functions: one type called survival reflexes are, not surprisingly, related to the baby's survival, and further assists with mother–child attachment. Survival reflexes (known as adaptive reflexes) include sucking/swallowing and rooting. When a baby sucks on a nipple or dummy the action soothes and provides the child with comfort. The *rooting* reflex is where, if one side of the baby's cheek or mouth is gently touched, the baby's head turns towards the touch and the mouth purses as if in search of a nipple to feed. Another important example, the *grasping* reflex – where the baby grabs a finger of an adult and holds on tightly to this – is seen to have a positive influence on the carer by helping to bond adult and child (Margulis, 2005).

**Survival reflexes**
Reflexes associated with early survival, also called adaptive reflexes.

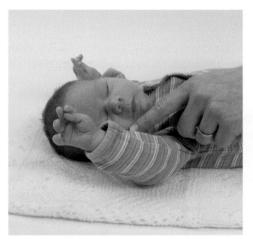

The rooting reflex.
*Source*: © Pearson Education Ltd / Tudor Photography.

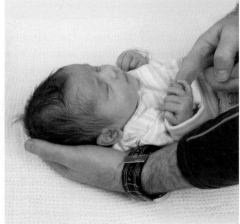

The grasp reflex.
*Source*: © Pearson Education Ltd / Tudor Photography.

## Retained primitive reflexes

Primitive reflexes (of which survival reflexes are a subset) are controlled by the lowest and most primitive (meaning first-formed) part of the human brain, the brainstem. Examples are the *swimming reflex* which enable a baby to be in a water environment by essentially blocking the throat, and the *stepping or walking reflex*; babies will make forward stepping movements when held upright and tilted forwards, with their feet on a firm surface.

**Primitive reflexes**
Automatic responses to stimulation, with no conscious thinking and are in no way learned.

In the falling reflex or *Moro reflex*, if the baby feels any sudden movement that affects the neck she suddenly extends arms and legs outwards then brings them into the body which is believed to have helped the baby cling to her mother in the days when the baby would have been carried around on the mother's back. These are 'throw-backs' to our evolutionary past and, rather than view them as reflexes that have outlived their usefulness, they should be seen as early preparations for later behaviours – perhaps as a basis for complex motor skills. To help explain this idea, let's look in some detail at some of these primitive reflexes that appear to

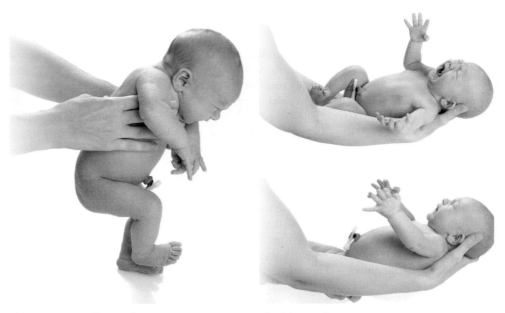

The stepping/walking reflex.
*Source*: © Pearson Education Ltd / Tudor Photography.

The Moro reflex.
*Source*: © Pearson Education Ltd / Jules Selmes.

have outlived their usefulness. The following is adapted from an article by chiropractor Keith Keen from Sydney, Australia, accessed at **www.headstarthealth.com.au/primitive.html** on 21 April 2013 and used with the permission of the author.

## Primitive reflexes – asymmetrical tonic neck reflex (ATNR)

The tonic neck reflex, where the baby's head and body turn to one side in an 'archer's position', should be fully present at birth and appears to assist the baby's active participation in the birthing process. The reflex continues after birth and plays an important part in the development of hand–eye–object co-ordination, and perception of distance. While the ATNR is uninhibited, the hand moves in conjunction with the head. This connection between touch and vision helps to establish distance perception and hand–eye co-ordination. By the middle of the first year of life this is normally accomplished and the ATNR, being no longer required, should be inhibited by habituation and integrated into a range of normal reactions.

If the reflex persists, the hand–eye connection makes co-ordinated crawling difficult. When walking, turning the head results in the straightening of the arm and leg on the same side, upsetting balance and the normal walking pattern. In early months, after the hand–eye relationship is established, ATNR locks vision on to anything which catches the attention, further reinforcing object and background perception. If ATNR is inappropriately retained, the child is easily distracted by anything that attracts the attention (check Table 6.1 for the kinds of behaviour associated with attention deficit hyperactivity disorder). With retained ATNR, difficulty may be experienced with visual, auditory and motor movement tasks which involve both left and right sides of the body, and establishment of dominant hand, leg or ear may be difficult. Turning the head can cause an image to momentarily disappear or parts of the visual field to be missed so visual tracking and judgement of distance may be affected.

The asymmetric tonic neck reflex.
*Source*: © Pearson Education Ltd / Tudor Photography.

**Table 6.1** Proposed areas of overlap between retained reflexes and ADHD symptoms

| Reflexes | Effect of retained primitive reflexes | ADHD symptoms |
|---|---|---|
| **Moro**<br>Emerges: 9–12 weeks *in utero*<br>Inhibited: 2–4 months after birth | Over-reactive<br>Hyperactivity, hypoactivity<br>Oculo-motor problems<br>Tense muscle tone, fatigue<br>Poor visual perception<br>Eyes stimulus bound, photosensitivity<br>Auditory confusion<br>Co-ordination difficulties<br>Anxious<br>Mood swings<br>Low self-esteem<br>Poor decision-making qualities | Impulsivity<br>Hyperactivity<br>Messy work<br>Inability to sit still<br>Inattentive<br>Easily distracted<br>Does not appear to listen<br>Clumsy<br>Anxious, social clumsiness<br>Inappropriate behaviour<br>Shy, withdrawn<br>Procrastinates, disorganised |
| **TLR**<br>Emerges: At birth<br>Inhibited: 2–4 months after birth | Poor balance<br>Easily disoriented<br>Problems re-establishing binocular vision | Poor sense of timing<br>Frequent careless mistakes |
| **ATNR**<br>Emerges: 18 weeks *in utero*<br>Inhibited: 3–9 months after birth | Poor eye tracking<br>Difficulty crossing visual midline – the notional boundary between left- and right-eye vision | Difficulty learning to read<br>Difficulty telling time<br>Left–right confusion |
| **STNR**<br>Emerges: 6–9 months after birth<br>Inhibited: 9–11 months after birth | Poor posture<br>Poor eye/hand co-ordination<br>Focusing difficulties | Problems sitting still in desk<br>Problems learning to swim<br>Problems with ball games |

*Source*: Taylor, M., Houghton, S. & Chapman, E. (2004). Primitive reflexes and attention-deficit hyperactivity disorder: Developmental origins of classroom dysfunction. *International Journal of Special Education, 19*(1), 23–37. Reproduced with permission.

## Primitive reflexes – fear paralysis reflex (FPR)

The FPR begins to function very early after conception and should normally be integrated before birth. It can be seen in the womb as movement of the head, neck and body in response to threat – a kind of 'freezing' when a threat is sensed. If FPR is retained after birth, it can be recognised by withdrawal from the social context, reticence at being involved in anything new, fear of different circumstances, the 'scaredy cat' child who bears the brunt of teasing by more adventurous children.

## Primitive reflexes – spinal galant reflex (SGR)

This reflex is normally integrated before the end of the first year of life. It appears to take an active role in the birth process, with movements of the hips helping the baby to work its way down the birth canal. In the newborn, stroking the lower back to one side of the spine will result in side flexion of the spine away from that side, with raising of the hip on the same side. Stimulation down both sides of the spine simultaneously will activate a related reflex, which causes urination. Children with retained SGR may have poor bladder control. As the low back region is stimulated by bed sheets, the involuntary voiding reflex may be elicited so the child may continue to wet the bed despite all attempts to stop. If the galant reflex remains present on one side only it may affect posture and walking gait, resulting in the appearance of a limp.

## Primitive relexes – tonic labyrinth reflex (TLR)

The TLR involves the sense of balance and position in space and the central cavity of the inner ear. When the neck is tilted backward the limbs straighten; when the neck is bent forward the limbs bend. The reflex should be fully developed in both positions from birth, and has done its job by the end of the first year of life. A child who has a retained TLR when starting to walk cannot acquire true walking and standing security, and may experience difficulty in judging distance, speed and space.

## Primitive reflexes – symmetrical tonic neck reflex (STNR)

• • • • • • • • • • • • • • • •
**Connect and Extend**
If bed wetting is associated with the retention of spinal galant reflex, what can prevent this troublesome and (for some) pernicious problem in late childhood? Read: Bennett, H. (2006). Does breastfeeding prevent nocturnal enuresis? *Pediatrics, 118,* 1802–1803.
• • • • • • • • • • • • • • • •

This reflex starts with the neck and arms extended and the legs flexed. As the neck flexes, the arms flex and the legs extend. This reflex interferes with reciprocal movement of the arms and legs as seen in crawling and walking. The STNR also interferes with using the hands when the head position changes. If it remains present in an older child, it can affect integration of upper and lower portions of the body, for example, when swimming; sitting posture – a tendency to slump when sitting at a desk or table; poor muscle tone; poorly developed hand–eye coordination; and an inability to sit still and concentrate.

Many of these reflexes are tested for as part of the checks made by midwives and health visitors in the first few hours and days of life. Why is presence of these primitive reflexes considered to be important, when babies 'grow out' of most of them in the first few months?

Reflexes are important indicators of normal development and health of the child's nervous system. In babies who have suffered brain damage, reflexes may be diminished, too pronounced, or remain after the period when they would normally disappear. Not all our reflexes leave us in the first year as those that have a protective role such as blinking, coughing or gagging stay with us throughout the course of life. As explained above, those reflexes that ought to disappear early in the neonate's development are sometimes retained and this has been found to have potentially serious implications for later learning. Table 6.1 shows suggested areas of overlap between four reflexes that are sometimes retained and the symptoms of attention deficit hyperactivity disorder (ADHD).

The *Controversy* feature below asks the question whether the unusual retention of reflexes really has a detrimental effect on classroom behaviour and learning (as is suggested in Table 6.1 which matches retained primitive reflexes and types of classroom dysfunction) or if this is all a 'storm in a teacup'.

## Controversy

### Does unusual retention of early childhood reflexes have an effect on future learning?

Already in this text we have identified a number of factors of environment and genetic make-up which can act jointly and severally to impede children's learning. Not so widely accepted is the potential impact of retained reflexes on later learning. Primitive reflexes are involuntary responses that a newborn has that include essential survival mechanisms in the first weeks of life. Development of primitive reflexes begins in the very early stages of foetal development to ensure the baby's survival after being born. They are controlled by the brainstem which is the primitive part of the brain and are executed without the involvement of other 'higher' parts of the brain, such as the motor cortex.

Primitive reflexes fulfil another role in providing a basis of future voluntary skill development, and functioning. Each reflex prepares for the next stage in development, and the central nervous system allows reflexes to disappear through a decreased response to repeated stimuli (habituation) or to be integrated in increasingly complex movements that are controlled by higher levels of the brain. When a cluster of reflexes which are delayed or aberrant persist, neuro-developmental delay exists which can only be improved by specific therapeutic programmes. Programmes involving specific physical, auditory or visual stimulation treatment gives the brain a 'second chance' to register the reflex inhibitory patterns that should have been in place at earlier stages of development (Goddard, 2005). A number of studies stretching back over 30 years confirm the impact of retained reflexes on academic achievement (e.g. Goddard Blythe, 2001; O'Dell & Cook, 1997; Faulkner, 1989) and identification and analysis of these retained early reflexes can be valuable tools in helping to promote learning for all children. Some examples of retained reflexes and the likely consequences for learning (drawing on the research studies) are given below.

### Primitive reflexes

Retention of the *Moro reflex* shows in the child's emotional profile through either being unusually withdrawn or easily and highly excitable to the point of being over-reactive or aggressive. Children show poor reactions to light and can be confused and alarmed by background noise. They dislike change. Retention of the *spinal gallant reflex* shows in constant fidgeting. Children also demonstrate poor concentration and have poor short-term memory. Retention of the *asymmetrical tonic neck reflex* affects balance, and also affects performance in physical skills that involve cross-patterning such as running and skipping. Children may have poor handwriting skills and visual difficulties.

The normal expectation is for these reflexes to disappear in the child's first year but their retention may be an underlying cause of learning difficulties: the types of difficulty which are very common in classroom situations and which impede learning. Difficulties, for example, may be seen with speech and language, physical skills, sensory perception, cognition, emotional and social maturity in children throughout the primary age and beyond into adulthood. The signs tend to become evident with children around 8 years of age and appear more frequently in boys.

A contrary argument is that the retention of primitive reflexes is only one factor affecting learning and academic achievement. There are of course many reasons why children do not achieve in school, and some studies argue that social and economic factors have a much greater influence than any other individual or set of related factors (e.g. Uline & Johnson, 2005).

Some scholars engaged in researching learning and the factors affecting academic achievement assert that discussion of the effect of retention of primitive reflexes is clouding the issue of underachievement with a small and not necessarily proven association between early reflexes and later classroom behaviours (e.g. Dichter *et al.*, 2010). They argue that such a discussion may provide an interesting diversion but makes little difference. Furthermore, some commentators assert that researchers, theorists and practitioners should concentrate their efforts much more on the causes of child poverty and social deprivation and the consequences of these for learning and achievement (e.g. Barnes & Horsfall, 2010).

What do you think? Do you think we should spend research time and resources on finding out more about the impact of retained reflexes on academic achievement, or view such research as a side issue? Spend some time debating this issue with your colleagues.

## Organised activity

What further characterises neonatal behaviour are organised patterns of daily activity. These are varying states of arousal over the entire 24-hour cycle. In a historic (1966) and classic explanation of the varying states, two researchers, psychoanalyst Dr Peter Wolff and Professor Heinz Prechtl of the Netherlands, classified patterns of infant behaviour into six different states of consciousness according to the baby's degree of wakefulness – although neonates spend approximately 70 per cent of their time asleep. The classification was reported by Dr Wolff in a paper in 1966. The six states suggest organised patterns in babies' internal systems but also show early individuality!

**Connect and Extend**

'Birth marks the beginning of the transition from external to internal self-regulation for infants. Acquiring regular sleep patterns, regulating crying and later, emotions are universal developmental tasks'. So begins the abstract of the paper: Meléndez, L. (2005). Parental beliefs and practices around early self-regulation. *Infants & Young Children: An Interdisciplinary Journal of Special Care Practices*, 18, 136–146. What part does the development of self-regulation have in other areas of development?

1. *Regular sleep*. This is complete rest. We can see slow regular breathing with non-rapid eye movements (NREM). Brain activity is slow. Non-rapid eye movements are when the eyes move around beneath the lids. Brain activity is on 'screen-saver' mode.

2. *Irregular sleep*. Here there is some rapid eye movement (REM) and some body movements. Breathing is irregular. Since so much of a newborn's time is spent asleep, REM becomes important to protect the babies' eyes (providing a water lubricant) and also to balance 'down-time' with time when they engage with their surroundings and stimulate their brains.

3. *Drowsiness*. In this state the baby's eyes are open and there maybe some general activity.

4. *Quiet alertness*. The baby shows interest in the immediate surroundings and some activity.

5. *Alert activity*. There are short bursts of movement.

6. *Crying*. An important type of early communication as well as signalling that the baby requires important physical needs to be met (like warmth, food and feeling safe).

Research (Sparrow, 2007; Saran, 2007) indicates that we may be pre-programmed to respond to a crying baby. It is interesting to note that obvious cross-cultural differences exist in responses to a crying infant. In most Western societies, the child is picked up by the adult, whereas, in other cultures, the practice of carrying the infant in pouches on the mother's back or front decreases crying because of increased warmth and sense of security. Therefore the child is already 'in contact' and does not need picking up.

Psychologist William James wrote in 1890 that a baby experiences the world as a 'blooming, buzzing confusion'. The famous Swiss psychologist Jean Piaget seems to have agreed: not until they are 2 years old do children fully appreciate that the world contains things that behave in predictable ways. In this chapter we set out to demonstrate that James and Piaget were wrong. How are we doing?

Once you understand these six patterns of newborn behaviour, the shifting world of the infant begins to make much more sense. By recognising the different states and realising when they occur and what the expected responses are in each state, parents and professionals can assess the general health of a baby and whether any developmental problems are emerging. How are these assessments made and when do they begin?

## Assessing newborns' capabilities and states

Assessments begin immediately after birth to allow an accurate diagnosis of the child's general health. Assessments identify what the child is capable of doing, which in turn can signal what might be needed. Two tests are commonly used for this. At a very early stage professionals use the **Apgar Scale** (Apgar, 1953) with its acronym A for appearance and heart rate, P for pulse, G for grimace and muscle tone, A for general activity and R for respiration. Scores are given on each of the five characteristics one minute and five minutes after birth. Scores of 7 or beyond indicate good health, 4–6 that some assistance is advisable and a score below 3 that the child is in serious danger.

The **Brazelton Neonatal Behavioural Assessment Scale** (Brazelton *et al.*, 1987) is a second widely used assessment that tests the baby's reflexes, changes in physical state and responsiveness to different stimuli. Both tests provide accurate information and are repeated to give professionals updated and accurate information. As primitive responses disappear or are

**Apgar Scale**
A scale used to assess a newborn's physical state after birth.

**Brazelton Neonatal Behavioural Assessment Scale**
A rating used to assess a newborn's reflexes and responsiveness after birth.

assimilated into higher-order behaviours, so more parts of the baby's brain begin to take control and to develop. Babies' brains do begin to 'flex their muscles' during the first year of life in complex and exciting ways, and it is important for us to know something about how the post-natal brain operates, develops, and to demonstrate how the brain is built for learning. This is what we will be discussing in the following section.

# A post-natal brain built for learning

## Cerebral composition

At birth, a newborn's brain weighs about 450 grams. As a fully mature adult it will be three times this weight. It grows at an astonishing rate: so much so that by the time a child is 3 years old, the brain is 75 per cent of its adult weight and by age 6 it is 90 per cent (Harris & Butterworth, 2002). So, fully grown, the brain weighs approximately 1500 grams or about 3lb, and is much more powerful than any computer we possess.

The things that we as humans are capable of (walking upright, reading and writing, manipulating tools and speaking languages) require a developed brain which is much larger in proportion to body size than other species. It has to be. There is a sort of developmental imperative to grow the largest and most able brain we can, and what controls all this growth and development is the brain itself – its own architect, quantity surveyor, builder and inspector. There are actually four 'brains': one at the top (cortex) used for higher thinking; one at the bottom, the brainstem, for the body's more basic functions like breathing; a central one for our emotions and sexuality; and finally a cerebellum or 'little brain' that deals with balance and posture (see Figure 6.2). The brain grows at the end of the spinal cord. The brain and spinal cord together make up our central nervous system.

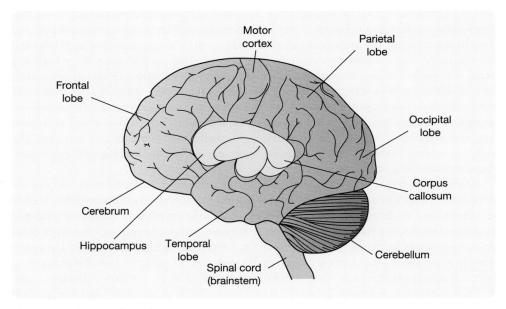

**Figure 6.2** The 'four brains'

Of course, all parts of the brain work together but it is useful to know which parts of the brain take the lead and in what circumstances.

**Cerebrum**
The two interconnected hemispheres of the brain.

**Cerebral cortex**
The outer layer of cells covering the brain's cerebrum and which is responsible for higher functioning.

• • • • • • • • • • • • • • • • •

**Connect and Extend**

There is an argument that 'left-brain' and 'right-brain' designations have no scientific basis, and scientific evidence of audio, visual and kinaesthetic learning styles is not strong: 'Neuroscience and education: Issues and opportunities. A commentary by the Teaching and Learning Research Programme' is available at **www.tlrp.org**.

• • • • • • • • • • • • • • • • •

**Temporal lobe**
Area of the brain that processes characteristics of sound, speech and balance.

**Occipital lobe**
Brain area responsible for processing colour, shape and movement.

**Parietal lobe**
Brain area that processes touch and taste sensations and provides information about spatial location.

**Frontal lobe**
Area of the brain responsible for higher functioning.

**Corpus callosum**
The bundle of fibres that connect both halves of the brain.

The brainstem with its 'reptilian' brain – the most basic part of the brain similar to the entire brain of a reptile – is the first part of our brain to develop and is responsible predominately for our survival. This is the area that governs the very basic 'flight or fight' scenarios such as unthinkingly stepping off the pavement and reacting instantly to a passing car by leaping backwards – flight. Its importance is in continuous monitoring of our situation for anxiety or stress which runs counter to all other thinking and learning. In a context where children feel under pressure, this lower brain function sends messages that do not allow the other parts of the brain to deal appropriately with the situation and assist the child to learn – scared children learn to be scared. The limbic system – a complex set of brain structures that is inside the cerebrum (see Figure 6.2) – takes responsibility for our emotions. This area acts as a gatekeeper by filtering out unhelpful feelings and directing attention to elements of importance. Its functions include long-term memory, calling up emotions from similar situations in the past. If learning in a particular context calls up unpleasant or stressful memories from a child's past learning, it is this system that will recall these same emotions again and again. Finally the neo-cortex containing two distinct hemispheres allows us to perform a range of mental functions.

Our main brain is made up of two hemispheres called the cerebrum and its outer layer, or cerebral cortex, gives it the commonly recognised normal brain shape and wrinkled appearance. The cerebrum has a crossover capacity so that both sides of our body communicate with each other. Take a common example of a child undertaking a writing task. Information coming into the left side about the task goes to the right hemisphere and information from the child's right hand holding the pen is controlled by the left motor cortex. Sensorimotor functions on the body's right side are controlled by the left hemisphere and vice versa. Each hemisphere of the cerebrum has four lobes – temporal, occipital, parietal and frontal – and two other association areas to the front and back that link up information from coming and going from the different parts of the brain. The temporal lobe processes characteristics of sound as well as speech and balance.

The occipital lobe is responsible for visual processing including colour, shape and movement while the parietal lobe processes touch and taste sensations and provides information about spatial location. The frontal lobe has a responsibility for the control of movement as well as carrying out important cognitive functions such as planning and organisation. All four lobes work together in an integrated way with other areas of the brain to organise past and present information. The association areas and take-up are the major parts of each lobe and are concerned with memory, personality and intelligence. Uniting both sides of the brain is a series of nerve fibres called the corpus callosum (interestingly this area is thicker in girls, which in part explains why girls learn to talk and read earlier than boys). Although the brain's two hemispheres do work together, it is common to separate out the functions of each hemisphere to explain its main function. In simple terms, the left hemisphere is that which deals with logical aspects that involve details, part information rather than whole picture and logic. The right hemisphere deals with holistic imaging, spontaneity and intuition. Figure 6.3 shows the respective functions of each hemisphere.

So what? Well first of all, the more we know about how a brain works the more likely we are to recognise patterns of development and learning, to match experiences to develop different kinds of learning and to discern preferences for different learning experiences. Earlier we explained that the cerebral cortex is the part of the brain that houses rational or reasoned functions. Brain research confirms that both sides of the brain (and much of the brain) are involved in nearly every human activity – just tapping a finger on the desk fires off millions of small electrical connections right across the brain. Remember that although most people have a dominant side, this dominance is a preference. When learning is new, difficult or 'upsetting' we prefer to learn in a certain way; and while no ability is isolated on one side of the brain, the characteristics commonly attributed to each side of the brain serve to inform us what ways of learning things would be more efficient. Just as it was more important for our purposes to determine

| Left | Right |
|---|---|
| Verbal, focusing on numbers, words and symbols | Visual, focusing on images, patterns |
| Analytical, led by logic | Intuitive, led by feelings |
| Process ideas sequentially, one step at a time | Processes ideas simultaneously |
| Like making lists and planning | 'Mind pictures' used to remember things |
| Likely to follow rules without questioning them | Enjoys touching and feeling actual objects |
| | Unlikely to read instruction manual before trying |

**Figure 6.3** Functions of the brain hemisphere
Some of the characteristics associated with left and right brain dominance.

that different parts of the brain have different functions rather than learn the exact function for each part, likewise it is not so much that we are biologically right brain or left brain dominant, but that we are more comfortable with the learning strategies characteristics of one over the other.

Having considered some of the physical components of the brain and the functions of its different areas, let us now look at what processes actually take place in it which leads on to the importance of early learning.

## Cerebral processes

As we said, the weight of a neonate's brain is about a third of adult size and looks very similar. The main parts – we called them the four brains – described above, are all present as are the 100 billion brain cells or **neurons** that make it up! Neurons are nerve cells that send and receive electrical impulses to and from all other parts of the brain and through this process form these other parts of the brain (Figure 6.4). At the top of the neurons are branch-like structures called **dendrites**. Signals pass between neurons or to one of the dendrites across the gap between the cells called the **synapse** and along the **axon** via neurotransmitters (Figure 6.5). The more dendrites at its head or terminals at the bottom of the neuron, the more connections with other neurons can be made. Shortly we shall see how early stimulation is essential to enable this whole process to take place and to assist in early learning (Als *et al.*, 2004).

Signals travel fastest in those neurons covered in a fatty layer called **myelin**. A second type of nerve cell, **glia**, helps to nourish the neurons in a process known as **myelination**. It is this process of encasing the neurons in this sheath of fat that makes the neuron a more effective transmitter. When axons are fully myelinated, they can send messages up to 12 times faster than before. Myelination begins in the prenatal period, about 6 months into pregnancy, which is around the same time as the foetus begins to respond to sound. At birth, those areas of the brain are directly responsible for breathing, heart beat and reflex activity of the neonate function because they are myelinated. The process increases quickly in early childhood, with myelination not complete until at least the late teens (Fischer & Rose, 1995) or perhaps even later.

**Neurons**
The nerve cells that send and receive electrical signals to the brain and the nervous system.

**Dendrites**
The part of the neuron that receives signals from other neurons and sends the information to the cell body.

**Synapse**
The gap between the end of one neuron and the dendrites of another.

**Axon**
A long thread-like part of a nerve cell, conducting impulses from the cell body.

**Myelin**
A fatty layer that covers neurons.

**Glia**
Cells whose function is to support neurons.

**Myelination**
The process by which the neurons of the central nervous system become covered in an insulating fatty layer (myelin) which allows an increase in speed of the electrical impulses.

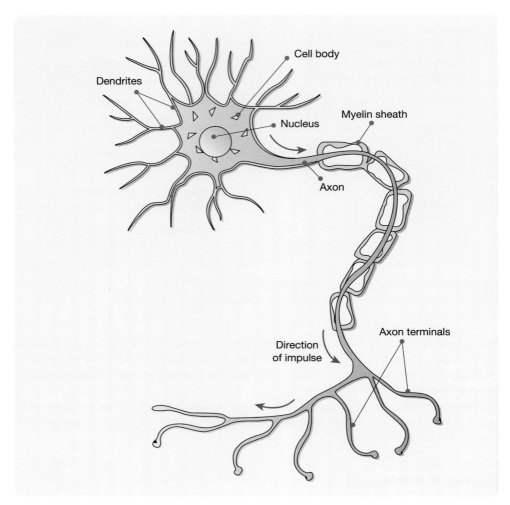

**Figure 6.4**  A brain cell or neurone

Neurons are nerve cells that send and receive electrical impulses to and from all other parts of the brain and throught this process from these other parts of the brain.

**Synaptogenesis**
The process of proliferation of the connections between neurons in early development.

**Synaptic pruning**
The process through which the brain rids itself of unused brain cells.

• • • • • • • • • • • • • • • • •
**Connect and Extend**
There is more information about the formation of the brain in the third section of Chapter 5 'Prenatal development' that precedes a discussion of foetal behaviour and learning. Why at 26 weeks do folds appear on the surface of the brain?
• • • • • • • • • • • • • • • • •

The process takes place from bottom to top which explains why we can walk before we can talk. It starts in the spinal cord, midbrain and hindbrains and finally in the forebrain, corresponding to increased use of this area of the brain for higher thinking and executive functioning as the child gets older.

Earlier research claimed that newborns have a much greater number of neurons than adults and by 12 months they have twice as many as adults (Huttenlocher, 1990) but more recent research in Denmark suggests that the number of neurons in developing parts of the brain are about the same (Larsen *et al.*, 2006). Neurons continue to make vital connections with others during the first year in a process known as **synaptogenesis**. Neurons that make successful connections with others remain while the brain rids itself of those neurons that are unsuccessful in making connection with others by **synaptic pruning**. It is a 'use it or lose' culture, with only the fittest surviving. Making connections is a useful way of thinking about one of the cornerstones of learning and cognition: the development of memory. Without memory a baby would not be able to store, retain and retrieve information – and it is information that makes the difference between thoughtful action and primitive reflexes. Research on early memory is so important we now 'spotlight' it in the *Focus on Theory* feature.

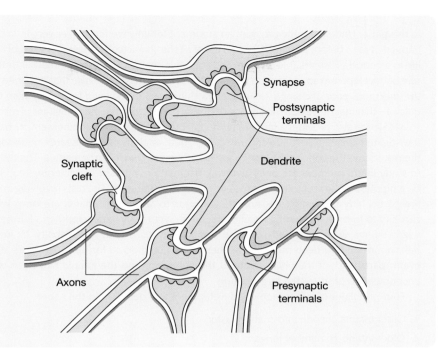

**Figure 6.5** Signal transmission

Signals pass between neurons or to one of the dendrites across the gap between the cells called the synapse and along the axon via neurotransmitters.

*Source*: www.sci-recovery.org

## Focus on Theory

### Infant Memory Development

What is your earliest memory? I think I remember sitting up in my pram outside a sweet-shop in Hoole, Chester. I also definitely remember upsetting my potty quite by accident and that my mother didn't see the funny side of it. The first memory is very hazy and in some ways I doubt it, as there were countless later times that I skulked outside the sweetshop gazing at the rows of bottled sweets in unashamed greed. The second is a definite as I can still remember the look of horror on my mother's face. Fortunately I remember nothing more about the consequences of my unfortunate 'accident'. Other than a sweetshop and an upset potty I hardly remember anything about the first four years of my life and this is not uncommon. In a paper 'Infant memory development: Implications for childhood amnesia', psychologist Harlene Hayne of the University of Otago writes:

> **When asked to recall their earliest personal memories, most children and adults have virtually no recollection of their infancy or early childhood. This phenomenon is commonly referred to as childhood amnesia. The fate of our earliest memories has puzzled psychologists for over 50 years, particularly in light of the importance of early experience in human development. Empirical research has shown that infants can both learn and remember very early in development making the ultimate fate of early memories even more mysterious.**
>
> **(Hayne, 2004, p 33)**

In this paper Harlene Hayne provides an argument for why we remember very little of what happened to us before the age of 3 or 4. First of all she characterises these first years of a child's life as a period of remarkable physical and cognitive change. She says 'at no other time is the rate of development so rapid or so dramatic' (p 33). She makes the case that it is quite simply the enormous pace of change – learning new things very quickly and forgetting them equally quickly – that means we have no chance of storing or retrieving the many millions of memories.

Ms Hayne also provides a fascinating study of the ways in which infant memory has been investigated over the past 60 years or so. Her meta-analysis of the research methods used, the results and the conclusions drawn are fascinating and well worth reading. The tasks used to study infant memory are ones involving habituation, operant conditioning (e.g. sucking on a nipple, kicking feet to make a mobile move) and imitation. The tests involving imitation are particularly interesting because they appear to show that infants are born with the capacity to imitate – including facial expressions – very early in development. Furthermore, when infants were provided with the opportunity to display their ability to imitate a behaviour that had been modelled to them, they could do so for up to 24 hours after the event, particularly if they had practised the behaviour and the infants had been verbally encouraged to produce the target action.

Four principles of infant memory development are identified in the paper:

1. Older infants encode information faster.

2. Older infants remember longer.

3. Older infants exploit a wider range of retrieval cues – e.g. a word that 'sparks' another word.

4. Forgotten memories can be retrieved through the presentation of a reminder – perhaps a smell or sound.

The argument continues that infant amnesia is not the result of having some kind of different memory. Rather that infant memories, because of the speed of information encoding (the first stage of creating a memory), do not provide sufficient time to create cues that allow for longer-term retrieval and the pace of synaptic pruning signals that forgetting is an instinctive drive. Harlene Hayne concludes:

> **If forgetting occurs within days or weeks during early infancy, it is hardly surprising that those memories are unavailable when we try to access them after intervals of years or decades! Over the course of development, however, the forgetting function gradually flattens, increasing the accessibility of a given memory even after very long delays.**

**(Hayne, 2004, pp 62–63)**

The full text of this paper is available at www.ballarat.edu.au/ard/bssh/school/nr521/childhood%20amnesia2.pdf

**Connect and Extend**

What do 4- and 5-year-olds remember about the first 2 years of life? Has childhood amnesia 'set in' at this early stage? Having spoken to 40 children, Emily Cleveland and Elaine Reese conclude that for events that happened before age 2, only around half of children's recall was accurate. For events that occurred after this age, over 75 per cent of children's recall was accurate. Complete forgetting of very early childhood has not yet occurred by age 5. Read this fascinating paper: Cleveland, E. & Reese, E. (2008). Children remember early childhood: Long-term recall across the offset of childhood amnesia. *Applied Cognitive Psychology, 22,* 127–142.

What else do we know about early memory and the brains of very young children? The brain of the neonate is perhaps best characterised by cortical areas that process different types of information and have different functions. Described earlier were the 'different' functions of the cerebrum, with both hemispheres becoming responsible for particular functions: the left responsible for functions including aspects of language and analytical thinking and the right for emotional expression and intuition. Remember that actions on the right side of the body are governed by the left hemisphere and those on the left side by the right side of the brain. **Lateralisation** is the process by which the brain's two halves become responsible for specialised functions. This also results in the child having a preference for using one side of the body over the other: a process which it is believed begins in the womb. This preference is not complete by birth but, by age 2, most children have a strong left- or right-hand preference which then continues.

**Lateralisation**
The process in which the brain's two halves become specialised and can carry out specific functions.

**Reflect**

There was a time when left-handedness was thought of as a sign of the devil. The Latin word *sinister* meaning 'left' is used in English for evil or threatening, while the Latin word for right is *dexter*, as in dexterity – a more positive connotation. In many primary schools in the twentieth century, left-handed children were discouraged from writing with their left hands. Is being left-handed a misfortune when learning to write, or is it a sign of greater intelligence and creativity?

**Connect and Extend**

An article from *Science Teacher* discusses the discovery of a gene that may contribute to a person's chance of being left-handed. The gene may also increase risk of schizophrenia. Find the article: Gene for left-handedness. *Science Teacher* 74, 16. Or, for a fascinating historic and classic treatise, read: Stromberg, E. T. & Stromberg, E. L. (1938). Left handedness as a factor influencing academic achievement. *Journal of Social Psychology.* Aug, 9(3), 335–341.

Although strong left- or right-hand preference implies that the brain somehow divides up work equally between both hemispheres, this is not truly the case. It is necessary for the brain to have such specialist functions to allow a greater range of abilities than if both sides performed the same functions. However, it should be remembered that the corpus callosum's role is to bridge the gap between the hemispheres and in this role many of the functions of the brain such as memory become integrated and connected. Communication between the hemispheres continues and accelerates between the ages of 3 and 6 (Giedd *et al.*, 1999), a critical period of brain development.

## Critical periods and brain plasticity

Research with patients who have suffered brain injuries has revealed the existence of critical periods for brain development. This is a period when recovery from damage is accommodated by the brain and allows constituent parts to organise themselves to carry out functions that the damaged regions are no longer capable of. The critical period extends to the first 6 years of life. After this the ability to organise diminishes due to increased lateralisation of the brain. For senses such as vision and audition, the critical period for development is very early because vital pathways are being laid down right from birth (Dubois *et al.*, 2006). Take, for example, a child of 2 whose opportunities to hear spoken language are severely restricted. If the child cannot hear sounds, then the ability to learn the mother language is compromised as will be the ability to learn other languages later on.

Brain scans (EEG and fMRI) have shown intensified frontal lobe activity at certain times in the early development of crawling, visual searching for objects in the environment and language in the preschool years (Dyet *et al.*, 2006) and later during the development of higher-order thinking in the upper primary and secondary school phases (Constable *et al.*, 2008).

This ability for periods of intense development demonstrates the brain's plasticity. Up to the middle of the last century, it was generally believed that the brain was 'hard-wired' and that it was impossible to alter development that was genetically pre-set. We now know this to be inaccurate. Our brains are constantly organising and reorganising from birth. Connections that are made early in life from experiences we have and from anticipating new experiences remodel and refine our genetic wiring. As previously noted, these changes take place in sensitive periods but also across the lifespan. This remarkable plasticity can also occur, as we have said, in situations where trauma or damage has taken place. For example, children with hearing impairments are still able to communicate because they utilise parts of their brain that are functioning normally. Figure 6.3 earlier showed that language is 'controlled' by the left side of the brain which, if damaged, could lead to communication difficulties. By using a sign language such as Makaton, with its physical motor component controlled by the right brain, children are able to process language through the right hemisphere and to better communicate.

So, brain development is a combination of maturation and experience and is a superb example of environment acting with genetics. Remember, although our brain development is not dissimilar to that of other mammals, it does take much longer to reach full maturity. If it were quicker, more human brain development would take place in the womb's very limited

**Plasticity**
The brain is flexible and adaptable.

**Makaton**
An international communication programme combining speech, hand actions and symbols.

environment. Development over extended time and through experience outside of the womb allows for a much larger cerebral cortex to develop, which is important for many of our advanced abilities and behaviours. Crucial amongst those behaviours is our ability to learn.

## Summary 2

Before moving on, let's summarise what we have learned in the middle section of this chapter:

- Reflexes are automatic responses to stimulation, with no conscious thinking, and are in no way learned.
- Primitive reflexes are controlled by the lowest and most primitive (meaning first-formed) part of the human brain, the brainstem.
- The set of reflexes include survival or adaptive reflexes (e.g. sucking and grasping).
- Other reflexes may have had their origins as behaviours for survival and are often adapted and subsumed into new learned behaviours.
- Almost all primitive reflexes outlive their usefulness and are inhibited and discarded.
- If a reflex is retained it can cause developmental and behavioural problems later on (e.g. spinal galant reflex and bed-wetting, or Moro reflex and ADHD).
- Patterns of infant behaviour have been identified into six different states of consciousness.
- Human babies have to spend more time developing their brains than other species.
- Brain research confirms that both sides of the brain (and much of the brain) are involved in nearly every human activity.
- Infant learning and memory involve processes of synaptogenesis (connection making) and synaptic pruning (discarding brain cells that are not making useful connections).
- Brain development is a combination of maturation and experience and is an example of environment acting with genetics.

### Connect and Extend

Review the theories section in Chapter 2 before reading the next section. Remember that theories allow us to explain phenomena, to predict, to provide a range of strategies to be used, and to understand the complex science of child development. Theories provide information that can help practitioners influence children's learning by providing developmentally appropriate practice, enable carers to optimise child-care environments, therapists to provide the most appropriate treatment, and parents to identify and interpret their children's behaviours.

# Early learning

So how do newborns and very young children learn? Clues to this were discussed in Chapter 5 and you may remember we said that foetuses seem to spend more time awake in the third trimester because their neurological organisation has improved. Even *in utero*, their growing brains seek stimulation by exploring their immediate environment. Also remember that foetal learning is largely through habituation where the child 'makes a habit' of attending to a new exciting stimulus and stops attending to sensations that have become boring, which suggests the foetus has a real capacity to acquire and remember information (DiPietro, 2005). As we discussed earlier in this chapter, babies are born retaining primitive reflexes which provide a basis for future voluntary skill development and functioning. The CNS allows reflexes to disappear through a decreased response to repeated stimuli – habituation – or to be integrated in increasingly complex movements that are controlled by higher levels of the brain. This is the first form of learning related to the ways in which new learning happens for everybody (those learning theories that we first discussed in Chapter 2) and now will look at this in more detail in relation to neonatal learning.

The title of this chapter *Neonatal Behaviour and Learning* gives a good clue as to where we go next. Early physical, cognitive and social/emotional development – the three domains of development – have a profound causal and 'reverse causal' relationship with learning that takes place in the first year of life; cognitive development provokes a need for learning, and learning creates further cognitive development.

In the section that follows look for the ways in which we integrate ideas about how:

- developing cognitive powers depends on appropriate learning experiences and at the same time, enables that learning to take place;
- to use the primitive reflexes as 'springboards' to higher cognitive development while learning to do without them;
- to make these ideas into a cohesive whole while reserving the individual requirements for physical, cognitive, social/emotional and learning development;
- ideas we have explored in the first half of this text 'work' with each other and with the themes of child development (continuity, heredity, training, contexts and activity – see Chapter 1).

Theories of how children learn are concerned with how learning affects change and development; how the environment influences a child's development; and how a child understands the world through experiences.

## Classical conditioning

Remember the behaviourist John Watson's view that children were passive recipients of experience and *tabula rasa* (a 'clean slate' – see Chapter 1) to be 'written on' by experience; that children play passive roles in their development and can be conditioned into being and behaving what parents and teachers want them to be. In Chapter 2 we discussed an infamous study (Watson & Raynor, 1920), in which a 9-month-old baby was trained to fear a rat after pairing this stimulus with loud banging sounds, so cried and turned away from the animal. Watson concluded that the environment explained development rather than innate emotions, tendencies or thinking capabilities. This was an example of classical conditioning as described by Russian physiologist Ivan Pavlov, in a famous study where he observed a dog salivating repeatedly in response to the clinking sound of food trays, because the dog associated the sound with the arrival of food. Follow-up work by Watson used these same principles to explain behaviours exhibited by children.

There is evidence from historic research by developmental psychobiologist Regina Sullivan and colleagues (1991) suggesting that complex associative learning – learning by classical conditioning – is seen in newborns within the first 48 hours of life. One-day-old awake infants received ten 30-second pairings of a citrus odour and tactile stimulation provided by stroking. Control babies received only the odour, only the stroking, or the stroking followed by the odour. The next day, all infants, in either the awake or sleep state, were given five 30-second bursts of the odour. The results indicate that only those infants who received the simultaneous pairings of the odour and stroking exhibited conditioned responding (head turning toward the odour) to the citrus odour; both awake and sleeping infants exhibited conditioned responses.

Learning by associating smell with survival reflexes appears to be a major part of learning in the first few days and weeks. Infants imprint on their mothers in the first instance owing to experiences in the womb such as the taste of mother's amniotic fluid. The CNS of very young and helpless infants is specialised for making the strongest possible attachment to their caregiver. During the first post-natal days, infants show a sensitive period for learning and are particularly susceptible to learning an attraction to their mother's odour. Infants form the attachment even if maltreated by the caregiver, so strong is the drive to form the attachment (Roth & Sullivan, 2005). Therefore both classical and operant conditioning (see below) break down when strong instincts are at play (Kirsch *et al.*, 2004) – in this case the survival instinct to form an attachment.

# Operant conditioning

**● ● ● ● ● ● ● ● ● ● ● ● ● ● ● ●**
**Connect and Extend**
Is it possible to train very young infants? Read a study investigating the effects of training preterm infants' kicking co-ordination to move a cot mobile: Heathcock, J. & and Galloway, J. (2007). The effects of movement training on performance in the mobile paradigm in infants born preterm. *Journal of Sport & Exercise Psychology, 29*, S84.
**● ● ● ● ● ● ● ● ● ● ● ● ● ● ● ●**

Young children 'operate' on the environment by voluntarily engaging in certain observable behaviours because of the effects of the behaviours. This type of learning involves an infant developing a new response to something that is happening to them because they like it and want it to happen again. So, the emphasis is on the consequences of behaviour and not simply pairing certain stimuli together as in classical conditioning. This is not something that is done to the infant; this is the infant learning to do something in order for a particular stimulus to be repeated when required by the baby. It will be helpful in the following discussion to bring to mind the work of B. F. Skinner that we first discussed in Chapter 2. He invented the 'operant conditioning chamber' which allowed him to measure learned responses of rats and birds pressing levers or pecking keys to obtain food or to stop loud noises (Slater, 2004).

There are four contexts of operant conditioning. Note the terms 'positive' and 'negative' are not used in their common sense, but rather 'positive' refers to something added or included, and 'negative' refers to something being removed or taken away.

1. *Positive reinforcement* occurs when a baby's behaviour is followed by a pleasant consequence. It could be argued that babies learn to cry when they feel hungry because that prompts the good feeling of being fed, so increases the frequency of crying when hungry. In Skinner's operant conditioning box experiment, a stimulus such as food or sugar solution was delivered when the rat engaged in a learned behaviour, such as pressing a lever.

2. *Negative reinforcement* occurs when a baby's response is followed by the removal of something unpleasant so increasing that behaviour's frequency. Again, it could be argued that a baby will cry when the nice warm wet feeling in her nappy has turned cold or is 'smarting' her nappy rash. A cry will bring mum or dad to remove the offending wetness and to apply soothing cream. In the Skinner box experiment, negative reinforcement was a loud noise continuously sounding inside the rat's box until it engaged in the learned behaviour, such as pressing a lever, when the loud noise was removed.

3. *Positive punishment* (a disturbing notion when applied to very small children) occurs when a baby's behaviour is followed by an unpleasant stimulus, such as introducing a loud noise, resulting in a decrease in that behaviour. The closest my young children got to a punishment was a loud clap of my hands (a shock) and a very firm 'No!' whereupon Rebecca would stop what she was attempting to do and her little face would dissolve into tears (quickly followed by a cuddle). Tom on the other hand would look at me as if I had finally 'lost it' then carry on regardless, until physically removed and diverted! In Skinner's box, it was an electric shock when the rat (expecting food) pressed the lever. The rat soon learned not to press the lever.

4. *Negative punishment* occurs when a baby's undesirable behaviour is followed by the removal of something nice, such as taking away a baby's toy resulting in a decrease in that behaviour. Well that is the theory. In practice the removal of a favourite toy as a negative punishment is generally greeted with an ear-splitting cacophony of screaming and wailing – much worse than the former undesirable behaviour. In this way a baby has learned to instantly change negative punishment into positive reinforcement because the toy is returned to mollify the infant!

**Reflect**  Most people would agree that it is wrong to punish a baby, but that punishment is an appropriate method of helping children develop a sense of right and wrong and to learn self-regulation. So at what stage of development is it OK to start punishing and what form should that punishment take? What effect does the use of some forms of punishment have on development?

So far this all sounds very behaviourist (because conditioning is the root of behaviourism) and seems to characterise babies' learning as little more than developing primitive responses: no higher order cognition, little conscious decision to set about learning. However, you may remember from Chapter 2 that social learning theory may be seen as a response to such criticism. Theorists (notably Julian Rotter, Albert Bandura and Edwin Sutherland) subscribe to a viewpoint, while accepting the role of conditioning in learning, that children also learn by watching and imitating others. Look below at the *Policy, Research and Praxis* feature for a detailed examination of how children learn in the early years and then we will discuss observational learning.

## Policy, Research and Praxis

### Learning from birth to 5: The revised framework for the early years foundation stage

The revised framework for children from birth to age 5 called the *Early Years Foundation Stage* (EYFS) became statutory in England in September 2012. It sets the standards for all early years providers to ensure that children learn and develop well and keep healthy and safe. The document is a slimmed down version of the earlier EYFS framework published in 2008 and responds to recommendations made in an independent review of the EYFS by Dame Claire Tickell (2011).

The framework is integral to policy drives to support families and demonstrates a commitment to promoting learning and teaching through a broad range of skills and knowledge to provide children with the foundation for good future progress into school and beyond. In its Introduction it states, 'every child deserves the best possible start in life and the support that enables them to fulfil their potential. Children develop quickly in the early years and a child's experiences between birth and age five have a major impact on their future life chances. A secure, safe and happy childhood is important in its own right. Good parenting and high quality early learning together provide the foundation children need to make the most of their abilities and talents as they grow up' (EYFS, 2012, p 2). There are new areas of learning and development which consist of three *Prime* areas of communication and language: physical development and personal and social development, included for their important role in igniting young children's curiosity and enthusiasm for learning and building their capacity to learn. For babies and very young children, this is the foundation upon which all later learning is built. These *Prime* areas are later applied and reinforced by four *Specific* areas of literacy: mathematics, understanding the world and expressive arts and design.

The framework makes it clear that all seven areas of learning are important and interconnected and that early years practitioners must consider a child's individual needs and interests and development stage to plan learning experiences. To support early educators' understanding of learning and development, non-statutory guidance aptly named *Development Matters* has been produced. This guides observational assessment of children and helps to inform on whether a child is showing typical development, may be at risk of delay or is ahead for their age. What are especially helpful are the three 'characteristics of effective learning' contained in this guidance which are identified as:

| Playing and exploring | Active learning | Creating and thinking critically |
|---|---|---|
| - finding out and exploring | - being involved | - having their own ideas |
| - playing with what they know | - keeping trying | - making links |
| - being willing to 'have a go' | - enjoying achieving | - choosing ways to do things |

The revised EYFS requires practitioners to assess learning and development and to share progress with parents in the prime areas between 22 and 36 months and later at the end when the child is 5. The framework recognises that learning begins from birth in the ways babies communicate with others, how they move and learn to socialise, and provides a framework for learning to progress through school and life.

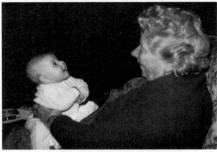

Isobel and Rebecca Hughes: nanny and granddaughter. Who is getting and giving the most pleasure here? Perhaps a smile is worth a thousand words.

*Source*: Malcolm Hughes.

At 1-year-old the smile has also fully developed.

*Source*: © Pearson Education Ltd / Jules Selmes.

# Observational learning

Psychologist Albert Bandura (1977) proposed that significant learning takes place by children choosing to watch other people who act as 'models'. (Remember the Bobo doll: a series of classic experiments when children watched an adult repeatedly punch and kick a Bobo doll.) No reinforcement of behaviour is necessary (nobody praised the children for kicking and punching the doll) for learning to take place but it is required to increase the probability of the behaviour being repeated.

Bandura regarded modelling as a powerful tool for learning that has both negative (aggressive behaviours) and positive (sharing, turn-taking, etc.) outcomes and he identified four sets of cognitive processes within observational learning (1989a):

1. *Attention* – the child notices something in the environment.

2. *Retention* – the child remembers what was noticed.

3. *Reproduction* – the child produces an action that is a copy of what was noticed.

4. *Motivation* – the environment delivers a consequence that changes the probability the behaviour will be performed again (reinforcement and punishment).

What contribution does observational learning make to development and cognitive development in particular? This may be best explained by making reference to the five themes of child development we identified in Chapter 1. In developmental terms, processes of attention, retention, reproduction and motivation become more sophisticated as children mature (the continuity theme of child development) and allow more effective self-regulation of behaviours (babies as 'active learners' theme). The theory acknowledges the influence of the environment on learning through the role played by models (the context theme), that the ability to observe and to mimic is a hard-wired ability (the heredity theme) and that this ability can be improved and developed (the training theme). One example of an observed behaviour, which is then copied, refined and experimented with by babies, is smiling.

Babies practise smiling *in utero*. How do we know? Well, remember the wonderful images created using Stuart Campbell's 3D and 4D techniques that we looked at in Chapter 5. Looking at Professor Campbell's book you see an engaging image of a foetus at 36 weeks who is giving the widest grin (Campbell puts this down to 'a happy thought') but we are not suggesting that unborn babies make the face of smiling in pleasure. Our view is that smiling is a social skill, one of the most powerful ways in which we communicate non-verbally and is (unlike babies grasping hold of a finger, which is engaging but purely a primitive reflex) a learned behaviour using the 'muscle-memory' of the face, practised in the non-social world (for most babies) of the mother's womb.

By a month old, a baby's expression is still pretty vague but becomes more alert, progressing to a social smile and responsive vocalisations at about 5 or 6 weeks (Sheridan, 1997). This is not surprising as almost every facial expression the baby sees is a much loved carer smiling at them – who can frown at a baby? Babies learn to respond to a smile and to communicate their own pleasure. Just look at the photograph of Rebecca winning over her grandmother Isobel. Rebecca has learned to do this by copying, but has also refined and improved her smile. We think you might agree that this is now 'a potent weapon'. No matter how delightful the smile is in a baby of Rebecca's age, it is also fleeting at this stage.

Development of the smile continues (the continuity theme). Different types of smiles were investigated by psychologist Alan Fogel and colleagues (2006) during two mother–infant games – peekaboo and tickle – at 6 and 12 months. Rather than a single smile expression that differs only in how wide the smile is (amplitude), the authors found a complex family of different smile expressions differing in their duration and amplitude in response to the playing of the game, the set-up (anticipation of the fun to come) and the climax of the game. Both the type of smiling and amplitude of smiling are controlled independently by the infant (babies as active learners) in relation to the context. These findings reveal developing systematic and context-specific nuances in infant smiles in the second-half of the first year.

**Connect and Extend**

This article provides practitioners with basic information to help them and parents become better able to recognise the expressive signals of the infants and young children in their care: Sullivan, M. & Lewis, M. (2003). Emotional expressions of young infants and children. *Infants & Young Children, 16,* 120.

# The importance of early experiences

We have already seen that early stimulation starts in the womb, but it is after birth when the influence of the environment really has its impact. Studies of animals in 'enriched environments' that have toys and mazes have shown positive effects on their neural development (Jones *et al.*, 1997). We could note that here many animal studies into 'enriched environments' really show animals in impoverished environments (i.e. standard laboratory cages), not enriched when compared with an animal's natural environment. For we humans, the adaptability of our brains creates more neural connections to meet the demands of the environment and this is especially true in critical periods. Conversely, a lack of stimulation restricts this dendritic growth, with neurons competing to connect with others in a 'use it or lose it' culture where only the fittest do survive. Childhood is the optimum time for neural development due to 'exuberant connectivity' (Diamond and Hopson, 1998, p 63). By making these connections, we are constantly making sense of the world around us. Early synaptic connections develop and refine our genetic wiring in a wonderful dynamic between inheritance and environment.

It is in the first 2–3 years that the vital foundations of thinking, language and personality are laid down. Early activities in post-natal life help to lay down the brain's hard-wiring. It is in those first few months of life that the brain is constantly organising itself and has the greatest plasticity talked about earlier. All essential processes in brain wiring are influenced by the experience that infants have: dendritic growth, synaptic formation and myelination. Once outside this stage, the ability to rewire and reorganise diminishes but does not disappear (Stiles, 2000).

Back in 1964, Benjamin Bloom revealed that 50 per cent of our ability to learn is developed by age 4 (Bloom, 1964). These are the ages when children's learning pathways are set down and all future learning built upon this base. Input is critical. In the preschool years this input is mostly provided by parents and family. These links still need to be continued as the child progresses into learning in crèches, nurseries and school settings.

**Summary 3**

We now summarise what you have learned in the final section of this chapter:

- Foetal learning is largely through habituation, where the child 'makes a habit' of attending to a new exciting stimulus and stops attending to sensations that have become boring.
- There is evidence from historic research by developmental psychobiologist Regina Sullivan and colleagues (1991) suggesting that complex associative learning – learning by classical conditioning – is seen in newborns within the first 48 hours after birth
- There are four contexts of operant conditioning: positive and negative reinforcement; and positive and negative punishment.
- Both classical and operant conditioning break down when strong instincts are at play, for example, the survival instinct to form an attachment despite the infant being abused by the caregiver.
- Significant learning takes place by children choosing to watch other people who act as 'models' – observational learning. There are four processes: attention, retention, reproduction and motivation. Learning to smile is an example of observational learning.
- It is after birth when the influence of the environment really has its impact.
- The research evidence informs us that the richer and the more varied a baby's early activities, and the more her developing brain is stimulated, the larger and more powerful it becomes.

## Conclusion

The 'miracle of child development' does not stop at birth, but carries on by building on our unique genetic wiring in a wonderful dynamic between inheritance and environment. In this chapter we have discussed a newborn's appearance and capabilities, with particular emphasis on the senses since these are the media for early learning. The processes, capacities and characteristics of successful early learning were discussed in detail, and we proposed that the neonate's brain is ideally set up to learn. Finally in this chapter, evidence for the importance of stimulating activities in early childhood was presented which have clear implications for educators, parents and carers. In Chapters 4–6 we have looked at the foundations of development, prenatal development and early integrated development and learning. We now move on to chapters dealing with individual aspects of development for children in their first 11 years: physical growth, sensory and perceptual development, cognition, language, emotions and personality, and the social and moral world of the child. But before we do, we need to confess something. Both of the authors hold very strong views about how children should be supported, encouraged and nurtured but we have tried not to proselytise about one correct way to be a good parent, carer or teacher. Not until now. In the remaining chapters you will find a ubiquitous theme: the vital importance of play and playing to the holistic development of children.

There is no better activity for learning and development than play. Consider again the stimulating experiences encouraged in the revised framework for the early years foundation stage explained in the *Policy, Research and Praxis* feature above; many of them relate to play activities. Watch any group of young children at play and you will see them using the environment around them as a learning centre of shapes, words, objects, sounds and people. Play is the vehicle for interactions (Wooldridge & Shapka, 2012), through which cognitive, social, emotional and physical development is enhanced. Play is an integrating mechanism, drawing on past experiences, making connections, exploring possibilities and making meanings (David, 1999). It is the natural curriculum of life (Jensen, 2000) in which children act out scenarios and future roles. The games that youngsters play become the real-world activities of adulthood, conquering fears, building physical capabilities and strengthening neurological structures.

Of course we are not alone in believing in the power of play. In the 2005 edition of the well-titled *The Excellence of Play*, early years' specialist Janet Moyles brings together 24 contributors to provide a powerful and passionate argument that children's experiences of play can create happier, more learned and better developed children in the present, and well-balanced contributing citizens in the future. We believe that the importance of play to continuing development is no less momentous once past the early years, and in the chapters ahead we will be making the case. First of all is Chapter 7 where we will explore the course and stages of physical and motor development and the factors that influence it, with a particular focus on childhood obesity, preschool and school physical education, and special needs. In the meantime, review the main headlines of this chapter in the *Summary Table*.

## Summary Table
### Neonatal Behaviour and Learning

### Childbirth (pp 150–152)

Human childbirth is divided into three stages of labour: dilation of the cervix brought about by contractions of the uterus; 'the pushing stage' – ejection of the infant; and ejection of the placenta. It is a potentially traumatic affair for baby and mother and the level of trauma can affect the development of the child. For example, oxygen starvation during birth and the resultant brain damage can result in cerebral palsy. Recent research shows that between 5 and 10 per cent of cases of cerebral palsy can be associated with obstetric experience.

### The characteristics and capabilities of newborns (pp 153–163)

Babies are well equipped for surviving, close to their mother in their new life outside the womb. They arrive with a range of reflexes, psychological and behavioural capabilities, and a voracious appetite to do and to know.

#### Sensory capabilities (pp 153–156)

They can experience the four taste sensations (salty, sour, bitter and sweet) and show a preference for sweet. A newborn's vision is poor, limited to objects only about 20 cm away (the distance between a nursing breast and mother's face). Newborns can distinguish the mother's voice from that of others, which suggests a familiarity from the time

spent *in utero*. Proprioception, which gives us an awareness of where our body is and what it is doing, is well developed from experiences *in utero* but the effects of environment can speed up the development of this vital sixth sense.

### Primitive reflexes (pp 157–161)

Primitive reflexes are automatic responses to stimulation, with no conscious thinking, and are in no way learned. These reflexes are controlled by the lowest and most primitive (meaning first-formed) part of the human brain, the brainstem and include survival or adaptive reflexes (e.g. sucking and grasping). Other reflexes may have had their origins as behaviours for survival and are often adapted and subsumed into new learned behaviours. Almost all primitive reflexes outlive their usefulness and are inhibited and discarded. However, if a reflex is retained beyond its period of usefulness, it can cause developmental and behavioural problems later on (e.g. spinal galant reflex and bed-wetting or Moro reflex and ADHD).

### Organised activity (pp 161–163)

Patterns of infant behaviour have been identified into six different states of consciousness: regular sleep; irregular sleep; drowsiness; quiet alertness; alert activity; and crying. All states of consciousness are needed to help develop an awareness of self and being able to control moving between the different states. By recognising the different states and realising when they occur and what the expected responses are in each state, parents and professionals can assess the general health of a baby and if any developmental problems are emerging.

## A post-natal brain built for learning
(pp 163–170)

Human babies have to spend more time developing their brains than other species. It is as if there is a developmental imperative to grow the largest and most able brain we can. Certainly brain research confirms that both sides of the brain (and much of the brain) are involved in nearly every human activity. Right from the start infant learning and memory involve processes of synaptogenesis (connection making) and synaptic pruning (discarding brain cells that are not making useful connections). So, brain development is a combination of maturation and experience and is an example of the environment acting with genetics.

## Early learning (pp 170–175)

Infant learning is largely through habituation, where the child 'makes a habit' of attending to a new exciting stimulus and stops attending to sensations that have become boring. The central nervous system allows reflexes to disappear through a decreased response to repeated stimuli – habituation – or to be integrated in increasingly complex movements that are controlled by higher levels of the brain. This is the first form of learning, not unrelated to the ways in which new learning happens for everybody.

### Classical conditioning (p 171)

There is evidence from historic research by developmental psychobiologist Regina Sullivan and colleagues (1991) suggesting that complex associative learning – learning by classical conditioning – is seen in newborns within the first 48 hours of life. One example is where a group of neonates (48 hours) were subjected to a citrus odour combined with the pleasurable experience of being stroked. Twenty-four hours later the infants turned to a repetition of the citrus odour, looking for the pleasure of another massage.

### Operant conditioning (pp 172–173)

This type of learning involves an infant developing a new response to something that is happening to them because they like it and want it to happen again. There are four contexts of operant conditioning: positive and negative reinforcement; and positive and negative punishment, but both classical and operant conditioning break down when strong instincts are at play. For example, infants will maintain their survival instinct to form a life-saving attachment to a principle caregiver despite the infant being abused by the same caregiver.

### Observational learning (pp 174–175)

Significant learning takes place by children choosing to watch other people who act as 'models'; this is called observational learning. There are four processes: attention, retention, reproduction and motivation, which become more sophisticated as children mature. The theory acknowledges the influence of the environment on learning through the role played by models. The ability to observe and to mimic is a hard-wired ability which can be improved and developed. Learning to smile is an example of observational learning.

## The importance of early experiences
(pp 175–176)

It is after birth when the influence of the stimulative experiences from the environment really has an impact. Conversely, a lack of stimulation restricts dendritic growth, with neurons competing to connect with others in a 'use it or lose it' culture where only the fittest survive. The research evidence informs us that the richer and the more varied a baby's early activities, and the more her developing brain is stimulated, the larger and more powerful her brain becomes.

## Going further

Eliot, L. (2001). *What's going on in there? How the brain and mind develop in the first five years of life.* New York: Bantam Books.
An excellent read charting the growth of early senses and linking into the nature–nurture debate.

Bruce, T. (2004). *Developing learning in early childhood.* London: Paul Chapman Publishing.
This book provides concise overviews of relevant research of early childhood development, and can be used as a contemporary reference book by a range of professionals. In particular, we recommend Chapter 1 for a discussion of critical and sensitive periods in cognitive development.

Diamond, M. (2005). *Magic trees of the mind*. London: Dutton.
This book provides a fascinating read on brain development and the role of early experience in forming the mind.

Moyles, J. (Ed.) (2010). *The excellence of play*. Maidenhead: Open University Press.
A text which strongly advocates the benefits of play for learning.

# Useful websites

http://www.ucl.ac.uk/medphys/research/borl/imaging/monstir/brain
Brain imaging of the neonatal brain is being developed at University College London, to help doctors diagnose and treat newborn babies suffering from brain injury. This occurs when breathing difficulties or other problems prevent the baby from receiving sufficient amounts of oxygenated blood during birth.

http://www.nhs.uk/news/2011/07July/Pages/young-baby-emotion-speech.aspx
Babies can tell sad voices at 3 months. A sample of 21 babies, aged 3 to 7 months old, was given a special type of MRI scan to measure the activity in different regions of the brain.

http://www.kcl.ac.uk/
In very premature babies, myelination can be particularly prone to damage. Scientists based at King's College London, scanned 14 healthy babies born at full term. The babies were scanned while asleep using a specially modified, quiet, baby-friendly MRI scanner. To build up a picture of their myelin development, the researchers scanned the infants monthly between 3 and 11 months. By the age of 9 months, myelination was visible in all brain areas and in some regions had developed to a near adult-like level.

# Chapter 7
## The Body and Physical Growth

### Overview

# Introduction

'Stop it Sanjit! Stop that – right now! Thank you!' Mrs Lawson slammed down her office window while still holding the gaze of the startled 6-year-old. The other children ran off squealing their celebration of playtime. Sanjit's discomfort lasted just a moment more. Dismissed by a slight jerk of his teacher's head, Sanjit skipped away to join his friends, reassured by the playful little glint in Mrs Lawson's eye that no permanent damage had been done. The new head teacher continued to gaze out over the school playground. She liked to take a break from the paperwork to spend a few minutes observing the hubbub of playful and learning activity taking place. Sometimes she took out a cup of coffee for the teacher on duty, and stayed for a quick chat – more often than not about the children. She knew almost all their names now – and more: their strengths and weaknesses, special needs, charming ways and the different triggers for giggles and tears. The school was a thorough mix of all kinds of children: different social and ethnic backgrounds, religious beliefs, colours, creeds, shapes and sizes.

Her practised eye followed the hundreds of different exciting things that were happening and the almost daily changes in the children. Their physical differences never ceased to amaze her as even those children in the same year group seemed to vary so much in height and build. Yet there were consistencies too. The younger pupils had lost much of the fat tissue associated with their time as toddlers, while many of the older children appeared tall and lean, or with the tell-tale signs of early obesity.

And there were so many different things going on. One small group had been kicking a ball, dodging in between and around everybody else – much against the playground rules. (There was a different playground for ball games.) Others chased friends, and several children were happily skipping with a large rope. In the play of others, there was jumping and galloping, and on the climbing frame, several children were confidently hanging upside-down and swinging from the bars as others looked on enviously! Yes, it was business as usual in the playground and Mrs Lawson resignedly returned to her paperwork, thinking about the children and what to do about the forbidden football. 'When I finish filling in these forms, I'll go and have a quiet word with Sanjit and his friends. That'll do the trick!'

Playtime at Mrs Lawson's school.

This opening imaginary scene is based on a conversation I had many years ago with a head teacher of an infant school in Milton Keynes, Buckinghamshire. She had mused about the many differences there were at her school as well as the amazing consistencies of the children's needs and responses. The story above depicts the differences that exist in the physical development of children of the same chronological age as well as showing the variation and range of their movement skills. These are two of the themes of the story of Mrs Lawson and Sanjit that are developed throughout this chapter.

But first, where have we got to in the bigger story that is this book? In the last chapter we established that children's holistic and integrated development builds on a unique genetic wiring in a wonderful dynamic between inheritance and environment – an environment explored through the senses. The processes, capacities and characteristics of successful early learning were discussed in detail, and we proposed that the neonate's brain is ideally set up to learn and take advantage of stimulating activities in early childhood.

In this chapter and those that follow we are going to differentiate between the classic aspects of human development – physical, sensory, cognitive, language, emotional and social – and so we begin by presenting information about children's general physical development. We then consider the changes in growth in the childhood years, including the factors that influence physical development such as the topical subject (and pernicious problem in developed countries) of childhood obesity. The development of motor skills is explained before finally considering the implications for motor skill performance with regard to school and community physical and health education.

## Chapter Objectives

By the time you have completed this chapter you should be able to answer the following questions:

- How is physical growth measured?
- What is the significance of measures of body mass index?
- What patterns of physical development are there and how do we account for individual and cultural differences?
- What is the relationship between early reflexes and later motor skills?
- How do children learn new skills that are obviously different from earlier ones?
- What role does the environment play in enabling motor patterns to emerge?
- Are some experiences better than others in facilitating new behaviours?
- What is the role of play in physical development?
- How important are school sport, physical education lessons and clubs?
- What are the advantages of an emphasis on outside activity and play?

# General physical development

The task of describing patterns in physical development is reasonably straightforward since there is predictability to the patterns in the childhood years. The infant/toddler years (birth to 2 years) are times of rapid physical development (remember the growth tables in Chapter 3). By 6 months, birth weight can have doubled and may have tripled by the end of the first year. Of course, growth continues but not as quickly as in the first year of life (see Figure 7.1). In the early childhood years (2–6 years), children's physical and cognitive capabilities are extended as they continue to learn about the world around them and discover what their bodies are capable of. The child who was once a cautious 2-year-old is now a risk-taking and

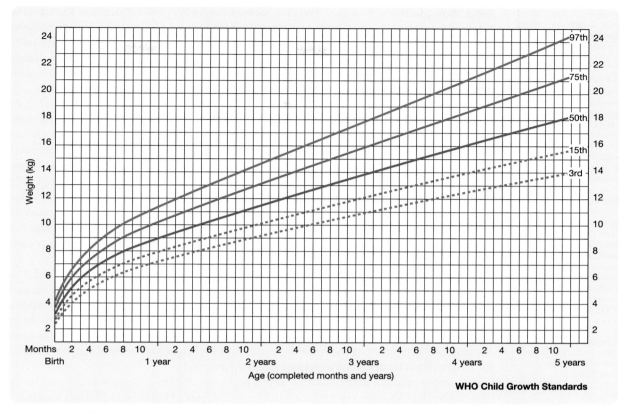

**Figure 7.1** World Health Organization growth standards for weight: girls, birth to 5 years

Notice the expected fast growth gain in the first six months.

*Source*: World Health Organization (2006). *WHO child growth standards: Methods and development*. Geneva: WHO (retrieved from **www.who.int/childgrowth/standards/en/**). Reproduced with permission.

adventurous 5-year-old anxious to show off a host of newly acquired movement skills, as the opening story of this chapter shows.

In the middle and late childhood years (6–11 years), physical growth slows down as this is a time to consolidate the movement skills acquired in the early years and to prepare the body for the tumult of puberty that is to follow shortly. Although general physical development follows a predictable path, the growth rate is not constant. Early acceleration is followed by a period of slowing down, then another period of acceleration. What are the reasons for these fluctuations? If development appears slower, is it giving children time to adjust to their own bodies and their different emerging physical capacities? How is physical growth measured and what terminology is used in its measurement? These are the some of the questions we will consider in the next sections of the chapter.

## Physical growth changes in childhood

Anthropometric measures assess height, weight, length and circumference of body parts. For example, at a visit to a clinic the doctor might measure around a patient's stomach using a tape measure colour coded green for measures that were healthy, yellow for measures over the safe levels of fat in that part of the body, and red for obese. This is an anthropometric measure. The doctor might also weigh her patient and measure standing height, then check a printed table on the consulting room wall to give her the patient's ratio between height and weight.

**Anthropometric measures**
Measurements used to assess physical growth: including height and weight measurements.

**Body mass index (BMI)**
Body weight (in kilograms) divided by height (in metres) squared.

● ● ● ● ● ● ● ● ● ● ● ● ● ● ● ● ● ●
**Connect and Extend**
There used to be regular medical examinations in UK schools which included height and weight checks. There is still disagreement about whether or not regular medical checks should continue. What do you think? For recent data, read: Ledergerber, M. & Steffen, T. (2011). Prevalence of overweight and obesity in children and adolescents from 1977 to 2009 – examination of the school medical data of more than 94 000 school-age children in the city of Basel (Switzerland), *Das Gesundheitswesen*. January, 73(1), 46–53.
● ● ● ● ● ● ● ● ● ● ● ● ● ● ● ● ● ●

**Somatotyping**
The classifying of children and adults according to body build.

**Physique**
The bodily structure, development and organisation of an individual.

**Ectomorph**
A person with a lean and delicate build of body and large skin surface in comparison with weight.

Ratios show a feature of growth as a relation between two anthropometic measures, e.g. standing height minus sitting height equals a measure of leg length, and a ratio can be formed between leg length and height. (Because young children have long torsos and short legs proportionally this can be a blunt but not inaccurate predictor of their adult height.) Ratios are valuable things to understand when discussing growth and physical development and one of the most commonly referred to is the body mass index (BMI).

The BMI is a commonly used medical ratio where weight is divided by the standing height squared. (Squaring is the standard method for turning negative values into consistently positive values because the product of two minus values – in the case of squaring $-2 \times -2$, say – is always positive, +4 or 4.) The BMI is regarded as the amount of adipose (fat) tissue expressed as percentage of total weight – a useful measure of how much fat there is in the body. We will be talking more about the significance of BMI ratios later in the chapter when exploring the troubling and fairly recent phenomenon of mass childhood obesity. BMI ratios are also valuable in taking into account different body shapes or builds that occur as a result of genotype (the genetic characteristics passed to us at the moment of conception). Table 7.1 gives the BMI chart for children aged 2–20. It is useful for paediatricians and other professionals to have these 'ready reckoners' to hand.

**Somatotyping** is how children and adults are classified according to their body build. The study of **physique** during periods of childhood growth permits understanding of growth and maturation differences in the physique (e.g. Ventrella *et al.*, 2008), although most studies have traditionally involved adult populations related to sporting success. Statements about physique that allow inferences about body size can be derived from anthropometric measures. For example, a child who is above the 75th percentile for height and below the 25th percentile for weight might be described as **ectomorph** (see Figure 7.2).

We need to sound a note of caution at this point. No one body shape is necessarily better or healthier than another. The BMI is a much better measure of fitness than having a long body and short legs. And we should not demonise fat unthinkingly. The human body needs fat for all sorts of body building and body repairing reasons. Children add weight steadily with age (check out Figure 7.1), with much of this increase due in the first instance to an increase in fat. Indeed, body fat increases from 16 per cent at birth to 30 per cent by the end of the first

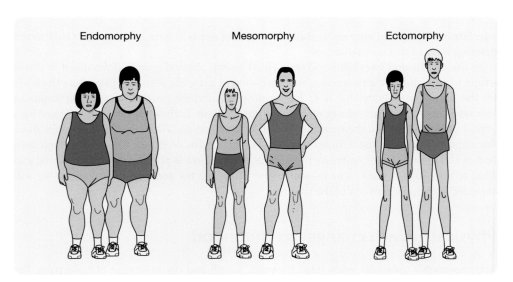

**Figure 7.2** Somatotyping

Somatotyping is a method of description and assessment of the body on three shape and composition scales: endomorphy (relative fatness), mesomorphy (relative musculoskeletal robustness) and ectomorphy (relative linearity).

*Source*: Robert O. Keel, University of Missouri–St. Louis (retrieved from **www.umsl.edu/~keelr/pics/somato3.jpg**).

**Table 7.1**  Body mass index chart for children aged 2–20

| Height | | Weight kg | 19.7 | 20.0 | 20.2 | 20.4 | 20.6 | 20.9 | 21.1 | 21.3 | 21.5 | 21.8 | 22.0 | 22.2 | 22.5 | 22.7 | 22.9 | 23.1 | 23.4 |
|---|---|---|---|---|---|---|---|---|---|---|---|---|---|---|---|---|---|---|---|
| | | lb | 43.5 | 44 | 44.5 | 45 | 45.5 | 46 | 46.5 | 47 | 47.5 | 48 | 48.5 | 49 | 49.5 | 50 | 50.5 | 51 | 51.5 |
| cm | inches | | | | | | | | | | | | | | | | | | |
| 76.2 | 30 | | 34.0 | 34.4 | 34.8 | | | | | | | | | | | | | | |
| 77.5 | 30.5 | | 32.9 | 33.3 | 33.6 | 34.0 | 34.4 | 34.8 | | | | | | | | | | | |
| 78.7 | 31 | | 31.8 | 32.2 | 32.6 | 32.9 | 33.3 | 33.7 | 34.0 | 34.4 | 34.8 | | | | | | | | |
| 80.0 | 31.5 | | 30.8 | 31.2 | 31.5 | 31.9 | 32.2 | 32.6 | 32.9 | 33.3 | 33.7 | 34.0 | 34.4 | 34.7 | | | | | |
| 81.3 | 32 | | 29.9 | 30.2 | 30.6 | 30.9 | 31.2 | 31.6 | 31.9 | 32.3 | 32.6 | 33.0 | 33.3 | 33.6 | 34.0 | 34.3 | 34.7 | | |
| 82.6 | 32.5 | | 29.0 | 29.3 | 29.6 | 30.0 | 30.3 | 30.6 | 31.0 | 31.3 | 31.6 | 32.0 | 32.3 | 32.6 | 32.9 | 33.3 | 33.6 | 33.9 | 34.3 |
| 83.8 | 33 | | 28.1 | 28.4 | 28.7 | 29.1 | 29.4 | 29.7 | 30.0 | 30.3 | 30.7 | 31.0 | 31.3 | 31.6 | 32.0 | 32.3 | 32.6 | 32.9 | 33.2 |
| 85.1 | 33.5 | | 27.3 | 27.6 | 27.9 | 28.2 | 28.5 | 28.8 | 29.1 | 29.4 | 29.8 | 30.1 | 30.4 | 30.7 | 31.0 | 31.3 | 31.6 | 32.0 | 32.3 |
| 86.4 | 34 | | 26.5 | 26.8 | 27.1 | 27.4 | 27.7 | 28.0 | 28.3 | 28.6 | 28.9 | 29.2 | 29.5 | 29.8 | 30.1 | 30.4 | 30.7 | 31.0 | 31.3 |
| 87.6 | 34.5 | | 25.7 | 26.0 | 26.3 | 26.6 | 26.9 | 27.2 | 27.5 | 27.8 | 28.1 | 28.4 | 28.6 | 28.9 | 29.2 | 29.5 | 29.8 | 30.1 | 30.4 |
| 88.9 | 35 | | 25.0 | 25.3 | 25.5 | 25.8 | 26.1 | 26.4 | 26.7 | 27.0 | 27.3 | 27.5 | 27.8 | 28.1 | 28.4 | 28.7 | 29.0 | 29.3 | 29.6 |
| 90.2 | 35.5 | | 24.3 | 24.5 | 24.8 | 25.1 | 25.4 | 25.7 | 25.9 | 26.2 | 26.5 | 26.8 | 27.1 | 27.3 | 27.6 | 27.9 | 28.2 | 28.5 | 28.7 |
| 91.4 | 36 | | 23.6 | 23.9 | 24.1 | 24.4 | 24.7 | 25.0 | 25.2 | 25.5 | 25.8 | 26.0 | 26.3 | 26.6 | 26.9 | 27.1 | 27.4 | 27.7 | 27.9 |
| 92.7 | 36.5 | | 23.0 | 23.2 | 23.5 | 23.7 | 24.0 | 24.3 | 24.5 | 24.8 | 25.1 | 25.3 | 25.6 | 25.9 | 26.1 | 26.4 | 26.7 | 26.9 | 27.2 |
| 94.0 | 37 | | 22.3 | 22.6 | 22.9 | 23.1 | 23.4 | 23.6 | 23.9 | 24.1 | 24.4 | 24.7 | 24.9 | 25.2 | 25.4 | 25.7 | 25.9 | 26.2 | 26.4 |
| 95.3 | 37.5 | | 21.7 | 22.0 | 22.2 | 22.5 | 22.7 | 23.0 | 23.2 | 23.5 | 23.7 | 24.0 | 24.2 | 24.5 | 24.7 | 25.0 | 25.2 | 25.5 | 25.7 |
| 96.5 | 38 | | 21.2 | 21.4 | 21.7 | 21.9 | 22.2 | 22.4 | 22.6 | 22.9 | 23.1 | 23.4 | 23.6 | 23.9 | 24.1 | 24.3 | 24.6 | 24.8 | 25.1 |
| 97.8 | 38.5 | | 20.6 | 20.9 | 21.1 | 21.3 | 21.6 | 21.8 | 22.1 | 22.3 | 22.5 | 22.8 | 23.0 | 23.2 | 23.5 | 23.7 | 24.0 | 24.2 | 24.4 |
| 99.1 | 39 | | 20.1 | 20.3 | 20.6 | 20.8 | 21.0 | 21.3 | 21.5 | 21.7 | 22.0 | 22.2 | 22.4 | 22.6 | 22.9 | 23.1 | 23.3 | 23.6 | 23.8 |
| 100.3 | 39.5 | | 19.6 | 19.8 | 20.1 | 20.3 | 20.5 | 20.7 | 21.0 | 21.2 | 21.4 | 21.6 | 21.9 | 22.1 | 22.3 | 22.5 | 22.8 | 23.0 | 23.2 |
| 101.6 | 40 | | 19.1 | 19.3 | 19.6 | 19.8 | 20.0 | 20.2 | 20.4 | 20.7 | 20.9 | 21.1 | 21.3 | 21.5 | 21.8 | 22.0 | 22.2 | 22.4 | 22.6 |
| 102.9 | 40.5 | | 18.6 | 18.9 | 19.1 | 19.3 | 19.5 | 19.7 | 19.9 | 20.1 | 20.4 | 20.6 | 20.8 | 21.0 | 21.2 | 21.4 | 21.6 | 21.9 | 22.1 |
| 104.1 | 41 | | 18.2 | 18.4 | 18.6 | 18.8 | 19.0 | 19.2 | 19.4 | 19.7 | 19.9 | 20.1 | 20.3 | 20.5 | 20.7 | 20.9 | 21.1 | 21.3 | 21.5 |
| 105.4 | 41.5 | | 17.8 | 18.0 | 18.2 | 18.4 | 18.6 | 18.8 | 19.0 | 19.2 | 19.4 | 19.6 | 19.8 | 20.0 | 20.2 | 20.4 | 20.6 | 20.8 | 21.0 |
| 106.7 | 42 | | 17.3 | 17.5 | 17.7 | 17.9 | 18.1 | 18.3 | 18.5 | 18.7 | 18.9 | 19.1 | 19.3 | 19.5 | 19.7 | 19.9 | 20.1 | 20.3 | 20.5 |
| 108.0 | 42.5 | | 16.9 | 17.1 | 17.3 | 17.5 | 17.7 | 17.9 | 18.1 | 18.3 | 18.5 | 18.7 | 18.9 | 19.1 | 19.3 | 19.5 | 19.7 | 19.9 | 20.0 |
| 109.2 | 43 | | 16.5 | 16.7 | 16.9 | 17.1 | 17.3 | 17.5 | 17.7 | 17.9 | 18.1 | 18.3 | 18.4 | 18.6 | 18.8 | 19.0 | 19.2 | 19.4 | 19.6 |
| 110.5 | 43.5 | | 16.2 | 16.3 | 16.5 | 16.7 | 16.9 | 17.1 | 17.3 | 17.5 | 17.6 | 17.8 | 18.0 | 18.2 | 18.4 | 18.6 | 18.8 | 18.9 | 19.1 |
| 111.8 | 44 | | 15.8 | 16.0 | 16.2 | 16.3 | 16.5 | 16.7 | 16.9 | 17.1 | 17.2 | 17.4 | 17.6 | 17.8 | 18.0 | 18.2 | 18.3 | 18.5 | 18.7 |

Note: Whenever a child's specific height or weight measurement is not listed, round to the closest number in the table.

*Source*: Centers for Disease Control and Prevention, chart: calculated body mass index (retrieved from **www.cdc.gov/growthcharts**).

year (Hauner *et al.*, 2009) and females have more body fat than males at all ages (Must *et al.*, 2005; Beaver, 2005).

**Reflect**  Why do girls have more body fat than boys? Are the reasons entirely physiological? Are they to do with reproduction? What advantages and disadvantages does more body fat offer to girls growing up?

## Body size

You may remember from the visit to the doctor referred to above that the most common measures of body size and growth are height and weight, and these measures, if plotted on a graph over the first 20 years of life, show an S-wave growth trend: growth acceleration during the prenatal stage and infancy, becoming slower in childhood and accelerating again during adolescence (see Figure 7.3). Because results for many thousands of children can be taken and

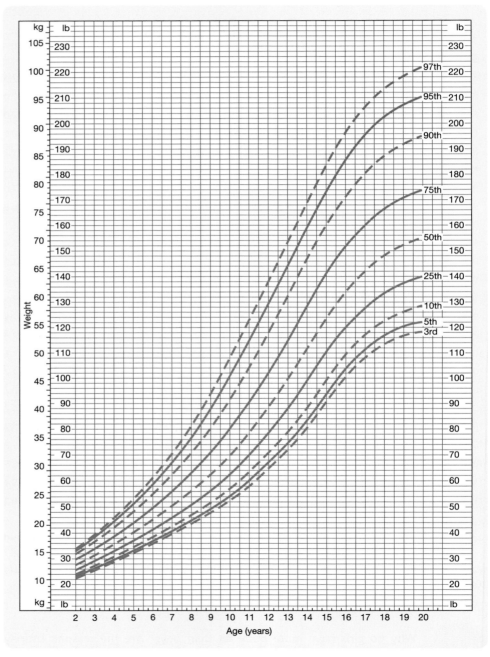

**Figure 7.3** S-wave growth trend weight-for-age percentiles: boys, 2 to 20 years

Growth is not a continuous straight line – rather growth follows the S-wave.

*Source:* allnutritionals.com (http://allnutritionals.com/growth_charts/growth_charts-3.gif).

aggregated, it is possible to predict how tall each child will be once fully grown and, to some extent, whether growth is occurring at the expected rate. Children at birth are approximately a third of their adult height, and by age 2 this rises to a half (Tandon *et al.*, 2012). Of course, physical growth as already stated is not a continuous straight-line function of growth over time (like a straight line on a graph). Rather, growth follows the S-wave mentioned above, so it is not always possible at every stage to predict what the final height for an individual will be. Nevertheless, it is interesting and important to know some of the common patterns of growth in childhood.

The weight of a newborn is on average 3.35 kg (7.4 lb) and doubles in the first 5 months. By the end of the first year it triples to 9.1 kg (20.5 lb); by 2 years to 12.5 kg (27.5 lb); and by age 5 to 18.3 kg (40.3 lb) (Kerkhof *et al.*, 2012; Kuczmarski *et al.*, 2000).

As one might expect, weight gains are seasonal, with most gains in the winter months, and are susceptible to lifestyle patterns, activity, calorific content of food, parental and peer pressures. Height and weight gains slow up in middle childhood until the growth spurt at puberty at 11–12 years on average for girls and a year later for boys (Arnett & Hughes, 2012; Kaltiala-Heino *et al.*, 2003; Coleman & Coleman, 2002; Finlay *et al.*, 2002).

## Body proportions

The rate of physical growth for different parts of the body varies. An infant's head appears larger than an older child's because the head is about a quarter of the total body length at birth to accommodate a near adult-sized brain. By age 6, the head is a sixth of total body length and by adulthood it is one-eighth of the total length of the body. Growth charts like Figures 7.1 and 7.3 show both continuous curves but also growth spurts. Parents observe differences almost overnight, particularly those applying to the long bones! Despite years of experience, teachers continue to be amazed to observe quite substantial growth increases when children come back to school after their summer holidays, although wise parents have often bought trousers and jumpers with extra-long legs and sleeves.

Two patterns of growth often referred to when assessing individual variation in the rate of physical development are cephalocaudal and proximodistal development. Cephalocaudal development refers to development from the head to the toes, i.e. head growth precedes arm growth, which precedes leg growth, since brain growth is rapid to allow the brain to steer developments around the whole body (and this begins at the prenatal stage). As we said earlier, the head becomes smaller proportionally as the torso and lower body grow. This is linked to sensory development because babies learn to use their upper limbs first, then their legs and feet later on.

Proximodistal development proceeds from the centre of the body outwards. Head and trunk development is advanced earlier than fingers and toes. The body's control centre, the central nervous system, lies along the body's central axis, and so functions at the core of the body develop before those at the extremities of hands and feet. This is usually the case but with one exception. In adolescence, young people's feet and hands grow larger, before leg and trunk growth in a kind of reverse of proximodistal trend. This gives the impression of awkwardness and a lack of co-ordination in many teenagers' actions. Excluding the adolescent period, proportions show similarity between the sexes in the early years but not so during puberty. In fact, as previously mentioned, girls and boys follow similar but not parallel patterns of growth, and, even though there are always individual differences, boys on the whole have more lean body mass than girls.

Around second birthdays, girls tend to be slightly taller and weigh less than boys, and this remains typical until puberty when boys catch up and surpass them in weight and height. The developed male physique is typically heavier due to increased muscle mass and larger bones. Boys' legs are longer, giving an obvious advantage in running. They have wider shoulders and the chest is deeper, providing a mechanical advantage in throwing and striking activities. The centre of gravity for females is lower than that in males, giving them better balance but a disadvantage in jumping.

**Cephalocaudal**
Growth that proceeds in sequence from the head to the toes.

**Proximodistal**
Development proceeding from the centre of the body outwards in sequence.

**Connect and Extend**
Can boys jump better than girls and does it matter? Read: Stodden, D., Langendorfer, S., Roberton, M. A. & Kelbley, L. (2007). Association between motor skill competence and health-related physical fitness. *Journal of Sport & Exercise Psychology*, 29, S45–S46. The purpose of this study was to examine the association between motor skill competence in three motor skills and six measures of health-related physical fitness. What similar studies can you find?

**Ossification**
The process through which
cartilage becomes bone.

**Skeletal age**
A way of estimating
physical maturity based on
the development of the
bones in the body.

**Growth plates**
The area of growing tissue
near the ends of the long
bones in children and
adolescents, also known as
epiphyseal plates or physis.

**Fontanelles**
Gaps in the skull that allow
the head of the baby to
pass through the birth
canal.

Alongside height and weight changes, internal changes take place in muscles and bones which are important for movement skills – the motor functions. Newborns have fewer bones in their extremities than older children and it takes until the end of the childhood period and into adolescence for all bones to be fully mature. Ossification, the process through which cartilage thickens to become bone, occurs rapidly in early childhood, beginning during the first 6 weeks *in utero* in the jaw and collarbone. Skeletal age is a measure of physical maturity and can be determined by X-ray to discover bone development. Different skeletal parts ossify at different ages as do the growth plates – the growing tissue near the ends of the long bones. Females have a more developed skeletal system than males. Even at birth, girls are more advanced than boys, typically by between 4 and 6 weeks. Measuring head size is frequently used by doctors in early development because the rate of growth of the skull is more consistent to accommodate a growing brain within (see Figure 7.4). Gaps in the skull called fontanelles, present before birth to allow a baby's head to squeeze through mother's dilated cervix, gradually close in the first 2 years.

Muscle tissue undergoes huge increases after birth. Two types of muscle fibre develop: *slow twitch*, which is associated with endurance, and *fast twitch*, associated with explosive power. By the end of the first year, these fibres are 30 per cent of adult size – and their size is believed to be mostly inherited. Although muscle fibres are present at birth, their constituency changes throughout the childhood period – gaining in length and thickness. Males have more muscle mass than females – a result of genetics, hormonal differences and the types of physical activity they engage in. This is also true for strength differences between girls and boys.

## Individual and cultural differences

The growth trends we have described are typical and predictable but individual variations are huge. While some girls may begin their pubescent spurt in the last year or two of primary schooling (9–11 years), others will not reach it before the second or third years of secondary school (12–14 years). There are of course social implications for the rate at which an individual child matures physically. According to one classic Swedish study, early maturing girls have fewer friends and are more likely to indulge in 'more adult' behaviours such as smoking, drinking and sex (Stattin & Magnusson, 1990). More recently it is found that early puberty is a risk factor for delinquency and presents a risk for aggressive behaviour in early adolescent girls (Mrug et al., 2008). That is not to say this is always the case as, again, context is an important factor. Not only are there individual differences in physical growth but also cultural ones. Take groups of 8-year-olds from different parts of the world and you would immediately see differences in their physical size. In South America and parts of India, Thailand and Burma, children are relatively small in stature. The United States and Northern Europe have the tallest children although growth norms need to be viewed with some caution (Berk, 2006). Ethnic groups within nation states also vary (e.g. Mathai et al., 2004), but evidence of these differences is a little thin on the ground.

Factors such as diet, climate, food and health are obvious ones to explain these differences apart from small genetic differences and adaptations. Interesting variations have been reported between urban and rural communities in many countries (e.g. Stephens, 2012), and global variations indicate that smaller children live in habitats across the world where famine and disease are common (UNICEF, 2012). It is clear that there are a number of factors that impact upon children's physical growth, and these factors are considered in the next section.

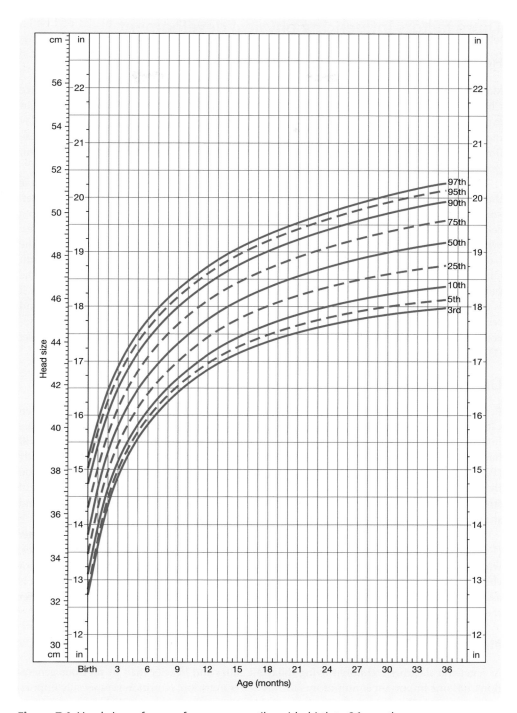

**Figure 7.4** Head circumference-for-age percentiles: girls, birth to 36 months

Measuring head size is frequently used by doctors in early development because the rate of growth of the skull is more consistent to accommodate a growing brain within.

*Source:* allnutritionals.com (http://allnutritionals.com/growth_charts/growth_charts-14.gif).

# Three factors influencing physical development

## Heredity

Many of the studies of heredity use twins as the basis for their data and conclusions (see Chapter 4 for much more information about twin studies). Identical twins, as you might expect, show broad similarity in their height and weight, whereas non-identical twins display more variation. Heredity sets limits but the environment has an important role in how these limits are reached, so when external factors such as diet and lifestyle are largely consistent, genetics is the prime determinant of physical development.

However, when contrasting weight and height, the more dominant influence for weight is the environment, and genetics tends to be the dominant determinant for body height. Yet, your genotype – your complete collection of genetic instructions for creating and replacing cells (refer to Chapter 5) – does affect all aspects of physical growth through the **hormones**. When stimulated by the adjacent **hypothalamus** region of the brain, the **pituitary gland** at the base of the brain releases hormones into the bloodstream, which trigger physical growth changes by cell division and by cell enlargement (see Chapter 4). The hormones from the pituitary gland act directly or stimulate other glands to release their hormones. In puberty it is the sex hormones – testosterone in boys and oestrogen in girls – that stimulate growth and sexual development. Menstruation appears to be primarily genetically controlled, but socio-economic factors such as nutrition, social class and family size all affect the timing of its onset (Herman-Giddens *et al.*, 2004).

**Hormones**
Chemicals in specialist cells that pass between other cells.

**Hypothalamus**
Part of the limbic system in the brain that, among other functions, is involved in eating and sexual responses.

**Pituitary gland**
A small ductless gland at the base of the brain secreting various hormones essential for growth and other bodily functions.

## Lifestyle factors

Regular participation in exercise, proper nutrition and healthcare means that children can grow healthily. Similarly, socioeconomic conditions such as housing and sanitation also influence this growth where poor housing, inadequate facilities and/or bad sanitation will have obvious negative effects on how children develop physically. An early Swedish study (Peck & Lundberg, 1995) found that a smaller adult size can be related to poor childhood living conditions. Links can be made with forced displacement from home and psychological stress, postulating that individuals have not been able to develop the resilience to stresses and strains imposed by their immediate environments (Clarkin, 2012).

Poor children in the UK breathe more polluted air and drink more contaminated water (Evans, 2004). Children who live in older houses with lead paint and lead-soldered pipes, which exist in many inner-city areas, have greater concentrations of lead in their blood. Poor children are at least twice as likely as non-poor children to suffer lead poisoning, which is associated with lower school achievement and long-term neurological impairment (Vivier *et al.*, 2011).

## Nutrition

As a general statement, children living today are taller and heavier than in previous generations and one important contributory factor is better nutrition. Nutrition is especially important in very early development when brain and body growth gains are at their most rapid (see Chapter 6). Proportionally, children breathe more air, drink more water, and consume more food than adults. This higher rate of intake means that children will receive higher doses of whatever contaminants are present in the air, water or food. Children aged 1–5 eat three to four times more per unit of body weight than the average adult (Bevelander *et al.*, 2012) and some children need food supplements to help to combat malnutrition. For example, a number of recent studies (e.g. Ojukwu *et al.*, 2010) building on an early classic study (Pollitt, 1994) report that iron supplements given to disadvantaged children led to improvements in growth since deficiencies in the amount of iron in the diet result in **iron-deficiency anaemia**: a condition

**Iron-deficiency anaemia**
Nutritional deficiency from inadequate amounts of iron in the diet.

that has negative influences on children's physical (and cognitive) development. Children of all socioeconomic groups can get what is often considered the best start by feeding on breast milk (Andres *et al.*, 2012), but over many years there has been a good deal of uncertainty about how deficiencies and contaminants affect the quality of breast milk (Pruitt *et al.*, 1983).

Although fashions change, breast-feeding is generally considered preferable to bottle-feeding because breast milk contains the correct nutritional balance for babies and is a complete food. Other foods given to babies such as rice water or commercial formula milk are open to the challenge that they fail to nourish properly and do not offer the same protection from infant illness (Barclay *et al.*, 2012). Alongside other advantages, breast-feeding provides a near-perfect food for brain development and importantly is a strong bonding mechanism between mother and baby. It also is easier for breast-fed infants to accept solid foods perhaps due to the variety of tastes the infant experiences from variety in the mother's diet.

The later slowing down of body growth after two years sees food consumption decline and a tendency for preschool children to be 'picky' eaters (Hendrix, 2008). As children mature, the social environment of mealtimes remains very important. Children learn the social rules and to eat the types of food they see their parents and other peers eating. Eating patterns established early may become very difficult to alter later. However, overly strict controls here can limit children's opportunities to develop self-control. While measures of weight and body composition reflect well-fed and healthy children and are obvious indicators of children's overall health status, over-nutrition can lead to serious physical and psychological problems. This is the very real threat of childhood obesity.

## Childhood obesity

**Welcome To Fat Land. Where the fries are extra large, the sodas are jumbo size and the jeans are 'baggy fit'.**

(Critser, 2003)

So says author Greg Critser in his exposé and biting attack on the obesity problem in the United States in his book entitled, *Fat Land. How Americans became the fattest people in the world*. However, obesity and specifically childhood obesity are not confined to the United States. Far from it – childhood obesity is now very much considered a global epidemic, with a number of European countries catching up with the United States (see Figure 7.5). According to estimates from the International Obesity Task Force (IOTS, 2012) reported in a number of IOTS journal articles (e.g. Lagerros & Rössner, 2011; Gross *et al.*, 2011; Emerson & Robertson, 2010), at least 155 million school-age children worldwide are overweight or obese of which 30–45 million children aged 5–17 are obese. Annual reports from the IOTS also indicates that 22 million children under 5 years are similarly affected – altogether 1 in 10 children. The figures for European countries are worrying. Up to 35 per cent of children in southern European countries are overweight. In Italy, 36 per cent of 9-year-olds are overweight or obese. In Crete, 39 per cent of all 12-year-olds are either obese or overweight, and in Spain the figure for children and adolescents is 27 per cent. Figures also show a steady increase in all developed countries in the past two decades. In the European Union, the number of overweight children is rising by about 400,000 each year. In Britain the number of children in the overweight and obese categories doubled during 2004 – in just one year. However, there is some evidence emerging that the rise in obesity has plateaued (Olds *et al.*, 2011).

There are a number of physical and psychological consequences of this ill health which are very clearly evident in the childhood years. These include coronary heart disease, Type 2 diabetes, raised blood pressure and joint pains. There are psychological problems connected with low self-esteem, concerns about body image, depression, which can lead to bullying in schools, and social exclusion (Curtis, 2008). The scale across the United Kingdom is such that, for the first time in history, some parents can be expected to outlive their children. Being an obese or overweight child comes at a high price.

**Obesity**
More than 20 per cent increase over average body weight, taking into consideration age, sex and body build.

**Connect and Extend**
Not everybody agrees about the definition of obesity and how to measure it in children. What other ways are used to assess weightiness? Read: Chen, S., Binns, C. & Zhang, Y. (2012). The importance of definition in diagnosing obesity. *Asia-Pacific Journal of Public Health*, March, 24(2), 248–262.

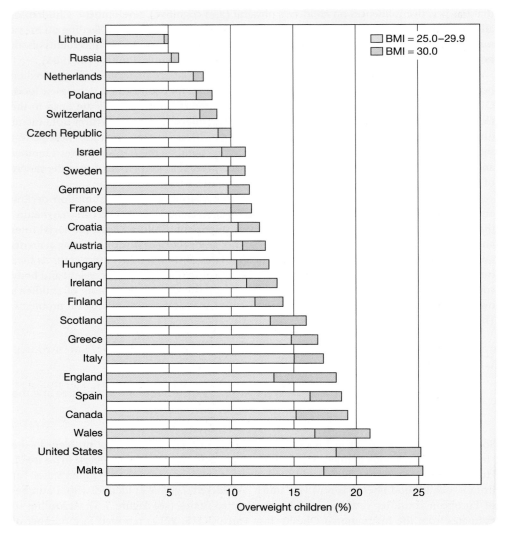

**Figure 7.5** Prevalence of overweight and obesity in schoolchildren aged 10–16 2001–2002
*Source*: Adapted from The International Association for the Study of Obesity (**www.iaso.org**). Reproduced with permission.

What actually is obesity? Obesity means that one's body weight has reached a point that causes a serious risk to health. As we mentioned earlier, degrees of 'over-weightiness' and obesity are calculated for adults by the BMI using this simple formula:

$$BMI = \frac{\text{Weight in kilograms}}{(\text{Height in metres} \times \text{Height in metres})}$$

**Reflect**   **Use the formula above to calculate your own BMI and the BMI of others who are willing to give their permission. If you have children of your own then calculate their BMI. For other children you would obviously need their permission and that of their parents. What does the BMI ratio mean in practice?**

Because children's BMI varies at different stages of development, various cut-off points are used to determine the significance of their BMI. However, a useful general rule is that you are overweight if your BMI index is greater than 20 per cent over the average body weight for somebody of your age, sex and body build. Adults with a BMI of 25–29.9 are considered overweight and 30.0 to be obese.

Potentially, there are a number of factors which contribute to increased risks of becoming obese, but the main causes of childhood obesity can be reduced to two: eating too much and exercising too little. Over-consumption of so-called 'fast foods', foods with high levels of saturated fats and sugary drinks, is likely to increase the risks of obesity, unlike fruit, vegetable fibre and low glycaemic foods. Many children (and adults also) take very little exercise, and are less likely to play running and chasing games outside or go swimming or cycling. A sedentary lifestyle in childhood is associated with increased risks in adulthood of coronary heart disease, Type 2 diabetes and raised blood pressure.

**Glycaemic foods**
Foods that contain carbohydrates that release glucose into the bloodstream.

However, both nature and nurture both play a role in childhood obesity. Findings of an early but classic study by researcher Albert Stunkard and colleagues (1990) of identical twins in Sweden indicated that the genetic contribution to obesity may be as high as 70 per cent. Similar contributions have been reported in more recent studies (Dudley *et al.*, 2008; Epstein *et al.*, 2007; Hampton, 2007). Four phenotypical factors (the interaction of genetic and environment) which contribute to childhood obesity were identified by physiologist Robert Malina and colleagues (2004):

- Biological – including heredity, sexual maturity and (lack of) proficiency in motor skills.
- Psychological – including self-efficacy, perceived barriers to activity and perceived competence.
- Social – including parental behaviours, attitude of peers, increased access to and attraction of TV and computer games.
- Physical – including domestic environment, availability of facilities and the climate, providing for less exercise.

**Self-efficacy**
Believing yourself to be capable of the desired outcome.

Parental obesity is a strong predictor of a child's obesity as an adult (AAP Committee on Nutrition, 2003) or, put more bluntly, obese children tend to have obese parents. If one parent is obese the risks are 40 per cent, rising to 80 per cent if both parents are obese. This evidence might suggest that genetics are the dominant factors in childhood obesity, but, as suggested by Malina *et al.* above, environmental factors must also be considered. Obesity in childhood may be understood as a family disorder. Family eating practices have been found to contribute to childhood obesity by a number of reports and articles, including exercise physiologist Lee Coyne (2008) which argue that children imitate parental eating behaviours and food choices from an early age. The *Policy, Research and Praxis* feature below explores the gap between policy and practice to address the problem of childhood obesity.

## Policy, Research and Praxis

### New thinking required on the problem of childhood obesity

The childhood years have recently become recognised as important ones for the prevention of obesity since physical activity patterns, eating habits and healthy lifestyle behaviours are largely formed during this period. It is these that help ensure good physical development in childhood and increase the likelihood of good adult health. Obesity remains high on the international political agendas and continues to influence policy. Research from Amsterdam University, as part of a European study (Van Stralen, 2012) into obesity prevention for children aged 4–6 years, shows variations in childhood obesity across countries.

In Belgium, Germany and Poland, less than 5 per cent of preschool children are obese. Figures for Bulgaria are at 6 per cent. In Greece and Spain, the rates are higher with 10 per cent of young children obese. In 2011, the Organisation for Economic Co-operation and Development (OECD, 2011) published *Health at a glance* which included data on overweight and obese populations across different countries. In the past 30 years in many developed countries, child obesity rates doubled and have doubled again. In emerging countries, the prevalence of obesity is rising, particularly in urban areas. A serious problem indeed and one that appears to require some fresh thinking.

In the UK, promises of new thinking followed. The White Paper, *Healthy lives, healthy people: Our strategy for public health in England* (Department of Health, 2010) set out the Government's new approach on public health and combatting obesity. The same year the Government's vision for a lasting legacy from the Olympic and Paralympic Games was published (Department for Culture, Media and Sport, 2010) and had as key themes harnessing the UK's passion for sport, increasing grass roots participation particularly by young people, and encouraging the whole population to be more physically active. In 2011, *Healthy lives, healthy people: A call to action on obesity in England* described more fully how obesity was to be addressed for the general public (Department of Health, 2011b). There is high political interest in promoting public health and tackling childhood obesity but just how serious is the problem? Data from the Health Survey of England's annual survey (NHS Information Centre, 2010) and Lifestyle Statistics (NHS Information Centre, 2012) provides an alarming picture for children aged 2 and older:

## Obesity

Around three in ten boys and girls were classed as either overweight or obese (31 per cent). 17 per cent of boys and 15 per cent of girls (aged 2 to 15) were classed as obese, a steady increase from 1995.

Around one in ten pupils in Reception class (aged 4–5 years) were classified as obese (9.4 per cent) and 1 in 5 pupils in Year 6 (aged 10–11 years) (19.0 per cent).

## Physical activity

A total of 41 per cent of respondents (aged 2+) said they made walks of 20 minutes or more at least 3 times a week. Some 20 per cent of respondents reported that they took walks of at least 20 minutes 'less than once a year or never'.

The most popular sports activities carried out by children aged 5 to 10 outside school hours were swimming, diving or life-saving. This was followed by football (36 per cent) and cycling or riding a bike (28 per cent).

A plethora of health promotion strategies have been implemented across the UK. School PE include weekly sessions on fundamental movement skills. Community sports clubs organise sessions for children in a variety of sports. Inter-school sport offer competitive sport for Primary aged children and are supported by sports co-ordinators and specialist PE staff from Secondary schools. There have been improvements to school dinners, advice given to children and families on eating healthily and being active. Despite this and many schemes to promote physical activity, childhood obesity continues to be a serious problem in the UK. The gap between policy and practice remains.

So, if children imitate parental eating behaviours and food choices from an early age, why is it that obesity is more common in urban and densely populated regions (Sjöberg *et al.*, 2008) and more common in winter months than in spring and summer (Our Children, 2005)? There is a strong connection between obesity and economic status. Lack of money and lack of knowledge about eating healthily and of what foods to buy among lower socio-economic groups increase the risks (Jain, 2004). In the UK, increased television viewing and time playing computer games can lead to reduced active leisure and increased snacking (Cardinal & Lumeng, 2007). TV advertisements which promote calorie-rich foods may tempt children to consume 'bad' foods that are high in salt, fat and processed sugars, and increased time watching TV leads to decreased time spent on physical activity. However, Valerie Burke and colleagues (2006) at the University of Western Australia found that excessive TV viewing was a **positive predictor** for obesity in boys, but a **negative predictor** in girls. It would seem that the more TV 12-year-old girls watch, the more likely they are to be thinner. Why might this be the case? Perhaps girls see lots of thin women on TV and this adds to the pressure to diet so that girls can look like their role models. However, overall the size of this effect was small and it was found that girls' other sedentary behaviours did predict a higher risk of obesity.

Schools have a role in reducing childhood obesity. In the United Kingdom a number of government initiatives are specifically targeting school-age children. Jamie Oliver's (a popular television chef and presenter) campaign at the end of the past decade to deliver healthy food to school-age children was on the whole largely successful. Whether it made a sustainable change to children's eating habits (and to those of their parents) remains to be seen but, at the time of writing, there is no evidence of any lasting legacy for this project.

Generally school-based interventions tend to promote physical activity and provide information about healthy eating habits. As evidence of the UK Government's commitment to tackle the rise in childhood obesity, a number of schemes were launched, jointly owned by the Department of Health, the Department for Education and Skills and the Department for Culture, Media and Sport. The National Healthy Schools programme (**www.wiredforhealth.gov.uk/** – now archived) outlined what it is to be a 'healthy school'; the Food in School (FiS) Programme incorporated various projects such as tuck shops, cookery clubs, vending machines and healthy lunch boxes. The School Fruit and Vegetable Scheme entitled all 4–6-year-olds to a free piece of fruit or vegetable each school day and the Physical Education, School Sport and Club Links programme aimed to mobilise the national culture in the United Kingdom and improve children and young people's access to sport and play networks.

**Positive predictor**
Where there is an increase in one variable, you can predict an increase in a second variable.

**Negative predictor**
Where there is an increase in one variable, you can predict a decrease in a second variable.

• • • • • • • • • • • • • • •
**Connect and Extend**
Connect to Liverpool John Moores University at **www.ljmu.ac.uk/** for details of the Active Schools Project (Zoe Butcher, Stuart Fairclough, Dave Richardson) – you may need to search the archive of the site. The aim of the project is to assess activity over the school day and to develop interventions that promote activity, through active transport, active breaktime, after-school clubs and physical education.
• • • • • • • • • • • • • • •

• • • • • • • • • • • • • • •
**Connect and Extend**
Extend your understanding of the importance of physical education in a school's curriculum by accessing Fairclough, S. J. & Stratton, G. (2005). Physical education makes you fit and healthy: Physical education's contribution to young people's activity levels. *Health Education Research, 20*, 14–23.
• • • • • • • • • • • • • • •

**Reflect** A number of UK Government initiatives on obesity have now been ended for financial and political reasons and their websites archived. Are there government-backed replacement schemes in current operation? Are such initiatives a real solution and what else could be done by governments and schools to combat the obesity epidemic?

A little earlier we said that one of the factors contributing to childhood obesity is perceived or real poor motor (movement) development or lack of physical skills. Understanding of how the body moves, including a theoretical framework for understanding movement (remember the usefulness of theory discussed in Chapter 1), requires knowledge of the theories of motor development, which is the subject of the next section.

Before moving on, let's summarise what we have learned so far:

- There are predictable patterns of physical development in the childhood years.
- The infant/toddler years (birth to 2 years) are times of rapid physical development.
- In the early childhood years (2–6 years), children's physical and cognitive capabilities are extended and in the middle and late childhood years (6–11 years), physical growth slows down.
- Anthropometric measures assess height, weight, length and circumference of body parts whilst ratios like the body mass index show a feature of growth as a relation between two measures.

**Summary 1**

- Because results for many thousands of children can be taken and aggregated, it is possible to predict how tall each child will be once fully grown, and whether growth is occurring at the expected rate. The growth trends are typical and predictable but individual variations are huge.

- Factors such as diet, climate, food and health are obvious ones to explain these differences, apart from small genetic differences and adaptations.

- Three factors influencing physical development are heredity, lifestyle factors including socioeconomic conditions, and nutrition.

- Childhood obesity is now considered a global epidemic. Obesity means that one's body weight has reached a point that causes a serious risk to health, which can be very clearly evident in the childhood years.

- Four factors contributing to childhood obesity have been identified: biological, psychological, social and physical.

# Theories of motor development

The study of motor development has re-emerged as one of the most active areas in child development research (e.g. Liu, 2012; Longmuir *et al.*, 2012; Vaivre-Douret *et al.*, 2010). For any theory to be robust in attempting to explain motor development, it must be able to explain the emergence of new skills that are not the same as those reflexive movements that are present at birth. What cannot be assumed is that the sequence of motor development is merely one of refining movements that are already present at, or even before, birth. Certainly, informal observations would tell us that many actions, such as taking hold of a crayon and drawing shapes that a 4-year-old finds easy, are not present at birth and have been acquired within a relatively short space of time. This conundrum raises a number of important questions that straightaway signal the complexity of motor development and the need for theory to attempt to provide solutions. Here are four of the questions we set out at the beginning of the chapter and which we will now address by looking at the major models, theories and perspectives:

- What is the relationship between early reflexes and later motor skills?
- How do children learn new skills that are obviously different from earlier ones?
- What role does the environment play in enabling motor patterns to emerge?
- Are some experiences better than others in facilitating new motor behaviours?

## Biological-maturation perspective

Between the 1930s and 1950s the biological-maturation perspective was the dominant discourse in motor development. The biological-maturation perspective views change as an internal process that is dictated by an individual's body clock. Advocates believe that, since development is the result of inheritance, no amount of stimulation can alter its course. Pioneering work by Arnold Gesell – a supporter of systematic observation of development – took the view (1954) that we develop in an ordered invariable sequence (marked by a number of motor development milestones) that is controlled by genetic factors. Gesell's work was specifically built on earlier work by Myrtle McGraw – a pioneer in the study of child development – who believed that maturation of the CNS was the catalyst for the emergence of new

**Connect and Extend**

Explore the connections between ideas of maturation, physical development and brain development (Chapter 6), read: Blakemore, S.-J. (2007). Why it's never too late to grow. *Times Educational Supplement*, 10 August, in the archive at **www.tes.co.uk/**

physical skills (1943). Based on these perspectives some teachers and parents believed that motor skills do not need to be taught explicitly; they will appear automatically as a child matures. Gesell's motor milestones are still widely used as a framework for the observation of motor development and it is worth checking these out on a reputable website.

## Information-processing perspective

The information-processing perspective is an analogy with a computer operating system (see Chapter 2; the section on learning theories), one based on the inputting and outputting of data. Input refers to information in the environment that is taken in via an individual's perceptual mechanisms. The information is interpreted and codified by the brain and acted upon by comparing new information to short-term and long-term memories, in turn resulting in decision-making. (This idea is developed in more detail in the next chapter.) So it is the CNS – which, as you may remember the brain is a part of – that organises the information and sends this to the peripheral nervous system (efferent organisation) to execute the movement as output. There are many variations on this theme of information processing as a model of motor development, but the most referred to of the information-processing theories are the following:

**Efferent organisation** Carrying away from a central part; specifically designating nerves that carry impulses away from a nerve centre.

- *Fitts & Posner's three-stage model (1967).* Stage 1, the *cognitive stage*, is typified by variable performance where the individual makes many gross errors, for example when learning to swing a golf club. This stage is about getting to understand the cognitive demands of the task. For example, all the aspects of a golf swing need careful checking each time: the stance, the grip, the shape of the back-swing, the head position at contact, the follow-through and finishing position.

  Stage 2, the *associative stage*, is when the individual tries for greater consistency in the movement. Many fundamentals are learned and relearned, with fewer errors. This stage is about skill refining. Individuals are usually able to detect their own errors and, with encouragement and support, can put the error right, but attention still needs to be given to one, some or all of the aspects of the new skill. For example, at this stage the toddler will fall over, but is less and less likely to do so once walking in many different contexts and as the main method of perambulation has been established.

  Stage 3, the *autonomous stage*, is when the skill is now automatic, not requiring the performer to focus attention on the mechanics of the action, so freeing up cognitive effort to attend to other aspects of the game or activity. Individuals by this stage can detect their own errors and correct them automatically as they go along. I often demonstrate this stage (or rather that the performer has not reached this stage) by asking a pre-warned student in one of my lectures to juggle three tennis balls while reciting the alphabet. Not a problem if you ask a student who can juggle, as both activities of juggling and reciting the alphabet require very little cognitive effort because they are thoroughly practised and mastered. Almost invariably, when I ask the performer to juggle three tennis balls and recite the alphabet backwards, then both the order of letters and the three balls are almost immediately lost. If I ask the student to juggle four balls, even a forwards alphabet is not usually attempted and the student returns to Stage 1, the *cognitive stage*.

- *Adams' closed loop theory (1971).* There are just two stages in this model. Stage 1 is the *verbal-motor stage*, which is almost equivalent to Paul Fitts and Michael Posner's initial stage. Jack Adams – a researcher in physical education – believed that the first stage does not have the total focus on cognitive dimension that Fitts and Posner ascribed in their model, but includes some involvement from the body – some kind of muscle memory. The second stage, the *motor stage*, has a cognitive component but is also automatic. In learning, a *perceptual trace* is developed which is the past memory of the successful movement, allowing a comparison to take place between the trace and the present movement and it allows

Success using diversification requires the correct selection of the appropriate implement and the motor skills necessary to wield the implement in dexterous ways – even a chocolate pudding lid.

*Source:* Malcolm Hughes.

**Connect and Extend**

For a discussion of how cognitive development relates to psychomotor development in children, read: Rhemtulla M. & Tucker-Drob, E. M. (2011) Correlated longitudinal changes across linguistic, achievement, and psychomotor domains in early childhood: evidence for a global dimension of development. *Developmental Science*, September, *14*(5), 1245–1254.

for correction of the movement. A memory trace is the control mechanism that begins movement. By stage 2, these traces are sufficiently strengthened to be used automatically.

On more occasions than I care to discuss, I drive a golf ball and the shot starts straight but then veers off to the right in a banana-shape called a 'fade'. I know I am swinging my club from in-to-out rather than out-to-in, and so before attempting the next drive will mentally and physically practise swinging the club, re-establishing the in-to-out shape – *the perceptual trace*.

- *Gentile's two-stage model (1972).* Developmental scientist Ann Gentile also developed a two-stage model of information processing. Stage 1 is about 'getting the idea of the movement' and this involves attending to relevant stimuli and not being distracted by non-relevant stimuli, e.g. scooping the right amount of chocolate pudding out of the bowl while ignoring the itch on the top of your head which could be alleviated with the spoon. Learners must also determine the appropriate movement patterns to adopt, for example, the different batting actions in baseball, cricket or rounders. The ball needs to be hit but the hitter has to adapt the movement for the bat they are holding.

  Stage 2 is the fixation/diversification stage, that is, where necessary, selecting what is needed to accomplish the goal. This needs to be done with consistency. The term 'fixation' refers to skills that are closed – no real decision to be taken, that is, tying a shoelace, tapping-in a putt; or 'bend it like Beckham' into the top right-hand corner from 20 yards out.

  Diversification refers to an open skill selection of a well-learned and rehearsed repertoire in order to successfully accomplish the goal. For example, a young child sitting in her high chair may be presented with a bowl of soup and three pieces of cutlery: a knife, fork and spoon. Successfully wielding each of these three requires both the correct selection of the appropriate implement – for example, a spoon – and the motor skills necessary to wield the spoon in dexterous ways to successfully transport the soup from the bowl into her mouth. Even more diversification may be required. A spoon can be used differently depending on the consistency of the soup, the shape of the bowl and spoon, and the social occasion. Best table manners require the tipping of the bowl and a scooping motion away from the soup eater – perhaps, on reflection, not a consideration for those obliged to sit in high chairs or those dealing with chocolate sauce for the first time!

- *Schmidt's schema theory (1975).* Behavioural scientist Richard Schmidt's theory arose from the problem that a number of theorists had with existing theories at the time, especially the idea of a closed loop, where feedback about an action is available each time. Schmidt argued that Adams's theory could not adequately explain fast movements and that movement must be controlled not by motor programmes, but by schemas. These are a set of generalised rules applicable to a set of movements, for example, throwing a ball into a hoop on the ground. On the first attempt a child may throw the ball too short, next time it is too long. By the third time the throw successfully lands in the target area. Thus the child is learning to associate the movement with distance and accuracy. With practice and repetition the schema is strengthened, eventually leading to highly skilled performance on this task. Schmidt's generalised motor schema is a general memory representation of the action and is responsible for controlling a set of actions (such as throwing, running). The motor response schema takes responsibility for the set of rules governing such actions and is context-specific.

Information-processing theories took over from maturation theories and were established as the accepted wisdom for several decades. There are some criticisms of this approach:

- While importance is given to memory, too much time is given over to this mental process. Too many examples exist in sports skills of there being little time available for schemas to happen. For example, when a tennis player receives the ball from a service at over 100 mph, there is insufficient time for the server to make the memory comparisons to previous movements and then execute a response based on this information.

- Past experience largely accounts for movement production. Information processing does not account for novel actions since these are not yet in the memory banks.

- The capacity to store and organise every single schema would require a massively sized storage space (however, advocates of information-processing theories suggest generalised motor programmes are modified for each specific situation).

## Ecological perspective – dynamic systems theory

Critics of information processing favour an ecological approach. The ecological approach originates from the mathematics of **dynamic systems**, which are patterns forming where future evolution is predictable from present states. Put another way, movement skills evolve from initial attempts, to fully automated and consistent mastery. How quickly such an evolution takes place and how far towards mastery an individual will get depends on what they are doing now – there are patterns of evolution which can be defined mathematically. Dynamic systems theory builds on the work of Soviet movement scientist Nikolai Bernstein (1967) and led to later studies of patterns of co-ordinated movement behaviour – taking a penalty kick in soccer (e.g. Caljouw *et al.*, 2004; Savelsbergh & Van der Kamp, 2000). As a view, dynamic systems theory emphasises developmental unfolding and, as such, differs from the maturational perspective describing stages which define when specific and sequential motor behaviours will occur. Dynamic systems theory suggests that motor co-ordination takes place by changes in the environment and the demands of a specific task. This theory proposes that development cannot be separated from the context in which a person develops.

Dynamic systems theory differs from the information-processing approach in a number of fundamental ways. Firstly, it places less importance on the role of memory. Instead, it proposes that what is important is the goal of any action. Movements are planned at an abstract level to achieve the goal then contextualised. Suppose you had never played basketball before but knew the aims of the game. The field of play provides many opportunities for various actions or what psychologist James Gibson (1979) referred to as 'affordances' (ways of doing things – more of this in the next chapter). If you were thrown the ball, you do not need to have played before to try the affordances of trying to project the ball in your hands into the basket above you. Such affordances are not the same for each person. Each player needs to actively seek out their own affordance in the context of the playing environment, usually by trial and error – a method of discovery. Explicit instruction is not always necessary.

A second difference for ecological psychologists is the role of the central nervous system. Movement is organised not solely in the CNS but at peripheral nervous system levels of touch and muscle movement in, for example, hands, eyes and feet. The executive orders provided by the CNS are broad, 'throw the ball', and the union of perception and action and hands and eyes together determine the specifics of how this is to be achieved. The argument against central processing is persuasive. How can our brain control so many muscles and joints, and produce movements in so many different environments? It would be too cumbersome to operationalise. This is known as the 'degrees of freedom' problem.

Advocates of dynamic systems theory propose that being able to operationalise arises from the properties of co-ordinated structures of muscles which are self-organising – for example, leg muscles that do not keep going back to the CNS for instructions. Look at the running techniques of the great sprinters. They are all different because of how each individual organises their individual movements. Environment also dictates difference. Children running in a

> **Dynamic systems**
> Movement defined and analysed by using mathematical terms, symbols and values.

**Connect and Extend**

Look at some video of sprinters, observe the differences and see whether there are movement principles in common. How much are these world-class sprinters thinking about what they are doing? (There are plenty of excellent clips on **www.youtube.com/** but don't stay away from the text for too long!)

school playground will all display variations that are dependent on the particular environmental conditions. (Think back to the opening scene of this chapter where there are many children running in a playground.) If the playground is wet, if there are other children to avoid, or the player has to keep control of the football, the runner must adapt the running technique to meet the demands of that particular situation. This is also how new motor patterns emerge: as older ones become less efficient, new patterns emerge that are not planned in detail beforehand but refined by the specific demands of the task and the situation.

Three main points might help you summarise the key points of dynamic systems theory research:

1. It is through self-organising properties in the body that movement emerges. Even the most simple of skills demands co-ordination of postural, perceptual and muscle systems.

2. As new patterns emerge and older ones become redundant, there may be discontinuities (periods of time) when motor performance is disrupted.

3. Muscle forces and mechanical interactions between muscle groups are influenced by overall intentions of the action, by body position, speed of limb, and direction and size of specific body segments being used.

Critics of the approach offer two arguments. Firstly, downplaying the role of memory leaves it difficult to believe there is no importance placed on internal representation. Movements are self-organising, yet surely memory must be involved?

Secondly, although as mastery is gained the role of cognitive processes is lessened, all actions do involve a cognitive element. Decisions need to be made, for example in a game: who to pass to, where to run, which shot to select.

As a relatively new theoretical position, dynamic systems theory has historically contributed to our existing knowledge of how early motor behaviours in particular are formed: stepping (Thelen & Ulrich, 1991); walking (Clark & Phillips, 1993); and clapping (Fitzpatrick *et al.*, 1996). As we shall now see, recent advances in neuroscience research (such as the plasticity of the brain and the holistic performance of the brain) have moved our understanding on from single idea explanations (like those stage models we discussed earlier of Adams, Gentile and Schmidt) towards connections between motor and cognitive performance, with multiple influences and levels in all motor acts.

**Reflect**   No one perspective can entirely explain skill acquisition or motor performance. Which perspective do you believe best explains it? Review the last three sections: biological-maturation perspective; information-processing perspective; ecological perspective. Which of these is most convincing for you?

## Linking motor and cognitive performance

Interest in relationships between motor and cognitive performance has existed for many years and been the source of much scholarly debate. In the sixteenth century, scientist and philosopher René Descartes asserted that the mind and body were separate, whereas in the last century Jean Piaget (first discussed in Chapter 1) held that motor and cognitive processes were inseparable (Piaget & Inhelder, 1966). In recent times the existence of an interdependent relationship between the two facets of development was put forward by psychologists Emily Bushnell and J. P. Boudreau (1993) who associated motor development with the onset of certain perceptual and cognitive capacities, for example, hand–eye co-ordination. Others have found some evidence of this association between cognitive and motor development while investigating impaired motor function – for example, paralysis (Hamilton, 2002) since these have been linked to later problems in attention and language acquisition. Some studies into ADHD (e.g. Bidwell *et al.*, 2011: Klimkeit *et al.*, 2004) and dyslexia (e.g. Viholainen *et al.*, 2006; Viholainen *et al.*, 2002) have strongly suggested links between cognitive and motor deficits. Neurobiological evidence linking the two has been found using functional brain imaging techniques: the cerebellum is involved in higher-order cognitive operations – memory and creativity (Hibi & Shimizu, 2012) where it was previously believed that its function was to regulate motor skills (Diamond, 2000). Findings from these and other studies would suggest that not just an association exists between cognitive and motor functions but that a profound relationship between the two may be mediated by attention (and yet in previous studies attention has not been controlled). The aim of the study in the *Focus on Theory* feature below was to investigate the relationship between aspects of motor and cognitive performance, independently of attention. This *Focus on Theory* shows that even the most carefully planned and crafted research can produce conflicting and confusing results.

**Attention**
The degree of focus on the task in hand measured in time.

## Focus on Theory

### Relation between cognitive and motor performance in 5–6-year-old children: results from a large-scale cross-sectional study

A Dutch study (Wassenberg *et al.*, 2005) investigated possible links between motor performance and cognitive development, using a sample of 378 children aged 5–6 years. The sample of 213 boys and 165 girls was large enough to control for the influence of sex. The age group was selected since little is known about higher cognitive processes of children in this age range – previous studies have focused on much younger children (Diamond, 2002) or those aged 7 and over (Anderson, 2002). Most importantly, the study worked on the premise that well-developed motor performance is a prerequisite for learning.

Cognitive tests measured verbal and perceptual abilities, and memory: the kinds of factors suggested by neuropsychologist Muriel Lezak and her colleagues (2004). The research protocol included at least one test suitable for the assessment of children of primary-school age with satisfactory validity and reliability. Quantitative and qualitative measures were used for the motor component, the former reflecting the acquisition of motor milestones and the latter capturing the acquisition of fundamental movement patterns (see Goh *et al.*, 2012 for an explanation). A score was calculated as an overall measure of cognitive performance, and a statistical analysis investigated the relationship between this overall measure and that of motor performance. Further statistical methods were then used to measure the nature of the specific relationship between motor and cognitive performance.

Overall, little significant relation was found between motor performance and cognitive development, which contradicts previous research, including that of Jean Piaget, who made an association between the two in the past. However, motor performance was found to be related to several specific cognitive measures for both boys and girls when that included paying attention to the task in hand; therefore paying attention and motor performance are related even though some interesting parallels between motor and cognitive development in 5–6-year-olds could not be ascribed to attention. It is not surprising, given the mixed findings of this study that the researchers call for further studies in other developmental periods to investigate similar parallels.

*Source*: Renske Wassenberg and colleagues from the University of Maastricht (2005). Relation between cognitive and motor performance in 5- to 6-year-old children: Results from a large-scale cross-sectional study. *Child Development*, 76, 1092–1103, at http://arno.unimaas.nl/show.cgi?fid=4670

The interpretation of the connection between cognition and motor performance remains, in part, open to question. Of course, we are on much firmer ground using scientific methods of observation to define the development of motor performance. Knowing the kinds of observation that have been made, and the results of typifying the ages at which different signs of motor development have been observed, helps parents, teachers and other practitioners to recognise that motor development is normal, or that there may be a situation with an individual child that requires further investigation. What can children do and at what ages should we look for motor skills to develop? It is to the models of motor development that we now turn.

# Motor development viewed as a staged model

Motor development is directly related to all other aspects of development. Earlier writers in motor development frequently suggested that motor development is a lifelong process and one that is revealed principally through changes in movement behaviour. These changes provide a 'window' through which to observe motor development and also provide clues to the underlying motor processes. A convenient way to view this is the hourglass model (Gallahue & Ozmun, 2005). This is a heuristic model that conceptualises the process of motor development through various stages across the lifespan. An adaptation of the model relevant to the birth to 11 age range appears in Figure 7.6.

**Reflexive movement phase**
The stage at which the first movements are evident. Reflexes are spontaneous sub-cortically controlled movements and are the first phase of development.

**Rudimentary movement phase**
The second stage in movement development occurring between birth to 2 years.

## Phases of motor development

Movements in the reflexive movement phase have already been discussed and cover the period in the womb and until a child is 1 year old. It is necessary that many of these early reflexive movements are phased out by the end of this period and, in reality, this is normally so by about 9 months. Then follows the rudimentary movement phase, spanning birth to age 2.

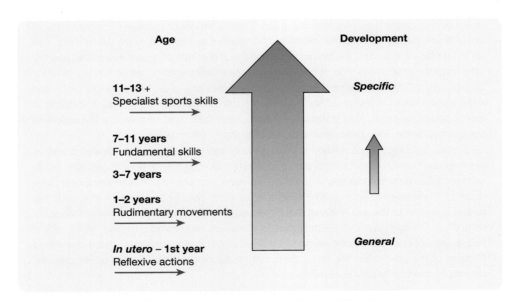

**Figure 7.6** Gallahue and Ozmun's stages of motor development (1998)

*Source*: Doherty, J. & Brennan, P. (2007). *Physical education and development 3–11. A guide for teachers.* Abingdon: Routledge. Reproduced with permission.

Many of these early movements co-exist with different reflexes but gradually *voluntary* movements are achieved through maturation of the infant's nervous system. Rudimentary movements are centred around postural control, manipulation and early locomotion. Maturation determines the sequence of the movements. Timing of their appearance is highly predictable but, as with all motor behaviours, shows great individual variation. Sitting and standing are arguably two highly significant motor achievements in this phase. Of great importance, too, is that these skills also signal the achievement of balance, which we will meet in the next chapter and which has a direct but often overlooked relationship to academic performance. Manipulation is discussed later under 'reaching and grasping'.

Mention infant locomotion and most people will assume the conversation is about walking. This is of course a major achievement and a motor skill that dominates our lives thereafter, but other forms of locomotion can be observed even earlier: commonly crawling (moving on hands and knees) and creeping (moving using arms while dragging the legs and stomach). The former occurs between 6 and 8 months and the latter from 8 to 10 months. Both skills involve important cross-patterning work of the arms and legs which develops hand–eye co-ordination, balance and encourages myelination of the CNS – all important ingredients for learning.

Between the ages of 2 and 7 is the fundamental movement phase which is characterised by children's exploration of their movement capabilities. These are the motor skills that are most commonly observed in playground activities. The skills can be conveniently grouped into three types and are shown below: locomotion skills that allow the body to move through space; stability skills involving axial movements and balance; and manipulation skills that allow the control of objects by hands or feet. The grouped skills are shown in Table 7.2.

The specialised movement phase is the period from 7 years to the onset of puberty extending up to children's final year in primary school or into their first years at secondary school. By this time the fundamental skills are well established and children now are eager to test out their capabilities in challenging situations. Fundamental motor skills are refined, combined and expanded upon in what physical educationalist Patricia Maude (1996) referred to as 'the skill hungry years'. Activities in the playground become more formalised and often resemble adult versions of games such as soccer, netball, hockey, basketball and tennis. Children in this phase are often highly motivated to perform physically and it is important that teachers capitalise on their enthusiasm. As noted above and earlier in the chapter, phases of movement development are defined by 'motor milestones'. What are these milestones? What should we be looking for?

**Table 7.2** Movement skills in the fundamental movement phase

| Stability skills | Locomotion skills | Manipulation skills |
| --- | --- | --- |
| Bending | Walking | Handling |
| Stretching | Running | Ball rolling |
| Twisting | Chasing | Kicking |
| Turning | Vertical jumping | Throwing |
| Reaching | Distance jumping | Catching |
| Swaying | Hopping | Trapping |
| Pushing | Galloping | Striking |
| Pulling | Sliding | Punting |
| Swinging | Leaping | Dribbling |
| Dodging | Skipping | Volleying |
| Rolling | Bouncing | Stopping |
| Balancing | Climbing | |

*Source*: Doherty, J. & Brennan, P. (2007). *Physical education and development 3–11. A guide for teachers.* Abingdon: Routledge. Reproduced with permission.

**Fundamental movement phase**
The third phase of movement development with movements such as throwing, catching, hopping, etc. Occurs between 2 and 7 years.

**Locomotion skills**
Motor skills that allow the body to move through space.

**Stability skills**
Those motor skills that include axial movements and balance.

**Manipulation skills**
Motor skills that allow the body to manipulate objects by using hands or feet.

**Specialised movement phase**
This phase occurs after the basic movement skills are in place. It is sports-specific and tends to be technique-oriented.

• • • • • • • • • • • • • • • •
**Connect and Extend**
Motor milestones are one tool for professionals to assess when something might be wrong. One sequence of motor milestones is learning to form sounds, babbling and then recognisable words. So what happens to the brothers and sisters of children with autism – often called 'the silent children'? Read: Iverson, J. & Wozniak, R. (2007). Variation in vocal–motor development in infant siblings of children with autism. *Journal of Autism & Developmental Disorders, 37*, 158–170.
• • • • • • • • • • • • • • • •

# Motor milestones

**Motor milestones**
Early and fundamental motor skills that appear in a relatively consistent sequence but with individual timing variations.

The old adage of 'You can't run before you can walk' remains true. The spontaneous, reflexive movements of the newborn are replaced within a child's first two years by the co-ordinated achievements of sitting, standing, walking and running; examples of **motor milestones**. These landmark accomplishments in motor development are reported for us in the ground-breaking work of early investigators such as Bayley (1935) and Shirley (1963), resulting in charting the sequence of motor skills and the typical age at which these are achieved.

Table 7.3 shows some of these skills and when they appear. What is also very apparent from this table is that an age range exists for the emergence of all these skills and that individual variation has been observed within a time frame of, for example, 3–6 months. Some children will walk by 12 months while others have just managed this by 18 months. There is no connection between a child who is late in sitting upright and the time when the child has mastered walking or running. As humans, we are well equipped from birth with a repertoire

**Table 7.3** Milestones in motor development

| Age | Gross and fine motor skills |
| --- | --- |
| Birth to 3 months | Holds head up voluntarily<br>Holds chest up with arm support in prone position<br>Rolls from side to side<br>Displays primitive reflexes |
| 3 to 6 months | Rolls from front on to back<br>Sits with support initially and then alone<br>Reaches out to touch nearby objects<br>Discovers properties of objects through touch |
| 6 months to 1 year | Sits down without support<br>Crawls<br>Creeps<br>Stands initially by holding on to objects then alone<br>Walks with support<br>Transfers objects from hand to hand<br>Picks up objects with thumb and finger |
| 1–2 years | Walks alone<br>Walks backwards<br>Pushes and pulls objects<br>Moves to music |

**Table 7.3** *Continued*

| Age | | | Gross and fine motor skills |
|---|---|---|---|
| 2–4 years | | | Walks up and down stairs<br>Runs with confidence<br>Balances on one foot<br>Rides a tricycle<br>Uses a slide alone<br>Throws and catches a ball<br>Draws crosses and circles |
| 5 years | | | Jumping skills quite proficient<br>Walks up and down stairs alternating feet<br>Performs forward rolls<br>Uses scissors safely<br>Copies shapes on paper with some accuracy<br>Draws a recognisable person |
| 6–8 years | | | Displays some skill in batting<br>Displays some skill in ball games<br>Swims<br>Can skip and play hopscotch<br>Writes cursively |
| 9–11 years | | | Much more adept in manipulative tasks<br>Shows skill in many sports and PE<br>Rides a bike with confidence |

of motor actions that assist in our survival but we don't start to try them out at the exactly the same time.

The milestones selected for inclusion in Table 7.3 are a mixture of gross and fine motor skills. Even though the development of these skills occurs in an integrated and holistic way, it is worth teasing apart some of these skills to understand what happens, how and why.

# The development of gross and fine motor skills

## Fine motors skills: reaching and grasping

Imagine the following scene. Uzma, a 9-month-old infant is investigating the contents of a cardboard box on her dining room floor. She uses one hand to tip the box slightly so as to get a good look at the contents. The other arm stretches out inside the box, her hand guided to the fluffy elephant at the bottom of the box. As her hand closes around the toy, she carefully lifts it out of the box to take a closer look at it. Uzma gives a beaming smile of satisfaction. Success!

This brief example is intended to show the importance of voluntary reaching and grasping: not only for motor development but also for cognitive development. Proficiency in reaching for objects enables Uzma to explore her immediate environment far more fully than mere observation of it. Developmental psychologists Bennett Bertenthal and Claes von Hofsten (1998) ranked it as one of the greatest achievements in a child's first two years, an idea supported by more recent studies (e.g. van Balen *et al.*, 2012; Babinsky *et al.*, 2012).

The motor action of Uzma is quite controlled but improvements in this skill reflect development from the coarse and inaccurate flinging actions as a newborn infant called **pre-reaching** (Lee *et al.*, 2008) to the accurate and co-ordinated action of the 9-month-old infant. Emergence of the new movement skill called **directed reaching** (Thelen *et al.*, 2001) can be observed in infants of 3 months and older which accompanies advances in visual abilities and the increased control of the head, neck and shoulders. By 7 months, infants show a preference to extend one arm at a time, replacing the earlier movement where two hands are extended together. After 9 months, reaching becomes much more precise and they no longer need to look at the outstretched hand when reaching for objects. This allows their attention to be diverted elsewhere. At this time too, they cup their hands in anticipation of the size and shape of the object they intend to grasp.

All of this may seem to take a rather long time but there is a reason for this. The actions of reaching and grasping are closely linked to development of infant perceptual capacities (as we discuss in detail in Chapter 8), in providing internal information on the location of the object, location of the hand in relation to the infant's body, distance of the object to be grasped and allowing the eyes to make the necessary finer adjustments to perform the action successfully.

**Pre-reaching**
Early stage of motor control where the infant has limited control over limbs.

**Directed reaching**
More advanced controlled action that is co-ordinated to specific targets.

• • • • • • • • • • • • • • • •
**Connect and Extend**
How are the different skills of reaching connected? For details of six experiments on infant reaching, read: Vishton, P. M., Ware, E. A. & Badger, A. N. (2005). Different Gestalt processing for different actions? Comparing object-directed reaching and looking time measures. *Journal of Experimental Child Psychology*, 90, 89–113.
• • • • • • • • • • • • • • • •

**Ulnar grip**
Early form of grasping where the fingers close against the palm.

**Pincer grasp**
More advanced grip using opposing index finger and thumb.

Pre-reaching: at 3 months reaching is still quite inaccurate.

*Source*: © Pearson Education Ltd / Tudor Photography.

Directed reaching: at 9 months, motor actions are much more co-ordinated.

*Source*: © Pearson Education Ltd / Jules Selmes.

It is interesting that objects that move tend to hasten pre-reaching more quickly than stationary objects. The actions are also closely linked to postural control (van Balen *et al.*, 2012) since pre-reaching is possible only when the trunk is supported in a sitting position upright which frees the arm up to extend outwards (at about 3 months). They are also related to the development of motor control in such a way that all parts need to be ready before they can work together efficiently, which is in keeping with the dynamic systems approach described earlier (Thelen *et al.*, 2001) and to the different experiences that a child may have.

As infants reach out, the ways in which they grasp objects alters. Classic work on grasping was carried out by Halverson (1931) that resulted in the compilation of a 10-stage scale of grasping development. It is to the credit of the researchers that their work continues to be referenced today. An ulnar grip replaces the grasp reflex present at birth, but is a rather coarse hold that combines the fingers and the palm. By 4–5 months infants can transfer an object from one hand to the other. Before the end of the first year, infants replace the ulnar grip with the superior pincer grasp where the thumb and forefinger are used together. This greatly improves the child's ability to pick up small objects and to manipulate them for further exploration. It is vital in painting and writing (which have a high motor component) by offering a more horizontal position for the brush or pencil and the use of the finger and thumb as guides with support from the second finger. Fine motor control is essential in the development of writing but can cause feelings of frustration and inadequacy if children are required to perform writing activities before fine motor control and adequate strength in the muscles of the wrist and hand are achieved.

*Handedness*, or a preference for one hand over the other, can be seen by age 3. Originally thought to be a side effect of brain lateralisation, it is now believed to develop in the womb (remember we discussed this in Chapter 5) where one side of the foetus's body develops faster than the other. This means that the hand you prefer as a 10-week foetus is probably the one you favour throughout your life (Hepper, 2004). Many motor actions tend to favour the use of one hand – imagine trying to learn to write using both hands at the same time. Children invariably choose the same hand to write or paint with but this may change according to the task, such as opening a door, carrying books and so forth. While most people are right-handed, about 10 per cent are left-handed. Remember there was a popular myth which considered these children are clumsy (right is *dexter* in Latin – dexterous) but in reality it is more likely that it is the children who fail to show hand preference that may be in need of support and intervention to improve their motor co-ordination.

The pincer grip: at 12 months, this girl can use her thumb and forefinger to pick up small objects.
*Source*: © Pearson Education Ltd / Jules Selmes.

By 7 years, children can write legibly.
*Source*: © Pearson Education Ltd / Jules Selmes.

**Reflect**

Do you consider being left-handed a disadvantage? How might left-handed children be disadvantaged at playgroup and school? Is there any advantage for children who are ambidextrous? Look to the *Connect and Extend* feature for some clues.

**Connect and Extend**

Is there disadvantage in being left-handed at school? Read: Hepburn, H. (2008). How a pen is mightier than prejudice. *Times Educational Supplement*, 1 February, available in the TES archive at **www.tes.co.uk/**

In the childhood years there is steady improvement in children's performance of fine motor skills due to improvements in brain and body capacity. Many of these are directly associated with their success in school – academically, physically and socially. At 3 years children can turn the pages of a book themselves, build a tower of more than six blocks and hold a pencil in a recognised writing position. By age 4 children colour inside lines, can copy square shapes and their use of scissors is improving. At 6 and 7 years, most children are proficient at tying their own shoelaces. They can write their first and last names legibly, fasten buttons and zips, and use a knife and fork correctly. In the remaining years of primary school (9–11 years), children can sew, use hand tools with precision and show much more neatness in their writing.

## Gross motors skills: the example of running

> Danni aged 11 is entered for the sprint race in the school sports day. He is a keen runner and this helps him in his PE lessons. In the weeks leading up to the event he has practised hard for the race. The day finally arrives. He crouches down and looks down the specially marked-out track. The sprint is 60 metres. Bang! The race has started. He gets a good start and is soon into his stride. His teacher has told him to keep his body straight and not to sway to the side. He extends his back leg, drives forward with his front knee, gets his front foot down quickly and uses his arms powerfully. He is running well! He flashes past the finish line in record time. The winner!

Running is a fundamental motor skill that begins approximately 6–8 months after children are able to walk. It is different from walking because it has a flight phase in which the feet make no contact with the ground for a short period. Younger children may demonstrate a running action as early as 2 or 3 years, but lack the control to stop and start with any efficiency. Between 5 and 8, improvements in form are readily detectable. In the later primary years, running variations become more obvious – dodging, showing variations in pace and direction and combining the running skill with another (e.g. carrying or travelling with a ball).

Observation of early or immature running reveals little flight phase, a short leg swing and no extension of the supporting leg. The swinging leg rotates out from the hip and the arms are barely used. As children mature and increase in strength and co-ordination, qualitative changes occur in the mechanics of the action: stride length increases, there is extension of hips and ankles, flight time is increased, the knee of the leading leg is lifted higher and the distance the support foot precedes the runner's centre of gravity decreases (Cappellini *et al.*, 2006).

One might expect to see further improvements in the skill in the later childhood period and into adolescence (7–13 years). Certainly running is central to most sports-related activities and a core element of many club and school-based PE programmes. Many children who regularly participate in sports or health-related exercise do show refinements in running form and speed, but when the skill is not practised regularly or when motivation to run is low, it is not uncommon for faults to appear in the running action. Inefficiencies in the angle of body lean, the positioning of the legs and balance difficulties related to the requirement to generate considerable force to execute the skill are all observable in this age group. Running fast is a function of stride rate and stride length, and since it is the latter that increases with age it is not unreasonable to assume that growth of the limbs accounts for some of the changes in speed in the childhood years.

As with fine motor skills, there is steady improvement in children's performance of gross motor skills in the childhood years, which have important implications for their socialisation with others, self-esteem and participation in school PE and sports. By 3 years, children can climb, balance on one foot, hop and walk up and down stairs alternating feet. At 4 most perform broad jumps and can throw a ball overhand. Between 5 and 6 children can skip and show some accomplishment in skating and using a scooter. They can kick a ball up to 6 metres and catch with some consistency. By 7 and 8, most fundamental motor skills are proficient and children have significantly developed their capacity to balance. Between 9 and 11, they demonstrate better perceptual-motor skills and co-ordination, decreased reaction times, increased strength and speed in the physical activities in which they engage in and out of school. These wide-ranging and exciting motor developments depend upon appropriate physical developments, and it is now worth noting the specifics of the dependence of one developmental aspect on another.

# Implications of physical development on motor performance

Components of physical development, that is, height, weight and physique, have implications for the performance of children's motor skills: for example, how head size affects balance or how hand size affects the manipulation of tools and equipment. Table 7.4 presents a number of such implications across the age range.

**Table 7.4** Physical development and its implications for motor skill performance

**Toddler/infant (0–2 years)**

- Length at birth affects the onset of independent walking (longer limbs walk earlier)
- Weight at birth affects the onset of independent walking (heavier babies walk earlier)
- Increased body size affects the performances of strength-related tasks (inconclusive evidence)
- Head size adversely affects balance

**Early childhood (2–6 years)**

- Excess body weight detrimental to self-propelling activities, e.g. running
- Weight is advantageous for the application of force to an object, e.g. throwing
- Perceptual-motor abilities developing but still problems in directions, timing, spatial awareness
- Basic motor skills are being learned. Bilateral activities (e.g. skipping) are difficult
- Cardiovascular systems prefer patterns of work and rest. Children need to be active!
- Dressing skills mostly in place
- Fine motor skills not yet mature
- Gross skills make rapid progress
- Poor posture evident

**Middle to later childhood (6–11 years)**

- Excess body weight detrimental to self-propelling activities, e.g. running
- Weight is advantageous for the application of force to an object, e.g. throwing
- Reaction time is still slow at 6. By 11 it is well established
- Children tire easily
- Visual mechanism is fully developed by the end of this period
- Fundamental motor skills are in place
- Practice is essential on motor skills to achieve proficiency
- Fundamental motor skills are refined to prepare for sports-specific skills (9 years +)

---

Before moving on, let's summarise what we have learned in the middle section of this chapter:

- For any theory of motor development to be robust it must be able to explain the emergence of new skills that are not the same as those movements that are present at birth.

- Between the 1930s and 1950s the biological-maturation perspective was the dominant discourse in motor development. This perspective views change as an internal process that is dictated by an individual's body clock.

- In the information-processing perspective information is interpreted and codified by the brain and acted upon by comparing new information to short-term and long-term memories, in turn resulting in decision-making.

**Summary 2**

- Four models of information-processing were explored: Fitts and Posner's three-stage model; Adams' closed loop theory; Gentile's two-stage model and Schmidt's schema theory (check back to see the differences).
- Major critics of information processing favour an ecological approach – specifically *dynamic systems* where movement skills evolve from initial attempts, to fully automated and consistent mastery (the emphasis is on automated).
- Neurobiological evidence links motor and cognitive performance by associating motor development with the onset of certain perceptual and cognitive capacities.
- Motor development is a lifelong process, revealed principally through changes in movement behaviour in four phases: reflexive (foetus to 1); rudimentary (birth to 2 – notice the overlap); fundamental (2 to 7); and specialised (7 to puberty). Three sets of skills develop in the fundamental stage: locomotion, stability and manipulation skills.
- The spontaneous, reflexive movements of the newborn are replaced within a child's first two years by the co-ordinated achievements of sitting, standing, and walking; these are examples of motor milestones.
- Motor milestones include the development of fine motor skills (reaching and gripping) and gross motor skills (sitting, walking and running).
- Physical development has implications for the development of motor performance: for example, longer limbs – walk earlier.

# Factors influencing motor development

Motor development follows a universal sequence, almost. Where there are cultural variations, this may be explained in part through genetic factors but not in entirety. African babies are more advanced in early skills than European counterparts by up to 5 months difference in the onset of walking (Gardiner & Komitzki, 2005). A more acceptable explanation is that any differences are also due to factors and customs within particular environments, for example in practices that encourage early or late development of motor skills. An example is child-rearing. In many African and West Indian cultures where infant motor development is quite advanced, great store is placed on the acquisition of sitting and walking. In Zambia, mothers carry their babies on slings on their backs but also provide much free time for them to explore their surroundings on the ground. The infants show advancement in their early motor skills. In Jamaica a practice called **formal handling** occurs whereby the infant is given massage and stretching exercises soon after birth to stimulate the body and to prepare for these important milestones. As the child matures, other propping and bouncing exercises are added for further stimulation. Because of this, the infants were found in an early study to sit and walk earlier than European children (Hopkins & Westra, 1988). Interestingly, Jamaican infants were not found to crawl any earlier than other cultures, which suggests the advancement is seen only in the skills that receive stimulation, in this case sitting and walking.

There is some evidence that cultural practices can slow down motor development. In a classic study by developmentalist Wayne Dennis (1960) of the motor development of Iranian orphans in very deprived circumstances – there was little opportunity for them to move freely – Dennis found this early practice delayed the onset of walking until well after the infants were 2 years old. He also noticed they adopted a shuffling motion and that they missed out the crawling stage completely. If there is little opportunity for early movement, motor milestones are delayed. However, once the deprivation is removed, the children make rapid advances in

**Formal handling**
Stretching and massage activities used by parents in some African and Jamaican communities to promote early walking.

• • • • • • • • • • • • • • • •
**Connect and Extend**
For a short article on the movements learnt by babies between 3 and 4 months to help them crawl, stand and walk, read: Honig, A. (2007). Born to move. *Parent & Child*, *14*, 25. Remember this is a magazine article and not an academic paper.
• • • • • • • • • • • • • • • •

motor development. The nomadic Ache people of Paraguay actively discourage their infants from crawling away from their mothers. As part of their travelling existence the children will later become involved in practices relevant to their culture and by age 9 their skills in climbing trees and wood chopping are in advance of most other children at that age. What does this tell us? It suggests that motor development is determined by both maturation and the environmental factors. If we accept this, then programmes of enhancement like stepping programmes do little to progress towards later milestones. The old saying 'they will all get there in the end' seems very relevant to infant motor development.

**Reflect**    It is common practice in many Western cultures to use aids such as baby bouncers to promote early walking in children. Is this helping children or will they walk when they are maturationally ready to do so? What is the evidence?

Differences between the sexes on the performance of motor skills before the age of 11 are minimal, although studies in the past 20 years have reported that boys outperform girls on gross motor skills like running and throwing and jumping (but not by much), and with the exception of balance (Thomas & Thomas, 2008). Qualitative development in the performance of motor skills (predominantly gross skills such as hopping, throwing, running, etc.) across the school years – and for both sexes – can be attributed to increases in body mass and height, physiological development and better neurological functioning. Biological differences between the sexes and their effect on motor performance have been discussed earlier, but their role is much diminished in the primary school years in contrast to the secondary school years where biomechanical factors, differences in body mass composition, and strength levels highlight the differences between boys and girls even further. In Chapter 6 we hinted at the importance of play activities in early cognitive development. Is this also the case for physical development? Do different play activities engaged in by boys and girls add to the differences in physical development and motor performance?

## The importance of play

Environmental factors have a role to play in influencing gender differences in motor development. Teachers (and parents) may have particular sex role expectations of children from a very early age, which determine what they play and how they play. Some studies (for example, Coakley, 2007) tell us that boys' involvement in sport is viewed as *de rigueur* in the road to adulthood, but this is not the case for girls. In fact, older girls' attitude towards sport can suffer if boys are allowed to join in with their sporting activities. Having to compete with boys and their growing edge on performance turns girls off competing at all (Lubans *et al.*, 2011). Commentators such as those writing in *The Journal of Physical Education, Recreation & Dance* (e.g. JOPERD, 2008) have argued that physiological and psychological differences must be taken into consideration before allowing boys to participate in girls' teams or allowing girls to participate in boys' teams. Certainly without targeted support at a societal level, girls' motivation to engage in physical activities and sports is reduced and consequently they never achieve their full potential with regard to skill and performance. Such concerns support societies which encourage girls to participate in what might be termed 'female-oriented' activities such as dance and gymnastics and boys in the 'male-oriented' team and contact activities like rugby and soccer. This view is challenged in many clubs and schools, where both sexes participate in a range of sports at recreational and competitive levels.

The social environment in which children grow up impacts upon individual motor skill proficiency by influencing values, knowledge and skills. The first environment children are exposed to is the family, which at this stage is the significant agent in the socialisation of children into activity and sport. Indeed, there are many ways in which parental attitudes and practices influence children's participation in physical activity and sport, including the provision of toys and sports equipment from an early age which helps children to become competent in motor skills. Messages from parents about the value they attach to physical activity and sport are absorbed by children. Words of praise from parents engender feelings of accomplishment from the child that encourage participation, whereas overt criticism and negativity undermine confidence and impair progress (Pagura *et al.*, 2006). In the middle and later childhood years, the influence of one's peers as a socialisation agent in sport and activity increases (Sabiston & Crocker, 2008). A lack of competency in motor skills becomes most obvious in these years and can lead to some children feeling excluded by their peers from play and sports (Hills, 2007).

Families who participate in physical activity, for example, by going to the swimming pool, playing tennis or walking, emphasise the importance attributed to such activities by parents. Activities engaged in together that include fun and variety promote positive attitudes and a huge variety of physical skills. Get out there and play!

Unfortunately in many modern societies parents harbour concerns about children's safety when playing outdoors. This is understandable and not to be trivialised. It does make more urgent those calls for safe and stimulating outdoor play spaces with a range of equipment that challenge growing bodies to climb, roll, scramble, swing, crawl and balance. When these play spaces do exist, children will play more (Tovey, 2007)!

In the following *Controversy* box we discuss the benefits of outdoor play and also raise the question of whether this area is afforded sufficient status in contemporary childcare practice.

- - - - - - - - - - - - - - - -

**Connect and Extend**

Unfortunately there are understandable and genuine concerns about children playing outside and the kinds of games allowed in the playground. Read the magazine article: Barker, I. (2007). Is it bonkers to ban conkers? 16 February 2007. *Times Educational Supplement* archive, 16 February, at **www.tes.co.uk**

- - - - - - - - - - - - - - - -

## Controversy

### Is outdoor play devalued in primary educational practice?

Four years ago I visited Blackawton Primary School in Devon. All children (and staff) bring a change of clothes to school so that they can go outside whatever the weather, and the children (though not the staff) are encouraged to climb the tall trees that form one of the boundaries of the school. When Dave Strudwick, the head teacher, pointed the trees out to me, I was astonished and excited that challenging physical outdoor play was so encouraged.

In the United Kingdom, however, changes to educational practice in the past 25 years have seen a steady decline in the emphasis placed upon outdoor learning and physical play. Factors include a strong shift towards a focus on children's literacy and numeracy development, a narrowed view of the purposes of education, the adoption of a top–down model that valued classroom learning whereas the outdoors was denigrated as a place to 'let off steam' with little academic contribution (Lindon, 2005). This was despite a strong tradition of early childhood pioneers such as Friedrich Froebel, Margaret McMillan and Susan Isaacs who placed outdoor play as central to education and care, and despite international recognition in the Forest schools of Norway and Reggio Emilia preschool settings in Italy. Barriers to provision for outdoor play include vandalism of outside facilities, management of the space and equipment, cost, restriction on space, storage of equipment, climate, safety and some reluctance on the part of staff to create such an area. Yet 25 years ago early childhood experts Geva Blenkin and Marian Whitehead stated, 'the most neglected and misunderstood dimension of the planned curriculum is the creation of an environment or setting in which education is to take place' (1988, p 35) and the creation of an area to encourage outdoor play seems to fit the bill.

The values of outdoor play are many. Quality outdoor environments are essential for children not least because virtually all areas of the school curriculum can be accessed through outdoor learning. Explorations of the weather develops scientific concepts; language is promoted through role-play (adventure stories, hiding games, building projects). Children's creativity is enhanced by large-scale painting, group artwork and exploring the sounds of the outside environment. Childhood experts such as Jane Drake (2001) found outdoor play built confidence and positive self-esteem and Melanie Nind (2001) found progress in nursery children's language developed from outdoor play. There are wide-ranging benefits of outdoor play for physical development gained through running, climbing, crawling and balancing, manoeuvring bikes and push-a-longs. Researcher Helen Bilton (2005) reported benefits that included improvements in risk assessment, the development of large muscle groups, heart and lung functioning and better general health. Also reported were fewer instances of challenging behaviour, more taking on responsibilities, extended concentration and a better attitude to learning.

Given this evidence, very recent practice in the United Kingdom has seen a revival in outdoor play provision and practice, and many young children now receive regular access to the outdoor environment – perhaps the case of Blackawton Primary School above is not so unusual, nor so controversial. However, this is not the case for older children. Integrated outdoor play areas seem confined to the under-5s. Given the many proven benefits of outdoor play, do you think it is given sufficient recognition and status?

For more information about Blackawton Primary School go to **www.our-school.org.uk/ blackawton** or web search using Blackawton Primary School.

## The influence of PE and school sport

Thirty-five years ago Rainer Martens, sports coach and writer, said:

> **Because of both the intrinsic and extrinsic appeal of sports, children discover them to be worthy of (such) commitment more so than many other activities. Sports also make a special contribution by teaching children to appreciate their bodies and the wondrous things they can do. The joy in a child's face when successfully hitting a ball for the first time – the inner satisfaction of mastering a complex skill – is beyond description.**

(Martens, 1978, p 15)

Few people would argue that sport and PE provide many opportunities for children to develop a range of motor skills and that teachers and sports coaches are important socialising agents for children. Despite the importance of very early home and family influences, the school remains the main institution in society for the development of skills and physical activity (Bowles & O'Sullivan, 2012). Yet up to fairly recently evidence highlights the decline in the status of sport (Walters *et al.*, 2009) and the marginalised position of PE and School Sport (sometimes referred to as PESS) in the school curricula of many countries throughout the world (e.g. Numerato, 2009). It could be argued that the highly successful London Olympics and Paralympics of 2012 have raised the profile of all sport in the UK and that there has been a sea change in attitudes towards athletes with disabilities.

There are many positive outcomes of PE and sport for children. Among benefits to health and the reduction in obesity trends (Wrynn, 2011), longevity, reduction of diseases and a better all-round quality of life have been reported (O'Connor *et al.*, 2012). There is strong evidence reporting increases in self-esteem, confidence and general well-being from regular participation in physical activity (Standage & Gillison, 2007). Schools, early years settings, playgroups and child-care settings can offer many opportunities to develop children's motor skills – within their daily programmes, curricula, at playtimes and in after-school activities. If policy makers fail to listen to the bulk of evidence on the positive effects of PE and school sport on children, there will be even greater concerns about children's health and their physical and psychological wellness in the future.

## Summary 3

We now summarise what you have learned in the final section of this chapter:

- Motor development follows a near-perfect universal sequence. Where there are cultural variations, this may be explained in part through genetic/cultural factors (e.g. Jamaican 'formal handling').
- There is some evidence that cultural practices can slow down motor development (e.g. Iranian orphans).
- Differences between the sexes on the performance of motor skills before the age of 11 are minimal.
- Environmental factors (e.g. family and gender expectations) have a role to play in influencing gender differences in motor development.
- In the middle and later childhood years, the influence of one's peers as a socialisation agent in sport and activity increases, but lack of motor development can lead to social exclusion.
- Opportunities for outside play are important – many would argue are vital.
- Despite the importance of very early home and family influences, school remains the main institution in society for the development of skills and physical activity.
- There is strong evidence of increases in self-esteem, confidence and general well-being from regular participation in physical activity.
- Schools, early years and child-care settings should offer many opportunities to develop children's motor skills within their curricula, at playtimes and in after-school activities.

## Conclusion

It was argued in this chapter that physical growth is a complex interaction of genetic and environmental factors. Although growth patterns in the childhood years show predictability, the growth rate is not constant. Early acceleration in the early childhood years is followed by a period of slowing down in middle childhood, followed by another period of acceleration in late childhood and into adolescence. While there are individual differences, there are also cultural differences. Genetics and evolutionary adaptations can explain this in part, but these are also due to factors such as diet, climate, food and general health. In many countries variations as a direct result of poverty have been reported.

Factors that influence physical development were discussed in this chapter in three categories: heredity; socioeconomic conditions; and nutrition. Nutrition is especially important in very early development when brain growth gains are at their most rapid. However, overnutrition can lead to serious physical and psychological problems. This was discussed as the real threat of childhood obesity. Alarming figures presented in this chapter show clearly that obesity is recognised as a global problem and a number of factors were discussed including parental obesity, economic status, decreased physical activity and increased screen viewing.

The chapter went on to point out how an understanding of how the body moves requires knowledge of the theories of motor development. The theoretical framework for understanding movement was presented in three key perspectives, and landmark accomplishments or motor milestones in movement phases were presented. An argument was presented for the importance of school sport and PE in providing opportunities for children to acquire and refine their movement skills. At the heart of this chapter was an attempt to associate physical and cognitive development. Although the evidence is unclear and some findings are contradictory, it is established that physical and cognitive development are clearly linked and mutually dependent. Development in both is strongly linked with opportunities for play both inside and outside, where children can take on the challenge of moving in challenging and exciting ways.

Cognitive development is also linked in profound and dependent ways with perceptual development – how we experience the world through our senses. In the next chapter we move on to consider the major milestones in perceptual development, to discuss how sensory/perceptual difficulties affect the learning process and acknowledge how the senses are involved in many aspects of learning and development. How do teachers and other practitioners maximise perceptual development to enhance pupil learning?

# Summary Table
## The Body and Physical Growth

## General physical development (pp 182–196)

There are predictable patterns of physical development in the childhood years. The infant/toddler years (birth to 2 years) are times of rapid physical development. In the early childhood years (2–6 years), growth slows a little but physical and cognitive capabilities are markedly extended. In the middle and late childhood years (6–11 years), physical growth slows down further in preparation for puberty.

### Physical growth changes in childhood (pp 183–188)

Anthropometric measures assess height, weight, length and circumference of body parts while ratios, like the body mass index, show a feature of growth as a relation between two measures. Because results for many thousands of children can be taken and aggregated, it is possible to predict how tall each child will be once fully grown, and whether growth is occurring at the expected rate. The growth trends are typical and predictable but allowance should be made for individual variations.

### Individual and cultural differences (pp 188–190)

Apart from small genetic differences and adaptations, factors such as diet, climate, food and health are obvious ones to explain individual and cultural differences. Three sets of factors influencing physical development are: heredity, lifestyle factors (including socioeconomic conditions) and nutrition.

### Childhood obesity (pp 191–195)

Childhood obesity is now considered a global epidemic. Obesity means that a person's body weight has reached a point that causes a serious risk to health. The threats to health of obesity are very clearly evident in the childhood years. Four factors that contribute to childhood obesity are: biological (e.g. genes or disability), psychological (losing confidence and interest), social (family eating patterns) and physical (lack of exercise and activity).

## Theories of motor development (pp 196–202)

For any theory of motor development to be robust it must be able to explain the emergence of new skills that are not the same as those movements that are present at birth. In fact, motor development is a lifelong process, revealed principally through changes in movement behaviour in four phases: reflexive (foetus to 1); rudimentary (birth to 2 – notice the overlap); fundamental (2 to 7); and specialised (7 to puberty). Three sets of skills develop in the fundamental stage: locomotion, stability and manipulation skills.

### Biological-maturation perspective (pp 196–197)

Between the 1930s and 1950s the biological-maturation perspective was the dominant discourse in motor development. This perspective views development as an internal process that is dictated by an individual's body clock.

### Information-processing perspective (pp 197–199)

In the information-processing perspective, information is interpreted and codified by the brain and acted upon by comparing new information to short-term and long-term memories. This results in decision-making. Four models of information-processing were explored: Fitts and Posner's three-stage model; Adams' closed loop theory; Gentile's two-stage model and Schmidt's schema theory (check back to see the differences).

### Ecological perspective – dynamic systems theory (pp 199–200)

Major critics of information processing favour an ecological approach – specifically *dynamic systems* where movement skills evolve from initial attempts to become fully automated, providing consistent mastery of the movement skill (the emphasis is on automated).

### Linking motor and cognitive performance (pp 200–202)

Neurobiological evidence links motor and cognitive performance by associating motor development with the onset of certain perceptual and cognitive capacities. This is also observed where there is significant disturbance to normal development of either motor or cognitive development.

## Motor development viewed as a staged model (pp 202–210)

### Motor milestones (pp 204–205)

The spontaneous, reflexive movements of the newborn are replaced within a child's first two years by the co-ordinated achievements of sitting, standing, and walking; these are examples of motor milestones.

### The development of gross and fine motor skills (pp 206–208)

Motor milestones include the development of fine motor skills (reaching and gripping) and gross motor skills (sitting, walking and running).

### Implications of physical development on motor performance (p 208)

Physical development has implications for the development of motor performance: quite simply, longer limbs walk earlier than shorter limbs.

## Factors influencing motor development (pp 210–214)

Motor development follows a near perfect universal sequence. Where there are cultural variations, this may be explained in part through genetic factors (e.g. Jamaican 'formal handling'). There is some evidence that cultural practices can slow down motor development (e.g. Iranian orphans). Differences between the sexes on the performance of motor skills before the age of 11 are minimal.

### The importance of play (pp 211–213)

Environmental factors (e.g. family and gender expectations) have a role to play in influencing gender differences in motor development. In the middle and later childhood years, the influence of one's peers as a socialisation agent in sport and activity increases, but lack of motor development can lead to social exclusion. Opportunities for outside play are important – many would argue they are vital.

### The influence of PE and school sport (pp 213–214)

Despite the importance of very early home and family influences, school remains the main institution in society for the development of skills and physical activity. There is strong evidence of increases in self-esteem, confidence and general well-being from regular participation in physical activity. Schools should offer many opportunities to develop children's motor skills within their curricula, at playtimes and in after-school activities.

# Going further

Pountney, T. (2007) Physiotherapy for children. Oxford: Butterworth-Heinemann Ltd.
The book is easy to read and would be an excellent study tool for students of physiotherapy, occupational therapy, speech language therapy, and for any clinician or practitioner working in the field of paediatrics or wanting to learn more about paediatrics.

Cooper, L. & Doherty, J. (2010) Physical development (supporting development in the early years foundation stage). London: Continuum.
The book makes a persuasive argument for the importance of outdoor play to the physical and motor development of young children.

Utley, A. & Astill, S. (2008) Motor control, learning and development. London: Taylor and Francis.
This book provides an overview of how the brain and nervous system control movement, and how new movements are learned and improved. The topics covered are important for anybody working as a teacher, coach or therapist.

O'Dea, J. A. & Eriksen, M. (2010) Childhood obesity prevention: International research, controversies and interventions. Oxford: OUP.
This book combines health education theory, research and practice to guide researchers, students, educators, community health workers and practitioners in the prevention of childhood obesity and the promotion of child and adolescent health and well-being.

# Useful websites

http://www.playforce.co.uk/combating-childhood-obesity/
Links to resources health initiatives and government schemes to combat obesity in children and young people.

http://www.education.gov.uk/schools/pupilsupport/pastoralcare/a0075278/healthy-schools
The Healthy Schools toolkit is designed to help schools to 'plan, do and review' health and well-being improvements for their children and young people and to identify and select activities and interventions effectively.

http://www.treloar.org.uk/physiotherapy-disabled-children
'The Treloar Trust provides education, care, therapy, medical support and independence training to young people with physical disabilities from all over the UK and overseas. Our aim is to prepare these young people for adult life, giving them the confidence and skills to achieve their full potential.'

http://www.kidsdevelopment.co.uk/HandednessInChildren.html
Very readable articles on right- versus left-handedness with some follow-up references.

# Chapter 8
## Sensory and Perceptual Development

**Overview**

# Introduction

Do you remember the photograph of Becca in the last chapter – the chocolate pudding incident? You might turn back to the image and revisit the joy of that captured moment before reading the following scenario.

*Asifa is approaching her first birthday. She is now able to sit up in her high chair and is very content looking around at people and things going on around her. When it comes to eating she is eager to do it by herself. This is not as easy as it sounds. The act of co-ordinating the spoon, the food and her mouth proves difficult. She is developing the sort of motor control to enable the spoon to reach her mouth successfully and her mental faculties are also developing to assist her in her task. There is one piece of the developmental jigsaw that does not quite fit yet. This is perception. Asifa needs to interpret a good deal of perceptual information in her immediate environment: she has to be aware that the spoon is in her right hand, she needs to estimate how far away the spoon is from her mouth and then using sight and knowledge of where her mouth is and the spoon as it travels to its destination to change the spoon's course if it is wrong. If she gets it right she eats. Get it wrong and the appetising pudding goes all over the place (and all over her face)!*

This word-scene shows Asifa involved in an everyday task that requires her to take in information about her surroundings and her position, that of the spoon, to think about this and to act. Perception is integral to almost every task that a child performs, acting as a bridge between the range of motor, social and cognitive challenges that are part of growing up. In Chapter 1 we asked the question 'What is the relationship between the different areas of development?' and argued that separating the domains of development is for the convenience of study only. In the last chapter we concluded that physical growth is a complex interaction of genetic and environmental factors. Individual difference due to biological inheritance and the effects of environment are mighty influences on development, and young children experience and perceive their environment through their senses.

In Chapter 1 we gave the example of Monique drinking from her cup for the first time and demonstrated how in that one successful act she could exhibit perceptual, physical, language and social development. We now argue that one domain of development that acts as 'the glue' defining and blending holistic child development is the development of perception through the senses. Perception precedes action, and requires action. Young children acquire new skills with guidance from information received by their perceptual faculties, organised and interpreted by the central nervous system. New actions result from play, discovery or observation, which then generate new information and perceptual development is refined and developed (Kanakogi & Itakura, 2010) providing new opportunities for physical, cognitive, emotional and language development.

This chapter begins by raising some questions about perception and clarifying some of the terms associated with the topic. It goes on to trace children's perceptual development through important milestones before addressing each of the senses in turn, explaining their role and how these develop across childhood. This leads to a discussion on sensory/perceptual difficulties relating to performance, and, finally, implications are presented for organising learning experiences that more fully involve the senses.

By the time you have completed this chapter you should be able to answer the following questions:

- What is perception and why do we need it?
- What is the difference between perception and sensation?
- What are the five main functions of perception?
- Is perceptive ability based on the brain being hard-wired or based on experience?
- How are perception, sensation and action linked?
- How does perception develop and what are the 'milestones'?
- What is intermodal co-ordination?
- What intervention programmes are available for perceptual development?
- What are the implications for learning of understanding the processes and development of perceptual development?

*Chapter Objectives*

**Reflect**

Review the questions above and note down what you think perception is. What are the key ideas for you and what might the implications be for children's learning of understanding the importance and processes of perceptual development?

# The science of perception

## What is perception and why do we need it?

'What is perception and why do we need it?' seems an obvious question to ask but the answer is perhaps not quite so obvious. The word 'perception' has a number of meanings and we use it in everyday conversation: 'That was perceptive of you'; 'What is your perception of what happened in that meeting?' Perception is understanding, and more. It is your understanding based on what you make of whatever it is you have seen or heard in the meeting. Being perceptive means to be observant, sensitive to what is happening and discerning about how you interpret what is happening. If I am observant, sensitive and discerning, I am likely to make comments about the situation that others might view as being perceptive. Let's use the three qualities of being observant, sensitive and discerning to model why we need to develop perception. During the following description and explanation of perception you should make reference to Figure 8.1.

We exist in an environment (light blue in Figure 8.1) that we can touch, see, hear, and so on. Our senses, the early development of which we explored in Chapter 6 are continually 'observing' or scanning what is happening – they are being observant and are very sensitive to changes in the information they are receiving (turquoise). A slight change in the colours of the image received by the cones at the back of the eye changes the messages being sent to the CNS. Yes, we are sensitive to millions of messages changing every second from the tips of our fingers and the balance mechanisms in our inner ear, and information about these changes is

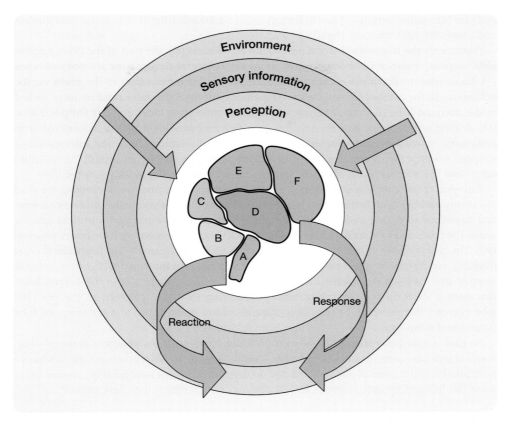

**Figure 8.1** A model of how perception relates to cognition and sensory information from the environment

The six senses receive information from the environment and these are passed to the central nervous system (CNS) which compares the information with stored sensations to discern their significance. The brain then reacts or responds through the CNS to create action or activity. (A–F: See pages 221–222 for details.)

continuously being sent to the CNS (straight arrows). Perceptive development allows us to discern the significance of each message. Information received is compared with the stored information of previous messages held in various parts of the brain (orange) and either the brain *reacts* – automatic impulsive behaviour – or *responds* – considers and formulates a response. Messages of reaction or response are then passed back through the CNS and the remote nerves to muscle receptors and we blink, jump, reach for a book or speak (curved arrows).

Where does this all happen in the brain and how? We will spend a good deal of time in the next chapter looking at cognition and the development of children's thinking, but for the time being a quick tour of the brain might help to explain how perception helps us to understand the information we have received.

The first part of the brain is the brainstem (A) sometimes referred to as the reptilian brain. You can find it deep down in the brain and it extends up from the top of the spinal cord. It is responsible for basic life support and controls heart rate and breathing, temperature and the digestion process. It is also responsible for keeping you alert to important information from your senses. This is the most reactive part of the brain responsible for the 'fright, fight or flight' response or acute stress response through the release of adrenaline from the adrenal glands. If threatened – perhaps by stepping off the pavement into the path of a speeding lorry – the immediate reaction from the brainstem (having been made aware through sound, sight and perhaps some additional sense of danger of the threat posed by the lorry) is to prepare the body for immediate action – either to fling yourself backwards (flight) or to stand your ground and physically fight the lorry (fight).

Fortunately the brainstem is right next to the cerebellum (B), the part of the brain responsible for poise, balance and body position. It also stores memories for basic learned responses – 'I know what to do in these circumstances'. It sends vital information to the brain via the brainstem. In the cerebellum will be stored memories of the sight and sound of 'lorry' linked to the occipital lobe (C) mainly made up of visual processing areas, the left temporal lobe (D) dealing with sound, and the parietal lobe (E) mainly with functions connected with movement, orientation and recognition – very useful for discerning a 'very near lorry travelling at speed towards me'. Normal reaction in this circumstance will be an instant 'Jump, don't fight!' and the adrenalin will allow the muscles to react sufficiently quickly – hopefully!

But what if the lorry is a good distance away? There may be some risk of crossing the road too slowly and being hit by the lorry, but there is plenty of time if you make the decision now. You have time to decide and to send the right information to your muscles to walk quickly across the road, and to your neck and eyes muscles to keep the oncoming lorry under observation. The frontal lobes of the brain (F) deal with the most integrated brain functions such as thinking, conceptualising and planning. If we need to make an informed and correct decision to cross the road – a considered and formulated response – then it is in the frontal lobes that such a decision will be taken, while continuing to make reference to the occipital lobe (vision), the parietal lobe (position, movement and recognition) and the temporal lobe (sound and memory).

So that is your perceptive ability – your understanding based on what you make of whatever it is you have seen, heard, felt, tasted or – well – sensed! To what extent are the newborn's perceptual abilities present and how quickly do they develop? Just how quickly can they make sense (by being observant, sensitive and discerning) of that which they have sensed?

## Theories of perception

Fascination with perceptual development of children is not new. In a compelling and very readable book *The Perceptual World of the Child*, the author Tom Bower (1983) argues that our perceptual system becomes more specified in the course of its development, operating in an increasingly restricted range of stimulation, but with a compensating increase in efficiency that allows more refined and precise discriminations with maturity. He believes, as we have asserted above, that perceptual development holds an important place in the overall framework of child development stating, 'the more we grow away from the perceptual world (towards the world of the mind), the more we are compelled to return to primitive certainties of perception' (p 85). The more deeply we think about the significance of a range of experiences, the more we need to return to those basic perceptions to check out that what we are thinking still makes sense. The components of perceptual development help us gather the information we need to make sense of ourselves and the things that happen to us. What are the components of perceptual development?

**Sensation** is the process through which sensory receptors detect information and transmit this information to our brains. Sensation is our ability to access information by responding to external stimulation via one or more of the senses. Information (or data if you prefer) is sent to the brain to be interpreted and then becomes **perception**. This is a further response from our brain and provides more structure to the information by giving it coherence. Perception is the bridge between our conscious mind and the external world. We have already seen how newborns can see and react to sounds, tastes, smells and touch, but can they make sense of it all? This is where perception comes in by interpreting information in the world immediately around them. The third stage is **cognition** (covered in the next chapter) which allows children to make decisions about the world and objects, events and people in it.

There is general agreement that our perceptual capacities fulfil five functions:

**Connect and Extend**

For a fascinating discussion of some of the issues of perception in relation to children's behaviour, connect to the final report on 'Children's activities, perceptions and behaviour in the local environment (CAPABLE)' on the project website at **www.cts.ucl.ac.uk/ research/chcaruse/**

**Connect and Extend**

Here is a useful preview of some ideas in Chapter 11. How do infants make sense of their parents' emotions? Do babies perceive when is a good time to demand attention? Read this short magazine article: Honig, A. (2006). Responding to your baby. *Parent & Child, 13,* 20–21.

**Sensation**
The process of detecting a stimulus event via a sensory system.

**Perception**
The processes through which we organise and interpret information from the senses.

**Cognition**
Knowing through the formation, memorisation and recall of ideas.

**Connect and Extend**

To extend your understanding of different meanings of 'perception', read: Kobayashi, H. (2010) Self-awareness and mental perception. *Journal of Indian Philosophy*, June, 38(3), 233–245.

1. They inform what to attend to in the environment.
2. They localise where objects are located.
3. They determine what the objects are.
4. They extract the relevant information from that received.
5. They retain the constancy of objects despite the retinal images altering.

However, there is less agreement about how these five functions develop. Traditional views on sensory and perceptual development have reflected stances adopted in the nature–nurture debate and the contrast between nativism (innate ideas) and empiricism (based on observation or experiment). The fundamental question in the debate is determining how much of what we perceive is innate (in some way hard-wired by our biology or as a matter of faith – 'placed there by God') and how much is the product of our experiences? There is no disputing the part that experience plays in perceptual development but the role of our innate perceptual capacities is also crucial. The early empiricists (remember John Locke and the mind as a blank slate) argued that perceptual capacities were constructed out of, and only out of, experience (nurture perspective). In partial contrast, Jean Piaget's theory of perceptual development (1969) suggests that perception is dependent upon intelligence which acts upon initial impressions by referencing these to previous experiences.

## Researching perception

Perception alone is not the source of one's knowledge since total dependence upon experience and only experience can cause misunderstanding, but knowledge relates to the whole development of a being, rather than information from the senses alone. Piaget's theory of perceptual development is largely one of reasoning (which we shall meet in Chapter 9) which is more about how children's cognitive faculties allow them to interpret their sensations. Piaget describes how children at different stages come to interpret their perceptions, but stresses the

Does the development of perception depend entirely on experience? If babies have no experience of falling how do they know not to go out over the visual cliff?

*Source*: Mark Richards / PhotoEdit Inc.

interactions between developing cognitive processes and experiences. In greater contrast are nativist views (by theorists such as Emmanuel Kant and Noam Chomsky) which argue that a newborn's perceptual capacities are already quite advanced (the nature perspective) and therefore not so dependent upon experience. For example, Chomsky argues that we are born with certain specialised genetically inherited psychological abilities that allow us to learn and acquire certain skills such as language (more of this in Chapter 10) and tell us not to venture out over a visual 'cliff' (see the nearby *Focus on Theory* feature). We have now established that there are two contrasting sets of theories about how perception develops. In the *Focus on Theory* feature we will focus on the work of two psychologists, James and Eleanor Gibson, and your challenge is to judge which view of the nature or nurture divide underpins their work.

## Focus on Theory

### Theories of perceptual development

Psychologist James Gibson's theory of perceptual development (1966) offered a direct contrast to the traditional theory of perception and argued that direct perception fails to include many of the vital elements that it claims to be about. His wife and fellow psychologist Eleanor Gibson later proposed (1969, 1988) that a close relationship exists between perception and action and suggested that it is impossible to study the two independently if the findings of such investigations are to be ecologically valid (taking account of how different factors are connected).

Both James and Eleanor Gibson propose interactionist approach that rejects the information-processing approach popular at the time in cognitive psychology. The interactionist approach championed the role of the central nervous system (CNS) in acting upon information about object and receiver through endless possible calculations. For James Gibson, it was the interactions of the individual with the environment that were important. These interactions allowed a vast number of possibilities through their **affordances**, all the possibilities that arise due to properties of whatever we interact with. This can be illustrated simply when a child catches a ball where the individual interaction with the ball and the environment provides many different situations and requires different motor solutions. These affordances constantly alter since the ball is moving and the child moves eyes and body in response to this. Gibson argued that such perception is active but, unlike information-processing theory, does not involve the child in inestimable calculations to discover in what direction or at what speed the ball will arrive into his hands. In a case like this, visual information flow directly on to the child's retina providing the information for perception.

The interactionist theory is a development theory because objects provide different information to those who receive it depending on the stage of development. Similarly, affordances may be perceived by exploiting **invariances** in the environment. These are the aspects that do not change in the environment. A playground slide affords the action of sliding because of its slope and smooth surface but does not alter no matter how many times you slide down it. Maturation brings about changes in how children perceive. With increased experiences, children learn to select the crucial elements in their sensory environments and their perceptual capacities become more focused and organised – very much the point that Tom Bower was making earlier.

More complex affordances are **compound variables** where information about relationships between objects is received rather than being reliant upon information about that object alone. In this way, the older or more experienced child is able to pick up higher-order relationships that the younger child is as yet unable to. Take as an example the differences

**Affordances**
Properties of objects that allow a variety of ways for an individual to interact with them.

**Invariances**
Those aspects in the environment that are constant.

**Compound variables**
Information not only about one particular variable, but about relationships between variables.

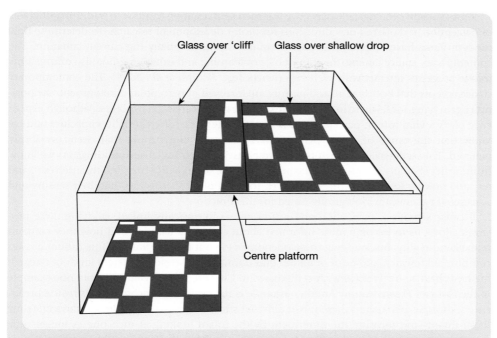

Figure 8.2  The difference between a deep drop and a shallow drop for Eleanor Gibson's 'visual cliff' experiment

*Source*: Gibson, E. J. & Walk, R. D. (1960). The 'visual cliff'. *Scientific American, 202*, 64–71.

when a 4-year-old runs in a game of chase to a 9-year-old in terms of the perceptual differences they glean from the environment. The younger child tends to run at the same pace in the game and ends up being caught very soon because s/he has not yet developed other strategies to run to avoid being caught. The older child would perceive the affordances in the game and use different running strategies to avoid being caught (such as changing direction or speed or waiting for just the right time to make the run). As this example illustrates, and as previously explained, James Gibson's interactionist theory is a development theory by virtue of the fact that, through development, older children abstract more complex information from objects or situations by exploiting the invariances in the environment. His is an influential theoretical model, but for something very practical we turn to the other half of the partnership.

Eleanor Jack Gibson's most famous work is that involving the 'visual cliff'. Her study (Gibson & Walk, 1960) involved the perception of infants, aged 6 to 14 months. The infants were placed on the centre platform (Figure 8.2) and their mothers would stand at either end of the platform successively and call to their children. Nearly all the infants refused to crawl out over the glass on the 'cliff' side, but nearly all of them were quite happy to crawl across the glass on the shallow side. From this study Gibson concluded that depth perception is developed at a very early age. How much of that development though is based on experience and how much on an intuitive dread of going over a 'cliff' is not known. The children seemed unwilling to explore the invariances of the glass surface – that they would not fall through it.

Reflect    At the top of Blackpool Tower in Lancashire, UK, is a glass floor. Many people walk across it looking down and some sit cross-legged gazing down hundreds of feet to the road below. I couldn't even look down. Are my perceptions working overtime or am I just scared? Is that the same thing?

• • • • • • • • • • • • • • • • •
**Connect and Extend**
Recognition of
face information by
3-month-olds may be
race-related, but short-term
familiarisation with
exemplars of another race
group is sufficient to reduce
the effect of recognising
others not of the same race.
A fascinating experiment is
described by Sangrigoli, S.
& De Schonen, S. (2004).
Recognition of own-race
and other-race faces by
three-month-old infants.
*Journal of Child Psychology
& Psychiatry*, 45,
1219–1227.
• • • • • • • • • • • • • • • • •

**Preference technique**
Method of study requiring
a child to show preference
for one stimulus over
another that is offered.

James Gibson's ecological perspective was seen as an exciting contrast to traditional theories of perception and offered new directions for motor development research. To determine how modern views have built on this theory, we now consider briefly the current situation. The contemporary stance accepts the importance of learning and experience but also affirms how innate processes interact with such experiences (e.g. Adolph *et al.*, 2003). The contemporary stance accepts that both nature and nurture are involved in perceptual development, the position again lying somewhere in the middle of these two polarised viewpoints. Although experience plays a vital role in perception, it is not the sole basis for creating its capacities and we know that the range of infant perceptual capacities is much more than were previously believed. This is especially true in infants' responses to their social surroundings. As we know from earlier chapters infants are well equipped for the social world they find themselves in and respond quickly to human voices and faces, for example. This suggests that their sensory and perceptual systems are biologically tuned for this function.

Because sensation, perception and action are so intrinsically linked, studying these processes allows us to become more informed about children's learning and how they come to understand reality. But studying these phenomena is not easy because infants cannot answer complicated research questions or fill out questionnaires! Therefore different kinds of research methods have to be used (as we first discussed in Chapter 3). We've already seen one example in the *Focus on Theory* feature. Another example is the **preference technique**. Using the preference technique, researchers present two different stimuli such as two pictures at the same time to an infant, and measure the time spent by the infant looking at each one. A longer time spent looking at one picture indicates a preference, which shows the ability to discriminate and may give clues as to why the infant finds that stimulus engaging.

When a stimulus such as a picture is presented on a number of occasions, the child loses interest in it and spends less time looking at it (remember the section in Chapter 6). This is known as habituation. If the stimulus is changed, the child displays interest in the new stimulus and looks at it for a longer time. If the infant looks at the second picture first, it can be inferred that discrimination is taking place. This is a useful technique for discovering what size of differences between two stimuli there has to be, for an infant to detect differences between them. Studies of this kind span both habituation and preferential-looking studies. Operant conditioning provides a third technique for data collection. Teaching an infant to turn her head (learned response) on hearing a particular sound when a moving toy provides the reinforcement allows researchers to change the sounds to find out if the infant will still turn her head. All these methods require researchers to provide information to one or more of the infant's senses, and before developing ideas about how perception develops we should check our understanding of the developing senses, building on what we learned earlier (see Chapter 5).

**Summary 1**

Before moving on, let's summarise what we have learned so far:

- Perception is the bridge between our conscious mind and the external world.

- The components (sensation, perception and cognition) of perceptual development help us gather the information we need to make sense of ourselves and the things that happen to us.

- Sensation is the process through which sensory receptors detect information and transmit this information to our brains.

- Cognition is knowing, through the formation, memorisation and recall of ideas.

- Perceptual systems fulfil five functions:
  1. they inform what to attend to in the environment;
  2. they localise where objects are located;
  3. they determine what the objects are;
  4. they extract the relevant information from that received; and
  5. they retain the constancy of objects despite the retinal images altering.

- One important question in the debate about how perception develops is determining how much of what we perceive is innate (in some way hard-wired or 'placed there by God') and how much is the product of our experiences?

- Piaget describes how children at different stages come to interpret their perceptions, but stresses the interactions between developing cognitive processes and experiences.

- Noam Chomsky argued that a newborn's perceptual capacities are already quite advanced (the nature perspective) and therefore not so dependent upon experience. He argues that we are born with certain abilities that allow us to learn language.

- Eleanor Jack Gibson's most famous work is that involving the 'visual cliff'. Nearly all the infants refused to crawl out over the glass on the 'cliff' side, and Gibson concluded that depth perception is developed at a very early age.

- Three research methods commonly used to measure perception development are preference technique, measures of habituation and training using operant conditioning.

- The three qualities of being observant, sensitive and discerning are needed to develop perception.

- Information about changes in the environment are continuously being sent to the CNS. Information received is compared with the stored information of previous messages held in various parts of the brain and either the brain reacts – automatic impulsive behaviour – or considers and formulates a response.

- Perception is what a person understands from what they sense.

# Making connections

## Connecting sensory and perceptual development

In the previous chapter you learnt that a newborn's motor skills are not especially well developed and this may have led to the common misconception that the same is true for their sensory-perceptual capacities. The majority of the basic sensory-perceptual systems are in place at birth as newborns are equipped to survive and to learn in the stunning new world in which they find themselves such a toolkit is indeed necessary. Table 8.1 confirms this and provides an overview of children's perceptual development in an interpretation of scientific observations by mum, and now grandmother, Sue Hughes remembering her daughter Stephanie's development. A more detailed discussion of these milestones follows.

**Table 8.1**  Milestones in sensory perceptual development

| Age | | Observations of sensory and perceptual development |
|---|---|---|
| Birth | 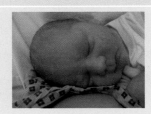 | I wasn't prepared for how 'knowing' a baby can be when first born. Before she was a week old my little Stephanie could recognise my voice when I spoke to her, although sudden noises do make her 'jump'. It's fascinating watching her respond to any movement or sound for that matter – she blinks! She likes brightly patterned things and her eyes follow something if I move it slowly in front of her, but it has to be quite close. She opens her eyes when I hold her upright but closes them tight when her brother Christopher shines a light into her face, naughty boy!<br><br>She even turns her head towards a light and seems to stare at bright shiny things. But the very best bit is the wonderful way she gazes at me when I am feeding or cuddling her, it gives me such an amazing feeling! |
| 1 month |  | Stephanie is 1 month old now and is growing in leaps and bounds! She can focus on things about 20–25 cm away. She stares at bold shapes, patterns, and bright shiny things and her eyes follow if you move a shiny thing quite slowly in front of her. The district nurse told me this is called 'tracking'. She can turn her head towards the window or the table lamp, and when she hears a noise, but she can't pinpoint where the noise is coming from yet. Christopher seems to get some fun out of making her jump because he's noticed she will 'freeze' or quiver, and blink, screw up her eyes, straighten her arms and legs, and fan out her fingers and toes – and bless her, sometimes she cries! But I can calm her down just by a little stroke of her hand or cheek, or with a soothing word.<br><br>She gets really excited when I talk quickly; she must know my voice really well now! She particularly likes me to sing so I am getting really good at all the old songs. She likes to hear lullaby music too. It's amazing that at just 1 month old, Stephanie can turn her head to look at me directly and I'm sure she is trying to imitate my smiles and frowns. She is truly a miracle! |
| 3 months |  | Our little bundle of joy is 3 months old now and I am fascinated by her progress. (I must be getting a bit of a bore about her.) Stephanie now responds when I say her name and she definitely moves her head to gaze at me when I walk around the room. She turns her head when someone else talks too, trying to see where they are, and gets excited when she hears someone coming, or the sound of her bath water running!<br><br>She loves to watch her toys when I move them in front or at the side of her and she's discovered her own hands now – she watches them and plays with her own fingers when she's lying on her back. The other day I experimented by showing her a photo of me and discovered she recognised me. Then she wrinkled her eyebrows and that made me laugh! |
| 6 months plus |  | Time just flies by, and Stephanie is now 6 months old. She is very alert now, smiles at me and mimics sounds and small movements I make. She reaches out to grab a toy with both hands and can hold quite small ones now, passing them from one hand to another, investigating I suppose. She does drop toys sometimes and I know when that's happened because she looks for it! She is definitely unhappy when I have to take something away from her though and now understands when I say 'no'!<br><br>She manages to change her position to see things clearly, even watches her dad quite carefully when he moves around the room. And if she can't see him she looks around to find out where he is.<br><br>It's wonderful now because Stephanie is starting to make sounds – she laughs, chuckles and squeals aloud, she has learnt to get my attention by babbling at me and has started saying 'mama' and 'dada'. I've noticed she makes different sounds when she wants different things, and there's even been a few times when I think she is trying to sing – well, babble tunefully anyway!<br><br>She has discovered herself in the mirror, and loves having conversations with this new little friend. I play peekaboo with her and patta-cake and she loves it! And Daddy's favourite little girl always waves goodbye to him now when he goes off to work in the mornings. |

**Table 8.1** *Continued*

| Age | Observations of sensory and perceptual development |
|---|---|
| 9 months<br> | Stephanie is 9 months old now – where is the time going? She now babbles loudly and tunefully to herself when she is not listening to everything going on around her. It's amusing to hear such a small person show annoyance or friendliness in her voice, especially when she shouts for attention. She will then listen to see if someone will go and see what is wrong, and if not, will shout again – learning already that 'if at first you don't succeed . . .'. Her vocabulary is growing, although slowly, but she does understand 'no' and 'bye-bye'.<br><br>It's fascinating to see the attention Steph now pays to what's going on and to people, especially if that person is prepared to play with her. She immediately stretches out to grasp a small toy that Daddy or Christopher gives her, and I've noticed that she has started grasping with one hand now instead of having to use both. She manipulates her toys with much interest passing them from one hand to the other, and pokes at small objects with her index finger – very inquisitive! The downside is that when she is finished with the toy she has to just drop it because she hasn't learned yet to put it down nicely. |
| 12 months<br> | Our little girl is now a year old and her remarkable progress continues. She now knows her own name and responds to it immediately, and she recognises familiar sounds and people coming towards her that she knows. We play a game of asking her to point to people, animals and toys that she knows, and she enjoys this.<br><br>Mealtimes are interesting now because Stephanie is getting to know different foods and knows the taste of salty, fatty and sweet foods. Playing with things is getting more complex for her – she can stroke, pat and turn objects in her hands, and recognise familiar things by touch alone. She has made a game of dropping and throwing toys forward deliberately, then pointing to them because she wants them back! When we want a quiet five minutes we turn on the television to watch a children's programme – she does enjoy this, thank goodness.<br><br>When we go out, Stephanie will sit for a long time just watching what's going on. Her visual memory is very good now, which is just as well because she sometimes finds things that I have lost! |
| 18 months<br> | Now she is 18 months old, our little Stephanie is beginning to show that she will be right-handed. We have been teaching her the different parts of her body and she can point to them now. She recognises herself in a mirror, and attempts to join in and sing nursery rhymes – hilarious! She also enjoys looking at simple children's books and points to the brightly coloured pictures. She has learned to build a tower with three cubes and can pick up small objects with just two fingers. And we were out the other day and she recognised her Gran coming down the road towards us! My mum was thrilled! |
| 2 years<br> | It's just 2 years since Stephanie was born and wow! This little person has developed at a fantastic rate and continues to learn new things every day. She recognises us and other familiar people in photographs after being shown them just once, but does not recognise her own photograph yet. She can now say 50 or so words and she talks to herself continually in long monologues when playing. She refers to herself by name which sometimes sounds funny, and is constantly asking the names of people and anything else around. She listens to general conversation with interest, and does try to join in sometimes.<br><br>Her dexterity is also improving – she can now build a tower of six or seven cubes, and holds a pencil towards its point using thumb and first two fingers. She still really enjoys picture books, and can turn the pages singly herself now. |

**Table 8.1** *Continued*

| Age | | Observations of sensory and perceptual development |
| --- | --- | --- |
| 3 years | | Stephanie was about 2¹/₂ years old when she started recognising herself in a photograph, and minute details in picture books. Now she has reached her third birthday the learning is getting more complex. She enjoys building towers of 10 cubes and bridges of 3 cubes; she can thread large wooden beads on a shoelace; and cuts with toy scissors. Now she can hold a pencil in the preferred hand and has good control so she can copy a circle, and the letters V, H and T; she can draw a person with head and one or two other features or parts. Her picture of me is not very flattering! Watching television is still a favourite pastime and Steph can now properly join in with the songs. She listens eagerly to stories and demands favourites over and over again – this can get a little boring! She is still continually asking questions – What? Where? Who? To be honest it can be a bit wearing. And although she can count up to 10 or more off by heart, she doesn't really understand any number beyond 2 or 3. |
| 4 years | | Our little girl is 4 now and I can't believe I will soon be taking her to school for the first time. She is very eager to learn and already can match and name the primary colours; she listens to and tells long stories with attention, although sometimes she confuses fact and fiction. She can draw a recognisable house and a person with head, legs and trunk (and usually enormous arms and fingers); and can build three steps with six cubes. Her speech is very good now – whole sentences and completely understandable. |
| 5 years | | Well, Stephanie is 5 and just about to start school. She is a bit 'ahead of the game' though because she can already match 10–12 colours; build four steps from ten cubes; copy squares and triangles; draw a recognisable man, with head, trunk, legs, arms, and features; and colour pictures neatly. Our little girl still loves to be read to or told stories and she acts them out in detail later, alone or with her friends. Some of her jokes are hilarious. |

*Sources*: Meggitt, C. (2006). *Child development: An illustrated guide* (2nd ed.). London: Heinemann; Sheridan, M. D. (1997). *From birth to five years. Children's developmental progress.* London: Routledge; Smith, P., Cowie, H. & Blades, M. (1999). Understanding children's development (4th ed.). Oxford: Blackwell Publishers. Interpreted by Sue Hughes remembering the first years of her daughter, Stephanie. Photos: © Stephanie Breen (birth; 1 month; 3 months; 6 months plus) and Richard Stagg (9 months; 12 months; 18 months; 2 years).

Babies use their mouths as the chief tool to explore objects.

*Source*: Stephanie Breen.

# The sensory perceptions

## Touch: haptic perception

Tactile sense is present at birth but is far from being fully developed. Touch is vitally important for young children. It is the sense that provides newborns with contact with their new world outside the womb. Nerve endings under the skin respond to sensations on and against the skin itself with hands, soles of the feet, the face and abdomen being particularly sensitive areas in young children (Honig, 2007). As we saw earlier, some early reflexes heavily involve the mouth and tongue, giving rise to rooting and sucking actions. While babies use their mouths as the chief tool to explore objects, this diminishes after about 6 months and is replaced by the hands, in keeping with development of reaching and grasping as the previous chapter described. Many older children still retain desires to touch objects. Observe a

**Haptic perception**
The process of recognising objects through touch.

story-time session in many primary classrooms and you will see children sitting listening while playing with small objects whilst others are stroking their own hair or the hair of the person in front of them. Touching and stroking can have a soothing effect and are another way of finding out about the object. Touch is a direct means to gain information about the environment and a critical part of cognitive development (Piaget, 1960). Stroking and gentle rubbing are well known treatments in a number of therapies and young children respond well – their therapeutic effects are well documented in the professional and research literature (e.g. Hernandez-Reif *et al.*, 2006, 2005).

Touch sensitivity is different for boys and girls (Noland & Rodrigues, 2012). Newborn girls are more sensitive to touch than boys. By middle childhood, boys' non-dominant side is more sensitive to touch than the dominant side, whereas girls show more symmetry and are equally touch sensitive on both sides of the body. Early contact between children and parents or carers in feeding or at play provides excellent opportunities for brain as well as emotional development (Honig, 2005). Early social handling is important in providing a socio-emotional bond, for stimulating intellectual growth and to reduce psychological stress. In an early classic study of young tactile contact, baby rhesus monkeys preferred a surrogate mother with a cloth body, to a 'mother' that provided milk but was just a face on a wire body (Harlow & Zimmerman, 1959) because the monkeys could cuddle up to the cloth body. This experiment showed the need for social touch in these animals. The same findings hold true for other mammals and that includes us.

## Taste and smell: gustatory and olfactory perception

Taste and smell perception in the developing infant are closely related to basic nutritional needs and the need to interact socially with 'significant' others. It is therefore important that these are in place at birth to enhance survival chances. Both systems also provide important sources of exploration and information, with many early discoveries (such as some of the differences between a hat and a sandwich) being made via the infant's mouth! In Chapter 5 we learned that taste is developed from the experiences *in utero* through the amniotic fluid. This may of course be evidence of prenatal learning rather than of innate capacity. Researching *in utero* tastes may provide clues about post-natal responses to teratogens, such as alcohol, for example. Mennella and Beauchamp (1996) found that breast-feeding babies accepted garlic if exposed to that very powerful taste via the mother's diet. Although this may not seem particularly relevant at first reading, it makes an important point: breast-feeding allows the infant to be familiar with the foods of the mother and so fit into the family culture. Exposure to different flavours in amniotic fluid and mothers' milk, probably underlie individual differences in food acceptability throughout the lifespan (Mennella *et al.*, 2004).

From birth, infants exhibit taste preferences and show a preference for sweet tastes by facial relaxation, and sucking harder and longer for sweet liquids (Fomon, 2000) and this develops in infancy. As many parents and teachers will know, children have an ability to communicate their food preferences! This is easily seen on infants' faces in ways similar to those of an adult, pursing their lips at a sour taste and relaxing the face muscles with sweet tastes (Mizuno *et al.*, 2004). The ability, however, helps the infant choose the sweet taste of the mother's milk over other foods and again is likely to be allied to the serious business of early survival.

**Connect and Extend**

Read an interesting study about the development of spatial awareness through haptic perception alone: the depiction of objects of people who are blind, through raised-outline drawings: D'Angiulli, A. (2007). Raised-line pictures, blindness, and tactile 'Beliefs': An observational case study. *Journal of Visual Impairment & Blindness*, 101, 172–177.

After 6 months, infants use hands to explore objects as their reaching and grasping skills improve.

*Source*: © Pearson Education Ltd / Jules Selmes.

Harlow and Zimmerman's classic study showed that baby rhesus monkeys preferred cuddling a cloth 'mother', rather than a wire 'mother' that provided milk.

*Source*: Nina Leen / Time & Life Pictures / Getty Images.

**Reflect**  There is no finer 'battleground' for parents and children than mealtimes. Why do you think this is? Why do children seem to have such strong views about the foods they will and will not eat; and what is so wrong with Brussels sprouts and Marmite? Is this a matter of survival?

A developed sense of smell may also be a legacy from the past in terms of its survival value in helping mother and baby identify each other. Olfactory discrimination allows infants to show preference for the mother's breast over those of another lactating mother (Todrank *et al.*, 2011) and is perhaps the first step in mother–child bonding. Results of another study (Marlier & Schaal, 2005) demonstrate that the odour of human milk is more attractive to human new-borns than formula milk and that this preference is independent of post-natal feeding experience. The same discriminatory capacity makes the infant turn away from unpleasant smells and towards pleasant ones. As early as 1976, psychologist John Rieser and colleagues found that infants turned away from the smell of ammonia. Apart from its role in alerting to dangers, smell also provides comfort. Toddlers can often be seen holding objects of comfort close to them where the familiar smell of the mother or their own familiar scent (an olfactory signature) provides comfort. Interestingly, this is less common in non-Western societies where children have more touch and olfactory contact with parents (Eliot, 1999).

## Hearing: auditory perception

At birth the ear is structurally complete and once the amniotic fluid is completely drained in the first few days after birth, the infant is capable of hearing, of discriminating sounds and perceiving similarities in sound. Without this, we would be unable to distinguish speech from any other array of sounds. Although neonatal hearing is good, improvement in perception happens quickly and approaches adult levels for the full range of sounds by 2 years (Saffran & Griepentrog, 2001). With younger children, some sounds must be louder by between 10 and 20 decibels for them to be heard owing to their inability to register low-pitched sounds. As mentioned earlier, it is common for adults to speak in higher tones or in 'motherese' (the slower and higher pitch talk used by mothers – and other adults – to talk to their baby) to capture attention. Simpler words and high intonation make it a suitable cadence for babies to follow and make it an ideal way to stimulate auditory perception. The term **infant directed speech (IDS)** is sometimes preferred to motherese as it is not only mothers who adapt their speech to babies!

**Infant directed speech (IDS)**
The slower and higher pitch talk used by mothers – and other adults – to talk to babies.

Have you noticed yourself turning your head to one side to listen to someone more carefully? Young children do this too. One classic study (Clifton *et al.*, 1994) showed that infants of 4 months placed in a dark room use auditory clues to help them locate a sound source. They also use clues when sleeping to pick up sounds in their environment. However, it takes a little time to perfect locating the source of a sound accurately. As they mature, young children's sound localisation improves and continues to do so throughout their preschool years (Werner, 2007). The ability to block out background noise is not so developed in young children and is not fully mature until they reach about 10 years. Busy early years care settings and classrooms are often noisy affairs and can easily overwhelm a child's auditory capacity: this can prohibit many children from picking up important instructions and explanations.

As we shall see in Chapter 10, auditory perception provides a wonderful base for language acquisition. Infants are especially sensitive to the human voice and can recognise their mother's voice soon after birth. By 6 months infants show matching and memory for the face–voice relations (Vogel *et al.*, 2012), without doubt a facility to encourage adult–child communication and further strengthen emotional bonding. They have an ability to discriminate speech sounds and have been found to discriminate between phonemes just as adults do, by categorising sounds into separate categories (Højen & Flege, 2006). (For example, 'hand'

and 'sand' are distinguished by one phoneme.) Development allows them to discriminate sound patterns. Earlier work by psychologist Sandra Trehub and her colleagues show that babies attend to sound patterns in music as early as 6 months (Trehub *et al.*, 1985). They can perceive and discriminate between all of the speech sounds in the world's languages but gradually lose the capacity to discriminate sounds not found in their native language (Bosch *et al.*, 2000). Since audition offers huge benefits to children's emotional, language and social development, fostering auditory perception in the home and preschool environment is important. Ways of doing this are suggested later in the chapter.

## Sight: visual perception

Unlike the other senses, vision is underdeveloped at birth. This is not a mistake: rather, we suggest it is such a complex and important sense that visual perception has to be waited for. Ours is a visual world, with half of what the cortex processes taken up with visual information (Sur & Rubenstein, 2005). In the womb there is no need for sight and so it is not surprising that the newborn arrives in this world with poor visual perception.

We said earlier that at birth, visual acuity (the ability to see detail) is within 20 centimetres and links were made to face recognition and emotional bonding between mother and child. Owing to early post-partum development in the eye structure allowing focusing at different lengths and in the cerebral cortex, this system improves rapidly and is comparable to that of adults from around 6 months (Gwiazda & Birch, 2001). Scanning improves with maturation of the control systems, and peripheral vision is used more frequently than depending on direct line vision by turning the head. Pathways in the brain promote colour discrimination quickly and by 2 months infants can discriminate colours across the spectrum, with older infants showing preferences for red, blue, green and yellow channels (witness the proliferation of these colours in toddler clothes and toys). They remember colours more than shapes, making colour one of the first abstractions.

Early findings by psychologist Robert Fantz (1961) showed that newborns prefer to look at patterns rather than dull stimuli and prefer more complex visual patterns as they get older. In school, peg boards, mosaics and patterns in artwork help children develop their competency with pattern-making and develop visual perception. The ability to perceive objects requires three-dimensional perception. **Size constancy** is the ability to perceive an object's size regardless of its distance from the observer and its size on the retina. Possibly present at birth, full proficiency is not attained until 10 or 11 years (Granrud, 2009). **Shape constancy**, or the ability to perceive an object's shape regardless of how it is oriented is established in the first few months, allowing infants to see parents' faces and other objects in the environment from different angles. **Face perception** is a special form of pattern perception. Infants prefer looking at complex patterns such as faces and by 3 months prefer human faces that have symmetrical features (Honda *et al.*, 2010). This is believed to be linked to the way they look at faces. Initially they scan the outside and later the internal features such as mouth, eyes and nose. They are more likely to remember the face of somebody who they associate with threatening behaviour (Kinzler & Shutts, 2008). Frequent interaction with parents and carers contributes to young children's face perception as well as supporting early social relationships.

The ability to judge distances of objects from themselves or from other objects, called **depth perception**, is another aspect of visual perception that infants must master early. In our three-dimensional world, the visual system provides important clues on the perception of depth and distance. The now-famous study (explained earlier) known as the 'visual cliff' (Gibson & Walk, 1960) tested this. In this study the researchers asked the mothers to encourage their infants to crawl across the 'cliff'. Infants of 6 months were reluctant to cross over, suggesting their perception of depth by this age is well developed. Later studies (e.g. Lin *et al.*, 2010) bear this out and also demonstrate the importance of crawling for young children in developing depth perception and other aspects of three-dimensional understanding such as remembering where objects are and finding hidden objects (Campos *et al.*, 2000). Movement experiences, for

**Size constancy**
Perception of an object's size is constant regardless of the distance away from the observer.

**Shape constancy**
Perception of an object's shape being constant even if movement alters its shape on the observer's retina.

**Face perception**
Infants seem to prefer the pattern of features of the face and can discriminate between the slightly different patterns of unique faces.

**Depth perception**
The ability to judge distances from, to or between objects.

**Proprioception**
The 'internal' sense the body has of position and balance, movement and posture, and which gives us an awareness of where our body is and what it is doing.

**Vestibular awareness**
The sense that provides information about balance and stillness.

● ● ● ● ● ● ● ● ● ● ● ● ● ● ● ●

**Connect and Extend**

Montessori classrooms aim to promote development and learning by sensory integration. View a short film (Davidson Films) on the legacy of Maria Montessori by searching **www.youtube.com**

● ● ● ● ● ● ● ● ● ● ● ● ● ● ● ●

**Kinaesthetic sense**
The human awareness of posture and movement of parts of the body with respect to each other.

**Kinaesthetic acuity**
The ability to match or detect differences between qualities such as location, distance, weight or speed.

**Kinaesthetic memory**
Memory capacity that allows reproduction of earlier movements.

example, on a variety of surfaces and on slopes, give much information about depth through cues which are vital for independent movement development of the young child.

## Proprioception

Using the same systems that sense touch, temperature and pain, **proprioception** is the 'sense' responsible for providing information about the position and movement of the body (see Chapter 6). Awareness of sensations comes from receptors in the muscles and joints as well as in the skin itself to provide information about the body at rest or in motion. The input from this sense is processed through **vestibular awareness** (chiefly concerned with the body's sense of balance) to keep the body upright and co-ordinate information from the other sensory systems to influence body movements. With infants, reaching and grasping are largely unconnected to vision, but are controlled by the proprioception system. Since the system also sends feedback to the brain, it monitors many common postures and positions and checks that they are appropriate for the environment. Of course, proprioception does not always work instantly and automatically. When older children appear temporarily clumsy and unco-ordinated, it is really a lag between the growing body and its proprioceptive system, usually at periods of growth spurts (Sigmundsson, 2003).

## Kinaesthetic sense

Similar to proprioception but differing in its role in providing directional and spatial advice is the **kinaesthetic sense** – awareness of own posture and movement of the body. It too receives input from muscles and tendons and the vestibular system. There are two aspects of kinaesthetic perception: **kinaesthetic acuity** and **kinaesthetic memory**. The former is the ability to match or detect differences in location, distance, weight and speed, such as detecting when one arm is raised higher than the other when the eyes are closed. The latter involves reproducing a movement such as removing a finger and with closed eyes placing it on exactly the same spot on the body or on another object as earlier. Kinaesthetic acuity approaches maturity by about age 8 and kinaesthetic memory not before about 12 years (Stuart, 2010; Ylonen & Cantell, 2009).

### The vestibular system

This is the second sensory system that receives information about the body from internal sources. It is located in the inner ear and constitutes three semicircular canals and two vestibular sacs that control our sense of balance and movement. It has enormous implications for everyday functioning as well as learning. It provides information on where children are in relation to gravity and other forms of acceleration, and so controls balance by sending messages about whether movements are fast, slow or at rest. Thus it has significant implications for the acquisition of early motor skills, such as rolling and crawling, and for sitting or standing still and moving around.

This sense develops prenatally to give the foetus direction about its movements in the womb and to prepare for birth; and, by birth, myelination (Chapter 4) has started to help the infant cope with making sense of the challenges and possibilities of 'normal' gravity. The vestibular system is a most important sensory system for core functioning with implications – apart from balance – for motor planning, hand–eye co-ordination, eye-tracking, fine motor control and learning (Granke, 2007). Its importance was highlighted by researcher Carla Hannaford (1995), who argued that every movement of a

The vestibular system controls balance and moving and is important for the acquisition of skills such as crawling.

*Source*: © Pearson Education Ltd / Jules Selmes.

young child stimulates this system, which in turn stimulates the brain for new learning – that physical movement (in this case what has come to be known as brain gym – organised movement to stimulate the brain) improves learning. The connections between perception and learning, and controversial views about the efficacy of Brain Gym are discussed later in this chapter.

So far we have discussed the senses as separate entities and you may have gained the impression that we experience the world about us through one sense at a time. Not so. We take in and make sense of information from more than one sense to understand and then act on the information, and this ability is believed to exist from a very early age. The way our senses are linked is the subject of discussion in the next section.

## Intermodal co-ordination

We are able to combine information across the senses through intermodal perception. Without the ability to integrate information using different senses, our perceptual capacities would be quite limiting. This is evident in our everyday experiences: for example, when we look at someone's mouth movements when they are talking we combine the two senses of vision and audition. When an alarm clock goes off, we look at the clock-face to check the time and hear the bell or buzzer simultaneously. Individual sense perceptions are sometimes referred to as modes of perception or sensory modalities.

> **Reflect**
>
> One of my son-in-law's favourite sayings when presented with a beautiful plate of food is 'The first taste is with the eyes!' Certainly the combination of visual and olfactory stimulant information 'gets the juices going' in anticipating the gustatory delights to come. What other everyday examples of intermodal co-ordination can you think of?

There are, of course, numerous examples of when sensory modalities work together purposefully. Imagine a 2-year-old playing with sand, pouring from one plastic container through the fingers of one hand into another container. Proprioception, vision and tactile perception are engaged here, auditory perception certainly and perhaps taste! In researching how infants co-ordinate information from their senses, researchers have adopted either an integrated perspective or a unified perspective. Let's explain. The integrated perspective acknowledges the uniqueness of each sense, and the task for the developing child is to learn how to integrate the separate systems. The unified perspective – which accords with the ecological perspective – acknowledges that senses 'unite' to present consolidated information about events or objects. Our perceptual systems identify patterns across different sensory modalities to understand what is happening and to react or to formulate a reaction.

Studies in sensory and perceptual development commonly match up two modalities. For example, in a classic study of newborns, researchers matched visual and tactile modalities and found that although the sample were all breast-fed babies, they all showed a preference for a pacifier they had briefly sucked on previously (Kaye & Bower, 1994). Clearly, babies showing a preference are displaying an innate capacity to recognise provoked by a brief experience – a kind of primitive learning. It is a plausible argument, and findings from other studies over the past 35 years have shown that brief experience may also explain certain behaviours. Experimental psychologist Elizabeth Spelke (1987) showed two films side by side (with accompanying soundtracks of a donkey and a kangaroo bouncing at different rates) to 4-month-old infants. When the films played only one soundtrack, the infants looked at the animal whose bouncing matched the sound of the 'correct' animal. Their ability does not come from significant previous experience. In another more recent study linking sound and

**Connect and Extend**

How much perception is there at birth? Some psychologists argue that infants start out with a relatively undifferentiated global or overall perception called 'amodal' perception. To find out how this works, read: Flom, R. & Bahrick, L. E. (2007). The development of infant discrimination of affect in multimodal and unimodal stimulation: The role of intersensory redundancy. *Developmental Psychology, 43*, 238–252.

**Intermodal perception**
Using sensory information from more than one sensory modality.

**Connect and Extend**

How do infants match faces and voices of unfamiliar people? A good example of this intermodal matching is given by: Bahrick, L., Hernandez-Reif, M. & Hom, R. (2005). The development of infant learning about specific face–voice relations. *Developmental Psychology, 41*, 541–552. You will need to access this article in your library.

vision, newborns were shown a toy in different locations associated with certain sounds. Psychologist Barbara Morrongiello and colleagues (1998) found that the babies showed increased attention when the sound came from locations other than that originally associated with the toy. It might be concluded that early learning uses information from more than one sensory source and this accounts for at least some of the new or learned behaviour.

Intermodal matching allows even very young children to use information from two different sensory modes to detect an object's distance and direction. Developmental psychologist Jeffrey Pickens in a study with 5-month-old children (1994) found they were able to match a film image of a train as it approached with the sound of its engine getting louder and the sound of the train diminishing as the train moved away. It is difficult to conclude whether this is as a result of an innate ability or experience. Experimental findings indicate that we may well be born with a capacity to transfer information from one sensory modality to another and, with added experience, this capacity increases with age. Very young children appear to be able to learn the 'rules' that govern the integration of sensory information and this is dependent upon both social and cognitive development and upon the types of experience the child encounters.

An excellent example of this is a more recent experiment (Curtindale *et al.*, 2007), during which 48 children and 48 adults performed auditory and visual vigilance tasks, measured for example by response times. Results showed that auditory tasks proved more difficult than visual tasks for both children and adults, responding to the sound took longer than responding to a visual clue. The relationship between sound and vision changed with age: performance of auditory and visual vigilance tasks was significantly correlated (see Chapter 3) for children but not for adults. Furthermore, temperament affected the behaviour of the children more so than the adults: temperament did not significantly predict performance in adults but it did for children. The temperament effects observed in children occurred in connection with the auditory task. So how we 'see' things and how we feel about our perceptions will change the ways in which we act.

## Perceptual-motor development

As cognitive neuroscientist Mary Immordino-Yang reported in 2008, a close relationship exists between perception and action, a point that we have certainly tried to emphasise earlier and in the previous chapter. Motor activity is an immediate way for children to learn about their world and to stimulate their perceptual development. It can be said with some confidence that motor performance affects perception and the development of perception affects motor performance. Development is understood by psychologists such as Dr Immordino-Yang to:

> involve cycles of perception and action – the internalization of interactions with the world and the construction of skills for acting in the world. From a neurobiological standpoint, new evidence suggests that neural activities related to action and perception converge in the brain in high-level sensory association and motor planning areas.

(Immordino-Yang, 2008, p 67)

This argument and conclusion is strengthened when looking at deficit models of development and learning. Children with deficits in perceptual performance – to make sense of the information we receive – also commonly have difficulties with motor tasks involving movement and manipulation. Problems in balance and co-ordination are exhibited by children in many classroom and care contexts (Getchell *et al.*, 2007) and can be traced to poor integration of movement and cognition. However, there are therapeutic techniques – for example, Brain Gym mentioned earlier – now being used by teachers and other practitioners to address some of the problems that become apparent in classrooms and early years settings. In the next section we will discuss some of these techniques and the implications for learning.

**Summary 2**

Before moving on, let's summarise what we have learned in the middle section of this chapter:

- The majority of the basic sensory-perceptual systems are in place at birth as newborns are equipped to survive and to learn.
- An overview of children's perceptual development is provided by well-known and commonly understood milestones.
- Nerve endings under the skin respond to sensations on and against the skin to gain information about the environment. Such information is a requirement for cognitive development.
- Stroking and gentle rubbing are well-known treatments in a number of therapies – the therapeutic effects are well documented in the literature.
- Taste and smell perception in the developing infant is closely related to basic nutritional needs and the need to interact socially with 'significant' others.
- Auditory perception enables us to distinguish speech from other sounds.
- Younger children are unable to hear low-pitched sounds so adults use 'motherese' – a slower, high-pitched style when talking to babies to stimulate auditory perception.
- The ability to block out background noise is not so developed in young children and is not fully mature until they reach about 10 years. Busy early years settings are often noisy affairs and can easily overwhelm a child's auditory capacity: this can prohibit many children from picking up important instructions and explanations.
- Visual perception is relatively underdeveloped at birth as there is no need for sight in the womb.
- Visual images take up half of the processing power of the brain and this takes time to organise.
- Colour perception, shape constancy and face recognition develop quickly, but size constancy is not fully mature until 10 or 11 years.
- Depth perception develops (surprisingly) quickly.
- Proprioception and the vestibular system provide information about the position and movement of the body, and kinaesthetic sense provides directional and spatial advice to the brain.
- Intermodal co-ordination integrates information from two or more sense perceptions (modalities), and studies into the development of perception will often match two or more modalities.
- A close relationship exists between perception and action – children with deficits in perceptual performance commonly have difficulties with perceptual-motor tasks.

# Implications for learning

## Brain Gym

By receiving and organising information from the senses and acting on this to formulate appropriate motor responses, intellectual and motor development are even more linked than was previously believed. Early studies of balance and locomotion using slopes and different surfaces confirm this, and have led to a host of screening and intervention programmes from the 1960s onwards (Ayres, 1972; Kephart, 1971). These and many more recent training programmes – some of which are referred to as brain gym – are in common use in many schools today. Although these are helpful in developing motor skills, claims about improvements in learning, as you will see, are not substantiated. That is not to deny that engaging in these programmes can develop perceptual skills applicable in the classroom, as, of course, learning certainly does demand something from perceptual development! However, the contemporary view is that such programmes may not live up to claims made by their creators about improvements in learning and specifically for those with learning difficulties (Hyatt, 2007). Typical features of these programmes include:

- gross and fine motor skills, such as bouncing on the spot and staying on the same spot, or using different fingers to press buttons assessing response times;
- hand–eye co-ordination;
- direction and laterality: for example, moving across the floor, maintaining posture and physical tension;
- multi-sensory training: for example, linking visual and auditory cues;
- crossing the midline: for example, repeatedly crossing arms or legs across the body's vertical midline;
- balance;
- recognition of sound rhythms and patterns;
- activities to promote self-esteem.

**Brain Gym**
A perceptual-motor programme designed to enhance the experience of whole-brain learning.

One intervention that is frequently witnessed in many primary schools and early years settings (and as we mentioned before) is **Brain Gym**.

## Controversy

### Does Brain Gym work?

Devised in the United States from work in the 1970s by pioneers in educational kinesiology Paul and Gail Dennison, Brain Gym is a movement-based programme which is widely used in many primary schools. The programme claims improvements in a range of learning and behaviour skills which are highly appropriate to children in schools and in everyday life. Claims include improvements in:

- memory;
- co-ordination and balance;
- posture;
- language development;
- academic skills (reading, spelling, thinking skills);
- stress management;
- increased energy.

Brain Gym takes a whole-brain approach to learning that allows learners to integrate information from a multi-sensory orientation through movement re-patterning. It claims to make immediate improvements in academic performance and behaviour by allowing learners to receive information and access parts of their brain previously not accessible to them. A series of specific movements *stimulate* the laterality dimension, which integrates both sides of the body and crossing the midline of the body, thus involving both left and right brain hemispheres and allowing proper focus, especially important for those children labelled with attention-deficit disorder (ADD), ADHD or inattentiveness. Brain Gym also claims to *relax* through a 'centreing' dimension that changes the physical state of the learner to that most suited to the particular situation. Movements have catchy titles – Cross Crawl, Alphabet 8s, The Owl, The Thinking Cap and Space Buttons – that the authors assert can unblock barriers to learning and enable the student to be free to learn (Dennison & Dennison, 1994). Impressive claims, but are they supported by research evidence?

Ben Goldacre writing in the newspaper the *Guardian* (2006) summarised a growing view amongst commentators in the learned journals (e.g. Maskell *et al.*, 2004) that Brain Gym is 'a vast empire of pseudoscience being peddled in hundreds of state schools up and down the country' and associated the programmes with telling children lies about science. Twenty years before, academic studies had argued that improvements in academic performance did exist, such as responding more quickly to a visual stimulus (Sifft & Khalsa, 1991); reducing errors in reading and increased memory (Donczik, 1994); improving static balance (Khalsa *et al.*, 1988) and, more recently, improving in concentration and speed in solving puzzles (Winkelmann, 2000). Critics might say there is no hard evidence for brain-based learning or that there is not sufficient evidence from these studies to judge. For example, in 2007, Keith Hyatt found in a review of the theoretical foundations of Brain Gym, and the associated peer-reviewed research studies, that empirical evidence failed to support the contentions of the promoters of Brain Gym.

Claims for the benefits of Brain Gym are still being made. For example, a preliminary report (2007) by Grace Archer and Buffy McClelland (published on the **braingym.org.uk** website) claims to have demonstrated in an experiment involving three groups of 25 12–13-year-olds that, after intervention, the Brain Gym group reading age increased significantly more than for both other two control groups. Final reading ages for the Brain Gym group were approximately 1 year better than control groups. Such claims continue to be tested by academic researchers (e.g. Miller & Robertson, 2011; Spaulding *et al.*, 2010; Miller & Robertson, 2010; Stephenson, 2009) and reported by commentators (e.g. Howard-Jones, 2008) because there are still hundreds, if not thousands of classrooms across the globe that use educational kinesiology as part of the daily school routine.

What do you think? Does Brain Gym live up to its bold claims?

**Dypraxia**
The partial loss of the ability to co-ordinate and perform purposeful movements like writing.

• • • • • • • • • • • • • • • •

**Connect and Extend**
What about the effect of training programs on problems with handwriting? Read: The effect of a computerised visual perception and visual-motor integration training program on improving Chinese handwriting of children with handwriting difficulties by Poon, K. W., Li-Tsang, C. W. P., Weiss, T. P. L. & Rosenblum, S. (2010). *Research In Developmental Disabilities*, November, 31(6), 1552–1560.

• • • • • • • • • • • • • • • •

Theories linking perceptual-motor programmes (such as Brain Gym) and improvements in academic performance are often criticised for their limited empirical support, but observation of perceptual-motor development can indicate a readiness for learning (Zafrana & Nickoltsou, 2000). This is particularly important for children in the early stages of formal education when skills such as reading, writing and basic numeracy are taught, and a case can be made that some forms of perceptual-motor training can help with readiness to learn for children with learning difficulties (Fusaro *et al.*, 2006). Take handwriting as an example. Handwriting is a complex skill and one that, despite technological advances, is still fundamental to most school systems. Indeed, much of the school day is spent in writing-related activities. It demands the kind of highly developed perceptual-motor development and honed fine movement skills with which many children with dyspraxia experience difficulties.

According to experts Gill Dixon and Lois Addy (2004), the perceptual and motor difficulties associated with handwriting for dyspraxic children are:

Handwriting is a complex skill and is fundamental to most school systems.

*Source*: © Pearson Education Ltd / Ian Wedgewood.

- poor pencil grip;
- abnormal posture;
- awkward position of paper in relation to the child;
- inaccurate hand–eye co-ordination;
- incorrect letter formation;
- incomplete letter formation;
- erratic sizing of letter forms;
- mixture of upper- and lower-case letters;
- poor alignment of writing on the page;
- lack of consistency in direction of ascenders and descenders;
- inconsistent spacing between words, either no spaces, too narrow or too wide;
- heavy or light pressure through the pencil.

If Brain Gym works – if it provokes advances in perceptual-motor development – and therefore improves learning and performance, it should be able to deal effectively with the perceptual and motor difficulties associated with handwriting. Therapeutic programmes and perceptual-motor exercises may assist some children when used by trained practitioners, but how can government policy reflect research into learning and encourage best practice for all children? The following *Policy, Research and Praxis* feature addresses this question.

## Policy, Research and Praxis

### Supporting learning and development for all children

Recent UK Government policy reflects that children deserve the very best chances in life and the very best start. This is true for not only children with perceptual and motor difficulties but for all children. The life chances of the two million children and young people in England who are identified as having a special educational need (SEN) are currently not good. Overly bureaucratic and confusing systems create obstacles for families with children who are disabled or have particular needs. Existing services not delivering the support necessary has led to frustration for many and contributes to a culture of low expectations and support needs that are identified much too late. Clearly there is a pressing case for change.

In England, the government response has been the publication of *Support and Aspiration: A new approach to special educational needs and disability. A consultation* (DfE, 2011). This is the catalyst for the most fundamental reforms to health and education services for SEN in the past 30 years. The vision for children with SEN or disabilities centres on supporting life chances; giving parents more confidence and control and transferring power to professionals in local communities. *Support and aspiration: A new approach to special educational needs and disability. Progress and next steps* was published a year later. This reported progress on each of the following five strands identified in the earlier document:

- *Early identification and assessment* – To identify children's needs a new early years progress check for children aged 2 was introduced as part of the revised Early Years Foundation Stage to identify problems and offer early support, and undertaken jointly between health and early years professionals. Free early education was extended to around 260,000 disadvantaged 2-year-olds and included children with special educational needs.

- *Giving parents more control* – To give parents greater control over the support for their family, £800 million was allocated for short breaks for families with disabled children through the Early Intervention Grant. Local authorities have been required to publish a statement of the services they offer families.

- *Learning and achieving* – To develop the knowledge and skills of teachers and other staff in supporting children and young people who are disabled or have SEN, schools have been encouraged to convert to academies to raise the achievement of all pupils. Materials have been developed on specific impairments to support continuing professional development. There is now a greater focus on special educational needs within standards for Qualified Teacher Status and sharpened accountability on the progress of the lowest attaining 20 per cent of pupils.

- *Preparing for adulthood* – To help give young people the opportunities and support to succeed in education, work and lead independent lives, an Education, Health and Care Plan is being developed for young people over 16 and up to 25.

- *Services working together for families* – To improve the ways services are provided locally, reforms to improve planning, commissioning and delivery of services have been introduced. Commissioned action research is looking specifically at how local authorities support disabled children and those with SEN.

Such policy drives offers a lot but it is set against a backdrop of dissatisfaction from many parents who previously did not receive the support they needed. Whether or not such a direction will change this situation, time will tell.

**Accelerated learning**
A brain-based approach to learning which matches teaching strategies to preferred learning styles: visual, auditory, kinaesthetic.

**Connect and Extend**
Why should we seek to accelerate learning? Is there any evidence that learning faster is necessarily better? Read Holt, M. (2002). It's time to start the slow school movement. *Kappan Professional Journal, 84*, 265–271.

Creating enriched sensory environments for all children is desirable but not always practical, although it is certainly common in teaching young children, children with learning difficulties and sensory impairments. Learning through the senses is predominant in the work of early years educationalist Elinor Goldschmied, based on her experiences in Italy and England (Goldschmied & Jackson, 1994). One idea of Goldschmied's pedagogy is to provide 'treasure baskets' containing natural materials such as pebbles, shells, fruit and items made of leather or fur. Treasure baskets allow young children to experience the properties of these items through their different senses and so accelerate their learning. Indeed, understanding that children need variety in their learning is a central message of **accelerated learning** (Lee & Horsefall, 2010; Smith & Call, 1999).

You will not be surprised to hear that accelerated learning is predicated on the notion that children do not learn in one modality only and therefore benefit from broad teaching approaches. You will also not be surprised to hear that such ideas are not unconditionally and universally accepted.

Enjoying cause and effect in a rich sensory environment, where the whole room is a 'treasure basket'.

*Source*: © Pearson Education Ltd / Jules Selmes.

## Summary 3

We now summarise what you have learned in the final section of this chapter:

- Intellectual and motor development are even more linked than was previously believed.
- Perceptual and physical training programmes are in common use in many schools today.
- Typical features of these programmes include gross and fine motor skills, hand–eye co-ordination, multi-sensory training, balance, recognition of sound rhythms and patterns and activities to promote self-esteem.
- The most well-known of these programmes is Brain Gym.
- There is no conclusive proof that Brain Gym promotes cognitive development or increases academic achievement, but improvements have been noted in some studies.
- Handwriting is a good example of where improvements in perceptual-motor development can have relatively speedy benefits.
- Kinesiologists argue for the importance of learning through active use of the senses.
- Lack of sensory-perceptual development is directly related to observable difficulties in many areas of academic performance.
- Accelerated learning – a brain-based approach to learning which matches teaching strategies to preferred learning styles: visual, auditory, kinaesthetic – is commonly used for young children, children with learning difficulties and with sensory impairments because of the multi-modality of the delivery.

## Conclusion

Children's basic perceptual capacities are almost universal but cultural differences do have some important effects. Culture provides a framework for how children interpret sensory input. A few examples illustrate this. Firstly, exposure to the sound patterns in a particular language increases sensitivity to detect the patterns inherent in that language. The consonants r and l are easy to discriminate in most languages with the exception of Chinese and Japanese. Five-year-old Ohta in Japan would find difficulty in discriminating between these sounds because there is no distinction between them in his language; we will take a closer look at this phenomenon later (see Chapter 10). Another example is that food preferences vary from culture to culture. In many Western cultures, eating rodents and small birds, beetles and bugs is considered undesirable, whereas in other cultures songbirds and crickets are considered delicacies. This leads to early taste preferences being established and the cultural differences are re-established for the new generation. How the environment around us is created has an effect upon our visual perception. Modern architecture favours lines, sharp angles and regular shapes. Road systems follow a similar pattern of linearity. This is often not the case in lesser developed countries which show a prevalence of curved lines. Findings from cross-cultural psychologists Marshall Segall and colleagues showed, in an early but important study (1966) on predicting vertical lines as the same or different lengths, that living in one type of environment can affect how we perceive depth and how we judge distances – important perceptions to operate effectively in any environment.

Today's environments are complex. It is commonplace in the United Kingdom to hear parents forbidding their children from playing outside because of the perceived dangers from traffic or strangers. Many children in the United Kingdom and Western Europe live in cramped urban environments that do not allow them freedom to explore their surroundings safely, or encourage natural play. Consequently, many children live sedentary lifestyles: they are taken to and from schools in cars and are not able to take in their surroundings as they would if walking; leisure pursuits centre around watching television or playing computer games. As we have seen in this chapter, children everywhere need varied and frequent movement experiences to stimulate their perceptual-motor development. They also need varied activities to stimulate all aspects of their perceptual development.

We began this chapter with a word scene describing a young child, Asifa, engrossed in the task of feeding herself with a spoon. Feeding herself required Asifa to take in information about her surroundings, her own position and that of the spoon. We stressed that perception is integral to self-feeding and, of course, almost every task that children learn and perform. Perception acts as a bridge between the motor, social and cognitive challenges that are all part of growing up. A distinction was made initially between sensation as the ability to register information in the external environment, and perception, or the ability to recognise and understand, and so act upon this information. Decision-making is a further response from our brains and provides more structure to external information by giving it coherence. This third element, cognition, is how we consider this information and execute a response. It is time now to identify the main theories of cognitive development and understand their application to education, particularly the factors that influence intelligence and how these relate to the concepts of giftedness, talent and creativity. Cognition is what sets reaction apart from decision-making, and the primitive proceed from the reasoned response. It is to Part 3 *Cognitive and Social Development*, and specifically Chapter 9 *Cognitive Development*, that we now turn.

## Summary Table
### Sensory and Perceptual Development

## The science of perception (pp 220-227)

The components (sensation, perception and cognition) of perceptual development help us gather the information we need to make sense of ourselves and the things that happen to us. Sensation is the process through which sensory receptors detect information. Perception is the bridge between our conscious mind and the external world, and cognition is 'knowing', through the formation, memorisation and recall of ideas. Perceptual systems fulfil five functions. They inform on what to attend to, determine what and where objects are, extract the relevant information, and retain the constancy of objects.

### What is perception and why do we need it?
(pp 220-222)

Perceptive ability is what a person understands from what they sense, and the three qualities of being observant, sensitive and discerning are needed to develop perception. Information about changes in the environment are con-tinuously being sent to the central nervous system and is compared with the stored information of previous messages held in various parts of the brain. Either the brain reacts with some automatic impulsive behaviour or considers and formulates a response.

### Theories of perception (pp 222-223)

The fundamental question in the theoretical debate about how perception develops is determining how much of what we perceive is innate (in some way hard-wired or 'placed there by God') and how much is the product of our experiences. Piaget describes how children at different stages come to interpret their perceptions, but stresses the interactions between developing cognitive processes and experiences. Noam Chomsky argued that a newborn's perceptual capacities are already quite advanced (the nature perspective) and therefore not so dependent upon experience. He argues that we are born with certain abilities that allow us to learn language.

### Researching perception (pp 223–227)

Three research methods commonly used to measure perception development are the preference technique, measures of habituation, and training using operant conditioning. Eleanor Jack Gibson's most famous experiment is that involving the 'visual cliff'. Nearly all the infants refused to crawl out over the glass on the 'cliff' side, and Gibson concluded that depth perception is developed at a very early age. This is an example of preference technique.

## Making connections (pp 227–237)

### Connecting sensory and perceptual development (pp 227–230)

The majority of the basic sensory-perceptual systems are in place at birth, as newborns are equipped to survive and to learn. What happens next, an overview of children's perceptual development, is provided by well-known and commonly understood milestones. These milestones are very useful checks for parents, carers, practitioners and teachers.

### The sensory perceptions (pp 230–235)

Taste and smell perceptions in the developing infant are closely related to basic nutritional needs and the need to interact socially with 'significant' others. Auditory perception enables us to distinguish speech from other sounds, and very young children are unable to hear low-pitched sounds. The ability to block out background noise is not so developed in young children and is not fully mature until they reach about 10 years. Visual perception is relatively underdeveloped at birth as there is no need for sight in the womb. However, colour perception, shape constancy and face recognition develop quickly. Proprioception and the vestibular system provide information about the position and movement of the body, and kinaesthetic sense provides directional and spatial advice to the brain.

### Intermodal co-ordination (pp 235–236)

Intermodal co-ordination integrates information from two or more sense-perceptions (modalities), and studies into the development of perception will often match two or more modalities. For example, a close relationship exists between perception and action (perceptual-motor development), so children with deficits in perceptual performance commonly have difficulties with perceptual-motor tasks.

## Implications for learning (pp 238–242)

Intellectual and motor development are even more linked than was previously believed. This has led to a growing use of perceptual and physical training programmes in many schools today. Typical features of these programmes include gross and fine motor skills, hand–eye co-ordination, multi-sensory training, balance, recognition of sound rhythms and patterns and activities to promote self-esteem.

### Brain Gym (pp 238–240)

The most well-known of these programmes is Brain Gym. There is no conclusive proof that Brain Gym promotes cognitive development or increased academic achievement, but improvements have been noted in some studies. For example, handwriting is a good example of where improvements in perceptual-motor development can have relatively speedy benefits.

## Going further

Parker-Rees, R. (2011) *Meeting the child in Steiner kindergartens: An exploration of beliefs, values and practices.* Abingdon: Routledge.
The Steiner kindergarten is widely admired as a model of good practice in early years provision and these essays show why. The perception–action–learning link is very evident.

Bremner, G. & Slater, A. (Eds) (2004) *Theories of infant development.* Oxford: Blackwell Publishing.
Part 1 of the book provides an in-depth consideration of perception and the developmental link between action and perception.

Fish, W. (2010) *Philosophy of perception: A contemporary introduction.* Abingdon: Routledge.
This book presents an account of the principal theories in the field, noting strengths and weaknesses, uncovering potentially problematic assumptions, and raising issues for further discussion.

Rizzolatti, G., Sinigaglia, C. & Anderson, F. (2007) *Mirrors in the brain: How our minds share actions, emotions, and experience.* Oxford: OUP.
In the early 1990s Giacomo Rizzolatti and his co-workers at the University of Parma discovered that some neurons had a surprising property. They responded not only when a subject performed a given action, but also when the subject observed someone else performing that same action. This is a fascinating book which includes important ideas on the link between perception and emotions.

# Useful websites

http://www.braingym.org.uk/
The website describes how the idea of Brain Gym had its beginnings in the learning challenges that Paul Dennison, creator of Educational Kinesiology, experienced as a child. The website also describes how the body is involved in all learning, whatever the subject or area, and a potential source of enhancement for learning skills.

http://www.acceleratedlearning.com/method/what_is.html
The Accelerated Learning Method is based on recent brain research because more has been discovered about how the human brain works in the past 25 years than in all history to date.

http://www.youtube.com/
Many clips of the visual cliff experiment.

http://www.montessori.org.uk/what_is_montessori/the_philosophy
Maria Montessori believed that children build on their own experiences of the world through their senses. She believed that teachers could help pupils extend this understanding by carefully designing interesting materials which the children were drawn to experiment with. She took each of the senses in turn. This website is a comprehensive summary of her work.

# Part 3
## Cognitive and Social Development

# Chapter 9
## Cognitive Development

### Overview

# Introduction

Teachers and parents say things like 'How thoughtless of you!' and 'Think hard about what you're about to do. Remember what happened last time!' Thinking seems to be a pretty important part of growing up and the key to staying out of trouble – but what is thinking? Thinking or cognition is how we consider information we perceive from our senses and formulate a response. Cognition sets apart considered decision-making from the way we instantly react to what is happening to us, and sets apart a reasoned response from a primitive process (fight-or-flight reflex). For a reasoned response we have to have enough time to 'weigh things up' by testing our ideas against memories of previous experiences before coming to a decision. In this chapter we will identify the main theories of cognitive development and understand their application to learning, particularly the factors that influence intelligence and how these relate to the concepts of giftedness, talent and creativity. Cognitive development is key to learning and learning promotes cognitive development, so you will need to be expert in how to encourage development in order to maximise learning. First of all consider this everyday scene:

> It is nearing the end of the lunch-time break in a primary school. Two of the children, Maria, aged 5 and Jodie, aged 9, skip into the dining hall, hot and thirsty after playing outside. They each want a drink of orange and approach the kitchen hatch where orange juice is normally poured out into beakers for the children. One problem: there are no beakers left for them on the table. The school cook, Mrs Leith, fetches a couple of beakers and a jug of juice. The beakers are not the usual beakers, however. One is a tall beaker and the other is a tumbler style that is much shorter and wider. Mrs Leith pours the juice into the tall beaker and it almost reaches the top. She then pours juice into the tumbler but it only seems to go up about half way. Maria, the younger of the two children, who was given the wider tumbler, exclaims, 'Hey, I need more juice. Jodie has got more than me!' 'Oh go on with you dear,' replies Mrs Leith, 'it's the same amount'. To prove her point, Mrs Leith goes back into the kitchen and brings out two of the normal beakers which are identical in shape and size. She asks Maria to pour the contents of the taller beaker into one of these beakers and the contents of the wider tumbler into the other beaker and asks the children to compare them. The level of juice in both beakers is the same. Jodie raises her eyes to the ceiling and turns to Maria, 'I could have told you that!'

What does this small story tell us? Nothing for certain about some children being more or less intelligent (though it was clever of Mrs Leith to demonstrate using other beakers rather than just telling – good pedagogy!). The opening word-scene of this chapter tells us that the thinking of children at different ages is qualitatively different. Maria at 5 years could not rationalise that the two beakers could contain the same amount of juice, one beaker being 'bigger' (taller) and the other 'smaller' (shorter and wider), whereas Jodie at 9 years was very obviously able to do this. Jodie was able to conceptualise that both beakers contained the same amount of liquid and was capable of thinking at a higher level than Maria.

In order to understand thinking and the developmental changes illustrated by these two children, we need to have some understanding of the theoretical frameworks of how children think. In this chapter we begin by explaining some of the relevant terminology and then discuss three important and defining perspectives on thinking and learning. The implications of understanding children's thinking and how this is exemplified in the home, care setting and classroom is invaluable to those tasked with caring for children of all ages, and especially important as young children begin their formal education.

By the time you have completed this chapter you should be able to answer the following questions:

- What is cognition?
- What is the difference between cognitive development and learning?
- What are the implications for children's learning of Piaget's cognitive development theory?
- How did Jerome Bruner enhance Lev Vygotsky's theory of sociocultural cognitive development?
- Is the human brain like a computer?
- What is intelligence and how is it measured?
- Can we 'fast-forward' children's intelligence?
- How should gifted and talented children be schooled?
- What are the implications for teaching and learning of understanding the importance and processes of cognitive development?

# Understanding cognition

In the past, cognition was generally described in terms of the involvement of mental structures and processes through which we acquire and use knowledge. However, contemporary views now associate cognitive processes and functions of the brain with our emotional states – a more holistic approach. Mental processes such as reasoning, remembering, solving problems and even daydreaming which constitute the vast area of cognitive effort, combine with social and emotional influences (see Chapters 11 and 12) to affect how we understand our world and act on our understandings.

**Cognitive development**
The changes in one's mental abilities that take place over the lifespan.

**Cognitive development** refers to the changes in one's mental abilities that take place throughout our lifespan. It is an enormous topic including attention, decision-making, memory, and critical and creative thinking – each with a vast research literature. You will need to follow the leads in the nearby *Connect and Extend* features to get as much as you can of a flavour of the complexity and richness of the topic, and we will guide you in throughout the chapter to look critically at the relevant research. We begin our explanation by critiquing three approaches to cognitive development that we first introduced in Chapter 2: (i) Piaget's cognitive-developmental theory, (ii) Vygotsky's sociocultural theory and (iii) information-processing theories. Then we discuss the implications of these theories and contemporary research contributions in each perspective for teaching early years and primary age children. Firstly, though, we need to be clear about what is cognition, what is learning and how they are connected.

Cognition is the act of knowing using mental processes such as imaging, remembering, understanding, generalising, finding reasons and causes, making inferences, decision-making, forming preferences, desires and intentions, planning and learning. At birth many of these cognitive functions are not yet developed. Much of the brain's activity is confined to the lower and rear parts of the brain (review the section in Chapter 8 – *What is perception and why do we need it?*), the brainstem and cerebellum (Figure 9.1). Visual auditory and movement received and processed in the occipital lobe, the left temporal lobe and the parietal lobe cause connective activity related to conceptualising and creativity across and throughout the brain, but particularly in the frontal lobes. Thinking processes move towards the higher and more forward parts of the brain. Biologically, cognitive processes are electrical pulses between the 100 billion brain cells or neurons (see the section in Chapter 6 *Cerebral processes* for a complete

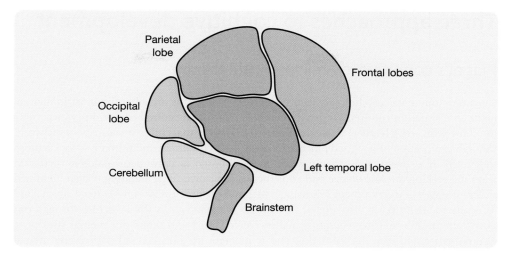

**Figure 9.1** Parts of the brain: a simplified schematic

explanation), and cognitive capacity is the number of connections that are made, and the speed and accuracy of those connections. Cognitive development is enormous in the first two years and continues throughout the lifespan.

Learning is one of the most important cognitive abilities and relies upon the recording, organising and retrieval of many millions of pieces of information, supported by a continuous stream of perceived information from the senses. Learning is based on conceptual understanding, knowledge and muscle skill memorisation and retrieval, replication or demand. Let us take learning multiplication tables as an example. Before learning tables (and, more importantly, being able to use them), we need an overlapping and complex understanding of the concepts of number: ordinal and cardinal properties, number names and (perhaps) symbols. Furthermore we need to know the pattern of sounds and symbols that make up each item in the multiplication table – 'four fives are twenty'. Lastly we need to be able to retrieve each item on demand, accurately and automatically. The level of accuracy and automaticity is often used as the test of how well we have learned our tables in thousands of classrooms every week of the school year.

Another example is learning to play a musical instrument. Watch a master of their instrument, such as Hilary Hahn playing – in her case – the violin. The whole process seems effortless, automatic and yet not mechanical. The instrument seems to be part of the player (you hardly see any photographs of the great violinists without their instruments). Try an Internet image search for a photograph of Hilary Hahn playing her violin. Just look at the relationship between her and her instrument. How did she get to be this good and how did she learn the skills of violin playing so well that it looks that natural, that easy? Many of the cognitive abilities of learning multiplication tables are the same: an overlapping and complex understanding of the concepts of notation; rhythm and pitch; note names and symbols. Furthermore she needs to know the pattern of sounds and symbols that make up each piece and she needs to be able to retrieve each item on demand, accurately and automatically. Here comes the big difference to writing or speaking the answer to 'What are four fives?' Those conceptual ways of knowing about music have to be transferred into physical actions that require the highest level of major and minor physical dexterity and skill. A finger of her left hand slightly out of place for one-tenth of a second, or without just the right amount of pressure on the fingerboard, will detract from the perfection of the performance. There is one highly developed part of the right brain which is super-developed in a master violinist: the area to do with controlling and sensing the fingertips of the left hand. Learning and practice, practice, and more practice have created accelerated cognitive development in one part of the brain. You will see many of the themes of this section reflected and referred to in what follows, but first let us return to cognition and cognitive development. What are the big ideas?

● ● ● ● ● ● ● ● ● ● ● ● ● ● ● ●
**Connect and Extend**
Children's drawings are thought to be a mirror of a child's representational development. This is a fascinating idea that is worth exploring by reading: Cherney, I., Seiwert, C., Dickey, T. R. & Flichtbeil, J. (2006). Children's drawings: A mirror to their minds. *Educational Psychology, 26,* 127–142.
● ● ● ● ● ● ● ● ● ● ● ● ● ● ● ●

# Three approaches to cognitive development

## Piaget's cognitive-developmental theory

Swiss developmental psychologist Jean Piaget (1896–1980) is arguably the most influential figure in research in children's cognitive development. Child-centred education (which views the child as an active learner) is deeply rooted to his theory that children learn about the world through exploration of it – good practice in many early childhood and primary school settings today. This is a constructivist theory which views children as active participants in their own learning, seeking out knowledge and constructing their own understanding. Piaget identified different stages of development following a hierarchical structure of 'simple to complex', and 'concrete to abstract'. He also argued that we do not start out as thinkers, but, through our developing motor and perceptual capacities, we construct and refine our mental structures. Central to thinking are the formation and refinement of concepts and particularly mental schemes. But what exactly are concepts and what are mental schemes?

## Concepts

**Concept**
A general category of ideas, objects, people, or experiences whose members share certain properties.

A **concept** is a category used to group similar events, ideas, objects or people. When we talk about a particular concept such as *student*, we refer to a category of people who are similar to one another – they all study a subject. Students may be old or young, in university or not; they may be studying drama or drawing, but they all can be categorised as students.

## Defining concepts

**Defining attributes**
Distinctive features shared by members of a category.

In early research, psychologists assumed that concepts share a set of **defining attributes**, or distinctive features. For example, books all contain pages that are bound together in some way. The defining attributes theory of concepts suggests that we recognise specific examples by noting key required features, in the case of books, bound pages. What about the concept of *bird*? Your first thought might be that birds are animals that fly, but is an ostrich a bird? What about a penguin or a bat? Earlier we talked about the concept of book, whose defining attributes were pages that are bound together in some way. But what about *e-books*? They do not conform to the defining attributes of *book* but rather those of *e-book*.

## Prototypes and exemplars

**Prototype**
Best or 'averaged' representative of a category.

Current views of concept learning suggest that we have in our minds a prototype of a bird – an image that captures the essence of each concept. A **prototype** is the best or most common representative of its category. For instance, the best representative of the 'bird' category for many Northern European people might be a robin, since it is a common garden bird, easily recognised and often depicted on Christmas cards. Other members of the category may be very similar to the prototype (sparrow) or similar in some ways but different in others (chicken or ostrich). At the boundaries of a category, it may be difficult to determine whether a particular instance really belongs.

## Exemplars

**Exemplar**
A specific example of a given category that is used to classify an item.

Another explanation of concept learning suggests that we identify members of a category by referring to an **exemplar**. Exemplars are our actual memories of specific birds, books or fruits that we use to compare with an item in question to see whether that item belongs in the same category as our exemplar. Prototypes are built from experiences with many exemplars. This happens naturally because memories of particular events tend to blur together over time, creating an 'average' or typical prototype from all the exemplars you have experienced.

## Concepts and schemas

In addition to prototypes and exemplars, there is a third element involved when we recognise a concept – our schematic knowledge related to the concept. How do we know that counterfeit money is not 'real' money, even though it perfectly fits our 'money' prototype and exemplars? We know because of its history. The 'wrong' people printed the money. So our schema of money is connected with concepts of crime, forgery, the treasury and many others.

Jacob Feldman (2003) – a psychologist working in the field of cognitive science – suggests a final aspect of concept learning, the simplicity principle. Feldman says that, when humans are confronted with examples, they induce the simplest category or rule that would cover all examples. Sometimes, it is easy to come up with a simple rule (triangles) and sometimes it is more difficult (fruit), but humans seek a simple way of collecting all the examples they perceive under one concept. Feldman suggests that this simplicity principle is one of the oldest ideas in cognitive psychology: 'organisms seek to understand their environment by reducing incoming information to a simpler, more coherent, and more useful form' (p 231).

Therefore **schemes** (or schemas) are organised ways of making sense of experience and are both sets of related concepts (money and forgery) and are 'co-ordinated systems of movements and perceptions, which constitute any elementary behaviour capable of being repeated and applied to new situations' (Piaget, 1962, p 274). Piaget believed that creating schemas is not a passive process, but one that involves active engagement and is dynamic – one that changes with age. As children grow older, they develop new schemes and refine existing ones and become better at developing and refining. As a result of applying a schema to an object, the child arrives at a generalisation about that object; in the case of a rattle, this object to an infant can be sucked, banged, shaken or thrown. First schemes are formed through sensorimotor perceptions and each brings with it understanding through the perceptual feedback that follows action. As the child grows older, internalisation of 'thought' in addition to action will provide feedback for refinement. Piagetian ideas of mental schemes were tested and built on throughout the remainder of the twentieth century. For example, Chris Athey (1990) explored the Piagetian notion of developing and refining schema, through her work observing children from 2 to 5 years. In *Extending Thought in Young Children* Athey analysed over 5000 observations collected during a 5-year Early Education Project at the Froebel Educational Institute. The text documents consistent 'forms of thought' used by young children and suggests how teachers can develop a greater knowledge of young children's thinking and learning. Of many examples given to illustrate young children's use of schema in building knowledge, this small extract shows developing schemas of the concept of rotation in children's play and is compiled from observations by teachers in Sheffield as part of their research.

> At a building site, Carl pointed out cement-mixers and wheels. On his return to school he was keen to see how the see-saw went around instead of up and down. Betty spun a bowl around, then a dish with dough in it on an old record player. She then found a clock and rotated its hands. Outside she ran around the climbing frame . . .
>
> Four boys chose wheels from the box and rolled these down some planks. Emma jumped up and began to twirl. The teacher sang, 'The wind blows high, the wind blows low, round and round the windmills go'.

(Athey, 1990, p 194)

A **mental representation** or way of depicting information internally takes place that allows the object to be compared with another or placed in a particular category. This is achieved through images or pictures (of cement-mixers and wheels) and concepts, or grouping together

**Connect and Extend**

For a full description and explanation of learning and teaching concepts, read: Chapter 8 in Woolfolk, A., Hughes, M. W. H. & Walkup, V. (2011). Complex cognitive processes. *Psychology in Education.* (2nd ed). Harlow: Pearson Education Limited.

**Schemes**
Repeatable patterns/ organised ways of making sense of an experience. They alter with age.

**Mental representation**
Way of depicting information internally, either as images or concepts.

things which are similar. Piaget argued that when children think in concepts they are also able to put labels to them (e.g. this is a pencil as an object to write or draw with), so they become thinkers and give meaning to their experiences in categories that are manageable and memorable to them. Thinking is an internalised action. For Piaget, the process of change in thinking from a sensorimotor activity to mental representations involves active processes. Such changes in the childhood years can be accounted for by two biological concepts: adaptation and organisation.

Adaptation refers to the construction of schemes arising from the direct engagement with the environment that allows us to adjust to the demands of our environment. Two processes are involved. In assimilation, current schemes are used to understand the external environment by integrating the environment into our mental structures. For example, when a child first sees a cat, the animal may be assimilated to an existing category, e.g. 'doggy'. Other people's responses when the child calls the cat a doggy would prompt the child to accommodate, to reorganise 'doggy' into two new concepts, 'doggy' and 'cat'. In accommodation, the child constructs new schemes when the current ones are redundant, by reorganising and amending cognitive strategies. A good example of an early scheme is grasping. A child will grasp a wooden brick using knowledge assimilated in an existing scheme. This works well except when the child sees a new object like a set of plastic keys. Their shape and size are different to the brick. In order to grasp the new object, the child must accommodate to the new object by changing grip. This in turn allows the new object to be successfully picked up and explored.

In organisation, the schemes or internal systems are organised and ordered and new networked systems established. Very young children will have a number of schemes that they will – as time goes by – be able to combine through the organisation process. Piaget believed that children continually organise schemes into more adaptive and complex ones. Often the two processes of assimilation and organisation take place at the same time (Kuschner, 2012). Adaptation does not occur in a linear fashion, but rather children move back and forward over time in a process called equilibration as they move from steady periods of relatively little change in assimilation to times of greater change in the accommodation state as they modify their existing schemes. Young children start with an initial map (scheme) and either add to it when an existing scheme is no longer fit for purpose, or demolish the existing scheme and reconstruct it. This process of equilibration is used to harmonise children's mental structures and the world around them. 'It is the process of achieving equilibrium, of finding a balance between those things that were previously understood and those that are yet to be understood' (Honstead, 1968, p 135). I think of this like a tightrope walker on a high wire. Everything is fine until a high wind blows, taking the performer out of balance and making her take account of the wind pressure to regain her perfect poise. It is the same with cognition. We are comfortable with our current schemes and all is well until a new and 'uncomfortable' experience makes us adapt our schemes to take account of the new experience. As a result of adapting to the wind, the tightrope walker becomes a more accomplished performer; as a result of new experience we develop our understandings about how the world works.

## Stages of development

In Piaget's theory, cognitive development is represented as unfolding in four stages:

- sensorimotor stage (birth to 2 years);
- pre-operational stage (2–7 years);
- concrete operational stage (7–11 years);
- formal operations stage (12 years upwards).

The sensorimotor stage (from birth to 2 years) is our first understanding of the world in which we assimilate information from the environment to the limited set of schemes we are

**Adaptation**
Constructing schemes as a result of engaging directly with the environment.

**Organisation**
The ways in which schemes are linked together in a connected network.

**Assimilation**
The absorption of a new idea or experience into a current schema.

**Accommodation**
Building new schemes when the existing ones appear redundant.

**Equilibration**
Adding to, or demolishing and reconstructing, existing schemes by using assimilation and accommodation.

**Sensorimotor stage**
The first stage in Piaget's model from birth to age 2 in which the child moves from an action-based way of understanding the world to thinking about it using symbols.

born with. A young child then accommodates those few schemes with experiences in a set of sub-stages that have been defined by observing what young children can do. So what can we expect an infant to be able to do at each sub-stage?

In sub-stage 1 (up to 1 month) simple reactions to the environment are formed in the reflexive schemes and behaviours of newborns (e.g. sucking, head turning). There is no actively controlled sensorimotor co-ordination and so an object that a child sees will not yet prompt movement to grasp it. Behaviours are innate but within hours of birth some reflexes become modified or accommodated through experience, for example, searching for the mother's nipple. In sub-stage 2 (2–4 months) reflexive actions are refined to suit the demands of the environment. The child actions a reflex, experiences it as pleasurable and repeats it, for example, thumb sucking or leg kicking. Nature and nurture are at work together and sensorimotor co-ordination is achieved largely through trial and error. In sub-stage 3 (4–8 months) secondary 'circular' reactions allow existing schemes to combine and we witness actions such as sitting up, reaching out for and playing with a rattle as actions that invoke a reaction outside the child's own body and involve objects or other people. At this stage, children like to copy sounds and facial expressions of others, which suggest there is some mental representation of their own features to know which part of their own face they are using. They enjoy games like peek-a-boo with an adult, even though they are as yet unable to join in fully (see Chapter 8 for a fuller discussion). If an action from the child like smiling affords a reaction from another person that the child enjoys, the action will very likely be repeated.

Sensorimotor sub-stage 1 (0–1 month): infants can turn their head to see object.
*Source*: © Pearson Education Ltd / Jules Selmes.

Sensorimotor sub-stage 4 (8–12 months): actions can be goal-directed, like this infant crawling decidedly to the toy.
*Source*: © Pearson Education Ltd / Jules Selmes.

**Reflect**

**Have you played peekaboo with a young child? Research suggests that this simple game is played in many cultures with similar routines (Fernald & O'Neill, 1993). It helps form ideas about an object's permanence, focuses attention that aids learning and helps with social skills. It can also help babies overcome anxiety about the adult carer disappearing. What have you noticed about the responses of young children to this game?**

During sub-stage 4 (8–12 months) the co-ordination of secondary circular reactions enables children to combine new actions that are both intentional and goal-directed. This is a time when an infant will intentionally drop a plastic beaker and deliberately takes hold of a rattle instead. Things of interest perhaps some distance away may prompt them to crawl in a very single-minded way towards them, ignoring all else in their way! The co-ordination of different schemes is nonetheless taking place and developing all the time. In sub-stage 5 (12–18 months), children solve simple problems and form better theories of the world by testing them out in practical ways. They display variety in actions already learned (e.g. grasping onto a building block and exploring it with hands and mouth now becomes banging the blocks together to make a loud noise). This is the stage they

Sensorimotor sub-stage 5 (12–18 months): developing object permanence.
*Source*: © Pearson Education Ltd / Jules Selmes.

Pre-operational stage (2–7 years): these children enjoy tipping water into beakers, and are learning about conservation of capacity.

*Source:* © Pearson Education Ltd / Jules Selmes.

**A-not-B search errors**
Mistakes made by 8–12-month-old children. When an object is moved from location A to B, they still look for it in the first location.

**Pre-operational stage**
The second stage in Piaget's model from age 2 to 7 years. It is characterised by an advancement in mental representation.

**Connect and Extend**
Harris and Kavanaugh (1993) found that 2–7-year-olds understood pretence. Read a more recent study with 1- and 2-year-olds by Bosco, F., Friedman, O. & Leslie, A. (2006). Recognition of pretend and real actions in play by 1- and 2-year-olds: Early success and why they fail. *Cognitive Development*, *21*, 3–10, available at **www.sciencedirect.com**

**Operations**
In the context of Piagetian accounts of cognitive development, operations are thinking or procedures that obey logical rules.

**Egocentric (1)**
In the context of Piagetian accounts of cognitive development, it is the belief that pre-operational thinking is thinking from a child's own perspective only.

further develop object permanence or understanding that objects still exist when they are not visible to them. If, as an example, a toy is placed in hiding place (A), and then obviously moved to hiding place (B), a child at this stage will search for it in the second location (they do not make **A-not-B search errors**).

In sub-stage 6 (18–24 months), developed abilities of mental representation allow a definite shift to symbolic thinking and the child is able to represent mentally happenings and ideas much more systematically. New combinations and more advanced mental experimentation take place, such as invisible displacement, an advancement in object permanence that permits objects to be found that have been moved while out of sight. Piaget conducted a similar experiment using a toy obscured from sight with a cloth to determine that infants have developed object permanence fully and will search for the toy in its correct place by this stage. During this sub-stage, development enables deferred imitation or copying the behaviour of models that are not visible, and the emergence of pretend play where children act out real and imaginary activities.

The **pre-operational stage** (from 2 to 7 years) or the pre-conceptual period is characterised by a marked increase in mental representation. Piaget believed that during this stage children increasingly use mental symbols to represent the world around them and this is evident in their use of language, drawings and in pretend play scenarios. Activities frequently observed in the unstructured play of children of this age such as tipping water into beakers, dressing up, building with blocks and role play are tremendously important for their cognitive development and are at the very heart of good practice in early childhood education. Progression of play in Piaget's stages is similar to the progression found by other researchers in the past thirty years or so (e.g. van Kuyk, 2011; Rubin *et al.*, 1983). At this stage pretend or symbolic play increases both in frequency and complexity (Nichols & Stich, 2000) and is increasingly more complex, requiring more sophisticated thinking, language and social skills.

 **Reflect**   Children in the 2–7 age range understand the concept of pretence (Harris & Kavanaugh, 1993). Researchers found that if you handed pre-operational children a towel and asked them to wipe up imaginary liquid that had been spilt, they did it. How can we account for this? Compare this finding with the research in the nearby *Connect and Extend* feature.

Piaget viewed this stage of children's thinking as being somewhat limited and rigid, seeming to place stress on what children cannot accomplish rather than what they can in this stage (psychologists and others call this a deficit model). He believed that pre-operational thought had definite limitations and children in this stage were incapable of thinking according to any logical structures or using **operations** (the procedures that obey logical rules). He viewed thinking in this stage as **egocentric**, or from the child's own perspective only. His stage theory fails to take account of the possible effects upon cognition of the thoughts and beliefs of other people. This is not to infer that Piaget thought pre-operational children are selfish, merely that their current understanding does not include that other people may have a different perspective on the world than they have.

His classic 'three mountains task' (Piaget & Inhelder, 1966) showed this. Here models of three mountains were placed on a table top – see Figure 9.2 – and chairs positioned at all four sides of the table. A child sat in one chair, and the experimenter placed a doll in each of the other three chairs one at a time. The child was asked to describe the doll's view of each

**Figure 9.2** Piaget's 'three mountains task'

This pasteboard model is one metre square and consists of three 'mountains' of various heights and colours. One is green, another brown, and the tallest grey with a white snow cap. A small red cross caps one of the mountains, and a small house another.

*Source*: Piaget, J. & Inhelder, B. (1967). *The child's conception of space* (pp 211–222). London: Routledge.

of the mountains. The child was then able to choose one of a set of drawings or cardboard cut-outs to match this. Piaget found that pre-operational children were not able to identify the doll's view from the three positions on the table. Only when children were in the later concrete operational stage was this possible. Subsequent studies that altered the original models to make them more distinctive (Borke, 1975) or made the task more comprehensible to the children (Hughes, 1975) found that children between 3 and 5 years old were competent in this task – findings that completely disagree with those of Piaget.

It was egocentrism, Piaget argued, that was responsible for children's **animistic thinking** during this stage, or the belief that objects can take on human qualities. For example, imagine Millie, aged 3 years, who in her nursery proudly explains that the stars look down at night and smile on all the people in the world, and the dolls she plays with become 'real' babies for her to look after. Her thinking and belief at this stage is pre-causal. Millie's responses to questions such as 'Why is it dark at night-time?', 'Why is grass green?' or 'Where does the wind go to?' appear egocentric because of the child's lack of knowledge of physical causes. Other limitations in pre-operational thinking are revealed in Piaget's well-known conservation experiments using glasses of different shapes filled with the same amount of liquid. Piaget challenged children to recognise that, even though an object may be altered in appearance, its basic properties are the same (remember the opening scene in this chapter about pouring juice into different shaped beakers). Classroom observation can confirm that conservation-type challenges involving number, length and capacity are typically mastered by children between 6 and 8 years and that any inability of children to conserve illustrates certain characteristics of pre-operational thinking.

Firstly, pre-operational thinking shows **centration** or a focus in on one characteristic of the task only (in the juice example this is on the height of the liquid in the beakers). Secondly, pre-operational thinking shows how children are confused by the appearance of the object and their perceptions of it compromised. (In the opening scene, Maria – aged

Exploring conservation of number. At 5 years old, this boy probably doesn't understand that both rows have the same number of sweets.

*Source*: © Pearson Education Ltd / Jules Selmes.

**Animistic thinking**
Thinking of young children typified by a belief that objects can take on human qualities.

**Centration**
Pre-operational thinking that focuses on one aspect of the task only.

Children in the concrete operational stage enjoy ordering objects based on size.

*Source*: Laura Dwight / PhotoEdit Inc.

**Reversibility**
The idea that a mental operation can be reversed by carrying out a second operation opposite to the first.

**Concrete operational stage**
The third of Piaget's four stages of cognitive development (between 7 to 11 years), this stage is characterised by children's use of logic to solve problems that apply to actual (concrete) objects or events, and not abstract concepts or hypothetical tasks.

**Seriation**
The ability to order objects quantitatively, e.g. by weight or length.

**Transitive inference problems**
The ability to seriate objects mentally on a quantitative continuum in order to achieve a solution.

5 years – believed the shorter beaker contained less juice and so loudly complained that she had been given less than Jodie!) Thirdly, pre-operational children cannot change direction in their thinking in a process Piaget called **reversibility**. In a conservation task, children could not imagine the liquid being poured back to fill the original container, or that a ball of clay, being rolled flat then broken up into small pieces can be rolled back into a ball of the same size. Piaget believed that by about the age of 7, children's brains developed a capacity to find causes, reasons and to attribute qualities and characteristics correctly. This was termed the 'concrete operational stage'.

The **concrete operational stage** in the later primary school years (from 7 to 11 years) represents a major milestone in children's cognitive development and in their interactions with the world around them. It is during this stage that conservation tasks can now be successfully accomplished and this is frequently observed by practitioners in many school-based achievements and out-of-school activities. For example, the ability to understand conservation is essential in number, shape, space and measure, and observations of children working on shape and measurement tasks provides a useful guide to the children's stage of cognitive development. Children in the concrete operational stage enjoy the success of organising objects such as coins and stamps into categories and can solve what Piaget termed 'class inclusion tasks'. These tasks relate to whole–part relations (the ball of clay) problems which Piaget argued that pre-operational children were unable to solve.

For example, if you show a 4-year-old a picture of two sub-classes of a larger class (showing five elephants and three bunny rabbits) and ask if there are more elephants or more animals in the picture, the child will say there are more elephants. Where the pre-operational child has difficulty in understanding the class of animals as well as the subsets, children in the later stage find this easier to understand. Another example of concrete operational ability that you can observe is the logical ordering of objects, perhaps by weight or length, called **seriation**. Successful seriation is also achieved by most 7-year-olds, in contrast to the more ad hoc ordering of counters or beans by many 5-year-olds!

Piaget (1967) concluded that cognition showing concrete operational ability such as seriation allows the solving of **transitive inference problems**. For example, in one experiment Piaget showed children various coloured sticks: stick A was longer than stick B which was longer than stick C. Which was longer, stick A or stick C? Solving this problem required mental inference in understanding that stick A was longer than B, that B was longer than C, and therefore that stick A must be longer than C. Findings showed that the majority of 8-year-olds accomplished this task successfully.

Children in middle childhood develop a better understanding of spatial reasoning than younger peers and cope well with geographical challenges such as calculating the distance between two points, giving directions accurately and constructing maps. They are comfortable with basic orienteering tasks involving map reading and computer tasks such as those involving the rotation of simple maps to find treasure in a fictitious castle. In the concrete operational stage children display inductive logic so use their own experiences to move to more general principles, thus teaching in practical ways (sometimes called play!) is highly effective pedagogy. In contrast, educational challenges that require children to use deductive logic (by beginning with a general principle and deduce hypotheses from this – extending from the concrete to the abstract) is one of the characteristics of the formal operations stage found in children of secondary school age, and is not addressed in detail here (but see the following *Connect and Extend* feature).

## Claims and critiques of Piaget's cognitive-developmental theory

From the 1960s, cognitive-developmental theory was the dominant paradigm in explaining cognition. It certainly provides a coherent theory of cognitive development that unites many areas in a way not previously attempted. Piaget's work prompted further research (replication of Piaget's original research tasks – e.g. Annesi, 2007) and new research (e.g. Siegler & Alibali, 2005) that has advanced our knowledge of how children think and learn. The impact of Piaget in psychology and in schooling remains evident in educational practice worldwide. He set the agenda for understanding how children think, was a skilled observer of young children and his work has been widely replicated, evaluated and criticised. Yet more recent research (e.g. Siegler & Alibali, 2005; Flavell *et al.*, 2002; Arterberry & Bornstein, 2001) calls into question some of his findings. It is argued that children at various ages are more cognitively developed than Piaget originally proposed. 'Were Piaget's theories correct or flawed?' is the question posed in the *Controversy* feature below. This *Controversy* is structured in a different way from those in previous chapters. In this *Controversy* we ask you to follow the references for a fuller reading of research that has challenged the Piagetian view on the identified issues. It is particularly interesting to read the various researchers' perspectives on the original work by Piaget.

**Connect and Extend**

For more explanation and examples of Piaget's fourth formal operations stage (in particular the pendulum task), read: Bond, T. (2004). Piaget and the pendulum. *Science & Education*, 13, 389–399.

## Controversy

### Were Piaget's theories correct or flawed? Consider the evidence

| Issue | Piagetian view | Criticism |
|---|---|---|
| Appearance of stages of cognitive development | Cognitive development appears in stages. Discontinuous. Largely unaffected by external factors. | More frequent assessment suggests more continuity. The stages are not as rigid (Flavell *et al.*, 2002). Cognitive abilities may be altered by training and experience (Siegler & Alibali, 2005). |
| Culture | General. Applies universally. | Cognitive competence and stage development is culturally relative and domain specific (Rogoff, 1998). |
| Social context | Little contribution to cognitive development. | Ignores social and emotional contributions. Piaget's theories are too independent and isolated (Meadows, 1995). |
| Egocentrism/ perspective taking | Perspective taking is not evident in very young children who are extremely egocentric. | Evident in the play of 2–3-year-olds (Brownell, 1990). Children of 4–5 can take others' perspectives (Newcombe & Huttenlocher, 2003). |
| Conservation | Pre-operational children cannot understand conservation. | Gelman (1972) 'the magic mice paradigm' experiment. Wynn (1990) on work with puppets with children $2\frac{1}{2}$- to $3\frac{1}{2}$-year-olds. Donaldson (1978) suggests otherwise providing the language used is understood. |
| Memory capacity | Young children have poorly developed memories. | Bhatt and Rovee-Collier (1996) study using a piece of string attached to a baby's leg while lying in a cot with a mobile suspended overhead. Found 3-month-olds remembered a week later. |

| Issue | Piagetian view | Criticism |
|-------|----------------|-----------|
| Deferred imitation | Proposed it not before 18 months. | Meltzoff (1988) study had 9-month-old infants watching adults pushing buttons on a box and producing sounds. |
| Imitation | Gradual process, not before 8–12 months. | Newborns can imitate tongues stuck out by an adult (Anisfeld, 1991). |
| Theory of mind | Is not evident in the pre-operational stage. | Gopnik and Slaughter (1991) showed young children beginning to understand that predicting what other people will do involve some understanding of the desires of other people. |
| Class inclusion (understanding part–whole relationships) | Appears around ages 7–8. | Hodkin's (1981) study on rows of Smarties sweets found it in children younger than this. Children of 3 months can categorise based on perceptual similarities (Arterberry & Bornstein, 2001). |

So was Piaget right about these issues of cognitive development or are his theories flawed?

**Theory of mind**
Being able to think of other people's mental states and construct theories about their thinking.

## Implications for teaching and learning

Although we want you to adopt your own critical stance on Piaget's work, we cannot leave this section without presenting what we consider to be the many positive contributions that Piaget's findings have made to our understanding of children's cognitive development and to learning. We present our own 'top 12' of ways Piaget's work has influenced education.

1. Learning requires an active construction of knowledge and children should engage actively with their school or nursery environment.
2. Discovery learning promotes learning by building up schemes and encourages later assimilation and accommodation – children 'doing' is better than teachers 'telling'.
3. Progression of ideas should move from concrete and practical to more abstract.
4. The teacher's role is to facilitate, to assist the child in discovery, questioning and speculating.
5. Understanding concept formation is vital for all learners (regardless of subject or age).
6. The notion of age-related stages should not become a 'straitjacket'. Mental age based on what a child can do may be more useful than chronological age in deciding provision.
7. Practical and verbal experience is necessary in the pre-operational thinking stage.
8. Curriculum planning should be more directly informed by understanding the significance of stages in children's cognitive development.
9. Thinking is a cumulative process. Lower-order schemes exist first that prepare for higher-order thinking later.
10. Teachers and practitioners should set tasks matched to the needs of pupils in a school or nursery curriculum designed to accommodate individual needs and rates of learning.
11. Readiness can determine the type of learning experiences provided.
12. Schools and other settings should provide appropriate experiences to foster cognitive development and children's natural desire to learn.

We have acknowledged and celebrated the contribution made by Jean Piaget to our understanding of cognitive development – and demonstrated the almost universal application of his theories to schools and other settings – but it is now timely to compare and contrast Piaget's research and theories with that of another hugely influential scientist, the Russian psychologist Lev Vygotsky.

# Vygotsky's sociocultural theory

Lev Vygotsky's social-constructivist approach offered a major alternative to Piaget in the period between 1920 and 1930 although his work did not appear in English, and therefore gain wider recognition, until the 1960s. The central principle of his theory argues that thinking is a socially constructed process. While Piaget saw children's cognitive development as an individual endeavour, Vygotsky stressed the social and environmental forces. Where Piaget took the view of a child as an experimental scientist, Vygotsky likened the child to an apprentice, acquiring knowledge and skills of a culture through interaction with those who already possess that knowledge and those skills. It is through our social interactions with those around us that we slowly move to becoming self-sufficient and independent learners and develop our intellectual capabilities; that development occurs from processes firstly on a social plane (i.e. between people) and then secondly in a psychological one (i.e. individually).

• • • • • • • • • • • • • • • • •
**Connect and Extend**
For an article defining quality in early years teaching, the 'leading activity' and 'amplification' of learning, read: Bodrova, E. & Leong, D. (2005). High quality preschool programs: What would Vygotsky say? *Early Education & Development, 16*, 435–444.
• • • • • • • • • • • • • • • • •

## The importance of language

We are born with limited cognitive functions (remember the elementary cognitive functions described in Chapter 6) and Vygotsky's view was that these functions are developed largely through the interventions of others in that community. Higher mental functions are enabled and developed though the use of language – the ultimate social tool as we shall see in Chapter 10. Tools such as language and number are the means by which cultures conceptualise and then transmit through childhood experiences abilities needed in adulthood such as categorisation, pattern-forming and problem-solving. So it is the child's social experiences that promote with category formation, whereby the identification of the critical attributes of objects or events can be organised. This is a progressive and iterative process since hierarchies of increased complexity are formed when concepts are subject to experiential influences. Increases in language capability change thinking. Language allows children to organise how they behave and to reflect on this. Vygotsky argued that when very young children interact with others they become more knowledgeable and this enables them to identify what tasks are accepted as culturally important. He believed that private speech – talking to yourself or what Piaget termed egocentric speech – was the foundation of higher thinking because it allowed children to plan, recall information and to solve problems. Consider a 4-year-old faced with the problem of sorting shapes by their colours. If you were to listen you would probably hear the child speaking to herself in order to work out how to solve the problem. Older children use the same strategy but will tend to speak inwardly – in their head (Askeland, 2012; Ostad & Sorensen, 2007).

By understanding this child's potential developmental level, her teacher can help her master skills.
*Source*: © Pearson Education Ltd / Jules Selmes.

## Zone of proximal development

Much of Vygotsky's work has direct implications for teaching and learning today. He believed that children actively develop their own knowledge at their own pace, but this process requires access to rich and stimulating environments. Rather than demeaning the role of teachers in

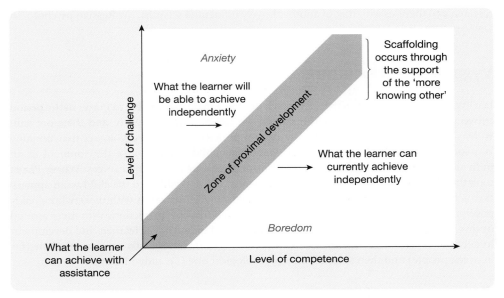

**Figure 9.3** How the zone of proximal development applies in the classroom

Teaching should be focused or targeted on the zone of proximal development or children will become bored or anxious.

*Source*: State of Victoria (Department of Education and Early Childhood Development), Australia (2007). *Student learning: literacy professional learning resource – key concepts*. Melbourne: DEECD (retrieved from **www.education.vic.gov.au/images/content/studentlearning/zpdgraph.jpg**).

children's learning, Vygotsky believed that instruction is as important as learning in a child's development. The function of teachers is to facilitate learning and this is made possible by structuring the learning environment to allow children's concepts and skills to develop. He stressed the necessity to attend to children's actual developmental levels (i.e. in terms of knowledge and skills mastered) and then move towards their potential developmental levels (which are knowledge and skills not yet mastered) at times when the child critically benefits from the help of adults or experienced peers. The **zone of proximal development** (ZPD) (Vygotsky, 1978) is 'the distance between the actual developmental level as determined by independent problem solving, and the level of potential development as determined through problem solving under adult guidance or in collaboration with more able peers' (Vygotsky, 1978, p 86). It might be understood best as a state of developmental readiness. Therefore, when planning, teachers and early years practitioners must focus or target their teaching and the planned experiences for the children on the zone of proximal development or children will become bored or anxious: see Figure 9.3. We draw your attention to the labelling of the axes *Challenge* and *Competence*. There is sometimes a temptation to consider ZPDs as critical periods when children can learn. This is not the case. It is much more helpful to think of a ZPD as a space for learning which children can explore between that which they already know, and that which they are capable of learning.

Vygotsky believed that a ZPD may differ according to individual children and that children with a more extensive ZPD have a greater capacity to be helped than those with a limited ZPD. Interestingly, and for us importantly, Vygotsky saw pretend play as a ZPD by which children advance their learning. By constructing make-believe scenarios children are grappling with internal ideas, coming to understand that thinking is separate from action and that their ideas can guide how they behave. Understanding that objects can represent other objects and that play has its own set of rules is developed, which helps their understanding of social norms. These ideas are supported by more recent findings (Yongho & Kellogg, 2007; Andresen, 2005).

**Zone of proximal development**
This is a state of developmental readiness defined as the gap between the actual developmental level and the level of potential development.

## Scaffolding

It is around 40 years since psychologists David Wood, Jerome Bruner and Gail Ross (1976) introduced the idea of 'scaffolding' to represent the way children's learning can be supported, where 'significant others' provide help at significant points and gradually remove the help as a child succeeds. Teachers must adjust and match their interventions to each individual's ZPD; it is the defining skill of a teacher to decide what kind of support is necessary, when to give the support and how much support is necessary for an individual. An example to illustrate this is a child trying to construct a floor jigsaw puzzle alone. Grappling with this task alone and having to work hard to complete it places the child in the ZPD. If the jigsaw is too difficult then the child will have gone outside her ZPD and a teacher might use simple language to help the child understand the task more fully and give support through skilled questioning and suggestions. This will raise the child's intellectual development to a new level and enable the jigsaw to be completed correctly. The involvement of the teacher at this stage is termed 'scaffolding'. Scaffolding is a very common practice in many school contexts – skilled teachers break down a task and adjust the level of assistance provided as the child proceeds – and examples can be both practical in nature (such as model design and building) and textbook-related (such as maths word problems).

## Guided participation

Barbara Rogoff and colleagues (1993) introduced the term 'guided participation' – one aspect of scaffolding – to mean children's interactions with adults that bridge children's understanding with that of the adults. Situations of guided participation vary across cultures. Observations by Rogoff and colleagues in rural Guatemala, in an Indian tribal village, an 'educated' urban community in the United States and in a semi-urban community in Turkey revealed distinct cross-cultural differences in child-rearing practices. In domestic tasks such as dressing or tying shoelaces, children in the first two communities observed a demonstration by the adults that typically used non-verbal instruction. Afterwards, the children did it for themselves, the adults being on hand if required to assist as they were occupied with their work in the nearby fields. This contrasted with the middle socioeconomic class in an urban North American community who preferred to provide more formal lesson-type instruction to teach these new skills and allowed their children to interact with them. The Turkish community was undergoing transition from a rural to an urban lifestyle, and used elements of both types of involvement. While all cultures provided guidance, this research shows that direct adult involvement is more likely to be found in urban communities where verbal skills are developed and parents may afford more time to child-rearing (Hamston & Love, 2003). In rural and developing communities, children learn typically through observing adults and becoming more involved in adult work patterns. Where the world of children markedly differs from that of their parents – for example, in access to information and communication technologies – guided participation is unlikely to be observed (Anastasiades *et al.*, 2008).

## Co-operative learning

It is not just parents or other 'significant' adults who can use scaffold learning in Vygotsky's theory. Scaffolding learners to competency also involves knowledgeable or skilful pupils helping less advanced ones. This takes place in contemporary classrooms and playgrounds when peers work together perhaps on a collaborative task in a process called co-operative learning. Most primary classrooms have furniture arranged in table groups to promote children's interactions with each other positively. If you spent 10 minutes observing well-structured and organised group work, you would see and hear children at any of these tables helping each other, learning from one another in pursuit of a common goal and without the direction of a teacher. This is a broader idea than Vygotsky's original view of ZPD where there is a single

**Scaffolding**
Role played by more knowledgeable others by which children can go beyond their zone of proximal development. Crucial to the idea is progressive withdrawal of support as learner's own competence increases.

● ● ● ● ● ● ● ● ● ● ● ● ● ● ● ●
**Connect and Extend**
To characterise some teaching approaches that can be identified as scaffolding and identifying further scaffolding strategies with particular reference to learning mathematics (geometry learning with 4- to 6-year-olds), read: Anghileri, J. (2006). Scaffolding practices that enhance mathematics learning. *Journal of Mathematics Teacher Education, 9*, 33–52.
● ● ● ● ● ● ● ● ● ● ● ● ● ● ● ●

**Guided participation**
Children's interactions with adults that bridge children's understanding with that of the adults.

**Co-operative learning**
Children work in small groups sharing a common goal in their learning.

**Connect and Extend**

For a study which supports assertions that, when pupils are allowed to pose questions and provide feedback to one another during peer collaboration, they help to place learning in their zone of proximal development, read: Gnadinger, C. M. (2008). Peer-mediated instruction: Assisted performance in the primary classroom. *Teachers & Teaching, 14*, 129–142.

**Reciprocal teaching**
Small groups having dialogue on a subject so that the level is beyond an individual's present capability but within ZPD.

child and another more expert child/adult. In co-operative learning, groups of children with varying degrees of expertise have been found to stimulate learning in each other (Tracey *et al.*, 2010; Doymus, 2008). Other research, while supportive of this, also indicates that co-operative learning is more effective when children had been trained in co-operative procedures – how to work together (Georgiadis *et al.*, 2011; Gillies, 2000) and the teacher has prior experience of working in this way (Oortwijn *et al.*, 2008).

## Reciprocal teaching

Peers as 'knowledgeable others' is integral to another important aspect of Vygotsky theory, that of reciprocal teaching. This involves using peers to promote dialogue at a level beyond an individual's capability but within their ZPD and has led to research studies over a number of years (e.g. Gnadinger, 2008; Rosenshine & Meister, 1994). Begun as a remedial strategy for reading, reciprocal teaching involves children in a group with a teacher where children take turns at leading dialogue so that the teaching exceeds the group's present capability but is within their respective ZPD. Commonly, the children would use techniques here such as asking questions, summarising, and predicting outcomes but again it does require training for both pupils and teachers for such teaching techniques to be effective.

## Implications for teaching and learning

Vygotskian theory has great potential for helping our understanding of cognitive development in social and cultural contexts, but, as with any other theory, it has some shortcomings. There is an obvious attention and value placed on language but there is a lack of emphasis on perceptual and motor capacities and how these influence cognitive change. There is an almost total focus on cultural factors that influence development but little in the original theory on development in other groups besides European middle classes. Finally, although some more recent research has investigated this issue, there is little in Vygotskian theory about how group dynamics and gender in collaborative learning affect development and learning.

Reciprocal teaching: working together on a task and sharing ideas helps children to develop within their ZPD.

*Source*: © Pearson Education Ltd / Ian Wedgewood.

Nevertheless, there are important implications of Vygotsky's work for education. One key factor is the important role of the teacher in structuring learning. In the United Kingdom as long ago as 1992, Robin Alexander, Jim Rose and Chris Woodhead (known then as the 'three wise men' of UK educational policy) criticised child-centred education (widely associated with the theories of Jean Piaget) and the notion of fixed stages development – again Piaget – which they believed led to lowered expectations, inhibited teacher interventions and confined the role of the teacher to 'facilitator'. They stated, 'More recent studies demonstrate what children, given effective teaching, can achieve . . . they show that learning is essentially a social and interactive process. They place proper emphasis on the teacher as teacher rather than facilitator. Such insights are, in our view, critical to the raising of standards in primary classrooms' (1992, p 14).

Vygotsky emphasised social influences and the role of the teacher on development in his social constructivist theory. Human functioning is socially evolved and uses socially cultural tools such as language, number, art, models and diagrams as part of a culture's shared knowledge. Children construct knowledge in a community with shared culture and it is through this social dimension that they develop as thinkers. A high level of competence is needed only in those skills that a society values, so, though cognitive potential may be universal, expertise is culturally determined (Joutsenvirta & Uusitalo, 2010; Nakashima & Vaddhanaphuti, 2006). Yet Vygotsky, perhaps and arguably (to the annoyance of the likes of Alexander, Rose and Woodhead) did not support children being taught sitting in rows or coached to pass tests – a cultural expectation in the United Kingdom. Children need to be active.

Lev Vygotsky stressed intellectual development rather than procedural learning. The activities selected in school are very important to challenge and extend learning, and should include meaningful and stimulating classroom activities in children's ZPDs – what has become known as 'personalised learning'. Teaching children at all stages should reflect many opportunities for pretend play and language development – which is seen as good practice in the early years but much less so, later on. Nevertheless, social context, shared pretend play and co-operative language development continue to be seen by a number of more recent theorists and researchers to be of singular importance in assisting in children's construction of concept. Notable among such researchers in the second half of the twentieth century is Jerome Bruner, who we have already referred to as one of the originators of the term 'scaffolding learning'.

 **Reflect**

Just a few lines ago we wrote 'A high level of competence is needed only in those skills that a society values', but what skills does our society value and how are those judgements reflected in the curriculum of our early years settings and primary classrooms? Do we teach in schools what we value in society?

## The legacy of Jerome Bruner

Influenced by Vygotsky, Jerome Bruner's social constructivist theory (1973) argued that the social environment and, in particular, our social interactions with others are fundamental to learning. Although critical of Piaget, his theory shares some commonalities with cognitive-developmental theory. Bruner (like Piaget) believed that learning is an active process and that children being naturally curious will adapt to their environment by interacting with it. He also shared the view that children's cognitive structures develop over time and become increasingly complex. He differed from Piaget in the importance he placed on language (which we return to in the next chapter) and was strongly influenced by Vygotsky in the belief that scaffolding allows children to move to qualitatively higher levels of thinking. Bruner theorised that children's intellectual development occurs in three modes, which are the ways in which they gain knowledge and understanding of the world. The *enactive mode* is represented through action so that by interacting with their environment children construct patterns of motor behaviour appropriate to their present needs. The *iconic mode* combines the latter stages of Piaget's sensorimotor and pre-operational stages. The thinker builds up mental images (icons) from past experiences and responds intuitively to what is perceived. In *symbolic mode* a child is much more able to symbolise ideas, including writing. The cognitive changes taking place at around the important years of 7–8 are greatly assisted by increased language capability.

An example of this is the unwillingness of many young boys to write. Six-year-old boys are notoriously unwilling to write down their ideas or to record the work they are doing. Even bright, sensitive, socially able children are often labelled as having a learning difficulty because 'it is like trying to get blood out of a stone' to get any writing done by many children before the age of 8. Yet in the UK we continue to not only demand that the curriculum is dominated by writing tasks but also say that children are failing because they are not yet at the symbolic mode of learning development. Can those who continue to expect all 6-year-old boys to spend long periods writing consider their teaching to be child-centred?

Although advocating a child-centred approach, the teacher's role was also important in Bruner's theory; teachers' interventions can advance learners' cognitive capacity. A teacher's role is to provide learners with understanding of a subject's concepts and structures, not just to transmit facts. It is this approach that enables children to go beyond what is transmitted or transferred, and to develop their own ideas. Bruner's **spiral curriculum** proposes that any subject can be taught to any child at any stage of development as long as it is developmentally appropriate, which is in contrast to Piaget's ideas about readiness to learn. This notion is very evident in the construction of curriculum frameworks in UK primary schools where concepts (such as conservation of capacity – the opening word-scene) are introduced early on, and then revisited throughout schooling.

The approaches we have discussed of Piaget, Vygotsky and Bruner, although with clear and important differences, all place the active developing child at the centre of the learning process. Other approaches adopt a different perspective and rely on explaining thinking through the processes involved. These are the information-processing approaches.

**Spiral curriculum**
Any subject can be taught to any child at any stage of development as long as it is developmentally appropriate.

## Information-processing theories of cognitive development

Information-processing (IP) theories focus on the process of cognition, in other words on the information available through the environment and how the brain processes it. They adopt a very different perspective from that of Piaget and Vygotsky. Advocates of IP theories believe we have psychological structures that explain behaviour outside culture and social relationships (Smagorinsky, 2001). This is the opposite of the nativist view expounded by Piaget. The IP perspective contains various theories – not just one integrated theory – and we are going to look at several important examples. What are the basic assumptions of these theories?

As we discussed in Chapter 2, IP theories hold that the mind operates like a computer. Even the language used reflects this: 'hardware' as the capacity of processing and 'software' as the strategies or programming used to allow efficient use of this information – we even talk about the brain being 'hard-wired' for certain cognitive capacities such as learning language. This analogy might well conjure up for you the image of the brain as a computer with many separate but connected units that have different functions: the hard disc; main processor; motherboard; sound card; graphics card; and network card. Analogous cognitive functions are auditory and visual, memory and attentional processes that encode and process information before providing some form of output through the central nervous system to the outer nervous system. One highly important function in the IP approach is that of memory. In IP theories, learning is dependent upon memory (as are most other cognitive capabilities).

Remember the 1993 Rovee Collier experiment (see earlier *Controversy* feature) with the baby in the crib and the ribbon tied to baby's foot: the requirements of the task – move your foot to move the mobile – was recalled by the infants, days after the first experience. IP theorists would argue that this experiment showed significant developmental changes in memory even at a very early age. Improvements in memory are evident by children with age, increasingly being able to encode, store and retrieve much greater amounts of information than at birth (Courage and Howe, 2004). From age 6, our brain's frontal lobes undergo a period of significant development mirroring a similar 'spurt' later in adolescence (Taylor *et al.*, 2012). Part of that development at 5 years results in improvements in metamemory and in the speed at which information is processed. Consider the difference between a 5-year-old and an 8-year-old taking part in a perceptual-motor task, tapping buttons in response to various stimuli presented – Xbox and PS3 games players, for example. Increases in accuracy and speed would in part result from age-related cognitive development as well as to the learned cognitive strategies and responses. In computer terms there is a much larger RAM (random access memory) and hard disc capacity in 8-year-olds than in 5-year-olds.

Developmental changes occur in how children deal with the content of information from the environment. In infants this is in low-level 'units' (would Piaget call them schemas?) that become more complex across domains of human knowledge and increase throughout the lifespan. IP theorists suggest that innate processes (the hard-wiring of the brain) manage the vastness of incoming data and provide a structure for storage and retrieval. Siegler and Alibali (2005) propose IP theories that make four assumptions.

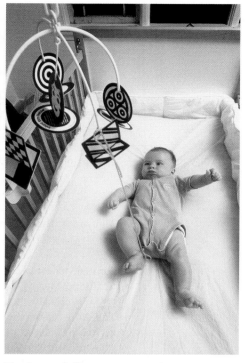

The Rovee Collier experiment shows that babies can remember what they learn (in this case that moving their foot will move the mobile).

*Source*: Michael Newman / PhotoEdit Inc.

1. Thinking is information processing – taken in and encoded in some way. It involves processes that change as children become more experienced.

2. The IP theories study change mechanisms. Children get better at thinking with age by their use of encoding, strategy construction, automatisation and generalisation as key mechanisms (important and discussed later).

3. Development is led by self-modification (building upon and modifying earlier knowledge) leading to higher levels of thinking. Children are active constructors here.

4. Task analysis is vital and allows an investigator – the learner – to understand what is necessary in solving a particular problem.

Furthermore, and importantly, general IP models assume that our brain's organisational structures are shared by everyone and that the functioning of memory is central and important, as is exemplified in the following models.

## Store model

IP theories liken memory to a store model, a model that views information as being held in three parts – the sensory register, short-term memory and long-term memory. The sensory register allows us to briefly store data. Try this – look at a television screen, then close your eyes and you should see a visual image trace for a brief time – the sensory register. The data then goes into our working memory (another name for the short-term memory). This operates on incoming data; auditory information goes into a phonological loop and visual information on to a visuo-spatial sketchpad (see Figure 9.4). Children from 9 to 12 have adult-like memories and use similar memory strategies (Rush *et al.*, 2011) but unfortunately for adults and children alike both the visuo-spatial sketchpad and the phonological loop are limited in capacity. Cognitive psychologist George Miller (1956) discovered the capacity of the phonological loop is seven letters or numbers (plus or minus two). Data are held for a short time only here, 15 to 30 seconds (Henry *et al.*, 2012). Information is either transferred into long-term memory

**Metamemory**
Knowing what strategies work best for an individual to memorise information and to retrieve information from the memory.

● ● ● ● ● ● ● ● ● ● ● ● ● ●
**Connect and Extend**
For a straightforward discussion of the different types of memory and links with the brain at the ages and stages of child development, read: Robinson, M. (2008). Child Development. *Nursery World*, 108, 20–24.
● ● ● ● ● ● ● ● ● ● ● ● ● ●

**Sensory register**
The sensory register hold sounds and images that last no more than about a second.

**Phonological loop**
A short-term store and retrieval system for sounds and words.

**Visuo-spatial sketchpad**
A short-term store and retrieval system for images and movements.

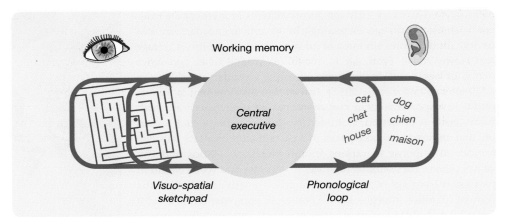

**Figure 9.4** The working memory
Images and audio cues are temporarily stored and either rehearsed and used, or lost.

through rehearsal or use, or it is lost. The long-term memory is a permanent store that has limitless capacity.

Strategies which allow data to be organised in efficient ways increase capacity. Examples are chunking information together, using mnemonics, using mental pictures or mental rehearsal techniques. Accomplished multilingual learners have greater short-term capacity than others (Biedroń & Szczpaniak, 2012). Of course, it is not clear whether greater capacity enables accomplishment as a multilinguist or whether learning a number of languages increases the capacity of the short-term or working memory. Which is the cause and which the effect? Some adults have no memory for number strings greater than 5 digits, even finding it difficult to repeat 6-figure phone numbers back correctly after just a few seconds. It also takes a huge amount of time to learn a new language to any kind of fluency. They just forget the words learned so carefully the day before.

One recent study examined individual differences in children's phonological and visuo-spatial short-term memory, and the relationship between short-term memory, attention problems and school achievement (Sarver *et al.*, 2012). The researchers found an association between length of the working memory and the ability to master new vocabulary and arithmetic facts such as multiplication tables. Children with a low-capacity short-term memory are more likely to be easily distracted and not to achieve as well as their peers. Getting new information to 'stick' and therefore transfer into the long-term memory takes much longer for learners such as this author.

Long-term memory is a permanent store and has limitless capacity and duration. It categorises information like a library so retrieval of information takes place along the lines of associations used to encode it initially. As children's knowledge of concepts develops, their long-term memory is able to organise information more efficiently. Nine-year-olds can find their way back from school better than 4-year-olds because they use their environmental cues better, take in salient features and remember significant objects in context. These three capacities, using environmental cues, taking in salient features and remembering significant objects, all develop with age and experience.

## Fuzzy trace theory

**Fuzzy trace theory**
Proposes a continuum exists in which we encode information from verbatim or literal representations to fuzzy representations.

An alternative view into how we solve problems assumes that not all our thinking demands precision. **Fuzzy trace theory** (Brainerd & Reyna, 1993) proposes that memory representations are on a continuum that ranges from verbatim representations to fuzzy and vague representations, and that we use both of these depending on the situation. For example, suppose you wanted to buy a coat. You might go to several shops and pick up a few coats and compare prices. The verbatim information you encode informs you of the exact price of each coat – but this takes greater effort to remember. In contrast the less specific information that the coat at the first shop is cheaper than the coat at any of the other shops is easier to remember and takes less effort. Which representation would be needed in deciding whether you have sufficient money to buy the coat?

The theory also distinguishes between how adults solve problems and the way children do. Children younger than 6 appear to use verbatim representations and children above this age encode using fuzzy representations. One reason for this – which fits well with an IP theory – is that the speed at which young children think is less efficient, causing them to get engrossed in detail so not permitting them to use other strategies to solve problems.

## Connectionism

Since the early 1990s there has been increased interest in connectionist approaches to cognitive development and learning (Westermann *et al.*, 2009; Zohar, 2006; Hughes & Longman, 2005; Myhill & Brackley, 2004; Askew *et al.*, 1997). We could probably write an entire book on the connectionist perspective, as we consider it has considerable and as-yet unresearched potential for understanding the interrelation (we might have said connection!) between cognition, learning and teaching styles across early years and primary schooling.

Connectionism has applications to language research and the use of computer programs to test models of development where programs simulate brain activity and the behaviour and networking of neurons. These models of neural networks attempt to explain how the brain functions and develops and how we learn (e.g. Ballabio & Vasighi, 2012). It is based on early ideas of a connection between stimulus and reaction (the S–R association), identified by behavioural psychologist Edward Thorndike (1913, 1932), considered to be one of the founding behaviourists. Thorndike was concerned with states of mind and how they changed with experience. For Thorndike learning results from associations forming between stimuli and responses. Such associations or 'habits' become strengthened or weakened by the nature and frequency of the S–R pairings. The thought pattern for S–R theory was trial-and-error learning in which some responses come to dominate others due to 'rewards'.

Thorndike's theory consists of three primary laws:

1. Law of effect – responses to a situation which are followed by a rewarding experience will be strengthened and become habitual responses to that situation.

2. Law of readiness – a series of responses can be connected together and automated to create a satisfying experience – indeed, rewards affect not only the connection that produced them but temporally adjacent connections as well.

3. Law of exercise – connections become strengthened with practice and weakened when practice is discontinued.

The classic example of Thorndike's S–R theory is a cat learning to escape from a box by pressing a lever. After much trial and error, the cat learns to associate pressing a lever (stimulus) with opening a door (reaction). The S–R connection is established because it results in a rewarding experience (escape from the box) and because the S–R pairing occurs many times (the law of exercise), is rewarded (law of effect) and forms a single automated sequence (law of readiness). Remember modern connectionism uses ideas of connected sets of microchipped circuits, and information and communications systems storing and instantly connecting trillions of bits of information. This is based on what we consider Thorndike's most important idea: intelligence is a function of the number of connections learned – much the same way as computer power is measured! And in much the way we see the interconnectedness of knowledge and concepts, the 'seamless robe' of experience that enables us to explore our sensory environments focus our perceptions and connect it all together with developing cognitive functions. If learning is about making connections, how should this be exemplified in the

**Connect and Extend**

Read a short article focusing on the influences of psychologist Edward Thorndike and philosopher, psychologist and educational reformer John Dewey on the educational system in the twenty-first century: Gibboney, R. & Kappan, P. D. (2006). Intelligence by design: Thorndike versus Dewey. *Phi Delta Kappan, 88*, 170–172.

learning experiences we provide for young children? Specifically, what would a connectionist classroom look like?

The following description of a connectionist classroom is based upon field notes made by one of the present authors who, as part of another project, visited a Year 3 classroom in a small rural primary school in Herefordshire. There was an Internet link, an interactive white-board (IWB), two digital slates or pads with wireless link to the computer driving the IWB, and two additional networked PCs in a resources corner of the room. The children were working in four groups on a collaborative task exploring adjectives and alliteration in poetry. Groups were of mixed reading ability and proficient readers were observed to be helping those who were having difficulties. The teacher and a classroom assistant were sitting with two of the groups.

The children's task was to make a collection in *Publish* from *Tizzy's First Tools* of images and text which showed the children's favourite examples of the use of descriptive alliteration. Children accessed books, web pages and CD-ROMs, annotated text and sketched their own ideas on paper, on the slates and onscreen. At intervals, activity was stopped by the teacher or by one of the pupils (by playing an animated fanfare and countdown on the IWB) in order to: review what groups were doing; what had been learned; ask for help on new ideas; celebrate achievement; or '. . . review work in progress, to reinforce key points emerging from individual and group work, and whole-class evaluation in plenary sessions' (Becta, 2004).

At the end of the session the presentation was uploaded to the school's external access server which the children could download at home later to show their parents what they had been doing and to make and personalise a copy for 'extra interest' work (the school's term for homework). The connections between the children as pupils (and teachers), the technologies, the ideas being explored, the contexts available, the schemas, concepts and skills being tried, rehearsed and perfected in this classroom provide a holistic view of an approach to learning and therefore cognitive development that is just 'scratching the surface' of what connectionist approaches may offer in the future. (Mal Hughes from unpublished field notes recorded 2008.)

**Reflect**  Review the nearby description of the connectionist classroom. What are the connections for you between what was happening in this classroom and the theories of Edward Thorndike – sometimes thought of as the 'father of connectionism'.

Other recent theories (in contrast to connectionism) include *Siegler's model of strategy choice* (1996) which offers an evolutionary perspective to cognition. This theory proposes that children use various strategies to problem solve. Through their different experiences, they select certain strategies over others. Those strategies that are not continued to be selected die. Experience of strategies that offer success is key here in selecting those to be used. Often in schools we can see children adding by 'counting' on their fingers. This has worked well for them in the past and so, if the numbers are viable, this strategy becomes selected. Speed and accuracy are important criteria for strategy selection. Once a strategy fails to offer the correct answer or is too slow to be useful, other strategies are needed. If new strategies are successful, children indirectly learn more about the concept. When they are taught to use a strategy that proves successful (e.g. to record multiple-stage mental addition calculations using a written algorithm), they abandon earlier ones – fingers – and adopt the new one – a quick 'sum' in the margin (Alibali, 1999).

**Neo-Piagetian theory**

A recent interpretation of Piaget's theory in an information-processing framework.

**Neo-Piagetian theory** (Case, 1992, 1998) concurs with the stages and qualitative changes in Piaget's cognitive development theory. Psychology researcher Robbie Case believes there are changes within each stage also resulting from changes in increased mental capacity. Cognitive structures in infancy are sensorimotor; in early childhood cognition relates to internal repre-sentations; and in later childhood, transformations of those representations.

For example, the Piagetian conservation of number task requires more than one cognitive strategy to be successful. Young children fail because they are unable to hold different pieces of information in their short-term memory at the same time. Preschool children can solve tasks in one to two steps; older primary-aged children hold information from previous experiences that allow them to go on to more complex tasks. Yet Case believes that changes in development result from changes to information-processing capacity in working memory or what he calls **m space**. Growth in capacity he argues is linked to how well children can use their limited memory capacity. This involves four processes.

**M space**
Capacity to retain information. Increases with age and experience.

1. *Encoding.* Maturation of the brain enables increases in speed of processing/operations and working memory over time. If six sweets are placed in a line in groups of two and children at Piaget's pre-operational stage are asked to count them they will do so one by one. Older children with their increased capacity with larger short-term memory will arrive at the answer faster and with fewer steps. Younger children cannot 'see' the whole picture as yet.

2. *Strategies* that free up mental capacity. Case sees merit in the strategies used by children that Piaget referred to. These are attractive as it links how schemes practised (assimilated) become automatic which then allow new constructions (accommodated).

3. *Automatisation* of knowledge leads to central conceptual structures. This allows more complex thinking which also frees up information-processing capacity and allows more advanced thinking. When ideas are fully formed, children can 'move up a level'. Preschool children understand stories in one dimension (e.g. what the story line is); by the early primary years several sub-plots can be understood and combined into a main plot. By later primary years children can handle multiple and overlapping storylines due to development in the conceptual structures – the higher, more forward parts of the brain.

4. *Generalisation* moves from being quite task-specific to more general. Here children learn to apply what they know in other contexts but this takes time. Take an example of conservation to illustrate this. A child pours liquid from one container to another and demonstrates understanding of height and width of the liquid and begins to create understanding of how liquid is conserved. Once automatic, a central conceptual structure of conservation is formed that enables that general concept to be applied to other similar situations.

The strengths of Case's theory are that it can account for changes in thinking from stage to stage. Increases in *m space* lead to better thinking in a new stage and are represented in a more complex way. It also accounts for Piaget's horizontal decalage, by which he meant that understandings appear specifically and at different times and are not mastered all at once – consistent with the IP view of developmental progression. Neo-Piagetian perspectives, which are a developing theory, already have shown applications to explaining dyslexic and reading difficulties (Snowling, 2000), and studies on academic skills using this approach have proved very valuable (e.g. teaching mathematics; Askew *et al.*, 1997). Drawbacks are that neo-Piagetian theory (like Piaget's own theories) avoids the biological underpinnings of how the brain functions and places little emphasis on the social or cultural influences of cognition. However, IP theories offer applications to early years and primary classrooms. Two examples: the emphasis IP theories place on memory helps to explain how young children's limited memory causes difficulties with many classroom and reading tasks; and teachers should encourage children to engage actively with their learning by using metacognitive strategies – testing out hypotheses and using imagery to see how their answers relate to 'real-life' situations.

**Horizontal decalage**
A term indicating that children can operate in different stages at the same time, in different kinds of tasks.

## General summary of all three approaches

Each of the three approaches – Piaget's cognitive-development theories, Vygotsky/Bruner's social-constructivist theories and information-processing perspectives – emphasise different factors contributing to development and learning. Piaget stressed individual interactions with

• • • • • • • • • • • • • • • • •
**Connect and Extend**

Nearby, we wrote 'Contemporary approaches and recent evidence from neurophysiology on the role of early explorations of objects via eye movements provide fresh ideas on how we think'. Access this recent evidence at: Johnson, S. P., Bremner, J. G., Slater, A., Mason, U., Foster, K. & Cheshire, A. (2003). Infants' perception of object trajectories. *Child Development*, 23, 461–483. Also, Bremner, G., Johnson, S., Slater, A., Mason, U., Foster, K., Cheshire, A. & Spring, J. (2005). Conditions for young infants' perception of object trajectories. *Child Development*, 76, 1029–1043.
• • • • • • • • • • • • • • • • •

the environment. Vygotsky emphasised social interactions and how children can learn with more experienced members in their culture. Information-processing theory illuminates mechanisms that lead to changes in thinking. In critiquing the three theories we suggest that none totally answers the problem of understanding cognition. No single approach can account for the complexity involved – though we think connectionism looks very promising. Yet each and everyone clearly contributes to our understanding of cognitive development. Progress, yes, but there is still some way to go. Contemporary approaches and recent evidence from neurophysiology on the role of early explorations of objects via eye movements (Johnson *et al.*, 2003; Johnson, 2001) provide fresh ideas on how we think, making new and valuable contributions to this fascinating field of study.

In this first section, the key approaches to understanding cognition were discussed and linked to an opening story at the start of the chapter – comparing the amount of orange juice in different-shaped beakers. The story clearly showed differences in thinking between two children of different ages, Maria and Jodie, but we then argued that these differences should not be linked to individual intelligence but to a different stage of cognitive development. That is not to say that intelligence might not have played some role because intelligence is linked of course to how well we can think. So what is intelligence, and how is it formed and developed?

## Summary 1

Before moving on, let's summarise what we have learned so far:

- Cognitive development refers to the changes in one's mental abilities that take place throughout our lifespan.

- Cognition is the act of knowing using mental processes such as imaging, remembering, understanding, generalising, finding reasons and causes and making inferences, decision-making, forming preferences, desires and intentions, planning and learning.

- Learning is one of the most important cognitive abilities and relies upon the recording, organising and retrieval of many millions of pieces of information, supported by a continuous stream of perceived information from the senses.

- Three approaches to cognitive development are Piaget's cognitive-developmental theory; Vygotsky's sociocultural theory; and information-processing theories of cognitive development.

- Piaget's cognitive-developmental theory is a constructivist theory which views children as active participants in their own learning, seeking out knowledge and constructing their own understanding. Central to thinking are the formation and refinement of concepts and, particularly, mental schemes.

- Piaget referred to adaptation as the construction of schemes arising from the direct engagement with the environment that allows us to adjust to the demands of our environment, and organisation as the ways in which schemes are linked together in a connected network.

- In Piaget's theory, cognitive development is organised into four stages:
  - sensorimotor stage (birth to 2 years);
  - pre-operational stage (2–7 years);
  - concrete operational stage (7–11 years);
  - formal operations stage (12 years upwards).

- The impact of Piaget in psychology and in schooling remains evident in educational practice worldwide.

- Vygotsky's social-constructivist approach offered a major alternative to Piaget. The central principle of his theory argues that thinking is a socially constructed process.
- The zone of proximal development (ZPD) is a time when the child critically benefits from the help of other adults or experienced peers.
- Vygotsky stressed the important role of the teacher in structuring learning.
- Bruner used Vygotsky's idea of 'scaffolding' to represent the way children's learning can be supported where 'significant others' provide help at significant points and gradually remove the help as a child succeeds.
- Information-processing theories focus on the process of cognition and hold that the mind operates like a computer.
- Information-processing theories liken memory to a store model: a model that views information as being held in three parts – sensory register, short-term memory and long-term memory.
- Modern connectionism uses ideas of connected sets of microchipped circuits and information and communications systems. This is based on Thorndike's most important idea: intelligence is a function of the number of connections learned, much the way we see the interconnectedness of knowledge and concepts.
- The neo-Piagetian theory of Robbie Case is a recent interpretation of Piaget's theory in an information-processing framework and includes encoding, strategies, automatisation and generalisation.

# The nature of intelligence

Here is a very short story:

At the nursery, Zara and Michelle show different interests and abilities. Zara enjoys dressing up and has a lively imagination. She loves to listen to stories and enjoys making up her own stories to tell her friends. Her favourite place is in the role-play area. Michelle is much quieter and will sit for ages engrossed in a puzzle. She seems not to need the company of others and will quite happily spend considerable time colouring in shapes and building towers with her bricks. To the observer, both children might be displaying different interests or talents but can we say that one child displays greater intelligence than the other?

The answer might be 'Well that depends on what you mean by intelligence?' A good question, and one which was the subject of debate during the past century. So much so that 52 professors (experts in intelligence) were brought together to agree a statement of conclusions that were to be considered 'mainstream among researchers on intelligence, in particular, on the nature, origins, and practical consequences of individual and group differences in intelligence' (*Wall Street Journal*, 13 December, 1994, p A18). Here is a précis of the first six of the twenty-five statements:

1. Intelligence is a very general mental capability that, among other things, involves the ability to reason, plan, solve problems, think abstractly, comprehend complex ideas, learn quickly and learn from experience.

2. Intelligence, so defined, can be measured, and intelligence tests measure it well.

3. Some intelligence tests require specific cultural knowledge (like vocabulary). Others use shapes or designs of universal concepts (many/few, up/down).

4. The IQ continuum, from low to high, can be represented well by the bell curve. Most people's scores cluster around the average (IQ 100): about 3 per cent score above IQ 130, and 3 per cent below IQ 70.

5. Intelligence tests are not culturally biased. Rather, IQ scores predict equally accurately.

6. The brain processes are still little understood: speed of neural transmission, glucose (energy) uptake, and electrical activity of the brain.

We would define intelligence as the capacity for cognition and for cognitive development but not everybody would think that definition to be sufficiently detailed or universally applicable. Fortunately we are not the only ones to attempt a definition of intelligence. For example, researcher Carolus Slovinec (2000) defines intelligence as 'the ability to recognise connections' (p 2).

Which of these definitions might apply to understanding the differences between Zara and Michelle? The answer is probably neither of them as intelligence is a very complex and abstract concept which includes many layers of ideas such as talents, interests and gifts, aptitude, ability and concentration. To begin to build a picture of intelligence, let's focus on intelligence that we are born with, what Cyril Burt, English educational psychologist called 'innate general cognitive ability' (1972, p 177). Is intelligence innate or can it be fostered through our experiences? In the controversial publication *The Bell Curve: Intelligence and class structure in American life* (1994) Richard Hernstein and Charles Murray boldly stated that intelligence was predominantly inherited and that little could be done through experiences to impact on it. There is strong evidence to counter this viewpoint as we shall see shortly! Early theories saw it as a general intelligence or 'g' that applied to almost everything we did, and as 's' or specific intelligence that was applicable to certain skills only. More recently the work of Goleman (1996) on emotional intelligence has popularised the idea that our ability to control our emotions is a feature of our intelligence (and we explore this in Chapter 11). In this section we look firstly at how intelligence is tested, and then at contemporary theories of it and address three important questions:

1. Is intelligence genetically determined or influenced by the environment?

2. How does intelligence influence academic performance?

3. Is intelligence fixed or does it change over time?

# Measuring intelligence – scales and tests

Why do we feel we need to measure how intelligent people are? Reasons for measuring intelligence include: to predict academic performance, to predict future employment, to assess general 'wellness' or to identify problems. Can we tell somebody's intelligence by looking at them? What does a highly intelligent person look like? Stereotypically, cartoons present intelligent individuals with huge heads and pronounced frontal lobes – 'a brain on legs' we might say. Nonsense! Or is it? We know that newborns with head circumferences over 35 cm will later typically score 7 points higher on intelligence tests. Bigger brains have increased capacity for information processing just as in a computer: not only is a bigger brain (or computer) better but it is also faster – evident in the storage and retrieval of information.

So how do we measure intelligence – by measuring children's heads? No. Psychologists assert that intelligence can be measured in more accurate ways. You may remember from Chapter 1 that we identified the beginnings of a scientific study of children as being marked by the work of G. Stanley Hall (1844–1924) and Alfred Binet (1857–1911). Hall employed a questionnaire on preschool children and was able to collect data on the nature of children's thinking by comparing responses by gender and ethnic origin (Hall, 1891b).

Within ten years, Frenchman and psychologist Alfred Binet had developed the first standardised intelligence test which was a scale systematically measuring higher-order thinking skills, memory, language and problem-solving abilities, unique to each individual. The Binet test was originally designed to identify children who were underachieving in mainstream schools. It was actually a battery of tests believed to represent the sorts of abilities typically demonstrated by children and to assess higher mental capacities such as reasoning and judgement making. The test has undergone a number of revisions and become the Stanford–Binet test to enable comparisons to be made between children of different intellectual capacities and at different ages, as well as allowing the testers to rank children according to IQ. Research identified the concept of mental age as being important in measuring intelligence, which led to the identification of an intelligence quotient (IQ). Thus, if an 8-year-old scores highly on the test, the results would be similar to the scores of an average 10-year-old, so the 8-year-old has a mental age of 10. The IQ is calculated using the following equation:

$$IQ = \frac{MA}{CA} \times 100$$

where MA = mental age and CA = chronological age. Therefore, an 8-year-old child with a mental capacity of a 10-year-old would have an IQ of 10/8 × 100 = 125. The test works well for older children who can attempt a range of tasks, but what about the very young?

Tests for babies are derived from observations and aim to record achievements in behaviour skills. However, progress is so accelerated in the very early years that making accurate measurements is difficult but nevertheless extremely valuable in diagnostic terms. Tests such as the 'Denver, Gesell and Bayley scales' assess a variety of skills at an early age and give a fairly accurate assessment of current cognitive capacity. However, these scales are not a good predictor of later academic success. Why? Because they are heavily reliant on motor and perceptual skills, that is, the ability to pick up a small plastic cube at 6 months does not correlate well with the types of (predominately verbal and spatial) tasks that measure intelligence later on. To measure intelligence in young children, the Bayley scales of infant development (Bayley, 1969) assess children between 1 month and 3$^1$/$_2$ months. The scales are useful in identifying health problems early but again are not reliable for predicting scholastic achievement because of their reliance on sensorimotor abilities.

The McCarthy scales of children's abilities (1972) cover the 2$^1$/$_2$ to age 8 period and provide measures in verbal, non-verbal, memory, spatial and motor skills. The Wechsler intelligence scales (2003) include the Wechsler Preschool and Primary Scale of Intelligence (WPPSI) and the Wechsler Intelligence Scale for Children (WISC). These scales produce IQs with a mean of 100 and measure knowledge and judgement through assessing reasoning, mathematical, verbal reasoning and spatial skills. Deviation IQ scores reflect the position of an average child of that age, computed using standard deviation to identify how far scores deviate from the norm. Since being updated (Wechsler, 2003), these scales reflect more recent findings in cognitive development.

These tests are used widely to identify strengths and weakness and as predictors of academic achievement. When used by skilled professionals they can provide insights into children's characteristic traits and motivation, identify children who have learning difficulties (usually accompanied by other assessment methods) and children who are gifted in one or more specific ways (which we address later). What about more general ability? Does a higher than mean average IQ score (100) suggest a higher general ability, and is that judgement specific to the society and culture in which the child is being reared?

Intelligence has a sociocultural context and has been found to vary across different societies. Therefore any comparisons of test results between different cultures should be viewed with caution. Indeed, tests are often criticised for being culturally biased. For example, cultures that are preliterate might do poorly on standard IQ tests; a person who is deemed to be a highly skilful dancer may be seen as possessing great intelligence in one culture but this would not translate as a sign of intelligence in many Western societies. Sarah Harkness and Charles Super (2001, 1992) in a Kenyan study reported that intelligence was related to the ability to perform family and parenting duties effectively. What one culture might view as intelligence, another might not.

**Stanford–Binet test**
Early intelligence test for school-aged children.

**Intelligence quotient**
How well one performs on a standardised test of intelligence relative to others of that age.

**Bayley scales of infant development**
Preverbal measure to assess general health and developmental milestones.

**Wechsler intelligence scales**
Both preschool and school-age tests of reasoning, mathematical and verbal reasoning and spatial skills.

**Deviation IQ scores**
IQ showing how far performance deviates from average performance of others of the same age.

**Reflect** Isobel, my mum, used to call it 'nouse' – but I've never seen it written down so I don't know how to spell it. I think I call it 'common sense'. Does common sense 'intelligence' exist? This is not related to scores on an IQ test but governs the sort of intelligence we need in everyday situations. Can you think of examples of this 'everyday' type of intelligence, and how is it formed and developed? What, cognitively, is happening? Is it the same as knowing your multiplication tables or playing the violin?

# Contemporary theories of intelligence

**Connect and Extend**

For a discussion of the influence of psychologists Lev Vygotsky and Howard Gardner to the theories and philosophy of education, read: Beliavsky, N. (2006). Revisiting Vygotsky and Gardner: Realising human potential. *Journal of Aesthetic Education, 40,* 1–11.

**Connect and Extend**

For a discussion of Howard Gardner's 'five minds for the future' and to hear Gardner talking about his theory of multiple intelligences, watch a video 'Howard Gardner's Five Minds for the Future' at **http://video. google.co.uk**. Why not attend a virtual lecture 'Future Minds' by Howard Gardner by searching the Web?

As we have seen, contemporary theories favour explaining intelligence in terms of the cognitive processes involved when we engage in intellectual activities. Central to this point of view is the notion that mental competence changes over time. Up to the 1970s, the Piagetian approach was the dominant discourse that proposed our innate ability to adapt to the environment and adapt our environment to suit us, reflecting how intelligent we were. Through maturation, processes of assimilation and accommodation accounted for the changes in cognitive development. Vygotsky (1978), as we have outlined in the previous section, held a different view and deemed that social influences and interactions with our environment were instrumental in shaping our intelligence. What do more recent views tell us about how intelligence is formed and developed?

The theory of multiple intelligences (Gardner & Seana, 2006; Gardner, 1999, 1998, 1993, 1983) was developed from Howard Gardner's observations of the many roles played by individuals in different cultures. He concluded there may be more than one underlying mental capacity which allows us to perform diverse roles: as teacher, doctor, accountant, dancer, and so on. He defined intelligence as 'the ability to solve problems or fashion products that are of consequence in a particular cultural setting or community' (1993, p 15) – which refers nicely back to the implications of the last paragraph. Each type of intelligence has its own development pathway and is therefore domain-specific. Gardner placed great store on cultural context and claimed that we display different combinations of multiple intelligences, and that different cultures place value on different intelligences. In the original theory there were seven 'intelligences' (linguistic, logical-mathematical, spatial, bodily-kinaesthetic, musical, intrapersonal and interpersonal) and an eighth, that of naturalist intelligence, was added in 1999. Today, Gardner has added a ninth, existential intelligence, which is concerned with our spirituality.

*Anderson's Theory of Intelligence* (1996) proposes a general intelligence which is non-domain specific. Psychologist John Anderson criticised Gardner's theory for being unclear whether intelligence is a process, a behaviour or a brain structure. Anderson's theory proposes that differences in intelligence arise from differences in inherent basic processing mechanisms which operationalise thinking and produce knowledge. Mechanisms are mostly universal although there are individual differences apparent in relation to speed. In other words, a person who is slow to process information is likely to be lower in intelligence than a fast processor. Through practice, new cognitive structures mature which lead to increased cognitive capacity, and speed is part of that capacity. If Gardner's theory leads some educationalists to question the content and structure of the school curriculum, Anderson's 'simple theory of complex cognition' proposes that changing the curriculum does not change the need for students to master the components of the curriculum. Anderson argues 'It is every bit as important to practice components of a "new look" curriculum [one based on Gardner's multiple intelligences theory] to achieve a high level of mastery as it was to practice the components of the "traditional" curriculum' (Anderson & Schunn, 2000, p 24). Whatever the nature of intelligence, we might all agree that there are significant differences in the ability of individuals to master the component parts of the curriculum – the subjects – no matter how that curriculum is structured. Anderson relates those differences to speed of cognition as a major component of capacity, and Gardner relates cognitive capacity to finding one or more aspects of the cultural domain to be easier for some individuals than for others. What accounts for those differences?

## Is intelligence genetically determined or influenced by the environment?

We want to answer this question with a bold statement – one that should not really come as a great surprise to readers at this point in the book. Both genetic and environmental influences, before and after birth, influence our intelligence. It is the interplay between nature and nurture again, rather than an 'either–or' situation. Any argument that proposes that innate factors predominate in accounting for intelligence must be viewed with caution since there are also a number of environmental factors that must be taken into account. However, can we know with any accuracy how much genetic and environmental influences affect intelligence? Fortunately, we can look to behavioural geneticist research to provide an answer to this question and particularly to twin studies.

Classic studies on identical twins show a 0.86 (very high) correlation between IQ scores (Plomin, 1990) for twins raised in a shared environment (which is perhaps not unexpected since the home, culture, education and socio-economic status will be the same for both children), the figure is 0.72 when identical twins are raised apart, although importantly the children here are together *in utero* – undoubtedly the most important time for brain development. For non-identical twins who have been raised together, the correlation figure is 0.60. If this figure is taken away from that relating to identical twins, it gives 0.26 as a representation of the added IQ correlation shared by identical twins with their 50 per cent shared genes. When doubled (to take account that only 50 per cent of the genes of identical twins are shared) to give 52 per cent, this gives a fairly accurate figure that, before taking cultural differences into account, genes are responsible for about half of our IQ – an important idea to hold on to and rehearse during the remainder of this section.

If we stay with the argument that IQ is not the only measure of intelligence, skills such as reading maps, spatial skills and even language skills have a high genetic dependence. Further evidence for this can be found in adoption study findings (Plomin *et al.*, 1988): adopted children share half their genes with their biological parents but none with their adoptive parents and none of their environment with the former but some of the environment with the latter. The evidence suggests that when the economics of biological and adoptive parents are similar, the intelligence of adopted children is closer to the biological parents, whereas when there is a stronger educational climate in adoptive homes, this has a significant effect upon measured intelligence.

Interestingly, there is a steady rise in IQ in the industrialised world with successive generations actually becoming smarter! This situation is known as the Flynn Effect (Sundet *et al.*, 2008; Flynn, 1987). Are we becoming more intelligent? One might argue that people today are well versed in taking IQ tests, but that does not account for such dramatic IQ increases. It cannot be due to genetics alone – this is not possible, so the answer must lie in the influence of the environment. Improvements in general health and nutrition, and universal education can and do account for improved IQ scores. Even our recently improved visuo-spatial skills coming from the technological 'advances' in our modern world – video games, computers, television, and so on – contribute significantly to increased IQ gains. The modern view tends to swing towards an agreement that, due to cultural changes at the end of the twentieth century, it is commonly held that around 40 per cent of our intelligence is influenced by genetics and 60 per cent by our environment (Plomin & Petrill, 1997).

# How does intelligence influence academic performance?

As we have seen in the last section, nature contributes to variance in intellectual functioning and this can often exaggerate nurture differences. A number of environmental (nurture) factors have been identified that impact upon intelligence and highly significant among these is the family. A secure and encouraging home environment in which children are encouraged to be self-reliant and actively discover their surroundings has been associated with higher levels of academic performance (Petrill & Deater-Deckard, 2004). Earlier studies showed that family size is also related: that the fewer children in a family, the more intelligent you are likely to be, although this effect is smaller than originally thought (Abdel-Khalek & Lynn, 2008). Schooling is an important factor such that high-quality education can increase IQ scores (Barber, 2005). Findings from some researchers working in school effectiveness have shown that a negative correlation exists between measures of social disadvantage and school achievement (Sunder & Uddin, 2007; Wagmiller *et al.*, 2006). Others claim that pupils from schools in economically deprived areas are more capable of high-order thinking than is generally assumed. They recommend a curriculum that is equal to that in more economically advantaged areas, built around powerful ideas and metacognitive skills (Leithwood & Steinbach, 2002).

Another important issue is that of achievement motivation. Children who give up easily on challenges are deemed to have learned helplessness, often have low self-esteem and lack strategies to deal with problems. In contrast, those who regularly master new ideas and skills – remember John Anderson's theory of intelligence – can set realistic goals for learning and performance on academic tasks and avoid negative self-images (Oyserman *et al.*, 2007; Dweck, 2001). Children with low self-esteem tend to view intelligence as fixed and unchangeable for them, whereas mastery-orientated children view intelligence as accruing knowledge that is gained from effort on their part. In other words, they believe that with hard work they can change their academic performances – become cleverer! Compounding the problem of not correctly assessing intelligence are a number of studies which show that traditional IQ testing may not measure accurately the intelligence of lower socioeconomic groups and some ethnic groups (Naglieri *et al.*, 2007; Rushton, 2002; Warner *et al.*, 2002).

Three cultural factors may be identified that influence this. Low scores can reflect cultural bias in the test, not intellect; there are still many issues arising from stereotypical views held by society about particular groups! Secondly, there may be difficulties due to language and/or values that are not matched to the particular group being studied (e.g. in IQ verbal reasoning tests). Thirdly, tests might not accurately measure contexts and real-life problems relevant to that group. It may be convenient to attribute poor scores on examinations to teaching alone but this is unrealistic. There are complex issues to address when teaching children in inner-city schools and encouraging positive attitudes to learning. Earlier attempts to address these issues has led to the notion of creating culturally and socially *resilient classrooms* (Rivera & Waxman, 2007), something to which we return in detail later (see Chapter 12).

Boys generally score better on spatial tasks.

*Source*: © Pearson Education Ltd / Ian Wedgewood.

Gender differences are another influencing factor. The female brain is not significantly different in size from the male brain (although boys' brains are slightly larger overall at birth), but there are striking differences between the two sexes in terms of intelligence. Differences created even before birth impact upon development with the responsiveness of girls' left-brain hemispheres giving them a language advantage, apparent in the first few months after birth. We know that, later on, girls on the whole tend to outperform boys on measures of reading, writing and language, whereas boys score well on non-verbal IQ tests, and many spatial tasks. It is not the slight difference in size that matters, but in how their respective brains are made up (Palmer, 2004). Girls use their brains more symmetrically and can engage both hemispheres more effectively via an enlarged corpus callosum in most activities (Bates, 2007). This enables better language skills which are often reinforced by their play choices in drawing, dressing up and social play. Boys favour gross motor activities such as jumping, climbing, kicking a ball and construction, which assist motor and spatial development (Günes & Nalçaci, 2006). In the currency of the classroom, language and literacy, as well as social skills, have high priority and girls will tend to prosper. Social pressures are exerted on boys and girls differently, both from inside and outside the family through TV advertising, stereotyping each gender and influencing play choices – and therefore cognitive development – from an early age (Strother, 2007).

**Reflect**

We gave our son dolls and our daughters construction toys, but it made no difference. Tom made guns out of bits of wood – so we gave up and bought him guns – and the girls liked making books and playing make-believe games with their dolls. Imagine! All the dolls were lined up in a make-believe classroom – and Emily is now a teacher! So, was it pointless to try and fight the 'hard-wiring', the social and developmental differences born of countless generations of Toms and Emilys?

## Is intelligence fixed or does it change over time?

The third question concerns the stability of intelligence. Traditionally intelligence was believed to be fixed at birth, largely because it was seen to be inherited. What happened subsequently to an individual was deemed not to influence intelligence to any significant extent. Evidence in the past 30 years derived from longitudinal studies shows improvements can be made in test scores from early to later testing (Antshel *et al.*, 2007). Measures on children of 8 years and older (Black *et al.*, 2007) give quite reliable results on scores in intelligence tests and later academic performance (Rindermann, 2008). Findings on infant attention (e.g. Martinez *et al.*, 2012) and on visual preferences (e.g. Flom & Johnson, 2011) have shown moderate correlations between early and later cognitive functioning, but results are in no way conclusive. Parental behaviours and children's personalities (Chapter 11) may also influence intelligence changes (Karass & Braungart-Rieker, 2004), all suggesting that intelligence can change over time.

Before moving on, let's summarise what we have learned in the middle section of this chapter:

- Intelligence is the capacity for cognition and for cognitive development.

- Alfred Binet developed the first standardised intelligence test which was a scale systematically measuring higher-order thinking skills, memory, language and problem-solving abilities, unique to each individual.

- Contemporary theories favour explaining intelligence in terms of the cognitive processes involved when we engage in intellectual activities. Central to this point of view is the notion that mental competence changes over time.

- Howard Gardner's original theory of multiple intelligences included seven 'intelligences' (linguistic, logical-mathematical, spatial, bodily-kinaesthetic, musical, intrapersonal and interpersonal) and an eighth, that of naturalist intelligence, was added in 1999. Today, Gardner has added a ninth, existential intelligence, which is concerned with our spirituality.

**Summary 2**

- In contrast to Gardner, John Anderson in his 'simple theory of complex cognition' proposes that changing the curriculum does not change the need for students to master the components of the curriculum.
- It is commonly held that around 40 per cent of our intelligence is influenced by genetics and 60 per cent by our environment.
- A number of environmental (nurture) factors have been identified that impact upon intelligence: family size, secure and encouraging home environment, school effectiveness, socioeconomic background, achievement motivation and gender differences.
- Intelligence can change over time; it is not fixed at birth.

# Developing intelligence

So far, we have presented an argument that both genetics and environmental factors contribute to intellectual functioning. This raises the question of the impact upon a child's IQ of specific programmes designed to foster academic functioning. Is it possible to speed up development and enhance intelligence? Reviewing the early evidence, cognitive psychologists Michael Howe and Harriet Griffey (1994) argued that in certain areas such as motor and language, early intervention programmes are beneficial. They also reported that the effects can be long-lasting. The reader must be cautious, however: parents who wish to turn their child into a genius overnight through **hot-housing programmes** may cause the child to miss out on other real-life experiences. A child of 12 may develop ahead of time the cognitive apparatus to gain a university degree, but, if it is at the expense of being able to share the interests and experiences of their peers, is there a trade-off, and is it worth it?

**Hot-housing programmes**
Specific programmes intended to accelerate cognitive devel opment.

As a result of the impact of Howard Gardner's theory, many schools now offer programmes of enrichment to help foster children's intelligence. These can be considered under the umbrella term of 'cognitive intervention programmes'. There have been many examples of such interventions attempted in the past 50 years, many based on an original enrichment programme **Head Start** begun in the mid-1960s in the United States for disadvantaged pre-school children – thus Head Start had both academic and social dimensions. Early gains were reported in cognitive development and social skills (Brooks-Gunn, 1995) but these proved to be short term and specific 'gains' in IQ vanished within several years. One reason for this might be that Head Start was begun too late – after many of the foundations of brain development are already laid through myelination and synaptogenesis. Critics of the programme argued that its emphasis on IQ improvement as an outcome did not reflect other broader factors such as social competence or mental health. The programme has had its success, however, and some early studies showed quite lasting IQ effects with children whose IQs were initially low (Brown & Grotberg, 1980).

**Head Start**
US programme of the 1960s for disadvantaged preschool children, which had both academic and social dimensions.

More recent programmes include the *SNAP™ Under 12 Outreach Project* for children with conduct problems (Augimeri *et al.*, 2007). The programme appears to be an effective cognitive-behavioural programme for antisocial children in the short term, with possible effects that extend into adolescence and adulthood. This is an example of the connections between cognition and personality in the social world – big issues for Chapters 11 and 12. A good example of a cognitive acceleration programme is in science education (Endler & Bond, 2008) in which Australian researchers report the result of using a version of the *Cognitive Acceleration through Science Education* (CASE) programme to address teacher-identified concerns about pupil competence in scientific enquiry. Similarly with younger children, researchers Julie Cattle and

Dorothy Howie (2008) report the efficacy of applying the CASE approach to children aged 6 and 7 years, and a number of researchers (Burton, 2007; Brown, 2004; Friedman, 2004; Mullrood, 2004; Tosey & Mathison, 2003) have looked at the role of *neuro-linguistic programming* (NLP) in classroom settings (see the *Focus on Theory* feature below).

Perhaps the most well-known intervention programme in the United Kingdom is the **Sure Start** programme aimed at disadvantaged areas (e.g. Jones *et al.*, 2008) to provide better outcomes for children, parents and local communities through combined health, social services and education agencies. Its principles championed the availability of child-care for all children, the improvement in health and emotional development for children and support for parents in building aspirations towards employment for themselves and their children.

In concluding whether such programmes do make a difference, all the evidence would suggest that they do influence children's IQ positively and especially for those children in poor environments. In the early days of the Head Start programme, Barnett *et al.* (1992) found that children on the programme showed higher IQ scores and were more likely to continue through school and enter better paid jobs. Programmes that seek to improve parent–child relationships and offer strong support for family functioning and that are resolute in aiming to enhance life chances have been found to be most successful in improving cognitive development and school performance (Ramey & Ramey, 2001).

Programmes that aim to promote the thinking abilities of school-age children have proven successful. These specify what is to be taught (subject content) and how it is to be taught (pedagogy). In the United Kingdom this allies with a government drive to emphasise quality in children's thinking as a way of raising educational standards and to prepare for lifelong learning. At the core of the programmes are the identification of mental skills that are transferable and that require learners to plan, describe and evaluate their own thinking and learning. Examples include *Instrumental Enrichment* (Schnitzer *et al.*, 2007); *Philosophy for Children* (Clegham, 2003); and the aforementioned *Cognitive Acceleration through Science Education* programme (Endler & Bond, 2008). Building on their success with secondary age children, King's College researchers Phillip Adey, Michael Shayer and Caroline Yates studied the effect of a programme aimed at accelerating the development of thinking processes in children aged 5 and 6 years. Findings of this study and the previously mentioned later study by Julie Cattle and Dorothy Howie (2008) are reported in the *Focus on Theory* feature.

**Sure Start**
UK state programme in disadvantaged areas aiming to provide better outcomes for children, parents and local communities.

• • • • • • • • • • • • • • • •
**Connect and Extend**
For an excellent paper which brings together a number of issues found at the end of this chapter, read: Daugherty, M. & White, S. (2008). Relationships among private speech and creativity in Head Start and low-socioeconomic status preschool children. *Gifted Child Quarterly, 52,* 30–39.
• • • • • • • • • • • • • • • •

## Focus on Theory

### Can teachers improve the thinking skills of young children? CASE – a case study!

#### What is CASE?

CASE (Cognitive Acceleration through Science Education) is an intervention strategy that is a combination of an enriched curriculum and improved teaching methods. The curriculum challenges children's present concepts of science and presents them with problems that they are unable to solve using their current strategies, therefore creating cognitive conflict. As part of the research a number of activities were devised – 32 lessons over 2 years – aimed at enhancing the pupils' thinking skills and so assist their learning as they progress through the school.

The theoretical bases behind CASE were developed by Phillip Adey and colleagues at King's College, London from the work of Piaget and Vygotsky. The lessons are designed to encourage the development of thinking from concrete to formal operations. Some of the types of reasoning (remember, called 'schemes' by Piaget) which characterise formal operations in science are:

- control and exclusion of variables;
- ratio and proportion;
- compensation and equilibrium;
- correlation;
- probability;
- classification; and
- formal models.

The CASE activities are designed to familiarise pupils with the apparatus (concrete preparation); provide 'events' which cause the pupils to pause, wonder and think again (cognitive conflict); encourage the pupils to reflect on their own thinking processes (metacognition); and show how this thinking can be applied in many contexts (bridging). These features – *the five pillars* of CASE – are described in detail by Phillip Adey and Michael Shayer (1994).

## The effect of CASE

The original and early study (1994) showed that cognition intervention programmes increased the development of thinking in older children in the first two years of secondary education (aged 12 and 13 years). A later study (Adey *et al.*, 2002) set out to discover whether this approach would show similar results for children of 5 and 6 years. The new study was based on three assumptions: that some general intellectual function occurs in children which is context-independent; that this function improves through interaction of nature and nurture; and that children's intelligence is flexible, which allows it be altered by a well-constructed intervention programme.

Some 338 children in ten experimental schools and five control schools were involved, and a baseline assessment was carried out to determine the current level of achievement. The strategy involved four steps:

1. cognitive conflict where the pupils were presented with a problem they were unable to tackle;
2. social construction wherein they were encouraged to discuss the problem with each other;
3. metacognition as a form of conscious reflection by the children on their thinking processes; and
4. development of a shared schema to develop the cognitive processes.

The actual intervention consisted of three introductory listening activities and 26 cognitive acceleration activities that six children undertook each day, so enabling a whole class to be involved by the end of the week. The activities included seriation of objects, classifying shapes, putting actions into a time sequence, spatial perception and causality.

What did the 2002 study find out? Firstly that the experimental group – those engaged in CASE activities – made significantly greater cognitive gains than the control group. Secondly that the gains made by girls were much greater than those of boys – a fascinating outcome that would surely bear more research! Finally, and importantly for the themes of this chapter, that cognitive gains appeared to be unrelated to linguistic or numeric abilities, entry age, receipt of free meals or ethnic group.

*Source*: Dudley Virtual Resource Centre at **www.edu.dudley.gov.uk/science/CASE2.html** for the general description of the CASE project.

Having identified and discussed the concept of intelligence and presented contemporary theories (chiefly Gardner's multiple intelligences work) that broaden the traditional view of it, the next section discusses how this is linked to notions of **giftedness**, talent and creativity. Why? Well, cognitive acceleration programmes used by schools are often targeted on children who are considered to have fallen behind in some way and need to be 'accelerated'. Other programmes are often administered – some from birth – by parents and other carers, not to help remediate a deficit but to help their children to become specially gifted or talented.

You have probably watched some parents showing their babies flashcards of objects and words, giving their precious infants baby massages every night or making sure they get their daily dose of Mozart or Bach. Of course, many of them would resist the idea that they wanted to teach their children to be gifted, because children who are considered gifted or talented often show the kind of cognitive development – the kind of thinking – that we would wish to see in all children. Yet highly developed cognitive skills do set gifted children, in particular, apart from their friends. Consider this example:

> Brad is a Reception (4–5-year-olds) class teacher who also lives in the small town where he teaches. He knows many of the parents and children in the local area, even before the children came into his class. One child, Emma, seems different. Brad has known Emma and her parents for several years and considers that there has always been something distinctive about Emma – something that was and is difficult to pin down. What is it? Brad knows that Emma spoke earlier than most other children, loved to listen to stories and could remember the smallest details a long time after the story – yet he has never before known a child to be so curious. She wants to find out about everything! Brad is also struck by the intense focus Emma is capable of in her play and the learning tasks in the classroom. She is tenacious and persistent, always staying with a challenge until she has solved it. What also impresses Brad is the different ways in which Emma sets about solving problems or challenges – so different from the other children in his class. She is obviously very intelligent and he speculates that perhaps Emma is one of those 'gifted' children he has read about.

## Giftedness, talent and creativity

### Giftedness

In schools, children like Emma might be labelled 'a bright spark', 'very able', 'talented', 'a high achiever' or just 'brainy', and yet each word or phrase may have a particular connotation, not necessarily related to the specific abilities of giftedness. There is no clear agreement about what giftedness means, but it is generally held that gifted children display qualities that set them apart from their peers. Educational psychologists Michael Martin and Cynthia Waltman-Greenwood (1995) offer the following common characteristics of gifted children which you might find useful:

- Curiosity – persistence, asking many questions. Have keen observational skills and a desire to learn quickly.
- Memory – such children have more developed memories and can retain a variety of information.
- Higher-order thinking skills – they can solve problems. They have an ability to understand complex concepts and to work in the abstract. They also can generate new ideas and solutions.
- Language – this is well developed from an early age, both through the vocabulary and ability to recount stories in great detail.

**Giftedness**
Characterised by an IQ of 130 or above. Individuals also show an exceptional talent in one or more areas.

**Connect and Extend**
For an interesting international perspective on differences in parenting between the parents of gifted children and the parents of non-gifted children, read: He Jing, Shi Jiannong and Luo Bin (2006). Parenting and children's cognitive development. *Gifted Education International*, 22, 86–100.

- Precociousness – gifted children attain development milestones early, e.g. walking, talking. They can have a specific talent in one area such as music or the expressive arts.

- Attention – they can concentrate intensely for long periods and display goal-directed behaviour.

- Social maturity – they will often seek out the company of older children and adults to converse with.

- Humour – this is usually well developed and gifted children can see humour in different situations.

Put another way, David George (consultant and member of the World Council for Gifted and Talented Children) offers this statement:

> **(they) perform well in academic subjects . . . are persistent, respond well to instruction, have good study skills . . . process information quickly, have better memories, have greater accuracy and are good at abstract thinking.**
>
> (George, 1997, p 37)

Giftedness may be considered as advanced development in either a single domain or in several domains (and thus links well to Gardner's multiple intelligences theory). In comparing gifted children with others, psychologist Camilla Benbow working with other colleagues (Park *et al.*, 2007; Lubinski *et al.*, 2001) has postulated that the underlying processes for the levels of thinking and performance in gifted children are not unique – not that different from other children – but it is in the way that gifted children use these cognitive skills that makes the difference – learned cognitive procedures. The neurological basis of giftedness is not entirely certain but is probably related to cognitive connective speed and capacity of memory recall. Gifted children's learning is different in a qualitative sense; thinking is divergent, it does not happen in a linear fashion and speed of learning is enormous. The *Policy, Research and Praxis* feature below provides a summary of current thinking in the UK about our most able pupils. After the feature we move on to look at the difference between giftedness and talent.

## Policy, Research and Praxis

### Genius encouraged or denied? Supporting more able children

Support for the most able children is a contentious issue for educators, pupils and parents, yet an important one for reasons of social mobility, inclusion and equal opportunities. It is also significant economically in an increasingly knowledge-based global society.

PISA results (OECD, 2010) show that UK standing is poor by international comparisons. English students are half as likely to reach the highest levels in maths compared to students from other developed nations, ranking 26th out of 34 OECD countries. Only 1.7 per cent of English students reached the highest level in maths, compared on average to 3.1 per cent across all OECD countries. The few high performing pupils in England predominately attend independent and grammar schools, with 'almost no pupils' achieving top levels from non-selective state schools. This is a worrying picture for the most able pupils from non-privileged backgrounds (Smithers & Robinson, 2012).

Why does the problem exist? There are a number of reasons. The actual concept of 'giftedness' is generally misunderstood. What does it actually mean for a child to be academically gifted? How is this viewed against one with talent in sport or the arts? Many checklists exist to help classify children with high abilities and yet teachers still complain that the highly able have become a neglected group in schools. Competing theoretical perspectives cloud the issue. Those taking a genetic stance argue for selecting only a few children for special provision, whilst others taking an environmental stance argue for educating all children to a high standard (Freeman *et al.*, 2010). There are objections to the gifted agenda as being exclusive, a lack of public interest and apathy from pupils themselves. Teachers are not always keen to identify young children as gifted because of concerns about early labelling. Gifted children can be pathologised as inherently damaged by their abilities. There are pragmatic difficulties like lack of funding, support from senior leaders, resources and staff capacity.

Policy and provision for the highly able is a hotch-potch of abandoned initiatives and unclear priorities (Smithers & Robinson, 2012). In their report the Welsh Inspectorate (Morgan *et al.*, 2012) found that the most more able pupils in primary schools are not challenged enough and that provision for them is too varied. Are there strategies to tackle the issue?

British businesses have recommended that teachers are given more freedom to tailor teaching to meet a child's individual needs (CBI, 2012). A number of proven strategies exist. Some schools have attempted to provide for their high attainers through setting or streaming arrangements, accelerated learning and extension activities. Others have concentrated on out-of-school activities like master classes, competitions and educational visits. Other features of effective practice include target setting, monitoring pupil progress, individualised/personalised approaches to learning, using experienced co-ordinators and providing support during the transition from primary to secondary schools.

More fundamentally, we should seek to improve our education system by looking at other jurisdictions, especially those in Europe where more pupils reach the highest levels of attainment.

Giftedness is generally understood in terms of possessing an IQ in excess of 130. If giftedness can be measured in this way, what about talent and creativity? Are there IQ scores related to these gifts? Let's try talent first.

**Connect and Extend**
For another helpful checklist of characteristics of gifted children, read: Manning, S. (2006). Recognizing gifted students: A practical guide for teachers. *Kappa Delta Pi Record, 42,* 64–68.

**Reflect**

The popular TV cartoon *The Simpsons* presents Homer's daughter Lisa as something of a child genius, but the depiction mirrors what are not uncommon experiences for gifted children growing up today: teased at home and patronised at school by adults. There are a number of complex emotional issues surrounding giftedness and we pose three questions:

1. How can we identify any particular social and emotional needs of gifted children?

2. Are intellectual needs more important than social and emotional ones?

3. Can gifted children successfully be challenged and supported in the context of mainstream education?

## Talent

Gardner's theory of multiple intelligences (see p 276) has another important contribution to make in this context, particularly to the literature of talent identification in schooling. Talent refers to performance that is outstanding in a particular field and its broad definition is similar to that of giftedness; see the nearby *Connect and Extend*. We will attempt a clear distinction. Giftedness is extraordinary ability in one or more so-called academic school subjects, and talent is defined as extraordinary ability in the performing aspects of the curriculum: sport,

• • • • • • • • • • • • • • • •
**Connect and Extend**

If you web search for talented pupils you are almost always referred to 'gifted and talented children' and if you use the Boolean search terms 'talented NOT gifted AND pupils' you will find the term talented being used as an alternative to gifted. Try it out for yourself. What does this tell you about our collective understanding of 'talent' and 'gift'?
• • • • • • • • • • • • • • • •

performance arts, dance, drama, music, art and design. In the United Kingdom, 'World Class Tests' have recently been introduced as a testing system in maths and/or problem-solving for upper primary and lower secondary pupils. This is intended to produce an international benchmark, to identify the top 10 per cent of 9–13-year-olds and to support teachers in understanding how special children in this category can be effectively challenged in ways that make the most of their particular talent(s). A national register of gifted and talented children is now in existence in the wake of much criticism that children with certain aptitudes and abilities have not been recognised or fully catered for with the current educational provision.

Talented pupils are found to be highly motivated (Mouratidis *et al.*, 2008); enjoy adventurous activity and have a good self-image (Graham & Robinson, 2007); have capacities of endurance and perseverance with highly developed perceptual capacities and motor skills (Visscher *et al.*, 2006); and developed conceptions of beauty, style, excellence, goodness, love, empathetic feelings, universal honesty and diligence (Vitkauskas, 2007). Armed with such an array of qualities it is not surprising, perhaps, that the rest of us look to talented (and gifted) individuals to be also the most creative people in our families, schools and wider society.

Children are naturally curious and playful and they often enjoy being creative.

*Source:* © Pearson Education Ltd / Jules Selmes.

## Creativity

What do you think of when you say someone is creative? We can all think of amazingly creative (and talented/gifted) people such as Shakespeare, Picasso, Brunel, Menuhin, Dickens and Mozart as famous individuals who have expressed their creative talents. Terms such as inventiveness, imagination or 'thinking outside the box' probably spring to mind and suggest a capacity which remains rather nebulous. Many definitions exist but the one proposed by educational strategist Bill Lucas (2001) reflects the notion of creativity involving more than one type of intelligence – like Gardner's work – as 'a state of mind in which all of our intelligences are working together'. We often hear adults referring to children as being 'creative', that their imaginations are fertile and that they seem to be insatiably inquisitive. Does this mean that children are more creative than adults? Certainly as play experts Joan Isenberg and Nancy Quisenberry (2002) remind us, children, if given the chance, are naturally curious and playful. Childhood may well be the foundation for creativity in later life where children can indulge their imaginations, their curiosity and playfulness before the realities and criticisms of everyday life put a ceiling on the 'freed-up' thinking and risk-taking that might allow fresh ideas to be created in adulthood.

The report of the UK National Advisory Committee for Creativity and Culture in Education (NACCCE, 1999) separates creativity into four processes. Firstly, it involves thinking and behaving imaginatively and, while recognising that imagination is a key feature, it also questions if all imaginative ideas are creative. Secondly, creativity must have purpose and be directed to the achievement of an objective (even if the objective changes over time). Thirdly, creativity must generate something that is original in relation to pupils' previous work or that of peers. Finally, the outcome must have value too and satisfy its intended purpose.

**Convergent thinking**
Thinking orientated towards the single solution to a problem.

Traditional IQ tests are not a useful measure of a child's creativity since they tend to encourage a focus on the 'right' answer and require **convergent thinking** orientated towards the single solution to a problem. In contrast, creativity tests encourage flexible thinking patterns of risk-taking and use divergent thinking that encourage multiple solutions and generations of new ideas almost without limit. As a concept, the previous two decades have seen a heightened focus in curriculum and pedagogy for policy-makers and practitioners. It is what psychologist

Anna Craft views as a 'changing landscape' (2005, p 15) arising from political, economic and social change and, in response to such change, what is considered significant in terms of educational achievement is also changing. Craft argues that knowledge alone is no longer adequate, and that creativity is critical to our survival as a species.

Of course, creativity is apparent in all children and every child should have opportunities to allow them to flourish. Teachers and early years practitioners are ideally placed in working closely with young people to identify and promote creative activities and therefore to influence the development of creativity, to see the genius in every child. Naturally there are some challenges here: undoing your own assumptions about creativity and intelligence and replacing these with more enlightened perspectives, and valuing creativity alongside test results and standards. Ken Robinson (Professor of Arts Education at the University of Warwick) sees it as a question of balance and comments further: 'everyone has creative potential but developing it requires a balance between skill and control and the freedom to experiment and take risks' (2001, p 45). True creative thinking has great rigour, and educators need to see the two as co-existing in the ways in which their pupils in school think and behave. Kemple and Nissenberg (2000) share this view and add that educators also need to communicate their understanding of creativity to parents and the wider community to challenge existing assumptions about talent and creativity.

---

We now summarise what you have learned in the final section of this chapter:

- To develop intelligence, Howe and Griffey (1994) argue that in certain areas such as motor and language, early intervention programmes are beneficial.

- Many schools now offer programmes of enrichment to help foster children's intelligence – cognitive intervention programmes.

- Cognitive intervention programmes include Head Start, the SNAP™ Under 12 Outreach Project, the Cognitive Acceleration through Science Education (CASE) programme, neuro-linguistic programming (NLP), and Sure Start.

- Programmes that aim to promote the thinking abilities of school-age children include Instrumental Enrichment and Philosophy for Children.

- Gifted children display qualities that set them apart from their peers: curiosity, memory, higher-order thinking skills, language, precociousness, attention, social maturity and humour.

- Giftedness is extraordinary ability in one or more so-called academic school subjects, and talent is defined as extraordinary ability in the performing aspects of the curriculum: sport, performance arts, dance, drama, music, art and design.

- Creativity can be thought of as a function of four processes: thinking and behaving imaginatively; being purposeful and directed to an objective; being original in relation to a pupil's previous work or that of their peers; and the outcome must satisfy its intended purpose.

**Summary 3**

# Conclusion

This chapter emphasised the importance of cognition to all other aspects of child development. Three key perspectives on cognition were presented and discussed. Piaget's cognitive-developmental theory adopts a constructivist viewpoint that sees children as active participants, seeking out knowledge and constructing their own understanding of their world. His identification of four stages of cognitive development and his examination of the changes in thinking in these different stages of development follow a hierarchical structure from simple to complex. While advancing our knowledge of children's thinking to an extent not achieved previously, there are a number of criticisms of Piaget's work that have led to alternative approaches.

Vygotsky's sociocultural theory offers a sociocultural approach to cognition in a theory that stresses social and environmental influences. Children are born with limited cognitive abilities (elementary mental functions) that are developed through interventions with others in their community. This allows higher mental functions which are mediated through the use of language and maths as symbolic tools. Vygotsky's work also has direct implications for contemporary teaching and learning. He believed that children develop their own knowledge at their own pace, actively (like Piaget), but it requires access to rich and stimulating environments. The role of the teacher is to facilitate learning and this is made possible by structuring the learning environment to allow children's concepts and skills to develop. A state of developmental readiness which he termed the 'zone of proximal development' exists where the child is unable to proceed alone and requires input from a significant other, namely an adult or experienced peer, who is able to scaffold learning and help the individual progress their learning to the next stage in ways outlined, including co-operative learning and reciprocal teaching. Through building upon this work and introducing the idea of a spiral curriculum where concepts are introduced early on and then constantly revisited through a child's school years, the influence of Jerome Bruner is to be seen in the curriculum frameworks in many primary schools today.

Presenting an alternative approach, information-processing theories work on the analogy of a computer: information comes in from the external environment, is acted upon by internal processes and results in action and output. General information-processing models assume that the brain's organisational structures are shared by everyone. More recent theories were also discussed that have largely built upon the three main approaches described and the reader invited to adopt a personal stance on which approach offered most appropriate interpretation of cognition. Applications were made throughout to classrooms and school-based learning.

The topic of intelligence was introduced and it was discussed how this has been traditionally measured. The research evidence suggests that around 40 per cent of our intelligence is influenced by genetics and 60 per cent by our environment. Secondly, in contrast to the traditional view, intelligence is not a fixed entity but can be improved by appropriate stimulation. A number of environmental factors were identified that impact upon scholastic achievement such as gender, culture, parental values, housing, diet and unemployment. Lastly, contemporary theories of intelligence were presented and supported by research evidence. Intelligence was linked to the concepts of giftedness, talent and creativity. Each of these was defined and discussed with applications suggested from educational research.

This has been a long and complex chapter but we trust you now have a clear idea of the importance of cognitive development in providing a basis for all the remaining domains of development that we will discuss in the final three chapters. Indeed, there is an intimate association, a symbiotic relationship between cognitive development and the subject of our next chapter, language development. In Chapter 10 we will discuss the four main components of language and how language develops in young children. We will also discuss some of the contemporary debates about literacy teaching in schools and early years settings. In the meantime you should review the questions posed at the beginning of this chapter: 'What is cognition?' and 'What is the difference between cognitive development and learning?' You should now be able to furnish expert answers!

# Summary Table
## Cognitive Development

## Understanding cognition (pp 250–251)

We define cognitive development as the changes in mental abilities that take place throughout the lifespan, and cognition is the act of knowing using mental processes such as imaging, remembering, understanding, generalising, finding reasons and causes and making inferences, decision-making, forming preferences, desires and intentions, planning and learning. Learning is one of the most important cognitive abilities and relies upon the recording, organising and retrieval of many millions of pieces of information, supported by a continuous stream of perceived information from the senses.

## Three approaches to cognitive development (pp 252–273)

### Piaget's cognitive-developmental theory (pp 252–261)

Piaget's cognitive-developmental theory is a constructivist theory which views children as active participants in their own learning, seeking out knowledge and constructing their own understanding. Important to the theory are the formation and refinement of concepts and, particularly, mental schemes through adaptation and organisation. Piaget referred to adaptation as the construction of schemes arising from the direct engagement with the environment that allows us to adjust to the demands of our environment, and organisation as the ways in which schemes are linked together in a connected network. In Piaget's theory, cognitive development is organised into four stages:

- sensorimotor stage (birth to 2 years);
- pre-operational stage (2–7 years);
- concrete operational stage (7–11 years);
- formal operations stage (12 years upwards).

The impact of Piaget in psychology and in schooling remains evident in educational practice worldwide.

### Vygotsky's sociocultural theory (pp 261–266)

Vygotsky's social-constructivist approach offered a major alternative to Piaget's theories. The central principle of Vygotsky's theory argues that thinking is a socially constructed process and that learning takes place when the learner is in their zone of proximal development (ZPD): times when the child critically benefits from the help of other adults or experienced peers. Indeed, Vygotsky stressed the important role of the teacher in structuring learning. Bruner used Vygotsky's idea of 'scaffolding' to represent the way children's learning can be supported where 'significant others' provide help at significant points and gradually remove the help as a child succeeds.

### Information-processing theories of cognitive development (pp 266–271)

Information-processing (IP) theories focus on the process of cognition and these theorists hold the view that the mind operates like a computer. IP theories liken memory to a store model: a model that views information as being held in three parts – sensory register, short-term memory and long-term memory. Modern connectionism uses ideas of connected sets of microchipped circuits and information and communications systems. This is based on Thorndike's most important idea: intelligence is a function of the number of connections learned, much the way we see the interconnectedness of knowledge and concepts. The neo-Piagetian theory of Robbie Case is a recent interpretation of Piaget's theory in an information-processing framework and includes encoding, strategies, automatisation and generalisation.

### General summary of all three approaches (pp 271–272)

## The nature of intelligence (pp 273–274)

Intelligence is the capacity for cognition and for cognitive development. Contemporary theories favour explaining intelligence in terms of the cognitive processes involved when we engage in intellectual activities. Central to this point of view is the notion that mental competence changes over time, and it is commonly held that only around 40 per cent of our intelligence is influenced by genetics and 60 per cent by our environment. A number of environmental (nurture) factors have been identified that impact upon intelligence: family size, secure and encouraging home environment, school effectiveness, socio-economic background, achievement motivation and gender differences.

## Measuring intelligence – scales and tests (pp 274–276)

Alfred Binet developed the first standardised intelligence test, which was a scale systematically measuring higher-order thinking skills, memory, language and problem-solving abilities, unique to each individual. To assess children between 1 month and 3½ months, the 'Bayley scales of infant development' are used. These scales are useful in identifying health problems early but again are not reliable for predicting scholastic achievement because of their reliance on sensorimotor abilities. The 'McCarthy scales of children's abilities' cover the 2½ to age 8 period and provide measures in verbal, non-verbal, memory, spatial and motor skills. The Wechsler intelligence scales include the Wechsler Preschool and Primary Scale of Intelligence (WPPSI) and the Wechsler Intelligence Scale for Children (WISC). These scales produce intelligence quotients with a mean of 100 and measure mathematical and verbal reasoning, and spatial skills.

## Contemporary theories of intelligence (pp 276-279)

Howard Gardner's original theory of multiple intelligences included seven 'intelligences' (linguistic, logical-mathematical, spatial, bodily-kinaesthetic, musical, intrapersonal and interpersonal) and an eighth, that of naturalist intelligence, was added in 1999. Today, Gardner has added a ninth, existential intelligence, which is concerned with spirituality. In contrast to Gardner, John Anderson in his 'simple theory of complex cognition' proposes that changing the curriculum does not change the need for students to master the components of the curriculum; mastery comes through practice.

## Developing intelligence (pp 280-283)

To develop intelligence Howe and Griffey argue that in certain areas such as motor and language, early intervention programmes are beneficial. Many schools now offer programmes of enrichment to help foster children's intelligence – these are termed cognitive intervention programmes. Examples of cognitive intervention programmes include Head Start, the SNAP™ Under 12 Outreach Project, the Cognitive Acceleration through Science Education (CASE) programme, neuro-linguistic programming (NLP) and Sure Start. Programmes that aim to promote the thinking abilities of school-age children include Instrumental Enrichment and Philosophy for Children.

## Giftedness, talent and creativity (pp 283-287)

Gifted children display qualities that set them apart from their peers: curiosity, memory, higher-order thinking skills, language, precociousness, attention, social maturity and humour. Giftedness is thought of as extraordinary ability in one or more so-called academic school subjects; and talent is defined as extraordinary ability in the performing aspects of the curriculum: sport, performance arts, dance, drama, music, art and design. Creativity can be thought of as a function of four processes: thinking and behaving imaginatively; being purposeful and directed to an objective; being original in relation to a pupil's previous work or that of their peers; and the outcome must satisfy its intended purpose.

## Going further

De Haan, M. & Johnson, M. H. (2012) **The cognitive neuroscience of development (Studies in developmental psychology).**
A collection of essays written by international experts in the field. It not only covers traditional topics such as language, attention and memory development, but also includes individual chapters covering the theories of neurocognitive development and methods of studying brain activity in young infants and children. There are additional chapters on hormonal influences on brain and behavioural development, gender differences in the brain, and genetic disorders.

Blakemore, S. J. & Frith, U. (2007). *The learning brain.* Oxford: Blackwell.
'Upbeat and fast-paced . . . when it comes to learning, it's all about the brain' (back cover quote from Prof. Michael S.

Gazzaniga, Dartmouth College). The book lacks academic citations and references but is a very good read.

Bruner, J. (1996). *The culture of education.* Cambridge, MA: Harvard University Press.
It is always valuable to return to the original texts of those most often quoted and cited. Jerome Bruner had an important impact on contemporary thinking about cognitive development and education.

Gopnik, A., Meltzoff, A. & Kuhl, P. (2002). *How babies think: The science of childhood.* London: Phoenix.
This is aimed at a popular audience. The authors draw on research in philosophy, psychology, computer science, linguistics and neuroscience to reveal what babies know and how they learn it.

Distin, K. (Ed) (2006) Gifted children: A guide for parents and professionals. London: Jessica Kingsley Publishers.

An exploration of the gifted mind and the social and emotional needs of gifted children and their families.

The authors give an insight into what is 'normal' for gifted children, acknowledge the difficulties they experience. Exceptional abilities in fields ranging from music and maths to linguistics and art are often complicated by poor social skills or dyslexia.

# Useful websites

http://www.potentialplusuk.org/

The website of Potential Plus UK, an independent charity established in 1967 which works with the whole family to support children with high learning potential. Their aim is to work with parents and carers to discover children's potential by nurturing their gifts and talents and to work with professionals to help gifted children succeed.

www.icn.ucl.ac.uk

The University College London Institute of Cognitive Science Researchers use imaging, EEG, TMS and patient studies to explore brain activity including executive function, social cognition, numeracy and language as well as a variety of developmental disorders including autism, dyslexia, dycaculia and prosopagnosia. Intriguing and authoritative.

www.med.harvard.edu/aanlib/home.html

'Provides a brain atlas' and an on-line lecture about fMRI scanning techniques with technical images of a 'normal' brain and a range of conditions.

www.funeducation.com/tests/KidsISIQ/
Kids-IQ-Testing.aspx

This is one of a large number of websites offering free on-line IQ tests. Take the results with a pinch of salt. Searching the web will provide other test opportunities.

# Chapter 10
## Language Development

**Overview**

*Staff at The Chestnut Nursery planned a special day when the emphasis would be on developing the children's language through activities around a common theme – the colour red. Everyone came dressed up: staff came in red clothes, sporting some amazing red wigs, and most of the children wore something red. The activities for the children were deliberately planned to stimulate the children's language with a starting point of 'redness'. There was red dye in the water trough, red play-dough, red plates and beakers, and various shades of red paint to use. Wherever possible all the equipment had been replaced with red alternatives, and stories, songs and rhymes had been chosen to match the theme. Thank goodness for 'The Little Red Hen'!*

*During the day each member of staff was allocated to a small group of children and many opportunities were taken to talk with the children, sometimes individually about 'red' as a colour, and about all the activities they engaged in. The intention was to listen carefully to children's language – what they said and the way they said it – and to make assessments of the language ability of each child.*

*At the end of the day, staff compared notes and it was agreed that all children had used many different types of language: explanations, narrative, questions, playful talk, etc. Of course some of the children had been a little withdrawn to begin with and several with English as an additional language had to be specially encouraged and supported. Nevertheless there was a general feeling that a language day had been a success and should be repeated regularly to help promote the language development of all the children. 'We've done red – what shall we do next?'*

You might consider it a little odd to plan a special language day like the 'red day' in our opening story. Surely every day in a school is a language day? How can you teach or learn except through communication? Let's just think about this! The vast majority of us have the capability of hearing and speaking; the usual way of communicating with those around us and almost every classroom in which we work or visit is full of language-based activities, irrespective of the subject or topic. The university students we now teach come in talking, carry on talking and go out talking. It's not just talking, it is writing as well. To illustrate this consider the following anecdote.

About eight years ago my 15-year-old youngest, Tom, complained – in the form of a question: 'Dad, why do they make us write in every lesson? Today I went to cooking [probably officially called food sciences] and all we did was write stuff. It was the same in physics, RE and even in PE; nothing but [expletive] writing all day. I hate [expletive] school!' Of course I carefully explained to Tom that writing is used in many lessons as a form of behaviour management; that (in my view) it is only during school inspections that teachers provide a variety of teaching and learning approaches; that it was just the same in my school days (not true, I went to a brilliant school) and that Tom should stop moaning because he had hated school from the age of 6 and his feelings were unlikely to change now. I also told Tom to 'Mind your language, young man!', but the irony was lost on him – probably because by then, and like many 15-year-olds, Tom had stopped listening.

By the end of Chapter 9 we had established the importance of cognitive development in providing a basis for all other domains of development including language development. As we said at the end of the last chapter, there is an intimate association, a symbiotic relationship between cognitive development and language development. In this chapter we will discuss this 'special' relationship by focusing on the four main components of language and how language develops in young children. We will also explore some of the contemporary debates about literacy teaching in schools and early years settings, and establish some of the reasons why the staff at The Chestnut Nursery were right to give special attention to the language development of the children on 'red day'.

By the time you have completed this chapter you should be able to answer the following questions:

- What are the main components of language?
- How do we learn to speak?
- What are the main theories of language acquisition?
- Is learning language an innate ability?
- What is the connection between brain, cognitive and language development?
- What is the sequence of language development and what can go wrong?
- What are the implications of learning two or more languages during the 'critical periods'?
- How do we learn to read and write?
- What are the implications for teaching and learning of understanding the importance and processes of language development?

# What is language and why is it so important?

**Language**
A system of sounds, symbols or gestures to communicate with others according to a set of agreed rules.

Becoming proficient with spoken language is without a doubt one of a child's most significant developmental milestones. The Latin word '*infans*' – from which the word 'infant' derives – means 'incapable of speech' and confirms speech is not a facility children are born with. They have to learn to speak and this is a really difficult thing to do as anybody who tries to learn a new language in later life will tell you! Yet in just a few years almost all children show themselves as competent communicators and capable readers with a good command of the spoken and written word. The speed at which language develops in the first years of life is extraordinary and it is the pace and scope of children's language and literacy development that raises some interesting questions. How do children acquire such an impressive vocabulary in relatively few years? How are the intricacies of grammar learned? How is it possible to learn to speak several languages from an early age? Are our brains hard-wired to make sense of and to produce speech, or does the environment and culture in which we grow up determine our linguistic competence? Let us begin answering these questions by defining what we mean by language and so perhaps discover something of its associated developmental complexity.

A definition of language by psychologist Martyn Barrett is: 'a code in which spoken sound is used in order to encode meaning' (1999, p 1). This is a useful starter and you should note this early reference to meaning. Language is an organised system of symbols, movements and sounds to communicate with others, according to a set of agreed rules for the oral, written or signed forms. The purpose of language is communication, and communication is a process by which information is transmitted and received. It can be verbal and auditory but it can also involve non-verbal communication such as gestures, facial expressions and body posture: very important ways of communicating with others and which we will deal with shortly. Language fulfils many purposes – it allows us to interact with others, to transmit information and to express our personal wishes. It can help us organise our thinking and actions, express emotions and even alter our emotional state.

**Communication**
A process by which information is transmitted and received.

**Non-verbal communication**
The types of communication that do not involve speech, including gestures, facial expressions and posture.

**Reflect**

Review the story (referred to in Chapter 1) of Victor the 'Wild Boy of Aveyron', at **www.feralchildren.com/** and the work of Jean-Marc Itard, who tried to transform the 'Wild Boy' into a civilised Frenchman. One area we asked you to concentrate on was that Victor only learned to speak at a very basic level and therefore found it difficult to associate with people normally. What effect did this lack of language have upon Victor's cognitive, emotional and social development?

Humans are the only species to use complex language. It is the thing that separates us from animals. Of course, animals do communicate with each other. Studies of dolphins reveal they use high-pitched sounds to communicate with each other and bees use their wings and flight patterns for the same reason. However, in the animal world, a single sound has one meaning and, unlike us, animals cannot combine sounds. We can create an endless variety of meanings that we are capable of communicating. All species appear to have just sufficient means to communicate in their particular environments and the reason for our elaborate speech is because we live in a sophisticated social world, where our survival was and is dependent upon complex communication. The evolutionary base for human language might – as Charles Darwin suggested in his 'survival of the fittest' theory – have evolved through various adaptations in order to sustain our survival as a species. Certainly, facility with language would have allowed our hunter-gatherer ancestors to protect themselves and to communicate in social groups, similar to those that we still seek out today. Another view is that language is a skill that developed as early humans learned a range of other sophisticated skills. We know that the areas in our brain controlling manipulation are those associated with speech. In the distant past, when the use of tools became a vitally important skill, could it also be possible that language evolved alongside?

**Reflect**

The British theoretical physicist Professor Stephen Hawking is widely acclaimed as one of the finest minds alive today and within known history (we've heard him referred to as a brain on wheels!). Professor Hawking can no longer speak, scribe or sign since acquiring a form of motor neuron disease in his third year at Cambridge University. Modern communication technologies enable him to communicate with the rest of us lesser mortals, and to 'speak' and write. How exciting is that? Would his contribution to the world have matched his cognitive power and potential without modern information and communication technologies?

## Non-verbal communication

Non-verbal communication (NVC) refers to the types of communication that do not involve speech. Its significance in the communication process is well documented in a range of quite recent publications (Knapp & Hall, 2007; Floyd & Guerrero, 2006; Freitas-Magalhães, 2006; Hargie & Dickson, 2004). Earlier, social psychologist Michael Argyle (1994, 1988) suggested (caution – with little empirical research support) that in some circumstances up to 93 per cent of 'messages received and understood' can be attributed to NVC. It is astonishing to think that people listen to only 7 per cent of what we actually say (although thinking back to my conversation with Tom – mentioned earlier – perhaps not quite so astonishing) and that the dominant way to communicate is with the body. Arguably, the first scientific study of non-verbal communication was Charles Darwin's book *The Expression of the Emotions in Man and Animals* (1872). He argued that all mammals show emotion reliably in their faces.

Perhaps the percentages above are less surprising given our evolutionary past and the typical 'grunting behaviour' of some teenage boys! It is important for us to understand and be able to interpret the NVC of young children as infants begin their communication with us by using non-verbal methods.

Some twenty years ago, six features of NVC were identified (Graddol *et al.*, 1994) and are still accepted as a useful guide:

1. Gestures, which allow a number of messages to be communicated as well as emotions and attitudes. Some of these, like fist-shaking to show anger and clapping to show approval, have virtually universal meaning.

2. Body contact ranging from a handshake to a hug while mostly universal, shows some cross-cultural variances. Touch is one of the earliest forms of human communication, with meanings given to length and pressure of touch and the touching of different body parts.

3. Posture is concerned with the orientation of the body: sitting, standing and lying down (with variations of each of these). Posture is often associated with temperament, as a person with a very upright posture is normally associated with a confident and outgoing temperament.

4. Proxemics is about one's personal space. When this distance between people is closest, the greater the range of non-verbal communication that goes with it. If a greater personal distance is routinely maintained there is a strong association with a shy and private disposition.

5. Gaze is the richest of all forms of NVC. Hiding the eyes suggests secrecy, and avoidance of another person's gaze suggests lack of confidence. We prefer to look at those we like and gaze is a common way to regulate interaction – we make eye contact with those with whom we wish to communicate with, but avoid it with those we do not.

6. Facial expressions are commonly associated with our emotions. For instance a raised eyebrow indicates surprise; knotted eyebrows and a pursed mouth that displays teeth indicate anger. As mirrors of our emotions these displays appear to be universal, although there are cultural as well as situational protocols called **display rules** which govern emotional expression. As we argue in the next chapter, crying and early smiling are inborn expressions of emotions – but children learn quite quickly how to display a whole range of different feelings.

• • • • • • • • • • • • • • • •
**Connect and Extend**
View a video of children listening to a story. We found some excellent examples on YouTube. What do the children's facial expressions and posture tell you about their feelings? What are they communicating?
• • • • • • • • • • • • • • • •

**Display rules**
Cultural and situational rules that indicate the appropriateness of emotional expression in particular contexts.

## Four components of language

As part of defining language, let us now look in more detail at its components. We present and briefly discuss what are generally considered the four components of language, since these terms provide a framework to help understand the scope and developmental requirements of human language.

**Phonology** is the system of meaningful sounds in a language. Core units of sound called **phonemes** are the smallest units of sound that can deliver a change in meaning. Examples of these are sounds like *ber* (b) and *ker* (c), found in words like 'bat' and 'cat'. Of course some phonemes are not always identically pronounced, for example the /t/ sound in the words *tin*, *stamp*, *water* and *bat*. These examples of /t/ are considered to be grouped under the same sound category despite the fact that in each word they are pronounced a little differently. That is, a phoneme may encompass several recognisably different speech sounds, called **phones**. In our example, the /t/ in *tin* is aspirated, [tʰ], while the /t/ in *stamp* is not. Developmental psychologists Stan Kuczaj and Heather Hill state that a phoneme is 'a set of sounds [phones] that are not physically identical to one another, but which speakers of a language treat as equivalent sounds' (2003, p 219). Remember phonemes alter meaning, so changing the initial phoneme produces *cat* rather than *bat*: very different meanings particularly if attempting to play table tennis.

**Phonology**
The study of sounds in a language.

**Phonemes**
The smallest parts of language that define or change meaning.

**Phones**
Speech sounds.

**Semantics** is a term which refers to how words are used in combinations to create different meanings. Effective communication has demands not only on the use of the correct word but also on how words are combined to create just the right meaning. Children's semantic knowledge increases throughout their school years, as we will see.

**Grammar** is about the structure of language necessary for constructing unambiguous sentences, important in communicating with others! Grammar includes the rules for the correct use of morphemes, which are language units that cannot stand alone as a complete word with a meaning – such as prefixes (for example *bi*) and suffixes (for example *ing*). Grammar also includes syntax, the principles and rules in which words are combined to form sentences.

**Pragmatics** is a term used for language conventions. Conventions govern the use of types of language for different purposes, for example, in formal conversation, making a speech or telling a joke, and in different contexts such as in the classroom, or the playground. Pragmatics include using different words with a similar meaning but are perhaps indirect and therefore require pragmatic inference to derive the intended meaning. For example, I might be invited into a stranger's house and blurt out, 'For goodness sake, get us a proper drink would you, I'm gasping!' or I might say 'Yes, what a warm day it is. I feel quite uncomfortable'. I hope that my host would infer that I needed a nice cold drink. Pragmatic inference is regarded as one of the most challenging aspects for language learners to grasp, and can be only truly learned with experience.

Given the importance of language one might assume that our ability to communicate effectively with others is universally advanced. Somewhat ironically, this is not the case. Research shows some disturbing signs that children's communication skills are below the level we might expect them to be. Consider this evidence for yourself in the *Controversy* feature.

**Semantics**
How words are used in combinations to create different meanings.

**Grammar**
The structure of language necessary for constructing unambiguous sentences.

**Syntax**
Specifies how words are combined into sentences.

**Pragmatics**
The conventions of language in different contexts.

• • • • • • • • • • • • •
**Connect and Extend**
Extend your knowledge of research on teacher/child interactions by assessing Myhill, D. (2006). Talk, talk, talk: Teaching and learning in whole class discourse. *Research Papers in Education, 21*, 19–41.
• • • • • • • • • • • • • • • •

## Controversy

### Are children today lacking in their basic communication skills?

Despite record amounts of money being spent on schooling in the United Kingdom and children attending formal early years schooling at younger and younger ages, we have a problem. In addition to considerable anecdotal evidence, findings from a number of studies support the view that children's communication skills are in decline. A UK survey of a sample of head teachers found that 74 per cent felt that children's speaking and listening skills had deteriorated in the previous 5 years (NLT/NAHT, 2001). More recently, an 'I CAN' poll found that 94 per cent of nursery staff were worried about the speech and communication of preschool children (2004). Even with the caution that the views of head teachers and nursery staff do not necessarily constitute empirical evidence (Chapter 3), any perceived decline in the communication skills of children is a worrying notion. Can we find reasons for this? The *Talk to Your Baby* project (NLT, 2005) identified a number of key factors.

This research showed that some parents failed to recognise how reliant some children were on their parents to encourage and promote good communication. Others did not connect talking to their children with the development of reading and writing skills. There was some evidence that teachers and nursery staff in the sample were not adequately trained to identify speech and language problems although the important role of speech and language therapists in preventing and treating language difficulties and their impact in settings in the most deprived areas was recognised.

A number of lifestyle factors which might contribute to a decline were identified. Changing work patterns have resulted in mothers having less time to communicate with their children by working longer hours. It is estimated that in the region of three-quarters of grandparents are now contributing to children's upbringing due to increases in working time of parents and the high cost of child-care. A reduction in the practice of families eating together at mealtimes has meant less time for family conversation to take place. Although studies have demonstrated that the time spent by parents with their children has increased in recent years (e.g. Fulkerson *et al.*, 2008; Gershuny, 2000), other studies have found that children report parents rarely or never play with them because they are too busy or tired to do so (e.g. Doliopoulou & Rizou, 2012). Television is deemed a major reason for a decline in language skills (Schmidt *et al.*, 2009). Long periods of viewing television each day are considered to erode time for socialisation (Jordan *et al.*, 2006) directly as well as creating constant background noise (Seo *et al.*, 2012) which has detrimental effects on children's listening skills. Studies have identified links between language and class that support earlier and similar findings in the United Kingdom and in the United States (e.g. Hart and Rilsey, 1995) which show that the vocabulary of children from professional parents is substantially more than children of working-class parents (Leseman, 2000) and this is the case in languages other than English (O'Toole & Fletcher, 2012).

Recent studies that we have cited here suggest that the message given to parents and practitioners to play and read with their children may not actually go far enough in addressing the problem of language deficiency. Scholars and researchers suggest that advice to parents and practitioners should inform them *how* they should do this. Some studies (e.g. Dalzell *et al.*, 2000) recommend additional training and resourcing so that early years practitioners can identify speech and language problems earlier, to create sensitive language classroom environments (like our story example at The Chestnut Nursery?) and be able to intervene much earlier to remediate deficiencies.

*Source:* National Literacy Trust (2005) *Why do so many young children lack basic language skills?* A discussion paper. Talk to Your Baby Campaign, NLT: London. **www.literacytrust.org.uk/talktoyourbaby/discussionpaper.pdf** (accessed 3 June 2008).

● ● ● ● ● ● ● ● ● ● ● ● ● ● ● ●

**Connect and Extend**

Find the full version of *Why do so many young children lack basic language skills?* A discussion paper from the National Literacy Trust (2005). Talk to Your Baby Campaign, NLT: London, at **www.literacytrust.org.uk/talktoyourbaby/discussionpaper.pdf**. What are the specific language deficiencies highlighted by the report? Review the full list of recommendations.

● ● ● ● ● ● ● ● ● ● ● ● ● ● ● ●

# Theories of language acquisition

## Is language innate or learned?

There is no unanimous or universal view of how human language is acquired and so in this section we present each of the main theories.

### Behaviourism

Psychologist B. F. Skinner in his book *Verbal Behavior* (1957) stated that one way in which learning takes place is through operant conditioning when behaviours are repeated and learned by being either rewarded or punished. He further argued that this is applicable to language learning just as for any other behaviour. In his view, two processes enable this: reinforcement and shaping. Children use words that are positively reinforced by parents and significant others who then gradually shape children's speech to mould it into adult-like communication. Babies play with sounds they can make – sometimes called baby babble. Even a close approximation to a common example of early baby babble – da-da-da-da – is seized on by a nearby doting adult, shaped and expanded into 'daddy' and reinforced with much smiling and nodding of the head. It also assists children to form longer phrases correctly. As an example, a child might say to a parent: 'Me play dollies.' The parent reinforces that s/he has understood what the child has said, and might respond, 'I would like to play with my dolls now. Is that right?' Reinforcement prompts the child to repeat the phrase by trying it out straightaway and in a different situation. Receiving immediate feedback and in any new context informs the toddler about the accuracy of the new phrase, which, in turn encourages its use. Some early studies support that reinforcement (systematic repetition perhaps with 'flashcards') can accelerate a child's vocabulary (Whitehurst & Valdez-Menchaca, 1988) but this is in general not a popular or accepted view of how complex language is acquired.

Most babies say their first recognisable word somewhere between 10 and 14 months, but more can show they understand the word or use NVC to indicate who or what they mean before this time, so that by baby's first birthday more than a quarter will have a usable vocabulary of six words of greeting and recognition (perhaps by gesture rather than spoken word). It is important for parents and carers to seize on, shape, expand and reinforce an infant's first few words in many everyday situations, such as going for 'a walk' or going shopping in the pushchair.

In the first part of a fascinating research study, Dr Suzanne Zeedyk and colleagues at Dundee University (Topping *et al.*, 2007) observed 2722 pairs of parents and young children in dozens of High Streets across Britain. She discovered that 62 per cent of the infants were in away-facing buggies, rising to 86 per cent in babies aged between one and two. The study found that the direction of the buggy had a significant impact on the child's behaviour, with 70 per cent of those in away-facing buggies remaining silent, compared with 43 per cent of those in forward-facing ones. In a second more detailed study of 20 mothers and their babies, researchers discovered the parents spoke an average of 15.50 sentences per minute when using toward-facing buggies, but just 6.11 in away-facing ones.

The results of the second study confirmed that mothers spoke more when travelling with their infants in toward-facing buggies; when they were in away-facing buggies, maternal speech dropped by half. They also showed that mothers and infants were both more likely to laugh in the toward-facing orientation, and that mothers were aware of and surprised by this overall change in communicative interactions with their babies. Finally, the results yielded further tentative evidence for the possibility that buggy orientation could influence child stress: infant heart rates fell slightly when moved into a toward-facing orientation, and they were also more likely to fall asleep in this orientation. The opportunities for reinforcement of early language when children are toward-facing is clear, but this is part of a behaviourist approach to reinforcing early language, and behaviourist approaches are not beyond criticism.

Criticisms of a behaviourist approach are that it demands a huge amount of time and does not account for the complexities of grammar nor for multifactorial language forms, since children typically experience quite simple language spoken to them by adults in what is known as **poverty of the stimulus** (Chomsky, 1957). Having words reinforced by a parent repeating and reshaping the first words of an infant is by itself insufficient to account for the speed at which infants acquire the complexities of language and the accelerated growth of vocabulary early in a child's life.

**Poverty of the stimulus**
Suggests that language heard by children is grammatically too simplistic to allow them to develop complex syntax.

## Social learning theory

Social learning theory (Bandura, 1989b) proposes that learning occurs indirectly through observational learning. Children listen to how others around them talk and, in doing so, observe the complexities in their phrases, and rules and conventions they use in conversation – and imitate these. This theory argues that it is through this process that rich vocabulary and complex grammar are acquired.

Undoubtedly, reinforcement (behaviourism) and imitation (social learning) are important processes in learning language, especially for word learning, but they remain incomplete systems in explaining language acquisition. In stark contrast to the above views, the nativist approach favours biological pre-programming. This approach argues that language is not learned but innate, emerging naturally through the maturation process. **Nativism** proposes that all languages have a similar structure. This approach was pioneered by linguist and philosopher Noam Chomsky, who asserted that because all languages are made up of

**Nativism**
A set of beliefs that favours the idea that much of our behaviour is due to biological pre-programming.

structures of nouns, verbs and adjectives, the ability to learn and produce language is innate. We are biologically predisposed to acquire language, born with the initial language connections already in place. However, infants must hear language to trigger this inborn biological facility (Christiansen *et al.*, 2012; Chomsky, 1957/1968).

Here is an example to illustrate this. A child growing up hearing Spanish as the common language will pick up the words and sentence structures of this language in the same way as a child hearing English will learn the nuances of this as their first language. Some experts argue that accent is formed in the first 3 years of life and some as early as the first year of life so that an infant raised in a Spanish-speaking environment then raised in a number of other language environments might well learn the other languages and so become multilingual, but will still speak Spanish with an authentic accent and other languages with a Spanish accent, no matter how slight. Remember at the beginning of the *Conclusion* to Chapter 8 we argued that exposure to the sound patterns in a particular language increases sensitivity to detect the patterns inherent in that language. We gave the example of the consonants *r* and *l*, which are easy to discriminate in most languages with the exception of Chinese and Japanese. Five-year-old Ohta in Japan would find difficulty in discriminating between these sounds because there is no distinction between them in his language. This is because even before babies can understand the meanings of words, they are paying attention to the sounds. They learn which types of sounds are more frequent than others and learn which combinations of sounds occur with each other. Baby babble is no random exercise. Rather, it is a conscious attempt to replicate the sounds and sound combinations of the speech that the baby has been listening to.

A language acquisition device (Chomsky, 1968) acts as the mechanism that allows new words and phrases not heard before to be produced. Cognitive scientist, and popular science author, Steve Pinker developed this idea with his emphasis on an innate language facility that guides our learning of language, and his proposal that language is universal. In his book *The Language Instinct* he writes that children 'actually reinvent' and learn language 'because they just can't help it' (1994, p 32). He proffers the view that we possess a basic common grammar and cites the pidgin languages first picked up in sugar plantations by adults as basic, functional work language, then developed as a 'creole' by children changing words and adapting phrases to create a fully inflected language suited to their own purposes. In doing so, he suggests that these children essentially developed a new language based on a recognisable structure that had many new words from various other languages added but which was still understood by the people in the plantations because it abided by a common grammatical structure.

Evidence in support of the nativist approach also comes from studies into sign language. For example, signing linguist Judy Kegl and her colleagues (1999) studied Nicaraguan deaf children who spontaneously devised their own sign language – based on signs individually developed in their own families, providing further evidence of the universality of language rules. Neuroscientific evidence provides support too. Studies using fMRI – functional magnetic resonance imaging is a procedure that measures brain activity – indicate that as humans we have a unique pattern of organising our language ability (e.g. Seghier *et al.*, 2011). Furthermore, we appear to 'tune in' to spoken language so that our early social context is very important as it provides opportunities for listening to the voices of others around us. We have already seen how babies in the womb attune to the mother's voice. Studies that propose the existence of critical periods (e.g. Chiswick & Miller, 2008), which we return to later, set time limits after which it is extremely difficult or even impossible to acquire language. Criticisms of this approach are, firstly, that there is a lack of evidence on precise identification of the linguistic functions of the parts of the brain that we know are connected with language use. Secondly, the approach may not explain the pace at which we learn language. If a 'language acquisition device' does exist, it raises the issue of why should it take so long for children to learn the rules of their own language – syntax, despite being exposed to excellent standard spoken English.

---

**Connect and Extend**

In Chapter 6 we said 'From birth they [babies] can distinguish between sound patterns such as loud sounds or angry words. Newborns appear to be pre-wired to respond positively to mother's voice but not to that of father.' Review the section on *Hearing* in Chapter 6 and the later section in the same chapter on *Observational learning* (Bandura).

## Interactionism

A third view, that taken by *interactionist* theorists, acknowledges the important role played by parents and other adults in providing social support and contexts for developing language (Bloom, 1998). Language development is accelerated when parents speak to a child in ways that match the child's understanding and knowledge (Tomasello, 2006). A **language acquisition support system (LASS)** (Bruner, 1983) is a set of strategies used predominantly by parents to foster language. One strategy we have met before in Chapters 2 and 9, *scaffolding*, encourages more advanced language by adults pitching language spoken at a higher level than the child is currently able to produce alone which provokes a learning effect. For example, in response to a young child's request/command, 'Mummy give book', a scaffolding parent might respond 'Would you like Mummy to give you this book?'

Early play is an important vehicle to promote early language and can provide LASS opportunities for parents, by providing children with labels for the objects in their play. So a parent might say to the 3-year-old playing with a plastic telephone, 'This is a lovely red telephone' and can then monitor the use of these words in this and future play with the telephone. Two further strategies used by parents and adults to support language are **infant-directed speech** or 'motherese' (Chan & Thompson, 2011) which we have met earlier. This occurs when adults speak to children more slowly, in a higher pitch, laying particular stress on certain syllables and repeating the words regularly. There is 'expansion and recasting' (Bohannon & Stanowicz, 1988). When parents use this strategy they take a simple statement of the child and expand it. For example, when the child says, 'cat runned', the parent might be heard to expand this phrase (see Figure 10.1) and recast it by saying 'Yes, Jess, the cat did run away, didn't she!' This gives important feedback on language accuracies. Expansion and recasting are importantly different and a very important distinction for you to understand. Expanding is simply filling out the child's utterance by repeating it complete with any missing bits, for example, 'cat runned' – 'Yes, the cat ran'. Recasting involves reordering the child's utterance, often by recasting it as a question and this often feels more conversational, less like a correction –

**Language acquisition support system (LASS)** A set of strategies used predominantly by parents to foster language.

**Infant-directed speech** A simplified speech style adopted by adults when talking to young children, using slower speech, repetition of words and higher pitch. Also called 'motherese'.

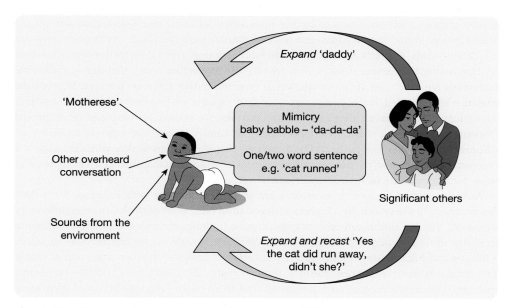

**Figure 10.1** Some combined processes of language acquisition

Owing to sensory and perceptive development an infant can take in and process auditory signals and then attempt to mimic the sounds; sometimes called baby babble. Significant others, like mother, father or siblings will often expand distinctive sounds to form words, e.g. 'daddy'. Later the infant will attempt one or two word 'sentences' which a significant other will scaffold by expanding and recasting into a fully formed sentence or question.

• • • • • • • • • • • • • • • •
**Connect and Extend**
What about motherese by
gesture? Read: Luef, E. &
Liebal K. (2012). Infant-
directed communication
in lowland gorillas (*Gorilla
gorilla*): Do older animals
scaffold communicative
competence in infants?
*American Journal Of
Primatology.* September,
74(9): 841–852.
• • • • • • • • • • • • • • • •

'cat runned' – 'Why did the cat run away?' and it also helps to break utterances up into their constituent parts, useful for learning a language.

It is argued that strategies like these in the *interactionist* approach can be effective due to the increased quality of the communication between parent and child. They do depend, however, on giving direct feedback and providing this feedback frequently. What about in a large family? Might it not be unreasonable to assume that the verbal skills of a child in a larger family might be considerably poorer than in the family with a single child – when, perhaps, LASS strategies are applied more consistently and more frequently than for a child in a much larger family?

We are moving towards providing an answer to the question whether our facility with language is innate or whether it is learned, but we are not quite ready to 'come clean'. First of all, we want to discuss whether there are areas of the brain which are critical and uniquely specialised for language acquisition and processing. If there are, then we might infer that we do have an innate language capacity. On the other hand, if language develops from general cognitive structures and processes stimulated by rich environments, then there is a strong case to conclude that language is a completely learned facility.

## Language and the maturing brain

At birth both left and right hemispheres of the brain are capable of developing language, and within each hemisphere neuro-scanning evidence indicates that different regions of the brain are involved. Two findings from an early study by Neville and colleagues (1998) are relevant to this debate. In their study, a group of deaf individuals were asked to view sign language and a group of hearing individuals to listen to the same message. When the hearing group were required to process language in their native language, regions in the left brain only were activated. However, interestingly, it was found that when the group of deaf individuals viewed sign language, there was activation in areas of the left and the right brain. This is known as the **equipotentiality hypothesis**, which proposes that both sides of the brain may be equally geared to language development. A second finding in the study was that there were different brain patterns in the responses of both groups when asked to read words that were grammatically significant in sentences, but showed similar patterns when reading semantically important words – aspects of language to do with meaning. From their evidence (and indeed after reviewing their research some 10 years on), the researchers concluded that grammatical features of language may be more attuned to experience than semantic features. This is clear evidence that the left brain is not the only side capable of processing language – which strengthens any argument that both nature and nurture impact on language development (Newman *et al.*, 2001). Such evidence does not totally negate the nativist approach of Chomsky and Pinker, but helps to build the case that the human facility with language is a combination of biological pre-programming and environmental influences. Let us look at some further evidence to support this claim.

As we argued in Chapter 6, newborns are well set up to deal with language from their development in the womb. By 32 weeks into gestation both sides of the brain react differently to sounds. The left side already shows specialisation for language which will help to make the newborn more responsive to human speech. We have already mentioned the way in which adults talk to babies using 'infant-directed' speech and how the rhythms and pitch of words and phrases assist in language acquisition (Francis *et al.*, 2004; Hollich *et al.*, 2000). Newborns tune into communication-related aspects around them when language becomes even more significant after birth: increased exposure helping to promote growth in the brain's neural systems. The growing brain allocates areas in the left rear to activities that involve word meaning, areas in the left front for processing word formation and grammar. (Perhaps a useful way to think of this is that the dictionary is at the back of the brain and the script is at the front!)

The chief processing areas of the brain are Broca's and Wernicke's areas (see Figure 10.2) but this is not exclusively so, since we now know that other areas are involved in language

**Equipotentiality hypothesis**
Proposes that areas in the left and right brain have the same potential, among other functions, for language.

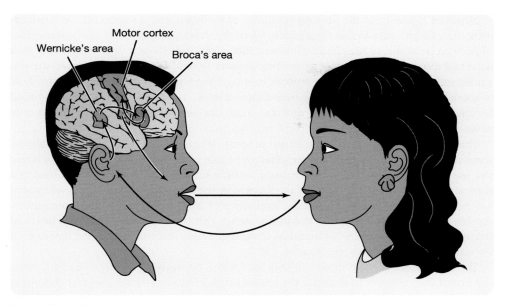

**Figure 10.2** Wernicke's and Broca's areas of the brain

When you hear a word spoken, the auditory signal is processed in your left temporal lobe (blue/green in Figure 9.1), which then sends it on to the nearby Wernicke's area. Here the signal is associated with the representation of a word stored in your memory; you retrieve the meaning of the particular word. We would formulate a reply in Broca's area.

production. These two areas divide language up according to syntax and semantics. Wernicke's area, situated in the left hemisphere of the brain deals with language comprehension and manages the sounds of individual words and what they mean – where sounds are processed. Broca's area, located in the frontal lobe, is responsible for language production and syntax – where actions including speech acts are planned. Broca's area is slower to develop and myelineate (up to 4 years) than Wernicke's area (18–24 months). Two-year-olds can follow instructions although they have not developed the capacity to respond to them verbally. Might the frustration at not being able to articulate their feelings account for what is commonly known as the 'terrible twos'?

Other evidence that language capacity is hard-wired into our brains is found in the brain's plasticity (refer to Chapters 6 and 9) and the not uncontentious idea of 'critical periods'. The early years in particular provide wonderful opportunities for the growth of neural pathways and developing language. As previously mentioned, infants love to babble using sounds (phones) that are particular, and sometimes peculiar, to their native language. In less than a year these seemingly random sounds become recognisable as common sounds (phonemes) in the mother tongue language.

Another persuasive argument about critical periods for language development is based on the premise that the brain is self-organising and makes compensations (the idea of plasticity) in the event of damage to its structures that still allow for language acquisition. An example, and a very famous example, was Helen Keller (1880–1968), who was deaf and blind from 19 months, yet mastered reading, writing and speaking with the patient and inspired teaching of a dedicated teacher, Anne Sullivan. What, perhaps, is less well known is that following her illness Helen's only communication was with Martha Washington, the 6-year-old daughter of the family cook, who was able to create a sign language with her, so that by the age of 7 – about the time Anne Sullivan became Helen's tutor – Helen had over 60 signs to communicate with her family. It has been suggested that Martha Washington's friendship and teaching during a critical period of cognitive development were crucial for Helen Keller's later extraordinary language development (Meshcheryakov, 1979).

However, it is not just the physical condition of the brain that is important. The environment that one grows up in also significantly affects the development of language, and the story of Isabelle from the 1930s clearly illustrates this point. Isabelle was discovered living in a darkened room with her mother as her only contact. When Isabelle was discovered she was almost seven years old and had no sense of language. She had been deprived of learning how to speak because of her mother being both deaf and mute. As a result, when authorities found her they believed that she was also deaf and mute like her mother, because she could only make noises.

• • • • • • • • • • • • • • • •
**Connect and Extend**
Web search to find other examples of deprived and feral children. Not all the stories you will find have a 'happy ending' like the nearby story of Isabelle, perhaps because some children are not found until they are older. Start with Genie, found in California in 1970.
• • • • • • • • • • • • • • • •

This was proven wrong when she started to speak. When Isabelle was first tested, at almost seven years old, her mental age was measured to be that of 19 month-old. By means of intensive teaching and a stimulating environment, Isabelle improved so much in 18 months that she was considered a child of 'normal' intelligence by the age of 8. Her language development had been rapid: by 8 she had learned a vocabulary of 2000 words; she could recite nursery rhymes; she could recount a story and make one up. This development meant Isabelle could create and share with others her world of imagination, not just confined to the language of the immediate and the concrete (Curtiss, 1977).

The story of Isabelle and those you may have found by engaging with the nearby *Connect and Extend* feature serves to illustrate the brain's plasticity at an early age and that childhood is a critical period for language development. After this time the capacity for full language development is diminished and (as we explained in Chapter 6) experiences in the first 2–3 years are especially crucial for language development.

There is plenty of evidence (e.g. Wehberg *et al.*, 2008) that girls talk earlier than boys and their vocabulary is larger. Their sentences tend to be longer at an earlier stage and show more variations in grammar. Girls make fewer verbal errors. It is widely thought that boys do catch the girls up – but do they ever really catch up? Are boys disadvantaged at school because of these differences?

In this section we have presented evidence that biology plays a major role in influencing linguistic capacity and that experience is also tremendously important. Remember, it is the quality of the experiences that has the most effect on linguistic capacity. Young children who are talked with have a larger vocabulary and tend to score higher on IQ tests. Perhaps this is obvious? Exposing children to different words and sentence structures really does make a difference. This difference has been found in many studies worldwide in the context of general language development, bilingualism and special needs (e.g. Hadjioannou & Loizou, 2011; Sénéchal *et al.*, 2008; Macrory, 2007; Fowler *et al.*, 2006; Fontaine *et al.*, 2006; Goldstein *et al.*, 2005; Vachha & Adam, 2005; Bar-Shalom, 2002; Aukrust, 2001). The studies cited also provide the answer to how best to promote language, and it is quite simple. To encourage better language skills later, include more talking and 'conversation', and read to very young children!

**Summary 1**

Before moving on, let's summarise what we have learned so far:

- Becoming proficient with spoken language is one of a child's most significant developmental milestones.
- Language is an organised system of symbols, gestures and sounds to communicate with others, according to a set of agreed rules for the oral, written or signed forms.
- Non-verbal communication (NVC) refers to the types of communication that do not involve speech. In some circumstances up to 93 per cent of 'messages received

and understood' can be attributed to NVC. Six features of NVC have been identified: gesture; body contact; posture; proxemics; gaze; and facial expressions.

- There are four components to language: phonology; semantics; grammar; and pragmatics.

- Psychologist B. F. Skinner stated that one way in which learning takes place is through operant conditioning when behaviours are repeated and learned by being either rewarded or punished. Children use words that are positively reinforced by parents and significant others who then gradually shape children's speech to mould it into adult-like communication.

- Social learning theory (Bandura, 1989b) proposes that learning occurs indirectly through observational learning. Children listen to how others around them talk and, in doing so, observe the complexities in their phrases, and rules and conventions they use in conversation – and imitate these.

- In stark contrast to the above views, the nativist approach favours biological pre-programming, which argues that language is not learned but innate, emerging naturally through the maturation process. Nativism was pioneered by linguist and philosopher Noam Chomsky, who asserted that because all languages are made up of structures of nouns, verbs and adjectives, the ability to learn and produce language is innate.

- Steve Pinker, building on Chomsky's notion of an innate language acquisition device that guides our learning of language, proposed that language is universal. In his book *The Language Instinct* he supports this view saying that children 'actually reinvent' and learn language 'because they just can't help it'.

- Interactionist theorists (e.g. Jerome Bruner) stress the language acquisition support system available to infants in which parents and others use scaffold learning by expanding and recasting baby babble and mimicked primitive words.

- The equipotentiality hypothesis proposes that both sides of the brain may be equally geared to language development but the left side shows specialisation for language and in the newborn is the side which is responsive to human speech.

- The growing brain allocates areas in the left rear (Wernicke's area) to activities that involve word meaning, areas in the left front (Broca's area) for processing word formation and grammar.

- Other evidence that language capacity is hard-wired into our brains is found in the brain's plasticity (e.g. it can self-organise after damage) and the idea of 'critical periods' during which certain experiences need to be perceived (e.g. difference between *l* and *r*) or the capacity is lost.

- It is the quality of early experiences that have the most effect on linguistic capacity. Children who are talked with early have a larger vocabulary and tend to score higher on IQ tests.

# The development of language

There are similarities across societies in the sequence of language development: a sequence that we will explain in this next section. The normal sequence of development starts with babbling sounds, goes on to using single words, then word pairs, and progresses to combinations of words and sentences with meaning and syntax that are understood in the context of one's own linguistic community. This is not just true for hearing children. Children who are deaf from birth learn sign language in a predictable sequence provided they have an early exposure to it. Let us take a closer look at the developmental sequence of language development.

# The sequence of language development

### 0–12 months – pre-linguistic stage

**Protodeclarative gestures**
Gestures intended as statements, to alert someone else's attention to something.

**Proto-imperative gestures**
Gestures intended to get another person to do something on the child's behalf.

**Categorical speech perception**
Phones are perceived as the same within a particular phonemic group.

From being born, babies produce sound and all parents learn early that a baby will cry to communicate a basic need! Yet much of this is not really about communication. It might be for amusement; early attempts to reproduce the sounds they hear around them, and it is very likely that these sounds are rehearsals for later speech. Hours after they are born, babies are able to distinguish speech from the other sounds around them but it will take some time before they speak in the terms we know it. Speaking involves many skills – control of face muscles including the tongue (the only muscle in the body unattached at one end!) and consciously thinking about (formulating in *Broca's area*) what it is they wish to say. All of this will take some months to acquire.

Much early communication is between child and parent or carer in the form of smiles, sounds and body movements. We call these 'pseudo-conversations'. Picture a mother talking to her baby. The child responds to mum's talk by gurgling and the dialogue continues in what researcher Kenneth Kaye once referred to as a time of 'shared rhythms and regulations' (1984, p 66). Psychologists Susan Goodwyn, Linda Acredolo and Catherine Brown's research (2000) highlighted the very early ways in which babies communicate by using signs. These signs reflect the child's own observations and personal experiences and as such are often quite individualistic. The interest grew from Susan Goodwyn's own daughter Kate, whom she observed rubbing her hands together as a baby when she saw a spider. Kate had observed her mother performing this action when Susan used to recite the nursery rhyme, *Incy Wincy Spider*, and so Kate was communicating her understanding in this physical expression.

Mother and baby taking turns smiling and cooing in a 'pseudo-conversation'
Source: Shutterstock.com / Oksana Kuzmina.

This little girl lets her mother know what she wants by pointing at it (a 'proto-imperative' gesture)
Source: Shutterstock.com / Angela Luchisniuc.

Inside a month the '*ooo*' or cooing sound can be distinguishable at pleasurable times like being bathed and changed: a baby's body rhythms help to establish a dialogue between adult and child. These early interactions reflect a sensitivity to each other that is later seen in turn-taking. After three months gestures play a more significant part in the adult–child communication. By 6 months infants use a pointing gesture to encourage others to attend to something, important in allowing them to learn about their world (Rohlfing *et al.*, 2012). These are termed **protodeclarative gestures**: those intended as statements or to alert someone else's attention, such as when a child points on seeing a dog and wants to tell the carer this. **Proto-imperative gestures** are those intended to get another person to do something on their behalf, for example, fetch their drinking cup from the table nearby. By 12 months, babies can follow the pointing of another. With maturity, gestures are combined with words and over time the amount of gestures is reduced as verbalisation increases.

Understanding of language develops early. **Categorical speech perception** is the term used to explain that infants perceive certain consonants in categories. Some *phones* are perceived by infants as being the same within a particular phonemic group. To illustrate, all *p* sounds are heard as one auditory signal, but all *b* sounds are the same, yet perceived as being in another group. Acoustically there is little between *b* and *p* (Hoff, 2001). This ability to discriminate very subtle differences in sounds occurs as early as 1 month and improves rapidly (Watson, 2000). Does this not add credibility to the nativist argument of pre-programming? Almost certainly, but environmental experiences, as we have argued, are also important. Remember we have used the example of the *l* and *r*, not separate sounds in some languages. Without exposure to the sounds of a language like *l* and *r*, this discriminatory ability is lost quickly – possibly within 9 months (Jusczyk *et al.*, 1993). The ability to discriminate between sounds is an important part of language development, but to discriminate between the significant speech sounds in a language demands time to acquire and considerable exposure to language. Nevertheless, children can segment speech and even recognise words in speech within the first year; findings by researchers Eric Thiessen and Jenny Saffran (2003) showed this developmental capacity occurring from 6 months.

At this 6 months milestone we hear babbling. Many people believe that babbling is an early attempt at meaningful communication. It is certainly an important stage in preparation for later linguistic skills. It is also universal. Babies all over the world babble sounds that appear in any language! They are practising language! Babbling is possibly genetically acquired and yet is modified by children imitating the sounds around them. This is the stage of pre-speech as children are not yet mature enough to make speech sounds. Parents love to guess about sounds their child makes, which could be parts of words, and will 'help out' by saying complete words – a form of early scaffolding and social interaction.

Cooing sounds heard within two months will, within a few more months, contain consonants *b*, *d*, *m*, *n* and *j* and transform into babbling. Finally in this phase we hear combinations of sounds that are heard as one or two repetitions of a syllable, such as *bababbba* in a process known as echolalia. By 10 months children can link words together in what is called 'variegated babbling' due to the mixing of syllables in various ways. By the end of the first year, most children are capable of producing all the vowel sounds and nearly half the consonants in English. They produce patterned speech, where strings of phonemes are combined, that resemble true speech but which is not yet recognisable speech.

As Alan Fogel (1993) suggested, the interactions between child and adult are like turn-taking improvisation of a jazz band. It involves knowing when to start and stop – turn-taking at 'speaking' and listening – each responding to the other through facial expressions, gestures and body rhythms in a mutually rewarding experience. The sequence of early sound production in the first year is ordered and similar across cultures, which, in turn suggests maturational improvement through changes in vocal structures and controlling brain architecture, accelerated by consistent patterns of sounds in the immediate environment.

## 1–2 years – first words

Cultural differences in pre-speech begin to appear by the middle of the second year. Toddlers can learn the names of people around them, pets and some significant objects like toys, in what is known as the naming explosion taking place between 12 and 18 months. Most children speak their first word between 10 and 15 months. By 18 months knowledge of over 150 words is quite common, and by 21 months this rises to about 200 words. This dramatic increase in children's understanding of word meaning and grammar is linked to cognitive advances that developmental psychologist Linda Smith (2000) says comes about by words being associated with each other as having perceptual similarities. Psychologist and teacher educator Lois Bloom (2000) attribute word learning to social cues such as pointing, while others, like cognitive scientists Thierry Nazzi and Alison Gopnik, emphasise the importance of the link between social and linguistic cues provided by adults. In a fascinating piece of research (2000), Nazzi and Gopnik found that children of 20 months will trust an adult speaker who misleads them and so give the same name to two very different looking objects!

**Connect and Extend**
To connect imitation and toy play to language ability, read: Toth, K., Munson, J., Meltzoff, A. & Dawson, G. (2006). Early predictors of communication development in young children with autism spectrum disorder. *Journal of Autism & Developmental Disorders, 36*, 993–1005.

**Patterned speech**
Strings of phonemes are combined that resemble true yet unrecognisable speech.

**Naming explosion**
Marked increase in vocabulary during the second year.

By 12 months social greetings such as *hi* and *bye* are added to a baby's growing repertoire as increased control over breathing and vocal cords (essential for speech) is linked to advances in cognitive development, which allow a child to relate words to an object or event. For example, 'ball' is now an object that rolls and bounces, and a **holophrase** or single word 'sentence' is developed to express a complete thought or sentence. The word 'dat' can mean 'I want that cup there' or when combined with a pointing gesture it might mean, 'What is it that I see?' Helped by adult scaffolding, this process becomes a valuable way of increasing a child's vocabulary. Those important first words are labels of familiar things, for example, milk, bath, which tells us that the type of words that are learned first have value. Naming words – nouns – account for almost two-thirds of the vocabulary of 1–2-year-olds because object names are simpler to encode (visualise) than verbs which require some understanding of the connections between the object and the action associated with it. However, a 2-year-old might confidently use the word 'climb', particularly if the action is one that is relevant to him or her. If this is an activity she enjoys, she will learn this word earlier than other words that are less relevant.

Two contemporary theories of how children acquire words are important in developing our knowledge of how language is acquired. The first is known as **fast mapping** (Spencer & Schuele, 2012). This is the process through which a child learns and, to some extent, understands a word after hearing it once or twice. Although this may seem like quite a feat, deeper inspection reveals that the word is spoken often in error and/or that the meaning of the word is not really fully understood. A second earlier theory is that of **syntactic boot strapping** (Basili *et al.*, 1997; Gleitman, 1990). This proposes that information is gained about a word from its use in a sentence. Often this is made possible by observing how others use the word and by being encouraged to see word and action connections in speech, e.g. the verb *to give* requires a couple of nouns as well, 'Shall we give the dog some food?'

Mistakes are common in this period. At times, the child is unable to interpret correctly the word spoken by the adult clearly enough and adults teach the wrong word. Instead of the word 'cow' they say '*moo moo*', and of course some sounds are easier than others to form. 'Poon' is much easier to pronounce than 'spoon', for example, because the consonant blend of *s* and *p* is not easy. Mistakes occur through **overextension** where the word's meaning is given to objects with similar properties. For example, 'doggie' is associated with the family canine pet but then extends to other similar animals with four legs and a tail, such as horses and cats. Word **underextensions** are less common. Underextensions are refusing to use a word, for example, *animal* in the belief that every animal has to have the same characteristics. 'That's not an animal, Mummy, that's a fish!'

## 2–3 years – the first sentences

After 12 months the infant's expanding repertoire of words have more meaning, and by 2 years infants know that meaning can be expressed in part by the order of the words, and that meaning can also be made more accurate by using more words. By 24 months, three to four word utterances are common. 'Telegraphic speech' occurs now by leaving out words that have not been noticed yet – at least enough to inform speech production. An example is the phrase, '*han shoo*' which means 'This is Hannah's shoe'. Children have progressed beyond single words to the beginning of grammar skills. Here they are finding out the rules of their own language and adjusting their speech to communicate with others. Here again language development is tied to cognitive development as a way of expressing understanding about the world. More neural connections (Chapter 9) are made, responding to stimuli which require and provoke more complex reactions and transforming the potential for language development in other areas of experience.

Adult scaffolding continues. A child of 20 months might say the single word like '*more*' referring to her cup of milk. The adult will often expand this word, and say 'Do you want some more milk'? Prepositions appear. Words are re-ordered, usually as questions, '*Where Han?*' (Where is Hannah?) or, negatively, '*No bath*' (I do not want to have a bath). Themes become evident:

---

**Holophrase**
A single word used to express a complete thought or sentence.

**Fast mapping**
The process through which a child learns and understands a word after hearing it once or twice.

**Syntactic boot strapping**
The idea that information is gained about a word from its context in a sentence.

●●●●●●●●●●●●●●●●●●

**Connect and Extend**
For a longitudinal study of fast mapping skills in normally developing children, 16–18 months of age, read: Gershkoff-Stowe, L. & Hahn, E. (2007). Fast mapping skills in the developing lexicon. *Journal of Speech, Language & Hearing Research, 50,* 682–697.

●●●●●●●●●●●●●●●●●●

**Overextension**
Where the word's meaning is given to objects with similar properties.

**Underextensions**
Refusal to use a word, for example, *animal*, in the belief that every animal has to have the same characteristics.

- *actions* with a corresponding phrase such as '*me stand*';

- *locations*, in the phrase '*cat in house*';

- *possession*, a phrase like '*mummy car*';

- *repetition* and the words '*more, more*' or '*gain*', '*gain*'; and

- *(dis)appearance*, for example, the phrase '*doggie gone*'.

It is during this period that the rules of grammar are acquired. You will remember that we said that grammar is about the structure of language necessary for constructing unambiguous sentences and includes syntax, the principles and rules in which words are combined to form sentences. However, even an elementary grasp of the rules of grammar can be problematic. The English language contains many irregularities and exceptions to the general rules. Children, in the beginning, typically produce correct irregular forms before they understand the nature of language rules. Then they ignore exceptions and adhere to what a rule says in what is called overregularisation – applying a regular rule to words that change irregularly. An example of this would be 'go' becomes '*goed*', rather than *went*, or '*drinked*' rather then *drank*. The same anomaly appears in word endings. Thus, 'mice' become '*mouses*', and so on since children learn that 's' and related suffixes always makes things plural.

**Overregularisation**
Applying a strict regularity rule to words that change irregularly.

So children are not only learning the rules but also need to learn the exceptions. There are still some errors in what is said. When aged 3, the past tense 'ed' applies to everything. '*I runned away*' is frequently heard and some other common syntax difficulties, but, overall, preschool children use correct language in adult-like sentence structures. Many opportunities exist for children to develop correct language in adult-like language structures naturally through play. Table 10.1 introduces the link between play and early language development in the period from birth to 3.

## 3–5 years and onwards

Children of this age understand and are understood by adults and peers. Their vocabulary increases to an impressive 1000 words and they confidently converse and use more complex sentences. Even the untrained ear can detect that children's sentences have become much more complex as they begin to display an understanding of formal (or adult) grammar rules and principles. This permits many more new types of expression. Tenses now exist for the first time, '*I banged a drum*' and fully formed questions like '*Where is my cup?*' The 'w' questions of *why, what, when, where* are increasingly heard at this age, linked to a seemingly insatiable desire for knowledge and deeper understanding: '*Why is the sky blue?*' for the tenth time provides a taxing time for parents! Advances in understanding and other speech types develop at such a pace that, by the time most children enter formal school by age 5, spoken grammar fundamentals are solidly in place.

Be mindful of the role of the environment in vocabulary development during early childhood. In a study of children of contrasting socio-economic classes, psychologists Zeheva Weizman and Catherine Snow (2001) investigated the home language environments of children aged 5, and the way that language is socially stimulated at home. There were two relevant findings to this investigation. Firstly, families that share the culture which informs school interactions provide a language environment more like that found in schools and, secondly, that by age 5, children's language experiences at home were positively related to their later vocabulary performance in school.

We explained earlier that *pragmatics* is the term referring to the practical use of language: for example, for conversation and for narrative. This is a significant aspect of communication for children of school age. Young children are better at conversations on a one-to-one basis. In larger groups they tend to interrupt or speak simultaneously more frequently. The social basis for language becomes more evident as schooling brings increased social contact and children have to adapt to the social requirements of the situation. Communication now is very much

**Table 10.1** Linking play and early language development

| Age range | | Play descriptions | Language descriptions |
|---|---|---|---|
| 0–10 months | | Explorations of immediate environment. Holding different shapes and banging them on a surface. | Using gestures and sounds to communicate. |
| 9–15 months | | Relating one object to another in play. Putting one brick on top of another. | Able to produce varied patterns of sound. |
| 11–18 months | | Use of pretend actions as parts of stories/rhymes. | First words. |
| 12–30 months | | Pretend actions that involve other people or objects (e.g. dolls, puppets). | Simple combinations. |
| 19–36 months | | Play sequences that involve others and modelling/construction materials. | Short sentences of 3, 4, 5 words. |

*Source*: Table adapted from Lindon, J. (2005). *Understanding child development: Linking theory and practice*. Abingdon, Oxon: Hodder Arnold. Photos: © Pearson Education Ltd / Jules Selmes (0–10 months); DK Images / Steve Gorton (9–15 months); Pearson Education Ltd / Lisa Payne Photography (11–18 months); DK Images / Dave King (12–30 months); Bananastock (19–36 months).

a two-way process and context requires that conversing with a friend in the playground is different from talking to an adult in the classroom. The requirement to listen and then respond in an appropriate way to a speaker is crucial, particularly if that speaker is a teacher! Children from 5 years onwards are acutely aware of the need to adjust their language to the listener, in terms of who this might be, that person's knowledge and what the speaker wishes that other person to know. The pragmatics of language – speech act theory (Holtgraves, 2008; Georgalidou, 2008) – argues that sentence formation is insufficient for real linguistic proficiency. Speakers' intentions and the listener's interpretation of intent are also necessary, and discerning intention and interpretation have to be learned.

Forms of speech develop during the primary years which are sophisticated and involve the figurative use of language and its conventions. The use of metaphor is one such convention that develops across childhood and another is humour. Humour is believed to be connected to advances in cognitive capacities (exaggerated mimicry or caricature, trick or practical joke) through increased knowledge (e.g. anecdote from common experiences) and also through increased linguistic skill (pun or outrageous contradiction).

Younger children are often unaware that they have not understood a message but from 6 onwards their critical listening skills improve considerably. For example, by the time they enter school, children's understanding of what is said is very literal. Over the course of a few years this will change. Sarcasm is lost on preschool children but begins to be understood by school-age children. Ten- and eleven-year-olds can readily identify it and relate to it.

**Reflect**

I was told at teacher training college never to use sarcasm with my pupils – but I did! I did use gentle (and sometimes not-so-gentle) sarcasm when I knew my pupil and I had a shared understanding that I was meaning the opposite of what I was saying. Of course perhaps this was more like irony than any attempt to wound the child, but it was often the most effective way of getting over my message. Surely, 'Smashing to see you on time again, John' is more effective than 'John, you are late'? – but I'm willing to be persuaded. Are there times when we shouldn't use sarcasm with children?

**Metalinguistic awareness** is the ability to know that language is a system of communication. This is evident quite early in childhood. By age 4, children already know that word labels are arbitrary, and by age 5 they have a good sense of the concept of what words are. This ability improves so that in the school years they manipulate language through puns, riddles and metaphors. Such ability allows thinking about how their own language can be best used in communication. It is a sophisticated level of language awareness and develops when language becomes more automatic to them. This ability has uses in a classroom context. When a teacher of 6-year-olds says to her especially noisy class, 'Gosh, you are very quiet today', many children of this age will be able to detect that the literal meaning is incorrect, either through her intonation and/or the context at the time, and many will recognise that the teacher in fact means the opposite.

**Metalinguistic awareness**
An ability to know about language and its characteristics as a system.

## When things go wrong with language

Although word articulation and syntax develop for individual children at different rates, when there is a significant delay to children achieving the milestones for language (see Table 10.2) this signals possible difficulties ahead. Specialist services such as those of a speech and language therapist may be able to correct difficulties if these are identified early on. Problems are in two forms. Firstly, speech disorders which range from being unable to articulate the '*r*' sound and the '*w*' sound to stuttering and stammering, which becomes evident in children between 2 and 4 years. Secondly, an inability to receive language input correctly or to express

**Table 10.2** Milestones in language acquisition and development

| Age | Language milestones |
|---|---|
| At birth | • Perceives speech of others<br>• Shows preference for human voices<br>• Cries frequently, showing some pitch variations |
| 1–6 months | • Cries become differentiated to indicate different needs<br>• Makes cooing and gurgling sounds. Greater range of vocal sounds now possible<br>• Listening skills greatly improved<br>• Laughs at things he/she finds amusing<br>• Recognises own name |
| 6–12 months | • Hearing developed to be able to locate sound sources with some accuracy<br>• Understands 'no'<br>• Babbling ('ba-ba-ba') that includes different vowel–consonant combinations<br>• Says ma-ma or da-da without meaning<br>• Tries to communicate by actions or gestures<br>• Tries to mimic sounds<br>• Utterances are recognisable as speech<br>• Enjoys 'language' games with adults |
| 12–24 months | • Achieves first word – may be earlier!<br>• Answers simple questions non-verbally<br>• Uses one-word 'sentences' (by 18 months)<br>• May form two-word 'sentences' (by 24 months) to label a person or object or 'more milk'<br>• Vocabulary of 4–6 words grows to 50 words – pronunciation not always clear<br>• Asks for common foods by name<br>• Makes animal sound like 'moo'<br>• Uses pronouns such as 'mine'<br>• Repeats words of interest<br>• 'Naming explosion'<br>• Increases participation and enjoyment in language games |
| 2–3 years | • Use of *what* questions<br>• Knows some spatial concepts such as *in* and *on*<br>• Knows pronouns: *you, me, her*<br>• Knows descriptive words: *big, happy*<br>• Uses question inflexion<br>• Uses plurals<br>• Forms three-word 'sentences' that include a verb |
| 3–5 years | • Easily copes with sentences of 4–5 words<br>• Increased use of pragmatics of language<br>• Applies language rules in everyday speech<br>• Overregularises<br>• Uses prepositions, negatives and imperatives<br>• Increased use of why questions |
| 5–8 years | • Understands time sequences (what happens/ed first, second, third, etc.)<br>• Carries out a series of three directions<br>• Understands and creates rhyming<br>• Engages in full conversation<br>• Uses more complex syntax in sentences (can be eight or more words in length)<br>• Uses compound and complex sentences<br>• Describes objects<br>• Uses imagination to create stories<br>• Applies pragmatics of language<br>• Develops metalinguistic awareness<br>• Has a vocabulary of 1000–2000 words on entering school which increases steadily<br>• Has enhanced understanding of metaphor and humour<br>• Learns to read and write |

oneself. The range here embraces children with hearing impairments, children with dyslexia, and elective mutes: those children who choose not to speak at all.

Aphasia is the term for language loss. This is a disruption in the ability to understand or produce spoken language. Children with damage to the lower left frontal lobe or Broca's area are shown as having difficulties in producing language . . . speak . . . ing . . . very . . . slow . . . ly . . . like . . . this. The effect is disjointed and lacking in sentence structure and grammar. 'Broca's aphasia' is caused by damage to the front of the temporal lobe and shows difficulties in language formation. Language that appears fluent but can have no meaning at all is caused by 'Wernicke's aphasia'. Situated between the visual cortex and Wernicke's area is the *angular gyrus*. This interprets visual information such as print into sounds and sends this data to Wernicke's area. Difficulties encountered by some children (and adults) are believed to arise in the angular gyrus where problems in segmenting words into sounds are encountered in a condition called dyslexia (Sumner *et al.*, 2013). It is estimated that between 4 per cent and 10 per cent of children are dyslexic and their difficulties range from poor word recognition, decoding and spelling to the retrieval of phonological information from long-term memory, perhaps stemming from deficits in speech perception or production. This has led to a proposal that the condition be defined as a core phonological deficit where it is recognised that poor phonology is related to underperformance in reading, regardless of cognitive ability. The *Policy, Research and Praxis* feature below provides a summary of current thinking in the UK about boys' underachievement in reading. After the feature we move on to look at milestones in language acquisition.

**Connect and Extend**

For an excellent summary of research and professional practice, read: Müller, P. (2012). The impediment that cannot say its name: Stammering and trauma in selected American and British texts. *Anglia – Zeitschrift Für Englische Philologie, 130*(1), 54–74.

**Aphasia**
The loss of ability to understand or express speech, owing to brain damage.

**Dyslexia**
A brain-based abnormal difficulty with reading and spelling, not explained as a general learning difficulty.

## Policy, Research and Praxis

### Closing the gender gap in boys' reading

The issue of boys underachieving in reading is a long-established trend in this country and internationally. A study involving 31 European countries into the impact on the acquisition of reading skills for 3–15-year-olds found that boys were one of the groups at risk of low achievement (EURYDICE, 2011). In schools in England, girls outperform boys on all National Curriculum reading tests. By age 7, the gap between boys and girls is already well established and continues to widen through to GCSE (Clark with Burke, 2012).

Data shows that the gender gap in reading enjoyment and reading frequency is also widening. Three out of four (76 per cent) UK schools are concerned about boys' underachievement in reading. There is still no government strategy to address the issue. In 2011 an estimated 60,000 boys failed to reach the expected level in reading at age 11 (Boys Reading Commission, 2012). The Commission report highlights that the 'reading gender gap' is widening and calls for action to be taken in homes, schools and communities.

Research has found that 1 young person in 3 does not have books of their own (33.2 per cent). Girls are more likely than boys to have their own books (7 in 10 girls compared with 6 in 10 boys) (Clark *et al.*, 2011). Studies continue to show the importance of having access to books for literacy development and for children to enjoy reading for pleasure. Reading is a fundamental life skill. It is essential for personal and social fulfilment. Reading well is a basic requirement for the social and economic demands of twenty-first century society (EURYDICE, 2011). Given its importance, what are the reasons for this gap and what can be done?

Three main causes can be identified. Firstly, at home, girls are more likely to be bought books and taken to the library. Mothers are more likely to support and role model reading, whereas male reading role models are often absent at home. Secondly, teachers' knowledge of attractive reading material for boys is often limited and boys may not be given the opportunity to develop as readers by experiencing reading for pleasure. The third reason is that male gender identities do not value reading as a mark of success. Peer pressure exerts a negative influence on boys who read (*ibid.*). There is no magic-bullet solution but successful strategies can also support girls who are disengaged or struggling. The Boys' Commission recommends:

- Schools should have access to an evidence framework to support boys' reading.
- Every child should be supported in school to develop as readers, including reading for enjoyment.
- Teachers should have an up-to-date knowledge of reading materials that will appeal to disengaged boys.
- Parents should be involved.
- Libraries should target children (particularly boys) least likely to be supported in their reading at home.
- Social marketing should be deployed to encourage parents to support boys' literacy.
- Every boy should have weekly support from a male reading role model.
- Parenting initiatives must specifically support literacy and fathers.
- A cross-government approach to literacy needs to be developed and coordinated.

The gender gap in reading is certainly a complex issue but one that urgently needs tackling.

Although it is possible as with other areas of development to ascribe ages to the achievement of language milestones, it is important to appreciate the substantial variation among individuals. However, knowing these milestones will help identify potential language difficulties such as dyslexia. Table 10.2 charts these milestones.

## Summary 2

Before moving on, let's summarise what we have learned in the middle section of this chapter:

- The sequence of language development is similar across societies and follows a recognisable pattern:
  - 0–12 months – pre-linguistic stage characterised by 'pseudo-conversations': smiles, sounds and body movements; protodeclarative and proto-imperative gestures; infants discriminating between and categorising similar sounds, and mimicking them in baby babble, first as echolalia and then patterned speech.
  - 1–2 years – first words which include *the naming explosion*, social greetings and holophrases (single word 'sentences'). Children acquire a vocabulary of 200 plus words by *fast mapping* and/or *syntactic boot strapping*, but mistakes occur because of overextension (doggie is applied to all small four-legged animals) and underextension (fish not considered to be animals).
  - 2–3 years – the first sentences appear where 3–4 word utterances using *telegraphic speech* are common. Themes become evident: actions like *'me stand'*; locations like *'cat in house'*; keeping possession, like *'mummy car'*; repetition *'gain'*, *'gain'*; and (dis)appearance, for example, the phrase *'doggie gone'*. Mistakes include overregularisation, e.g. 'go' becomes *'goed'*.
  - 3–5 years and onwards – children's vocabulary increases to an impressive 1000 words. Tenses now exist for the first time, *'I banged a drum'* and fully formed questions like *'Where is my cup?'* The 'w' questions of *why, what, when, where* are increasingly heard at this age, e.g. 'Why is the sky blue?'

- By the time children go to school they are aware of the need to adjust their language to the listener, and discerning intention and interpretation have to be learned. They use metaphor, humour and can identify sarcasm, developing metalinguistic awareness to manipulate language.

- Although word articulation and syntax develop for individual children at different rates, when there is a significant delay to children achieving the milestones for language, this signals possible problems ahead.

- Aphasia is the term for language loss: disruption in the ability to understand or produce spoken language. Teachers and others need to be aware of unreasonable developmental delay and disruption, as speech and language therapists may be able to correct difficulties if these are identified early on.

# Language development – different contexts and different forms

## Bilingualism: learning and speaking two languages

Multilingualism in early years and school settings is the norm nowadays. Parents might speak a different language at home, and exposure to television and the World Wide Web increases children's exposure to more than one language. The European Union encourages its citizens to learn other European languages, and since 1 January 2007 the number of its official working languages has risen to 23. In addition there are over 60 regional minority languages spoken in its countries. Modern languages are included in the secondary-school curriculum in England, and since 2010 all children aged 7–11 have the opportunity to learn another language. In England and Wales, the National Languages Strategy sets out the vision for increasing the nation's language potential and views it as 'a lifelong skill to be used in business and for pleasure, to open up avenues of communication and exploration, and to promote, encourage and instil a broader cultural understanding' (DfES, 2002b, p 5). Increasingly, many children in our schools can converse in two languages and are required to speak with one language in the home and another in school. A person who is fluent in two languages is **bilingual**.

**Bilingual**
Fluency in two languages.

The term refers either to acquiring two languages together from the outset (simultaneous bilingualism) or to learning a second after the first language has been mastered (successive bilingualism). It is sometimes said that the older you are, the more difficult it is to learn another or a new language. One reason why adults may have such difficulties with learning a second language is the lessening of plasticity in the mature adult brain; the connections have become hard-wired. Therefore, the task of learning another language in addition is made not impossible but considerably more difficult. Learning a new language involves the same areas of the brain as those that are responsible for making our first sounds, but the key word here is *learning*. Below about the age of 5, the area of the brain responsible for speech and for grammar (Broca region) is shared between the two or more languages being used. Young children process different languages as if they were one language: they do not discriminate between words of different languages. When learning a language after this time, this area divides and separates so that other regions of the brain are used for the learning function. Thus, learning languages at an early age facilitates the learning of a second language more easily. For children who are simultaneous bilinguals, refinement in both languages comes from the brain's wiring and the opportunities to hear and use both languages. If a child's parents speak two different

• • • • • • • • • • • • • • • •
### Connect and Extend
This study reports tension between children's use of the home language and reluctance to use it in a primary school setting. Read: Pagett, L. (2006). Mum and Dad prefer me to speak Bengali at home. *Literacy*, *40*, 137–145.
• • • • • • • • • • • • • • • •

**Code switching**
The ability of a bilingual child to switch comprehension and output from one language to the other depending on their audience.

**Bilingual education**
Educational programmes that teach two languages simultaneously.

languages the child must decide which language to converse in when talking to each parent, although may use words in one language when speaking to another in a process known as code switching because both sets of words retain meaning.

Clearly, there are educational implications for children learning two languages. One advantage is that it assists with cognitive advancement (Kenner, 2008). It has been found to enhance reading skills (Cummine & Boliek, 2013), and the well-known psychologist Laura Berk states that 'the benefits of being bilingual are so significant that goals of schooling should aim to make all children bilingual through systematic bilingual education and thus foster the cognitive, language and cultural enrichment of the nation' (2012, p 388). Yet, if the benefits are so significant, why are Berk's views not universally held? Are there drawbacks and disadvantages to learning more than one language at an early age?

In the last decade of the twentieth century being bilingual was regarded as the reason for language delay in some children and for difficulties that migrant children experienced in language learning. The evidence indicated that below $2^{1}/_{2}$ years the vocabulary of mono- and bilingual children are about the same (Pearson *et al.*, 1993). However at 5 years, the mother-tongue vocabulary of children learning two or more languages is smaller than that of monolingual children (Gupta, 1997). The good news is that this gap soon closes and the bilingual children catch up. It has also been found more recently that there was a tie between toddlers learning two languages (simultaneous bilingualism) and improved development in grammatical competence (Conboy & Thal, 2006). Is the situation the same for other literacy skills? Are there advantages or indeed disadvantages for learning writing in being able to converse in a second language? The *Focus on Theory* feature below considers this issue.

## Focus on Theory

### Writing and bilingualism

In *Could they do better? The writing of advanced bilingual learners of English at Key Stage 2* (Office for Standards in Education, 2005), bilingual pupils are defined as those who have had all/most of their education in the United Kingdom, whose English oracy is indistinguishable from that of pupils with English as their first language, but whose writing shows features related to their language background.

This report draws upon growing evidence that advanced bilingual learners do not achieve their full potential in UK primary schools. The research was undertaken to complement other recent research that identified features of language in which pupils learning English as an Additional Language (EAL) were less confident than peers who had English as their first language (Cameron & Besser, 2004).

In 2004, Her Majesty's Inspectors (HMI), the governmental body which at the time officially monitored educational standards in England and Wales, visited 21 primary schools in 18 local education authorities in England to carry out the research. There were two criteria for school selection: schools needed to demonstrate good or improving standards of attainment in writing for pupils across the schools and by minority ethnic pupils, and that staff understood issues relating to writing and the particular needs of advanced bilingual learners. Data from standardised test results revealed that, in comparison with learners of similar ability, minority ethnic pupils were underachieving in writing. The pattern was evident across the primary-age range but was more marked for pupils aged 7–11 (Key Stage 2). This suggested that some schools may underestimate the potential of able pupils with EAL and that bilingual learners might be disadvantaged as their oracy masks a need for writing support. Methods of data collection were varied and comprised classroom observation, scrutiny of pupils' writing, discussion with pupils and the English co-ordinator and school senior management, documentation reviews and the analysis of performance data of minority ethnic pupils. The report identified the following key findings:

- All schools valued pupils' linguistic diversity but only half the sample took steps to build upon this in teaching writing.
- Only a small percentage of schools were sufficiently aware of the improvement needs of advanced bilingual learners in writing.
- Few school policies were explicit about pupil writing needs in early and advanced stages of language acquisition.
- Two-thirds of the schools had achievement needs for bilingual pupils that were too low.
- Specialist staff were used in only half of the schools.
- Effective provision included environments that were rich in literacy. Two-thirds of schools gave adequate attention to pupils' experiences or set realistic contexts for writing.
- Bilingual learners benefited from speaking and listening to other pupils, from whom they developed confidence, organised their ideas and increased their vocabulary.

In concluding, the research team made a list of recommendations for future work in schools that prioritises the need for schools to be more aware of the needs of bilingual pupils. These findings support other research findings that bilingual learners are underachieving in writing in the latter primary years in UK schools. Why might this be? Well, perhaps there is also bound to be a cultural difference between children who speak other languages at home and those who speak only English both at home and at school. Writing ability is surely influenced by depth of experience of the culture of English as well as by more technical knowledge and skills.

**Family literacy**
The term referring to the interrelated literacy practices of parents, children and others at home, and the educational programmes that recognise the family dimension for children's literacy learning.

**Emergent literacy**
The way in which children construct literary knowledge by means of their everyday experiences.

• • • • • • • • • • • • • • • • •
**Connect and Extend**
For results which highlight the importance of phonological processing abilities (PPA), read: Anthony, J., Williams, J., McDonald, R. & Francis, D. (2007). Phonological processing and emergent literacy in younger and older preschool children. *Annals of Dyslexia, 57,* 113–137.
• • • • • • • • • • • • • • • • •

## Literacy (reading and writing)

The advantages of exposing children to rich oral language in the home from an early age is unequivocal, and supported throughout the research, professional and educational literature. Family literacy (Nutbrown, 2006) that includes parent-to-child conversations, children experimenting with words and rhythms, listening to and telling stories and having opportunities to develop language in pretend play, provides important building blocks for children's future literacy.

The past 20 years, certainly in the United Kingdom, have seen a shift away from the focus on oracy and story-telling as a key feature of early education to emergent literacy that includes meaningful literacy (i.e. reading and writing) activities in the school curriculum which reflect children's familiar experiences. Writing is a skill that parallels children's development of reading. Of the two activities, writing is by far the more difficult for children to acquire proficiency in. Why? For one thing there are the mechanics of holding a tool and moving it with proficiency on a page. Feedback is less immediate than with conversation, and rules of grammar, spelling and punctuation are clearly more tested in writing than speaking (Knoch, 2011).

Success with reading offers many advantages. Children in the majority of industrialised countries are surrounded by print: written symbols are everywhere in books, signs, labels on the food we eat, text on the television. It is therefore no surprise that preschool children's understanding of the structures of written language (eye-scanning

Encouraging a joy of reading with young children.
Source: © Pearson Education Ltd / Jules Selmes.

The phonics approach advocates teaching children to read by teaching them to connect sounds with letters or groups of letters.

*Source*: © Pearson Education Ltd / Jules Selmes.

**Connect and Extend**

For a review of the 'great debate or reading wars' over basic skills approach versus whole-language approach, read: Do children who acquire word reading without explicit phonics employ compensatory learning? Thompson, G.; McKay, M., Fletcher-Flinn, C., Connelly, V., Kaa, R. & Ewing, J. (2008). Issues of phonological recoding, lexical orthography, and fluency. *Reading and Writing*, July, *21*(5), 505–537.

direction, words as separate items of text) is quite advanced and precedes their learning to read or write. However, there are several different ways in which children's understanding of literacy differs from that of adults. To preschoolers, single letters can stand for whole words. They are yet to discover that letters are parts of words that are linked to sounds. Common to this age group is a reliance on sounds in letters (LAFNT is 'elephant' or a favourite: tewingm) and to learn later that letters can have more than one sound (e.g. 'a' in mat and 'a' in face). By about 8 years, practice and appropriate comprehensive strategies improve decoding and comprehensive skills so that a shift from learning to read to reading to learn occurs.

What is considered the best approach to teach reading? We know that school-age children make use of a variety of strategies to help them decode print – such as sounding words out, working it out from the context or asking the teacher or adult to tell them (Siegler, 1996), but what is the best way to teach reading? The debate on which is the better approach – sometimes referred to as 'the reading wars' – rages on. Advocates of a basic skills approach champion the use of phonics, which involves teaching children to connect sounds with letters, or groups of letters. Children are systematically taught to blend the sounds of letters together to produce approximate pronunciations of unknown words. The skills are practised in graduated reading materials that begin by decoding simple sounds and progress steadily to more complex reading materials in a highly structured way.

In opposition, supporters of a 'whole-language approach' claim a child-centred approach and argue vehemently that children learn to read best by exposure to text in complete form. This includes poems, lists and stories as these forms of text motivate children and encourage them to appreciate language in real-life activities.

What does the research tell us? There was some early strong support that a mixing of both methods is preferable, especially introducing the holistic approach early and then progressing on with phonics (Pressley *et al.*, 2001; Jeynes & Littell, 2000). However, decoding and building up sounds allow children to see relationships between letters and sounds that they can make use of with words they have not seen before. It is argued that when this process becomes automatic it frees up working memory to assist with higher-order comprehension processes. Yet it is also argued that the whole-language approach stimulates interest because reading is promoted as a relevant and realistic experience.

In England, a national independent review into the teaching of reading (Rose, 2006) recommended that systematic phonic work should be taught discretely as this is considered the most effective approach for decoding (reading) and encoding (writing and spelling). Although many academics and classroom practitioners do not disagree with the recommendations in the report, many dispute that a phonics approach should be the only approach to teach reading. However, and on balance, we think that a phonics-based approach to the teaching of reading works better for the majority of children and so we now present five research-based elements of reading and eight building blocks of phonemic awareness.

## The five elements of reading

The whole-language approach claims that children learn to read best by reading poems and stories.

*Source*: © Pearson Education Ltd / Ian Wedgewood.

These five elements of reading are defined by teacher-educator Bonnie Armbruster and her colleagues (2001):

1. 'Phonemic Awareness is the ability to hear, identify and manipulate the individual sounds – phonemes – in spoken words' (p 4).

2. 'Phonics is the understanding that there is a predictable relationship between phonemes (the sounds of spoken language) and graphemes (the letters and spellings that represent those sounds in written language)' (p 4).

3. 'Vocabulary refers to the words we must know to communicate effectively. In general, vocabulary can be described as oral vocabulary or reading vocabulary. Oral vocabulary refers to words that we use in speaking or recognise in listening. Reading vocabulary refers to words we recognise or use in print' (p 34).

4. 'Fluency is the ability to read a text accurately and quickly. When fluent readers read silently, they recognise words automatically. They group words quickly to help them gain meaning from what they read. Fluent readers read aloud effortlessly and with expression. Their reading sounds natural, as if they are speaking' (p 22).

5. 'Comprehension is the reason for reading. If readers can read the words but do not understand what they are reading, they are not really reading' (p 48).

The five elements of reading are and should be taught concurrently. However, we would argue that phonemic awareness does support the teaching and learning of the other elements and the ability to spell. In Table 10.3 we present the building blocks of phonemic awareness.

**Connect and Extend**
Mums and dads reading to their very young children is important! What evidence is there? Read: Fletcher, K., Cross, J., Tanney, A., Schneider, M. & Finch, W. (2008). Predicting language development in children at risk: The effects of quality and frequency of caregiver reading. *Early Education & Development, 19*, 89–111.

**Reflect** Do you remember learning to read? Which do you consider the best strategy for teaching reading in order to meet children's individual needs and to promote reading? What evidence do you have to defend this viewpoint?

**Table 10.3** The building blocks of phonemic awareness

| | Description | Example |
| --- | --- | --- |
| **Phoneme isolation** | Helping children recognise individual sounds in a word | Adult: 'What's the first sound in *fit*?' Child: 'The first sound is /f/' |
| **Phoneme identity** | Recognising the same sound in different words | Adult: 'What sound is the same in *sit, sun,* and *sand*?' Child: 'The first sound is the same. The first sound is /s/' |
| **Phoneme categorisation** | Recognising that one word in a sequence of words is different from the others | Adult: 'Which word doesn't belong – *fall, fan, bug*?' Child: '*Bug*. It doesn't begin with /f/' |
| **Phoneme blending** | Listening to a sequence of separately spoken phonemes and combining them to form a word | Adult: 'What word is /s/ /i/ /t/?' Child: '/s/ /i/ /t/ is sit' |
| **Phoneme segmentation** | Breaking a word into its separate sounds and saying each sound while tapping out or counting the sounds | Adult: 'How many sounds do you hear in *drum*?' Child: '/d/ /r/ /u/ /m/. There are four sounds' |
| **Phoneme deletion** | Recognising the word that remains when a phoneme is removed | Adult: 'What is *train* without the /t/?' Child: '*Train* without the /t/ is rain' |
| **Phoneme addition** | Making a new word by adding a phoneme to another word | Adult: 'What word do you have if you add /s/ to *mile*?' Child: '*Smile*' |
| **Phoneme substitution** | Substituting one phoneme for another to make a new word | Adult: 'The word is *run*. Change the /n/ to /g/. What's the new word?' Child: '*Rug*' |

*Source:* Adapted from Armbruster, B. B., Lehr, F. & Osborn, J. (2001). *Put reading first: The research building blocks for teaching children to read.* Washington, DC: National Institute for Literacy (**www.nifl.gov/nifl/publications.html**).

As we mentioned earlier, a literacy-rich home environment is great preparation for reading and writing, especially so for children in economically disadvantaged homes (Van Steensel, 2006). We would also argue that parents and other carers should be made aware of the *five elements of reading* and particularly the *eight building blocks of phonemic awareness* (see nearby *Connect and Extend* and Table 10.3) so that reading stories at home and in other care settings can be even more purposeful and worthwhile. What other factors apply? There is a good deal of recent evidence that British boys are lagging behind girls, particularly when it comes to literacy (Carrington & McPhee, 2008; Montgomery, 2008; Lindsay & Muijs, 2006; Francis, 2006). Indeed, concerns about the literacy attainments of boys are considered an important area of government concern.

## Summary 3

We now summarise what you have learned in the final section of this chapter:

- Increasingly, many children in our schools can converse in two (or more) languages and are required to speak with one language in the home and another in school.

- Learning a new language involves the same areas of the brain as those that are responsible for making our first sounds.

- Young children process different languages as if they were one language: they do not discriminate between words of different languages.

- Young simultaneous bilinguals use code switching to swap effortlessly from one language to another.

- The advantages of exposing children to rich oral language in the home (family literacy) from an early age is unequivocal, and supported throughout the research, professional and educational literature.

- There has been a shift away from the focus on oracy and story-telling as a key feature of early education to emergent literacy that includes meaningful literacy (i.e. reading and writing) activities in which children construct literary knowledge by means of their everyday experiences.

- Advocates of a basic-skills approach to teaching reading champion the use of phonics, which involves teaching children to connect sounds with letters, or groups of letters.

- In opposition, supporters of a whole-language approach claim a child-centred approach and argue vehemently that children learn to read best by exposure to text in complete form.

- The five elements of reading are phonemic awareness, phonics, vocabulary, fluency and comprehension.

- The eight building blocks of phonemic awareness are isolation, identity, categorisation, blending, segmentation, deletion, addition and substitution.

- Writing is a skill that parallels children's development of reading. Of the two activities, writing is by far the more difficult for children to acquire proficiency.

- Currently in the United Kingdom there are concerns about attainment in literacy, particularly that of boys who appear to be lagging behind the girls, but school inspectors and government advisers have identified strategies to improve boys' performance in writing.

# Conclusion

Remember in the anecdote at the start of the chapter when I said to my son Tom, 'Mind your language, young man', when he complained (with associated expletives) that every lesson at school was a writing lesson. It is true and widely accepted, even by Tom, that almost all learning is language-based and that in a child's life acquiring language is rated at the top of the list of important developmental milestones. Cognitive and language development are closely associated, and the ability to communicate is one of the surest ways we have to assess how well children are developing in more general terms. Our message is clear to all those who aspire to teach and support the learning of young children: 'Mind their language and mind it well!', just as the staff at The Chestnut Nursery were right to give special attention to the language development of the children on 'red day'.

We have traced the predictable course of language development that begins in the pre-linguistic stage with 'pseudo-conversations' between child and adult that comprise smiles, sounds and body movements. Later there is cooing and babbling and the first words appear after 10 months or so. A naming explosion takes place between 12 and 18 months, so much so that by 18 months, two-word sentences appear and by 24 months, three and four-word utterances are common. By five years, children's vocabulary has increased to 1000 words, and they can confidently converse and use more complex sentences, display an understanding of formal grammar rules and principles and develop metalinguistic awareness. Metalinguistic ability improves throughout the school years in that children are increasingly able to manipulate language through puns, riddles and metaphors, and use more complex linguistic structures.

Language development depends upon interrelated literacy practices of parents, children and others taking place in homes and educational programmes. In this chapter we have highlighted the importance of the family dimension in children's literacy learning, as early exposure to rich oral language from an early age is well supported in the research and educational literature. The importance of a rich literary home environment as preparation for reading and writing in schools is well documented and is especially so for children in economically disadvantaged homes.

In the final chapters we deal with the affective domains of development, emotions, personality, and children's social and moral development. We will begin with the development of personality: to explore temperament and the 'big five' personality types; to appreciate the link between emotions and cognition in the development of self-knowledge and understanding of emotions in other people; and to know how important personal attachments are formed. For now and before moving on, we suggest you review the questions about language development we asked at the beginning of this chapter using the *Summary Table* that follows.

## Summary Table
### Language Development

### What is language and why is it so important? (pp 294–298)

Becoming proficient with spoken language is one of a child's most significant developmental milestones. Language is an organised system of symbols, movements and sounds to communicate with others, according to a set of agreed rules for the oral, written or signed forms.

Non-verbal communication (NVC) refers to the types of communication that do not involve speech. Six features of NVC have been identified: gesture; body contact; posture; proxemics; gaze; and facial expressions. In some circumstances up to 93 per cent of 'messages received and understood' can be attributed to NVC. There are four components to language: phonology, semantics, grammar and pragmatics.

# Theories of language acquisition
(pp 298–305)

## Is language innate or learned? (pp 298–302)

Psychologist B. F. Skinner stated that one way in which learning takes place is through operant conditioning when behaviours are repeated and learned by being either rewarded or punished. Children use words that are positively reinforced by parents and significant others who then gradually shape children's speech to mould it into adult-like communication. Social learning theory (Bandura, 1989b) proposes that learning occurs indirectly through observational learning. Children listen to how others around them talk and, in doing so, observe the complexities in their phrases, and rules and conventions they use in conversation – and imitate these.

In contrast to the above views, the nativist approach favours biological pre-programming, which argues that language is not learned but innate, emerging naturally through the maturation process. Nativism was pioneered by linguist and philosopher Noam Chomsky, who asserted that because all languages are made up of structures of nouns, verbs and adjectives, the ability to learn and produce language is innate. Steve Pinker, building on Chomsky's notion of an innate language acquisition device that guides our learning of language proposed that language is universal. In his book *The Language Instinct* he supports this view saying that children 'actually reinvent' and learn language 'because they just can't help it'.

Interactionist theorists (e.g. Jerome Bruner) stress the language acquisition support system available to infants in which parents and others use scaffold learning by expanding and recasting baby babble and mimicked primitive words.

## Language and the maturing brain (pp 302–304)

The equipotentiality hypothesis proposes that both sides of the brain may be equally geared to language development, but the left side shows specialisation for language and in the newborn is the side which is responsive to human speech. The growing brain allocates areas in the left rear (Wernicke's area) to activities that involve word meaning and areas in the left front (Broca's area) for processing word formation and grammar.

Other evidence that language capacity is hard-wired into our brains is found in the brain's plasticity (e.g. ability to self-organise after damage) and the idea of 'critical periods' during which certain experiences need to be perceived (e.g. the difference between *l* and *r*) or the capacity is lost. It is the quality of early experiences that have the most effect on linguistic capacity. Children who are talked with early, have a larger vocabulary and tend to score higher on IQ tests.

# The development of language (pp 305–315)

## The sequence of language development
(pp 306–311)

The developmental sequence of language development is similar across societies and follows a recognisable pattern:

- 0–12 months – pre-linguistic stage characterised by 'pseudo-conversations': smiles, sounds and body movements; protodeclarative and proto-imperative gestures; infants discriminating between and categorising similar sounds, and mimicking them in baby babble, first as echolalia and then patterned speech.

- 1–2 years – first words which include the naming explosion, social greetings and holophrases (single word 'sentences'). Children acquire a vocabulary of 200 plus words by fast mapping and/or syntactic boot strapping but mistakes occur because of overextension ('doggie' is applied to all small four-legged animals) and underextension (fish not considered to be animals).

- 2–3 years – the first sentences appear where three or four word utterances using telegraphic speech are common. Themes become evident: actions like *'me stand'*; locations like *'cat in house'*; keeping possession, like *'mummy car'*; repetition *'gain'*, *'gain'*; and (dis)appearance, for example, the phrase *'doggie gone'*. Mistakes include overregularisation, e.g. 'go' becomes *'goed'*.

- 3–5 years and onwards – children's vocabulary increases to an impressive 1000 words. Tenses now exist for the first time, *'I banged a drum'*, and fully formed questions like 'Where *is* my cup?' The 'w' questions of *why, what, when, where* are increasingly heard at this age, e.g. 'Why is the sky blue?'

By the time children go to school they are aware of the need to adjust their language to the listener, and discerning intention and interpretation have to be learned. They use metaphor and humour, can identify sarcasm, and continue to develop metalinguistic awareness to manipulate language.

## When things go wrong with language (pp 311–314)

Although word articulation and syntax develop for individual children at different rates, any unreasonable delay to children achieving the milestones for language signals possible developmental delay in some form. Aphasia is the term for language loss: disruption in the ability to understand or produce spoken language. Teachers and others need to be aware of unreasonable developmental delay and disruption, as speech and language therapists may be able to correct difficulties if these are identified early on.

## Language development – different contexts and different forms (pp 315–320)

### Bilingualism: learning and speaking two languages (pp 315–317)

Increasingly, many children in our schools can converse in two (or more) languages and are required to speak with one language in the home and another in school. Learning a new language involves the same areas of the brain as those that are responsible for making our first sounds, so young children process different languages as if as they were one language: they do not discriminate between words of different languages. Young simultaneous bilinguals use code switching to swap effortlessly from one language to another.

### Literacy (reading and writing) (pp 317–318)

The advantages of exposing children to rich oral language in the home (family literacy) from an early age are unequivocal and supported throughout the research, professional and educational literature. There has been a shift away from the focus on oracy and story-telling as a key feature of early education to emergent literacy that includes meaningful literacy (i.e. reading and writing) activities in which children construct literary knowledge by means of their everyday experiences.

Advocates of a basic-skills approach to teaching reading champion the use of phonics, which involves teaching children to connect sounds with letters, or groups of letters in opposition. Supporters of a whole-language approach claim a child-centred approach and argue vehemently that children learn to read best by exposure to text in complete form.

### The five elements of reading (pp 318–320)

The five elements of reading are phonemic awareness, phonics, vocabulary, fluency and comprehension and the eight building blocks of phonemic awareness are isolation, identity, categorisation, blending, segmentation, deletion, addition and substitution. Writing is a skill that parallels children's development of reading. Of the two activities, writing is by far the more difficult for children to acquire proficiency. Currently in the United Kingdom there are concerns about attainment in literacy, particularly that of boys who appear to be lagging behind the girls but school inspectors and government advisers have identified strategies to improve boys' performance in writing.

. . . . . . . . . . . . . . . . . . . . . . . . . . . . . . . . . . . . . . . . . . . . . . . . . . . . . . . . . . . . . . . . . . . . . . . . . . . . . . . . . . . . . . . . . .

## Going further

Roskos, K. A., Tabors, P. O. & Lenhart, L. A. (2009) Oral language and early literacy in preschool: Talking, reading, and writing (Preschool Literacy Collection). 2nd revised edition. Toronto: International Reading Association.
Based on brain science, this useful and practical guide is authoritative and accessible to all who are interested in early language development.

Eide, B. L. & Eide. F. F. (2011) The dyslexic advantage: Unlocking the hidden potential of the dyslexic brain. London: Hay House.
Neuro-learning experts Drs Brock and Fernette Eide describe an exciting new brain science that reveals that people with dyslexia have unique brain structure and organisation.

Oates, J. & Grayson, A. (Eds) (2004) Cognitive and language development in children. Oxford: Blackwell.
This book gives a comprehensive and accessible account of how thinking and language develop during childhood.

It starts by considering cognition and language in infants and continues to weave together these two areas in subsequent chapters that cover aspects of their development through childhood.

Rumsey, J. M. (Ed) & Ernst, M. (Ed) (2009) Neuroimaging in developmental clinical neuroscience. Cambridge: Cambridge University Press.
This book will enable you to understand the mechanisms underlying basic language development, and become familiar with current knowledge and hypotheses concerning the neural bases of language disorders.

Tomasello, M. (2003) Constructing a language – A usage-based theory of language acquisition. Harvard, MA: Harvard University Press.
Up-to-date research with strong emphasis on the theories behind language acquisition.

# Useful websites

http://www.nhscareers.nhs.uk/explore-by-career/
allied-health-professions/careers-in-the-allied-
health-professions/speech-and-language-therapist/
This page describes the role of a speech and language
therapist. SLTs assist children (and adults) who have the
following types of problems: difficulty producing and using
speech; difficulty understanding language; difficulty using
language; difficulty with feeding, chewing or swallowing; a
stammer; a voice problem.

http://acecentre.org.uk/
ACE is a charity working with people of all ages who find
challenges in effective communication because of physical
impairment, language disorder or learning disability.

http://ec.europa.eu/public_opinion/archives/ebs/
ebs_243_en.pdf
Useful website on language and language learning within
the European Union. There is an excellent report with
two main themes: the long-term objective for all EU
citizens to speak two languages in addition to their mother
tongue and lifelong language learning starting from a very
early age.

http://www.literacytrust.org.uk
Website of the National Literacy Trust. Contains a treasury
of useful resources and articles.

# Chapter 11
## Emotions and Personality

# Introduction

So far in Part 3 of *Child Development: Theory and Practice 0–11* we have explored the themes and theories of childhood through two principal aspects of development, cognition and language. A recurrent theme of Chapters 9 and 10 was the importance of the family dimension to child development and this focus on early familial experiences will also hold true for our two remaining chapters, emotional and social development – but first a story.

*'Mum, Mum – I've been angry and surprised, but Miss said that I was the best at being disgusted'. Eight-year-old Lee scooted across the playground to where his mother waited with some of the other parents for the end of school. Mum paused in rocking the pram – holding Lee's complaining baby sister – to catch hold of a coat and lunch box thrust in her general direction. Lee buried his head under the pram sunshade and the little grumbles changed to giggles of happiness. What joy little Sarah and her brother found in each other's company and shared play! Lee's mother was intrigued. 'Go on then, why were you disgusted?' So on the way home Lee recounted what had happened that afternoon.*

*After lunch the class returned to their classroom to find that their teacher Madame Martine had placed an impressive looking top-hat on one of the tables. She explained that they were all going to play a game called Emotion Charades. The top hat – used as the 'choosing hat' in class – contained separate pieces of paper on which were written the name of an emotion: fear, happiness, anger, sadness, disgust, surprise. Madame Martine asked one of the children to pick out one of the pieces of paper and to act out the emotion while she read aloud a short four-line poem that expressed that emotion. The other children then had to guess what the emotion was. After several turns the class were split up into teams to continue the activity themselves by choosing an emotion and getting children in another team to guess it. The game concluded with Madame Martine reading more short poems to the whole group and asking the children to identify the emotions from her tone of voice, her expression and posture.*

*'Some of them were dead easy' boasted Lee to his mum, 'but there were a few tricky ones. Nobody got "dread" but Amy chose "excitement" – and we all thought she just wanted to go to the toilet!'*

Emotional maturity is an aspect of child development that is often overlooked. The attainment of milestones in other areas, such as motor skills and language tend to be diligently monitored by parents and medical practitioners but less attention is paid to important affective domains of childhood. Our emotions develop rapidly in childhood and form an integral part of our daily lives. They are a vital foundation on which are built all other mental skills, mostly through social interactions with those close to us and, like the relationship between Lee and his little sister in the story above, well before language is acquired. From birth, we display a range of emotions and can communicate our feelings to those around us. Consider the emotional expressions of a baby: peer over the cot and smile and you will often be rewarded with a beaming smile back. Go away, and the next moment that smiling face can instantly transform. Babies can change from happy and smiling little darlings to screaming bundles of woe in what seems like a split second, and parents soon learn to interpret different cries variously meaning hunger, boredom, loneliness, pain or discontentedness. Body language and, in particular, a child's facial expressions provide an accurate mirror of a child's emotional state, and, as we get older, while body language (non-verbal communication – Chapter 10) continues to reflect our inner feelings, we also use words and phrases to describe how we feel. Toddlers are able to express a much greater range of emotions than babies, and school-age children develop important skills of emotional regulation which are essential for social interactions, collaboration and co-operation in the classroom and playground.

This chapter begins by considering the nature of emotions and the theories that allow us to interpret our own feelings and the expressed emotions of others. We look at how emotions develop; the first emotions to appear and later more complex ones, and point out the milestones in this development. Later we introduce important concepts of emotional literacy and emotional

**Affective domains**
Aspects of development that are to do with feelings and emotions.

intelligence and show their practical application in the classroom. We then examine personal attachment and review its key theories before considering implications of personal attachments in relation to child-care and schooling. The final section in the chapter considers personality and temperament.

**Chapter Objectives**

By the time you have completed this chapter you should be able to answer the following questions:

- What are the main theories of emotional development?
- How do we learn to express our emotions and learn to understand the emotions of others?
- What is emotional intelligence?
- How do young children use social referencing?
- What are the theories of attachment?
- How do we judge the quality of attachment and what happens when things go wrong?
- What are the 'big five' personality types?
- How can temperament be linked to social, cultural and schooling contexts?
- What are the implications for teaching and learning of understanding the importance and processes of emotional development, personality and temperament?

# Understanding emotions

What then do we understand by emotions? In the opening story, a range of different emotions were acted out in a charade game and it is likely that it would be the extremes of physical behaviour on show! But emotions are more than just physical mechanisms to tell others how we are feeling. They are behaviours that direct our thinking and subsequent actions in response to events. When defining emotion it is common to include three components (for example, Saarni *et al.*, 2006b). Firstly, there is a *physiological* component. When our emotions run high, our hearts beat faster and we perspire. Secondly, there is an intellectual *subjective* component which allows us to judge our emotions (e.g. 'Today I feel happy'). Thirdly, there is an *expressive* component which communicates our feelings to others: obvious in facial displays of smiling, crying, frowning, and so on.

Development expert Michael Lewis (2002) writes that emotions and their development are tied to cognitive development. It is not simply learning by experience but thinking through understandings that have developed through experience. For example, imagine a toddler tottering towards an unguarded fire in a room. She receives a sharp instruction from a vigilant adult, 'Stop, don't go near that fire! It is hot!' Without having to feel the pain of the fire, the toddler builds thinking that will protect her: a base for future behaviour and learning. Of course emotions also influence present health and wellness. There is now general understanding that stress causes a range of health-related problems including raised heart rate and blood pressure, digestive problems, cardiovascular diseases and some cancers.

A study by Gunnar (2000) on infants adopted in Canada, previously exposed to acute stress from living in deprived circumstances in Romanian orphanages, found that children who spent longer in orphanage care had significantly high levels of cortisol (the stress hormone) and food-related disorders. Children's emotional development is predominantly about communicating feelings and learning to interpret the emotions of other people. In this sense, being able to express and control one's emotions is important for a child's well-being, social acceptance and success. For example, in order to make new friends, we must appear friendly and interested in other people, express happiness and use cues to interpret the emotions of other people.

## Theoretical approaches to understanding emotions

A quick tour of theoretical approaches to understanding emotional development reveals some differences. From a cognitive perspective, theorists such as Alan Sroufe (e.g. Sroufe *et al.*, 2007) link emotional development to children's developing understanding of the world. Sroufe argues that understanding is acquired through the development of mental representations or schemata (as discussed in Chapter 9 with particular reference to Piagetian theory). Take the example of the toddler and the fire above. After the warning, part of the toddler's schema of fire will now include 'something that people are anxious about' and 'hot'. As 'anxious' and 'hot' have particular meanings for the toddler, both are assimilated into 'fire' and give new meaning to 'fire'.

The maturational perspective takes the view that emotions are products of our biology. The social aspect of emotions is well illustrated in the early work of psychologist Paul Ekman in the early 1970s which revealed cross-cultural similarities in our facial expressions. Basic emotional expressions such as fear, happiness and anger have the same meaning across many cultures although some cultures overlay different display patterns and rules for the expressing or masking of emotions (Ekman, 1972). Similarly and in the same decade, clinical psychologist Carroll Izard's work argues that emotions are inborn and developed through adaptation (1979). Watch a very young baby react to a sharp taste like a lemon: the child will roll up her lips and wrinkle her nose at the unpleasant experience – not a learned response, rather it is innate. Advocates of this perspective argue that the timing of the first appearance of emotions is linked to cognitive development and the experiences that a child might have. This suggests some common ground between the two views, that certain emotions are shown by infants of a few months old and that they proceed in an ordered fashion, although there is disagreement as to when exactly certain emotions appear.

Theorists advocating a learning perspective emphasise that the interactions a child has with the environment that includes people account for emotional development. Take the example of a young child playing with his mother in the garden when a large and unfamiliar dog suddenly appears. The child observes the adult's response, which on this occasion might be one of fear. Later, the child will imitate and replicate the behaviour observed on that occasion and express a fear of dogs in similar circumstances. The emotion (i.e. fear) was prompted by a direct experience. Recently, the functionalist perspective (Saarni *et al.*, 2006a) combines features of the cognitive and learning perspectives by emphasising how actions are a function of emotions connected to experiences. Imagine the pride of a 9-year-old when asked to read out in a school assembly a poem she has written herself. The child finds the experience highly motivating, will want to share it with others and to later recall the emotions attached to her 'big moment'. A functional perspective maintains that the ways we respond to events such as this determine how much we wish to repeat the experience in future.

## Expressing emotions

From the foregoing description of four theoretical perspectives it can be argued that emotional development is a combination of biology and environment, the recurrent themes of 'nature and nurture'. We know that our emotions are universal and we have a long evolutionary history in which emotional behaviours have become gradually adapted to surroundings and circumstances.

• • • • • • • • • • • • • • • • • •
**Connect and Extend**

For an explanation of some baby facial expressions, read: Gil, S., Teissèdre, F., Chambres, P. & Droit-Volet, S. (2011). The evaluation of emotional facial expressions in early postpartum depression mood: A difference between adult and baby faces? *Psychiatry Research*, 186(2–3), 281–286.
• • • • • • • • • • • • • • • • • •

Happiness and surprise are two of the 'basic emotions' that are shown universally by infants.

*Source:* Stephanie Breen.

This idea accords with a dynamic systems perspective that supports how children adapt skills into more efficient systems as their goals and experiences alter (as discussed in Chapter 6). Emotions may be universal but can be expressed in different ways. Let's start with the very young.

Although we cannot precisely know how a baby is feeling, the best we can do is to judge those emotions which are expressed. Facial expressions provide reliable information on the emotional state of infants. The Maximally Discriminative Facial Movement system (MAX system) devised by Carroll Izard (1979) provides a still popular means of classifying emotional expression in young children by identifying facial movements and matching these to basic feelings.

What then are the **basic emotions** (or primary emotions)? There are six emotions which universally appear in children between 2 and 7 months and are predominantly observable in their facial expressions. These are:

- anger;
- disgust;
- fear;
- happiness;
- sadness;
- surprise.

Table 11.1 presents these six basic emotions and commonplace situations where and how these might be expressed.

**Basic emotions**
Anger, disgust, fear, happiness, sadness and surprise. These emotions emerge from about 2 months onwards. They are generally believed to have a biological foundation.

## The development of emotions

An infant's basic emotions at birth may be reduced simply to two main bipolar states: orientation to stimulation that is pleasurable, and withdrawal from stimulation that is not pleasurable.

**Table 11.1** The basic emotions and situations where these are observable

| Emotion | Situations where observable |
|---------|------------------------------|
| Anger | <ul><li>Removal of an object or toy</li><li>Brief separation from carer</li><li>Imposed nap times</li></ul> |
| Disgust | <ul><li>Getting rid of objects in the mouth</li><li>Response to unpleasant taste or smells</li><li>Later food preferences</li></ul> |
| Fear | <ul><li>Stranger anxiety</li><li>Unfamiliar settings</li><li>Falling</li></ul> |
| Happiness | <ul><li>Expressing delight in mastery of a skill</li><li>Encouraging immediate others to show affection</li><li>Bonding between infant and parent</li></ul> |
| Sadness | <ul><li>Showing a response to pain</li><li>When an object (or toy) is taken away</li><li>Separation</li></ul> |
| Surprise | <ul><li>New tastes</li><li>Loud noises</li><li>Changes in appearance</li></ul> |

Within a few months emotional expressions are differentiated further and the 'basic six' emotions of happiness, sadness, anger, fear, disgust and surprise are observable. Let us now examine each of these in more depth.

Happiness is evident by 3 months, although many parents report seeing a 'half smile' at birth. In response to gentle rocking movements to soothe, the softness of the mother's voice, to a full stomach after a feed and to calming sounds, a full smile is observed from 3 to 6 weeks. This is called the social smile. This smile is usually directed to the face of the mother, father or sibling, believed to be due to an in-built interest in the human face and is often accompanied by cooing sounds to show pleasure. Infants laugh at around 4–7 months, corresponding with an increase in their cognitive abilities to process information in their environment. A game of peek-a-boo between a parent and child at this age is sure to evoke smiling and laughter.

Sadness is not as commonly observed in infants as anger. It is observed usually when something they enjoy is taken away from them. Observe a mother playing with a child of this age, making eye contact, smiling and talking. The child responds well but the moment the mother turns her face away or gets up to leave, we see the expression of this emotion. It is frequently combined with the infant crying. Expressions of anger are not uncommon from 4 months onwards as infants react to different situations around them and become frustrated with events in these interactions. If you were to hold an infant's arms to the side of the child's body too long, you would be sure to trigger this response from the child! Such an expression of anger increases in intensity and frequency with age as young children acquire the capacity for intentioned behaviour and being able to control this emotion, and the effects of associated actions, will take time.

Disgust is readily seen as a response to some foods. This is a defensive reflex that makes the child spit out food that tastes unpleasant or turn away things that smell horrible. Surprise is seen in the first 6 months when expected events are changed. One early study observed the emotion when infants saw an undersized adult walking towards them when they might have been expecting a child or normal sized adult (Lewis & Brooks-Gunn, 1982) – the children were clearly not expecting to see this. Wariness as an early indicator of fear is evident by 3 months and becomes most apparent from about 6 months onwards. Its expression is certainly linked to developing knowledge because in order to be frightened there must be some comparison made to the 'fearful' event and another event. It is most common in stranger anxiety or the expression towards strangers they are not familiar with. As cognitive capacity increases, children are able to better discriminate between potentially threatening situations and the caring situations provided by parents and others. One example is Israeli infants raised in kibbutzim (co-operative settlements) where there was constant fear of terrorist attacks. Infant fear of strangers was more marked than in children raised elsewhere (Saarni et al., 2006b).

These are the six basic emotions, which we see evidence of in the first 6 months of an infant's life. Although there is some association with cognitive development at this age phase, this is mostly in terms of perceptual abilities and memory. The next set of emotions we meet requires more sophisticated cognition.

Late in the infant's second year what are termed complex emotions emerge. These are the emotions of embarrassment, shame, guilt, pride and jealousy and are often called the *self-conscious emotions*, owing to the association they have on the child's developing sense of self. Consciousness in terms of thought or action is not apparent until the latter months of a child's second year since it is linked to the development of intellectual faculties. You might remember that Piaget characterised this stage as a time when children are first able to make mental representations of themselves, and other people and events. The classic 'rouge test' (Amsterdam, 1972) confirms this link to cognitive development. The test requires a child to sit in front of a mirror for a brief period. A red dot is then placed on the child's nose and s/he is then encouraged to look again into the mirror. Children younger than 15 months seem not to make the connection between the image they see in front of them and the motor patterns required to bring a hand to their 'own' nose but all normally developing children can do so by 24 months due to the increased capacity to see the mirror image as a representation of self (Lewis & Brooks-Gunn, 1979).

**Social smile**
An intentional smile first seen in infants at around 6 weeks.

● ● ● ● ● ● ● ● ● ● ● ● ●
**Connect and Extend**
For an explanation of face-to-face communication between birth and 3 months, read: Lavelli M. & Fogel, A. (2005). Developmental changes in the relationship between the infant's attention and emotion during early face-to-face communication. *Developmental Psychology, 41*, 265–280.
● ● ● ● ● ● ● ● ● ● ● ● ●

**Complex emotions**
Embarrassment, shame, guilt, pride and envy. These secondary emotions appear late in the second year.

As with other areas of child development, the onset of language allows for a more precise measure of the level of understanding that a child has reached. Research findings (e.g. Hsieh, 2011) show language which refers to the emotions is used by children between 2 and 3 years, with a substantial increase after their third birthday in associated vocabulary. The emotions of embarrassment, jealousy and empathy (considered in more depth later in the chapter) are possible only with the development of **self-awareness**. The emotions of pride, guilt and shame appear as children begin to have an understanding of rules and goals and assess their thoughts and actions against social norms and expectations as **self-evaluative emotions**.

The link between emotions and cognition can be seen in the development of self-knowledge, that is, 'this is me' type knowledge (e.g. Fernández, 2013). Preschool children make use of straightforward emotional self-labels like 'I am happy' and 'I am sad' and locate their emotions in events, objects and people of significance. They talk excitedly about their approaching birthday or a new pet. School-age children show more understanding of their emotions and of the emotions of others, more sophistication in their emotional responses and less desirable social behaviours such as deceit, as their capacity to understand and manage their emotions increases.

The psychologist H. Rudolph Schaffer talks about this developing understanding and capacity as developing 'emotional competence' (2006, p 148), an umbrella term for the ability to interpret our own and other's emotions and respond appropriately. Citing and re-framing the work of Carolyn Saarni (1999) he lists the following components of emotional competence:

- an awareness of one's own emotional state;
- an ability to discern the emotions of other people;
- an ability to use culturally appropriate language in describing emotions;
- a capacity for sympathetic involvement in others' emotional experiences;
- an ability to see inner emotional states as different to outer emotional expressions;
- a capacity to cope with distressing emotions;
- an awareness that relationships can be defined by how emotions are communicated;
- feelings of being in control of one's emotional experiences.

Vital to many of the components of emotional competence above is **emotional self-regulation**. These are strategies used to adjust our emotional state and to allow us to achieve our goals. Such capacity is limited in young children and they tend to rely on carers to intervene on their behalf. So, for example, an infant who is frightened by the sudden appearance and abrupt behaviour of an unfamiliar adult will seek solace in soothing and gentle words from the carer to relieve the distress. By 12 months when many infants are more mobile, they can approach or withdraw from unpleasant situations but the role of the parent/carer remains to avoid excessive distress for the child. Research has shown that if children become too stressed too often, it is more difficult for carers to pacify them, for children to learn to soothe themselves and increases the chances of an anxious temperament (Macedo *et al.*, 2011).

By the third and fourth years, children can verbalise their emotions, 'bad doggie' or 'scary monster'. Although children are now at a stage to control their feelings actively more effectively, this is also a time to develop more long-standing fears. Parents often have to deal with their child's nightmares or help them come to terms with the dark – possibly when characters they know from books and television haunt their already vivid imaginations. It's not just fiction. Real situations affect children's emotions early in their lives. Television news reporting a tsunami disaster, the September 11th attacks in the United States and many other national and local events can provoke fear in children. Parents can contribute very positively to helping their children regulate their fear about disasters by talking such events through with them and attaching messages of sympathy and reassurance to these conversations.

Children of school age have to make rapid gains in emotional self-regulation. This is a time of new anxieties: pressures of daily 'tests' in physical and academic achievement, and

**Self-awareness**
The explicit understanding that 'me' exists as a separate individual with private thoughts, and that other people are similarly self-aware.

**Self-evaluative emotions**
The emotions that depend on knowledge of 'self' and of social norms of behaviour.

**Emotional self-regulation**
Strategies used to adjust our emotional state to allow us to achieve our goals.

• • • • • • • • • • • • • • • •
**Connect and Extend**
We all want children to become self-motivated and feel responsible for their own actions. How can carers and practitioners contribute to making this happen for all children? Read: Szente, J. (2007). *Empowering young children for success in school and in life. Early Childhood Education Journal*, 34, 449–453.
• • • • • • • • • • • • • • • •

comparisons of accomplishments with peers have direct impact on feelings of self-worth as well as a broadening understanding of the realities of the world. By age 10, adaptive strategies to manage their emotions are well established to such an extent that they gain a sense of emotional self-efficacy, a position where they are in control of their emotions which helps them adopt a positive approach to emotional challenges, including those they undoubtedly will meet later.

The work of Daniel Goleman popularised most recently in his book *Emotional Intelligence: Why it can matter more than IQ*, 10th Anniversary Edition (2006), has attracted widespread interest among educators. **Emotional intelligence** is best thought of as being aware of one's own emotions and those of others, and being sufficiently motivated to develop relationships. The argument for emotional intelligence put forward by Goleman was that traditionally it has been intellectual achievement which has been the priority in schools. He argues that this skew to academic achievement results in a kind of 'one-sidedness', where a child might be achieving academically but is less developed emotionally. Of course, developing emotional intelligence is problematic because it is so multifaceted, and conventional cognitive performance remains the main focus in most schools.

**Emotional intelligence** An awareness and understanding of one's own emotions and of others' emotions, and being motivated to develop relationships.

## Emotional knowledge and understanding the emotions of others

Emotional understanding in preschool children also allows them to identify emotional cues of others and to connect cause and consequence to those signals with some accuracy. For instance, a 4-year-old can remember and act on the memory that an angry playmate is capable of hitting out. They may also realise that when someone is reminded of a sad event, this makes that person feel sad again. Substantial advances in understanding other people's emotions are made in middle childhood. At 8–9 years of age children can show two same-valence emotions about two different targets at the same time (where valence is either a positive or negative nature of the emotion). An 8-year-old can feel angry that she was hit by Tom and disappointed that the teacher didn't notice. A 10-year-old might say, 'I'm a bit disappointed about my maths test result but I'm really excited about going to Tom's birthday tonight' (opposite valence to two targets). By about 11 or 12 years old, children believe they can feel opposite emotions to the same target, 'That film made me feel happy and sad at the same time'.

 **Reflect** In families that regularly discuss their feelings, children are better able to judge others' emotions, primarily because doing this provides opportunities for cognition, for children to reflect on their own experiences. They are also able to transfer knowledge of what they have experienced to other contexts. What might these contexts be for a preschool child and for a child of school age?

Not all children are equally adept at reading other people's emotions, and a typical primary classroom will have many different levels of emotional knowledge and understanding. Unpopular children show much less emotional understanding and this incapacity may be part of the reason for their unpopularity. In an early longitudinal study on economically disadvantaged children, Carroll Izard and colleagues (1997) found that the children who showed more knowledge of others' emotions were those who were socially accepted in school and presented fewer behaviour problems. Intervention programmes can help children to develop their emotional competence. It is on this premise that curriculum and leadership interventions for primary-age children can develop, which may include lessons designed to help with children's emotional expression and assist them with skills in forming social relationships. Results of evaluations of changes in children following such programmes in comparison to control groups are very positive (e.g. Cortes & Greenberg, 2007; Riggs *et al.*, 2006):

**Connect and Extend**
No all children understand their own emotions. Many need some help. One intervention that seems to work is a course (known as PATHS) for preschool children in Head Start. To find out more, read: Cortes, R. & Greenberg, M. (2007). Improving young children's social and emotional competence. *Journal of Primary Prevention, 28,* 67–91.

- improved self-control;
- improved understanding and recognition of emotions;
- increased ability to tolerate frustration;
- use of more effective conflict-resolution strategies;
- improved thinking and planning skills;
- decreased anxiety/depressive symptoms (teacher report of special needs pupils);
- decreased behaviour problems (teacher report of special needs pupils);
- decreased symptoms of sadness and depression (child reports – special needs); and
- decreased report of behaviour problems, including aggression (child reports).

A key feature of the PATHS curriculum referred to in the nearby *Connect and Extend* feature is the relationship between cognitive and affective understanding and real-life situations. Helping children to understand their emotions, and to think about their actions and the effects of these on other people, lays a firm base for developing advanced strategies of emotion regulation. There is certainly potential for including more work on emotional development in the primary school curriculum, and one very helpful perspective in framing schools' responses to identifying and intervening in the emotional development of children is emotional literacy.

**Emotional literacy**
The ability to express one's feelings and understand other people's emotions.

**Emotional literacy** (Steiner, 2003; Steiner & Perry, 1997) is another term used to describe our ability to express personal feelings and understand other people's emotions. Despite other pressures on schools, there has certainly been a shift away from an almost exclusive focus on cognitive development and physical health to one where emotional, social and mental health is now addressed. It is worth mentioning here that in September 2007, 'Personal, Social and Emotional Development' moved to the top of the list of 'Areas of Learning' in the UK Curriculum Guidance for the Foundation Stage (England) and has stayed there in the Early Years Foundation Stage (England).

UK initiatives such as Lifeskills teaching and Healthy Schools aim to teach pupils about self-esteem and decision-making as part of personal, social and health education (PSHE), and more recently a defined curriculum area of citizenship (to be covered in the next chapter) highlights a new interest in emotional and social issues for school-age pupils. As with the PATHS programme, early evaluations have shown that implementing courses in emotional and social development bring about better learning, problem-solving abilities, communication and empathy, with wide-ranging benefits in mental health for both individuals and for society (Formby, 2011; Wells *et al.*, 2003; Catalano *et al.*, 2002). In her book, *Developing the Emotionally Literate School*, Katherine Weare (2004) summarises much of this work for a UK audience and has conveniently drawn together competencies associated with emotional literacy under three headings of (1) Self-understanding. (2) Understanding, expressing and managing emotions and (3) Understanding social situations and making relationships.

## Social referencing

So far in this chapter we have argued that children's expression of their emotions is linked to their ability to interpret other people's emotional cues and that skill at interpreting emotional expressions of other people appears at an early age. Now it is time for another short story.

Nanette, aged 11 months, is busily playing with some brightly coloured plastic rings on the floor of the living room when the door-bell rings. Her mother goes out to answer the door and returns moments later with her friend Jo. In the meantime, Nanette clutches one of the rings firmly and looks anxiously towards the door. As she enters the room again, Nanette's mother says, 'Nanette, I want you to meet Jo'. Nanette looks intently at this new person, as if trying to work out who she is and what she is here to do. She then looks across at her mother, who is smiling. Cautiously, Nanette reaches

Social referencing – baby Niamh checks her mother's reaction when a stranger visits.
*Source*: Edward and Ella Hogan.

out her hand with the ring on it to show it to Jo who says, 'Hi Nanette. That is a lovely yellow ring you have'. Taking a further glance at her mother, Nanette fully extends her arm and breaks into a beaming smile.

**Social referencing** is the term that refers to reliance on someone else's emotional reaction to assess a new or uncertain situation. In the example above, Nanette used her mother's facial expressions to help her work out how she should respond to this new person. In a similar way, a child new to playgroup will keep close to her carer or keep the carer in view. If the carer moves away, the child will adjust position to access the carer's facial cues. This capacity begins by about 6 months when infants carefully study the facial expressions or listen to the tone of voice of adults around them.

It is time for another personal anecdote. When Niamh Hogan was 7 months old (we all first got acquainted at the beginning of Chapter 1 – check back for a picture of her) I picked her up and cuddled her. Being a writer about child development (and more importantly a time-served parent) I propped her on my arm with her face level with mine. We are not strangers but I hadn't seen her in a little while. I talked to Niamh using 'motherese' and much repetition. She studied my reading spectacles and my beard, reaching to grab, then swivelled hard to see her mother's face. Ella smiled broadly and called her a good girl. She turned back to me, smiled and continued to try to wrestle my glasses from my nose. Social referencing had successfully taken place. As a postscript to this story, we were playing with a toy parrot. Niamh sucked the beak (still exploring with her mouth) and became fascinated by my repetition of the initial sound (pa, pa, pa, pa, pa, pa), particularly as it included a small explosive exhalation which made her blink. She studied my mouth very carefully and for quite some time. I was thrilled to see her storing up that sound for later playful mimicry.

Studies (e.g. Soussignan *et al.*, 2009; Striano & Rochat, 2000) confirm that the emotional expressions of carers influence young children's reactions to strangers and ways in which they play with unfamiliar toys. In an earlier study, Boccia and Campos (1989) showed 8-month-old children reacting in a friendly way to a stranger when the mothers showed warm facial expressions, and not so when the expressions displayed worry. Emotional signals from fathers

**Social referencing**
A reliance upon someone else's emotional reaction to make sense of a new or uncertain situation.

have also been shown to provide important cues (Kokkinaki, 2009) and those from care workers (Stryker, 2012).

A second source of evidence for the existence of social referencing comes from the studies using visual cliffs designed to test depth perception (which we discussed earlier in Chapter 8), modifying the visual cliff apparatus to study how infants monitor the facial expressions of mothers. These studies have shown that the babies look to their mothers for clues to the new situation when they are approaching the part of the cliff apparatus that seemed to disappear. In a classic study by James Sorce and colleagues (1985), mothers were positioned opposite their infant so that their face could be seen clearly. When the mothers were asked to show a happy face, the majority of infants did move onto the visual cliff and when other mothers were asked to show a frightened face, none of their children ventured across the 'cliff'. This clearly showed how the infants relied on and interpreted their mother's facial expressions to determine their actions. Further evidence of social referencing can be found in the work of psychologist Louis Moses and colleagues (2001) with infants less than 2 years of age who were given unfamiliar toys. This study showed the positive vocalisations of the adults (e.g. 'Nice!') or negative (e.g. 'Yuk!') determined the children's behaviour towards the strange toy. These experiments show how cues provided by adults and interpreted by infants help children to guide their own reactions, responses and feelings. From 2 years of age, another important capacity begins to develop which enables young children to interpret and 'share' other people's feelings, and this capacity is a deliberate cognitive act.

**Reflect**  Is social referencing just a childhood phenomenon? Can you think of times when you have been in new situations and you too were uncertain about what to do and how to feel? Did you observe other people's reactions and did their reactions help you assess the situation?

## Social cognition

**Empathy** is about understanding emotions by taking another person's perspective or responding in a similar way, and is an important capacity in social interactions. Such an important social capacity is dependent on **social cognition** (which is developed as a major topic in Chapter 12). It requires an understanding of 'self' as different from 'others', associated with the development of self-awareness – which takes place around 2 years. Initially empathy is shown by hugging or sensitive facial expressions and then as children's language develops an astute 5-year-old might be heard saying something like, 'Mummy, you are sad today. It will be OK.' Throughout the school years these kind of empathetic statements increase in complexity. Children gain understanding of a wider range of emotions, and their skill of identifying cues linked to these emotions also increases to a stage where children show empathy with people suffering poverty and disaster (Nickols & Nielsen, 2011; Hoffman, 2000). The role of parents is interesting and influential here. Parents who show sensitivity and sincerity towards their children as preschoolers are likely to have children who respond similarly to the distresses of others, into late childhood and adolescence (Rieffe *et al.*, 2010). Conversely, insensitive, punitive or neglective parents have a negative effect on the development of empathy in pre-school children, revealed in behavioural inhibition (Cornell & Frick, 2007) and expressions of fear and anger outbursts (Rodriguez & Richardson, 2007).

Speaking of anger outbursts, we have already noted that babies are capable of expressing their feelings. They have a basic need, a survival function, to feel emotionally connected to other people; they need to bond with others and to form relationships. With young children, this need is directed towards adults around them who are closest to them, normally parents and, in particular, mothers. In the early months it is the physical contact and communication that goes on between parent and child that creates this vital bond. Although there is no two-

**Table 11.2** Milestones in emotional development

| Periods of development | Emotional expressions and understanding |
|---|---|
| Birth to 6 months | Appearance of the primary emotions<br>Cries to signal a physical need<br>The 'social' smile is present<br>Copies facial expressions of others<br>Engages in interactive synchrony |
| 6 months to 1 year | Primary emotions much more apparent<br>Social referencing evident<br>Expressions of anger and fear increase, in particular stranger anxiety<br>Some emotional regulation (control) apparent |
| 1–2 years | Self-conscious emotions now evident<br>Language development allows verbal expressions of emotions<br>Temper outbursts in the 'terrible twos' period – possible frustration with inability to express more complex emotions |
| 3–6 years | Can describe causes for and consequence of own emotions<br>Empathetic responding developing |
| 7–11 years | Understands that thoughts can control emotions<br>Strategies for self-regulation of emotions are now internalised<br>Increased and developed empathy for strangers<br>Aware that expressions of others may not be a true reflection of emotion<br>Able to fake display of own emotions (aged 10+) |

way verbal communication with the youngest children as yet, the desire to connect is still very evident. Watch a mother peering down at an infant in a cot. She smiles and coos and speaks warmly. The child responds through smiles and leg kicking. The adult responds with even more eye contact, more cooing and some tickles. This 'dialogue' of turn-taking is called **synchrony**: the interactions in the first year of life where both parent and infant engage in watching, copying and responding to each other. It is for the child's parents that the warmest smiles of affection are reserved, and with whom the closest bonds are made. In future years, the nature of synchrony changes (although there is still a good deal of watching and copying going on), as children become emotionally attached to others of importance around them, principally their peers. It is to the nature of emotional attachment that we now turn in the next section. In advance of this and to conclude this section of the chapter, we present in Table 11.2 the major milestones of emotional development from birth to age 11.

**Synchrony**
Among other uses, describes early interactions which parents and infants engage in by watching and copying and responding to each other.

Before moving on, let's summarise what we have learned so far:

- Emotions are behaviours that direct our thinking and subsequent actions in response to events.

- Emotions include three components: *physiological* – a physical reaction or feeling; *subjective* – judging one's own emotional state; and *expressive* – communicating by expression, posture and word.

- Children's emotional development is predominantly about communicating feelings and learning to interpret the emotions of other people.

- Theoretical approaches to emotional development include cognitive perspectives – understanding of the world and how 'things' work; maturational perspectives – expressions of common emotions appearing at the same time; learning perspectives – emotions are a result of our lived experiences; and functional perspectives which maintain that the ways we respond to events determine how much we wish to repeat the experience in future.

- Babies begin by expressing (and we presume feeling) six basic or primary emotions: happiness, sadness, anger, disgust, surprise and fear.
- Late in the infant's second year, complex emotions (or self-conscious emotions) emerge: embarrassment, shame, guilt, pride and jealousy.
- The emotions of embarrassment, jealousy and empathy are possible only with the development of self-awareness.
- The emotions of pride, guilt and shame appear as children begin to have an understanding of rules and goals.
- Emotional self-regulation are strategies used to adjust our emotional state and to allow us to achieve our goals. Such capacity is limited in young children and they tend to rely on carers to intervene on their behalf.
- Emotional intelligence is best thought of as being aware of one's own emotions and those of others, and being sufficiently motivated to develop relationships.
- Social referencing is the term that refers to reliance on someone else's emotional reaction to assess a new or uncertain situation.
- Emotional expressions of carers influence young children's reactions to strangers and ways in which they play with unfamiliar toys.
- Empathy is dependent on social cognition and about understanding emotions by taking another person's perspective or responding in a similar way.
- Milestones in emotional development include social referencing, the development of empathy and evidence of social cognition – thoughts can control emotions.

# Attachment

It is the first day at nursery for 3-year-old Dani Coates. There are quite a few 'new' parents and children making their way into the bright and stimulating building, each excited and a little anxious about what to expect. The staff at the nursery have laid out various toys and activities for the children to investigate with their parents. Minutes later, parents and children are happily engaged in exploring the many tabletop activities on offer, the colourful board books in the book corner and the tools in the sand and water troughs. There are many shared activities between parents, nursery staff and the children. Too soon it is time for the parents to leave. Most parents give their children a cuddle and a reassuring few words, and then quietly leave. Dani's mum tries to do this, even though she knows from earlier experiences of leaving Dani that this is not going to be easy.

As Mrs Coates tries to say goodbye, Dani tenses up. He is clearly distressed. He cries out, he sobs, he holds on desperately to his mother. She struggles to know what to do, extricates herself and moves to the door – the crying continues. She goes back to comfort him. When she again tries to leave, Dani again lets out some fearsome cries. He cannot bear to be separated from her.

**Attachment**
Personal connection that produces a desire for contact and a distress on separation.

In the section that follows we shall find out why Dani is making such a fuss, but first we need to talk about the important concept of attachment. **Attachment** refers to emotional ties to the special people who offer us comfort and in whose company we feel happiest. Berger (2001) sees it in terms of both a desire for social contact and a distress on being separated from another person (Dani's behaviour in the story above). While attachment theory can and does relate to any point in one's life, it is normally associated with the early years and acknowledged to be vital for forming good relationships in later life. Parent–infant interactions, especially those made in the very early days, build a very special kind of intimate relationship. These interactions or **synchronised routines** are those everyday but vital practices that go on between parent and child. They include paying attention to the baby's physical or emotional states and being sensitive to these, and not overstimulating the infant at an inappropriate time when the baby is tired. This is also a time when both learn about each other and learn to interpret each other's signals. Synchronised routines have been likened to a kind of dance (Isabella, 1993) where both partners practise their routine to help build a reciprocal relationship of understanding. How does 'the dance' help in forming attachments and when are the key moments?

One of the most influential early accounts of the development of attachment is by Rudolph Schaffer and Peggy Emerson in 1964. They studied 60 babies at monthly intervals and in the infants' own homes for the first 18 months of life (remember from Chapter 3 that this form of research is known as a longitudinal study). Patterns were identified for the development of an attachment using evidence of when a baby showed separation anxiety.

Schaffer and Emerson discovered that baby's attachments develop in the following sequence:

- **Birth to 6 weeks – asocial stage**. Babies do not act in a social manner and respond to people in much the same way as everything else. They do not show social recognition of an individual (they of course respond to their main caregiver).

- **After 6 weeks – indiscriminate attachments**. The newborn will attach to any human. Most babies respond equally to any caregiver.

- **After 4 months – preference for certain people**. Infants learn to distinguish primary and secondary caregivers but accept care from anyone.

- **After 7 months – special preference for a single attachment figure**. The baby looks to particular people for security, comfort and protection. S/he shows fear of strangers (stranger fear) and unhappiness when separated from a special person (separation anxiety). Some babies show stranger fear and separation anxiety much more frequently and intensely than others, but nevertheless they are seen as evidence that the baby has formed an attachment. This has usually developed by 1 year of age.

- **After 9 months – multiple attachments**. The baby becomes increasingly independent and forms several attachments.

The study indicated that attachments were most likely to form with those who responded accurately to the baby's signals, not necessarily the person with whom they spent the most time. Schaffer and Emerson called this 'sensitive responsiveness'. Many of the babies had several attachments by 10 months, including attachments to grandparents, siblings and neighbours. The mother was the main attachment figure for about half of the children at 18 months and the father for most of the others. The most important factor in forming attachments is not who feeds and changes the child but who plays and communicates with him or her.

A critical point is reached by 7–8 months, which coincides with two problem areas in a child's emotional development. The first of these, as mentioned, is *stranger anxiety* – a child's reaction to someone unfamiliar appearing. Most infants respond quite positively to a stranger until they have made their first attachment. It is after this that their wariness increases, then declines by about ten months. *Separation anxiety* occurs when children are separated from a parent/carer. It is usually accompanied by distress signals of crying, clinging or trying to follow. This appears on average at around 8 months and reaches a peak by 18 months. It declines gradually by the time children enter school. This is exactly the type of attachment we saw earlier with Dani and his mother, from whom he could not bear to be separated. While his mother was there and engaging in the activities in the nursery with him, Dani was happy. The

**Synchronised routines**
Simplified action sequences created by mother and infant together, such as feeding and dressing.

• • • • • • • • • • • • • • •
**Connect and Extend**
How do children and parents see the transition from early years settings to school? The differences in their perspectives make fascinating reading. Find: Fabian, H. & Dunlop, A.-W. (2006). Outcomes of good practice in transition processes for children entering primary school, available at **http://unesdoc.unesco.org**
• • • • • • • • • • • • • • •

• • • • • • • • • • • • • • •
**Connect and Extend**
To help chart the developmental sequences of children's independent and interdependent behaviour, read: Raeff, C. (2006). Multiple and inseparable: Conceptualizing the development of independence and interdependence. *Human Development*, 49, 96–121.
• • • • • • • • • • • • • • •

moment she got up to leave him with strangers he became anxious and unable to cope. Let us look to the theories of attachment to help explain this common problem.

## Theories of attachment

*Learning theory of attachment* (e.g. Dollard & Miller, 1950) suggests that attachment is a set of learned behaviours. The basis for the learning of attachments is the provision of food. An infant will initially form an attachment to whoever feeds it. They learn to associate the feeder (usually the mother) with the comfort of being fed and, through the process of classical conditioning, come to find contact with the mother comforting. The child responds with smiles and coos to stay close to such reinforcement or cries to attract the carer's attention, and through the process of classical conditioning learns to repeat successful actions in order to get the things they want.

*Cognitive-developmental theory of attachment* places emphasis on intellectual development. Attachment requires understanding of the differences between friends and strangers since it is with the former that stable and lasting relationships are formed. It requires a level of the intellectual ability to distinguish one person from another. An emphasis on cognitive development accords with developing the capacity to determine object permanence, which holds that if, as far as an infant is concerned, a person ceases to exist when he or she disappears from view, attachment with that person would be impossible. This is true as attachment really accelerates from about 9 months onwards, the time when object permanence is being understood. The theory asserts that children form attachments with the most interesting and intellectually challenging happenings in their lives and from developing an increasingly organised conception of their social world (Fraley & Marks, 2011).

*Ethological theory of attachment* (sometimes called the evolutionary theory) holds that we are born with innate tendencies for carers and children to form attachments: a view associated with adaptive behaviours and the survival of our species. This view proposes that parents and

others are biologically disposed to respond in a positive way to the emotions expressed by children and many studies confirm this phenomenon (e.g. Vatne *et al.*, 2012; Wood & Gustafson, 2001). What adult can ignore the cry of a baby in distress? Early work with animals supports this (as we discovered in Chapter 2). You may remember Konrad Lorenz who, in a classic and now historic study with goslings (1937), reported that very young goslings would follow any object that moved in a process he termed 'imprinting', a kind of inborn learning where some species will follow and become attached to a moving object. His findings showed that this behaviour does not have to be taught but is automatic, and there is a definite critical period that limits it. The birds in his study followed their food provider and sought the protection provided by the 'mother' to increase their survival chances.

Although humans do not imprint in the same way, we have inherited characteristics that encourage contact with other humans. Large rounded eyes, a large forehead and soft features (Kewpie doll appearance) are characteristics that encourage contact between child and mother by making the infant appear loveable to the carer (Hahn *et al.*, 2013). Lorenz did argue that there was a critical time following birth for attachments to be made: the time was immediately after a child is born. He said that if attachments are not made in this period, then attachment will not happen. This has important ramifications for newborns who are separated from their mothers at birth, for example, when medical complications occur.

Celluloid Kewpie dolls were manufactured from 1913 onwards and featured large rounded eyes, a large forehead and soft, rounded features.

*Source*: Alamy Images / Ashley Whitworth.

**Reflect** Sara was separated from her newborn baby Mollie, born premature and by emergency Caesarean section, whilst both received medical attention. Will this separation impede future attachment between the two? Some developmentalists argue against the existence of a critical period after birth, yet anecdotal evidence (supported by Konrad Lorenz) would indicate that separation can create physical and psychological barriers which adversely affect attachment. What is your view?

Early reflexive responses (Chapter 6) are also an aid to attachment between child and parent. Behaviours such as rooting and grasping are believed to help bonding through the closeness of the contact behaviours. So too do cooing, babbling and smiling, which indicate baby's affection for a carer, reinforce caring activities and increase likelihood that a carer will want to be with this contented and responsive little individual. The ethological theory argues that the key to attachment is the bond between parent and child seen in the adult's sensitivity to the child's signals. The theory also predicts that children will become most strongly attached to parents who respond best to their signals. In time, these interactions form expectations about future interactions with others and build an internal working model of the relationship between the child and the parent. When signals are interpreted responsively, the child builds a model of the parent as a trustworthy individual and the child of being competent and worth the parent's responsiveness. The model provides the guide for all close relationships in the future (Beebe *et al.*, 2012).

John Bowlby's work in the middle part of the twentieth century (1969) was highly significant in offering a comprehensive ethological theory of attachment, and indeed his work has influenced modern thinking on loss and grief (e.g. Wijngaards-de Meij *et al.*, 2007; Field, 2006). Bowlby's view was that a sense of security was at the heart of emotional attachment. In his attachment theory, he argued that a mother has a genetic blueprint that programmes her to respond to her baby in a positive way. The synchrony of action between the two produces attachment. This innate bond initially to one individual, in what he called *monotropy*, is the strongest bond of all and is unique between mother and child – different from all others. His theory opposed the Freudian view that attachment arises out of parental gratification of a child's basic needs, briefly described below. Instead, he highlights the role of parents in fostering early attachments, while maintaining that a strong predisposition exists for infants to attach to one primary carer. It is what he considered the reciprocal nature of these relationships that are vital for attachments to form over longer periods of time.

Although highly influential (we have spent some time exploring it), the ethological view is not without critics. There is general consensus that the existence of a critical period for human attachment is not true although lack of early contact between carer and child can create an obstacle for attachment. We believe that children can attach to people other than the mother and that the mother is not always the main attachment figure. In the past 30 years, Bowlby's earlier view of fathers having only minimal influence on the emotional development of the child has also been refuted (e.g. Flouri, 2008; Guishard-Pine, 2006; Kenrick, 1994; Parke, 1981).

*Psychoanalytic theory of attachment* proposes that a child's physical needs create psychological tensions, creating a drive to reduce the tension. Hunger is one such need and the child seeks to reduce that need by signalling the need to be fed. A carer who satisfies the need by providing food becomes associated with the satisfaction and pleasure when that need is met. Freudian theory (Chapter 2) places great emphasis on oral satisfaction such as that received by sucking or placing objects into the mouth. In this way, a carer who feeds is for that time a baby's primary object of security, a point further supporting the view that different strengths of attachment are possible in the early stages.

Influential psychologist Erik Erikson (Chapter 2) believed that feeding practices influenced the strength of attachments but he also held the view that the general responsiveness to the

**Internal working model** Expectations arising from early care experiences about carers which become a model for later close relationships.

● ● ● ● ● ● ● ● ● ● ● ● ● ● ● ● ●
**Connect and Extend**
The attachment baby and a mother feel is very important and mothers can deepen that attachment in powerful ways. To give you a fuller understanding, read: Laible, D. (2004). Mother–child discourse in two contexts: Links with child temperament, attachment security, and socioemotional competence. *Developmental Psychology, 40,* 979–992.
● ● ● ● ● ● ● ● ● ● ● ● ● ● ● ● ●

child – the psychosocial theory – is more important than the act of feeding. Responsiveness promotes trust, the establishment of which to Erikson was a primary and elemental task in infancy. In his theory, Erikson postulates that adults who have difficulty in forming mutual-trust relationships learned in infancy not to trust their carers.

It is now recognised that although feeding is an important time in which attachment takes place it is not the only or necessarily defining time. Much of what was proposed in the psychoanalytic approach was supplanted by Bowlby's findings – notably, and as we have presented, the idea that an infant forms an attachment to the mother because she is able to gratify the child's needs for physical comfort and reassurance. We consider attachment not as a psychological drive but, in line with the ethological approach, as part of an ongoing secure set of relationships that is built up initially between a child and the mother and then significant others.

At this point let me recap the four attachment theories in this way:

1. Learning theory (Reward me and I will love you).
2. Cognitive-developmental theory (I need to know you are there).
3. Ethological theory (I am born to love you).
4. Psychoanalytic theory (You feed me so I love you).

Although markedly different, each of the theories has a contribution to make to our understanding of attachment. Learning theorists inform us of the importance of this aspect in a child's emotional development. Cognitive theorists have emphasised the importance of the timing of attachments. Ethologists have contributed the value of children being active in the process in order to utilise their already pre-programmed ability to form attachments and to form these with different people in our lives. Finally, psychoanalysts highlight the need to understand mother–child interactions in the attachment process.

Research into attachment subsequent to the development of these attachment theories, notably Michael Rutter's research (1981) on early separation, the work of René Spitz – maternal deprivation in orphanages (1971) – and Mary Ainsworth's study of parent–child communication have all been influenced by these four theoretical approaches, and attachment remains very much a topical issue today. For example, the 'Strange Situation' test (Ainsworth *et al.*, 1978), the experimental protocol that Mary Ainsworth devised, continues to be widely used (e.g. Grandgeorge *et al.*, 2011) along with other naturalistic methods.

**Strange Situation**
A series of separation and reunion events that determine the quality of infant–carer-attachment.

Strange Situation is an experimental protocol that provides a measure of infant attachment to the mother through a series of eight brief separation and reunion events which allows the quality of infant–parent (or carer) attachment to be assessed. The intention of these episodes is to simulate parent–child interactions and to determine to what extent the infant uses the parent as a base to explore the environment. Strange Situation gives a most useful means to judge the quality of an infant's attachment, as Table 11.3 illustrates. Each 22-minute episode is videoed from behind one-way mirrors.

Studies using this measure report four common types of attachment (typical percentages of infants are from Barnett & Vondra, 1999). The first three were the original tripartite typology and a fourth, Type D, was added later by Ainsworth as a catch-all for behaviours that did not fit into the first three types:

- *Type A. Insecure avoidant attachment*. Infants do not show distress at separation and often deliberately ignore their mothers. Relationships with the stranger tend to show some sociability or avoidance (typically 15–25 per cent of 12–18-month-olds).
- *Type B. Secure attachment* is where the child explores the immediate environment with confidence. The infant is distressed when the parent leaves but reacts warmly to her in her return. With the mother present, the child is confident with the stranger (typically 60–75 per cent of 12–18-month-olds).

**Table 11.3** Parent–child interactions and attachment behaviours

| Episode | Attachment behaviours |
| --- | --- |
| Parent and child are left alone in the playroom | |
| The parent sits close by as the child plays | Parent offers a secure base – infant initiates |
| A stranger enters the room. Talks to the parent | Stranger anxiety |
| The parent leaves the room. The stranger comforts the child if distressed | Separation anxiety |
| The parent returns. Offers comfort to the child if required. The stranger leaves | Reunion |
| Parent now leaves the playroom | Second separation anxiety |
| The stranger re-enters and comforts the child | Comforting |
| The parent returns. Comforts the child if necessary and tries to interest the child in the toys. | 2nd reunion |

*Source*: Based on Ainsworth, M. D. S., Blehar, M., Waters, E. & Wall, S. (1978). *Patterns of attachment: A psychological study of the Strange Situation*. Hillsdale, NJ: Erlbaum. Reproduced with permission of Taylor & Francis.

- *Type C. Insecure ambivalent or resistant attachment*. Infants remain close to the mother and do not tend to explore. Distress at her leaving is replaced by ambivalence on her return. They stay quite close but resist physical contact with her on return. An anxiety towards the stranger is also evident (typically 10–15 per cent of 12–18-month-olds).
- *Type D. Disorganised/disoriented attachment* is where infants display most distress. Their behaviour is either one of resistance to the parent or avoidance. When reunited the infants are strongly confused, uncertain whether to approach the mother or avoid her (typically 10–15 per cent of 12–18-month-olds).

Attachment theory is relevant to different age phases when a lifespan approach to developmental psychology is adopted, because, as we shall see, early experiences provide the blueprint for future relationship experiences. For the moment let us return to the same nursery where we met Dani earlier. We saw how Dani was very dependent upon his mother and that he could not cope well with her leaving him. Looking around the nursery at other 3-year-olds, we can also see a very different picture of attachment.

## Early attachment and its consequences

Matti skipped ahead of her mother into the nursery, smiling and confident. Matti loved to do puzzles and she had a go at four or five different ones in the room. As she moved about the room she acknowledged the other children around her. She spoke to several of them and even helped another girl with her puzzle. When it was time for her mother to leave, Matti hugged her and waved goodbye. She watched her leave the room and then carried on with her puzzle.

A very different type of early attachment is obvious here. The account of Matti, the master puzzle solver, illustrates the typical behaviour of children in new situations who are securely attached to parent(s). Securely attached children, like Matti, are stable, happier and are more sociable with their peers and adults, including those unfamiliar to them (Yoon Phaik *et al.*, 2006). There are academic implications here too. Such children have longer periods of sustained concentration and are better at problem-solving (Granot & Mayseless, 2001). They tend to be popular with teachers and show fewer behavioural problems in class (JAACAP, 2006).

Studies show a correlation between early attachment and later cognitive and social adjustment – although other factors (e.g. divorce, illness) are also powerful influences, especially in early adolescence (e.g. Bohlin *et al.*, 2000). If a child of 12 months shows the sort of anxious behaviour in the Strange Situation experiment, does this behaviour prophesy similar anxiety in later years? Since the majority of studies have found a positive link between early attachment and later development, a number of useful points can be made from findings. Children who are able to make strong attachments in very early childhood, later will typically:

- cry less when separated from a parent or carer;
- be more quickly and easily comforted on the return of the parent or carer;
- engage in more pretend play;
- be less prone to attention deficit problems;
- appear more persistent in problem-solving situations;
- show greater flexibility in controlling their personal feelings;
- benefit from stimulation of parent or carer and show this in relation to gains in cognitive, social and language development;
- demonstrate autonomy;
- be popular with peers and adults;
- be less aggressive; and
- be at a lower risk of being bullied in school.

• • • • • • • • • • • • • • • • •
**Connect and Extend**
Internationally adopted children have increased risk of developmental and behavioural difficulties. This article reviews the literature: Welsh, J., Viana, A., Petrill, S. & Mathias, M. (2007). Interventions for internationally adopted children and families. *Child & Adolescent Social Work Journal, 24,* 285–311.
• • • • • • • • • • • • • • • • •

These very positive behaviours paint a picture of young children growing into balanced sensitive and trusting individuals who approach life situations with confidence. For children like Dani whose early attachments are not strong, the picture is less rosy.

## What are the factors that influence attachment?

There are a number of factors that have been found to have an impact on attachment, which we have grouped under five main headings.

### Cross-cultural differences

Cross-cultural differences exist in attachment and come about principally from differences in child-rearing beliefs and practices. Japanese parents rarely leave their children with other carers and consequently these children do not easily form attachments to others. When separated from the mother figure, they show distress at her leaving. They stay quite close but resist physical contact with her on return. In contrast Israeli children raised on kibbutzim are used to sleeping without their parents being present. Generally across the world, it is widely reported that most children display secure attachment and parents are most comfortable when their children remain close to them (Jin, 2012; Rothbaum & Pott, 2000; van Ijzendoorn & Sagi, 1999).

Secure attachments are usually made between young children and their parents, despite variation in child-bearing practices across cultures.

*Source:* © Corbis.

### Parental characteristics

Parental characteristics, which include the giving of emotional support, being sensitive to a child's moods and needs, and having a positive attitude, are found to produce secure, attached children (Coplan *et al.*, 2008). Infants who display resistant attachment have parents who are inconsistent in their caring (Wearden *et al.*, 2008) and those who show disoriented attachment tend to fear strangers, but might also be attracted to them because of personal experiences in their past – they may have been neglected or abused (Iy, 2006). Babies who receive intrusive and overwhelming attention become anxious and develop a resistant reaction to such care. When this 'smothering care' is inconsistent, babies can experience frustration and develop heightened dependence. Maternal illness, depression and poor treatment of a child by the mother are also factors associated with insecure attachments. The 'goodness of fit model' (Thomas & Chess, 1977) is a match between a child's temperament and parental patterns of child-rearing. When the match is optimised, and caring fits with the individual child's temperament, there is secure attachment (Raymond *et al.*, 2010). If the fit results in stressed or inflexible parenting that does not accommodate a child's personal temperament traits, this leads to an insecure attachment and mother–child conflict (Laible *et al.*, 2008b). We will further explore the notion of 'goodness of fit' at the end of this chapter.

## Child characteristics

Child characteristics also contribute to the forming of attachments. Behaviour traits in babies that make them appear unreactive, slow or irritable can potentially alienate carers. These traits are common in low-birth-weight babies, often attributed to illness or the mother's stimulant addiction in pregnancy (see Chapter 5). Psychologist Jerome Kagan's (1989) **temperament hypothesis** suggests that it is children and not parents who are the chief architects of their attachment behaviours. Kagan suggests that Strange Situation experiments with young children measure individual differences in temperament more than the quality of infant-care attachment. At the same time as Kagan was postulating this hypothesis, Frits Goossens and Marinus van Ijzendoorn (1990) argued that, since most children are strongly attached to one person and insecurely attached to another, this pattern would not be possible if attachment was totally based on the child's temperament. Today, there is much more agreement in favour of the view that although a child's temperament is a factor it is parents (and carers) who are the main architects of infant attachment (e.g. Pace *et al.*, 2011).

**Temperament hypothesis**
Proposes that attachment behaviours are strongly linked to temperament.

## Family circumstances

Family circumstances provide another influencing factor. Attachment insecurity is consistently linked in the literature to unemployment, divorce, financial difficulties and other stressors in family life, any and all of which can interfere with sensitive and consistent parenting. For many parents, struggling to balance the role of parent and employee has its own stresses. In a study by psychologist Cynthia Stifter and colleagues (1993), mothers working full time reported factors such as tiredness and general harassment, which appeared to risk positive relations with their children. Yet when mothers want to work, but out of necessity must remain at home, this too may have a negative effect on their child's emotional development – discussed in the *Controversy* feature later. Related to all the factors that affect attachment (and as we shall see later, arguably most important of all) is the quality of care that a child receives, whether from the mother or in various care settings. When caring is really poor and fails to meet the needs of children, considerable disruption to the child's emotional well-being results, most obviously in cases of neglect and child abuse (Rikhye *et al.*, 2008). Quality care involves collaboration between parents and carers, working together to providing what developmental psychologists Sandra Scarr and Judith Dunn referred to as a 'consistent and agreeable world for the child' (1987, p 187). Researchers over the past 20 years have consistently come to similar conclusions (e.g. Poehlmann, 2005; O'Connor & Croft, 2001; Franco & Levitt, 1998; Ochiltree, 1994).

The upcoming *Policy, Research and Praxis* feature provides a summary of current thinking in the UK about how to support children's well-being. After the feature we move on to look at the importance of multiple attachments.

• • • • • • • • • • • • • • •
**Connect and Extend**
For an investigation of working mothers' self-reported feelings of guilt, read: Guendouzi, J. (2006). The guilt thing: Balancing domestic and professional roles. *Journal of Marriage & Family*, 68, 901–909.
• • • • • • • • • • • • • • •

## Policy, Research and Praxis

### Genius joined-up policy to support children's well-being

Recent government policy places significant emphasis on early intervention to reduce health and educational inequalities and give all children the best start in life. Policy documents encourage health professionals to put social and emotional well-being at the heart of their work with vulnerable children (DH, 2009; DH, 2011), and it is the cornerstone of early years education and learning (DfE, 2012).

Many factors impact on children's social and emotional well-being, and knowledge of these can help professionals assess the needs of and risks to individual children and their families more effectively. Children in disadvantaged families are more likely to experience adversity such as mental illness, neglect, abuse and domestic violence. Consequently, they are more likely to experience emotional and behavioural problems that negatively impact on their development (Shonkoff & Phillips, 2000). Professional services which support children during their early years are generally not well integrated either at the strategic or local level (Allen, 2011a; Field, 2010). The level and quality of early child-care and education services varies and the most disadvantaged children are more likely to get the worst provision (Ofsted, 2010). Interventions to address social and emotional needs vary widely. Some have been proven to be effective, whilst others have not and, where evidence-based interventions are used, they are not always implemented effectively (Allen, 2011b; Field, 2010).

In 2008, the National Institute for Health and Clinical Excellence (NIHCE) produced guidance on promoting the social and emotional well-being of children in primary schools. Recommendations were made that schools adopt 'whole school' approaches to developing children's social and emotional well-being. These included, for example, creating conditions that support positive behaviours for learning and forming relationships with other people; having safe and emotionally secure environments that prevent bullying, and that support be given to all pupils and, where appropriate, to parents and carers. It recommended a curriculum that integrates social and emotional skills within all subjects (e.g. problem-solving, coping, conflict management/resolution and understanding and managing feelings) and that teachers are trained to identify and assess the early signs of anxiety, emotional distress and behavioural problems in primary-age children.

Recent policy attention has been directed to how interventions can reduce the risks to vulnerable children and promote the social and emotional well-being of the under-5 age group. NIHCE guidance (2012) made four recommendations covering home visiting, early education and childcare which were to:

1. Adopt a 'life course perspective', recognising that disadvantage before birth and in a child's early years can have life-long, negative effects.

2. Focus on the social and emotional well-being of vulnerable children as the foundation for their healthy development and to offset the risks relating to disadvantage.

3. Aim to ensure universal, as well as targeted services to provide the additional support all vulnerable children need.

4. All of the above in conjunction with local child safeguarding policies.

A number of themes are consistent across policy documents: a more explicit focus on promoting the social and emotional well-being of children; appropriate indicators for early identification of those children and families who are at risk or already experiencing problems; and the importance of providing early evidence-based intervention services that respond to local needs.

## Multiple attachments

Attachments made to people other than the main carer, or **multiple attachments**, mean children are less dependent on one person only. Children can attach securely to both parents (Kochanska *et al.*, 2008) and to other carers who may be part of multiple, concurrent, non-parental child-care arrangements (Morrissey, 2008). Being 'forced' to make multiple attachments appears to help children as long as arrangements made are 'consistent and agreeable'.

However, multiple attachments can be forced by circumstances such as parental death, illness and divorce, and the nature of those circumstances can bring about serious effects for children. Family researcher Martin Richards in a series of studies and reports over the past 20 years (e.g. 2003, 1995) has established that following the break-up of their parents' marriage there are higher incidences of children with lower levels of academic attainment, adjustment problems, higher incidences of depression and who found it harder to form close relationships. Of course, the effects were age-dependent.

In their earlier study on the effects of divorce on children, Monica Cockett and John Tripp (The Exeter Family Study, 1994) found that children in reordered or blended families (i.e. those where parents had married again and taken on a step-family) had more problems in school, difficulties making friends and low self-esteem. Their study continues to be widely cited in support of any argument that the re-forming of family arrangements can be very disruptive for children at any stage of development. The more a child is disrupted as a result of marital break-ups, the worse the outcomes for emotional development and, so, much depends on the quality of any new attachments made.

**Multiple attachments**
Attachments to more than one person, usually the other parent, grandparents, siblings and care-givers.

## Judging the quality of attachment

Is it possible to judge the quality of attachments? One answer to this is Mary Ainsworth's security technique (*ibid.*) in which she observed that when children are securely attached to one person (remember the work of John Bowlby) it is that person who serves as a firm base for the infant to explore the environment.

Mary Ainsworth's findings and subsequently those of others (e.g. Fraley & Spieker, 2003) inform us that mothers who are sensitive to their child's needs have children who form secure attachments (like Matti from the earlier story), while those who are less consistently sensitive to their children's needs have insecurely attached children (like Dani). Such findings have been recently criticised by some scholars (e.g. Gojman *et al.*, 2012), while findings from cross-cultural studies show differences in the spread of attachment types A, B and C (DiTommaso *et al.*, 2005). Despite such criticisms, the Strange Situation remains a powerful way of studying attachment in the early years and of predicting future sociability. For children of 2 years up to school age and above, the **Attachment Q-set** is another measure in use (e.g. Warfield *et al.*, 2011). This measure involves an observer and a set of 90 descriptors of attachment behaviours and has the great advantage of allowing naturalistic observation or those used in natural environments such as playgroups and nurseries, rather than the laboratory setting of the Strange Situation. (However, it is worth noting that the Strange Situation was originally designed to be an experiment in as natural a setting as possible.)

**Attachment Q-set**
A technique of assessing attachment security of infant–carer used frequently in natural settings.

**Reflect**

**Knowing about developmental milestones sometimes creates problems. Over-anxious parents and practitioners can look for signs of development too soon and start to panic if a particular child is late talking or is not 'normal' in some way. Working mothers in particular can suffer from guilt about going out to work or spending time away from their children. Is it true that all children get there in the end and parents should not over-react? How do we *know* when there is a potential problem?**

**Maternal deprivation hypothesis**
Bowlby's claim that serious damage would occur to a child's emotional development if the attachment between child and mother was severed in the first years of the child's life.

**Deprivation**
The effect of a poor or loveless attachment figure.

**Privation**
The term used with reference to the total absence of an attachment figure.

• • • • • • • • • • • • • • • •
**Connect and Extend**
For an interesting and not unproblematic account of the effect of maternal deprivation on the behaviour of children, read: Mackintosh, V., Myers, B. & Kennon, S. (2006). Children of incarcerated mothers and their caregivers. *Journal of Child & Family Studies*, 15, 579–594.
• • • • • • • • • • • • • • • •

# When things go wrong with attachment

As previously referred to, John Bowlby's pioneering work on attachment was hugely influential in advancing our understanding of the bond between parent and child. His observations in the 1930s and 1940s of children in orphanages led to forming his maternal deprivation hypothesis – that serious damage would occur to a child's development if the attachment between child and mother was severed in the first years of the child's life. Historic studies on rhesus monkeys (Harlow *et al.*, 1971) showed that when these animals were reared with no contact whatsoever with any other animal or human (some ethical problems here!) they played much less, spent time rocking back and forward in a corner and, when they did meet other monkeys later on, cowered in their presence and avoided them. Subsequent research has revealed the complexity of separation situations. For example, Barbara Tizard's research in the 1970s (e.g. Tizard & Hodges, 1978) on children in residential care has important messages for us today in identifying that a high turnover in care staff can affect some children's abilities to form lasting relationships in later life. Later research with ex-institutionalised orphans (Fisher *et al.*, 1997) identified that understimulation of the children seen in these environments and/ or the lack of maternal care was a significant factor in their developmental difficulties. However, psychiatrists Thomas O'Connor, Michael Rutter and colleagues from the University of Birmingham (2000), while investigating maternal separation in Romanian orphans, concluded that not all children suffer similar effects from separation from the main attachment figure and that factors such as the child's age and temperament, and the duration of the separation were important. Earlier, Sandra Scarr and Judith Dunn (1987) concluded that the mother is not necessarily the key attachment figure. They found that psychological damage suffered by children in institutions was due to a deficit in human contact and stimulation, not from the absence of a mother figure. What has been concluded from studies over the past 30 years is that children raised in settings where there is a lack of stimulation from carers do encounter problems in their physical, social, intellectual and emotional development (e.g. Bhattacharjee, 2008; Cermak & Groza, 1998; Grusec & Lytton, 1988).

Maternal separation is now understood as deprivation, whereas privation is the term used with reference to the complete absence of an attachment figure: circumstances like those experienced by the orphan children of Romania (O'Connor *et al.*, 2000; McIlveen & Gross, 1998). This distinction is important since the former is linked to the effects of separation from the attachment figure and the latter to never attaching in the first instance. Deprivation in the short term may be hours, days or weeks such as can happen when a child starts nursery for the first time, mother has to go into hospital or away on business, or perhaps later when children start boarding school. Such events can be distressing for many children. Most distress seems to occur between the ages of 7 months up to 3 years, with boys showing most signs of distress. Two possible explanations for this perceived distress at this age are that a child might feel him/herself abandoned by the mother (who it is felt) may or may not return, and secondly that there may be a lack of understanding by the child of a phrase like, 'I'll be back in a few days'.

Privation is when there is no attachment formed. John Bowlby's findings led him to view these early experiences to be the cause of individuals developing as 'affectionless characters'. A similar portrayal was suggested by Michael Rutter (1981) who described personality traits in adulthood of individuals who in childhood experienced early privation: being without guilt, avoiding rules and unable to form lasting relationships with others.

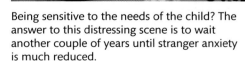

Being sensitive to the needs of the child? The answer to this distressing scene is to wait another couple of years until stranger anxiety is much reduced.

*Source*: Marmaduke St. John / Alamy Images.

Can we moderate the effects of such privation? A wealth of evidence suggests that early experiences are of central importance in determining brain development and later outcomes (e.g. Eluvathingal *et al.*, 2006). Longitudinal research traces children's developmental pathways from early privation to outcomes in maturity (e.g. Shaffer & Sroufe, 2005; Schaffer, 1996). The evidence suggests that, while early privation can seriously affect development, this is not always the case. There are many factors to be considered here such as the paucity of the experiences, the period when these occurred and the resilience of the individual children concerned. Children suffering from early (de)privation can and do make up this deficit in later life; critical factors appear to be the quality of the care experiences and the stimulation that children receive in helping to offset the effects of early negative experiences.

Mary Ainsworth's original tripartite categories of attachment – *Insecure Avoidant* (Type A), *Secure* (Type B) and *Insecure Resistant* (Type C) and the later category *Disorganised* (Type D) category (previously referenced and discussed) are extremely helpful, but we should not accept that every child neatly fits into one of the categories. Even in the best of theories some exceptions to the rule can be ignored, yet it is by exploring the exceptions that more accurate reflection on existing models and schema occurs. In the *Focus on Theory* feature below, we present an important classic paper which provides a reflection on attachment types as identified in a number of earlier studies and makes some interesting comments on the Type D category, particularly atypical attachments.

## Focus on Theory

### Atypical attachments in infancy and early childhood

To look at the nature of research in the context of emotional development and in particular attachment theory, we focus on Douglas Barnett and Joan Vondra's paper 'Atypical attachment in infancy and early childhood among children at developmental risk' (1999) which uses Mary Ainsworth's original categories of attachment – *Insecure Avoidant* (Type A), *Secure* (Type B) and *Insecure Resistant* (Type C) and the later *Disorganised* (Type D) category. Barnett and Vondra identify sets of behaviours judged *not* to meet criteria in Ainsworth's categories. The research methods adopted include a meta-analysis of results in other studies and a thorough exploration of the typology created as a result of Strange Situation methods.

Their main concern is that once a really useful and universally accepted category system is developed there is a tendency for researchers to observe that all cases will fit into the categories; some cases are actually only very approximate fits and others are ignored exceptions. While Type D attachment is the most commonly equated with atypical behaviours, the authors point out that to make this association exclusively would be a mistake; atypical behaviours can be observed in all types of attachment and they are important. Atypical behaviours can tell us more about the effect of the whole familial context (nurture) and the influence of the child's characteristics (nature).

Barnett and Vondra also make a very useful distinction between the supportive and important relationships between infants and play leaders or teachers that are not 'attached relationships', and true attachment with one or two primary caregivers. They define an attached relationship as a psychological consideration by the infant of the attached caregiver as a source of safety and comfort at times of distress – hence the two potential distresses in Strange Situation of the mother leaving and the introduction of a stranger.

Infants displaying Type D (disorganised/disoriented) are thought to lack consistent coping strategies and lack a 'readily observable goal, intention, or explanation' (Main & Solomon, 1990, p 122). Fear of the carer distinguishes this category from all the others and it is fear that may disturb infants, resulting in disorganised behaviours in the Strange Situation. Observation reveals these children to freeze or move very slowly, and at times are attracted to move towards a stranger – all atypical behaviours in the context of Strange Situation. An earlier study by Carlson *et al.* (1989) revealed the high incidence of adult psychiatric problems from children who had suffered some form of abuse from their caregiver in childhood. In their study, Radke-Yarrow and colleagues (1995) found 23 per cent of infants of mothers with depression and 42 per cent with manic depression had Type D attachments. Lyons-Ruth and Jacobvitz (1999) videotaped the interactions of mothers diagnosed with manic depression with their 18-month-old infants and found a consistent failure on the part of the mothers to respond to infant signals: again characterised by Type D attachments. These behaviours, many of which were discrete and in some cases unique, were considered by Barnett and Vondra to be characteristic of the relationship between caregiver and child rather than a simple reflection of the quality of any general attachment formed. To fit the description of being atypical there had to be strong and frequent manifestation of: contradictory behaviours, sometimes simultaneous; misdirected and incomplete movements; anomalous postures; disorientation and apprehension of the parent.

What is proposed in the paper is the conclusion that Type D attachment is highly disadvantageous for children. The insecure attachments in Type A and C categories, while impacting moderately on development, do not have the potential disastrous consequences of a young child developing a Type D attachment – no well-organised attachment at all – with their principal caregiver.

*Source*: From Barnett, D. & Vondra, J. I. (1999). Atypical attachment in infancy and early childhood among children at developmental risk. *Monographs of the Society for Research in Child Development, 64*(3), 1–24.

## Child-care and its influence on attachment

More questions are raised by the kind of findings we have highlighted in the *Focus on Theory* feature. For example, is the kind of attachment more to do with the personality of the main carer or that of the child, and what kinds of child-care result in what kinds of attachments? Do children form Type B attachments when Mum stays at home and type D attachments when left at the nursery 12 hours a day, six days a week? Here is another story.

This scene takes place outside a daycare centre which boasts that it offers early learning opportunities for children from birth to five years. It also boasts opening hours each day from 7 a.m. to 7 p.m. A large four-wheel drive vehicle screeches to a halt outside the front of the building one morning and a smartly dressed man alights, slams the car door firmly shut and strides around the car to extricate a bundle from the back seat. He is obviously a man in a hurry. The bundle is in fact a tiny baby. The man steamrolls into the building and in less than a minute he returns to the car minus the baby. Having deposited the baby in the daycare centre, he screeches away.

This story is an abridged version of one that appears in *Raising Babies* (2005) by Australian psychologist Steve Biddulph, and we include it to raise the very important issue of child-care and its impact on the emotional security and development of young children. There is no suggestion that this experience is in any way typical of child-care by be-suited drivers of four-wheel-drive cars but is a situation Steve Biddulph witnessed and shares with readers. Debates around the short- and long-term effects of child-care on children are of immense interest to parents, carers, educators and policy-makers.

In England, the establishment of a National Childcare Strategy in 1997 was a turning point in policy related to young people and signalled the UK Government's commitment to the regulation of and standards of care for young children. As part of this strategy, Sure Start

**Connect and Extend**

Can governments make any difference to child poverty? Many politicians aspire to make a difference, but how do we give life chances to those at the bottom of the socioeconomic order of society? This article discusses and evaluates the UK Government's drive to end child poverty. Read: Ball, S. & Vincent, C. (2005). The 'childcare champion'? New Labour, social justice and the childcare market. *British Educational Research Journal, 31*, 557–570.

(see **www.surestart.gov.uk**) became the first UK Government-funded programme (in 1999), supporting families with children up to 14 years of age. Working with various agencies in health, social services and education, it seeks to achieve better outcomes for parents, children and local communities. Some 524 programmes continue in operation in England, involving 400 000 children in disadvantaged areas. Relevant to this discussion are two of the programme's stated aims: first of all, to improve children's health and emotional development and, secondly, an increase in the availability of child-care for all children. Start-up grants are available for childminders and nurseries as well as after-school care, aiming to increase both the quantity and quality of child-care. Research of this initiative has shown some mixed findings. Its early national evaluation (NESS, 2004) found considerable progress in parenting and family support as seen through children's emotional and social development. Positive improvements in language development for 2-year-olds and a reduction in parental anxiety were also found (Harris *et al.*, 2003). Other scholars were and are less convinced and view Sure Start as a hotchpotch of contradictory policies, a result of a century of weak policy-making and financial ambivalences (Lloyd & Harrington, 2012; MacNeill, 2009; Penn, 2005).

Child-care takes different forms: childminding where a child is cared for at the home of another person; babysitting where individual children are cared for in their own home by someone other than a relative; care provided by relatives in their homes; and group daycare in which children attend a setting such as a nursery or private or community daycare centre.

Time spent in the various settings varies considerably. Some children spend several hours over a week, while for others 8 a.m. to 6 p.m. five days a week is not uncommon. Some studies (e.g. Shulman *et al.*, 1998; Woodard & Fine, 1991) report no significant detriments for children in their middle primary school years who care for themselves after school while their parent(s) finish work. Does this hold true for younger or older children? The critical factor here appears to be the quality of the experiences and the stimulation that children receive in helping to offset the effects of early negative experiences. The *Controversy* feature below asks the question: are young children in child-care from an early age at greater risk of developmental problems than those who remain at home, or is it a healthy separation? Let us consider the evidence.

A bright nursery setting with toys, mobiles and lots of colour. Children here are engaged in play, and adults are interacting with the children.

*Source:* © Pearson Education Ltd / Jules Selmes.

## Controversy

### Is child-care a good alternative to family care?

Findings from a number of studies about this issue may, on first reading, appear contradictory. In the United Kingdom, the Effective Provision of Pre-School Education Project (EPPE, 2004) found positive effects of high-quality preschool provision for children between 3 and 7 years on intellectual and socio-behavioural development (Sylva *et al.*, 2003). Earlier research found academic attainment better for children who attended daycare settings than those that stayed at home and this was more marked for children from low-income families (e.g. Andersson, 1992). A later Swedish study (Broberg *et al.*, 1997), involving children under 2 years and attending child-care settings, showed gains in social, cognitive and emotional competence in later childhood and adolescence. Conversely, Jay Belsky and colleagues (2001) found that children who spent in excess of 30 hours in daycare per week were reported by their teachers to be less co-operative and more aggressive to their peers. Earlier, Baydar and Brooks-Gunn (1991) found that children in full daycare (20 hours a week and more) displayed insecure attachment as measured by the Strange Situation procedure. What sense do we make of these seeming contradictions?

There are many factors to be considered before we reach a decision about the validity and reliability of these research findings: the temperament and age of the children; the home environments including family income; the type of care studied; time spent in the care and the stability of the care arrangements are all influencing factors. As we have hinted before, we believe there is one decisive factor in the evidence: the quality of the care provided. This is not a new thought specific to children in the UK.

The extensive National Institute of Child Health and Human Development study (NICHD, 1999) in the United States found that child-care alone did not contribute to infant insecurity. Insecurity was raised when there was insensitive care at home and in care settings, when children were exposed to indifferent care for long hours and when there were many different arrangements for care. In care settings deemed to be of high quality, children who have attended these have more social skills than children attending settings of inferior quality (Claessens & Chen, 2013). Where there is poor-quality care either at home or in external settings, children score lower on tests of cognitive and social skills (NICHD, 2001). Too long periods in care increases aggression (Watamura *et al.*, 2003) – although 'only children' can cope better than others with extended care. High-quality care is the answer (Lamb & Ahnert, 2006). The quality of the relationship between carer and child is essential and the key determinant of quality care provision.

Alison Clarke-Stewart and Virginia Allhusen's research (2005) found that secure attachments to carers existed when levels of training of staff was high. Other indicators of quality they identified include staff-to-child ratios that are low, with informed and well-qualified staff who have knowledge of child development and child-rearing practices. Trained staff interact effectively (play) with children and offer activities that promote regular communication and respect. In high-quality settings the relationships between staff and parents are very positive. The physical environment is stimulating both indoors and outdoors and a daily timetable shows flexibility and variety. Local and national standards of care are rigorously adhered to.

In summary, then, child-care is seen by some as a good alternative to family care with many positive developmental outcomes possible. It is quality of the relationship between carer(s) and child which are the determinant.

What do you think? Can child-care ever be thought of as a good alternative to family care?

**Summary 2**

Before moving on, let's summarise what we have learned in the middle section of this chapter:

- Attachment refers to emotional ties to the special people who offer us comfort and in whose company we feel happiest in terms of both a desire for social contact and a distress on being separated from another person.

- Attachment begins with synchronised routines – everyday but vital practices that go on between parent and child. They include paying attention to the baby's physical or emotional states, being sensitive to these and learning to play together.

- Attachments were most likely to form with those who responded accurately to the baby's signals, not necessarily the person with whom they spent the most time. Schaffer and Emerson called this 'sensitive responsiveness'.

- There are four main theories of attachment theory: *learning* – through the process of classical conditioning babies learn to repeat behaviours in order to get the things they want; *cognitive* – requires understanding of the differences between friends and strangers since it is with the former that stable and lasting relationships are formed; *ethological* holds that we are born with innate tendencies for carers and children to form attachments; *psychoanalytic* proposes that a child's physical needs create psychological tensions, creating a drive to reduce the tension.

- Children who are able to make strong attachments in very early childhood grow into balanced, sensitive and trusting individuals who approach life situations with confidence.

- Five factors which influence attachment are: cross-cultural differences; maternal characteristics; child characteristics; family circumstances; multiple attachments.

- The quality of attachments can be judged by security theory using a technique known as the Strange Situation procedure to judge how securely children are attached to one person and that person serves as a firm base for the infant to explore the environment.

- There are four types of attachment: insecure avoidant; secure avoidant; insecure ambivalent and disorganised/disoriented attachment.

- Attachments can go wrong when there is maternal deprivation or privation. Other factors are the child's age, temperament and the duration of the separation.

- Child-care is seen by some as a proper alternative to family care: it is quality of the relationship between carer(s) and child which is important.

# Personality

## Children's personalities and the 'Big Five'

It was the end of the first week in the Autumn Term and Mr Crane, the teacher, was building a mental picture of the 8-year-old children in his class. It was always very exciting finding out about them as people – not just ticks in a markbook.

There were the extroverts, Mike and Jen: boisterous and loud, willing to have a go at anything and generally getting their own way. There was Lewis, the opposite – shy, who seemed to find new situations difficult and easily got lost in the crowd. Abdul just seemed very content in an untidy sort of a way and would happily engage in whatever he had to without a fuss. Marj was meticulous in her work; always neat and tidy and thorough. Bella, who was very capable indeed, perhaps highly intelligent if a little intense, always wanting to find out more but was not very popular with the others in the class.

'The usual suspects this year!' thought Mr Crane.

This imaginary story illustrates a common scene in any classroom at the beginning of a school year. Having some knowledge of the different personality traits in the class assists a teacher to understand children's behaviour in the classroom and playground, and provides a more rounded picture of each individual child – much more than academic grades. **Personality** is the term used to refer to the differences in the ways in which people relate to objects or other people around them, describing 'enduring individual differences in behaviour' (Bee, 2000a, p 259). For 75 years or so psychologists have identified and referred to five major personality traits – known as the **Big Five** – formed from early research into adult personality (Thurstone, 1934) and used as the basis for much subsequent research and discussion (e.g. Kappe & Flier, 2012). There is evidence that these traits are reliable and applicable to personalities in childhood and adolescence (Slobodskaya, 2007) and are good predictors of behaviour (Hong *et al.*, 2008). The five traits are: extroversion, conscientiousness, agreeableness, neuroticism and openness. These traits are relatively stable across cultures (McAdams & Pals, 2006) and have been found to be stable in longitudinal studies (e.g. Prinzie & Deković, 2008). In the discussion that follows do bear in mind that each of the personality traits are scales; an individual could be really extroverted and just a little neurotic and it would be wrong to label children as wholly one personality trait or another. We have summarised the key features and qualities of each trait (Table 11.4) and indicated how children might behave. Annotations in italics are included as comments on the implications of each type of personality.

**Personality**
Differences in the ways in which people relate to objects or other people around them.

**Big Five**
The personality traits of extroversion, conscientiousness, agreeableness, neuroticism and openness.

**Connect and Extend**
How do young personalities of 6–9-year-olds change – one of the critical periods of childhood for emotional development? Read a 3-year longitudinal study of personality characteristics by Prinzie, P. & Deković, M. (2008). Continuity and change of childhood personality characteristics. *Personality & Individual Differences*, 45, 82–88.

**Table 11.4** Features and qualities of 'Big Five' personality types and some educational implications

| Personality type | Key features | Types of behaviour |
|---|---|---|
| Extroversion | The degree of active engagement a child has with its surroundings. Extent of social interactions with others | Outgoing Confident Enthusiastic |
| *Children at the high end of this scale are the star performers in any class. Teachers learn their names first in a new class because they are noticeable quickly. They are confident and will put themselves forward in a group or in a new situation.* | | |
| Conscientiousness | The ability to control impulses | Responsible Thorough |
| *Children at the high end of this scale display control. They act responsibly in class and approach their work and school life in general seriously. They are the archetypal model pupils.* | | |
| Agreeableness | Warmth and sincerity | Affectionate Generous Interested in others |
| *Children at the high end of this scale are the popular children. They tend to be liked by peers and by adults for their genuineness and sincerity.* | | |
| Neuroticism | Experiencing the world as a struggle | Anxious Unstable |
| *Children at the high end of this scale struggle with school. They worry about relationships, exams and their academic performance throughout their school lives.* | | |
| Openness | Complexity and depth in relation to experiences in life | Curious Original |
| *Children at the high end of this scale are honest in all that they undertake. Often they have many interests in and outside of school.* | | |

As we saw in Chapter 6, a combination of genetics and early experiences allow children to form 'a lens' through which they look at the world around them. Even by the end of the first year, parents will be able to describe the personality type of their child quite accurately: whether he or she is shy, social, boisterous, confident and so on. Such knowledge is of course invaluable later in school – as the story of Mr Crane and his new class suggests – and allows teachers to describe an individual child more holistically in terms of their attitudes, attributes and behaviours. When a child is labelled as shy and another as confident, what is being referred to is the child's temperament. This is the topic we turn to next.

**Temperament**
A matrix of core qualities apparent in infancy that inform a child's future personality.

## Temperament and personality

Most researchers agree that temperament and personality are not exactly the same although in many books the terms are often used interchangeably. Temperament may be thought of as a kind of matrix of core qualities apparent in infancy that inform a child's future personality. It is allied to emotions and in broad terms can be thought of as the characteristics of a person's emotional nature – hence it is included in this chapter. Several definitions, like that of Mary Rothbart and John Bates who define temperament as 'constitutionally based individual differences in emotional, motor, and attentional reactivity and self-regulation' (1998, p 108), link temperament to the emotions, and stress the processes of attention and self-regulation in how one's temperament is constructed. It is certainly not fixed as the term 'constitutionally based' might imply in the definition above, as a child's temperament will undergo some degree of developmental change. Even so, identifying trajectories of both personality and social–emotional development are possible from measurement of its characteristics because there is evidence that shows that stability in temperament exists from infancy to adulthood.

For example, a classic longitudinal study by Diana Guerin and colleagues (1997) tracked children with 'difficult' temperaments from 1$^1$/$_2$ to 12 years using parental reports initially and then reports from teachers. The research team found correlations between the stable temperament of these children at home and throughout school, with behaviours that included short attention spans and hostility. Stability in temperament means that anxious toddlers tend to become anxious teenagers. The young child who refuses to accept new food as an infant is likely to show the same anxieties and difficulties on entering nursery and later may have difficulties in adjusting to life as an adolescent.

Differences in temperament characteristics are somewhat similar to the 'Big Five' personality dimensions. From a number of existing models (see also Rothbart *et al.*, 2000; Buss & Plomin, 1984; Kagan *et al.*, 1984) describing the important dimensions of temperament, the one provided by Alexander Thomas and Stella Chess (1986) is most commonly used by researchers. Their model describes nine dimensions organised into three groups, classifying infants as: the easy child, the slow-to-warm-up child and the difficult child.

The *easy child* has a positive approach to life. As a baby this child sleeps well and has regular cycles. This child is happy and social and adjusts to life quite easily, smiles at strangers, is not phased by setbacks, and adapts to novelty (40 per cent of children identified in the original sample). The *slow-to-warm-up child* shows less radical reactions to life, either positively or negatively. This child is reluctant to respond to newness at first but gradually accepts it over time. Initial responses to new stimuli tend to be negative (15 per cent identified in the original sample). The *difficult child* reacts badly to change. As a baby and toddler he/she is more irritable, sleeps badly and is slow to develop regular cycles in sleeping or eating. This child responds badly to change and novelty, often displays tantrums and treats strangers with suspicion (10 per cent identified in original sample). Of course, many children do not neatly fit into just one of the above categories – the remaining 35 per cent in Thomas and Chess' study showed a significant mixture of temperament traits.

Psychologist Avshalom Caspi (1998) has linked temperament to the Big Five personality types by creating five dimensions. These are presented in Table 11.5 linked to common behaviours

**Table 11.5** Temperament and observable behaviours in children and some educational implications

| Temperament dimension | Observable behaviours |
|---|---|
| High activity | Vigorous movement patterns<br>Possible extrovert tendencies later |
| *Children with high scores in this dimension are highly active in care settings and classrooms. These children never seem to be still for a moment. They enjoy movement and need to express themselves by moving about through the school day.* | |
| Inhibition and anxiety | Not meeting eye gaze, nail-biting<br>Possible neuroticism later |
| *Children with high scores in this dimension tend to withdraw from new and uncertain situations. They are reluctant to start school and leave their parent(s). They continue to shun exposure and find talking about themselves or their work, or speaking or reading in assembly stressful.* | |
| Positive emotionality | Drawn towards new objects and people<br>Agreeable demeanour |
| *Children with high scores in this dimension are positive to new experiences in care settings and school. They are popular.* | |
| Negative emotionality | Responds with anger and fuss to many situations<br>Has a low threshold of tolerance |
| *Children with high scores in this dimension are less positive to new experiences in school. They become distressed quickly when they do not understand.* | |
| Task persistent | Remains focused<br>Can sustain attention and effort<br>Open to new experiences |
| *Children with high scores in this dimension are good academic achievers who concentrate and see challenges through to completion.* | |

and to this we have added an annotation commenting on the educational implications of each dimension (in italics). Although this is not an exhaustive list of all temperament traits, these five dimensions provide a useful way of classifying variations in an individual's traits. In a similar way to our earlier discussion of personality types, knowing these temperament traits can assist teachers to understand children more holistically and help them account for some behaviours of children they witness daily in the classroom. Although it may be tempting to assume that these traits are stable across all cultures, this is not the case. Differences among cultures are apparent as the first few months of a child's life show. For example, in two early studies, Navaho babies were found to be less excitable than white American newborn babies (Chisholm, 1989) and Chinese newborn babies to be less vocal and less active than white American babies (Kagan *et al.*, 1994). More recently, significant cultural differences in temperament were found between European (Swedish and German) subjects and Iranian subjects (Richter *et al.*, 2007) and in temperament-based preferred learning styles between Palestinian children and US children (Oakland *et al.*, 2007).

Such findings argue quite convincingly that some cultural variations exist. They also suggest that differences observable in newborns are probably due to both cultural and biological factors. Indeed, individual differences which are at the core of temperament research are generally received as being both genetically and culturally based. Some researchers (recently Nyman *et al.*, 2009; Plomin, 2000) take the view that temperament aspects such as shyness, activity levels and sociability are inherited. Findings from behaviour genetic studies favour such a biological basis of temperament but also testify to important environmental factors that shape an individual's temperament. Since any biological tendencies are shaped by early experiences, the effect of temperament on how we behave is best understood (not surprisingly by now!) as an interaction of nature and nurture.

**Connect and Extend**

Connect with Chapter 2 – Erikson's theory of human development, temperament, families and cultures – by reading: Tu, T. & Lash, M. (2007/2008). Don't tell me no; I tell you no!: Facilitating self-control in infants and toddlers. *Childhood Education, 84*, 79–84, available through your library.

# Linking temperament and social context

We mentioned earlier in the chapter Alexander Thomas and Stella Chess's work on how early emotional development influences later development and links a child's temperament and his or her social environment. The 'goodness of fit' hypothesis (Thomas & Chess, 1977) is the match between a child's temperament and the environment, and it is the link between the two that determines a child's eventual personality. The theory suggests that if their environment suits a child's temperament and is 'a good fit', then a child will grow and develop with a well-adjusted personality. Children's individual temperaments evoke different reactions from parents (and also their other carers, teachers and peers). Children described as 'easy' fit in well at school and make friends easily. However, parents of a boisterous child may have great difficulties in coping with such a child and over-rigid caring on the part of parents – in an attempt to provide structure for the child – may have just the opposite effect. As a consequence this inflexibility may make the child even more difficult for those parents to manage. Over-controlling behaviour towards the child is relatively ineffectual in altering how the child behaves and results in reinforcing the undesirable aspects of the child's temperament.

Returning to differences in cultures, parental expectations differ here too. In Western societies there is a strong drive from many parents to get their children to sleep through the night from an early age and not to disrupt the sleep of parents (many of whom work full time) and to master skills such as dressing and toileting, which are viewed as culturally important milestones of development. In many rural societies across the globe, this drive is not evident and so the home environment places less of these kinds of pressures on children. Cultural differences give rise to expectations that lead to differences in parenting styles that in turn affect children's development. It is worth making the link here with Bronfenbrenner's ecological model introduced in Chapter 1. Cultural values play a powerful role in shaping what parents worry about and what they will try and control in their child's behaviour. One aspect of temperament which we in Western cultures consider helps to define personality is shyness. Time for another anecdote.

I remember – foolishly and in ignorance – demanding that a child from a Chinese background should 'Look at me when I'm talking to you!' when ticking off a teenage boy for some slight misdemeanour. I did not understand that it was considered rude in his culture to make eye-contact with an elder and that the young chap was showing his deference and respect. I just thought he was shy or rude or both! What I didn't understand was the difference between anxious shyness (involuntary behaviour) and regulated shyness (culturally taught behaviour) and the role of culture in shaping the expression of children's shy behaviour (Yiyuan *et al.*, 2007). This is important. I hadn't grasped that some behaviours are 'dead giveaways' to temperament and that others are culturally situated and should be treated with care and respect. It is not just understanding about temperament, personality and emotional development, it is judging when that understanding applies.

## Goodness of fit
A match between child-rearing practice and the individual child's temperament.

● ● ● ● ● ● ● ● ● ● ● ● ● ● ● ●
**Connect and Extend**
For an article which discusses the factors that affect classroom education including cultural differences, language, dialect or economic difficulties, read: Landsman, J., Moore, T. & Simmons, R. (2008). Reluctant teachers, reluctant learners. *Educational Leadership*, 65, 62–66.
● ● ● ● ● ● ● ● ● ● ● ● ● ● ● ●

# Linking temperament and learning styles

The popularity of the 'goodness of fit' model stems from a common acceptance of learner differences in temperament and personality and how these differences are likely to influence preferred learning styles. Remember that the notion of preferred learning styles is based upon the work of behavioural analyst David Kolb, developed over many years and published in 1984. Working with a colleague, Roger Fry, Kolb developed a model of effective experiential learning based upon four different abilities (see Table 11.6): ability to learn through active 'concrete' experimentation; ability to reflect upon observations and to learn from them; ability to form abstract concepts; and to learn through active experimentation.

Ideally we would all have high ability in each of these areas but this ideal is rarely true. Almost all of us develop an orientation – by experience of success and as some function of our

**Table 11.6** Kolb's learning styles, learning abilities and characteristics

| Learning style (and possible temperament dimension) | Combination of learning abilities | Description of characteristics and preferred activities |
|---|---|---|
| **Converger**<br><br>Task persistent? | An ability to form abstract concepts and to learn through active experimentation | • Strong in practical application of ideas<br>• Can focus on deductive reasoning to solve specific problems<br>• Unemotional<br>• Can narrow interests |
| **Diverger**<br><br>Positive emotionally? | An ability to learn through active 'concrete' experimentation, to reflect upon observations and to learn from them | • Strong in imaginative ability<br>• Good at generating ideas and seeing things from different perspectives<br>• Interested in people<br>• Broad cultural interests |
| **Assimilator**<br><br>Inhibition and anxiety? | An ability to reflect upon observations and to learn from them, and to form abstract concepts | • Strong ability to create theoretical models<br>• Excels in inductive reasoning<br>• Concerned with abstract concepts rather than people |
| **Accommodator**<br><br>Extrovert? | An ability to learn through active 'concrete' experimentation and to learn through active experimentation | • Greatest strength is doing things<br>• More of a risk taker<br>• Performs well when required to react to immediate circumstances<br>• Solves problems intuitively |

*Source*: Adapted from Tennant, M. (1997). *Psychology and Adult Learning* (2nd ed.). London: Routledge. Reproduced with permission.

temperament – towards one or more of these abilities of learning. By associating the four different learning abilities in different combinations, Kolb and Fry created the idea of four preferred learning styles: converger, diverger, assimilator and accommodator. Psychologist Mark Tennant has usefully associated for us the four learning styles with the combinations of learning abilities and preferred learning activities. We have added suggestions for matching up temperament dimensions and associated behaviours for you to think about and critique.

You may have noticed that we have not attempted to place the 'negative emotionally' temperament dimension into Table 11.6. Why not? Well, children who display anger, fuss and intolerance (which characterise a negative temperament) are unlikely to engage in learning activities. An unhappy child is not learning and, until we deal with the causes and the effects of a negative emotional response, then it is unlikely that children will do well at pre-school or school or engage in the learning activities. School refusers and truants (those who absent themselves from school without or with the knowledge of the main caregiver) during adolescence are often drawn from those who exhibit negative emotional temperament characteristics from infancy (Laible *et al.*, 2008a).

Goodness of fit is not about labelling children in particular categories or parents as weak or strong, but in helping all carers to understand how changes in their own behaviours and attitudes can result in improvements in a child's emotional development. Such an idea as we have put forward in Table 11.6 has not received universal acceptance, but, in the absence of further research, it offers a useful tool to explain how temperament interfaces with behaviour. Application in classroom situations can begin by raising awareness that a knowledge of the biological/ecological basis of individual difference and temperament can help practitioners turn away from negative attitudes towards children's motivation and achievement, and towards interventions and methods that work with individual differences – authentic personalised learning.

**Summary 3**

We now summarise what you have learned in the final section of this chapter:

- Personality is the term used to refer to the differences in the ways in which people relate to objects or other people around them, describing 'enduring individual differences in behaviour' (Bee, 2000a, p 259).

- Psychologists have identified and referred to five major personality traits known as the 'Big Five': extroversion, conscientiousness, agreeableness, neuroticism and openness.

- Temperament may be thought of as core qualities of a person's emotional nature apparent in infancy that inform a child's future personality.

- There is evidence that shows that stability in temperament exists from infancy to adulthood.

- Thomas and Chess (1986) describe nine dimensions of temperament organised into three groups, classifying infants as: the easy child, the slow-to-warm-up child and the difficult child.

- Avshalom Caspi (1998) has linked temperament to the Big Five personality types by creating five dimensions: high activity; inhibition and anxiety; positive emotionally; negative emotionally; task persistent.

- Temperament is our biological tendencies shaped by our early experiences.

- The 'goodness of fit' hypothesis (Thomas & Chess, 1977) is the match between a child's temperament and the environment and it is the link between the two that determines a child's eventual personality.

- Knowledge of the biological/ecological basis of individual difference and temperament can help educators use teaching methods that work with individual differences – authentic personalised learning.

## Conclusion

When we talk about somebody giving 'an emotional response' this tends to be accusatory. We appear to be saying that they have not thought through what they are saying or how they are behaving. And yet, is not the expression of how we are feeling an act of cognition rather than a reflex? Although the basic emotions – including sadness and anger – appear 'hard-wired' and culture-resistant, all babies very quickly learn much more complex feelings. Furthermore, they associate emotions and behaviours with responses that they learn from those with whom they make their first important attachments. They learn to control their feelings and their reactions, and this 'emotional intelligence' – understanding feelings and the behaviour of others – is the key idea in emotional development.

Emotions may be explained through a combination of biology and environment – biologically pre-programmed since they tend to appear at the same times, but it is also true that they are shaped by experiences in the environment. From an initial set of six basic emotions a child comes to possess a more complex system, so that by the age of 3 emotions become differentiated, and the ways they are expressed are personal to the child. Security of attachment relates to any point in one's life, but is normally associated with the very early months and years, and acknowledged to be vital for subsequent relationships. The effect of temperament on behaviour is best understood as an interaction of biology and the cultural and social environment, and temperament can be related to preferred learning styles and a child's success at pre-school settings and school.

One of the key concerns for teachers, early years health professionals, and parents is the extent to which we can support children through the difficult crucial times for the development of personality and temperament. One key time is the first experiences that young children have of separation from the main carer(s) and the substitution of concurrent and multi-context child-care arrangements. As long as those settings are what developmental psychologists Sandra Scarr and Judith Dunn referred to as a 'consistent and agreeable world for the child' (1987, p 187), then things look very positive for healthy emotional development. Where this is not the case, then from early schooling through adolescence the likelihood is that children will exhibit some elements of emotional and behavioural difficulties, which at the extreme will stifle cognitive development and progress at school and inhibit opportunities to take their place in the social and moral world. It is to the complex world of the moral society that we now turn for the final chapter in *Child Development: Theory and Practice 0–11.*

In Chapter 12 we will learn how a child's social world develops from first relationships with parents, to contact and relationships with others, recognise the importance of play in developing children's social skills, identify the three major socialisation influences on children and understand children's moral development through expressions of prosocial and antisocial behaviours. We will also draw together the themes and theories of child development and take a long hard look at how we have been able to bring together research and practice in child-care and education. For the time being we leave this chapter with a couple of questions for you to think about – can we practise feelings and expressing emotions in the way that the children were doing in Madame Martine's class of 8-year-olds? Or were the children coming to a shared social understanding and agreement of how some emotions are best controlled and expressed? Was Lee really best 'at being disgusted', why did nobody get 'dread', and did Amy really want to go to the toilet?

## Summary Table
### Emotions and Personality

## Understanding emotions (pp 328–338)

Emotions are behaviours that direct our thinking and subsequent actions in response to events and include three components: *physiological* – a physical reaction or feeling; *subjective* – judging one's own emotional state; and *expressive* – communicating by expression, posture and word. Children's emotional development is predominantly about communicating feelings and learning to interpret the emotions of other people.

## Theoretical approaches to understanding emotions (p 329)

Theoretical approaches to emotional development include: cognitive perspectives – understanding of the world and how 'things' work; maturational perspectives – expressions of common emotions appearing at the same time; learning perspectives – emotions are a result of our lived experiences; and functional perspectives which maintain that the ways we respond to events determine how much we wish to repeat the experience in future.

## Expressing emotions and the development of emotions (pp 329–333)

Babies begin by expressing six basic or primary emotions: happiness, sadness, anger, disgust, surprise and fear. Late in the infant's second year, complex emotions (or self-conscious emotions) emerge: embarrassment, shame, guilt, pride and jealousy. The emotions of embarrassment, jealousy and empathy are possible only with the development of self-awareness, and pride, guilt and shame appear as children begin to have an understanding of rules and goals.

### Emotional knowledge and understanding the emotions of others (pp 333–334)

Emotional self-regulation are strategies used to adjust our emotional state and to allow us to achieve our goals. Such capacity is limited in young children and they tend to rely on carers to intervene on their behalf. Emotional intelligence is best thought of as being aware of one's own emotions and those of others, and being sufficiently motivated to develop relationships.

### Social referencing and social cognition (pp 334–337)

Social referencing is the term that refers to reliance on someone else's emotional reaction to assess a new or uncertain situation. Emotional expressions of carers influence young children's reactions to strangers and ways in which they play with unfamiliar toys. The development of empathy is dependent on social cognition by taking another person's perspective or responding in a similar way. Milestones in emotional development include social referencing, the development of empathy and evidence of social cognition – that our thoughts can control our emotions.

## Attachment (pp 338–353)

Attachment refers to emotional ties to the special people who offer us comfort and in whose company we feel happiest. It is measured in terms of both a desire for social contact and a distress on being separated from another person.

### Theories of attachment (pp 340–343)

There are four main theories of attachment theory: *learning* – through the process of classical conditioning babies learn to repeat behaviours in order to get the things they want; *cognitive* – requires understanding of the differences between friends; *ethological* holds that we are born with innate tendencies for carers and children to form attachments; *psycho-analytic* proposes that a child's physical needs create psychological tensions, creating a drive to reduce the tension. There are four types of attachment: insecure avoidant, secure avoidant, insecure ambivalent and disorganised/disoriented attachment.

### Early attachment and its consequences (pp 343–347)

Attachment begins with synchronised routines – everyday but vital practices that go on between parent and child. They include paying attention to the baby's physical or emotional states and being sensitive to these. Parents and children also learn to play together in a series of regular and practised games – remember the importance of play to children's development and learning at all ages. Attachments were most likely to form with those who respond accurately to the baby's signals – sensitive responsiveness – not necessarily the person with whom they spend the most time. Children who are able to make strong attachments in very early childhood grow into sensitive and trusting individuals who approach life situations with confidence. Five factors which influence attachment are: cross-cultural differences; maternal characteristics; child characteristics; family circumstances; multiple attachments.

### Judging the quality of attachment (pp 347–352)

The quality of attachment can be judged by security theory using a technique known as the Strange Situation procedure to judge how securely children are attached to one person and how that person serves as a firm base for the infant to explore the environment. Attachments can go wrong when there is maternal deprivation or privation. Other factors are the child's age, temperament and the duration of the separation. Child-care is seen by some as a proper alternative to family care: it is quality of the relationship between carer(s) and child which is important.

## Personality (pp 353–359)

Personality is the term used to refer to the differences in the ways in which people relate to objects or other people around them, describing 'enduring individual differences in behaviour' (Bee, 2000b, p 259). Psychologists have identified and referred to five major personality traits known as the 'Big Five': extroversion, conscientiousness, agreeableness, neuroticism and openness.

### Temperament and personality (pp 355–357)

Temperament is core qualities of a person's emotional nature apparent in infancy that inform a child's future personality: our biological tendencies shaped by our early experiences. Thomas and Chess (1986) describe nine dimensions of temperament organised into three groups, classifying infants as: the easy child, the slow-to-warm-up child and the difficult child. Avshalom Caspi (1998) has linked temperament to the Big Five personality types by creating five dimensions: high activity; inhibition and anxiety; positive emotionally; negative emotionally; task persistent.

### Linking temperament, social context and learning styles (pp 357–359)

The 'goodness of fit' hypothesis (Thomas & Chess, 1977) is the match between a child's temperament and the environment, and it is the link between the two that determines a child's eventual personality. Knowledge of the biological/ ecological basis of individual difference and temperament can help educators use teaching methods that work with individual differences – authentic personalised learning.

# Going further

Golding, K. S. *et al.* (2012) Observing children with attachment or emotional difficulties in school. London: Jessica Kingsley Publishers.
This book provides an observation checklist which enables practitioners to identify behavioural patterns in children with social and emotional difficulties, to analyse the emotional difficulties underlying these behaviours and to establish what kind of help and support the children need.

Ekman, P. (2004). *Emotions revealed.* London: Phoenix. Written by a leading authority on facial expressions, this book provides ideas and insights into understanding children's emotions. Chapter 1 on emotions across cultures is particularly informative.

Goleman, D. (2006). *Emotional intelligence: Why it can matter more than IQ*, 10th anniversary edition. New York: Bantam Books.
This has fast become a classic text. It makes a convincing case for the promotion of emotional intelligence over IQ!

Bahman, S. & Maffini, H. (2008) Developing children's emotional intelligence. London: Continuum Education.
The authors of this book provide practical tools and techniques that you can use with children to successfully develop their emotional intelligence.

# Useful websites

www.circle-time.co.uk
From Jenny Mosley consultancies. Interactive materials for practitioners to use.

www.nelig.com
Website from UK combining information from organisations associated with promoting emotional literacy in education.

www.wiredforhealth.gov.uk/healthy.healsch.html
National Healthy School Standard is a government scheme in the United Kingdom. It views schools as settings to improve mental health and emotional wellness of children. In the United Kingdom, approximately 14 000 schools are involved.

www.feel.org/articles/multiple_intelligences.html
Site containing information to deepen your understanding of multiple intelligences and links to emotional literacy.

www.personalityresearch.org/papers/pendry.html
A research site which makes strong theoretical and practical links between personality and ethological attachment theory.

www.standards.dfes.gov.uk/primary/publications/banda/seal/
Seal stands for 'Social and emotional aspects of learning'. It is a curriculum resource to help primary schools develop children's social, emotional and behavioural skills. The UK Government has endorsed this material and it is now used in many primary schools in England.

# Chapter 12
## The Social and Moral World of the Child

## Overview

# Introduction

In the last chapter we learned that, although the basic emotions – such as fear and happiness – appear 'hard-wired' and culture-resistant, all babies very quickly learn much more complex feelings associated with their first important attachments. Moreover, young children begin to understand the feelings and the behaviour of others: key ideas in the development of their temperament and personality. Where emotional development is distorted, then we can predict with some confidence that children will exhibit elements of emotional and behavioural difficulties. Such difficulties inhibit opportunities to 'enjoy and achieve', 'make a positive contribution' and 'achieve economic well-being' – three of the five outcomes for children in the Every Child Matters approach launched by the UK Government in the 2004 Children Act that we introduced in the first chapter. It is to the complex social and moral world of the child that we now turn for the final chapter in *Child Development: Theory and Practice 0–11*. As usual we begin with a story.

> *Lin Yan is just about to begin her first day in Meadowbank Junior School. Her parents have recently moved into the area and have found a school that they believe will be ideal for their rather shy daughter. Meadowbank is known for its friendly ethos and for the value it places on children 'getting along well' with one another. The class teacher makes Lin Yan feel very welcome. She has a place for her coat with her name above it and the children have made her a special welcome card. During the morning, the teacher encourages her to join Hannah and Seetal at the computer. They soon invite Lin Yan to have a go. She is a little anxious at first but soon uses the mouse to click and drag icons on the screen with considerable skill, and together they answer all the on-screen questions correctly! The other children are very impressed and tell others that 'Lin is great at maths'.*
>
> *At break-time, other girls come over to meet Lin Yan. They have been watching her across the classroom and want to know more about her. They are full of questions and soon find they have some common interests, including dance. Lin Yan shows the girls some basic moves of Chinese classical dance and everybody is impressed with her grace and balance. The girls try to copy and there is a lot of laughter and smiles. On the first day at her new school, Lin Yan has made new friends and learned that being good at something can be helpful in starting and building relationships with others.*

In this story Lin Yan wanted to make friends with other children in her new class and they were keen to get to know her and be her friend too. Humans desire to be with other humans – we are curious about others and seek the interest and security of being part of a family, a group, and a wider society. It is through being in groups that children learn about the practices and values of the society in which they live. Experiences in childhood in various social groups play an important part in making us who we are and who we become. Through this **enculturation** process, children acquire knowledge, skills and behaviours so that they can 'enjoy and achieve', 'make a positive contribution' and 'achieve economic well-being'. For Lin Yan, the experiences on her first day at school were positive, and knowledge and skills gained on this important occasion will stand her in good stead in making new relationships in the future.

**Enculturation**
A process by which people learn about the practices and values of the society in which they live.

Social development is linked to other aspects of development: early sensory and cognitive development being especially closely connected. A newborn infant is unable to differentiate between strangers and friends and not yet ready to communicate with others by smiling and gesturing – skills reliant upon interpreting the signals of other people. Yet two years on, the same child is capable of showing deep attachment towards others, can communicate with others in quite sophisticated ways, and shows the beginnings of prosocial behaviour (as opposed to anti-social behaviour). Initial social experiences are principally those determined by immediate family members, but as social beings children seek out other people, form relationships and engage with them in various social activities.

The achievement of important mobility milestones such as crawling and walking combined with early utterances, gestures and facial expressions enables a child to come into contact with

**Nexus**
A bonded or connected group of individuals.

more people and be understood by those immediately around. An increasing ability to communicate with different people becomes vital for a child as they form a social **nexus** of peers and other adults that they meet in their steadily expanding social world.

This chapter begins by charting social development, from the close relationships with those in the immediate environment, to starting school and beyond. It stresses the importance of play experiences in fostering social skills and behaviours, introducing the concept of play as 'social chess'. Issues connecting social and cognitive development – social cognition – which incorporates personal feelings, notions of self and self-identity, theory of mind and social identity are explored and discussed in the context of three main social influences of family, peers and school. In the final section we discuss moral development, largely through pro- and antisocial behaviours common in school contexts.

## Chapter Objectives

By the time you have completed this chapter you should be able to answer the following questions:

- What are the main theories of social development?
- What is the role of play in socialisation?
- How do we come to understand the motives and intentions of others?
- What is the social influence of family, peers and schools?
- How do children develop a sense of right and wrong?
- What are prosocial behaviours and how do we promote them in schools?
- How should we deal with forms of aggressive behaviour, including bullying?

# Human sociability and the need for nexus

## The early social world of the child – first relationships

Young children are already part of a social system before they are born. Remember in Chapter 10 how a baby is capable of discriminating its mother's voice in the womb? This means that fairly soon into life outside of the womb babies can orient themselves – sense and know that others are separate to them – to social situations and to other people. Of course, physical bonding in the first moments after a child is born is important, but bonding and the first indications of attachments also includes reacting to the sound of mother's voice and excited by other voices too. Babies' social development is much more sophisticated than just meeting their primary needs of warmth, hunger and security alone and much more than just physical contact.

**CONSPEC mechanism**
A brain system that passes on information about face processing to the cortex and directs an infant's gaze to the human face.

**Person permanence**
Understanding that a person still exists even when no longer in view.

Although early reflexes such as those used in grasping and rooting link babies immediately to their carers, it is the rapidly developing sensory capabilities that provide information to assist in recognising aspects of other people that are different. The perceptual systems of babies are already geared up to orienting themselves to others, differentiating by smell, sound and look. We have already said how important faces are for babies (Chapter 8), even to newborns and that we appear to be hard-wired to make sense of facial structures and symmetrical patterns. Developmentalists Mark Johnson and John Morton (Johnson, 2000; Johnson & Morton, 1991) believe that as a species we are pre-wired to process faces. They propose we are born with a conspecific face recognition system (**CONSPEC mechanism**), which is a brain system that passes on information about the structure of the human face to the brain cortex for further analysis, sufficient to direct the infant's gaze to another person's face for the purpose of comparison. After 2 months babies take interest in other babies, and we can observe children of this age gazing at each other (Rubin *et al.*, 1998). In Chapter 11 we discussed the infant smile as perhaps the first and most potent form of early communication. Young children smile and look towards others around them and use smiling as an important social signal, looking for clear responses; others respond to the babies' smiles, with motherese, babbling, cooing and returning smiles. Interaction is further promoted through adult–baby games and helps with the child's understanding of turn-taking. A baby also learns (as we have argued from Chapter 2 and throughout) by imitation, for example, clapping hands, and sticking tongues out in simple games which contribute to an infant's growing repertoire of social actions. Psychologist Maria Rhode (2005) suggests that the reason *why* babies can imitate is precisely for the purpose of communication; mouth opening, blinking and tongue protrusion are all part of a desire even in 45-minute-old newborns to communicate with others.

Psychologist Alan Fogel (Fogel & Garvey, 2007; Fogel, 1993) describes this interaction between child and adult as coregulation, which includes the many ways in which people change their actions anticipating or responding to those of another. This interaction can be best thought of as a verbal and non-verbal conversation (with nods, eye contact, etc.). It is frequently seen in rituals that mothers and fathers (usually) develop during feeds where parents engage with young baby's natural rhythms of behaviour. The use of language by speaking in a higher pitch, exaggerating tone, speaking slowly, using long pauses and repetition allows a parent to adjust to baby's likes and dislikes.

During the first 6 months, parent and child begin to respond to each other in what is termed primary intersubjectivity. This includes a response by an infant to their parent's sensitive communcation, as is shown when the infant looks up intently at her face and responds with movements of face and hands in rhythmical patterns. Later, when these exchanges of sounds, gestures and movements involve objects or toys, it is termed secondary intersubjectivity (Cortina & Liotti, 2010). The baby recognises that objects and events can be shared between them by grasping, giving and taking, drawing attention to an object and demanding it. Mums and dads teach their baby the routines at their special shared times which become their joint-action formats (also referred to as synchronised routines in Chapter 11). These joint-action formats are developed when sharing a picture book, feeding and during bath time, dressing and nappy changing routines. They are simplified action sequences created by and used by parents to develop early language (Smith & Fluck, 2000; Bruner, 1975).

A relevant aspect of an infant's development is person permanence: the idea previously mentioned that a person still exists even when no longer in view. This is a significant development in beginning to form relationships (connected to advances in cognitive capacity), such that if mother is not in the room she can be looked for, called for, and, once she returns, welcomed back. Research into social referencing (Chapter 11) tells us that after 7 months a child will look to the mother/ parent and check their reaction, to guide their actions and reactions to strangers. This is becoming a thinking, reasoned response to the social environment and such advances in social development during the first year are rapid. Simple relationships with parents (usually the mother) are immensely important for developing social skills as is much greater awareness of other children. By 2 years self-conscious emotions are evident and language development allows verbal expressions of emotions, although (as noted in Chapter 11) temper outbursts in the 'terrible twos' period may be the result of frustration, an inability to express more complex emotions. What happens next?

Increased language skills in the preschool years open up new communication opportunities with others; greater mobility allows

Using a book as an object – secondary intersubjectivity – in a joint action format. Mother is scaffolding her child's experience and learning, because the child cannot do this alone.

*Source:* © Pearson Education Ltd / Jules Selmes.

----

**Connect and Extend**

We remember faces of threatening over non-threatening individuals. When does this begin? To find out, read: Kinzler, K. D. & Shutts, K. (2008). Memory for 'mean' over 'nice': The influence of threat on children's face memory. *Cognition, 107,* 775–783.

**Coregulation**
A joint development of the way in which infants and parents make up the rules for how they will behave together during shared activities, particularly feeding to start with.

**Primary intersubjectivity**
Person-to-person responses between infants and carers through language/sounds, actions, gestures and facial expressions.

**Secondary intersubjectivity**
Person-to-person responses between infants and carers through objects and shared events, like a shared book or exchanging toys.

**Joint-action formats**
Simplified action sequences created by infants and carers that are repeated regularly and to a set pattern, for example, nappy changing or getting ready for bed.

Children waiting their turn with the skipping rope demonstrate social participation.

*Source*: © Pearson Education Ltd / Jules Selmes.

exploration of a larger environment and cognitive advances enable children to view others as separate to themselves, with interests and intentions that might be different from their own. By 3 years, an infant starts to accommodate to their mother's and other's needs. This is not an overnight process and young children can appear very **egocentric**. However, by school age, a child has built abstract models of the adult–child and child–child relationships using an internal schema based on (hopefully) trust and approval, the social experiences of being cared for by grandparents, fathers and older siblings. Between 3 and 5 years, social participation increases outside of the family as well. Beginning nursery school exposes them to a larger circle of others of their age than previously, and activities connected with nursery school and other outside interests such as beginner swimming, gym and dance clubs foster social interactions in a range of new settings and locations.

Pre-school children can and do take the lead, initiating interactions with others and are therefore less dependent on adults to structure experiences for them. They have an understanding of the rules of simple games and shared activities. This is a time when prosocial behaviours such as turn-taking and sharing with others become very evident based on early joint-action formats, so that in nursery school and other play settings you might observe children waiting for their turn on the climbing frame or sitting with friends and sharing a jug of juice at break times. Indeed, progress in children's social development is perhaps most obvious when watching them play together; play, an important topic to which we now turn with another short story.

**Egocentric (2)**
The self is not yet constructed as something separate from others – commonly thought of as a self-centred view of the world.

## Children's play and social experiences

In the playgroup Anna, aged 4, has arranged some red plastic cups, saucers and plates. She carefully and thoughtfully put them on a tablecloth on the floor with the help of one of the play workers. Are there enough plates and cups? Is the pattern of plates and cups the same for each place setting? It is a tea party and Anna has invited her best friends to come for tea. A few moments later the children are happily chattering away, pouring cups of tea for themselves and pretending to eat the plastic cakes that are neatly set on the plates.

> Outside the classroom in the playground, Mo and Jon Paul are engaged in what appears to be wrestling. Mo has hold of Jon Paul's shoulders, while Jon Paul has his arms locked tightly around Mo's waist. There is much tussling, some pushing and shoving but all good-natured and part of a shared make-believe game. Jon Paul is swung around and spins off before he sets off, chasing Mo across the playground.

Both scenes describe typical children's play behaviours and neither is a scene of children engaged in formal classroom learning – yet who could not argue that learning is taking place? Imagine the language associated with both situations. Conceive of what the children are learning about relationships with the other children and about themselves: physical skills, language and the self-regulation of their emotions. Most certainly both episodes are powerful learning experiences. Other common early years play activities such as sand and water play and play on large outdoor apparatus promotes creativity, social skills and language development.

Traditional views have linked the functions of play with survival through the development of hunting and building skills (Laaksoharju *et al.*, 2012) and caring behaviours (Wentzel, 2003). Some of the great theorists of psychology explored the importance of play for language, cognitive and social development. Lev Vygotsky viewed play as important in building up mental structures using culturally specific tools, such as language. Albert Bandura saw play as rehearsal and preparation for skills in later life. Jean Piaget allied play to the development of cognition, as an activity that only higher mammals can participate in. Combined together, these perspectives have led to a belief amongst early years practitioners that play advances intellectual skills through the association of play with the development of problem-solving and symbolic thinking (Jacobse & Harskamp, 2012). Imagine two children in school trying to finish a puzzle. The children are learning together and having fun. Their social development is enhanced by taking turns, sharing the pieces and working in tandem using trial-success-and-error and other **heuristics** to solve the puzzle. The sharing of ideas – sometimes in argument – and explanations require metaphors and connected thinking to be used: 'it's a bit like . . .' and 'don't you remember . . . ?' are often heard when older children are trying to get the other person to understand something. The seed of such advanced thinking is often to be found in the logic of play talk heard in playgroup.

**Heuristics**
Methods for learners to solve problems or find out things for themselves.

Different types of play have been identified related to different developmental phases in a child's life. Jean Piaget identified five types of play which are hierarchical in terms of their cognitive complexity and organised into three levels (1951).

- Level 1:
  1. *Functional play* begins in the sensorimotor stage, through a repetitive motor activity such as banging a wooden brick on a table.
  2. *Physical activity play* is active play that combines large body movements, exercise play and rough and tumble play. Others (e.g. Loprinzi *et al.*, 2012; Pellegrini & Smith, 1998) have identified three phases of physical activity play, beginning with leg kicking and arm waving of babies, to the exercise play involving running and jumping, and finally the rough-and-tumble play that becomes apparent from age 3 through adolescence, and involves children in friendly play-fighting and chasing games with peers. Play-fighting and chasing is common in playgrounds, and despite views of playground supervisors, it does not generally lead to genuine fights (Gartrell & Sonsteng, 2008). A mitigating plea 'It's just a game, Mrs Peters. We're only playing!' is usually accurate.
- Level 2:
  3. *Constructive play*, using materials such as wooden blocks, bricks and other 3D shapes, and is a common feature in many nurseries and daycare centres.
- Level 3:
  4. *Symbolic play* (otherwise known as fantasy, dramatic or pretend play). This appears around 15 months and embraces pretend play with role-playing, social participation play (more on this coming up) and responding to stories. Well-established social roles are acted out using social permission and information requests, directives and assistance

appeals overheard or observed in the 'adult world' (Griswold, 2007). In their earlier longitudinal study of children playing at home, Wendy Haight and Paula Miller (1993) found that 75 per cent of pretend play was social involving mothers initially and later with peers. Pretend play is also imitative – children replicate what is observed in social interactions, that is, feeding or dressing the baby, gossiping, talking on the phone. At this age children adapt and make more use of their imagination to perform pretend actions themselves, than with toys like a teddy bear in what Piaget called **decentration** (Garcia & Pastor, 2006). For example, a child's motor action of raising a cup to drink can be decentred so that teddy can be given a drink and then later that teddy can raise the cup to give himself a drink. Later children can act out scenarios without any objects and can mime what they are doing and using. Play can and often does include an imaginary 'friend' (although this idea usually disappears by about age 10).

5. Piaget's final category was **formal games**. This type of play takes the form of any game with a rule structure. It includes ball games, traditional games, board games, and would nowadays include video and console games. Such activities usually have a physical component and varying degrees of social interaction.

Sociologist Mildred Parten in the first systematic study of children's play behaviours in nursery (1932) identified a hierarchy of six categories of social participation play, which underscore some forms of play as a social experience (in brackets below are the age ranges associated with the play preferences in Parten's original sample):

1. Unoccupied behaviour – perhaps sitting and thinking.

2. Onlooker behaviour – where the child attends to something interesting in what other children are doing but does not join it.

3. Solitary play – takes place alone and is play that is different from that of others around (most 2- to $2^1/_2$-year-olds).

4. Parallel play – where children play alongside but not with another child. There is little or no verbal interaction but children playing alongside each other often use imitation as an effective way of showing interest in what the other child is doing (most $2^1/_2$- to $3^1/_2$-year-olds).

5. In associative play, children may share materials or resources but there is no adoption of alternate roles in the scenario or working collaboratively (most $3^1/_2$- to $4^1/_2$-year-olds).

6. Finally, co-operative play which becomes more frequent after age 5 includes playing games or model making together.

The first four of these categories are more non-social participation play. Parten's work clearly showed how children's activity appears to become more social as they get older and that their play becomes more interactive and more likely to involve others. The latter two categories of associative and co-operative play are considered as social play, and Parten found these types of play were most frequently displayed by age 5, a finding supported by more recent research (e.g. Chazan, 2009). However, we think caution should be adopted if attempting to use the original modal values (in brackets above) in a **normative** fashion. Remember from Chapter 3 that normative values can be applied to all children but there is little evidence in this case for practitioners in play settings to look for similar age ranges irrespective of the sample chosen. Casual observation over many years leads us to expect to see a good deal of solitary and parallel play in many groups of 4-year-olds. Also, contemporary researchers tend to view these categories as too simplistic and have turned their interest to reasons why children play alone (Molina *et al.*, 2004) and the educational attainments of children engaging in solitary and parallel play (Coplan *et al.*, 2004).

**Decentration**
The ability to focus simultaneously on several aspects of an activity.

**Formal games**
Play that takes the form of any game with a rule structure.

**Normative**
A form of assessment where an individual's or group's results are compared with a much larger set of results in a standardised test.

• • • • • • • • • • • • • • • • •
**Connect and Extend**
Can types of social interaction define stages in friendship? Read Erwin, P. (2008). Childhood friendships. *Nursery World*, 4 March, 19–22. Compare and contrast the three stages in the development of children's friendship in this reading (egocentric, sociocentric and empathetic) with other categorisations such as those of Piaget and Parten.
• • • • • • • • • • • • • • • • •

Associative and co-operative play promotes social development by sharing and talking together. Which is going on here?

*Source*: Richard Stagg.

**Reflect**

Parten's modal values for associative and co-operative play would lead us to expect most children to be engaging in social participation play by the age of 5. Children of this age happily play side-by-side but generally ignore each other. From your experience or research, do you think that most 5-year-olds engage in social participation play?

Despite our reservation about Parten's modal values, her work is a splendid starting point for many practitioners when observing young children at play. The notion of a social play hierarchy has supported the work of other pioneers of childhood education in the past century such as Froebel, Isaacs and Steiner, all of whom influenced the position of play in the early childhood curriculum today. The importance of play in the early years curriculum today is also vehemently defended by many contemporary advocates (e.g. Guilfoyle & Mistry, 2013; Howard *et al.*, 2006; Moyles, 2005; de Boo, 2004; Bruce, 2001; Lindon, 2001). However, research into play has tended to focus on its cognitive outcomes (interesting that it is an activity that only higher mammals and humans can participate in), and the benefits of sociability and social competence are less studied but still well established (e.g. Kordt-Thomas & Lee, 2006; Broadhead, 2001). Play is obviously a prime medium for creating social networks among children, allows a child to learn about themselves, to explore relationships with others, to express their emotions, act out social roles and to learn cultural values (Bernstein & Tamis-Lemonda, 2007).

Building on the work of Mildred Parten, Professor of Playful Learning (what a splendid title!) Pat Broadhead's social play continuum (2001) proposes that play moves from associative through social, highly social and on to co-operative play. In this progression, Broadhead's observations of children in nurseries reveals that play becomes both socially and cognitively more demanding. Regarding the relationship between the cognitive and affective dimensions of play, she states, 'Social and co-operative interactions provide emotional outlets and individual satisfaction along with intellectual challenge, hence their inherent attraction to children' (2001, p 33). The idea of social interaction as intellectual challenge is supported by psychologist Richard Bailey who considers play as children's 'social chess'; the notion is presented in the *Focus on Theory* feature.

**Connect and Extend**

For an article focusing on the advantages associated with children's play, read: Sterling Honig, A. (2006). What infants, toddlers, and preschoolers learn from play: 12 ideas. *Montessori Life*, *18*, 16–21.

## Focus on Theory

### Play as children's social chess

Richard Bailey's paper (2002) draws on research from developmental and evolutionary psychology, primatology (study of primates) and studies of autistic children. It is a form of meta-research: a commentary (originally a contribution to a symposium on children's play), drawing on connected ideas from a number of different fields. He begins with the assertion that we live in complex social environments and as such it is not unreasonable to use the label of 'social chess' (Humphrey, 1984) in describing our very complicated social interactions.

In chess, a good player will not only plan several moves ahead for himself but also try to anticipate the other person's moves. Success is dependent upon how many future moves a player can anticipate. A chess master will also be able to dissemble their own intentions and see through their opponent's attempts to hide their cunning plans. In social interactions, the extent to which children can correctly guess what is coming up and can see through attempts to hide others' intentions is a good test of social development.

Chess as a metaphor for children's social interactions is attractive as their social interactions involve both co-operative and competitive transactions and the creation and recreation of friendship networks. However, the metaphor may be also inadequate in capturing the intricacies of childhood social exchange for two reasons suggested by developmental psychologist Simon Baron-Cohen (1995). Firstly, not all of children's social interactions are competitive and, secondly, the game of chess demands an intensity of thinking and effort which contrasts with the ease with which children's social exchanges take place. On entering primary school, most children have mastered the skills of being able automatically to interpret the behaviour of others in terms of what they are thinking and planning. They are well on the road to being masters of social chess.

As suggested earlier, at the heart of much social interaction lies the ability to work out the other person's mental states – a kind of mind-reading. Without such ability one would be blind to the thinking, desires and intentions that underlie other people's behaviour. This condition, suggests Baron-Cohen, is 'mindblindness', or the inability to mind-read. Children's psychopathologist Peter Hobson (2002) further contributes to the status of mind-reading in cognition while others (Harris & Leevers, 2000) highlight its role in pretend play.

In pretend play children create imaginary conversations with make-believe characters and play out fictional roles in their play. These behaviours have led Richard Bailey to believe that play is a precondition for the development of mind-reading skills. His argument is that through play children distinguish what is real from what is unreal, develop skills of self-awareness and are discerning of the intentions of other children: abilities which underpin the development of mind-reading skills. Evidence is cited (Perner *et al.*, 1994) that children whose social play is more frequent and of high quality progress more quickly to a mature theory of mind than children who do not. This is the key point of the paper.

In concluding the paper, Bailey recognises the pivotal place of mind-reading skills in enabling children to develop social expertise. He argues that at every stage of an infant's development, social intelligence is unmatched by any other facet of cognitive development. Although he does not categorically state that play alone prompts mind-reading skills, he argues that play provides an activity dimension for children that is not replicated anywhere else in their lives. Bailey cites Nicholas Humphrey (1986) who argues that all kinds of play allow children to experiment with their feelings and identities, in ways that extend an inner knowledge of what it is to be human.

The previous section and the *Focus on Theory* feature discuss how play contexts provide children with many opportunities to foster social development. Now it is time to explore how children think about their own motives and those of other people. This is what is known as 'social cognition' (mentioned in Chapter 11 in the context of emotional development) and it bridges both social and cognitive development. What are the defining aspects of social cognition?

**The Twenty Statements Test (Humphries & Jobson, 2012).**

How would you describe yourself? Write down your 20 answers to the question, 'Who am I?' Afterwards, reflect on your answers. What do they say about your personality, temperament, behaviour, interests and values? Is this really who you think you are? Perhaps you might like to show the list to somebody else and see whether your idea of who you are is the person they think you are.

# Self and self-concept

Perhaps you found the above *Reflect* activity difficult, or relatively straightforward. Nevertheless, doing the activity will help in getting you to explore and make judgements about your own identity. Part of social cognition is concerned with how we think of ourselves. The subjective 'I' implies an understanding of one's personal qualities and characteristics, our individual skills, beliefs and values. The psychologist William James, writing over a century ago, drew our attention to a notion of 'self' which had two complementary features: 'I self' – that I am separate from others around me and in control of my own actions and thoughts – this is self-awareness; 'me self' – self as object, recognising the individual traits and characteristics we hold true about ourselves that make us special. The notion of 'self' in this chapter embodying these two elements proposes an early awareness of self that gradually develops from concrete into a more organised abstract view of personal and social characteristics and capabilities.

A sense of self is an important milestone in children's social development. Children reaching this developmental marker show that they think of themselves as distinct from other people around them. It is linked to *person permanence* through an infant understanding that another person exists in time and space beyond that which the infant can perceive (discussed earlier in this chapter) and, more importantly, that the infant recognises their own continuing existence despite another person not being present at that moment. I can interact with myself, control what I do and think, think through what I am doing, and decide to carry on or do something different. (We will return to this notion later when discussing the moral world of the child.)

The idea of self as an active observer of oneself may be an appropriate one to begin with in exploring the course of social development in relation to social cognition. Early researchers such as sociologist Charles Cooley at the beginning of the nineteenth century used the metaphor of a looking glass to describe the notion of self, believing that what was shown in the mirror reflected the inner self outwardly. He and others believed that *self* is built up through the social interactions babies encounter, through observing themselves interacting with those around them.

You may remember that very young babies are incapable of recognising themselves when looking in a mirror, yet, within several months, they can be seen smiling and noticing how what they do is reflected back in the mirror. Being able to do this is another milestone in human social development – interesting that no other species apart from several primates have the perceptual and cognitive abilities for this! If at around 12 months you were to show a child a picture of themselves they would look at it for a slightly longer time than if shown a picture of another of the same age. In a few more months, many will be able to attach verbal labels like their own name to make this distinction greater. By 2 years, they perceive themselves as distinct from others and the sense of self-recognition is established. At this age, their sense of possessing something that is definitely theirs is strong enough to express a claim on a toy or favourite book with a vocal 'mine!' This is a further stage on, signalling an elementary understanding of things permanent – things remaining the same over time.

In early childhood, children's perceptions of who they are rests predominately on external representations, that is, what they look like, what they can do, where they live, and so on. Over time, researchers have capitalised on methods that involve young children looking into mirrors such as in the 'rouge test' (mentioned in Chapter 11) and at photographs, in order to assess this self-recognition (Lewis & Brooks-Gunn, 1979). To recap this test, infants from 9–24 months were placed in front of a mirror and a dab of rouge placed on each child's nose. Each child was then placed in front of the mirror again and observed. Findings were that most children smiled and pointed to the mirror but the effect varied with age. The results of the mirror test indicated that infants of 20 months had a growing sense of self-recognition: there was recognition that what a child of this age saw in the mirror was a representation of themselves. Later studies with video representations and photographs (Povinelli *et al.*, 1996) show that young children have some understanding of self in an immediate sense, but their capacity to connect an earlier image of themselves with the one currently presented is limited. As children get older and their cognitive capacities increase, they define themselves more through abstract internal representations. The Twenty Statements Test (which is the one we asked you to do earlier) supports this empirically (Humphries & Jobson, 2012).

This test requires 20 answers to the 'Who am I?' question, and highlights the relationships between self-concept and developing cognitive abilities. Children of 8 will give answers about their name, age, where they live and describe their physical characteristics. They articulate their competencies in positive terms, 'I am good at maths', as well as negatively, 'I am not very good at speling.' Eleven-year-olds, in addition, make more evaluative statements about how well they perform in activities such as sport and music, what their likes and dislikes are and their popularity among peers. Between 8 and 11 years the ability to make social comparisons increases where children judge their own abilities and appearance against others. Understanding of self accelerates forward rapidly in the middle childhood years, at a time when they interact with many more people than previously. This is a time when membership of particular groups assumes much greater importance: for example, sports clubs, music groups and so on (Damon, 2000). As this is a time for comparing themselves with others, this is also the time when they find out how their own worth is decided – their self-esteem.

## Self-esteem

The term is concerned with comparing ourselves with others in an evaluative way. The relationship between the image of who we are (real self) and who we would like to be (ideal self) was the basis of psychotherapist Carl Rogers's pioneering work on self-esteem (1961). If both images are compatible, then one has good self-esteem. Compatibility is reliant upon both *unconditional positive regard* from others and *self-actualisation* or being able to fulfil all that we are capable of achieving. Both are interrelated. With younger children, it might be argued that their perceptions of themselves are unrealistic and exaggerated: 'I am the best runner ever' or 'I am the best reader in the whole school'. As their cognitive capacities increase, children in middle childhood are more able to more finely differentiate their self-image.

Rogers further argued that self-esteem is crucial for general wellness and that parenting is important in developing children's self-esteem. This latter point is also made in a classic text *The Antecedents of Self-esteem* (Coopersmith, 1967) studying self-esteem in 9 to 10-year-old boys. Psychologist Stanley Coopersmith found that positive regard for parents was a key factor in the development of self-esteem and that clear boundaries laid down by parents were high predictors of positive self-esteem in their children. A close relationship between parent and child fosters high self-esteem and links between positive parenting styles and high self-esteem in children is borne out across cultures (Bagley *et al.*, 2001). Good self-esteem is found in children who have experienced involved and loving parenting, whereas those with low self-esteem are found in children with authoritarian or rejecting parents.

Judgements about self are important for current and future psychological adjustment. Imagine when 3-year-old Jenna finishes her jigsaw and proudly looks to her mum to comment on the achievement. The way in which her mother reacts (hopefully all smiles, words of praise and encouragement) will have an impact on the development of Jenna's self-esteem. Research by Herbert Marsh and colleagues (1991) found that 5–7-year-olds made judgements about themselves related to their physical appearance, physical ability, peer and parent relationships, reading, maths and overall school attainment. Interestingly, self-esteem is generally high in early childhood but takes a slight down-slide for many children temporarily in middle childhood. There are various factors that account for this trend. Firstly earlier self-judgements are likely to be unrealistic. No comparisons are made when little Jenna gets all that praise and smiles. As far as Jenna is concerned she is the master puzzler of the world, and quite right too! However, when comparisons are made – much more common in middle childhood – with other children, and when the outcome is deemed to be negative, this often has an adverse effect on levels of self-esteem that can last for some time. Such **social comparisons** provide immediate 'mirrors' to reflect the worth of what you can do and how well you are doing it, in comparison with others. Hence, we come to evaluate our own abilities and values.

**Social comparisons**
How individuals define themselves with reference to the skills, interests and values held by others.

 **Reflect**  Do children who have good self-esteem do well at school because of good self-esteem, or does doing well at school increase self-esteem? Think back through your own time at school. What subjects did you like or dislike? What subjects were you good at or not so good? Is there any connection? When and why did you start to dislike/'fail' at some subjects?

Other factors of course affect the perception of self-esteem. Studies on academic achievement (e.g. Burden & Burdett, a motivational analysis of successful learning of pupils with dyslexia) have shown that children who are academically successful at school have a positive self-image. Psychologists Josee Jarry and Amy Kossert (2007) found positive correlations between satisfaction about girls' body image and their self-concept. Studies reveal clear distinctions between the sexes. Girls report higher self-concept scores on general academic performance and reading in particular, while boys are more positive in physical ability (Tannenbaum, 2008) maths and ICT (Sáinz, & Eccles, 2012). There are cultural variations in the notion of self. In a classic piece of research Henriëtte Van den Heuvel and colleagues from the University of Amsterdam (1992) asked Moroccan, Turkish and Dutch children to describe themselves. Responses showed a greater emphasis was placed on family and community by the Moroccan and Turkish children than on the individual. It is easy to think of self-concept as something which 'belongs' to the holder, whereas it actually represents a relationship between the person and the expectations of the culture in which they are raised.

Low self-esteem is associated with difficulties in children with loneliness (Cava *et al.*, 2007) and depression (Plunkett *et al.*, 2007). An outcome of having low self-esteem that emerges in middle childhood is **learned helplessness** (Derharmi, 2013; Akca, 2011). This is a belief that one can do little to affect one's control over one's environment. Helpless children are resigned in their belief that success is due to ability and not effort, and they believe their own ability is low either generally or in a particular area, and fixed for them. It is a kind of self-perpetuating prophecy and as a consequence such children often perform poorly in school tests. In contrast, children who believe in themselves are persistent in their efforts in meeting difficulties and believe that with effort they will be successful (Zimmermann, 2000). They focus on **learning goals** and seek out strategies to attain goals, and to capitalise on their ability by making greater effort. One interesting and regrettable example is how helplessness and gender affect attainment in mathematics. Earlier findings from Jacquelynne Eccles and colleagues (1991) were that girls do not achieve as highly as boys and were less confident in their own abilities – a finding subsequently established in many more recent studies (e.g. Bloomfield & Soyibo, 2008; Ojala & Talts, 2007; Elias *et al.*, 2007). Parental expectations of girls' lower achievement in maths may again result in a self-fulfilling prophesy that results in girls not achieving their potential in this subject.

**Learned helplessness**
A belief that one can do nothing to affect one's control of one's environment.

**Learning goals**
Targets related to specific skills, knowledge or understanding.

**Connect and Extend**
Girls do not achieve as highly as boys and are less confident in their own abilities (e.g. Bloomfield & Soyibo, 2008). For a discussion of factors affecting girls learned helplessness in mathematics, read: Ai, X. (2002). Gender differences in growth in mathematics achievement. *Mathematical Thinking & Learning*, 4, 1–22.

## Understanding others

A second key aspect of social cognition is being able to understand what other people think, that is, perceiving their mental states. By age 2 children see themselves as being part of a large social world and understand that they play definite roles in this. A developing theory of mind allows those self-conscious emotions to be developed which are linked to understanding of how others perceive us. In the previous chapter we saw how the primary emotions (e.g. happiness, sadness, surprise and anger) are followed by secondary emotions of guilt, embarrassment, envy and empathy. An interesting early study by Doris Bischof-Kohler at the University of Zurich (1988) featured a researcher who was 'sad' because teddy's arm had fallen off and this 'tragic' event was used to assess the empathy of infants from 16 to 24 months. This study and others (Roth-Hanania *et al.*, 2000; Stipek *et al.*, 1992) found close links between the level of self-recognition and the expression of empathy. Between ages of 3 and 4 preschool children reach an important milestone in their development and acquire a developed theory of mind. This term describes how our mental state – our desires, beliefs and intentions – explains our behaviour. The importance of theory of mind in relation to social development lies in enabling children to understand the social world in which they live. The theory of mind also develops sharing and co-operating with others and these behaviours closely mirror the development of self as an active chooser of appropriate behaviour. Let's take a closer look at this idea, focusing on earlier work done in the 1980s and 1990s, a 'rich seam' of work on the developing theory of mind.

According to Henry Wellman (1990) theory of mind for children of 2 years of age can be termed a *desire theory* since by this age children have a simple understanding of other people's desires and base their reactions to others on this new perceptive proficiency. By 3, a child can add a perception of beliefs to their desire theory and so can make more sophisticated predictions. However, children do not yet understand that beliefs can also be false, but by 4 they understand that beliefs held might also be untrue. This means that children can now act on their own representations of reality, rather than reality itself. This is an important step forward since it means that children are aware of deceptive behaviour.

Psychologist Joan Peskin's study (1992) using a friendly and a mean puppet found that children under 4 have little understanding of deceit. This new and important understanding is a *representational* theory of mind. Testing it involves the classic **false-belief task** (Wimmer & Perner, 1983). This involves a child watching a friendly puppet place a toy into a blue box. The puppet then goes away. A second mean puppet is seen to take the toy from the box and put it elsewhere (e.g. into a basket). The friendly puppet returns. The researcher then asks the child to state where the friendly puppet will look for the toy. Findings indicated that most 3-year-olds chose wrongly, while most 4-year-olds answered correctly. The researchers argued this was due to 3-year-olds' beliefs about reality which differed from the 4-year-olds' who understood the friendly puppet held a false belief and acted on this belief. Other researchers have found similar results using dolls and marbles in what is known as the 'Sally-Anne task' – where two dolls 'hide' a marble from each other (Baron-Cohen *et al.*, 1985) and the 'Smarties task' where a Smartie tube contains pencils rather than sweets (Perner *et al.*, 1987).

What are the implications for such findings in understanding how children make sense of their social experiences? Firstly, that significant advances are made in theory of mind between the ages of 3 and 4 as stated. Secondly, other research (e.g. Wright & Mahfoud, 2012; Perner *et al.*, 1994) shows that children from large families tend to be more advanced in their development of theory of mind. It is not unreasonable to speculate that this may well be due to increased social interaction among siblings, therefore that 'only' children may require additional socialisation at this key stage. A third implication is the importance of the role played by parents in advancing this development (Galende, 2012) not only in providing for family socialisation but also in making provision for their children to have a rich and varied social life in the wider community. In summary then, what research does exist in this area points to a symbiotic relationship between the positive influence of theory of mind on children's socialisation, helping them to form relevant mental images of themselves, and socialisation promoting the development of a healthy theory of mind essential for important social situations such as forming friendships (Bauminger *et al.*, 2010; Keenan & Harvey, 1998). Do these processes work in the same way for everybody? Are there individual and cultural identities that make a difference? In the next section we move on to the concept of social identity.

**False-belief task**
A test which identifies whether or not a child is able to represent what another person knows, when this is different from what the child knows.

• • • • • • • • • • • • • • • •

**Connect and Extend**

To explore different forms of self-regulation and understanding of false belief, read: Jahromi, L. & Stifter, C. (2008). Individual differences in preschoolers' self-regulation and theory of mind. *Merrill-Palmer Quarterly*, 54, 125–150.

• • • • • • • • • • • • • • • •

Before moving on, let's summarise what we have learned so far:

- Young children smile and look towards others around them and use smiling as an important social signal, looking for clear responses: adults and siblings respond to the babies' smiles, babbling and cooing with motherese and by returning smiles.

- Interaction between child and adult is coregulation, which includes the many ways in which individuals change their actions anticipating or responding to those of another.

- Joint-action formats or *synchronised routines* are simplified action sequences created by the mother.

- Lev Vygotsky viewed play as important in building up mental structures. Albert Bandura saw play as a rehearsal of, and preparation for skills in later life. Jean Piaget allied play to the development of cognition. Mildred Parten identified a hierarchy of six categories of social participation play – playing (or not) with others.

- Social cognition includes two key aspects: knowing yourself and knowing others.

- Knowledge of 'self' has two components: *I self* – that I am separate from others around me and in control of my own actions and thoughts – this is self-awareness; *me self* – recognising the individual traits and characteristics that make us special. It is the *who* of who we are.

- Our self-esteem is *how* we are in comparison with others, how we evaluate ourselves in comparison to others and *learnt helplessness* is a belief that one can do little well or effectively. Helpless children believe that success is due to ability, that their own ability is fixed.

- We develop a *theory of mind* which, among other abilities, allows us to predict what others are going to do. The *false-belief task* is a test that infants have formed a theory of mind.

**Summary 1**

# Social identity and influence

## Theories of social identity

Two of the strands of research into social identity are **ethnic identity** and gender identity. Ethnic identity is described as 'an awareness of being a member of a specific ethnic group combined with a sense of belonging to that group' (Schaffer, 2006, p 84). Developmental psychologist H. Rudolph Schaffer argues that ethnic identity has four components:

**Ethnic identity**
An awareness of and a sense of belonging to a particular ethnic group.

1. *Salience* refers to the extent to which ethnicity is perceived as being important in one's self-concept.
2. *Ideology* refers to how the people in that ethnic group are regarded.
3. *Centrality* refers to how individuals define themselves according to their ethnicity.
4. *Regard* refers to positive and/or negative feelings in relation to ethnicity.

Under 2 years of age children show little understanding of differences between ethnic groups. By age 4 children are able to label pictures of individuals of different skin colour, and by age 5 have a sense of their identity according to a particular ethnic group. Between 5 and 7, children show ethnic preferences and constancy – in that they believe a person's ethnicity will not change or become influenced by physical appearances (Schaffer, 2006).

Gender identity refers to an individual's perception of their own gender. Appreciating our own gender is a major part of understanding who we are. Behavioural differences can be apparent as early as the first 2 years. This is seen at home, in playgroup or school settings through children's preferences for same-sex companions and preferences for particular toys and activities (Serbin *et al.*, 2001).

Research in this area, as we shall see, indicates the existence of some psychological differences between boys and girls, but we should avoid making overgeneralisations; it is necessary to be aware of pseudo-differences due to popular beliefs and cultural myths. Differences in self-esteem are socially constructed – 'an invented idea within a particular society or culture' – but other perceived differences, say, in cognition, are often the result of applying stereotypical attitudes to learning settings. For example, notions that cognitive abilities of boys outweigh those of girls in mathematics are refuted by many studies over the past 20 years (Marks, 2008; Berube & Glanz, 2008; Opyene-Eluk & Opolot-Okurut, 1995; Hyde *et al.*, 1990), and over time researchers have found no gender differences existed in the results of IQ tests (e.g. Furnham *et al.*, 2005; Keenan & Shaw, 1997).

There is, however, some evidence of differences in specific abilities. Girls have better percep-tual speed (Gilbert, 2008), fine motor skills and do better on verbal tests (Strand *et al.*, 2006). Boys are better on spatial (Reynolds *et al.*, 2008) and abstract mathematical tests (Liu *et al.*, 2008) and these differences are evident in the early school years (Penner & Paret, 2008). Girls walk, talk and generally reach most developmental milestones earlier than boys and do better at school. Regarding differences in emotional expressiveness, this was found to be greater in emotions stereotypically associated with each gender. Females showed greater warmth and more fear while males displayed greater anger and pride (Brechet, 2013; Hewahi & Baraka, 2012). Yes, there are some differences between the sexes, but to what extent are these differ-ences in social behaviours the result of 'hard-wired' sex differences in the brain?

There are differences between sexes, in terms of brain structure, and Dr Louann Brizendine in her book *The Female Brain* (2008) details the differences and the possible causes. Areas in the brain responsible for language (mentioned in Chapter 10), namely the Broca's and Wernicke's regions, are more active in females, giving girls advantages in communication over males. The corpus callosum, which bridges left and right brain hemispheres, in females is thicker, allowing them to co-ordinate both brain hemispheres well. Higher levels of oestrogen in females encourage girls to manage social situations much more calmly and fairly, while boys are more aggressive and seek social dominance through their higher levels of testoster-one. Before we get too carried away with the notion that the female brain and physiology are very different from those of males, it might be helpful to consider the extent to which gender identity is more a consequence of many learned differences in social behaviours. What do the theories tell us about acquired gender identities? There are two sets to consider: cognitive learning theories and social learning theories.

*Cognitive-developmental theories* such as that proposed by Kohlberg (1966) argue that gender concept is gradually acquired over time. Gender identity comes first and is followed by the construction of other schema. In the first three years *gender labelling* takes place where children become aware of their own gender. They attach labels to other people such as Mummy, Daddy, boy, girl. *Gender stability and consistency*, which can take up to age 7, is the stage in which the permanency of gender takes place where children understand that, even if one changes physical appearance through clothes or hairstyles, this does not change the gender. This has been extended into **gender schema** theory (Knobloch-Westerwick & Hoplamazian, 2012), which proposes that children come to understand about gender by constructing a schema or, in other words, a cognitive structure that informs them about the world. They build this up by seeking out information about their own sex first – an own-sex schema that is the basis for how they behave in gender-typical ways: for example, boys play gun fights and girls play with

**Connect and Extend**

Naima Browne has some interesting information on the differences between girls' and boy's brains, including the T (testosterone) factor, in her book: *Gender Equity in the Early Years* (2004). Maidenhead: Open University Press.

**Gender schema**
The mental structures that organise information relevant to gender.

dolls. Such schemas provide children with powerful ways of organising their social world. It shows children prefer other children to show gender-stereotypical behaviour that conforms to their own view or schema (Warin, 2000), apparent in any decision a child takes to choose one playmate rather than another in a group.

Social learning theories (learning by imitating others – Bandura, 1986) of gender concept reject stages of cognitive development in favour of knowledge acquired through increased opportunities for learning experiences. To explain, an 8-year-old boy at his first football match watches dad cheer on Manchester United. The child will replicate this behaviour. Social cognitive theory (Bussey & Bandura, 1999), which expands the original theory of Albert Bandura (see Chapter 2) emphasises that multiple social factors impact on a child's identity. Psychodynamic theories stress the importance of the family context. For example, Sigmund Freud's theory of personality development proposed that social development was affected by relationships with important others and at different stages of development.

No single approach adequately explains gender socialisation. Elements of each approach hold true. What is certain is that there are a number of factors that influence it: advertising, television, books, peers, experiences in schools, all encourage such categorisation. Play research shows the importance of peer attitudes and behaviours. Play is clearly more social with children of the same sex than with children of the opposite sex (Colwell & Lindsey, 2005). Girls are more passive when playing with boys, and boys often ignore instructions from girls and become more dominant and competitive (Manwaring, 2008; Tulviste & Koor, 2005). As pre-schoolers, both sexes are more likely to continue with behaviour if there is a positive reaction from a same-sex peer, and to discontinue a behaviour if the reaction is negative (Nakamura, 2001). With preschool children the tendency to play with peers of the same sex is striking and their tendency is to form same-gender groups (Kurtz–Costes et al., 2011). Psychologist Eleanor Maccoby in her earlier research recorded these observations about same-gender differences in children's play:

> **Boys play in somewhat larger groups on the average and their play is rougher . . . and it takes up more space. . . . Girls tend to form close, intimate friendships with one or two other girls, and these friendships are marked by sharing of confidences. . . . In male groups there is more concern with issues of dominance.**
>
> (Maccoby, 1990, p 516)

Certain academic subjects are viewed by teachers and parents as either masculine (mathematics) or feminine (reading) (Marks, 2008). Boys dominate classroom interactions (Bulotsky-Shearer et al., 2008) and are the cause of most classroom disturbances. Teachers give boys more attention (Beaman et al., 2006). They ask boys more questions and in return receive more in-depth feedback (Aukrust, 2008). Girls are the cause of fewer discipline problems and are much less likely to drop out of school early (Cook, 2006). They follow rules more readily and tend to get more acceptance from teachers, who certainly in primary schools tend to be mostly female (Carrington & McPhee, 2008; Carrington et al., 2007). It can be argued that the culture of schools is very much in favour of those who conform to rules, study hard and cause minimum disturbance, rather than those who are boisterous, independent and who appear unmotivated and uninterested in lessons (Myhill & Jones, 2006). There are huge implications for children (and especially boys) about schools as gender (in)appropriate places of learning. If the differences between the sexes at school are so apparent and from such an early age, then the causes of such differences must lie elsewhere, perhaps the family.

It is important to confirm straightaway that parents do have a persuasive influence upon gender identity. Parental attitudes are influenced by their own beliefs about masculinity and femininity, and messages given to children are both explicit and implicit. Parents – fathers in particular – play more roughly with boys and talk to them differently (Flanders et al., 2009). Typically girls are given domestic tasks such as cooking and cleaning and boys mow lawns, take out rubbish and mend things (Penha-Lopes, 2006). A study by family researcher Susan McHale and colleagues (2001) found that boys prefer to explore their surroundings, sports

**Connect and Extend**

Read about the development of gender schemas in: Giles, J. & Heyman, G. (2005). Young children's beliefs about the relationship between gender and aggressive behaviour. *Child Development*, 76, 107–121.

**Connect and Extend**

To understand much more about the effect of school culture on gender differences, track down Pam Jarvis's (2007) work on bio-cultural models of play in: Monsters, magic and Mr Psycho: A biocultural approach to rough and tumble play in the early years of primary school. *Early Years*, 27, 171–188.

Is she engaging in gender-appropriate behaviour?

*Source*: Catherine Yates.

and construction while girls showed preferences for writing and dance. In the past parents have been observed to pressurise and reward both boys and girls when they play with gender-appropriate toys and even punish when they play with cross-gendered toys. Why might parents punish boys for playing with dolls, for dressing up or for playing with girls? Research in the 1970s (e.g. Tauber, 1979; Whitam, 1977) suggested there are six 'childhood indicators' of later adult male homosexuality: (1) interest in dolls, (2) cross-dressing, (3) preference for company of girls rather than boys in childhood games, (4) preference for company of older women rather than older men, (5) being regarded by other boys as a sissy, (6) sexual interest in other boys rather than girls in childhood sex play. It was found that the stronger one's homosexual orientation, the greater was the number of childhood indicators. Is punishing boys for playing with dolls likely or typical today, or in this respect do we live in different times? What is the effect of different family contexts? In the section to follow we look at the influence of the family on a child's socialisation in more depth.

## The social influence of the family

**Socialisation**
The process by which parents can influence their children's attitudes and behaviours to fit those expected within a given society.

Families are social networks of relatives providing protection and increased survival chances for members of the group. The family also fulfils important social functions – providing emotional support for those in the network, establishing and maintaining culturally appropriate social order and educating the young to be competent members of that community. From the beginning of a child's life, the family exerts a tremendous and enduring effect upon a child's social development. The experiences that families have together are much more lasting than those a child will have with others and influence all aspects of a child's development: language, cognition, gender identity and emotional development. The family is the prime instrument for socialisation in childhood, and parents' influence on the socialisation of their children will reflect their own attitudes and values, social class, education, religious beliefs and their individual adult personal traits.

Socialisation is the process by which parents ensure that their children conform in attitudes and behaviours to those expected within their own society – and this is a two-way process: the family actively shapes the child, and children actively shape the family's beliefs, behaviours and attitudes. Overheard during a radio interview was the following neat turn of phrase: 'Before my wife and I started our family we wrote down six principles of child-rearing to guide our future behaviour. I now have six children and no principles!' Seriously, families change over time and these changes come to be reflected in each member.

Furthermore, families do not exist in isolation but are influenced by the wider social, cultural and physical environments and events within them. **Systems theory** provides an extremely useful way of understanding the complex structure of the family and is relevant to this discussion for two reasons. Firstly, it centres the child in the network of interacting relationships initially of the family and later the wider community and economic, educational social and political influences. The word 'interacting' is key as it implies a reciprocal interaction which is mutually beneficial to parent and child. Secondly, it views the family as a dynamic and self-regulating group of individuals that require the child to adapt to newness and change. A systems model referred to earlier in this book (Bronfenbrenner, 1989) proposed ecological development as a series of concentric circles.

In Figure 12.1, the innermost circle contains the *microsystem*: people with which the child has immediate early contact such as parents, grandparents and siblings. The second layer, the

**Systems theory**
A framework by which one can analyse and/or describe any group that work in concert.

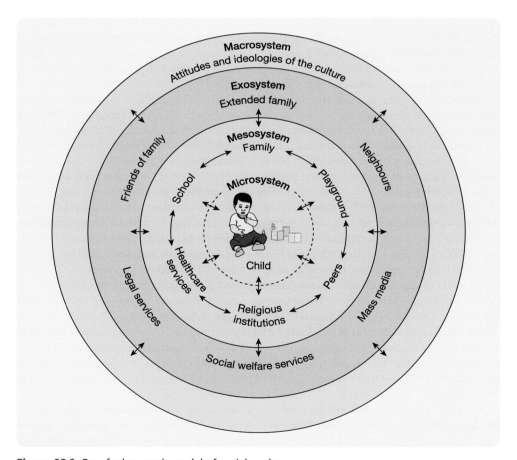

**Figure 12.1** Bronfenbrenner's model of social ecology

Beginning with parents and moving through and between Urie Bronfenbrenner's concentric circles – or social systems – is a good way of describing children's social development.

*Source*: Adapted from J. Garabino & Associates (1982). *Children and families in the social environment.* New York: Aldine. Reproduced with permission.

*mesosystem*, is the child's own developing system of social contacts at school, the wider family and other friends. The *exosystem* is usually the parents' own network of friends and neighbours that influence the child due to their direct involvement with the family. Next comes the *macrosystem*, referring to the wider social and cultural influences of the neighbourhood, schools within which both *micro-* and *exosystems* are embedded. Beginning with parents and moving outward through Urie Bronfenbrenner's concentric circles – or social systems – is a good way of describing children's social development.

How do parents socialise the young child? At the heart of the relationship between child and parent is attachment, the topic discussed in the previous chapter. This is the bond that exists between the two even before birth and is the cornerstone for subsequent relationships. Early attachment means that from the earliest moments parents, grandparents and siblings hold, cuddle affectionately and praise the child's smallest achievement. Their use of praise extends through the many milestones in development – sitting up, the first step, holding a cup and the first word. Language is a powerful medium for shaping desirable social behaviours. Praise is used to reward what is seen to be socially acceptable, and commands used to check behaviour with an emphatic 'No!' So the first way that parents help to socialise children is through the reinforcement of behaviour. A second way is through modelling the kinds of behaviour that parents wish to see replicated by their children. Modelling is a powerful medium for learning. A 5-year-old observing a parent preparing a meal will see the social significance of meals for the family, will note the gender behaviour of the parent, witness positive behaviours such as turn-taking in the kitchen and share in the grateful and positive comments (hopefully) made to the meal provider. If the same child observes a display of aggression and verbal abuse when a parent is watching a football match on television, or watching a more overtly violent activity, is the resultant connected child behaviour more or less likely to be socially desirable (e.g. Coyne *et al.*, 2004)?

Attachment operates as a two-way system. The children of parents who are loving and show genuine warmth are secure in themselves, develop high self-esteem (mentioned before) and know how to give and return affection. They understand their parents' behaviours towards them and can internalise parental standards more easily than those of inconsistent or rejecting parents. Tense environments and harsh physical punishment are confusing for children and make the learning of socially accepted norms difficult. In families with weak parents, it is the child who often takes control and the family becomes dysfunctional (Barnett and Hunter, 2012; Martin & Martin, 2000). Subsequent direction of the child to self-regulating behaviour and to adopting socially responsible behaviour is compromised. In contrast, when parents are consistent in their own behaviour and behaviour towards their children and to the disciplining of their children, children are more likely to internalise the standards of these parents (Holden, 1997). Over time, successful shaping of social behaviour becomes less directive and parents engage the child in more discussion and active reasoning about behaviour and decision-making. There is more 'behaviour bargaining' between parent and child in later childhood as social and intellectual skills develop. The style of parenting adopted influences children's socialisation, and so it would be helpful at this point to think about parenting styles. An early and influential typology describing different styles of parenting was developed by Eleanor Maccoby and John Martin (1983). The typology extended an original model by the influential clinical and developmental psychologist Diana Baumrind (1973) and is shown in Table 12.1.

As Table 12.1 shows, *authoritative* parenting – built upon love and respect for the child – results in children usually having higher self-esteem and is linked to greater social competence. Authoritative parenting is firm but fair, and features willingness to listen to children and respect their viewpoint. Children in these relationships tend to comply and are likely to do so again in the future. Studies of this parenting style show high degrees of children's competence in task persistence, co-operation, achievement, motivation and academic success in childhood through to adolescence (Kiuru *et al.*, 2012; Aunola *et al.*, 2001; Mackey *et al.*, 2001).

**Connect and Extend**

Do good parents make their children go to bed? Read: Tse, L. & Hall, W. (2008). A qualitative study of parents' perceptions of a behavioural sleep intervention. *Child: Care, Health & Development*, 34, 162–172.

**Table 12.1** Parenting styles and their relations to behaviour outcomes

| Style of parenting | Descriptors |
|---|---|
| Authoritative | Parents in control<br>Clear boundaries set<br>Expectations of socially accepted behaviour<br>Children show high self-esteem |
| Authoritarian | Emphasis on control<br>Unrealistic demands on children<br>Unresponsive to needs<br>Children have low self-esteem |
| Permissive | Indulgent parents<br>Also warm and tolerant<br>Children display immaturity or aggression<br>Dependent |
| Uninvolved | Neglecting<br>Children have difficulties forming relations with others<br>Antisocial |

**Reflect**

Imagine you are in a supermarket. What goes through your mind when you see a parent shouting at a crying child? In the next aisle is an 'I want . . . !' child loudly demanding sweets and chocolate – how did that happen? What might be happening to the children of the parents found chatting in the groceries aisle, having lost track of where their children are?

Within the family, it is not only parents who have a socialisation role to play. In modern White British cultures few grandparents live with the main family, but in many others such as Swedish, Spanish, Greek and Italian, Japanese and Korean cultures, grandparents are very much part of the family home. Interaction with grandparents provides many opportunities for intergenerational learning. They transmit information, inform about family histories and past times. They provide emotional and often financial support, and can offer the kind of consistent authoritative style of 'parenting' that hassled and stressed working mums and dads find difficult.

Time spent with brothers and sisters also provides opportunities for learning appropriate family – social – behaviour. We know that order of birth has an effect here. For a time, first-born children enjoy their parents' complete attention but, on the downside, expectations from parents tend to be higher for first-borns and there is more pressure for them to achieve academically. The eldest child in a family uses parents as a model for social behaviour and younger children use both their parents and older **siblings**. Relationships with siblings provide an important context for helping children learn to resolve personal conflicts in the comparatively safe environment of the home (Harwood, 2008). Sibling rivalry – resentment and competition is natural – is less of an issue when parents have good relationships with each other and with each of the children. However, life-changing episodes such as divorce and bereavement in families also impact on children's social development and, as we will soon discuss, the type of child-care they experience outside the home. How can professionals work with parents and families to enhance the influence of the social development of children? The following *Policy, Research and Praxis* feature provides a summary of current thinking in the UK. After the feature we move on to look at how **peers** can also be important agents in the socialisation process.

**Siblings**
Children having one or more parents in common.

**Peers**
Others of roughly the same age and developmental level.

## Policy, Research and Praxis

### Working together with parents and families

Strong, stable families are the bedrock of any society. The 'family' has evolved over time and is one of society's oldest institutions. It continues to adapt and re-adapt to economic changes and the challenges of modern living. In 2010 there were an estimated 50.8 million people living in families in the United Kingdom (ONS, 2010). Family structures are changing and we now see a greater diversity in family types across many societies, not just in the UK. What happens within a family has more impact on a child's well-being and development than any other single factor (DSCF, 2010).

The family is *the* prime instrument for socialisation in childhood. Children's life trajectories are significantly influenced by what happens in their first three years. The experiences in the home environment and the parenting they receive have a direct and long-lasting effect on their life chances. The learning environment provided by parents begins even before a child is born, and, since almost three-quarters of a young child's life is spent with the family and wider community, the home becomes the significant learning environment. Negative experiences put young children at a serious disadvantage compared to their peers. Poor experiences affect a child's brain development directly, making children more prone towards disaffection, low self-worth and disruptive behaviour as they grow up.

All families can face challenging times and some have particular needs or circumstances which make them more vulnerable and in need of support. Intervention strategies have claimed to put the needs of the child at the centre, but support for children needs to be embedded in support for families and parents. Since *Every Child Matters* was published (DfES, 2004b), multi-agency practice and better partnership working has sharpened data-sharing amongst agencies to ensure better safeguarding procedures and information sharing (CSJ, 2010). Recently there have been more changes to policy to provide better support for families. The Coalition Government's vision for families in the Foundation years is set out in the document *Supporting Families in the Foundation Years* (DFE/DH, 2011). In sum this vision aims to:

- support new parents as they make the transition to parenthood, through pregnancy and then in the important first few months after birth;
- have better working together of professional services with clear understanding of child development needs;
- bring in new arrangements for more flexible parental leave and support for flexible childcare so that parents can balance their working and family responsibilities;
- make online and helpline family-support services accessible to fathers and mothers (see **www.education.gov.uk/childrenandyoungpeople/families**);
- increase take-up of parenting and relationship programmes as well as family learning programmes;
- repurpose local community Children's Centres to serve the most disadvantaged families and enable parents and communities to have more say in their running.

The current UK Government policy is that all young children, whatever their background or current circumstances, deserve the best possible start in life and must be given the opportunity to fulfil their potential.

**Connect and Extend**

Many consider that smacking children teaches them to be violent. Others think that 'sparing the rod' results in tearaway teenagers. Read: Silverstein, M., Augustyn, M., Young, R. & Zuckerman, B. (2009). The relationship between maternal depression, in-home violence and use of physical punishment: what is the role of child behaviour? *Archives of Disease In Childhood, 94*(2), 138–143.

# The social influence of peers

Although the influence of parents and siblings are typically the most influential in the socialisation of children, relationships with peers are also important. Peer friendships are powerful influences on children's conformity (Keddie, 2004). In contrast to the hierarchical relationship that exists between parent and child, peer relationships tend to be on a more equal footing and provide opportunities to acquire and refine social skills and understanding with more give-and-take. Piaget argued that children's interactions with peers help reduce a child's natural egocentrism by requiring them to accept and work with the views of others. Remember, Lev Vygotsky also talked about scaffolding by more experienced peers thereby enabling the child to internalise a new level of thinking through this form of social interaction. The point is that children who are sociable – with developed social skills – make friends easily and enjoy school. Let's first focus on this point. Friendship among peers is central to children's social development and competence. We know that the time children spend with peers and their understanding of friendship alters with age. In early childhood little time is spent in the company of peers, yet by the time they begin school this rises to approximately 30 per cent of the 'working week' (Mashburn, 2008).

What does it mean to be a 'friend'? Selecting from a large volume of research and drawing upon the earlier work of psychologists Andrew Newcomb and Catherine Bagwell (1995), we have identified four features of friendship:

1. *Reciprocity*. Young children learn to call play companions 'friends' because a 3-year-old considers a friend is someone to spend time with and share your toys or an activity.

2. *Intense social activity*. Children of school age look for qualities in a friend that are less transitory than when they were very young. They play for longer and their co-operative play shows more complex levels of engagement than before. Friendships for older children become more lasting and can be taken up after a period of no contact.

3. *Conflict resolution* is the third feature. Friends help each other to work out problems between them – they share and take turns – and to respect the differences.

4. *Effective task performance* is the fourth identified feature of friendship. Friends plan joint actions, co-operate and collaborate to solve problems more accurately and work together to reason things out, presenting a joint outcome.

Relationships with peers begin early. Infants are genuinely interested in others even though interactions with others are limited by their intellectual, physical and language capabilities for the present. At 2 months, infants seeing another child of approximately the same age react in a different way from that observed in contact with the mother. By 6 months, there is an increase in non-verbal communication between two children. They lean towards each other, smile and even touch. Bolder children in a matter of a few months will even crawl towards a peer, curious to find out more about this strange person with similar features, shape and size. By 18 months they show preference for those children they wish to play with (Shin, 2010; Beaver *et al.*, 1999).

As children mature and their intellectual, language and physical development advances, their sphere of involvement increases to include a larger network of peers. They are beginning to understand rules of social intercourse. The *microsystem* (in Bronfenbrenner's model, referred to earlier) operates as the first level of interaction with others, providing opportunities for peer contact as well as with parents and siblings. Between 2 and 3 years, peer interactions become longer and more frequent due to advances in development. Most friendships will be with a peer of the same sex. Although not having the intensity of later relationships, these early friendships are still important for experiencing and learning sharing, turn-taking and co-operating. Children of this age imitate others and recognise when others imitate them. At the end of this preschool period, social dominance hierarchies (Boyce, 2004) are evident. These rank an individual in terms of their dominance in a group and are particularly important for boys' one-to-one and group friendships (Geary *et al.*, 2003). While many social skills are acquired in this period, it is predominately parents who control the social opportunities of children in the early childhood years.

In middle childhood, there is a definite increase in desire to play with peers and be in their company. The focus for developing relationships with others changes from the aim of playing with others in early childhood to being accepted 'as one of the gang' in the years from 7 to 11. Gossiping about others is a common form of communication and provides one way of becoming accepted socially. Friends of school age are reported to be more attentive, relaxed and mutually responsive to each other (Man Chow & Buhrmester, 2011) than during pre-school years. Common interests such as cinema, television programmes, sport, music and clothes continue to dominate relationships and form the basis for creating friendship groups, and groups become much larger as children make contact with a greater and more diverse group of peers.

Children become involved in a range of social activities in and out of school that expand this social exposure even further, but separation of the sexes continues. Girls play with girls and boys play with boys, a pattern that crosses cultures. Boys' drive to dominate and desire to compete physically (Martin-Matillas *et al.*, 2011) may discourage male–female friendships. As we have discussed, girls construct their own rules and social codes and listen to each other's suggestions about these, whereas boys avoid talking about relationships. The commonly heard 'She's my best friend' signals friendship pairs called **reciprocal friendships**. This close friend-ship with one other, usually a peer, gradually extends in the school years to children counting five or so peers as close friends (Uusitalo-Malmivaara & Lehto, 2013). Sex differences are evident here too. Whereas girls show preference for one or two close friends, boys develop more friendships but these tend to be less intimate. As children prepare for the next stage of educa-tion in secondary schools, displaying friendships in public becomes important (Griswold, 2007), although displays of friendship are practised during the preschool years (Hruska, 2007).

Sharing, co-operating, dealing with conflict, listening to worries and curbing aggressive behaviour are some of the ways in which peers are socialising agents. According to social learn-ing theory – you may remember from earlier – parents use the tools of modelling and re-inforcement to socialise children, and so do peers. Social comparison provides an immediate way of forming self-image and a 'yardstick' for children to compare themselves with others. This is important to help children understand that others share their problems too and that their experiences are normal and a natural part of growing up. Imitating appropriate beha-viours is most common in early childhood and occurs in a number of ways. Often a younger child will imitate the behaviours modelled by an older peer in preference to an adult, viewing these behaviours as more relevant: for example, sharing a toy with a child of the opposite sex. It is a powerful means of learning new skills and about different social rules. Later, children quickly learn the unwritten rules of the classroom and the playground. Whilst this behaviour can be positive, it is not always the case. Children observing aggressive behaviour on the part of an experienced and older peer will copy what is seen (and we come to this later in the chapter). This has implications for the reasons that make one child popular, and therefore likely to be a happy, resilient learner and another child not popular with all the likely out-comes of that sad circumstance. So why are some children popular and others unpopular?

Let's talk about measuring popularity first. A common way to gauge popularity is by using **sociometric techniques**. These are used by researchers as tools to measure status within peer groups, and teachers are now finding them very useful in the classroom. Psychologists Kenneth Rubin and Robert Coplan using sociometric techniques identified five categories of peer acceptance that remain a useful framework for identifying unpopular and popular children (1992).

1. *Popular* children are those rated as most liked and who hold high status in a group.

2. *Controversial* children can either be liked or disliked depending on the circumstances and the personalities making up a group.

**Reciprocal friendships**
Mutually supportive and close friendships with one other peer.

**Sociometric techniques**
Tools to measure relationships, status and social acceptance in a group.

3. **Rejected** children are least liked and include sub-groups of aggressive rejected and non-aggressive rejected.

4. **Neglected** children score low on being the most liked but tend to score low on being liked least too.

5. **Average** children are middle of the road. They are not as well accepted as popular children nor disliked as much as rejected children.

Peer popularity is the result of a number of factors – even children's names are a consideration here and seem to have been for some considerable time (Crozier & Skliopidou, 2002; McDavid & Harari, 1966). There is also a strong correlation between physical attractiveness and peer acceptance. The factors of attractiveness, sporting abilities, prosocial behaviours (we come to these later) and personal possessions are important, because children associate these factors with friendliness and social competence (Meisinger *et al.*, 2007; Babad, 2002). Children in the *Popular* category have more opportunities to acquire even more social skills – a kind of win–win situation. They display greater prosocial skills and use strategies that indicate their willingness to be friendly. A phrase like 'Do you want to play too?' invites others to join in. Communicating and instigating social interactions are important skills of social acceptance, and, where there are intellectual disabilities or cognitive dysfunctions such as ADHD, then winning social acceptance can be a challenge (Scholtens *et al.*, 2012; Fiasse & Nader-Grosbois, 2012).

Even *Average* children who can manage their emotions and control their behaviours tend to be more positive and as such their interactions with others are on the whole also positive. Pope and Bierman (1999) found that children excluded others who were easily irritated or got upset when things went wrong. Thus *Popular*, *Controversial* and *Average* children have the kinds of social–emotional skills that unpopular classmates do not have. *Popular* children (and in the right circumstances *Controversial* and *Average* children) are those who are friendly, co-operative and helpful. They have high self-esteem, are socially competent, and successful academically and in outside school activities (Chen *et al.*, 2001). Rejected children display inappropriate social behaviours such as aggression in a behaviour–rejection cycle (Lansford *et al.*, 2010). Typically these are the children arguing with others or engaging in rough-and-tumble fighting in the playground, although it should be noted that researchers have recently identified more complex configurations of popularity: *aggressive–unpopular*; *aggressive–popular*; and *prosocial–popular* (Estell, 2007), so it would be unwise to always associate aggressive behaviour with unpopularity. We will come back to the idea of the *popular–aggressive* configuration later. Ignored children display least aggression and engage in solitary play and other inconspicuous activities. In general, unpopular children – those who have difficulties in socialising with others – can struggle academically, are likely to play truant, be depressed and to drop out of school (Estell *et al.*, 2008).

Parents play an important role in helping their child form relationships with peers. Many studies confirm that children who form successful early attachments with their parents or carers are those who will form good relationships with other children (Fallu *et al.*, 2010; Sroufe *et al.*, 1999). This is in no small way due to the opportunities provided in early relationships to learn social skills of communication, turn-taking and sharing, and so on and for parents to model social competence. Popular children with good prosocial behaviours have parents who are authoritative (as we have discussed earlier), who involve children in discussion and respond to them in caring ways. Parents are able to influence their children's social development through the types of social and family activities in which they engage. These can include eating meals together as a family, getting together with friends who have children of a similar age, involving children from an early age in regular wider family events, enrolling children in play groups, crèches and day-care settings, and local organisations and clubs in later childhood years. Such involvement provides multiple opportunities to develop a range of social skills with a range of age groups, to elicit positive responses from others and provide effective models of behaviour in social situations.

• • • • • • • • • • • • • • • •
**Connect and Extend**
For a case study of a 4-year-old child who developed the hurtful habit of saying to her friends and younger sister, 'You're not my friend', unless they did exactly as she wished, read: Greenberg, P. (2006). You're not my friend! *Parent & Child*, 13, 22.
• • • • • • • • • • • • • • • •

> **Reflect**
>
> You may have noticed children who have few or no friends and appear very shy and withdrawn. There could be a number of reasons for children being ignored. What indicators can you list that identify a 'shy' child? How is this type of child particularly disadvantaged? What could you do to help?

# The social influence of schools and the media

Among other determinants, two more sets of factors influence the social development of children: schools and the media – and we begin with schools. Cross-cultural studies show that schools influence how children organise their thinking and are therefore a vehicle for how children understand the world (Salmon, 2008; Prokop *et al.*, 2007; Kazlauskienė, 2007). Schools are important influences in extending children's social networks because schooling places many demands on children that affect all aspects of their development: how children communicate, how they behave, how they make progress in learning in different subjects. Schools also influence moral and social development (Woolfolk *et al.*, 2012), as we explore in the next section.

Socially the transition from preschool to school is significant and one that impacts upon future school experiences. Making a successful transition requires being able to cope with being separated from parents for longer periods of time, becoming more independent and self-controlled, and acquiring many new social skills. Here, the earlier experiences within the family and with peers are highly influential. Certain aspects of the school environment can help ease this transition in and through school, socially and intellectually. For example, smaller schools can offer a stronger sense of personal identity and more chance of children being given positions of responsibility (Tajalli & Opheim, 2005). When class sizes are also small, teachers report having more time for pupils and that having fewer pupils in class facilitates group work more easily, discourages bad behaviour and fosters individual learning (Englehart, 2007). However, there is evidence gathered over the past 35 years that, within the range of about 25–34 pupils, class size seems to have little, if any, decisive impact on the academic achievement of most pupils (Januszka & Dixon-Krauss, 2008; *Education Digest*, 1978). Perhaps it is a matter of age. It could be argued that younger children in smaller teaching groups may get more individual help with the basic skills needed for success at school. Early successes in the 'basics' of reading, writing and mathematics allow pupils to express themselves more freely and be seen by their peers to engage fully with the curriculum (Leopold, 2008; Eldridge, 2008). That is the point perhaps: being seen in positions of responsibility, and being seen to succeed in the abilities and skills that schools emphasise in the activities they offer, provides a context in which healthy social development can be encouraged.

Teachers also act as agents of social development. Social development is fostered when teachers link academic achievement to the emotional climate in classrooms, involving pupils continually in the learning process, setting clear learning goals matched to individual needs, with regular personalised feedback (Tomlinson, 2005). Teachers should have high expectations – termed being a 'warm demander' (Ware, 2006) – of all pupils since this is connected with motivation, success and achievement (Ross *et al.*, 2008). Young children pay little attention to the achievements of their peers. However, as they grow older, comparison with others, and judgements from parents and teachers influence how they feel about themselves, their feelings about their academic competency and about their self-worth. **Achievement motivation** is when pupils desire to be successful and want to feel pleasure in performing well, and this impacts directly on self-esteem. Pupils who are mastery-oriented, in other words who have clear learning goals which they have set for themselves (Sungur, 2007) and who focus on improving their skills and knowledge, tend to be successful. In contrast, helpless children (remember the idea of learned-helplessness) have **performance goals** rather than learning

**Connect and Extend**

The cry of 'This is boring!' challenges every teacher. This article highlights 10 key principles from brain science for creating a passion for learning: Strother, M. A. (2007). A mind for adventure. *Reclaiming Children & Youth*, 16, 17–21.

**Achievement motivation**
A desire on the part of learners to be successful and to measure themselves against external standards and to feel pleasure in performing well.

**Performance goals**
Targets comparing performance of the individual with those in the same class or age group.

goals, are overconcerned with how they appear to others and try to avoid negative judgements on their ability by not engaging with the learning activities – 'This is boring' – or by disrupting the class.

Teachers can also plan for teaching and learning strategies that have a high degree of social involvement. Co-operative learning strategies are where pupils are placed in small groups and work together on a common goal; this is found to have a positive impact on self-esteem, attitudes towards peers and to school generally (Woolfolk *et al.*, 2012; Gillies & Boyle, 2008). **Peer collaboration** is similar but generally involves two students working together. **Peer tutoring** is a method of teaching in which a more experienced child tutors a less experienced pupil. Both participants benefit from this technique and the more experienced pupil particularly gains from the experience of 'being the teacher' and helping others. The use of peer tutoring can impact positively on the social behaviour, academic achievement and self-esteem of pupils with behavioural problems. These strategies involve pupils in active learning in the classroom, promote autonomy, give pupils responsibility and foster feelings of self-worth and mastery (McMaster *et al.*, 2008, 2006).

There are other factors that influence children's socialisation. The content and tone of a good deal of children's literature influence role divisions, stereotyping men as assertive and independent, and women as dependent and passive (Shachar, 2012). Popular television programmes will often portray men as decisive and strong and women as gentler and more emotional. Stereotyping effects of television are significant and occur from an early age. How early? Well babies of 6 months can attend to television, although consistent and focused viewing does not usually occur under 12 months of age and patterns of viewing are less led by the content of programmes and more by visual features, patterns, faces, music and animation. What is surprising perhaps is how early patterns of television viewing are established. In a study published in 2005, Darcy Thompson and Dimitri Christakis found the following using data from 2068 children under 3 years of age. Mean hours of television viewing per day were as follows: 0.9 hours a day for children under 12 months of age, 1.6 hours a day for children 12 to 23 months of age, and 2.3 hours/day for children 24 to 35 months of age. The higher number of hours of television watched per day was associated with both an irregular naptime schedule and an irregular bedtime schedule. What might be the social and educational benefits of watching this amount of TV? Table 12.2 summarises the positive and negative effects, based on Thompson and Christakis's 2005 study.

Items in Table 12.2 are only a small selection of possible effects but nevertheless they serve to characterise television as a mixed blessing. The variety of television programmes that children watch, including educational and family programmes, cartoons and children's films, can have both positive and negative influences on their social development. Serious breaches of 'safe' periods – programmes with adult themes – are far more worrying and may possibly warp normal social development. There are some more subtle concerns as well. For example, how much of the programmes they watch do children of different ages actually understand? Can children distinguish truth from fiction, in what is known as **magic window thinking** (Denman, 1952) and does it matter? Does television watching inordinately impact on time available for playing with friends or engaging in other social activities? Despite these concerns and a number of other potentially negative influences, opportunities to co-view television with parents and significant others can encourage critical and evaluative communication skills and enhance social-cognitive development.

Nowadays in the United Kingdom, computers are almost universally a part of homes and schools, and many children from an early

**Peer collaboration**
Classroom learning technique involving two students working together to achieve a particular goal.

**Peer tutoring**
A method of teaching in which an older more experienced child tutors one who is younger and/or less experienced.

**Magic window thinking**
Beliefs held by young children that what is seen on television is reality.

How well these boys perform compared with each other is likely to influence their self-esteem and social development.

*Source*: © Pearson Education Ltd / Jules Selmes.

**Table 12.2** Possible social and cognitive effects of television viewing on children

| Possible positive effects of television | Possible negative effects of television |
| --- | --- |
| Motivates and helps with reading development through programmes specifically targeted at young children | Too much viewing can impede reading progress; there is no time for reading |
| Increases language development through vocabulary, alphabet letters, simplified language | Can produce negative attitudes towards certain ethnic groups, particularly if children watch television outside of 'safe' periods |
| Helps with mathematical development, e.g. numbers, counting and problem-solving shown in real-life contexts | Can influence the formation of gender roles and stereotypes |
| Assists with children's sharing and turn-taking abilities. Modelled in children's programmes | Can produce negative attitudes towards sexual relationships, such as aggressive sexual behaviour, particularly if children watch television outside of 'safe' periods |
| Examples of good television role models can be used to educate children in prosocial behaviour | Can increase aggressive behaviour even if watching during 'safe' periods |
| Time spent co-viewing with parents and other siblings is productive social time – a common experience | Certain advertisements may create poor life choices or impede normal healthy development (e.g. fast food, cost and types of toys) |
| Explanation of programme content and meaning by parents or older siblings helps with developing positive social values | Produces a false sense of 'reality' about the world |

*Source*: Thompson, D. A. & Christakis, D. A. (2005). The association between television viewing and irregular sleep schedules among children less than 3 years of age. *Pediatrics, 116*, 851–856.

age have access to them in their bedrooms. Schools and parents will willingly invest in educational programs to enhance children's education, and yet practitioners and parents alike feel anxious about the content of some programs and games, and, in particular those available on the Internet. As with television viewing, there are possible social detriments to unregulated access to computers and the Internet but there are also many potential cognitive and social benefits. Computer-aided learning (CAL) allies educational possibilities of technology with children's specific needs. Important benefits have been shown in higher-order thinking for computer-based work in schools. Skills of reflection, metacognition and enhanced creativity are claimed and academic gains are especially evident with young children and children with learning difficulties (Yang *et al.*, 2007). Aids to communication have potential benefit for many children in their social development.

In classrooms or computer suites it is common to observe pairs or small groups of children clustered around a computer, happily chatting away about what they are doing and pointing to something on the screen. Working in pairs and in small groups is a powerful vehicle for learning when collaborative activities engage children in the task and with each other. There is evidence across the primary-age range of greater collaboration when using computers than with other school tasks (Rosé, 2013; Svensson, 2000). However, it should be noted that educationalist Pat Broadhead's research shows highest levels of collaboration in open-ended activities, for example, playing with sand and water (Broadhead, 2004). Perhaps it is the nature of well-designed open-ended activities using computers that provokes high-quality collaboration. Children discuss, collaborate, solve problems and co-construct knowledge by engaging in exactly the type of social interactions consistent with Vygotsky's theory of 'scaffolding' learning (discussed in Chapter 2) (Schraw, 2007). Children working with a peer in this way show persistence and positive attitudes to learning (Miller *et al.*, 2006) and it encourages helpful ways of conflict resolution (Hubal *et al.*, 2008).

At home and in school children communicate with others in chat rooms, synchronous messaging systems and through email. This may seem like a very social activity but research

**Connect and Extend**

How does cyberbullying reach victims in their own homes? If the machine isn't on, then the bullying can't happen. Read: Anderson, T. & Sturm, B. (2007). Cyberbullying: From playground to computer. *Young Adult Library Services*, 5, 24–27.

Shoot them before they shoot you! Many parents worry about the possible negative outcomes of playing violent video games.
*Source*: © Pearson Education Ltd. / Tudor Photography.

with adolescents has found substantial use of the Internet in this way can have negative effects on emotional and social development by displacing face-to-face social activity with family and friends (e.g. Young, 2008). Many parents harbour deep anxieties about unsupervised access their children might have to the Internet and the potential for cyberstalking and bullying (Stomfay-Stitz & Wheeler, 2007). Children also play interactive games, with friends. Some of these simulation games, although fostering spatial skills and attention, have violent plots that involve shooting and fighting enemies, appealing mostly to boys, and have negative outcomes associated with racial stereotyping and aggression (Kassis, 2007; Eastin & Griffiths, 2006). However, it is these play contexts and more traditional games of the playground and nursery that raise important matters of right and wrong. Learning the difference between right and wrong and understanding the effects of our actions on others form an important part of our social development, and it is to the moral world of the child that we now turn.

Before moving on, let's summarise what we have learned in the middle section of this chapter:

- Two strands of social identity were considered: ethnic identity and gender identity.
- Ethnic identity is important in one's self-concept, and depends on how the ethnic group are defined and regarded.
- Gender identity refers to an individual's perception of their own gender. Behavioural differences can be apparent as early as the first two years.
- There is, however, some evidence of differences in specific abilities. Girls walk, talk and generally reach developmental milestones earlier than boys and do better at school.
- Language regions are more active in females, giving girls advantages in communication over males.

Summary 2

- Cognitive-developmental theories are about construction of schema – the basis for behaviour in gender-typical ways, for example, boys play gun fights and girls play with dolls.
- Knowledge of gender is acquired through increased opportunities for children to observe others and imitate them – social learning theory.
- With preschool children the tendency to play with peers of the same sex is striking.
- Boys dominate classroom interactions and are the cause of most classroom disturbances. Girls are the cause of fewer discipline problems and are much less likely to drop out of school early.
- The family is the prime instrument for socialisation in childhood, and parents' influence on the socialisation of their children will reflect their own attitudes and values, social class, education and religious beliefs.
- Beginning with parents and moving outward through Urie Bronfenbrenner's concentric circles – or social systems – is a good way of describing children's social development.
- Children's social skills and self-esteem are a function of parenting style, with the authoritative style coming out on top.
- Peer friendships are powerful influences on children's conformity and tend to provide opportunities to acquire and refine social skills with more give-and-take.
- Schools are important influences in extending children's social networks and forming how children communicate, how they behave, and how they make progress.
- Co-operative learning strategies such as *peer collaboration* and *peer tutoring* have a positive impact on self-esteem, attitudes towards peers and to school generally.
- Children's literature, television, video games and the Internet can affect children's social and moral development but not always positively.

# Moral development: right or wrong?

In assembly the headteacher, Mrs Tranter, was telling the children a story. It was about a boy who had stolen a large loaf of bread from a shop to give to a friend whose family had very little money, and who were hungry. The headteacher showed the school a large and appetising-looking loaf. She then told another story about a girl who stole a small biscuit from a bakery because she liked cream biscuits. The girl was not hungry but she did like to eat cream biscuits. Mrs Tranter showed the children a small biscuit and asked the children which of the two children was most naughty. All the young children in the Reception class (aged 4–5) agreed that it was wrong to steal and since the loaf was large compared with only one small cream biscuit, they thought that the boy was the naughtiest.

When the older children (9–11) in the school were asked, their answer was different. Their view was that the act of stealing for selfish gains was worse than stealing to give to someone else, even if what was stolen was not as large.

This story illustrates the difference in moral thinking between young and older children: in this case the fine moral judgements involved in appreciating the notion of doing the wrong thing for the right reason. In this section, we will further explore the moral thinking of young children in the Piagetian pre-operational stage and see how it differs to that of older children who have acquired operational thought. From the outset we can establish that moral and social development are closely connected since the relationships we have with other people influence how we act, and how we act is very often determined by social contexts. But how best to define what we mean by moral development? One concise and much quoted definition of moral development is 'the process by which children adopt and internalise the rules and expectations of society and develop a sense of right or wrong' (Dwyer and Scampion, 1995, p 254). We begin this section with the theoretical frameworks underpinning the development of right and wrong, with particular emphasis on the theories of Piaget and Kohlberg.

Each society has rules and standards of behaviour it deems as acceptable for its citizens. Although these vary according to culture, there is universal consistency in the belief that standards of behaviour should be communicated to children so that they will learn and practise these as they get older. Messages and expectations about what is 'right' and 'wrong' are initially communicated by parents – those who first shape children's moral views and standards of behaviour. Later, early years professionals and teachers become powerful influences on children's moral behaviour and development. As children grow older, they acquire a fuller knowledge and understanding of self, and become more able to self-regulate their actions and thinking. They move from depending upon external controls to their own internal control of their behaviour. Child psychologist Jenny Lindon views children's understanding of right and wrong as a combination of three aspects of their development (2005, p 206):

1. *Social relationships*. Babies are born as social beings so their understanding of rights and wrongs – their sense of morality – is grounded in relationships with other people.

2. *Moral behaviour*. Young children have no concept of adult moral judgements but do recognise adult disapproval.

3. *Moral reasoning and judgement*. Older children come to understand – related to increased cognitive ability – 'why' something should be done and that good behaviour is a related series of making the 'right' decisions.

Let us now turn to the theories to find out what they can contribute to our understanding of moral development.

## Theories of moral development

In his psychodynamic theory, Sigmund Freud (1935) emphasised internalising standards of moral behaviour. His account combines both social factors – largely through the influence of parents – and biological factors though an inbuilt natural desire to act in certain ways. A focus in psychodynamics is the connection between emotional states in a child's unconscious mind (see Chapter 2) as they relate to early childhood developments and processes. According to Freud's theory, the *super-ego* at age 3–5 (the phallic stage) drives an attraction towards a parent of the opposite sex (the *Oedipus* complex in boys and the *Electra* complex in girls). This leads to a perception of the other parent as a rival and to associated feelings of guilt, hostility and a fear of being punished if the attraction is discovered.

A process of identification is used to maintain parents' affections, and this leads to the development of conscience embracing the moral standards of the identified parent or *ego ideal*. This process of identification accounts for the regard of children for those who establish moral standards by the correction of wrongdoings – the 'punishing parent'. It also accounts for the bond that exists between an assertive parent and child and associated feelings of pride when behaviours are displayed in accordance with parental moral values – the 'rewarding parent' – almost always, according to Freud, the same-sex parent.

Freud's claims are now generally considered as unrealistic. For instance, his claim that boys have stronger superegos than girls and, as such, are less likely to behave inappropriately, is unsubstantiated and probably refuted by parents and teachers everywhere! Another example

**Psychodynamic theory**
The explanation of how psychological forces shape human behaviour.

is Freud's claim that children learn moral standards from the same-sex parent. How is it then that children raised in one-parent families can and usually do exhibit appropriate moral behaviour? Furthermore, Freud's focus on guilt as a primal driver of conscience receives little support nowadays. Although guilt is important in motivating moral actions, it is not the sole force in encouraging appropriate and acceptable behaviour. Children are capable of internalising rules much earlier than Freud proposed (by age 2 in some cases, and by 3 many will comply with requests from parents and carers to put away toys and tidy up) and contrary to his notion of children being morally mature by about 6, moral development continues throughout childhood years and into adulthood. These concerns aside, the role of emotions as a base for moral development, the importance placed on the role of parents and early attachments are still relevant in contemporary psychodynamic research (e.g. Taylor *et al.*, 2007).

• • • • • • • • • • • • • • • • •
**Connect and Extend**
Do young children have a conscience? Read: Kochanska, G., Forman, D. R., Aksan, N. & Dunbar, S. (2005). Pathways to conscience. *Journal of Child Psychology & Psychiatry*, 46, 19–34.
• • • • • • • • • • • • • • • • •

In his social learning theory, Canadian psychologist Albert Bandura (1977) placed emphasis on moral behaviours. These he believed were the acquired internal standards of how to behave and are developed through cognitive representations of what children observe and process. Moral behaviours are built on explanations of moral conduct from parents and other figures in authority. He proposed, therefore, that values can be learned just as other behaviours and skills can, largely through the processes of modelling and imitation. Like Freud, Bandura believed that parents serve as powerful models of influence for children's moral development. The use of reprimands shapes children's behaviour as they respond to these and other punishments administered by adults. Reinforcements through praise, demonstrations of approval and tangible rewards increase the frequency of desirable behaviour reoccurring. One possible criticism of Bandura's work is that behaviours such as sharing or helping another child do not happen frequently enough to be reinforced, so that 'reinforcers' are not powerful enough to explain adequately the scope and rapid development of these kinds of moral behaviours in childhood. What other explanation might there be? Is it something to do with a move from external rewards or punishments to internal values? How are those values established?

Both social learning theory and psychodynamic theory help us to understand that moral development is a gradual process of conforming to societal standards and norms. This process progresses from a focus upon the self to a focus on others and, with increased maturity, moves from external rewards or punishments to internal standards of morality. Today, by far the most commonly accepted theories of moral development within this framework are those offered by Piaget and by Kohlberg, which we will now consider.

## The cognitive-developmental perspective

Psychologist Jean Piaget was the first to develop an account of moral development in a systematic manner (1932). He applied his theory of cognitive development, which we have already met, to developing his theory of moral development. In this theory he stressed the importance of moral reasoning, or an ability to think through answers to questions such as 'Should I take these sweets if my friend wants me to?' Such a question requires considerable reasoning ability (and hence closely linked to cognitive maturity) and a capacity to consider another's feelings and perspectives.

His theory arose in the main from his observations of children playing a formal game, for example, marbles, and how the game prompted questions about the rules. What are the rules? Where did they come from? Have the rules changed? In marbles, children construct and monitor their rules away from adult influences and, Piaget believed, games like marbles are important in the development of moral knowledge. His theory has two stages and proposes that children pass through recognisable and qualitatively different stages.

Stage 1 is the *heteronomous stage*. This pre-moral stage covers the period from birth to the end of the preschool years. During this time there is little understanding of rules. For example, in attempting to play a simple board game like draughts, a child of this age would be more concerned with finding out how the pieces could be used in different ways than with systematically playing to rules. In the game of marbles, preschool children while enjoying a fun activity are often unaware of the existence of rules for the game. At the concrete operations stage at 7 years, they become aware of rules but not in conventional terms in that children believe the rules are unchangeable. Actions are only evaluated in terms of the consequences and morals are deemed the property of *heteronomous* others in authority (*'hetereo'* meaning 'by others') which must be obeyed. A child of 5 will be often heard to say, 'My mum says that . . .', or a child coming home and announcing, 'My teacher says . . .'. In these cases the child is adamant that what the parent or teacher says is definitely not to be questioned!

By age 9 and in the second stage, that of *autonomous morality*, children realise that rules can be altered and are arbitrary. Actions are judged by intentions (feeding a hungry family with a stolen loaf of bread) rather than consequences, and an adherence to authority figures is now seen to be no longer necessary. Of course, in the real world, rule breaking is not always wrong or punished. By 9 or 10 years and beyond, children's thinking becomes much more flexible. They can focus attention in a number of different directions which allows them to evaluate the application of rules and intentions of transgressors in particular situations. Remember from the last chapter that children are able at this age to empathise with others. In the cups story, which is coming up shortly, accidents are not judged with the same severity as intentional acts. The child who, as part of a deliberate act, breaks one cup deserves a greater punishment than the child who accidentally breaks several cups. Young children would consider both breakages 'naughty'.

A second way Piaget developed his theory was by listening to children's responses to short stories containing a moral dilemma – like the one we told at the beginning of this section. In these stories, a main character commits an act of transgression. The story of John (A) and the story of Henry (B) illustrate the moral dilemmas behind the stories and are taken from the account of Piaget's investigations published as *The Moral Judgment of the Child* (1932):

A. A boy called John is in his bedroom and is called down for dinner. He goes into the dining room where there is a chair behind the door. On the chair is a tray with 15 cups on it. John could not have known that the tray was behind the door. He goes into the room and knocks over the tray, breaking all the cups.

B. A boy called Henry tried to get some jam from a cupboard one day while his mother was out. He climbed onto a chair and reached out. The jam was too high and he was not able to reach it. While he was trying, he knocked over a cup. The cup fell down and broke.

The moral dilemma is this: Henry broke a cup while stealing jam. By accident, John broke 15 cups, but is this worse? Young children in the *moral realism* stage judge that the more things are broken, the naughtier the act and the more severe the punishment should be. John broke more cups, therefore young children would think he committed the naughtier act. For children in this stage, the fact that Henry tried to deceive his mother is less important. By ages 8–9, in the *autonomous morality* stage, children's views change. The child who broke the cups by accident should not be punished because they now believe that the act was an accident – no fault is attributable – and that the child who broke the cup whilst engaged in an act of deceit is worse than the one who broke 15 by accident. Their moral development has moved on, and in short the punishment should fit the crime.

## Kohlberg's stage theory

Kohlberg's stage theory of moral development (1969) was heavily based on Piagetian theories and was linked to children's moral reasoning abilities. He too allied a child's cognitive capacity with the capacity for moral thinking, yet was more concerned with reasoning than children's understanding of right and wrong. It is a theory more about moral principles than moral behaviours. It is based on his observations of how children solve hypothetical problems, that is, the 'what if' type questions, and proposes that the reasons children give for their moral decisions change with age. Lawrence Kohlberg identified six stages that span three levels of

**Table 12.3**  Kohlberg's six stages of moral development

| Level 1: Preconventional morality | |
| --- | --- |
| Stage 1:<br>Obedience and punishment orientation | Makes moral decisions purely on the basis of self-interest. Will disobey rules if he thinks he can do so without getting caught. |
| Stage 2:<br>Hedonistic and instrumental orientation | Recognises that others have needs, but prioritises her own needs over those of others. |
| **Level 2: Conventional morality** | |
| Stage 3:<br>Good boy/good girl | Makes decision on the basis of what will please others and is very concerned to keep friends. |
| Stage 4:<br>Law and order | Looks to society as a whole for guidelines about moral decisions. Thinks of rules as absolute, inflexible and unchangeable. |
| **Level 3: Postconventional morality** | |
| Stage 5:<br>Social contract | Recognises that rules are social constructions – agreements that can be changed or ignored when necessary. |
| Stage 6:<br>Universal ethical principle | Adheres to a small number of universal abstract principles that transcend specific rules. Answers only to inner conscience. |

*Source*: Based on Kohlberg, L. (1984). *Essays on moral development (Vol. 2). The Psychology of Moral Development*. San Francisco, CA: Harper & Row.

moral reasoning (see Table 12.3), which he argued are common to all but are not presented as age-specific. He recognised that there would be individual differences as to when children pass through each stage and that some people, even as adults, never reach the highest level.

Most children up to the age of 10 have preconventional morality; Stages 1 and 2 of the six stages. At the first level, Stage 1 is *obedience and punishment orientation*. Children respond to rules, imposed by authority figures. They submit to authority. So the child being reprimanded by a teacher in school for a misdemeanour will generally accept this telling-off. They obey rules to avoid being punished and decide, if it is wrong, then the wrong doing should be punished. Stage 2 is *hedonistic and instrumental orientation*. Children now seek rewards for their actions. They can behave well for their own gains and judge rightness if it benefits them. They also engage in negotiation, so a school-age child might be heard to say, 'I will learn my spellings for tomorrow if I can watch the television programme afterwards'.

**Connect and Extend**

For information about evoking and teaching kindness to others based on schema developed by Lawrence Kohlberg, read: O'Malley, W. (1998). Kindness, *America, 178*, 10.

Like Piaget, Kohlberg made extensive use of story-telling (as we have in the last couple of chapters) to investigate moral reasoning, exemplified in his famous story of Heinz who buys drugs for his dying wife (Kohlberg, 1984). A précis of the story is that a woman is near to death but there exists a drug that could save her life. It is very expensive. In the town, the local chemist has a supply but is charging ten times the correct price for it. The woman's husband, Heinz, tried to borrow money from people he knew, but could not raise enough cash to buy it. He even pleaded with the chemist to let him pay some money in advance but the chemist refused. Heinz then considered breaking into the store to steal the drug for his dying wife.

If we take this story and apply it to the children under 10, that is, in the first two stages of Kohlberg's theory, what dilemmas would we find? Children in *obedience and punishment orientation* of Stage 1 would say that Heinz should steal the drug because to let his wife die is wrong but also he should not steal it because he would be sent to prison. At this level of preconventional morality, children believe strongly that stealing is wrong because those in authority say it is. Right and wrong are determined by what will or will not be punished. At Stage 2, *hedonistic and instrumental orientation*, children would say that Heinz should steal it because his wife needs it to live but also he should not steal it because if he got caught he could go to prison and his wife would die anyway. At this second level of preconventional morality, right and wrong is determined by the rewards it brings and by what other people want if there is a reciprocal relationship.

**Reflect** How would you apply Stages 3–6 of Kohlberg's model to Heinz and the drugs? Kohlberg's theory places emphasis on being able to view the world from another's perspective. Think back to Chapter 11. Does Kohlberg's stage theory fit with what you learned about the development of empathy?

The theories of Piaget and Kohlberg make influential contributions to our understanding of moral development. We now know that children act as moral beings in search of 'truths' of right and wrong and that new moral understandings are built from experiences in various social encounters. These understandings have also led current researchers to explore moral reasoning in new dimensions such as gender and culture (e.g. Sachdeva *et al.*, 2011; Wilgus, 2009; Reinke *et al.*, 2008) through the observation of children's behaviour in nurseries and schools. It is to the topic of pro- and antisocial behaviour that we now turn.

## Pro- and antisocial behaviours

It seems that each generation bemoans the moral standards and low levels of social behaviour of the next one. Certainly children's behaviour today is a major concern for class teachers, and, by anecdote, amongst teacher-trainers, by far the most consistent reason why trainees on the teacher training courses fail their examination of professional practice. All too often in the last few days of a teaching practice teachers will say, 'I'm sorry but he cannot pass. He just can't control the class.' This is a common situation by anecdote and reflected in some studies (e.g. Preece, 1979) but needs some sound and more recent empirical research to support this important idea.

A 'difficult' class can make lessons a tiring ordeal for any teacher, whether a trainee or not, and constantly having to deal with incidences of disruptive and challenging behaviour can ruin even the best planned lessons. Fortunately the majority of children do behave well in schools and have done so for some time. The inspectors of the UK Office for Standards in Education (OfSTED) rated classroom behaviour as good or excellent in 92 per cent of primary schools in England (Steer, 2005). This is a reassuring finding; yet, it remains necessary to recognise that the behavioural climate of all classrooms depends upon the behaviours of each and all of the persons who are present (Galanes & Carmack, 2013). What kind of personal behaviours lead to good or excellent classroom behaviour?

Prosocial behaviour and interactions are important for all societies and it is not surprising that promoting prosocial behaviour is of concern to educators, politicians and to policy makers in many countries. Of course, the family provides a significant learning context for developing prosocial values and behaviours: relationships within the family, parenting styles, sharing in home chores and helping to look after siblings are all important foundations for moral development and it can begin early in life.

**Prosocial behaviour** Intentional, voluntary behaviour intended to benefit another person for which there is no reward expectation.

As observed in the last chapter, infants under 12 months use gestures and expressions to communicate with others, including sharing interesting objects with others. Infants notice that other children nearby are distressed and when mobility allows will approach another child or adult and share some of the distress. By 3 years children will offer specific help, perhaps a sticking plaster to an adult with a cut finger. They may also offer a favourite toy or blanket as a comfort, demonstrating some understanding about how others are feeling. A 3-year-old will pat the hand of his weeping mother and may be heard to say, 'Mummy sad.'

In the first 3 years there are many other examples of prosocial behaviours to be seen: children sharing toys and food, offering verbal assistance, and involving others in helping:

like directing an older brother to fetch a younger sibling's rattle. Expressions of prosocial behaviour change with age. In general, children engage in more prosocial behaviours as they get older (Bureau & Moss, 2010). The pattern of prosocial behaviour is also stable over time; thus a child who shows abundant examples of prosocial behaviours at age 3 is likely to continue to do so as an adolescent and adult and, if anything, this increases as perceptive abilities improve with age. As children more accurately understand what is happening around them, they respond to situations less aggressively and with more prosocial behaviours. There appears to be little gender difference, although girls have a slight edge in tending to others, and in their comfort-giving and instrumental helping. Girls in the main consistently show a little more empathy – see below – than boys (Dadds *et al.*, 2008), but one does need to view such findings with some caution since expectations and gender stereotyping make it a complex area.

**Altruism**
Acting with a selfless
concern for others.

Two elements of prosocial behaviour can be identified. These are empathy and altruism. Empathy has been discussed previously: to recap, it is defined as a willingness to tune into the feelings of others and having a sensitivity to other people's feelings. It is therefore a vicarious response requiring an appreciation of how others are feeling and a sympathetic response to their needs. Altruism is defined as acting with a selfless concern for others. Altruistic behaviour is behaviour intended to help someone else, without any expectation of reward and sometimes at some cost to the 'giver'. Altruistic children can regulate their own feelings well, tend to be the most popular children, display better social skills and are more self-assured. Neither empathy nor altruism develop naturally but arise out of positive early experiences as we have described. One important contributor to how children develop altruistic natures is through prosocial moral reasoning.

For over fifteen years (e.g. with Lee, 2013; 1998), psychologist Nancy Eisenberg has developed a progression in children's prosocial reasoning, which begins with a preoccupation about their own needs in what she called *hedonistic orientation*. This is 'help only if it benefits self'. Let's consider an example of a child being asked to visit an elderly neighbour to deliver some cake for tea. Through this example we can explore Eisenberg's different stages in prosocial moral reasoning. In the first category of *hedonistic orientation*, a child might think to herself, 'I won't visit old Mrs Evans because I want to play at my friends''. This stage is followed in middle childhood by the *needs-of-others orientation* stage, where concerns for others are shown although these may conflict with a child's own feelings. A child in this stage of reasoning might think, 'I need to visit Mrs Evans because I have been asked to, though her house smells funny'. There then follows an *approval and interpersonal orientation* stage which is associated with seeking approval from others. An older child might say to herself 'I have done a good job in taking the cake next door. My parents will be pleased with me'. In late primary school and early secondary school comes the *self-reflective, empathetic orientation* stage where the child tries to put him- or herself in another person's shoes. A child of 11 or older might think, 'I feel good about taking the cake around to see Mrs Evans. She's old and lonely'. A final stage of *internalised values orientation* is included and applicable to adolescents whose justification for helping is also based on values and responsibilities – to ignore these would undermine one's own self-respect: 'It is right to take the cake around and stay for a visit. We should judge our society by how well we treat the elderly and vulnerable'.

There are a number of reasons why some children demonstrate more prosocial behaviours than others and therefore move more smoothly through the stages of prosocial moral reasoning. An emphasis on genetic determinants in general receive little support, although we have already seen how temperament is integral to how children respond emotionally to others. Social learning theory tells us that reinforcement is important, that is, giving rewards for sharing – sweets, money and verbal praise – all increase the likelihood of these behaviours being replicated. Social learning theory also points to other factors: the importance of modelling and imitation (again, Eisenberg & Fabes, 1998), parenting styles and child-rearing practices, secure attachments and warm supportive families, where assertive parents (warm demanders) are less inclined to use controlling techniques to discipline children (Strayer & Roberts, 2004).

When parents, carers and teachers express disappointment with antisocial behaviours, explain why such behaviour is wrong and give reasons why other behaviours are preferable, it is likely to lead to more positive moral behaviour. As an example, when 5-year-old Jemma hits out at her friend Lucy a reaction like, 'Don't do that Jemma (assertive)! That makes me very sad (seeking empathy). That really hurt Lucy and you wouldn't like it if she did that to you, now, would you (moral reasoning)? Now say sorry and the two of you go and help Martin with the toys (preferable behaviours)' is likely to be an effective teacher intervention. **Induction** techniques like this are really convincing and powerful.

One way of understanding the development of prosocial and antisocial behaviours is a social development model originally developed by social psychologists Richard Catalano and David Hawkins (1996), now often referenced, which suggests that similar paths lead to both prosocial and antisocial behaviours. The model is shown in Figure 12.2.

The pathways model suggests that factors such as sex, race, age and socio-economic status determine the social opportunities that are available. Children recognise that some activities are available and become involved with positive or problem behaviour related to those activities. Importantly children also interact with either 'good' people or 'bad' people related to those activities. So a child who is coerced into shoplifting begins to practise an antisocial behaviour and to interact with petty criminals, while another who is invited to sing in the church choir begins to practise a prosocial behaviour and to interact with church members. How can schools engage children in prosocial behaviours and so set them on the *positive path*?

**Induction**
Disciplining where the effects of bad behaviour on others are communicated to the child.

• • • • • • • • • • • • • • • •
**Connect and Extend**
Teachers interact more with disruptive and the underachieving pupils: Reay, D. (2006). 'I'm not seen as one of the clever children': Consulting primary school pupils about the social conditions of learning. *Educational Review, 58,* 171–181.
• • • • • • • • • • • • • • • •

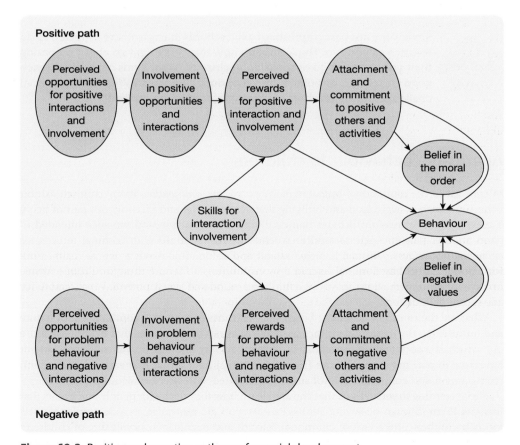

**Figure 12.2** Positive and negative pathways for social development

*Source:* Catalano, R. F. & Hawkins, J. D. (1996). The social development model: A theory of antisocial behavior. In J. D. Hawkins (Ed.), *Delinquency and crime: Current theories* (pp 149–197). New York: Cambridge University Press.

# Promoting prosocial behaviour in schools

In UK schools the development of prosocial behaviour is more usually seen as being part of citizenship skills. Until recently attention to citizenship in the curriculum was uneven, and systematic planning to ensure pupils are adequately prepared for their social, political, economic and cultural place in modern society was not common. This situation is changing rapidly. Since 1998 when the first commissioned study into citizenship began (Kerr, 1999), there have been rapid advances in policy and practice of citizenship education. From 2000, primary and secondary schools in England had to teach citizenship as part of the statutory National Curriculum – supported by subsequent governmental guidance on how to encourage young people to become involved in decision-making processes (DfES, 2004). Schools in England are expected to prepare their young people to take an active role in society and become 'good citizens'. Children are also expected to learn about citizenship by experiencing it in action, by the ways in which they are taught and the ways in which their school lives are organised. *Education for Democratic Citizenship* became a goal of education policies in Europe (Bîrzéa *et al.*, 2004) and a study (EURYDICE, 2005) found components of citizenship learning in the legislation of the majority of European countries. The year of 2005 was designated as the European *Year of Citizenship through Education* and the European Commission developed a programme entitled *Citizens for Europe* to run from 2007 to 2013. What, then, is citizenship education for young people? The term, originally proposed by Crick *et al.* (1999), has been interpreted in broad terms that range from including children in the decision-making of the school, to debating issues and making a contribution to the local community through activities such as volunteering.

**Reflect**  Review the last paragraph about what schools in England are expected to do to teach citizenship. Think through how teachers might go about preparing their young people to become 'good citizens'. What kinds of activities teach good citizenship, or political and economic awareness? What are the special challenges facing teachers of young children in this context?

# Aggressive behaviour in children

In contrast to the aspirational outcome *making a positive contribution*, many children exhibit behaviours such as aggression and bullying that are antisocial and certainly not part of being a good citizen. Aggression includes name-calling and acts of physical violence intended to harm another person. Aggressive children tend to become adults with criminal records for antisocial behaviours: criminal damage, assault and so on. This is not a new thought. Work with boys in inner-city London described by criminologist David Farrington (1995) identified troublesome behaviour in young childhood as one of seven potential risk factors for adolescent delinquency.

What are the causes of antisocial behaviour? The answer is again a combination of nature and nurture. On the nature side is increased testosterone (the hormone that males have more of), which is associated with increases in physical activity and aggressiveness. Temperament has a role to play too. Many studies (e.g. Martel, 2012) have found that early problems with temperament and emotional control strongly correlated with later behaviour problems.

Social learning theory tells us that children learn how they deal with people and events that frustrate them through observing adults. Parents who are aggressive serve as similar models for their children, and a lack of emotional warmth and insufficient monitoring of children's activities – ineffective discipline – increases the likelihood of children behaving aggressively at home and in school. Smacking or verbally abusing children as a punishment is not a long-term solution – and serves only as an instant expression of parental frustration and anger.

Children who experience parental violence are likely to repeat the behaviour away from their parents' view and likely to replicate this behaviour as parents. The now famous Bobo doll experiment in social learning conducted by psychologist Albert Bandura and colleagues (1963), where children viewed violent behaviour towards a clown doll on a video and then replicated this behaviour while playing with the doll shortly afterwards, is an excellent example of such imitation. Children who use aggression to get their own way will continue to do so again and again, and such behaviours are reinforced by scenes of violence, damage, and mayhem on the media (Erwin & Morton, 2013; Fedorov, 2005; Villani, 2001). As children spend more time in front of televisions and games consoles, the greater the influence these have on children, particularly in middle childhood when children are specially able to 'absorb' violent and antisocial behaviour and often view it as acceptable. The relationship between television and aggressive behaviours has been well documented for some time (e.g. Anderson *et al.*, 2003; Huesmann *et al.*, 2003).

There are two forms of aggression: instrumental aggression is used to achieve an end, for example, gaining possession of a toy that someone else has hold of, and hostile aggression is intended to hurt a person or group deliberately, for example, through name-calling and inflicting physical pain. Aggression can be reactive when children and adults act in self-defence to an attack; or it can be proactive, where force is used to dominate another, such as in bullying. There are developmental trends to it. By age 2, we can see instrumental aggression towards objects. There is also kicking out at another person, for example, as part of a refusal to share toys. This type of early aggression is instrumental in the sense that its intention is to stop another from getting what they want and is not intended to hurt. By age 4, there is a much greater verbal aggression with taunting and name-calling. Around this age boys are more physical in their aggressive displays, while girls tend to gossip and exclude others from their play – a culture-transferable phenomenon (Innes, 2006).

Between the ages of 6 and 11 energies are channelled into sport and physical activities and children are by now more able to resolve their disputes by sharing with others. Physical aggression declines but is often replaced by verbal abuse. In schools, children learn the rules of acceptability of displaying aggression. The difference between a preschool child and a school-age child is that the preschooler will display hostile aggression to get back the ball from another child; the schoolchild directs aggression to someone he or she does not like (McEachern & Snyder, 2012).

Fortunately not all of what appears to be aggressive behaviour in school (and, in particular, in school playgrounds) is what it appears to be. In fact, as we previously discussed, most fights are play, and few turn into real fight situations. What was interesting is that many teachers generalise from a small number of aggressive pupils (Romi *et al.*, 2011). They worried that what they saw might turn into real fights. Children, on the other hand, knew the behaviour was not typical of everyone and that only a small minority of children demonstrated real hostile aggressive behaviours. As we said before, playground play-fights and rough-and-tumble play is seen as having a positive side; it is an important way that some children form and learn about relationships. Vivien Paley (2004) in a study on superhero play in the kindergarten reported that she came to realise from her observations that what she saw was not aggressive behaviour, rather they were conflict resolutions over issues mostly about space. But aggressive behaviour should not be ignored because it is a typical trait of the school bully and, yes, it is time to address a form of social behaviour that dominates the school life of far too many of our children and – if we take the views of many social commentators seriously – the offices and workplaces of the adult world. Acts of physical hostility, taunting and teasing are for some children in schools almost a part of the daily school ritual and influence how and with whom they form relationships. The ethos of any school is negatively affected by *bullying*, with both bullies and victims perceiving the schools to be a non-safe place to be (Nansel *et al.*, 2003). So what is bullying?

Bullying is a form of antisocial behaviour that emerges in the behaviours of some school-age children. It is the predominant form of peer-group aggression in school years. Particular

**Instrumental aggression**
Aggression used to achieve an end, for example, taking possession of a toy from someone else.

**Hostile aggression**
Aggressive behaviour intended to hurt a person or group deliberately, for example, through name-calling.

**Reactive aggression**
Aggression in response to an attack.

**Proactive aggression**
The use of force to dominate another.

children are targeted to become victims of physical and/or verbal assaults. Bullying is use of force on another person and in most cases the force is never countered or challenged. This idea is reinforced by a an often quoted definition from Barry Schneider, Professor of Psychology, that bullying is 'aggression directed repeatedly and specifically towards a specific victim who, in most cases, is weaker than the bully' (2000, p 106). Bullying is also psychological when a child is deliberately excluded from a peer group, or threatening when demands are made for money or other possessions.

Bullies are usually unpopular children, and it is generally agreed that they have a deficiency in some aspect(s) of normal social development. This is not to suggest that these children are coarse and unintelligent. Bullies soon realise that using physical and/or verbal threats on others can be an easy means of getting their own way. Bullies are skilled at manipulating the emotions of others and possess a well-developed theory of mind in being able to cajole others to carry out the bullying upon others and avoid detection themselves (Wei & Chen, 2012). As to the victims, consequences can be far-reaching. Lack of confidence and self-worth, guilt, further alienation from peers, anxiety attacks and truancy and relationships problems in later life are common. Again, genetics and factors in a child's environment account for 'victimness'. Victims of bullying are singled out because they are easy targets: usually physically inferior, often rejected by peers and not disposed or likely to defend themselves against the bully's attacks (Davies, 2011).

Advances in technology may have led to increased opportunities for communication but they have also led to another and modern form of bullying known as – as we mentioned before – cyber bullying. One form of this, 'happy slapping', is a craze where young people use cameras on their mobile phones to video physical attacks on their victims – including teachers (Chan *et al.*, 2012). The extent of this new phenomenon, usually involving older children, has led to a number of incidents of younger children being assaulted in school playgrounds, or on their way to or from school. Mobile phone-related bullying can take other forms as well, including threats by instant messaging, anonymous text messages and even web links to Internet sites advertising personalised abuse. Playground taunts are one thing – a reprehensible phenomenon and one to be challenged and expunged – but when the insult is sent far and wide, the level of humiliation for the victim is inestimable (Griezel *et al.*, 2012).

## Controversy

### Can bullying be stopped by punishing those responsible or are there better solutions?

The complexities of bullying in schools mean that occurrences of teasing and name-calling, even some forms of physical abuse like pushing and punching, are often reported as isolated incidents, and this can mask the scale of systematic bullying. Subsequent punishments of those incidents often fail and this leads to an escalation of the occurrence, and even greater levels of fear and humiliation for the victim. Revenge attacks and making the victim known to a much wider community are not uncommon. Victims are not capable of stopping the abuse so it is to other methods that we must look for solutions to this escalating problem.

In response to media publicity, schools in England are now compelled to have a policy in place that identifies how they keep their pupils safe and the strategies they use. Let's be clear. It is the responsibility of teachers and other care professionals to stop bullying and not to claim that they are powerless or that this is some kind of socially normal behaviour. Anti-Bullying Week – UK (**http://antibullyingweek2012.org/**) takes place in November each year, raises the awareness of the problem and sends a very clear national message that bullying is unacceptable. There are guides for parents to ask questions and receive answers to frequently asked questions about bullying and violence. Small-scale school projects managed by pupils themselves are another effective strategy for regional awareness. One example is Bully Free Zone (Onderdonk, 2007), a peer-support programme operating in schools in the North East of England. Bully Free Zone offers training and support for children, parents and teachers in primary and secondary schools. To counter cyber bullying, various software packages have been developed that identify key words associated with abuse and can block messages on school servers. Other schools have set up confidential telephone numbers so that bullying can be reported by text message. It is again worth bringing to mind that one of the five outcomes for children as part of the Every Child Matters agenda is to 'stay safe', which itself has five aims:

- Safe from maltreatment, neglect, violence and sexual exploitation.
- Safe from accidental injury and death.
- Safe from bullying and discrimination.
- Safe from crime and antisocial behaviour in and out of school.
- Have security, stability and are cared for.

To ensure safety for children from bullying, discrimination and antisocial behaviour, schools and local authorities have adopted a range of policies and practices. For example, anti-bullying practices include counselling, mentoring schemes with older children, circle-time sessions for younger children, mediation and peer support. Talking to an adult, walking away and talking to the bully are further strategies that have received much support from children. Intervention strategies such as teaching children to respect other's rights, establishing clear rules about acceptable behaviour in class, explicitly teaching negotiating skills, providing praise to reward positive behaviour from children, adults setting good examples by being good role models and enlisting parental help to change bullies and victims' behaviour are all ways to solve this problem. A number of intervention programmes exist (e.g. Ttofi & Farrington, 2012), many of which incorporate strategies as those outlined and have all shown a reduction in bullying through them. Punishing the bully is not a long-term solution; positive action is.

However, there is an argument that we are all over-reacting. It could be said that it is human nature for some individuals to be more extrovert than others, and that bullying is showing a form – some might argue, a distorted form – of leadership. We need leaders to show the weaker ones what to do and to keep them out of trouble. How are we going to recognise individuals with stronger personalities if they are not allowed to show any signs of leadership? By identifying some people as 'victims' we establish them as victims, label them as victims and make them feel like victims. It could also be argued that some teachers physically and psychologically bully pupils and that these are the successful classroom disciplinarians (Demanet & Van Houtte, 2012). Military discipline is based upon bullying (although service chiefs would deny this). Isn't it precisely because bullying in some form or another is so widespread in schools, social groups and businesses that it should be considered a social norm to be checked in its more extreme forms? Of course, some individuals can take this too far – bullying in the extreme is always frightening – but we shouldn't over-react.

What do you think? Is it the responsibility of teachers and other care professionals to stop bullying and not to claim that this is some kind of socially normal behaviour?

**Summary 3**

We now summarise what you have learned in the final section of this chapter:

- Moral (understanding of right and wrong) and social development are closely connected.
- There is universal consistency in the belief that standards of behaviour should be communicated to children so that they will learn and practise these as they get older.
- Psychodynamic theory (Freud) emphasises internalising standards of moral behaviour by combining the influence of parents and biological factors through an inbuilt natural drive to act in certain ways.
- Social learning theory (Bandura) emphasises moral behaviours built on personal explanations of moral conduct from parents and other authority figures.
- The cognitive-developmental perspective (Piaget) stresses the importance of moral reasoning, a capacity to consider another's feelings and perspectives.
- Lawrence Kohlberg constructed six stages that span three levels of moral reasoning which, he argued, are common to all but are not presented as age-specific.
- Prosocial behaviour has two elements: empathy and altruism.
- Empathy is a willingness to tune into the feelings of others – a sensitivity to other people's feelings. Altruism is defined as acting with a selfless concern for others.
- In our schools prosocial behaviour is more usually termed 'citizenship skills'.
- Schools in England are expected to prepare their young people to become 'good citizens' by how they are taught and the ways in which their school lives are organised.
- Aggressive children tend to become adults with criminal records for antisocial behaviours: criminal damage, assault and so on.
- Parents who are aggressive serve as similar models for their children, and ineffective discipline increases the likelihood of children being aggressive at home and in school.
- Bullying is a form of antisocial behaviour that is the predominant form of peer-group aggression in school years.
- Anti-bullying practices include counselling, mentoring schemes with older pupils, circle-time sessions for younger children, mediation and peer support.

## Conclusion

Remember the story of Lin Yan at the start of this chapter, who wanted to make friends with other children in her new class, and they too were keen to get to know her and be her friend. Lin Yan was an example of one person's desire to be with other people – we are curious about others and seek the interest and security of being part of a family, a group, and a wider society – it is part of what makes us human. Being successful at being part of a family or a group takes practice and we have to learn prosocial behaviours which are the key to popularity and acceptance.

Even before they are born, children are part of a social system. Their brains are 'hardwired' to want to be with others and this is established through early bonding with the mother/carer in a relationship that is much more than feeding and protection. Important social signals are given off that a child readily responds to and builds upon – imitating facial expressions, hand gestures and cooing and giggling are all part of the desire to communicate with others. By school age, the child builds up more abstract models of the adult–child relationship based on trust and approval. Play is an important means for children to explore their surrounding world through first-hand experiences and provides a platform to rehearse future roles, act out personal agendas and experiment with new physical, social, emotional and intellectual skills.

Social cognition is the term referring to thinking about personal feelings and those of other people. The first of these includes an understanding of 'self': the *I self* and the *me self* and of self-esteem, concerned with comparing ourselves with others in an evaluative way. We learn to comprehend others by understanding their desires, beliefs and intentions through developing a theory of mind – the term describing how our mental states explain our behaviour. Being able to understand oneself and others is also related to social identity which embraces ethnicity and gender.

Identified and discussed in the chapter were three main influences upon children's socialisation – chiefly the family. Authoritative parenting in which there was fairness and clear boundaries results in children developing high self-esteem and social competence. Friendship among peers is central to children's social development and competence. In early childhood less time is spent in the company of peers, yet by the time they begin school the percentage of time is sharply increased. A third agent of socialisation is the school. Although the priority is the development of cognitive skills, there is no doubt that having a supportive school ethos is increasingly important. Peer tutoring and collaborative learning are examples of strategies with a high degree of social involvement that have been proven to be effective for learning.

Although the rules and standards of behaviour deemed acceptable vary according to culture, there is consistency in the belief that standards of behaviour must be communicated to children. Prosocial behaviours begin early, largely influenced by the socialisation experiences provided by parents and carers. Children who show good prosocial behaviours tend to be the most popular children, display better social skills and are more self-assured. Social difficulties experienced in childhood predict similar difficulties in adulthood, and bullying as a form of antisocial behaviour which, though emerging in the behaviours of some school-age children, often continues into adolescence and beyond. Evidence suggests that interventions such as counselling and mentoring schemes, pupil mediation and peer support are more effective in preventing bullying than punishing offenders.

Will Lin Yan grow up to be a bully? I don't think so. Even on our momentary acquaintance through the story at the beginning of the chapter, she seems to have all that it takes to develop successful prosocial behaviours, display impressive social skills and be self-assured even when meeting new people. Supportive and attentive parents have placed her carefully in a school with a caring ethos that places high value on children's social and emotional development and she can dance beautifully, which is one of the most important socialising activities and social mood changers. Will Lin Yan grow up to be a bully? She doesn't seem the type.

This is not only the conclusion of Chapter 12 but also of our book. In the Preface we commended you to the study of children, childhood and child development and we trust you have taken every opportunity to follow the *Connect and Extend* features.

In the last 7 months we have all come a long way. *Child Development: Theory and Practice 0–11* has brought us from the very beginning of Niamh's life when she was just a few hours old, to the marvellous picture opposite taken by her swimming teacher, Helen Whittle. Gaze a few moments at the miracle of what Niamh has already become and consider the complexity and completeness of her physical, perceptual, cognitive, emotional and social development to date, and marvel at what is to come for her. She is well on her way to being confident, capable and

Here's Niamh putting it all together, and at just 7 months, look what she can do!
*Source*: Edward and Ella Hogan.

self-sufficient, in what is just the beginning of her journey through life. During our journey in writing this book she has been a source of wonder and an inspiration.

What is equally wondrous is the potential there is for you, the reader, not to think 'job done' – no – take every opportunity to further enhance and enrich your understanding of the theory and practice of child development so that, no matter what role or roles you fulfil later, *Child Development* has been a good beginning for you to becoming an expert in children and childhood. There is no finer aspiration.

# Summary Table
## The Social and Moral World of the Child

## Human sociability and the need for nexus
(pp 366–377)

### The early social world of the child – first relationships (pp 366–368)

Fairly soon after birth infants can socially orient themselves to social situations and to other people. Young children smile and look towards others around them and use smiling as an important social signal. Adults and siblings respond to babies' smiles, babbling and cooing with motherese and by returning smiles. Interaction between child and adult includes joint-action formats or synchronised routines – simplified action sequences created by the mother, such as sharing a book, feeding and dressing routines.

### Children's play and social experiences (pp 368–372)

Lev Vygotsky viewed play as important in building up mental structures. Albert Bandura saw play as a rehearsal of, and preparation for skills in later life. Jean Piaget allied play to the development of cognition and identified five types of play:

1. Functional play – banging a brick.
2. Physical activity play – arm waving and rough-and-tumble.
3. Constructive play – using three-dimensional shapes and apparatus.
4. Symbolic play – pretend play by imitating.
5. Formal play – games with rules.

Mildred Parten identified a hierarchy of six categories of social participation play – playing (or not) with others:

1. Unoccupied behaviour – perhaps sitting and thinking.
2. Onlooker behaviour – where the child attends to what other children are doing.
3. Solitary play – takes place alone and is different from that of others.

4. Parallel play – where children play alongside but not with another child.
5. Associative play – children may share materials or resources.
6. Co-operative play – includes playing games or model-making together.

### Self and self-concept (pp 373–374)

Social cognition includes two key aspects: knowing yourself and knowing others. Knowledge of 'self' has two components: *I self* – that I am separate from others around me and in control of my own actions and thoughts – and the *me self* – recognising the individual traits and characteristics that make us special.

### Self-esteem (pp 374–375)

Our self-esteem is *how* we are in comparison with others, how we evaluate ourselves in comparison to others, and learned helplessness is a belief that one can do little well or effectively. Helpless children believe that success is due to ability, that their own ability is low and fixed for them.

### Understanding others (pp 375–377)

We develop a theory of mind which allows us to predict what others are going to do. The false-belief task is a test that infants have formed a theory of mind.

## Social identity and influence (pp 377–392)

Two strands of social identity currently exist: ethnic identity and gender identity. H. Rudolph Schaffer argues that ethnic identity has four components:

1. Salience – the extent to which ethnicity is important in one's self-concept.
2. Ideology – how the people in that ethnic group are regarded.
3. Centrality – how individuals define themselves.

4. Regard – positive and/or negative feelings in relation to ethnicity.

Gender identity refers to an individual's perception of their own gender. Behavioural differences can be apparent as early as the first two years. Girls walk, talk and generally reach developmental milestones earlier than boys and do better at school. Furthermore, language regions are more active in girls, giving them advantages in communication over boys. Girls use more parts of the brain, which accounts for their being better at multitasking.

### Theories of social identity (pp 377–380)

There are two sets of acquired gender identities to consider: cognitive learning theories and social learning theories. Cognitive-developmental theories argue that gender identity comes first and is followed by construction of schema – the basis for behaviour in gender typical ways, for example, boys play gun fights and girls play with dolls. Social learning theories is knowledge of gender acquired through increased opportunities for observing others and imitating them. With preschool children the tendency to play with peers of the same sex is striking. Boys dominate classroom interactions and are the cause of most classroom disturbances. Girls are the cause of fewer discipline problems and are much less likely to drop out of school early.

### The social influence of the family (pp 380–384)

The family is the prime instrument for socialisation in childhood, and parents' influence on the socialisation of their children will reflect their own attitudes and values, social class, education and religious belief. Beginning with parents and moving outward through Urie Bronfenbrenner's concentric circles – or social systems – is a good way of describing children's social development. Children's social skills and self-esteem comes from parenting style, with the authoritative style coming out on top.

### The social influence of peers (pp 385–388)

Peer friendships are powerful influences on children's conformity and tend to provide opportunities to acquire and refine social skills with more give-and-take. Newcomb and Bagwell (1995) have identified four features of friendship:

1. Reciprocity – someone to spend time with and share your toys or an activity.
2. Intense social activity – children of school age look for specific qualities in a friend.
3. Conflict resolution – friends help each other to work out problems between them.
4. Effective task performance – friends plan joint actions, co-operate and collaborate to present a joint outcome.

Rubin and Coplan have identified five categories of peer acceptance:

1. Popular children are those most liked and who hold high status.
2. Controversial children can either be liked or disliked depending on the circumstances.
3. Rejected children are least liked and include sub-groups of aggressive rejected and non-aggressive rejected.
4. Neglected children score low on being the most liked but tend to score low on being liked least too.
5. Average children – not accepted as popular children nor disliked as much as rejected children.

### The social influence of schools and the media (pp 388–392)

Schools are important influences in extending children's social networks and forming how children communicate, how they behave and how they make progress. Co-operative learning strategies such as *peer collaboration* and *peer tutoring* have a positive impact on self-esteem, attitudes towards peers and to school generally. Children's literature, television, video games and the Internet can affect children's social and moral development but not always positively.

## Moral development: right or wrong? (pp 392–404)

Moral (understanding of right and wrong) and social development are closely connected since the relationships we have with other people influence how we act, and how we act is very often determined by social contexts. There is universal consistency in the belief that standards of behaviour should be communicated to children so that they will learn and practise these as they get older.

### Theories of moral development (pp 393–397)

Psychodynamic theory (Freud) emphasises internalising standards of moral behaviour by combining the influence of parents and biological factors though an inbuilt natural drive to act in certain ways. Social learning theory (Bandura) emphasises moral behaviours developed through cognitive representations of what children observe and process, and built on personal explanations of moral conduct from parents and other authority figures. The cognitive-developmental perspective (Piaget) stresses the importance of moral reasoning, requiring considerable reasoning and a capacity to consider another's feelings and perspectives.

It is in two stages:

1. *Heteronomous* – a pre-moral stage from birth to the end of the preschool years. There is little understanding of rules – consequences and morals are deemed the property of *heteronomous* (others) in authority.

2. *Autonomous morality* – rules can be altered and are arbitrary; actions are judged by intentions rather than consequences. Adherence to authority figures is now seen to be no longer necessary.

Lawrence Kohlberg constructed six stages that span three levels of moral reasoning which, he argued, are common to all but are not presented as age-specific:

1. Makes moral decisions purely on the basis of self-interest.
2. Recognises that others have needs, but prioritises her own needs.
3. Makes decision on the basis of what will please others.
4. Looks to society as a whole for guidelines about moral decisions – laws and rules.
5. Recognises that rules are social constructions – that can be changed or ignored.
6. Answers only to her inner conscience – a small number of universal abstract principles.

## Pro- and antisocial behaviours (pp 397–400)

Prosocial behaviour is defined as 'intentional, voluntary behaviour intended to benefit another' (Eisenberg, 1992, p 3) and has two elements: empathy and altruism. Empathy is a willingness to tune into the feelings of others – a sensitivity to other people's feelings. Altruism is defined as acting with a selfless concern for others.

## Promoting prosocial behaviour in schools (p 400)

In UK schools prosocial behaviour is more usually termed 'citizenship skills'. Schools in England are expected to prepare their young people to take an active role in society and become 'good citizens' by experiencing it in action, by the ways in which they are taught and the ways in which their school lives are organised.

## Aggressive behaviour in children (pp 400–403)

Aggressive children tend to become adults with criminal records for antisocial behaviours: criminal damage, assault and so on. This is not a new thought. Parents who are aggressive serve as similar models for their children, and a lack of emotional warmth and insufficient monitoring of children's activities – ineffective discipline – increases the likelihood of children behaving aggressively at home and in school. *Instrumental aggression* is used to achieve an end, for example, gaining possession of a toy, and *hostile aggression* is intended to hurt a person or group deliberately. Bullying is a form of antisocial behaviour that is the predominant form of peer-group aggression in school years. Anti-bullying practices include counselling, mentoring schemes with older pupils, circle-time sessions for younger children, mediation and peer support. Punishing the bully is not a long-term solution; positive action is.

# Going further

Arnett, J. and Hughes, M. (2012) Adolescence and emerging adulthood: A cultural approach. Longman. Where next for your study and scholarship? What happens after childhood? This book takes up where *Child Development 0–11* finishes and is co-written by Mal Hughes, one of the authors of this text. It covers the period from 12 to 25 years and offers a cultural and cross-cultural dimension on the study of developmental psychology. Harlow: Pearson Education.

Rose, C. (2011) *Self awareness and personal development: Resources for psychotherapists and counsellors.* Basingstoke: Palgrave Macmillan. Resources and support for qualified therapists and trainees as well as for other professionals who are engaged in the process of becoming more self-aware as part of their professional development.

Benson, J., Benson, J. B. & Haith, M. M. (2009*) Social and emotional development in infancy and early childhood.* Oxford: Academic Press. Provides a resource for researchers and clinicians interested in social psychology and personality covering such areas as adoption, attachment, birth order, effects of day care, discipline and compliance, divorce, emotion regulation, family influences, preschool, routines, separation anxiety, shyness, socialisation, and the effects of television.

O'Moore, M. (2010) *Understanding school bullying: A guide for parents and teachers.* Dublin: Veritas Publications. This book explains the serious consequences of bullying for the victims, the bullies and society. The author places a strong emphasis on prevention and intervention at primary, secondary and tertiary level. Practical steps are provided, especially for parents and teachers, as to how they can make a real difference in reducing the widespread and serious level of victimisation and bullying in our schools today.

Santer, J., Griffiths, C. & Goodall, D. (2007). *Free play in early childhood.* London: National Children's Bureau.
A comprehensive review of the developmental, social and emotional implications of children's play from birth to age 7.

## Useful websites

https://ssl.bbc.co.uk/labuk/experiments/personality/
You can take part in the 'Big Personality test'.

http://www.statistics.gov.uk/hub/people-places/people/identity/index.html
For the most up-to-date UK national statistics on ethnic and gender identity – plus a good deal more.

http://www.education.gov.uk/schools/teachingandlearning/curriculum/a00199700/spiritual-and-moral
Explicit opportunities to promote pupils' moral and social development are provided in religious education and the UK non-statutory framework for personal, social and health education (PSHE) and citizenship. A significant contribution is also made by school ethos, effective relationships throughout the school, collective worship and other curriculum activities.

www.bullying.co.uk
Online bullying website providing advice, information and support.

# References

AAP (American Academy of Pediatrics) Committee on Nutrition (2003). Prevention of pediatric, overweight and obesity. *Pediatrics*, *112*, 424–430.

Abdel-Khalek, A. M. & Lynn, R. (2008). Intelligence, family size and birth order: Some data from Kuwait. *Personality & Individual Differences*, *44*, 1032–1038.

Adey, P. & Shayer, M. (1994). *Really raising standards: Cognitive intervention and academic achievement*. London: Routledge.

Adey, P., Robertson, A. & Venville, G. (2002). Effects of a cognitive acceleration programme on Year 1 pupils. *British Journal of Educational Psychology*, *72*, 1–25.

Adey, P. S., Shayer, M. & Yates, C. (1995). *Thinking science: The curriculum materials of the CASE Project*. London: Thomas Nelson and Sons.

Adgent, M. A. (2006). Environmental tobacco smoke and sudden infant death syndrome: a review. *Birth Defects Research Part B: Developmental and Reproductive Toxicology*, February, *77*(1), 69–85.

Adolph, K., Vereijken, B. & Shrout, P. E. (2003). What changes in infant walking and why. *Child Development*, *74*(2), 475–497.

Ainsworth, H. F., Unwin, J., Jamison, D. L. & Cordell, H. J. (2011). Investigation of maternal effects, maternal-fetal interactions and parent-of origin-effects (imprinting), using mothers and their offspring. *Genetic Epidemiology*, *35*(1), 19–45.

Ainsworth, M. D. S., Blehar, M., Waters, E. & Wall, S. (1978). *Patterns of attachment: A psychological study of the Strange Situation*. Hillsdale, NJ: Erlbaum.

Akca, F. (2011). The relationship between test anxiety and learned helplessness. *Social Behavior and Personality*, *39*(1), 101–111.

Akobeng, A. K., Ramanan, A. V., Buchan, I. & Heller, R. F. (2006). Effect of breast feeding on risk of coeliac disease: a systematic review and meta-analysis of observational studies. *Archives of Disease in Childhood*, *91*, 39–43.

Alexander, C. (2006). Introduction: Mapping the issues. *Ethnic and Racial Studies*, May, *29*(3), 397–410.

Alexander, R., Rose, J. & Woodhead, C. (1992). *Curriculum organisation and classroom practice in primary schools: A discussion paper*. London: DES.

Alibali, M. W. (1999). How children change their minds: Strategy change can be gradual or abrupt. *Developmental Psychology*, *35*, 127–145.

Allen, G. (2011a). *Early intervention: smart investment, massive savings*. London: The Cabinet Office.

Allen, G. (2011b). *Early intervention: the next steps*. London: The Cabinet Office.

Alm, B., Wennergren, G., Norvenius, G., Skjærven, R., Øyen, N., Irgens, L. M., Helweg-Larsen, K. & Lagercrantz, H. (1999). Caffeine and alcohol as risk factors for sudden infant death syndrome. *Archives of Disease in Childhood*, *81*, 107–111.

Als, H., Duffy, F. H., McAnulty, G. B., Rivkin, M. J., Vajapeyam, S. & Mulkern, R. V. (2004). Early experience alters brain function and structure. *Pediatrics*, *113*, 846–858.

Altwicker-Hámori, S. & Köllő, J. (2012). Whose children gain from starting school later? – evidence from Hungary. *Educational Research and Evaluation*, July, *18*(5), 459–488.

Amsterdam, B. (1972). Mirror self-image reactions before age two. *Developmental Psychology*, *5*, 297–305.

Anastasi, A. (2007). *Differential psychology – Individual and group differences in behaviour*. Anastasi Press.

Anastasiades, P. S., Vitalaki, E. & Gertzakis, N. (2008). Collaborative learning activities at a distance via interactive videoconferencing in elementary schools: Parents' attitudes. *Computers & Education*, *50*, 1527–1539.

Anderson, C. A., Berkowitz, L., Donnerstein, E., Huesmann, L. R., Johnson, J., Linz, D., Malamuth, N. & Wartella, E. (2003). The influence of media violence on youth. *Psychological Science in the Public Interest*, *4*(3), 81–110.

Anderson, J. R. (1996). *ACT: A simple theory of complex cognition*. Cambridge, MA: Harvard University Press.

Anderson, J. R. & Schunn, C. D. (2000). Implications of the ACT-R Learning Theory: No magic bullets. In R. Glaser (Ed.), *Advances in instructional psychology* (Vol. 5). Mahwah, NJ: Erlbaum.

Anderson, P. (2002). Assessment and development of executive function (EF) during childhood. *Child Neuropsychology*, *8*, 71–82.

Andersson, B. (1992). Effects of day-care on cognitive and socioemotional competence of thirteen-year-old Swedish schoolchildren. *Child Development*, *63*, 20–36.

Andres, A., Cleves, M. A., Bellando, J. B., Pivik, R. T., Casey, P. H. & Badger, T. M. (2012). Developmental status of 1-year-old infants fed breast milk, cow's milk formula, or soy formula. *Pediatric*, June, *129*(6), 1134–1140.

Andresen, H. (2005). Role play and language development in the preschool years. *Culture & Psychology*, *11*, 387–414.

Anisfeld, M. (1991). Neonatal imitation. *Developmental Review*, 11, 60–97.

Annesi, J. J. (2007). Relations of age with changes in self-efficacy and physical self-concept in pre-adolescents participating in a physical activity intervention during afterschool care. *Perceptual & Motor Skills*, 105, 221–226.

Antshel, K. M., Faraone, S. V., Stallone, K., Nave, A., Kaufmann, F. A., Doyle, A., Fried, R., Seidman, L. & Biederman, J. (2007). Is attention deficit hyperactivity disorder a valid diagnosis in the presence of high IQ? Results from the MGH Longitudinal Family Studies of ADHD. *Journal of Child Psychology & Psychiatry*, 48, 687–694.

Apgar, V. (1953). A proposal for a new method of evaluation in the newborn infant. *Current Research in Anaesthesia and Analgesia*, 32, 260–277.

Areepattamannil, S. (2012). First- and second-generation immigrant adolescent's multidimensional mathematics and science self-concepts and their achievement in mathematics and science. *International Journal of Science & Mathematics Education*. June, 10(3), 695–716.

Argyle, M. (1988). *Bodily communication*. London: Methuen.

Argyle, M. (1994). *The psychology of interpersonal behaviour* (5th ed.). London: Penguin.

Aries, P. (1962). *Centuries of childhood*. New York: Vintage Books.

Armbruster, B. B., Lehr, F. & Osborn, J. (2001). *Put reading first: The research building blocks for teaching children to read*. Washington, DC: National Institute of Child Health and Human Development and US Department of Education. Available online at www.nifl.gov/nifl/publications.html

Arnett, J. J. & Hughes, M. W. H. (2012). *Adolescence and emerging adulthood. A cultural approach*. Harlow: Pearson Education.

Arora, C. M. J. (2006). Elective home education and special educational needs. *Journal of Research in Special Educational Needs*, 6, 55–66.

Arterberry, M. E. & Bornstein, M. (2001). Three-month-old infants' categorization of animals and vehicles based on static and dynamic attributes. *Journal of Experimental Child Psychology*, 80, 333–346.

Askeland, M. (2012). Sound-based strategy training in multiplication *European Journal of Special Needs Education*, May, 27(2), 201–217.

Askew, M., Brown, M., Rhodes, V., Wiliam, D. & Johnson, D. (1997). *Effective teachers of numeracy in primary schools: Teachers' beliefs, practices and pupils' learning*. Paper presented at the British Educational Research Association (BERA) Conference, University of York.

ASRM (2003). The American Society for Reproductive Medicine Age and Fertility: A Guide for Patients ASRM, Birmingham, AL, 2003. March of Dimes. Archived from the original on 30 January 2009. Retrieved 2/5/09.

Athey, C. (1990). *Extending thought in young children. A parent–teacher partnership*. London: Paul Chapman Publishing.

Augimeri, L., Farrington, D., Koegl, C. & Day, D. (2007). The SNAP™ Under 12 Outreach Project: Effects of a community based program for children with conduct problems. *Journal of Child & Family Studies*, 16, 799–807.

Aukrust, V. G. (2001). Agency and appropriation of voice – Cultural differences in parental ideas about young children's talk. *Human Development*, 44, 235–249.

Aukrust, V. G. (2008). Boys' and girls' conversational participation across four grade levels in Norwegian classrooms: Taking the floor or being given the floor? *Gender & Education*, 20, 237–252.

Aunola, K., Stattin, H. & Nurmi, J.-E. (2001). Parenting styles and adolescents' achievement strategies. *Journal of Adolescence*, 23, 205–222.

Autti-Rämö, I., Autti, T., Korkman, M., Kettunen, S., Salonen, O. & Valanne, L. (2002). MRI findings in children with school problems who had been exposed prenatally to alcohol. *Developmental Medicine & Child Neurology*, 44, 98–106.

Avalos, L., Kaskutas, L., Block, G., Abrams, B. & Li, D-K. (2011). Does lack of multinutrient supplementation during early pregnancy increase vulnerability to alcohol-related preterm or small-for-gestational-age births? *Maternal and Child Health Journal*, 15(8), 1324–1332.

Ayres, A. J. (1972). *Southern California sensory-motor integration tests*. Los Angeles: Western Psychological Services.

Babad, E. (2002). On the conception and measurement of popularity: More facts and some straight conclusions. *Social Psychology of Education*, 5, 3–30.

Babinsky, E., Braddick, O. & Atkinson, J. (2012). Infants and adults reaching in the dark. *Experimental Brain Research*, 217(2), 237–249.

Bader, D., Kugelman, A., Boyko, V., Levitzki, O., Lerner-Geva, L., Riskin, A. & Reichman, B. (2010). Risk factors and estimation tool for death among extremely premature infants: A national study. *Pediatrics*. Apr, 125(4), 696–703.

Bagley, C., Bertrand, L., Bolitho, F. & Mallick, K. (2001). Discrepant parent–adolescent views on family functioning: Predictors of poorer self-esteem and problems of emotion and behaviour in British and Canadian adolescents. *Journal of Comparative Family Studies*, 32, 393–403.

Bailey, R. (2002). Playing social chess: Children's play and social intelligence. *Early Years*, 22, 163–173.

Bailey, R. & Dismore, H. (2005). Physical education and school sport: The international Sport in Education Project (SpinEd). *African Journal for Physical, Health Education, Recreation and Dance*, 11(1), 1–5.

Ballabio, D. & Vasighi, M. (2012). A MATLAB toolbox for self organizing maps and supervised neural network learning strategies. *Chemometrics and Intelligent Laboratory Systems*, August, 118(3), 24–32.

Balluz, L. S., Kiesak, S. M., Philen, R. M. & Mulinare, J. (2000). Vitamin and mineral supplement use in the United States: Results for the third national health and nutrition examination survey. *Archives of Family Medicine*, 9, 258.

Baltes, P. B., Reese, H. W. & Lipsitt, L. P. (1980). Life-span developmental psychology. In L. R. Goldberg, M. R. Rosenzweig & L. W. Porter (Series Eds), *Annual Review of Psychology*, Vol. 31 (pp 65–110). Palo Alto, CA: Annual Reviews.

Bandura, A. (1977). *Social learning theory*. Englewood Cliffs, NJ: Prentice-Hall.

Bandura, A. (1986). *Social foundations of thought and action. A social cognitive theory*. Englewood Cliffs, NJ: Prentice-Hall.

Bandura, A. (1989a). Human agency in social cognitive theory. *American Psychologist, 44*, 1175–1184.

Bandura, A. (1989b). Social cognitive theory. In R. Vasta (Ed.), *Annals of child development. Vol. 6. Theories of child development: Revised formulations and current issues* (pp 1–60). Greenwich, CT: JAI Press.

Bandura, A., Ross, D. & Ross, S. A. (1963). Imitation of film-mediated aggressive models. *Journal of Abnormal and Social Psychology, 66*, 3–11.

Bangerter, A. & Heath, C. (2004). The Mozart effect: Tracking the evolution of a scientific legend. *British Journal of Social Psychology, 43*, 605–623.

Barber, N. (2005). Educational and ecological correlates of IQ: A cross-national investigation. Intelligence. May, *33*(3), 273–284.

Barclay, L., Longman, J., Schmied, V., Sheehan, A., Rolfe, M., Burns, E. & Fenwick, J. (2012). The professionalising of breast feeding – Where are we a decade on? *Midwifery, 28*(3), 281–290.

Barker, B. A. & Newman, R. S. (2004). Listen to your mother! The role of talker familiarity in infant streaming. *Cognition, 94*, B45–B53.

Barker, D., Law, C., Egger, P., Dada, O., Delgado, H., Kylberg, E., Lavin, P., Tang, G.-H., von Hertzen, H. & Shiell, A. (2001). Body size at birth and blood pressure among children in developing countries. *International Journal of Epidemiology, 30*, 52–57.

Barker, D. J. P. (2012). Developmental origins of chronic disease. *Public Health*, March, *126*(3), 185–189.

Barnes, J. & Horsfall, P. (2010). It's your life: Developing a community of learners to combat social deprivation. *Education Review*. Summer, *22*(2), 17–26.

Barnett, D. & Vondra, J. I. (1999). Atypical attachment in infancy and early childhood among children at developmental risk. *Monographs of the Society for Research in Child Development, 64*, 1–24.

Barnett, D. W., Macmann, G. M. & Carey, K. (1992). Early intervention and the assessment of developmental skills: Challenges and directions. *Topics in Early Childhood Special Education, 12*, 21–43.

Barnett, R. & Hunter, M. (2012). Adjustment of siblings of children with mental health problems: Behaviour, self-concept, quality of life and family functioning. *Journal of Child and Family Studies, 21*(2), 262–272.

Baron-Cohen, S., Leslie, A. M. & Frith, U. (1985). Does the autistic child have a 'theory of mind'? *Cognition, 21*, 37–46.

Baron-Cohen, S. (1995). *Mindblindness: An essay on autism and theory of mind*. Cambridge, MA: MIT Press.

Barrett, M. D. (Ed.) (1999). *The development of language*. London: Psychology Press.

Barrs, M. & Cork, V. (2001). *The reader in the writer*. London: Centre for Language in Primary Education.

Bar-Shalom, E. (2002). Tense and aspect in early child Russian. *Language Acquisition, 10*, 321–337.

Basili, R., Della Rocca, M. & Pazienza, M. (1997). Contextual word sense tuning and disambiguation. *Applied Artificial Intelligence, 11*(3), 235–262.

Bates, E. A. (2004). Explaining and interpreting deficits in language development across clinical groups: Where do we go from here? *Brain and Language, 88*, 248–253.

Bates, T. C. (2007). Fluctuating asymmetry and intelligence. *Intelligence, 35*, 41–46.

Bauminger, N., Solomon, M. & Rogers, S. (2010). Predicting friendship quality in autism spectrum disorders and typical development. *Journal of Autism and Developmental Disorders, 40*(6), 751–761.

Baumrind, D. (1973). The development of instrumental competence through socialization. In A. Pick (Ed.), *Minnesota Symposium on Child Psychology* (Vol. 7, pp 3–46). Minneapolis: University of Minnesota Press.

Baumrind, D. (1993). The average expectable environment is not good enough: A response to Scarr. *Child Development, 64*, 1299–1317.

Baydar, N. & Brooks-Gunn, J. (1991). Effects of maternal employment and child-care arrangements on preschoolers' cognitive and behavioral outcomes: Evidence from the Children of the National Longitudinal Survey of Youth. *Developmental Psychology, 27*, 932–945.

Bayley, N. (1935). The development of motor abilities during the first three years. *Society for Research in Child Development, 1*(1), 1–26.

Bayley, N. (1969). *Bayley scales of infant development*. New York: HarperCollins.

Baylis, P. & Snowling, M. (2012). Evaluation of a phonological reading programme for children with Down syndrome. *Child Language Teaching and Therapy, 28*(1), 39–56.

Beaman, R., Wheldall, K. & Kemp, C. (2006). Differential teacher attention to boys and girls in the classroom. *Educational Review, 58*, 339–366.

Beaver, D. (2005). The continuing battle of the bulge! *Palaestra, 21*, 4–7.

Beaver, M., Brewster, J., Jones, P., Keene, A., Neaum, S. & Tallack, J. (1999). *Babies and Young Children. Book 1: Early Years Development*, 2nd ed. Cheltenham: Stanley Thornes.

Becker, R. & Wegner, R.-D. (2006). Detailed screening for fetal anomalies and cardiac defects at the 11–13-week scan. *Ultrasound in Obstetrics and Gynecology, 27*, 613–618.

Becta (2004). Getting the most from your interactive whiteboard: A guide for primary schools. Coventry: Becta.

Bee, H. L. (2000a). *The developing child*. London: Allyn & Bacon.

Bee, H. L. (2000b). *Child and adolescent development*, 9th ed. Boston, MA: Pearson Custom Publishing.

Beebe, B., Lachmann, F. M., Markese, S., Buck, K. A., Bahrick, L. E., Chen, H., Cohen, P., Andrews, H., Feldstein, S. & Jaffe, J. (2012). On the origins of disorganized attachment and internal working models: Paper II. An empirical microanalysis of 4-month mother–infant interaction. *Psychoanalytic Dialogues, 22*(3), 352–374.

Bell, R. (2008). Trends in birth weight in the North of England. *Human Fertility* 2008, *11*(1), 1–8.

Belsky, J., Weintraub, M., Owen, M. & Kelly, J. (2001). Quantity of child care and problem behaviour. In J. Belsky (Chair), *Early childcare and children's development prior to school entry*. April. Symposium, Biennial Meetings of the Society for Research in Child Development, Minneapolis.

Berger, K. S. (2001). *The developing person through the lifespan* (5th ed.). New York: Worth Publishers.

Berk, L. E. (2006). *Child development* (7th ed.). Boston, MA: Allyn & Bacon.

Berk, L. E. (2012). *Child development* (9th ed.). Boston, MA: Allyn & Bacon.

Bernet, W., Vnencak-Jones, C. L., Farahany, N. & Montgomery, S. A. (2007). Bad nature, bad nurture, and testimony regarding MAOA and SLC6A4 genotyping at murder trials. *Journal of Forensic Science*, November, *52*(6).

Bernstein, M. & Tamis-Lemonda, C. S. (2007). Infants at play: Development, functions, and partners. In A. Slater & M. Lewis (Eds), *Introduction to infant development* (2nd ed.). Oxford: Oxford University Press.

Bernstein, N. (1967). *The coordination and regulation of movements*. Oxford: Pergamon.

Bertenthal, B. L. & von Hofsten, C. (1998). Eye, head, and trunk control: The foundation for manual development. *Neuroscience and Biobehavioral Reviews*, *22*, 515–520.

Berube, C. & Glanz, J. (2008). Equal opportunity: Reframing gender differences in science and math. *Principal Leadership: High School Edition*, *8*, 28–33.

Bevelander, K. E., Anschütz, D. J. & Engels, R. C. M. E. (2012). Social norms in food intake among normal weight and overweight. *Appetite*, *58*(3), 864–872.

Bhatt, R. S. & Rovee-Collier, C. (1996). Infants' forgetting of correlated attributes and object recognition. *Child Development*, *67*, 172–187.

Bhattacharjee, Y. (2008). Tracking and tackling deprivation's toll. *Science*, *319*, 1028–1029.

Biddulph, S. (2005). *Raising babies. Should under 3s go to nursery?* London: HarperThorsons.

Bidwell, L. C., McClernon, F. J. & Kollins, S. H. (2011). Cognitive enhancers for the treatment of ADHD. *Pharmacology, Biochemistry and Behavior*, *99*(2), 262–274.

Biedroń, A. & Szczepaniak, A. (2012). Working memory and short-term memory abilities in accomplished multilinguals. *The Modern Language Journal*, June, *96*(2), 290–306.

Bilton, H. (Ed.) (2005). *Learning outdoors. Improving the quality of young children's play outdoors*. London: David Fulton Publishers.

Binet, A. (1916). *The development of intelligence in children: The Binet–Simon scale*. Baltimore: Williams & Wilkins.

Bîrzéa, C., Kerr, D., Mikkelsen, R., Froumin, I., Losito, B., Pol, M. & Sardoc, M. (2004). *All-European Study on Policies for Education for Democratic Citizenship*. Strasbourg: Council of Europe.

Bischof-Kohler, D. (1988). Uber der Zusammenhang von Empathie und der Fahigkeit, sich im Spiegel zu erkennen. *Schweizerische Zeitschrift fur Psychologie*, *47*, 147–159.

Bischof, H-J., Geißler, E. & Rollenhagen, A. (2002). Limitations of the sensitive period for sexual imprinting: neuroanatomical and behavioral experiments in the zebra finch (Taeniopygia guttata) *Behavioural Brain Research*, *133*(2), 317–322.

Blaasaas, K. G., Tynes, T. & Lie, R. T. (2004). Risk of selected birth defects by maternal residence close to power lines during pregnancy. *Occupational and Environmental Medicine*, *61*, 174–176.

Black, M. M., Dubowitz, H., Krishnakumar, A. & Starr, R. H. (2007). Early intervention and recovery among children with failure to thrive: Follow-up at age 8. *Pediatrics*, *120*, 59–69.

Black, S. E., Devereux, P. J. & Salvanes, K. G. (2011). Too young to leave the nest? The effects of school starting age. *The Review of Economics and Statistics*. May 2011, *93*(2), 455–467.

Blackburn, C. M., Bonas, S., Spencer, N. J., Coe, C. J., Dolan, A. & Moy, R. (2005). Parental smoking and passive smoking in infants: Fathers matter too. *Health Education Research*, *20*, 185–194.

Blakemore, S. J. & Frith, U. (2005). *The learning brain: Lessons for education*. Oxford: Blackwell.

Blenkin, G. M. & Whitehead, M. (1988). Creating a context for development. In G. M. Blenkin and A. V. Kelly (Eds), *Early childhood education. A developmental curriculum*. London: Paul Chapman Publishing.

Blok, H. (2004). Performance in home schooling: An argument against compulsory schooling in the Netherlands. *International Review of Education*, *50*, 39–52.

Blondel, B. & Kaminski, M. (2002). Trends in the occurrence, determinants, and consequences of multiple births. *Population Trends in Perinatal Health*, *26*, 239–249.

Blondel, B., Macfarlane, A., Gissler, M., Breart, G. & Zeitlin, J. (2006). Preterm birth and multiple pregnancy in European countries participating in the PERISTAT project. *BJOG: An International Journal of Obstetrics and Gynaecology*, *113*, 528–535.

Bloom, B. S. (1964). *Stability and change in human characteristics*. New York: Wiley.

Bloom, L. (1998). Language acquisition in its developmental context. In D. Kuhn & R. S. Siegler (Eds), *Handbook of child psychology: Vol. 2. Cognition, perception, and language* (pp 309–370). New York: Wiley.

Bloom, L. (2000). The intentionality model of language development: How to learn a word, any word. In R. Golinkoff, K. Hirsh-Pasek, L. Bloom, L. Smith, A. Woodward, N. Akhtar, M. Tomasello & G. Hollich (Eds), *Becoming a word learner: A debate on lexical acquisition*. New York: Oxford University Press.

Bloomfield, D.-P. & Soyibo, K. (2008). Correlations among Jamaican 12th-graders' five variables and performance in genetics. *Eurasia Journal of Mathematics, Science & Technology Education*, *4*, 63–69.

BMJ (2006). What are the risks for couples with a balanced structural chromosome abnormality? *British Medical Journal, 332.*

Bone, J. (2010). Metamorphosis: play, spirituality and the animal. *Contemporary Issues in Early Childhood*, December, *11*(4), 402–414.

Boccia, M. & Campos, J. J. (1989). Maternal emotional signals, social referencing, and infants' reactions to strangers. In N. Eisenberg (Ed.), *New directions for child development: No. 44. Empathy and related emotional responses.* San Francisco: Jossey-Bass.

Bohannon, J. N. & Stanowicz, L. (1988). The issue of negative evidence: Adult responses to children's language errors. *Developmental Psychology, 24*, 684–689.

Bohlin, G., Hagekull, B. & Rydell, A. (2000). Attachment and social functioning: A longitudinal study from infancy to middle childhood. *Social Development, 9*, 24–39.

Boomsma, D., Willemsen, G., Dolan, C., Hawkley, L. & Cacioppo, John (2005). Genetic and environmental contributions to loneliness in adults: The Netherlands twin register study. *Behavior Genetics*, November, *35*(6), 745–752.

Borke, H. (1975). Piaget's mountains revisited: Changes in the egocentric landscape. *Developmental Psychology, 11*, 240–243.

Bosch, L., Costa, A. & Sebastian-Galles, N. (2000). First and second language vowel perception in early bilinguals. *European Journal of Cognitive Psychology, 12*, 189–221.

Bower, T. (1983). *The perceptual world of the child.* London: Fontana Press.

Bowes, J., Harrison, L., Ungerer, J., Simpson, T., Wise, S., Sanson, A. & Watson, J. (2004). Child care choices: A longitudinal study of children, families and child care in partnership with policy makers. *Australian Educational Researcher*, December, *31*(3), 69–86.

Bowlby, J. (1958). The nature of the child's tie to his mother. *International Journal of Psycho-Analysis, 39*, 350–373.

Bowlby, J. (1969). *Attachment and loss. Vol. 1. Attachment.* New York: Basic Books.

Bowles, R. & O'Sullivan, M. (2012). Rhetoric and reality: The role of the teacher in shaping a school sport programme. *Physical Education and Sport Pedagogy, 17*(3), 303–316.

Boyce, W. (2004). Social stratification, health, and violence in the very young. *Annals of The New York Academy Of Sciences, 1036*(1), 47–68.

Boyle, E. M., Poulsen, G., Field, D. J., Kurinczuk, J. J., Wolke, D., Alfirevic, Z. & Quigley, M. A. (2012). Effects of gestational age at birth on health outcomes at 3 and 5 years of age: Population based on cohort study. *British Medical Journal, 344*, e896.

Bradley, B., Fleck, A. & Osei, E. K. (2006). Normalized data for the estimation of fetal radiation dose from radiotherapy of the breast. *British Journal of Radiology (BJR), 79*, 818–827.

Brainerd, C. J. & Reyna, V. F. (1993). Mere memory testing creates false memories in children. *Developmental Psychology, 32*, 467–478.

Brazelton, T. B., Nugent, J. K. & Lester, B. M. (1987). Neonatal behaviour assessment scale. In J. D. Osofsky (Ed.), *Handbook of infant development*, 2nd ed. New York: Wiley.

Brechet, C. (2013). Children's gender stereotypes through drawings of emotional faces: Do boys draw angrier faces than girls? *Sex Roles*, 2013, Preprints, 1–12.

Brill, M. T. (2007). *Down's syndrome.* New York: Marshall Cavendish Benchmark.

British Psychological Society (2006). *Code of ethics and conduct.* Leicester: BPS.

Brizendine, L. (2008). *The female brain.* New York: Morgan Road Books.

Broadhead, P. (2001). Investigating sociability and cooperation in four and five year olds in reception class settings. *International Journal of Early Years Education, 9*, 25–34.

Broadhead, P. (2004). *Early years play and learning: Developing social skills and cooperation.* London: Routledge Falmer.

Broberg, A. G., Wessels, H., Lamb, M. E. & Hwang, C. P. (1997). Effects of day care on the development of cognitive abilities in 8 year-olds: A longitudinal study. *Developmental Psychology, 33*, 62–69.

Bronfenbrenner, U. (1979). *The ecology of human development: Experiments by nature and design. Cambridge*, MA: Harvard University Press.

Bronfenbrenner, U. (1989). Ecological systems theory. In R. Vasta (Ed.), *Annals of child development* (Vol. 6, pp 187–249). Boston, MA: JAI Press, Inc.

Bronfenbrenner, U. & Evans, G. W. (2000). Developmental science in the 21st century: Emerging theoretical models, research designs, and empirical findings. *Social Development, 9*, 115–125.

Bronfenbrenner, U. & Morris, P. A. (1998). The ecology of developmental processes. In W. Damon & R. M. Lerner (Eds), *Handbook of child psychology: Vol 1: Theoretical models of human development* (pp 993–1028). New York: Wiley.

Brooks-Gunn, J. (1995). Children in families in communities: Risk and intervention in the Bronfenbrenner tradition. In P. Moen, G. H. Elder & K. Lescher (Eds), *Examining lives in context* (pp 467–519). Washington, DC: American Psychological Association.

Brown, B. & Grotberg, E. H. (1980). Head Start: A successful experiment. *Courier 30*, 337–344.

Brown, N. (2004). What makes a good educator? The relevance of meta programmes. *Assessment & Evaluation in Higher Education, 29*, 515–533.

Brownell, A. (1990). Peer social skills in toddlers: Competencies and constraints illustrated by same-age and mixed-age interaction. *Child Development, 61*, 836–848.

Bruce, T. (2001). *Learning through play: Babies, toddlers and the foundation years.* London: David Fulton.

Bruner, J. S. (1966). *Toward a theory of instruction.* Cambridge, MA: Harvard University Press.

Bruner, J. S. (1973). *Beyond the information given: Studies in the psychology of knowing.* Oxford: W. W. Norton.

Bruner, J. S. (1975). From communication to language: A psychological perspective. *Cognition, 3*, 255–287.

Bruner, J. S. (1983). *Child's talk: Learning to use language.* Oxford: Oxford University Press.

Bruner, J. S. & Haste, H. (Eds) (1987). *Making sense: The child's construction of the world*. New York: Methuen.

Bryant, G. A. & Barrett, H. C. (2008). Vocal emotion recognition across disparate cultures. *Journal of Cognition and Culture*, 2008, 8(1–2), 135–148.

Bryson, B. (2003). *A short history of nearly everything*. Toronto: Doubleday.

Buckley, S. & Sacks, B. (2001). *An overview of the development of children with Down's syndrome (5–11 years)*. Southsea: The Down's Syndrome Educational Trust.

Bugental, D. B. & Goodnow, J. J. (1998). Socialization processes. In W. Damon (Series Ed.) & N. Eisenberg (Vol. Ed.), *Handbook of child psychology: Vol. 3. Social, emotional, and personality development*, 5th ed. (pp 389–462). New York: Wiley.

Bukatko, D. & Daehler, M. W. (2001). *Child development: A thematic approach*, 4th ed. Boston, MA: Houghton Mifflin.

Bulmer, M. (2003). *Francis Galton: Pioneer of heredity and biometry*. Baltimore: Johns Hopkins University Press.

Bulotsky-Shearer, R., Fantuzzo, J. W. & McDemont, P. A. (2008). An investigation of classroom situational dimensions of emotional and behavioral adjustment and cognitive and social outcomes for Head Start children. *Developmental Psychology*, 44, 139–154.

Burden, R. & Burdett, J. (2005). Factors associated with successful learning in pupils with dyslexia: A motivational analysis. *British Journal of Special Education*, 32(2), 100–104.

Bureau, J. & Moss, E. (2010). Behavioural precursors of attachment representations in middle childhood and links with child social adaptation. *British Journal Of Developmental Psychology*, 28(3), 657–677.

Burke, M. J., Drasgow, F. & Edwards, J. E. (2004). Closing science–practice knowledge gaps: Contributions of psychological research to human resource management. *Human Resource Management*, 43, 299–304.

Burke, P. J. (2003). *Advances in identity theory and research*. New York: Kluwer Academic/Plenum.

Burke, V., Beilin, L. J., Durkin, K., Stritzke, W. G. K., Houghton, S. & Cameron, C. A. (2006). Television, computer use, physical activity, diet and fatness in Australian adolescents. *International Journal of Pediatric Obesity*, 1, 248–255.

Burt, C. L. (1972). Inheritance of general intelligence. *American Psychologist*, 27, 175–190.

Burton, D. (2007). Psycho-pedagogy and personalised learning. *Journal of Education for Teaching*, 33, 5–17.

Bushnell, E. & Boudreau, J. P. (1993). Motor development and the mind: the potential role of motor abilities as a determinant of aspects of perceptual development. *Child Development*, 64, 1005–1021.

Buss, A. H. & Plomin, R. (1984). *Temperament: Early developing personality traits*. Hillsdale, NJ: Erlbaum.

Buss, D. M. (1995). Evolutionary psychology: A new paradigm for psychological science. *Psychological Inquiry*, 6, 1–30.

Bussey, K. & Bandura, A. (1999). Social cognitive theory of gender development and differentiation. *Developmental Review*, 106, 676–713.

Bwire, R., Freeman, J. & Houn, F. (2011). Managing the teratogenic risk of thalidomide and lenalidomide: An industry perspective. *Expert Opinion on Drug Safety*, 10(1), 3–8.

Caljouw, S. R., Van der Kamp, J. & Savelsbergh, G. J. P. (2004). Timing of goal-directed hitting: Impact requirements change the information movement coupling. *Experimental Brain Research*, 155, 135–114.

Cameron, L. & Besser, S. (2004). *Writing in English as an additional language at Key Stage 2*. Nottingham: DFES Publications.

Campbell, S. (2004). *Watch me grow: A unique, 3-dimensional week-by-week look at your baby's behaviour and development in the womb*. London: Carroll & Brown.

Campbell, S. (2005). *Your pregnancy day by day: Watch your baby grow every day as you enjoy a healthy pregnancy*. London: Carroll & Brown.

Campos, J. J., Anderson, D. I., Barbu-Roth, M. A., Hubbard, E. M., Hertenstein, J. J. & Witherington, D. (2000). Travel broadens the mind. *Infancy*, 1, 149–219.

Cappellini, G., Ivanenko, Y. P., Poppele, R. E. & Lacquaniti, F. (2006). Motor patterns in human walking and running. *Journal of Neurophysiology*, 95(6), 3426–3437.

Cardak, B. A. (2004). Education choice, neoclassical growth, and class structure. *Oxford Economic Papers*, 56, 643–666.

Cardinal, T. M. & Lumeng, J. C. (2007). Too much tube time? *Zero to Three*, 28, 31–36.

Carpendale, J. I. M. & Lewis, C. (2004). Constructing an understanding of mind: The development of children's social understanding within social interaction. *Behavioral and Brain Sciences*, 27, 79–96.

Carlson, V., Cicchetti, D., Barnett, D. & Braunwald, K. (1989). Disorganised/disoriented attachment relationships in maltreated infants. *Developmental Psychology*, 25, 525–531.

Carrington, B., Francis, B., Hutchings, M., Skelton, C., Read, B. & Hall, I. (2007). Does the gender of the teacher really matter? Seven- to eight-year-olds' accounts of their interactions with their teachers. *Educational Studies*, 33, 397–413.

Carrington, B. & McPhee, A. (2008). Boys' 'underachievement' and the feminization of teaching. *Journal of Education for Teaching*, 34, 109–120.

Case, R. (1992). Neo-Piagetian theories of child development. In R. J. Sternberg & C. A. Berg (Eds), *Intellectual development* (pp 161–196). New York: Cambridge University Press.

Case, R. (1998). The development of conceptual structures. In W. Damon (Series Ed.) & D. Kuhn & R. S. Siegler (Vol. Eds), *Handbook of child psychology: Vol. 2, Cognition, perception, and language*. New York: Wiley.

Casey, B. J. & Richards, J. E. (1988). Sustained visual attention in young infants measured with an adapted version of the visual preference paradigm. *Child Development*, 59, 1514.

Caspi, A. (1998). Personality development across the life course. In N. Eisenberg (Ed.), *Handbook of child psychology: Vol. 3. Social, emotional, and personality development* (5th ed., pp 311–388). New York: Wiley.

Catalano, R. F. & Hawkins, J. D. (1996). The social development model: A theory of antisocial behavior. In J. D. Hawkins (Ed.), *Delinquency and crime: Current theories* (pp 149–197). New York: Cambridge University Press.

Catalano, R. F., Berglund, L., Ryan, A. M., Lonczak, H. S. & Hawkins, J. (2002). Positive youth development in the United States: Research finding on evaluations of positive youth development programmes. *Prevention and Treatment*, (5), Article 15. Available at: http://journals.apa.org/prevention/volume5/pre0050001a.html

Cattle, J. & Howie, D. (2008). An evaluation of a school programme for the development of thinking skills through the CASE@KS1 approach. *International Journal of Science Education*, 30, 185–202.

Cava, M. J., Musitu, G. & Murgui, S. (2007). Individual and social risk factors related to overt victimization in a sample of Spanish. *Psychological Reports*, 101, 275–290.

Ceciliani, A., Bardella, L., Grasso, M. L., Zabonati, A. & Robazzo, C. (2008). Effects of a physical education programme on children's attitudes and emotions associated with sport climbing. *Perceptual & Motor Skills*. June, 106(3), 773–784.

Centre for Social Justice (2010). *Green Paper on the Family*. London: CSJ.

Cermak, S. & Groza, V. (1998). Sensory processing problems in post-institutionalized children: Implications for social work. *Child & Adolescent Social Work Journal*, 15, 5–37.

Chan, C. (2011). Bridging research and practice: Implementing and sustaining knowledge building in Hong Kong classrooms. *International Journal of Computer-Supported Collaborative Learning*, June, 6(2), 147–186.

Chan, R. S. & Thompson, N. S. (2011). Whines, cries, and motherese: Their relative power to distract. *The Journal of Social, Evolutionary, and Cultural Psychology*, May, 5(2), 131–141.

Chan, S., Khader, M., Ang, J., Tan, E., Khoo, K. & Chin, J. (2012). Understanding 'happy slapping'. *International Journal of Police Science and Management*, 14(1), 42–57.

Chang, A. B., Wilson, S. J., Masters, I. B., Yuill, M., Williams, J., Williams, G. & Hubbard, M. (2003). Altered arousal response in infants exposed to cigarette smoke. *Archives of Disease in Childhood*, 88, 30–33.

Chasiotis, A., Kiessling, F., Winter, V. & Hofer, J. (2006). Sensory motor inhibition as a prerequisite for theory-of-mind: A comparison of clinical and normal preschoolers differing in sensory motor abilities. *International Journal of Behavioral Development*, 30, 178–190.

Chazan, S. (2009). Observing play activity: The children's developmental play instrument (CDPI) with reliability studies. *Child Indicators Research*, 2(4), 417–436.

Chen, X., Chen, H. & Kaspar, V. (2001). Group social functioning and individual socioemotional and school adjustment in Chinese children. *Merrill-Palmer Quarterly*, 47, 264–299.

Chi, M. T. H., Bassok, M., Lewis, M. W., Reimann, P. & Glaser, R. (1989). Self-explanations – how students study and use examples in learning to solve problems. *Cognitive Science*, 13, 145–182.

Child, D. (2004). *Psychology and the teacher*. London: Continuum.

Chisholm, J. S. (1989). Biology, culture, and the development of temperament: A Navaho example. In J. K. Nugent, B. M. Lester & T. B. Brazelton (Eds), *The cultural context of infancy: Vol. 1. Biology, culture, and infant development*. Norwood, NJ: Ablex.

Chiswick, B. & Miller, P. (2008). A test of the critical period hypothesis for language learning. *Journal of Multilingual and Multicultural Development*, 29(1), 16–29.

Chomsky, N. (1957). *Syntactic structures*. The Hague: Mouton.

Chomsky, N. (1968). *Language and mind*. New York: Harcourt Brace & World.

Christiansen, M. H., Conway, C. M. & Onnis, L. (2012). Similar neural correlates for language and sequential learning: Evidence from event-related brain potentials. *Language and Cognitive Processes*, 27(2), 231–256.

Claessens, A. & Chen, J. (2013). Multiple child care arrangements and child well being: Early care experiences in Australia. *Early Childhood Research Quarterly*, 28(1), 49–61.

Clark, C., Woodley, J. & Lewis, F. (2011). *The gift of reading in 2011: Children and young people's access to books and attitudes towards reading*. London: National Literacy Trust.

Clark, C. with Burke, D. (2012). *Boys' Reading Commission. A review of existing research to underpin the Commission*. London: National Literacy Trust.

Clark, J., Craig, L., McNeill, G., Smith, N., Norrie, J. & Devereux, G. (2012). A novel dietary intervention to optimize vitamin E intake of pregnant women to 15 mg/Day. *Journal of the Academy of Nutrition & Dietetics*. Feb, 112(2), 297–301.

Clark, J. E. & Phillips, S. J. (1993). A longitudinal study of the intra-limb coordination in the first year of independent walking. *Child Development*, 64, 1143–1157.

Clarke-Stewart, K. A. & Allhusen, V. D. (2005). *What we know about childcare*. Cambridge, MA: Harvard University Press.

Clarkin, P. F. (2012). War, forced displacement and growth in Laotian adults *Annals of Human Biology*, 39(1), 36–45.

Clegham, P. (2003). *Thinking through philosophy*. Blackburn: EPSL.

Clifton, R. K., Rochat, P., Robin, D. J. & Berthier, N. E. (1994). Multimodal perception in the control of infant reaching. *Journal of Experimental Psychology: Human Perception and Performance*, 20, 876–886.

Coakley, J. (2007). *Sport in society: Issues and controversies*, 9th ed. Boston, MA: McGraw-Hill.

Cockett, M. & Tripp, J. (1994). Children living in disordered families. *Social Policy Research Findings*, No. 45. York: Joseph Rowntree Foundation.

Cohen, L., Manion, L. & Morrison, K. (2007). *Research methods in education*, 6th ed. London: Routledge Falmer.

Coleman, L. & Coleman, J. (2002). The measurement of puberty: A review. *Journal of Adolescence*, 25, 535.

Colwell, M. & Lindsey, E. (2005). Preschool children's pretend and physical play and sex of play partner: Connections to peer competence. *Sex Roles*, 52, 497–509.

Conboy, B. T. & Thal, D. J. (2006). Ties between the lexicon and grammar: Cross-sectional and longitudinal studies of bilingual toddlers. *Child Development*, 77, 712–735.

Confederation of British Industry (CBI) (2012). *First Steps. A new approach for our schools.* London: CBI.

Conner, P., Westgren, M., Marsk, A., Gustafsson, S. & Kublickas, M. (2012). Combined ultrasound and biochemistry for risk evaluation in the first trimester. *Acta Obstetricia et Gynecologica Scandinavica*, January, *91*(1), 34–38.

Constable, R. T., Ment, L. R., Vohr, B. R., Kesler, S. R., Fulbright, R. K., Lacadie, C., Delancy, S., Katz, K. H., Schneider, K. C., Schafer, R. J., Makuch, R. W. & Reiss, A. R. (2008). Prematurely born children demonstrate white matter microstructural differences at 12 years of age, relative to term control subjects: An investigation of group and gender effects. *Pediatrics*, *121*, 306–316.

Cook, D. G., Peacock, J. L., Feyerabend, C., Carey, I. M., Jarvis, M. J., Anderson, H. R. & Bland, J. M. (1996). Relation of caffeine intake and blood caffeine concentrations during pregnancy to fetal growth: Prospective population based study. *BMJ (British Medical Journal)*, *313*, 1358–1362.

Cook, G. (2006). Boys at risk: The gender achievement gap. *American School Board Journal*, *193*, 4.

Cooke, R. W. I. & Foulder-Hughes, L. (2003). Growth impairment in the very preterm and cognitive and motor performance at 7 years. *Archives of Disease in Childhood*, *88*, 482–487.

Coopersmith, S. (1967). *The antecedents of self-esteem.* New York: W. H. Freeman.

Coplan, R. J., Prakash, K., O'Neil, K. & Armer, M. (2004). Do you 'want' to play? Distinguishing between conflicted-shyness and social disinterest in early childhood. *Developmental Psychology*, *40*, 244–258.

Coplan, R. J., Arbeau, K. A. & Armer, M. (2008). Don't fret, be supportive! Maternal characteristics linking child shyness to psychosocial and school adjustment in kindergarten. *Journal of Abnormal Child Psychology*, *36*, 359–371.

Cornell, A. H. & Frick, P. J. (2007). The moderating effects of parenting styles in the association between behavioral inhibition and parent-reported guilt and empathy in preschool children. *Journal of Clinical Child & Adolescent Psychology*, *36*, 305–318.

Cortes, R. & Greenberg, M. (2007). Improving young children's social and emotional competence. *Journal of Primary Prevention*, *28*, 67–91.

Cortina, M. & Liotti, G. (2010). The intersubjective and cooperative origins of consciousness: An evolutionary-developmental approach. *Journal of the American Academy of Psychoanalysis and Dynamic Psychiatry*, *38*(2), 291–314.

Côté, S., Tremblay, R. E., Nagin, D., Zoccolillo, M. & Vitaro, F. (2002). The development of impulsivity, fearfulness, and helpfulness during childhood: Patterns of consistency and change in the trajectories of boys and girls. *Journal of Child Psychology and Psychiatry (formerly Journal of Child Psychology and Psychiatry and Allied Disciplines)*, *43*, 609–618.

Cotterill, R. (2003). CyberChild a simulation test-bed for consciousness studies. *Journal of Consciousness Studies*, *10*, 31–45.

Courage, M. L. & Howe, M. L. (2004). Advances in early memory development research: Insights about the dark side of the moon. *Developmental Review*, *24*, 6.

Coussons-Read, M., Okun, M. & Simms, S. (2003). The psychoneuroimmunology of pregnancy. *Journal of Reproductive and Infant Psychology*, *21*, 103–112.

Cox, J. E., Buman, M. P., Woods, E. R., Famakinwa, O. & Harris, S. K. (2012). Evaluation of raising adolescent families together program: A medical home for adolescent mothers and their children. *American Journal of Public Health.* Oct, *102*(10), 1875–1885.

Coyne, L. L. (2008). Childhood obesity – problems/solutions. www.centralhome.com/childhoodobesity.htm, accessed 5 May 2008.

Coyne, S. M., Archer, J. & Eslea, M. (2004). Cruel intentions on television and in real life: Can viewing indirect aggression increase viewers' subsequent indirect aggression? *Journal of Experimental Child Psychology.* July, *88*(3), 234–253.

Craft, A. (2005). Changes in the landscape for creativity in education. In A. Wilson (Ed.), *Creativity in primary education.* Exeter: Learning Matters.

Crawford, D. A. (2002). Keep the focus on the family. *Journal of Child Health Care*, *6*, 133–146.

Crick, N. R., Werner, N. E., Casas, J. F., O'Brien, K. M., Nelson, D. A., Grotpeter, J. K. & Markon, K. (1999). Childhood aggression and gender: A new look at an old problem. In D. Bernstein (Ed.), *Gender and motivation: Nebraska Symposium on Motivation*, Vol. 45 (pp 75–141). Lincoln: University of Nebraska Press.

Critser, G. (2003). *Fat land. How Americans became the fattest people in the world.* London: The Penguin Group.

Crncec, R., Wilson, S. & Prior, M. (2006). The cognitive and academic benefits of music to children: Facts and fiction. *Educational Psychology*, *26*, 579–594.

Crockenberg, S. C. & Leerkes, E. M. (2004). Infant and maternal behaviors regulate infant reactivity to novelty at 6 months. *Developmental Psychology*, Nov, *40*(6), 1123–1132.

Crozier, W. R. & Skliopidou, E. (2002). Adult recollections of name-calling at school. *Educational Psychology*, *22*(1), 113–124.

Cummine, J. & Boliek, C. (2013). Understanding white matter integrity stability for bilinguals on language status and reading performance. *Brain Structure and Function*, (Preprints), 1–7.

Curtindale, L., Laurie-Rose, C., Bennett-Murphy, L. & Hull, S. (2007). Sensory modality, temperament, and the development of sustained attention: A vigilance study in children and adults. *Developmental Psychology*, *43*, 576–589.

Curtis, P. (2008). The experiences of young people with obesity in secondary school: Some implications for the healthy school agenda. *Health & Social Care in the Community*, *16*(4), 410–418.

Curtiss, S. (1977). *Genie: A psycholinguistic study of a modern-day 'wild child'.* New York: Academic Press.

Dadds, M. R., Hunter, K., Hawes, D. J., Frost, A. D. J., Vassallo, S., Bunn, P., Merz, S. & El Masry, Y. (2008).

A measure of cognitive and affective empathy in children using parent ratings. *Child Psychiatry & Human Development, 39*, 111–122.

Dalzell, V. P., Msall, M. E. & High, P. C. (2000). Parental attitudes of television and videocassette viewing of children aged birth to 36 months. *Journal of Developmental and Behavioural Pediatrics, 21*, 390.

Damon, W. (2000). Setting the stage for the development of wisdom: Self-understanding and moral identity during adolescence. In W. S. Brown (Ed.), *Understanding wisdom: Sources, science, and society* (pp 339–360). Philadelphia: Templeton Foundation Press.

Darwin, C. R. (1877). A biographical sketch of an infant. *Mind. A Quarterly Review of Psychology and Philosophy, 2*(7) (July), 285–294.

David, T. (Ed.) (1999). *Young children learning*. Buckingham: Open University Press.

Davies, B. (2011). Bullies as guardians of the moral order or an ethic of truths? *Children & Society, 25*(4), 278–286.

Davis, R. A. (2011). Brilliance of a fire: Innocence, experience and the theory of childhood. *Journal of Philosophy of Education*, May, *45*(2), 379–397.

Davis, S., Gervin, D., White, G., Williams, A., Taylor, A. & McGriff, E. (2013). Bridging the gap between research, evaluation, and evidence-based practice. *Journal of Social Work Education*. Winter, *49*(1), 16–29.

de Almeida, M. D. V., Pinho, S., Stewart-Knox, B., Parr, H. J. & Gibney, M. J. (2006). An overview of findings from a six-country European survey on consumer attitudes to the metabolic syndrome, genetics in nutrition, and potential agro-food technologies. *Nutrition Bulletin, 31*, 239–246.

de Boo, M. (Ed.) (2004). *The early years handbook. Support for practitioners in the Foundation Stage*. Sheffield: Geography Association.

DeCasper, A. J. & Spence, M. J. (1986). Prenatal maternal speech influences newborns' perception of speech sounds. *Infant Behavior and Development, 9*, 133–150.

De Gangi, G. & Kendall, A. (2007). *Effective parenting for the hard-to-manage child: A skills-based book*. London: Routledge.

Deans, A. (Ed.) (2007). *Your pregnancy bible*. London: Carroll & Brown.

Del Giudice, M. (2011). Alone in the dark? Modeling the conditions for visual experience in human fetuses. *Developmental Psychobiology*, March, *53*(2), 214–219.

Delogu, F., Nijboer, T. & Postma, A (2012). Encoding location and serial order in auditory working memory: Evidence for separable processes. *Cognitive Processing*, Preprints, 1–10.

Demanet, J. & Van Houtte, M. (2012). The impact of bullying and victimization on students' relationships. *American Journal of Health Education, 43*(2), 104–113.

Denman, F. (1952). *Television, the magic window*. New York: Macmillan.

Dennis, W. (1960). Causes of retardation among institutionalized children: Iran. *Journal of Genetic Psychology, 96*, 47–59.

Dennison, P. E. (2010). *Brain Gym: Teacher's edition* (Revised). Ventura CA: Edu-Kinesthetics Inc.

Dennison, P. E. & Dennison, G. E. (1994). *Brain Gym. Teacher's edition (Revised)*. Ventura, CA: Edu-Kinesthetics.

Department for Culture, Media and Sport (2010). Plans for the Legacy from the 2012 Olympic and Paralympic Games. Available at: www.culture.gov.uk/publications/7674.aspx

Department for Education (2013). *More great childcare. Raising quality and giving parents more choice*. London: DfE.

Department for Education, Department of Health (2011). *Supporting families in the foundation years*. London: Department for Education.

Department of Health (2009). *Healthy child programme: pregnancy and the first five years of life*. London: Department of Health.

Department of Health (2010). *Healthy Lives, Healthy People: Our Strategy for Public Health in England*. Available at: www.dh.gov.uk/en/Publicationsandstatistics/Publications/PublicationsPolicyAndGuidance/DH_121941

Department of Health (2011a). *Healthy lives, healthy people: A tobacco control plan for England*. London. HMSO.

Department of Health (2011b). Healthy lives, healthy people: A call to action on obesity in England. Available at: www.dh.gov.uk/en/Publicationsandstatistics/Publications/PublicationsPolicyAndGuidance/DH_130401

Department of Health (2012a). Giving all children a healthy start in life. Available at www.dh.gov.uk/health/2012/05/start4life/ (accessed 30.10.2012).

Department of Health (2012b). Healthy lives, healthy people: Improving outcomes and supporting transparency – A Public Health Outcomes Framework. Available at: www.dh.gov.uk/en/Publicationsandstatistics/Publications/PublicationsPolicyAndGuidance/DH_132358

Derbyshire, S. W. G. (2010). Foetal pain? Best *Practice & Research Clinical Obstetrics & Gynaecology, 24*(5), 647–655.

Derhami, V. (2013). Similarity of learned helplessness in human being and fuzzy reinforcement learning algorithms. *Journal of Intelligent and Fuzzy Systems* (Preprints).

Desforges, C. (2004). Researchers have got lost in thought whilst practitioners have gone missing in action. *NERF Bulletin, 1*, 15.

Deutscher, B., Fewell, R. R. & Gross, M. (2006). Enhancing the interactions of teenage mothers and their at-risk children: Effectiveness of a maternal-focused intervention. *Topics in Early Childhood Special Education*. Winter, *26*(4), 194–205.

DfE (2011). *Support and aspiration: A new approach to special educational needs and disability. A consultation* (2011). London: DfE.

DfE (2012). *Support and aspiration: A new approach to special educational needs and disability Progress and next steps*. London: DfE.

DfE (2012). *Statutory framework for the early years foundation stage*. Runcorn: DfE Publications.

DfES (2002a). *Student achievement in England: Results in reading, mathematical and scientific literacy among 15 year-olds from the OECD PISA 2000 study*. London: National Statistics.

DfES (2002b). *Languages for all: Languages for life. A strategy for England*. Nottingham: DfES Publications.

DfES (2003). *Every child matters* (green paper). London: TSO.

DfES (2004). *Pupil participation guidance: Working together – giving children and young people a say*. Available online at www.teachernet.gov.uk/wholeschool/behaviour/participationguidance

DfES (2004a). *Every child matters: Next steps*. London: DfES Publications.

DfES (2004b). *Every child matters: Change for children*. London: DfES Publications.

DfES (2006). *The early years foundation stage*. London: DfES Publications.

Diamond, A. (2000). Close interrelation of motor development and cognitive development and of the cerebellum and prefrontal cortex. *Child Development, 71*, 44–56.

Diamond, A. (2002). Normal development of prefrontal cortex from birth to young adulthood: Cognitive functions, anatomy, and biochemistry. In D. T. Stuss & R. T. Knight (Eds), *The frontal lobes* (pp 66–503). London: Oxford University Press.

Diamond, M. & Hopson, J. (1998). *Magic trees of the mind*. New York: Dutton.

Dichter, G. S., Benning, S. D., Holtzclaw, T. N. & Bodfish, J. W. (2010). Affective modulation of the startle eyeblink and postauricular reflexes in autism spectrum disorder. *Journal of Autism & Developmental Disorders*, July, *10*(7), 858–869.

Diego, M., Field, T., Hernandez-Reif, M., Vera, Y., Gil, K. & Gonzalez-Garcia, A. (2007). Caffeine use affects pregnancy outcome. *Journal of Child & Adolescent Substance Abuse, 17*(2), 41–49.

DiPietro, J. A. (2005). Neurobehavioral assessment before birth. *Mental Retardation & Developmental Disabilities Research Reviews, 11*, 4–13.

DiPietro, J. A., Hodgson, D. M., Costigan, K. A. & Johnson, T. R. B. (1996). Fetal antecedents of infant temperament. *Child Development, 67*, 2568–2583.

DiTommaso, E., Brannen, C. & Burgess, M. (2005). The universality of relationship characteristics: A cross–cultural comparison of different types of attachment and loneliness in Canadian and visiting Chinese students. *Social Behavior and Personality, 33*(1), 57–68.

Dixon, G. & Addy, L. (2004). *Making inclusion work for children with dyspraxia*. London: Routledge Falmer.

DoE/Early Education (2012). *Development matters in the early years foundation stage*. London: Early Education.

Doliopoulou, E. & Rizou, C. (2012). Greek kindergarten teachers' and parents' views about changes in play since their own childhood. *European Early Childhood Education Research Journal*, March, *20*(1), 133–147.

Dolk, H., Nichols, R. & EUROCAT Working Group (1999). Evaluation of the impact of Chernobyl on the prevalence of congenital anomalies in 16 regions of Europe. *International Journal of Epidemiology, 28*, 941–948.

Dollard, J. & Miller, N. E. (1950). *Personality and psychotherapy*. New York: McGraw-Hill.

Donczik, J. (1994). Brain exercise improves reading and memory. *Brain Gym Journal, XV*, Nos. 1 & 2. Translated by C. M. Grimm & S. Wong (2001), *Die Sprach-heilarbeit, 39*, 297–305.

D'Oosterlinck, F., Broekaert, E., De Wilde, J., Bockaert, L. F. & Goethals, I. (2006). Original article. Characteristics and profile of boys and girls with emotional and behavioural disorders in Flanders mental health institutes: A quantitative study. *Child: Care Health & Development, 32*, 213–224.

Doymus, K. (2008). Teaching chemical equilibrium with the jigsaw technique. *Research in Science Education, 38*, 249–260.

Draganova, R. L., Eswaran, H., Lowery, C. L., Murphy, P., Huotilainen, M. & Preissl, H. (2005). Sound frequency change detection in fetuses and newborns. An agnetoencephalographic study. *NeuroImage, 28*, 354–361.

Drake, J. (2001). *Planning children's play and learning in the foundation stage*. London: David Fulton.

Drozd, K. F. (2004). Learnability and linguistic performance. *Journal of Child Language, 31*, 431–457.

DSCF (2010). *Support for All. The families and relationships* Green Paper. London: HMSO.

Dubois, J., Hertz-Pannier, L., Dehaene-Lambertz, G., Cointepas, Y. & Le Bihan, D. (2006). Assessment of the early organization and maturation of infants' cerebral white matter fiber bundles: A feasibility study using quantitative diffusion tensor imaging and tractography. *NeuroImage, 30*, 1121–1132.

Dudley, O., McManus, B., Vogels, A., Whittington, J. & Muscatelli, F. (2008). Cross-cultural comparisons of obesity and growth in Prader–Willi syndrome. *Journal of Intellectual Disability Research, 52*, 426–436.

Duff, C. (2010). Towards a developmental ethology: Exploring Deleuze's contribution to the study of health and human development. *Health*, November, *14*(6), 619–634.

Dweck, C. (2001). Caution – praise can be dangerous. In K. L. Frieberg (Ed.), *Human development 01/02* (pp 105–109). Guilford, CT: Dushkin/McGraw-Hill.

Dwyer, D. & Scampion, J. (1995). *A Level psychology*. London: Macmillan.

Dyet, L. E., Kennea, N., Counsell, S. J., Maalouf, E. F., Ajayi-Obe, M., Duggan, P. J., Harrison, M., Allsop, J. M., Hajnal, J., Herlihy, A. H., Edwards, B., Laroche, S., Cowan, F. M., Rutherford, M. A. & Edwards, A. D. (2006). Natural history of brain lesions in extremely preterm infants studied with serial magnetic resonance imaging from birth and neuro-developmental assessment. *Pediatrics, 118*, 536–548.

Eastin, M. S. & Griffiths, R. P. (2006). Beyond the shooter game. *Communication Research, 33*, 448–466.

Eccles, J., Jacobs, J., Harold, J., Yoon, K., Amerbach, A. & Freedman Doan, C. (1991). *Expectancy effects are alive and well on the home front: Influences on, and consequences of parents' beliefs regarding their daughters' and sons' abilities and interests*. Presented at the annual meeting of the American Psychological Association, San Francisco, CA.

*Education Digest* (1978). A summary of research on class size. *Education Digest, 44*, 26–28.

Eisenberg, N. & Fabes, R. A. (1998). Prosocial behavior. In W. Damon (Ed.), *Handbook of child psychology: Vol. 3. Social, emotional, and personality development* (5th ed., pp 701–778). New York: Wiley.

Ekman, P. (1972). Universal and cultural differences in facial expressions of emotion. In J. Cole (Ed.), *Nebraska Symposium on Motivation* (pp 207–282). Lincoln: University of Nebraska Press.

Elaziz, K. M. A., Sabbour, S. M. & Dewedar, S. A. (2010). A measles and rubella (MR) catch-up vaccination campaign in an Egyptian University: Vaccine uptake and knowledge and attitudes of students. *Vaccine, 28*(47), 7563–7568.

Elbert, T., Pantev, C., Weinbruch, C., Rockstroh, B. & Taub, E. (1995). Increased cortical representation of the left hand in string players. *Science, 270*, 305–307.

Eldridge, G. (2008). The importance of self-regulation skills. *International Educator, 22*, 21.

Elias, H., Mahyuddin, R., Abdullah, M. C., Roslan, S., Noordin, N. & Fauzee, O. (2007). Emotional intelligence of at risk students in Malaysian secondary schools. *International Journal of Learning, 14*, 51–56.

Eliot, L. (1999). *What's going on in there? How the brain and mind develop in the first five years of life.* London: Penguin.

Elley, W. B. (1992). *How in the world do students read? IEA study of reading literacy.* The Hague: The International Association for the Evaluation of Educational Achievement.

Eluvathingal, T. J., Chugani, H. T., Behen, M. E., Juhász, C., Muzik, O., Maqbool, M., Chugani, D. C. & Makki, M. (2006). Abnormal brain connectivity in children after early severe socioemotional deprivation: A diffusion tensor imaging study. *Pediatrics, 117*, 2093–2100.

Emerson, E. & Robertson, J. (2010). Obesity in young children with intellectual disabilities or borderline intellectual functioning. *International Journal of Pediatric Obesity, 5*(4), 320–326.

Endler, L. & Bond, T. (2008). Changing science outcomes: Cognitive acceleration in a US setting. *Research in Science Education, 38*, 149–166.

Englehart, J. M. (2007). The centrality of context in learning from further class size research. *Educational Psychology Review, 19*, 455–467.

EPPE (2004). *Final Report.* Effective provision of pre-school education project. Nottingham: Department for Education and Skills/Sure Start.

Epstein, L. H., Leddy, J. J., Temple, J. L. & Faith, M. S. (2007). Food reinforcement and eating: A multilevel analysis. *Psychological Bulletin, 133*, 884–906.

Erikson, E. H. (1963). *Childhood and society.* New York: W. W. Norton.

Erwin, E. & Morton, N. (2013). Exposure to media violence and young children with and without disabilities: Powerful opportunities for family–professional partnerships. *Early Childhood Education Journal* (Preprints), 1–8.

Estell, D. B. (2007). Aggression, social status, and affiliation in kindergarten children: A preliminary study. *Education & Treatment of Children, 30*, 53–72.

Estell, D. B., Farmer, T. W., Pearl, R., Van Acker, R. & Rodkin, P. C. (2008). Social status and aggressive and disruptive behavior in girls: Individual, group, and classroom influences. *Journal of School Psychology, 46*, 193–212.

EURYDICE (2005). *Citizenship education at school in Europe. Country reports.* Brussels: European Commission.

EURIDYCE (2011). *Teaching reading in Europe: Contexts, policies and practices*, Brussels: European Commission.

Evangelou, M., Sylva, K., Kyriacou, M., Wild, M. & Glenny, G. (2009). *Early years learning and development literature review.* Research Report DCSF-RR176. London: DCSF.

Evans, G. W. (2004). The environment of childhood poverty. *American Psychologist, 59*, 77–92.

Evans, M. I. (2006). *Prenatal diagnosis.* New York: McGraw-Hill.

EYFS (2012). Statutory Framework for the Early Years Foundation Stage. London: DfE. Also available online at https://www.education.gov.uk/publications/standard/AllPublications/Page1/DFE-00023-2012.

Fallu, J. S., Janosz, M. M., Brière, F. N., Descheneaux, A. A., Vitaro, F. F. & Tremblay, R. E. (2010). Preventing disruptive boys from becoming heavy substance users during adolescence: A longitudinal study of familial and peer-related protective factors. *Addictive Behaviors, 35*(12), 1074–1082.

Fanta, C. H. (2009). Asthma. *The New England Journal of Medicine 360*(10), 1002–14.

Fantz, R. L. (1961). The origin of form perception. *Scientific American, 204*, 66–72.

Farrell, M. (2006). *The effective teacher's guide to moderate, severe and profound learning difficulties practical strategies.* London: Routledge.

Farrington, D. P. (1995). The development of offending and anti-social behaviour from childhood: Key findings from the Cambridge Study in Delinquent Development. *Journal of Child Psychology & Psychiatry, 36*, 929–964.

Fasouliotis, S. J. & Schenker, J. G. (2000). Ethics and assisted reproduction. *European Journal of Obstetrics, Gynecology, and Reproductive Biology, 90*, 171–180.

Faulkner, P. (1989). The detection of neurophysiological factors in children with reading problems. Paper presented at the second International Conference on Children with Neurodevelopmental delay. Chester, UK.

Favaro, A., Tenconi, E. & Santonastaso, P. (2006). Perinatal factors and the risk of developing anorexia nervosa and bulimia nervosa. *Archives or General Psychiatry, 63*, 82–88.

Fechner, G. T. (1860/1966). *Elemente der Psychophysik.* Breitkopf & Härtel, Leipzig (reprinted in 1964 by Bonset, Amsterdam); English translation by H. E. Adler (1966). *Elements of psychophysics.* New York: Holt, Rinehart & Winston.

Fedorov, A. V. (2005). School students and computer games with screen violence. *Russian Education & Society, 47*(11), 88–96.

Feldman, J. (2003). The simplicity principle in human concept learning. *Current Directions in Psychological Science*, *12*, 227–232.

Fernald, A. & O'Neill, D. K. (1993). Peekaboo across cultures: How mothers and infants play with voices, faces, and expectations. In K. MacDonald & D. Pelligrini (Eds), *Parent–child play: Descriptions and implications* (pp 259–286). New York: SUNY.

Fernández, J. (2013). Self-deception and self-knowledge. *Philosophical Studies*, *162*(2), 379–400.

Fiasse, C. & Nader-Grosbois, N. (2012). Perceived social acceptance, theory of mind and social adjustment in children with intellectual disabilities. *Research in Developmental Disabilities*, *33*(6), 1871–1880.

Field, F. (2010). *The foundation years: Preventing poor children becoming poor adults. The report of the independent review on poverty and life chances*. London: HM Government.

Field, N. P. (2006). Unresolved grief and continuing bonds: An attachment perspective. *Death Studies*, *30*, 739–756.

Fifer, W. & Moon, C. (2005). Prenatal development. In A. Slater & G. Bremner (Eds), *An introduction to developmental psychology*. Oxford: Blackwell Publishing.

Figueiredo, B., Costa, R., Pacheco, A. & Pais, A. (2007). Mother-to-infant and father-to-infant initial emotional involvement. *Early Child Development and Care*, *177*(5), 521–532.

Finlay, F. O., Jones, R. & Coleman, J. (2002). Is puberty getting earlier? The views of doctors and teachers. *Child: Care, Health & Development*, *28*, 205–209.

Fischer, G., Jagsch, R., Eder, H., Gombas, W., Etzersdorfer, P., Schmidl-Mohl, K., Schatten, C., Weninger, M. & Aschauer, H. N. (1999). Comparison of methadone and slow-release morphine maintenance in pregnant addicts. *Addiction*, *94*, 231–239.

Fischer, K. W. & Rose, S. P. (1995). Concurrent cycles in the dynamic development of the brain and behaviour. *SRCD Newsletter*, Fall, 3–4, 15–16.

Fisher, L., Ames, E. W., Chisholm, K. & Savoie, L. (1997). Problems reported by parents of Romanian orphans adopted to British Columbia. *International Journal of Behavioral Development*, *20*, 67–82.

Fitzgerald, N., Stewart, D. & Mackie, C. (2002). A qualitative study of drug education in secondary schools in Northeast Scotland: Background and methodology. *Drugs: Education, Prevention & Policy*, 2002, *9*(3), 253–265.

Fitzpatrick, P., Schmidt, R. C. & Lockman, J. J. (1996). Dynamical patterns in the development of clapping. *Child Development*, *67*, 2691–2708.

Flanders, J. L., Leo, V., Paquette, D., Pihl, R. O. & Séguin, J. R. (2009). Rough-and-tumble play and the regulation of aggression: An observational study of father–child play dyads. *Aggressive Behavior*, *35*(4), 285–295.

Flavell, J. H., Miller, P. H. & Miller, S. A. (2002). *Cognitive development*. Upper Saddle River, NJ: Prentice-Hall.

Flom, R. & Johnson, S. (2011). The effects of adults' affective expression and direction of visual gaze on 12-month-olds' visual preferences for an object following a 5-minute, 1-day, or 1-month delay. *British Journal of Developmental Psychology*, March, *29*(1), 65–85.

Flouri, E. (2008). Fathering and adolescents' psychological adjustment: The role of fathers' involvement, residence and biology status. *Child: Care, Health & Development*, *34*, 152–161.

Floyd, K. & Guerrero, L. K. (2006). *Nonverbal communication in close relationships*. Mahwah, NJ: Lawrence Erlbaum Associates.

Flynn, J. R. (1987). Massive IQ gains in 14 nations; What IQ tests really measure. *Psychological Bulletin*, *101*, 171–191.

Fogel, A. (1993). *Developing through relationships: Origins of communication, self, and culture*. Chicago, IL: University of Chicago Press.

Fogel, A. & Garvey, A. (2007). Alive communication. *Infant Behavior & Development*, *30*, 251–257.

Fogel, A., Shapiro, A. F., Hui-Chin, H., Nelson-Goens, G. C. & Secrist, C. (2006). Effects of normal and perturbed social play on the duration and amplitude of different types of infant smiles. *Developmental Psychology*, *42*, 459–473.

Fomon, S. J. (2000). Taste acquisition and appetite control. *Pediatrics*, *106*, 1278.

Fontaine, N., Torre, D. L. & Grafwallner, R. (2006). Effects of quality early care on school readiness skills of children at risk. *Early Child Development & Care*, *176*, 99–109.

Ford, R. P. K., Schluter, P. J., Mitchell, E. A., Taylor, B. J., Scragg, R. & Stewart, A. W. (1998). Heavy caffeine intake in pregnancy and sudden infant death syndrome. *Archives of Disease in Childhood*, *78*, 9–13.

Formby, E. (2011). It's better to learn about your health and things that are going to happen to you than learning things that you just do at school: Findings from a mapping study of PSHE education in primary schools in England. *Pastoral Care in Education*, *29*(3), 161–173.

Fowler, J. (1971). *Stages of faith*. San Francisco, CA: Harper and Row.

Fowler, W., Ogston, K., Roberts, G. & Swenson, A. (2006). The effects of early language enrichment. *Early Child Development & Care*, *176*, 777–815.

Fraley, R. C. & Marks, M. J. (2011). Pushing mom away: Embodied cognition and avoidant attachment. *Journal of Research in Personality*, *45*(2), 243–246.

Fraley, R. C. & Spieker, S. J. (2003). Are infant attachment patterns continuously or categorically distributed? A taxometric analysis of strange situation behavior. *Developmental Psychology*, *39*, 387.

Francis, A. L., Ciocca, V. & Ma, L. (2004). Effects of native language experience on perceptual learning of Cantonese lexical tones. *The Journal of the Acoustical Society of America*, *115*(5), 2544.

Francis, B. (2006). Heroes or zeroes? The discursive positioning of 'underachieving boys' in English neo-liberal education policy. *Journal of Education Policy*, *21*, 187–200.

Francis, B. & Mills, M. (2012). Schools as damaging organisations: instigating a dialogue concerning alternative models of schooling. *Pedagogy, Culture & Society*, July, *20*(2), 251–271.

Franco, N. & Levitt, M. J. (1998). The social ecology of middle childhood: Family support, friendship quality, and self-esteem. *Family Relations, 47*, 315–321.

Franco, P., Chananski, S., Szliwowski, H., Dramaiz, M. & Kahn, A. (2000). Influence of maternal smoking on autonomic nervous system in healthy infants. *Pediatric Research, 47*, 215–220.

Freeman, J., Raffan, J. & Warwick, I. (2010). *Worldwide provision to develop gifts and talents. An international survey. Research report.* Reading, Berkshire: CFBT Education Trust.

Freitag, C. M. (2007). The genetics of autistic disorders and its clinical relevance: A review of the literature. *Molecular Psychiatry, 12*(1), 2–22.

Freitas-Magalhães, A. (2006). *The psychology of the human smile.* Oporto: University Fernando Pessoa Press.

Freud, S. (1935). *A general introduction to psychoanalysis.* Translated by J. Riviare. New York: Modern Library.

Freud, S. (1962). *Three essays on the theory of sexuality*, trans. James Strachey. New York: Basic Books.

Friedberg, J. W., Kim, H., McCauley, M., Hessel, E. M., Paul, S., Fisher, D. C., Nadler, L. M., Coffman, R. L. & Freedman, A. S. (2005). Combination immunotherapy with a CpG oligonucleotide (1018 ISS) and rituximab in patients with non-Hodgkin lymphoma: increased interferon-alpha/beta-inducible gene expression, without significant toxicity. *Blood, 105*, 489–495.

Friedman, S. (2004). Learning to make more effective decisions: Changing beliefs as a prelude to action. *Learning Organization, 11*, 110–128.

Fulkerson, J. A., Story, M., Neumark-Sztainer, D. & Rydell, S. (2008). Family meals: Perceptions of benefits and challenges among parents of 8- to 10-year-old children. *Journal of the American Dietetic Association.* April 2008, *108*(4), 706–709.

Furnham, A., Moutafi, J. & Chamorro-Premuzic, T. (2005). Personality and intelligence: Gender, the Big Five, self-estimated and psychometric intelligence. *International Journal of Selection and Assessment, 13*(1), 11–24.

Fusaro, J. A., Shibley, I. A. & Wiley, D. A. (2006). Learning disabilities and performance on the Pennsylvania system of school assessment. *Perceptual & Motor Skills, 102*, 760–766.

Gabutti, G., Rota, M. C., Salmaso, S., Bruzzone, M., Bella, A. & Crovari, P. (2002). Epidemiology of measles, mumps and rubella in Italy. *Epidemiology and Infection, 129*, 543–550.

Galanes, G. J. & Carmack, H. J. (2013). 'He's really setting an example': Student contributions to the learning environment. *Communication Studies, 64*(1), 49–65.

Galende, N. (2012). The role of parents' distancing strategies in the development of five-year-old children's theory of mind. *Early Child Development And Care, 182*(2), 207–220.

Galeote, M., Soto, P., Sebastián, E., Rey, R. & Checa, E. (2012). Vocabulary acquisition in children with Down syndrome: Normative data and developmental trends. Infancia y Aprendizaje, February, *35*(1), 111–122.

Gallahue, D. L. & Ozmun, J. (2005). *Understanding motor development: Infants, children, adolescents, adults*, 6th ed. Boston, MA: WCB/McGraw-Hill.

Garay, J. P. & Gray, J. W. (2012). Omics and therapy – A basis for precision medicine. *Molecular Oncology*, April, *6*(2), 128–139.

Garbarski, D. & Witt, W. P. (2013). Child health, maternal marital and socioeconomic factors, and maternal health. *Journal of Family Issues.* Apr, *34*(4), 484–509.

Garcia, Mª. D. & Pastor, E. (2006). Dimensions for analysing shared parent–child play interaction and management. *Infancia y Aprendizaje, 29*, 177–190.

Garcia-Mila, M., Gilabert, S. & Rojo, N. (2011). El cambio estratégico en la adquisición del conocimiento: la metodología microgenética. Strategy change in knowledge acquisition: The microgenetic methodology. *Infancia y Aprendizaje*, May, *34*(2), 169–180.

Gardiner, H. W. & Komitzki, C. (2005). *Lives across cultures: Cross-cultural human development.* Boston, MA: Allyn & Bacon.

Gardner, H. (1983). *Frames of mind: The theory of multiple intelligences.* New York: Basic Books.

Gardner, H. (1993). *Frames of mind.* London: Heinemann.

Gardner, H. (1998). A reply to Perry D. Klein's 'Multiplying the problems of intelligence by eight'. *Canadian Journal of Education, 23*, 96–102.

Gardner, H. (1999). *Intelligence reframed: Multiple intelligences for the 21st century.* New York: Basic Books.

Gardner, H. & Seana, M. (2006). The science of multiple intelligences theory: A response to Lynn Waterhouse. *Educational Psychologist, 41*, 227–232.

Garmendia, J. V. & De Sanctis, J. B. (2012). Perspectives of new therapies for endometriosis. Recent patents on endocrine. *Metabolic & Immune Drug Discovery, 6*(3), 218–223.

Gartrell, D. & Sonsteng, K. (2008). Promote physical activity – It's proactive guidance. *Young Children, 63*, 51–53.

Gaston, A., Cramp, A. G. & Prapavessis, H. (2012). Pregnancy – should women put up their feet or lace up their running shoes?: Self-presentation and the exercise stereotype phenomenon during pregnancy. *Journal of Sport & Exercise Psychology.* Apr, *34*(2), 223–237.

Geary, D. C. & Bjorklund, D. F. (2000). Evolutionary developmental psychology. *Child Development, 71*, 57–65.

Geary, D. C., Byrd-Craven, J., Hoard, M. K., Vigil, J. & Numtee, C. (2003). Evolution and development of boys' social behavior. *Developmental Review, 23*, 444–470.

Gelman, R. (1972). Logical capacity of very young children: Number invariance rules. *Child Development, 43*, 75–90.

Gentile, A. M. (1972). A working model of skill acquisition with application to teaching. *Quest, 17*, 3–23.

Georgalidou, M. (2008). The contextual parameters of linguistic choice: Greek children's preferences for the formation of directive speech acts. *Journal of Pragmatics, 40*, 72–94.

George, D. (1997). *The challenge of the able child.* London: David Fulton.

Georghiades, P. (2004). From the general to the situated: Three decades of metacognition. *International Journal of Science Education, 26*, 365–383.

Georgiadis, F., Koutsouri, A. & Zisimos, A. (2011). Educational interventions on 'Otherness': Cooperative learning through intercultural children's literature in Muslim minority schools in Greece. *Journal of Muslim Minority Affairs*, March, *31*(1), 31–48.

Gershuny, J. (2000). *Changing times: Work and leisure in postindustrial society*. Oxford: Oxford University Press.

Gesell, A. (1928). *Infancy and human growth*. New York: MacMillan Company.

Gesell, A. (1954). The ontogenesis of infant behaviour. In L. Carmichael (Ed.), *Manual of child psychology*. New York: Wiley.

Getchell, N., Pabreja, P., Neeld, K. & Carrio, V. (2007). Comparing children with and without dyslexia on the movement assessment battery for children and the test of gross motor development. *Perceptual & Motor Skills, 105*, 207–214.

Gewirtz, J. L. & Peláez-Nogueras, M. (1992). B. F. Skinner's legacy to human infant behavior and development. *American Psychologist, 47*, 1411–1422.

Gibson, E. J. (1969). *Principles of perceptual learning and development*. New York: Appleton-Century-Crofts.

Gibson, E. J. (1988). Exploratory behaviour in the development of perceiving, acting, and the acquiring of knowledge. *Annual Review of Psychology, 39*, 1–41.

Gibson, E. J. & Walk, R. D. (1960). The 'visual cliff'. *Scientific American, 202*, 64–71.

Gibson, J. J. (1966). *The Senses considered as perceptual systems*. Boston: Houghton Mifflin.

Gibson, J. J. (1979). *The ecological approach to visual perception*. Boston, MA: Houghton Mifflin.

Giedd, J. N., Blumenthal, J., Jeffries, N. O., Rajapaske, J. C., Vaituzis, C. & Liu, H. (1999). Development of the corpus callosum during childhood and adolescence: A longitudinal MRI study. *Progress in Neuro-Psychopharmacology and Biological Psychiatry, 23*, 571–588.

Gilbert, J. (2008). Reading between the lines: Gender may matter. *ESL Magazine, 61*, 16–20.

Gillies, R. M. (2000). The maintenance of co-operative and helping behaviours in co-operative groups. *British Journal of Educational Psychology, 70*, 97–111.

Gillies, R. M. & Boyle, M. (2008). Teachers' discourse during cooperative learning and their perceptions of this pedagogical practice. *Teaching & Teacher Education, 24*, 1333–1348.

Gingras, J. L., Mitchell, E. A. & Grattan, K. E. (2005). Fetal homologue of infant crying. *Archives of Disease in Childhood – Fetal and Neonatal Edition, 90*, F415–F418.

Glasson, E. J. (2004). Autism linked to birth problems. *Archives of General Psychiatry, 61*, 618–627.

Gleitman, L. R. (1990). The structural sources of verb meanings. *Language Acquisition, 1*, 3–55.

Gnadinger, C. M. (2008). Peer-mediated instruction: Assisted performance in the primary classroom. *Teachers & Teaching, 14*, 129–142.

Goddard, S. (2005). *Reflexes, learning and behaviour: A window into the child's mind: A non-invasive approach to solving learning and behavior problems*, 3rd rev. ed. Eugene, OR: Fern Ridge Press.

Goddard Blythe, S. (2001). *Neurological dysfunction as a significant factor in children diagnosed with dyslexia*. Proceedings of the 5th International British Dyslexia Association Conference, University of York, UK.

Goh, H-T., Kantak, S. & Sullivan, K. (2012). Movement pattern and parameter learning in children: Effects of feedback frequency. *Research Quarterly for Exercise & Sport, 83*(2), 346–352.

Gojman, S., Millán, S., Carlson, E., Sánchez, G., Rodarte, A., González, P. & Hernández, G. (2012). Intergenerational relations of attachment: A research synthesis of urban/rural Mexican samples. *Attachment & Human Development, 14*(6), 553–566.

Goldberg, T. & Weinberger, D. (2004). Genes and the parsing of cognitive processes. *Trends in Cognitive Sciences, 8*, 325–335.

Goldschmied, E. & Jackson, S. (1994). *People under three: Young children in day care*. London: Routledge.

Goldstein, B. A., Fabiano, L. & Washington, P. S. (2005). Phonological skills in predominantly English-speaking, predominantly Spanish-speaking, and Spanish–English bilingual children. *Language, Speech & Hearing Services in Schools, 36*, 201–218.

Goleman, D. (1996). *Emotional intelligence*. London: Bloomsbury.

Goleman, D. (2006). *Emotional intelligence: Why it can matter more than IQ*, 10th anniversary edition. New York: Bantam Books.

Goodwyn, S., Acredolo, L. & Brown, C. (2000). Impact of symbolic gesturing on early language development. *Journal of Nonverbal Behavior, 24*, 81–103.

Goossens, F. A. & van Ijzendoorn, M. H. (1990). Quality of infants' attachments to professional caregivers: Relation to infant–parent attachment and day-care characteristics. *Child Development, 61*, 832–837.

Gopnik, A. & Slaughter, V. (1991). Young children's understanding of changes in their mental states. *Child Development, 62*, 98–110.

Gould, J. L. & Keeton, W. T. (1996). *Biological science*, 6th ed. New York: Norton.

Graddol, D., Cheshire, J. & Swann, J. (1994). *Describing language*, 2nd ed. Buckingham: Open University Press.

Graham, L. B. & Robinson, E. M. (2007). Project adventure and self concept of academically talented adolescent boys. *Physical Educator, 64*, 114–122.

Grandgeorge, M., Deleau, M., Lemonnier, E. & Hausberger, M. (2011). The Strange Animal Situation Test. *Anthrozoos, 24*(4), 393–408.

Granke, J. (2007). Doors of perception: Sensory integration for Montessori classrooms. *NAMTA Journal, 32*, 231–243.

Granot, D. & Mayseless, O. (2001). Attachment security and adjustment to school in middle childhood. *International Journal of Behavioral Development, 25*, 530–541.

Granrud, C. (2009). Development of size constancy in children: A test of the metacognitive theory. *Attention, Perception, and Psychophysics, 71*(3), 644–654.

Goldacre, B. (2006). Brain Gym exercises do pupils no favours. *Guardian*, 18 March.

Green, N. (2006). Everyday life in distance education: One family's home schooling experience. *Distance Education, 27*, 27–44.

Griezel, L., Finger, L. R., Bodkin-Andrews, G. H., Craven, R. G. & Yeung, A. S. (2012). Uncovering the structure of and gender and developmental differences in cyber bullying. *Journal of Educational Research. 105*(6), 442–455.

Griswold, O. (2007). Achieving authority: Discursive practices in Russian girls' pretend play. *Research on Language & Social Interaction, 40*, 291–319.

Gross, R., Brammli-Greenberg, S., Rabinowitz, J., Gordon, B. & Afek, A. (2011). Disparities in obesity temporal trends of Israeli adolescents by ethnic origin. *International Journal of Pediatric Obesity, 6*(2), p. e154–e161.

Grusec, J. E. & Lytton, H. (1988). *Social development: History, theory and research*. New York: Springer-Verlag.

Guerin, D. W., Gottfried, A. W. & Thomas, C. W. (1997). Difficult temperament and behavior problems: A longitudinal study from 1.5 to 12 years. *International Journal of Behavioral Development, 21*, 71–90.

Guilfoyle, N. & Mistry, M. (2013). How effective is role play in supporting speaking and listening for pupils with English as an additional language in the Foundation Stage? *Education 3–13, 41*(1), 63–70.

Guishard-Pine, J. (2006). Men in black families: The impact of fathering on children's development. *Race Equality Teaching, 24*, 45–48.

Güneş, E. & Nalçaci, E. (2006). Directional preferences in turning behavior of boys and girls. *Perceptual & Motor Skills, 102*, 352–357.

Gunnar, M. D. (2000). Early adversity and the development of stress reactivity and regulation. In C. A. Nelson (Ed.), *Minnesota Symposia on Child Psychology* (vol. 31, pp 163–200). Hillsdale, NJ: Erlbaum.

Gupta, A. F. (1997). When mother-tongue education is not preferred. *Journal of Multilingual and Multicultural Development*, November, *18*(6), 496–506.

Guralnick, M. J., Hammond, M. A., Connor, R. T. & Neville, B. (2006). Stability, change, and correlates of the peer relationships of young children with mild developmental delays. *Child Development, 77*, 312–324.

Gwiazda, J. J. & Birch, E. E. (2001). Perceptual development: Vision. In E. B. Goldstein (Ed.), *Blackwell handbook of perception* (pp 636–668). Oxford: Blackwell.

Hadjioannou, X. & Loizou, E. (2011). Talking about books with young children: Analyzing the discursive nature of one-to-one booktalks. *Early Education and Development*, January, *22*(1), 53–76.

Hahn, A. C., Xiao, D., Sprengelmeyer, R. & Perrett, D. I. (2013). Gender differences in the incentive salience of adult and infant faces. *The Quarterly Journal of Experimental Psychology, 66*(1), 200–208.

Haight, W. L. & Miller, P. J. (1993). *Pretending at home: Early development in a sociocultural context*. Albany: State University of New York Press.

Hainline, L. & Abramov, I. (1992). Assessing visual development: Is infant vision good enough? In C. Rovee-Collier & B. L. P. Lipsitt (Eds), *Advances in infancy research*, Vol. 7. Norwood, NJ: Ablex.

Hall, G. S. (1891a). The contents of children's minds on entering school. *Pedagogical Seminary, 1*, 139–173. (Chapter 1).

Hall, G. S. (1891b). *The new movement in education*. New York.

Halverson, H. M. (1931). An experimental study of prehension in infants by means of systematic cinema records. *Genetic Psychology Monographs, 10*, 107–286.

Hamer, R. D. & Norcia, A. M. (1994). The development of motion sensitivity during the first year of life. *Vision Research, 34*, 2387–2402.

Hamilton, S. S. (2002). Evaluation of clumsiness in children. *American Family Physician, 66*, 1435–1440.

Hampton, T. (2007). Common gene variant linked to obesity. *JAMA: Journal of the American Medical Association, 297*, 2063–2064.

Hamston, J. & Love, K. (2003). Reading relationships: Parents, boys, and reading as cultural practice. *Australian Journal of Language & Literacy, 26*, 44.

Hannaford, C. (1995). *Smart moves. Why learning is not all in your head*. Arlington, VA: Great Ocean Publishers.

Harakeh, Z., Scholte, R. H. J., Vries, H. de & Engels, R. C. M. E. (2005). Parental rules and communication: Their association with adolescent smoking. *Addiction, 100*, 862–870.

Hargie, O. & Dickson, D. (2004). *Skilled interpersonal communication: Research, theory and practice*. Hove: Routledge.

Hargreaves, D. H. (1996). *Teaching as a research based profession: Possibilities and prospects*. London: Teacher Training Agency.

Harkness, S. & Super, C. (1992). Parental ethnotheories in action. In I. E. Siegel (Ed.), *Parental belief systems: The psychological consequences for children*. Hillsdale, NJ: Erlbaum.

Harkness, S. & Super, C. M. (2001). Culture and parenting. In M. H. Bornstein (Ed.), *Handbook of parenting* (2nd ed.). Hillsdale, NJ: Erlbaum.

Harlow, H., McGaugh, J. L. & Thompson, R. F. (1971). *Psychology*. San Francisco, CA: Albion Publication Company.

Harlow, H. F. & Zimmerman, R. R. (1959). Affectional responses in the infant monkey. *Science, 130*, 421–432.

Harris, F., Law, J. & Kermani, S. (2003). *The second implementation of the Sure Start language measure*. London: City University.

Harris, M. & Butterworth, G. (2002). Developmental psychology: A student's handbook. Hove: Psychology Press.

Harris, P. & Leevers, H. (2000). Pretending, imagery and self-awareness in autism. In Baron-Cohen, S., Tager-Flusberg, H. & Cohen, D. J. (Eds), *Understanding other minds: Perspectives from developmental cognitive neuroscience*. Oxford: Oxford University Press.

Harris, P. L. & Kavanaugh, R. D. (1993). Young children's understanding of pretense. *Monograph of the Society for Research in Child Development, 58*.

Harrison, P. J. & Owen, M. J. (2003). Genes for schizophrenia? Recent findings and their pathophysiological implications. *Lancet*, *361*, 417–419.

Hart, B. & Rilsey, T. R. (1995). *Meaningful differences in the everyday experience of young American children*. Baltimore, MD: Paul H. Brookes.

Harwood, D. (2008). The teasing phenomenon: Preschool siblings' experiences with teasing within their relationships. *Canadian Children*, *33*, 10–16.

Hauner, H., Vollhardt, C., Schneider, K. T., Zimmermann, A., Schuster, T. & Amann-Gassner, U. (2009). The impact of nutritional fatty acids during pregnancy and lactation on early human adipose tissue development. *Annals of Nutrition & Metabolism*, *54*(2), 97–103.

Hayne, H. (2004). Infant memory development: Implications for childhood amnesia. *Developmental Review*, *24*, 33–73.

Hedlund, G. & Lindberg, M. (2012). New steering methods in regional policy – Transforming the alliance of 'state feminism'. *Women's Studies International Forum*, May, *35*(3), 166–172.

Heffner, L. (2004). Advanced, maternal age – How old is too old? *New England Journal of Medicine*, *351*(19), 1927–29.

Hendrix, M. (2008). Picky eaters. *Exchange*, *180*, 90–92.

Henry, L. A., Messer, D., Luger-Klein, S. & Crane, L. (2012). Phonological, visual, and semantic coding strategies and children's short-term picture memory span. *The Quarterly Journal of Experimental Psychology*, October, *65*(10), 2033–2053.

Hepper, P. (2004). *Do human embryonic movements build brain symmetries?* FENS Forum Abstracts, vol. 2. Forum of European Neuroscience, Lisbon, July.

Hepper, P. G. (1996). Foetal memory does it exist? *Acta Pediatrica*, Supplement *416*, 16–20.

Herman-Giddens, M. E., Kaplowitz, P. B. & Wasserman, R. (2004). Navigating the recent articles on girls' puberty in pediatrics: What do we know and where do we go from here? *Pediatrics*, *113*, 911–917.

Hernandez, D. C. (2012). Gestational weight gain as a predictor of longitudinal body mass index transitions among socioeconomically disadvantaged women. *Journal of Women's Health*, *21*(10), 1082–1090.

Hernández-Martínez, C., Canals Sans, J. & Fernández-Ballart, J. (2011). Parents' perceptions of their neonates and their relation to infant development. *Child: Care, Health & Development*. Jul, *37*(4), 484–492.

Hernandez-Reif, M., Field, T., Largie, S., Diego, M., Manigat, N., Seoanes, J. & Bornstein, J. (2005). Cerebral palsy symptoms in children decreased following massage therapy. *Early Child Development & Care*, *175*, 445–456.

Hernandez-Reif, M., Field, T., Largie, S., Mora, D., Bornstein, J. & Waldman, R. (2006). Children with Down's syndrome improved in motor functioning and muscle tone following massage therapy. *Early Child Development & Care*, *176*, 395–410.

Hernstein, R. J. & Murray, C. (1994). *The bell curve: Intelligence and class structure in American life*. New York: Free Press.

Herrero, C., Martínez, R. & Villar, A. (2012). A newer human development index. *Journal of Human Development and Capabilities*, May, *13*(2), 247–268.

Herwig, R., Aanstad, P., Clark, M. & Lehrach, H. (2001). Statistical evaluation of differential expression on cDNA nylon arrays with replicated experiments. *Nucleic Acids Research*, *29*, e117.

Hewahi, N. & Baraka, A. (2012). Emotion recognition model based on facial expressions, ethnicity and gender using back propagation neural network. *International Journal of Technology Diffusion (IJTD)*, *3*(1), 33–43.

Hibi, M. & Shimizu, T. (2012). Development of the cerebellum and cerebellar neural circuits. *Developmental Neurobiology*, *72*(3), 282–301.

Hill, J. & Maughan, B. (2001). *Conduct disorders in childhood and adolescence*. Cambridge: Cambridge University Press.

Hills, L. (2007). Friendship, physicality, and physical education: An exploration of the social and embodied dynamics of girls' physical education experiences. *Sport, Education & Society*, *12*, 335–354.

Hobson, P. (2002). *The cradle of thought*. Basingstoke: Macmillan.

Hodkin, B. (1981). Language effects in assessment of class-inclusion ability. *Child Development*, *52*, 470–478.

Hoff, L. (2001). *Acoustic characterisation of contrast agents for medical ultrasound imaging*. Dordrecht: Kluwer Academic Publishing.

Hoffman, M. L. (2000). *Empathy and moral development*. New York: Cambridge University Press.

Højen, A. & Flege, J. E. (2006). Early learners' discrimination of second-language vowels. *Journal of the Acoustical Society of America*, *119*, 3072–3084.

Holden, G. W. (1997). *Parents and the dynamics of child rearing*. Boulder, CO: Westview Press.

Holding, S. (2002). Current state of screening for Down's syndrome. *Annals of Clinical Biochemistry*, *39*, 1–11.

Hollich, G. J., Hirsh-Pasek, K. & Golinkoff, R. M. (2000). Breaking the language barrier: An emergentist coalition model for the origins of word learning. *Monographs of the Society for Research in Child Development*, *65*(3), Serial 262.

Holmes, L. B. (2011). Human teratogens: Update 2010 *Birth Defects Research Part A: Clinical and Molecular Teratology*, *91*(1), 1–7.

Holst, M., Eswaran, H., Lowery, C. L., Murphy, P., Norton, J. D. & Preissl, H. (2005). Development of auditory evoked fields in human fetuses and newborns: A longitudinal MEG study. *Clinical Neurophysiology*, April, 1–7.

Holtgraves, T. (2008). Automatic intention recognition in conversation processing. *Journal of Memory & Language*, *58*, 627–645.

Honda, Y., Nakato, E., Otsuka, Y., Kanazawa, S., Kojima, S., Yamaguchi, M. K. & Kakigi, R. (2010). How do infants perceive scrambled face: A near-infrared spectroscopic study. *Brain Research*, *1308*(6), 137–146.

Hong, R. Y., Paunonen, S. V. & Slade, H. P. (2008). Big Five personality factors and the prediction of behavior: A multitrait–multimethod approach. *Personality & Individual Differences*, *45*, 160–166.

Honig, A. S. (2007). The power of sensory experiences. *Early Childhood Today*, *21*, Issue 6.

Honig, A. S. (2005). Crying out loud. *Parent & Child*, *13*, 27–28.

Honstead, C. (1968). The developmental theory of Jean Piaget. In J. L. Frost (Ed.), *Early childhood education rediscovered*. New York: Holt, Rinehart & Winston.

Hooiveld, M., Haveman, W., Roskes, K., Bretveld, R., Burstyn, I. & Roeleveld, N. (2006). Adverse reproductive outcomes among male painters with occupational exposure to organic solvents. *Occupational and Environmental Medicine*, *63*, 538–544.

Hopkins, B. & Westra, T. (1988). Maternal handling and motor development: An intracultural study. *Genetic Psychology Monographs*, *14*, 377–420.

Horne, R. S. C., Ferens, D., Watts, A.-M., Vitkovic, J., Lacey, B., Andrew, S., Cranage, S. M., Chau, B., Greaves, R. & Adamson, T. (2002). Effects of maternal tobacco smoking, sleeping position, and sleep state on arousal in healthy term infants. *Archives of Disease in Childhood Fetal and Neonatal Edition*, *87*, F100–F105.

Horwitz, S. (2005). The functions of the family in the great society. *Cambridge Journal of Economics*, *29*, 669–684.

Howard, J., Jenvey, V. & Hill, C. (2006). Children's categorisation of play and learning based on social context. *Early Child Development and Care*, *176*(3), 379–393.

Howard-Jones, P. (2008). Exploding myths. *Times Educational Supplement*. 4/11/2008, Issue 4783, special section, 36–37.

Howe, M. & Griffey, H. (1994). *Give your child a better start*. London: Michael Joseph.

Hruska, B. (2007). Part I: Advancing the conversation: 'She my friend': Implications of friend ideologies, identities, and relationships for bilingual kindergarteners. *Multicultural Perspectives*, *9*, 3–12.

Hsieh, F. I. (2011). The conceptualization of emotion events in three formosan languages: Kavalan, Paiwan, and Saisiyat. *Oceanic Linguistics*, *50*(1), 65–92.

Hubal, R. C., Fishbein, D. H., Sheppard, M. S., Paschall, M. J., Eldreth, D. L. & Hyde, C. T. (2008). How do varied populations interact with embodied conversational agents? *Computers in Human Behavior*, *24*, 1104–1138.

Huesmann, L. R., Moise-Titus, J., Podolski, C. L. & Eron, L. (2003). Longitudinal relations between children's exposure to TV violence and their aggressive and violent behaviour in young adulthood: 1977–1992. *Developmental Psychology*, *39*, 201–221.

Hughes, M. (1975). Egocentrism in pre-school children. The University of Edinburgh: Unpublished doctoral thesis. Edinburgh.

Hughes, M. W. H. (2011). Developmental psychology and education. In Gillibrand, R., Lam, V. & O'Donnell, V. L. *Developmental Psychology* Harlow: Pearson Education.

Hughes, M. W. H. & Longman, D. (2005). *Interactive digital display boards and class teaching: Interactive or just another epidiascope?* British Educational Research Association Conference, University of Glamorgan, 15–17 September.

Huizink, A. C., Robles de Medina, P. G., Mulder, E. J. H., Visser, G. H. A. & Buitelaar, J. K. (2003). Stress during pregnancy is associated with developmental outcome in infancy. *Journal of Child Psychology and Psychiatry (formerly Journal of Child Psychology and Psychiatry and Allied Disciplines)*, *44*, 810–818.

Hulse, G. K., Milne, E., English, D. R. & Holman, C. D. J. (1998). Assessing the relationship between maternal opiate use and antepartum haemorrhage. *Addiction*, *93*, 1553–1558.

Humphrey, N. (1986). *The inner eye*. London: Vintage.

Humphrey, N. (1984). *Consciousness regained*. Oxford: Oxford University Press.

Humphries, C. & Jobson, L. (2012). Short report: Influence of culture and trauma history on autobiographical memory specificity. *Memory*, *20*(8), 915–922.

Huttenlocher, P. R. (1990). Morphometric study of human cerebral cortex development. *Neuropsychologia*, *28*, 517–527.

Hyatt, K. J. (2007). Brain Gym: Building stronger brains or wishful thinking? *Remedial & Special Education*, *28*, 117–124.

Hyde, J. S., Fennema, E. & Lamon, S. J. (1990). Gender differences in mathematics performance: A meta-analysis. *Psychological Bulletin*, *107*, 139–155.

Immordino-Yang, M. H. (2008). All smoke and mirror neurons: Goals as sociocultural and emotional organizers of perception and action in learning. *Mind, Brain & Education*, *2*, 67–73.

Iñiguez, C., Ballester, F., Amorós, R., Murcia, M., Plana, A. & Rebagliato, M. (2012). Active and passive smoking during pregnancy and ultrasound measures of fetal growth in a cohort of pregnant women. *Journal of Epidemiology & Community Health*, *66*(6), 563–570.

Innes, P. (2006). The interplay of genres, gender, and language ideology among the Muskogee. *Language in Society*, *35*, 231–259.

International Human Genome Sequencing Consortium (2001). Initial sequencing and analysis of the human genome. *Nature*, *409*, 860–921.

IOTS (2012). www.iaso.org/resources/obesity-data-portal/ (accessed 14 October 2012).

Isabella, R. A. (1993). Origins of attachment: Maternal interactive behaviour across the first year. *Child Development*, *64*, 605–621.

Isenberg, J. P. & Quisenberry, N. (2002). *Play: Essential for all children*. A Position Paper of the Association for Childhood Education International. Olney, MD: Association for Childhood Education International.

Ivanov, V. K. & Geake, J. G. (2003). The Mozart effect and primary school children. *Psychology of Music*, *31*, 405–413.

Iy, A. (2006). Attachment: Stability and change across the life span. *Infancia y Aprendizaje*, *29*, 9–23.

Izard, C. E. (1979). The maximally discriminative facial movement scoring system. Unpublished manuscript, University of Delaware.

Izard, C. E., Schultz, D. & Ackerman, B. P. (1997). *Emotion knowledge, social competence, and behaviour problems in disadvantaged children.* Paper presented at the biennial meeting of the Society for Research in Child Development, Washington, DC.

JAACAP (2006). Thinking about children's attachments. *Journal of the American Academy of Child & Adolescent Psychiatry*, *45*, 848.

Jackson, C. S. & Tlauka, M. (2004). Route-learning and the Mozart effect. *Psychology of Music*, *32*, 213–220.

Jacobse, A. & Harskamp, E. (2012). Towards efficient measurement of metacognition in mathematical problem solving. *Metacognition and Learning*, *7*(2), 133–149.

Jain, A. (2004). *What works for obesity? A summary of the research behind obesity interventions.* BMJ Knowledge. London. www.unitedhealthfoundation.org/obesity.pdf

Jakupcak, M. (2003). Masculine gender role stress and men's fear of emotions as predictors of self-reported aggression and violence. *Violence and Victims*, *18*(5), 533–541.

Januszka, C. & Dixon-Krauss, L. (2008). Class size: A battle between accountability and quality instruction. *Childhood Education*, *84*, 167–170.

Jarry, J. L. & Kossert, A. L. (2007). Self-esteem threat combined with exposure to thin media images leads to body image compensatory self-enhancement. *Body Image*, *4*(1), 39–50.

Jarvis, C. (2004). *Physical examination & health assessment*, 4th ed. St Louis, MO: Elsevier.

Jegelevičienė, S. (2012). The influence of prematurity on the language development of an extremely low birth weight infant: Case analysis. *Special Education*, Issue 2, 201–215.

Jensen, A. (2000). Review of: *Apes, language and the human mind*, by S. Savage-Rumbaugh, S. G. Shanker and T. J. Taylor. *Notes on Linguistics*, *3*, 38–40.

Jeynes, W. H. & Littell, S. W. (2000). A meta-analysis of studies examining the effect of whole language instruction on the literacy of low-SES students. *Elementary School Journal*, *101*, 21–33.

Jin, M. (2012). Maternal sensitivity and infant attachment security in Korea: Cross-cultural validation of the Strange Situation. *Attachment & Human Development*, *14*(1), 33–44.

Johnson, E. I. & Easterling, B. (2012). Understanding unique effects of parental incarceration on children: Challenges, progress, and recommendations. *Journal of Marriage and Family*, April, *74*(2), 342–356.

Johnson, F., Pratt, M. & Wardle, J. (2012). Dietary restraint and self-regulation in eating behavior. *International Journal of Obesity* (formerly *International Journal of Obesity and Related Metabolic Disorders*), May, *36*(5), 665–674.

Johnson, M. H. (2000). Functional brain development in infants: Elements of an interactive specialization framework. *Child Development*, *71*, 75–81.

Johnson, M. H. & Morton, J. (1991). *Biology and cognitive development: The case of face recognition.* Oxford: Blackwell.

Johnson, S. P. (2001). Neurophysiological and psychophysical approaches to visual development. In A. F. Kalverboer & A. Gramsbergen (Eds), *Handbook of brain and behaviour in human development. IV. Development of perception and cognition.* Amsterdam: Elsevier.

Johnson, S. P., Bremner, J. G., Slater, A., Mason, U., Foster, K. & Cheshire, A. (2003). Infants' perception of object trajectories. *Child Development*, *23*, 461–483.

Jones, H. G. (2007). Life expectancy. *Kenyon Review*, *29*, 154–172.

Jones, K., Daley, D., Hutchings, J., Bywater, T. & Eames, C. (2008). Efficacy of the Incredible Years Programme as an early intervention for children with conduct problems and ADHD: Long-term follow-up. *Child Care, Health & Development*, *34*, 380–390.

Jones, T. A., Klintsova, A. Y., Kilman, V. L., Sirevaag, A. M. & Greenough, W. T. (1997). Induction of multiple synapses by experience in the visual cortex of adult rats. *Neurobiology of Learning and Memory*, *68*, 13–20.

JOPERD (2008). If an interscholastic sport is not offered for boys (e.g., volleyball), should the boys be allowed to participate on the girls' team? *The Journal of Physical Education, Recreation & Dance*, *79*, 12–16.

Jordan, A., Hersey, J., McDivitt, J. & Heitzler, C. (2006). Reducing children's television-viewing time: A qualitative study of parents and their children. *Pediatrics.* November 1, 2006; *118*(5), 1303–1310.

Joutsenvirta, M. & Uusitalo, L. (2010). Cultural competences: An important resource in the industry–NGO Dialog. *Journal of Business Ethics*, *91*(3).

Judd, S. J. (2007). *Congenital disorders sourcebook.* Detroit, MI: Omnigraphics.

Jurkowski, J., Mills, L. G., Lawson, H., Bovenzi, M., Quartimon, R. & Davison, K. (2012). Engaging low-income parents in childhood obesity prevention from start to finish: A case study. *Journal of Community Health* (2012) Preprints, 1–11.

Jusczyk, P. W., Friederic, A. D., Wessels, J., Svenkerund, V. Y. & Jusczyk, A. M. (1993). Infants' sensitivity to the sound patterns of native language words. *Journal of Memory and Language*, *32*, 402–420.

Kagan, J. (1989). *Unstable ideas: Temperament, cognition, and self.* Cambridge, MA: Cambridge University Press.

Kagan, J., Arcus, D., Snidman, N., Feng, W. Y., Hendler, J. & Greene, S. (1994). Reactivity in infants: A cross-national comparison. *Developmental Psychology*, *30*, 342–345.

Kagan, J., Reznick, J. S., Clarke, C., Snidman, N. & Garcia-Coll, C. (1984). Behavioral inhibition to the unfamiliar. *Child Development*, *55*, 2212–2225.

Kagitcibasi, C. (2012). Sociocultural change and integrative syntheses in human development: Autonomous-related self and social-cognitive competence. *Child Development Perspectives*, *6*(1), 5–11.

Källén, K. (2001). The impact of maternal smoking during pregnancy on delivery outcome. *The European Journal of Public Health*, *11*, 329–333.

Kaltiala-Heino, R., Kosunen, E. & Rimpelä, M. (2003). Pubertal timing, sexual behaviour and self-reported depression in middle adolescence. *Journal of Adolescence*, *26*, 531.

Kanakogi, Y. & Itakura, S. (2010). The link between perception and action in early infancy: From the viewpoint of the direct-matching hypothesis. *Japanese Psychological Research*, *52*(2), 121–131.

Kangas, S., Määttä, K. & Uusiautti, S. (2012). Alone and in a group: Ethnographic research on autistic children's play. *International Journal of Play*, March, *1*(1), 37–50.

Kao, G. (2000). Psychological well-being and educational achievement among immigrant youth. In D. J. Herandez (Ed.), *Children of immigrants: Health, adjustment, and public assistance*. Washington, DC: National Academy Press.

Kappe, R. & Flier, H. (2012). Predicting academic success in higher education: what's more important than being smart? *European Journal of Psychology of Education*, *27*(4), 605–619.

Karass, J. & Braungart-Rieker, J. M. (2004). Infant negative emotionality and attachment: Implications for preschool intelligence. *International Journal of Behavioral Development*, *28*, 221–229.

Kassis, W. (2007). Uncontrolled or unbridled? An Aristotelian classification coupled with Fritz's thesis concerning the competence to control violence among extensive users of violence-oriented computer games. *Zeitschrift für Paedagogik*, *2*, 223–242.

Katz, J., West, K. P., Khatry, S. K., LeClerq, S. C., Christian, P., Pradhan, E. K. & Shrestha, S. R. (2001). Twinning rates and survival of twins in rural Nepal. *International Journal of Epidemiology*, *30*, 802–807.

Kay, J. (2006). *Managing behaviour in the early years*. London: Continuum International Publishing Group.

Kaye, K. (1984). *The mental and social life of babies*. Chicago, IL: University of Chicago Press.

Kaye, K. L. & Bower, T. G. R. (1994). Learning and inter-modal transfer of information in newborns. *Psychological Science*, *5*, 286–288.

Kazlauskienė, A. (2007). Statistical skills in the content of education in Lithuania and foreign countries. *Pedagogy Studies*, *87*, 107–111.

Keddie, A. (2004). Research with young children: The use of an affinity group approach to explore the social dynamics of peer culture. *British Journal of Sociology of Education*, *25*(1), 35–51.

Keenan, K. & Shaw, D. (1997). Developmental and social influences on young girls' early problem behaviour. *Psychological Bulletin*, *121*, 95–113.

Keenan, T. (2002). *An introduction to child development*. London: Sage.

Keenan, T. & Harvey, M. (1998). What's in that child's mind? *New Zealand Science Monthly*, *9*, 6–8.

Kegl, J., Senghas, A. & Coppola, M. (1999). Creation through construct: Sign language emergence and sign language change in Nicaragua. In M. DeGrasf (Ed.), *Language creation and language change: Creolization, diachrony and development*. Cambridge, MA: MIT Press.

Kellman, P. J. & von Hofsten, C. (1992). The world of the moving infant: Perception of motion, stability, and space. In C. Rovee-Collier & L. P. Lipsitt (Eds), *Advances in infancy research*, Vol. 7. Norwood, NJ: Ablex.

Kember, S. (2001). Resisting the new evolutionism. *Women: A cultural review*, *12*, 1–8.

Kemmis, S. (2010). Research for praxis: knowing doing. *Pedagogy, Culture & Society*, March, *18*(1), 9–27.

Kemple, K. M. & Nissenberg, S. A. (2000). Nurturing creativity in early childhood education: Families are part of it. *Early Childhood Education Journal*, *28*, 67–71.

Kennedy, E. J. & Flynn, M. C. (2003). Training phonological awareness skills in children with Down syndrome. *Research in Developmental Disabilities*, *24*(1), 44–57.

Kenner, C. (2008). Bilingual learning for second and third generation children language, *Culture and Curriculum*, August, *21*(2), 120–137.

Kenrick, D. T. (1994). Evolutionary social psychology: From sexual selection to social cognition. *Advances in Experimental Social Psychology*, *26*, 75–121.

Kephart, N. C. (1971). *The slow learner in the classroom*. Columbus, OH: Merrill.

Kerkhof, G. F., Leunissen, R. W. J. & Hokken-Koelega, A. C. S. (2012). Early origins of the metabolic syndrome: Role of small size at birth, early postnatal weight gain, and adult IGF-I. *The Journal of Clinical Endocrinology & Metabolism*, *97*(8), 2637–2643.

Kerr, D. (1999). Changing the political culture: The advisory group on education for citizenship and the teaching of democracy in schools. *Oxford Review of Education*, *25*, 25–35.

Khalsa, G. C. K., Morris, D. & Sifft, J. M. (1988). The effects of educational kinesiology on the static balance of learning-disabled students. *Perceptual and Motor Skills*, *67*, 51–54.

Kim, M. (2011). Play, drawing and writing: A case study of Korean–Canadian young children. *European Early Childhood Education Research Journal*, December, *19*(4), 483–500.

Kintraia, P. Ia, Devdariani, M. G., Kokhiia, M. I. & Mikadze, S. I. (2006). Diagnostic value of particularities of circadian rhythms of sleep–wake cycle in early ontogenesis. *Georgian Med News*, *138*, 7–9.

Kinzler, K. D. & Shutts, K. (2008). Memory for 'mean' over 'nice': The influence of threat on children's face memory. *Cognition*, *107*, 775–783.

Kirsch, I., Lynn, S. J., Vigorito, M. & Miller, R. R. (2004). The role of cognition in classical and operant conditioning. *Journal of Clinical Psychology*, *60*, 369–392.

Kiuru, N., Aunola, K., Torppa, M., Lerkkanen, M., Poikkeus, A., Niemi, P. & Nurmi, J. (2012). The role of parenting styles and teacher interactional styles in children's reading and spelling development. *Journal of School Psychology*, *50*(6), 799–823.

Klahr, D. & Wallace, J. G. (1976). *Cognitive development: An information processing view*. Hillsdale, NJ: Lawrence Erlbaum Associates Inc.

Klimkeit, E. I., Sheppard, D. M., Lee, P. & Bradshaw, J. L. (2004). Bimanual coordination deficits in attention deficit/hyperactivity disorder (ADHD). *Journal of Clinical and Experimental Neuropsychology*, *26*, 999–1010.

Knapp, M. L. & Hall, J. A. (2007). *Nonverbal communication in human interaction* (5th ed.). Wadsworth: Thomas Learning.

Knobloch-Westerwick, S. & Hoplamazian, G. (2012). Gendering the self. *Communication Research*, *39*(3), 358–384.

Knoch, U. (2011). Investigating the effectiveness of individualized feedback to rating behavior – a longitudinal study. *Language Testing*, *28*(2), 179–200.

Knyazev, G. G., Slobodskaya, H. R., Safronova, M. V. & Kinsht, I. A. (2002). School adjustment and health in Russian adolescents. *Psychology, Health & Medicine*, 7, 143–155.

Kochanska, G., Aksan, N., Prisco, T. R. & Adams, E. E. (2008). Mother–child and father–child mutually responsive orientation in the first 2 years and children's outcomes at preschool age: Mechanisms of influence. *Child Development*, *79*, 30–44.

Kohlberg, L. (1966). A cognitive-developmental analysis of children's sex-role concepts and attitudes. In E. E. Maccoby (Ed.), *The development of sex differences*. Stanford, CA: Stanford University Press.

Kohlberg, L. (1969). Stage and sequence: The cognitive-developmental approach to socialization. In D. A. Goslin (Ed.), *Handbook of socialization theory and research* (pp 347–380). Chicago, IL: Rand McNally.

Kohlberg, L. (1984). *Essays on moral development (Vol. 2). The psychology of moral development*. San Francisco, CA: Harper & Row.

Kokkinaki, T. (2009). Emotional expressions during early infant–father conversations. *European Journal of Developmental Psychology*, *6*(6), 705–721.

Kolb, D. A. (1984). *Experiential learning*. Englewood Cliffs, NJ: Prentice-Hall.

Kordt-Thomas, C. & Lee, I. (2006). Floor time rethinking play in the classroom. *Young Children*, *61*, 86–90.

Kristensen, J., Vestergaard, M., Wisborg, K., Kesmodel, U. & Secher, N. J. (2005). Pre-pregnancy weight and the risk of stillbirth and neonatal death. *BJOG: An International Journal of Obstetrics and Gynaecology*, *112*, 403–408.

Kuczaj, S. A. & Hill, H. M. (2003). The development of language. In A. Slater & G. Bremner, *An introduction to developmental psychology*. Oxford: Blackwell Publishing.

Kuczmarski, R. J., Ogden, C. L., Grummer-Strawn, L. M. *et al.* (2000). *CDC growth charts: United States*. Advance Data from Vital and Health Statistics, No. 314. Hyattsville, MD: National Center for Health Statistics.

Kumpel, B. M. (2012). Pregnancy immunology and maternal alloimmune responses *ISBT Science Series*, *7*(1), 68–71.

Kunagaratnam, N. & Loh, S. (2010). Parental concerns regarding a centre-based early intervention programme for Down syndrome in Malaysia: A case study. *Asia Pacific Education Review*, December, *11*(4), 489–496.

Kunešová, M., Vignerová, J., Pařízková, J., Procházka, B., Braunerová, R., Riedlová, J., Zamrazilová, H., Hill, M., Bláha, P. & Šteflová, A. (2011). Long-term changes in prevalence of overweight and obesity in Czech 7-year-old children: Evaluation of different cut-off criteria of childhood obesity. *Obesity Reviews*, *12*(7), 483–491.

Kurtz-Costes, B., DeFreitas, S. C., Halle, T. G. & Kinlaw, C. R. (2011). Gender and racial favouritism in Black and White preschool girls. *British Journal of Developmental Psychology*, *29*(2), 270–287.

Kuschner, D. (2012). Play is natural to childhood but school is not: The problem of integrating play into the curriculum. *International Journal of Play*, December, *1*(3), 242–249.

Kwalombota, M. (2002). The effect of pregnancy in HIV-infected women. *AIDS Care*, *14*, 3, 431–433.

Laaksoharju, T., Rappe, E. & Kaivola, T. (2012). Garden affordances for social learning, play, and for building nature–child relationship. *Urban Forestry & Urban Greening*, January, *11*(2), 195–203.

Lagerros, Y. T. & Rössner, S. (2011). Managing obesity – from childhood and onwards. *International Journal of Pediatric Obesity*, *6*(1), Supplement 1, 74–78.

Lai, C.-Y. & Wu, C.-C. (2006). Using handhelds in a jigsaw cooperative learning environment. *Journal of Computer Assisted Learning*, *22*, 284–297.

Laible, D., Eye, J. & Carlo, G. (2008a). Dimensions of conscience in mid-adolescence: Links with social behavior, parenting, and temperament. *Journal of Youth & Adolescence*, *37*, 875–887.

Laible, D., Panfile, T. & Makariev, D. (2008b). The quality and frequency of mother–toddler conflict: Links with attachment and temperament. *Child Development*, *79*, 426–443.

Lamb, M. E. & Ahnert, L. (2006). Childcare and youth programs. In W. Damon & R. L. Lerner (Gen. Eds) and K. A. Renninger & I. E. Sigel (Vol. Eds), *Handbook of child psychology: Vol. 4. Child psychology and practice*. New York: Wiley.

Lamerz, A., Kuepper-Nybelen, J., Bruning, N., Wehle, C., Trost-Brinkhues, G., Brenner, H., Hebebrand, J. & Herpertz-Dahlmann, B. (2005). Prevalence of obesity, binge eating, and night eating in a cross-sectional field survey of 6-year-old children and their parents in a German urban population. *Journal of Child Psychology and Psychiatry (formerly Journal of Child Psychology and Psychiatry and Allied Disciplines)*, *46*, 385–393.

Lansford, J. E., Malone, P. S., Dodge, K. A., Pettit, G. S. & Bates, J. E. (2010). Developmental cascades of peer rejection, social information processing biases, and aggression during middle childhood. *Development and Psychopathology*, *22*(3), 593–602.

Larsen, C. C., Bonde Larsen, K., Bogdanovic, N., Laursen, H., Graem, N., Samuelsen, G. B. & Pakkenberg, B. (2006). Total number of cells in the human newborn telencephalic wall. *Neuroscience*, *139*, 999–1003.

Lavezzi, A. M., Ottaviani, G., Mauri, M. & Matturri, L. (2007). Biopathology of the dentate-olivary complex in sudden unexplained perinatal death and sudden infant death syndrome related to maternal cigarette smoking. *Neurological Research*, *29*(6), 525–532.

Lawlor, D. A., Clark, H., Ronalds, G. & Leon, D. A. (2006). Season of birth and childhood intelligence: Findings from the Aberdeen children of the 1950s cohort study. *British Journal of Educational Psychology, 76*, 481–499.

Leary, S., Ness, A., Emmett, P. & Smith, G. D. (2005). Maternal diet in pregnancy and offspring height, sitting height, and leg length. *Journal of Epidemiology & Community Health, 59*, 467–472.

Lee, B., Gardner, R., Dal, H., Svensson, A., Galanti, M., Rai, D., Dalman, C. & Magnusson, C. (2012). Brief report: Maternal smoking during pregnancy and autism spectrum disorders. *Journal of Autism & Developmental Disorders.* Sep, *42*(9).

Lee, C. (2007). *Resolving behaviour problems in your school: A practical guide for teachers and support staff.* London: Paul Chapman.

Lee, E., Zhou, Q., Eisenberg, N. & Wang, Y. (2013). Bidirectional relations between temperament and parenting styles in Chinese children. *International Journal of Behavioral Development, 37*(1), 57–67.

Lee, H. M., Bhat, A., Scholz, J. P. & Galloway, J. C. (2008). Toy-oriented changes during early arm movements. *Infant Behavior and Development, 31*(3), 447–469.

Lee, N. & Horsfall, B. (2010). Accelerated learning: A study of faculty and student experiences. *Innovative Higher Education, 35*(3), 191–202.

Legerstee, M., Anderson, D. & Schaffer, A. (1998). Five- and eight-month-old infants recognize their faces and voices as familiar and social stimuli. *Child Development, 69*, 37–50.

Leithwood, K. & Steinbach, R. (2002). Leadership for especially challenging schools. In B. Davies & J. West-Burnham (Eds), *Handbook of educational leadership and management.* London: Pearson.

Leopold, W. (2008). Early academic skills best predictor of school success. *International Educator, 22*, 4.

Leseman, P. (2000). Bilingual vocabulary development of Turkish preschoolers in the Netherlands. *Journal of Multilingual and Multicultural Development,* March, *21*(2), 93–112.

Leviton, A. (1998). Heavy caffeine consumption in pregnancy, smoking, and sudden infant death syndrome. *Archives of Disease in Childhood, 79*, 291.

Lewis, M. (2002). Early emotional development. In A. Slater & M. Lewis (Eds), *Introduction to infant development.* Oxford: Oxford University Press.

Lewis, M. & Brooks-Gunn, J. (1979). *Social cognition and the acquisition of self.* New York: Plenum Press.

Lewis, M. & Brooks-Gunn, J. (1982). The self as social knowledge. In M. D. Lynch, A. Norem-Hebeisen & J. Gergen (Eds), *Self-concept: Advances in theory and research* (pp 101–118). Cambridge, MA: Ballinger.

Lewontin, R. C. (1976). Race and intelligence. In N. J. Block & G. Dworkin (Eds), *The IQ controversy.* New York: Pantheon Books.

Leyens, J. Ph., Camino, L., Parle, R. D. & Berkowitz, L. (1975). Effects of movie violence on aggression in a field setting as a function of group dominance and cohesion. *Journal of Personality and Social Psychology, 32*, 346–360.

Lezak, M. D., Howieson, D. B. & Loring, D. W. (2004). *Neuropsychological assessment.* New York: Oxford University Press.

Li, Y. (2009). Iron deficiency and its impact on academic achievement *China Agricultural Economic Review,* May, *1*(3), 245–259.

Liebert, R. M. & Baron, R. A. (1972). Short term effects of television aggression on children's aggressive behavior. In J. P. Murray, E. A. Rubinstein & G. A. Comstock (Eds), *Television and Social Behavior,* Vol. 2, *Television and Social Learning.* Washington, DC: United States Government Printing Office.

Lin, Y., Reilly, M. & Mercer, V. S. (2010). Responses to a modified Visual Cliff by pre-walking infants born preterm and at term. *Physical & Occupational Therapy in Pediatrics, 30*(1), 66–78.

Lindbohm, M.-L., Ylöstalo, P., Sallmén, M., Henriks-Eckerman, M.-L., Nurminen, T., Forss, H. & Taskinen, H. (2007). Occupational exposure in dentistry and miscarriage. *Occupational and Environmental Medicine, 64*, 127–133.

Lindon, J. (2001). *Understanding children's play.* Cheltenham: Nelson Thornes.

Lindon, J. (2005). *Understanding child development. Linking theory and practice.* Abingdon: Hodder Arnold.

Lindsay, G. & Muijs, D. (2006). Challenging underachievement in boys. *Educational Research, 48*, 313–332.

Little, C. M. (2011). Genetics and twins. *Newborn and Infant Nursing Reviews,* December, *11*(4), 185–189.

Liu, O. L., Wilson, M. & Insu, P. (2008). A multi-dimensional Rasch analysis of gender differences in PISA mathematics. *Journal of Applied Measurement, 9*, 18–35.

Liu, T. (2012). Motor milestone development in young children with autism spectrum disorders: An exploratory study. *Educational Psychology in Practice, 28*(3), 315–326.

Livingstone, T. (2005). *Child of our time.* London: Bantam Press.

Lloyd, N. & Harrington, L. (2012). The challenges to effective outcome evaluation of a national, multi-agency initiative: The experience of Sure Start. *Evaluation, 18*(1), 93–109.

Longmuir, P. E., Banks, L. & McCrindle, B. W. (2012). Cross-sectional study of motor development among children after the Fontan procedure. *Cardiology in the Young, 22*(4), 443–450.

Lopes, P. N., Brackett, M. A., Nezlek, J. B., Schütz, A., Sellin, I. & Salovey, P. (2004). Emotional intelligence and social interaction. *Personality and Social Psychology Bulletin, 30*, 1018–1034.

Loprinzi, P. D., Cardinal, B. J., Loprinzi, K. L. & Lee, H. (2012). Parenting practices as mediators of child physical activity and weight status. *Obesity Facts, 5*(3), 420–430.

Lorenz, K. Z. (1937). The companion in the bird's world. *Auk, 54*, 245–273.

Lorenz, K. (1974, © 1966). *On aggression.* A. Harvest (Ed.). New York: Harcourt Brace Jovanovich.

Love, P. (2012). Informal theory: The ignored link in theory-to-practice. *Journal of College Student Development*, March, *53*(2), 177–191.

Lubans, D. R., Morgan, P. J. & McCormack, A. (2011). Adolescents and school sport: The relationship between beliefs, social support and physical self-perception. *Physical Education & Sport Pedagogy*. Jul, *16*(3), 237–250.

Lubienski, C. (2000). Whither the Common Good? A critique of home schooling. *Peabody Journal of Education*. April, *75*(1–2), 207–232.

Lubienski, C. (2003). A critical view of home education. *Evaluation & Research in Education*, *17*, 167–178.

Lubinski, D., Webb, R. M., Morelock, M. J. & Benbow, C. P. (2001). Top 1 in 10,000: A 10-year follow-up of the profoundly gifted. *Journal of Applied Psychology*, *86*, 718–729.

Lucas, B. (2001). Creative teaching, teaching creativity and creative learning. In A. Craft, B. Jeffrey & M. Liebling, *Creativity in Education*. London: Continuum.

Lumey, L. H. (1992). Decreased birthweights in infants after maternal in utero exposure to the Dutch famine of 1944 to 1945. *Pediatric and Perinatal Epidemiology*, *6*, 240–253.

Lyons-Ruth, K. & Jacobvitz, D. (1999). Attachment disorganization: Unresolved loss, relational violence and lapses in behavioral and attentional strategies. In J. Cassidy & P. Shaver (Eds), *Handbook of attachment* (pp 520–554). New York: Guilford Press.

Maccoby, E. E. (1990). Gender and relationships: A developmental account. *American Psychologist*, *45*, 513–520.

Maccoby, E. E. & Martin, J. A. (1983). Socialization in the context of the family: Parent–child interaction. In E. M. Hetherington (Ed.), *Handbook of child psychology: Vol. 4. Socialization, personality, and social development* (pp 1–101). New York: Wiley.

Macedo, A. A., Marques, M. M., Bos, S. S., Maia, B. R., Pereira, T. T., Soares, M. J. & Azevedo, M. H. (2011). Mother's personality and infant temperament. *Infant Behavior and Development*, *34*(4), 552–568.

Mackey, K., Arnold, M. K. & Pratt, M. W. (2001). Adolescents' stories of decision making in more and less authoritative families: Representing the voices of parents in narrative. *Journal of Adolescent Research*, *16*, 243–268.

MacNaughton, G. & Rolfe, S. A. (2004). The research process. In G. MacNaughton, S. A. Rolfe & I. Siraj-Blatchford, *Doing early childhood research. International perspectives on theory and practice*. Maidenhead: Open University Press.

MacNeill, V. (2009). Forming partnerships with parents from a community development perspective: Lessons learnt from Sure Start. *Health & Social Care in The Community*, *17*(6), 659–665.

Macrory, G. (2007). Constructing language: Evidence from a French–English bilingual child. *Early Child Development & Care*, *177*, 781–792.

Maecker, B., Anderson, K. S., von Bergwelt-Baildon, M. S., Weller, E., Vonderheide, R. H., Richardson, P. G., Schlossman, R. L., Menezes, I. A., Xia, Z., Munshi, N. C., Anderson, K. C., Nadler, L. M. & Schultze, J. L. (2003). Viral antigen-specific CD8+ T-cell responses are impaired in multiple myeloma. *British Journal of Haematology*, *121*, 842–848.

Magnusson, L. L., Wennborg, H., Bonde, J. P. & Olsen, J. (2006). Wheezing, asthma, hay fever, and atopic eczema in relation to maternal occupations in pregnancy. *Occupational and Environmental Medicine*, *63*, 640–646.

Magos, K. (2012). '. . . , But I cannot do research': action-research and early childhood teachers. A case study from Greece. *Teachers and Teaching: Theory and Practice*, June, *18*(3), 331–343.

Main, M. & Solomon, J. (1990). Procedures for identifying infants as disorganized/disoriented during the Ainsworth Strange Situation. In M. T. Greenberg, D. Cicchetti & E. M. Cummings (Eds), *Attachment in the preschool years: Theory, research, and intervention*. Chicago, IL: Chicago University Press.

Makagon, M. M., McCowan, B. & Mench, J. A. (2012). How can social network analysis contribute to social behavior research in applied ethology? *Applied Animal Behaviour Science*, May, *138*(3–4), 152–161.

Malina, R. M., Bouchard, C. & Bar-Or, O. (2004). *Growth, maturation, and physical activity*. Champaign, IL: Human Kinetics.

Man Chow, C. & Buhrmester, D. (2011). Interdependent patterns of coping and support among close friends. *Journal of Social and Personal Relationships*, *28*(5), 684–705.

Manios, Y. (2012). The 'ToyBox-study' obesity prevention programme in early childhood: An introduction. *Obesity Reviews*, 13: 1–2. doi: 10.1111/j.1467-789X.2011.00977.x

Manwaring, J. S. (2008). Wendy or Tinkerbell? *Teaching Exceptional Children*, *40*, 60–65.

Marcus, D. (2006). A review of perinatal acute pain: Treating perinatal pain to reduce adult chronic pain. *The Journal of Headache and Pain*, *7*(1), 3–8.

Margulis, J. (2005). *Why babies do that: Baffling baby behavior explained*. Minocqua, WI: Willow Creek Press.

Marks, G. N. (2008). Accounting for the gender gaps in student performance in reading and mathematics: Evidence from 31 countries. *Oxford Review of Education*, *34*, 89–109.

Marlier, L. & Schaal, B. (2005). Human newborns prefer human milk: Conspecific milk odor is attractive without postnatal exposure. *Child Development*, *76*, 155–168.

Marmet, C., Shell, E. & Aldana, S. (2000). Assessing infant suck dysfunction: Case management. *Journal of Human Lactation*, *16*, 332–336.

Marrow, A. F. (1969). *The practical theorist: The life and work of Kurt Lewin*. New York: Basic Books.

Marsh, H. W., Craven, R. G. & Debus, R. (1991). Self-concepts of young children 5 to 8 years of age: Measurement and multidimensional structure. *Journal of Educational Psychology*, *83*, 377–392.

Marsh, J. & Millard, E. (2000). *Literacy and popular culture*. London: Paul Chapman Publishers.

Martel, M. M., Gremillion, M. L. & Roberts, B. (2012). Temperament and common disruptive behavior problems in preschool. *Personality & Individual Differences.* *53*(7), 874–879.

Martens, R. (1978). *Joy and sadness in children's sports*. Champaign, IL: Human Kinetics.

Martin, D. & Martin, M. (2000). Understanding dysfunctional and functional family behaviors for the at-risk adolescent. *Adolescence, 35*, 785.

Martin, J. A., Hamilton, B. E., Sutton, P. D., Ventura, S. J., Menacker, F. & Munson, M. L. (2003). Births: Final data for 2002. *National Vital Statistics Reports*, Vol. 52(10). Hyattsville, MD: National Center for Health Statistics.

Martin, M. & Waltman-Greenwood, C. (1995). Giftedness. In M. Martin & C. Waltman-Greenwood, *Solve your child's school-related problems*. New York: National Association of School Psychologists.

Martin-Matillas, M., Ortega, F., Chillon, P., Perez, I., Ruiz, J., Castillo, R., Gomez-Martinez, S., Moreno, L., Delgado-Fernandez, M. & Tercedor, P. (2011). Physical activity among Spanish adolescents: Relationship with their relatives' physical activity – The AVENA Study. *Journal of Sports Sciences, 29*(4), 329–336.

Martinos, M., Matheson, A. & De Haan, M. (2012). Links between infant temperament and neurophysiological measures of attention to happy and fearful faces. *Journal of Child Psychology & Psychiatry*. Nov, *53*(11), 1118–1127.

Martin, R. P., Dombrowski, S. C., Mullis, C., Wisenbaker, J. & Huttunen, M. O. (2006). Smoking during pregnancy: Association with childhood temperament, behavior, and academic performance. *Journal of Pediatric Psychology, 31*, 490–500.

Mashburn, A. (2008). Quality of social and physical environments in preschools and children's development of academic, language, and literacy skills. *Applied Developmental Science, 12*(3), 113–127.

Maskell, B., Shapiro, D. R. & Ridley, C. (2004). Effects of Brain Gym on overhand throwing in first grade students: A preliminary investigation. *Physical Educator*. Late Winter, *61*(1), 14–22.

Masser, B., Grass, K. & Nesic, M. (2007). 'We like you, but we don't want you' – The impact of pregnancy in the workplace. *Sex Roles*. Nov, *57*(9–10), 703–712.

Masson, J. (2006). The Climbié Inquiry – Context and critique. *Journal of Law and Society, 33*, 221–243.

Mathai, M., Schramm, M., Baravilala, W., Shankar, V., Antonisamy, B., Jeyaseelan, L. & Bergstrom, S. (2004). Original article. Ethnicity and fetal growth in Fiji. *Australian and New Zealand Journal of Obstetrics and Gynaecology, 44*(4), 318–321.

Mathers, S., Ranns, H., Karemaker, A., Moody, A., Sylva, K., Graham, J. & Siraj-Blatchford, I. (2011). *Evaluation of the Graduate Leader Fund Final Report*. Research Report DFE-RR144. London: DfE.

Matthews, G., Deary, I. J. & Whiteman, M. C. (2003). *Personality traits*. Cambridge: Cambridge University Press.

Matthews, S. (2006). Imaging pulmonary embolism in pregnancy: What is the most appropriate imaging protocol? *British Journal of Radiology (BJR), 79*, 441–444.

Maude, P. (1996). Differentiation in physical education. In E. Bearne (Ed.), *Differentiation and diversity in the primary school*. London: Routledge.

Mayo, J. (2001). Life analysis: Using life-story narratives in teaching life-span developmental psychology. *Journal of Constructivist Psychology*, 1 January, *14*(1), 25–41.

McAdams, D. P. & Pals, J. L. (2006). A new Big Five. *American Psychologist, 61*, 204–217.

McCabe, D., Roediger, H. & Karpicke, J. (2011). Automatic processing influences free recall: Converging evidence from the process dissociation procedure and remember–know judgments. *Memory & Cognition*, April 2011, Vol. 39 Issue: Number 3, 389–402.

McCrae, R. R., Costa, P. T. Jr, Ostendorf, F., Angleitner, A., Hrebrikova, M., Avia, M. D., Sanz, J., Sanchez-Bernardos, M. L., Kusdil, M. E., Wood-field, R., Saunders, P. T. & Smith, P. B. (2000). Nature over nurture: Temperament, personality, and lifespan development. *Journal of Personality and Social Psychology, 78*, 173–186.

McDavid, J. W. & Harari, H. (1966). Sterotyping of names and popularity in grade-school children. *Child Development, 37*, 453.

McEachern, A. & Snyder, J. (2012). Gender differences in predicting antisocial behaviors: Developmental consequences of physical and relational aggression. *Journal of Abnormal Child Psychology*. *40*(4), 501–512.

McGraw, M. B. (1943). *The neuromuscular maturation of the human infant*. New York: Columbia University Press. (Reprinted by Hafner, 1963).

McHale, S. M., Updegraff, K. A., Helms-Erikson, H. & Crouter, A. C. (2001). Sibling influences on gender development in middle childhood and early adolescence: A longitudinal study. *Developmental Psychology, 37*, 115–125.

McIlveen, R. & Gross, R. (1998). *Developmental psychology*. Abingdon: Hodder & Stoughton.

McIntyre, D. (2005). Bridging the gap between research and practice. *Cambridge Journal of Education, 35*, 357–382.

McKelvie, P. & Low, J. (2002). Listening to Mozart does not improve children's spatial ability: Final curtains for the Mozart effect. *British Journal of Developmental Psychology, 20*, 241–258.

McKinney, P. A., Fear, N. T. & Stockton, D. (2003). Parental occupation at periconception: findings from the United Kingdom Childhood Cancer Study. *Occupational and Environmental Medicine, 60*(12), 901–909.

McMaster, K. L., Fuchs, D. & Fuchs, L. S. (2006). Research on peer-assisted learning strategies: The promise and limitations of peer-mediated instruction. *Reading & Writing Quarterly, 22*, 5–25.

McMaster, K. L., Shu-Hsuan, K., Insoon, H. & Cao, M. (2008). Peer-assisted learning strategies: A 'Tier 1' approach to promoting english learners' response to intervention. *Exceptional Children, 74*, 194–214.

Meadows, S. (1995). Cognitive development. In P. E. Bryant & A. M. Colman (Eds), *Developmental Psychology*. London: Longman.

Medlin, R. C. (1991). Homeschooled children's social skills. *Home School Researcher*, *17*(1), 1–8.

Meisinger, E. B., Blake, J. J., Lease, A. M., Palardy, G. J. & Olejnik, S. F. (2007). Variant and invariant predictors of perceived popularity across majority-Black and majority-White classrooms. *Journal of School Psychology*, *45*, 21–44.

Meltzoff, A. N. (1988). Infant imitation and memory: Nine-month-olds in immediate and deferred tests. *Child Development*, *59*, 217–225.

Menias, C., Elsayes, K., Peterson, C., Huete, A., Gratz, B. & Bhalla, S. (2007). CT of pregnancy-related complications. *Emergency Radiology*, *13*, 299–306.

Mennella, J. A. (2007a). Sweet taste and development. In Smith, G., Smith, D. & Firestein, S. (Eds), *Handbook of the senses: Olfaction and taste*. San Diego, CA: Elsevier.

Mennella, J. A. (2007b). Taste and smell. In Shweder, R., Bidell, T., Dailey, A., Dixon, S., Miller, P. & Modell, J. (Eds), *Chicago companion of the child*. Chicago, IL: University of Chicago Press.

Mennella, J. A. & Beauchamp, G. K. (1996). The human infants' response to vanilla flavors in mother's milk and formula. *Infant Behavior and Development*, *19*, 13–19.

Mennella, J. A., Griffin, C. E. & Beauchamp, G. K. (2004). Flavour programming during infancy. *Pediatrics*, *113*, 840–845.

Mennella, J. A. & Jagnow, C. (2001). Prenatal and postnatal flavor learning by human infants. *Pediatrics*, *107*, e88.

Meshcheryakov, A. (1979). *Awakening to life*. Moscow: Progress Publishers.

Miller, A. L., Seifer, R., Stroud, L., Sheinkopf, S. J. & Dickstein, S. (2006). Biobehavioral indices of emotion regulation relate to school attitudes, motivation, and behavior problems in a low-income preschool sample. *Annals of the New York Academy of Sciences*, *1094*, 325–329.

Miller, D. J. & Robertson, D. P. (2010). Using a games console in the primary classroom: Effects of 'brain training' programme on computation and self-esteem. *British Journal of Educational Technology*. Mar, *41*(2), 242–255.

Miller, D. J. & Robertson, D. P. (2011). Response to Logie and Della Sala: Brain training in schools, where is the evidence? *British Journal of Educational Technology*. Sep, *42*(5).

Miller, G. A. (1956). The magical number seven, plus or minus two: Some limits on our capacity to process information. *Psychological Review*, *63*, 81–97.

Mills, C. & Mills, D. (1998). *Britain's early years*. London: Channel 4 Television.

Milunsky, A. (1992). *Heredity and your family's health*. Baltimore, MD: Johns Hopkins University Press.

Mizuno, K., Fujimaki, K. & Sawada, M. (2004). Sucking behavior at breast during the early newborn period affects later breast-feeding rate and duration of breast-feeding. *Pediatrics International*, *46*(1), 15–20.

Molina, M. G., Coplan, R. & Younger, A. (2004). A closer look at children's knowledge about social isolation. *Journal of Research in Childhood Education*, *18*(2), 93–104.

Mondloch, C. J. & Maurer, D. (2004). Do small white balls squeak? Pitch–object correspondences in young children. *Cognitive, Affective & Behavioral Neuroscience*, *4*, 133–136.

Monk, D. (2003). Home education: A human right? *Evaluation & Research in Education*, *17*, 157–166.

Montgomery, D. (2008). Cohort analysis of writing in Year 7 following two, four and seven years of the National Literacy Strategy. *Support for Learning*, *23*, 3–11.

Morgan, S. J., Newton, L. & Waldron, J. (2012). *Supporting more able and talented pupils in primary schools*. Cardiff: Estyn. Her Majesty's Inspectorate for Education and Training in Wales.

Morleo, M., Woolfall, K., Dedman, D., Mukherjee, R., Bellis, M. & Cook, P. (2011). Under-reporting of foetal alcohol spectrum disorders: An analysis of hospital episode statistics. *BMC Pediatrics*, *11*(1), 14–14.

Morrissey, T. W. (2008). Familial factors associated with the use of multiple child-care arrangements. *Journal of Marriage & Family*, *70*, 549–563.

Morrongiello, B. A., Fenwick, K. D. & Chance, G. (1998). Crossmodal learning in newborn infants: Inferences about properties of auditory–visual events. *Infant Behavior and Development*, *21*, 543–554.

Moses, L. J., Baldwin, D. A., Rosicky, J. G. & Tidball, G. (2001). Evidence for referential understanding in the emotions domain at twelve and eighteen months. *Child Development*, *72*, 718–735.

Mouratidis, A., Vansteenkiste, M., Lens, W. & Sideridis, G. (2008). The motivating role of positive feedback in sport and physical education: Evidence for a motivational model. *Journal of Sport & Exercise Psychology*, *30*, 240–268.

Moyles, J. R. (Ed.) (2005). *The excellence of play* (2nd ed.). Buckingham: Open University Press.

Mrug, S., Elliott, M., Gilliland, M. J., Grunbaum, J. A., Tortolero, S. R., Cuccaro, P. & Schuster, M. (2008). Positive parenting and early puberty in girls: Protective effects against aggressive behavior. *Archives of Pediatrics & Adolescent Medicine*, *162*(8), 781–786.

Mullrood, R. (2004). The role of NIP in teachers' classroom discourse. *ELT Journal: English Language Teachers Journal*, *58*, 28–37.

Murcott, A. (2002). Nutrition and inequalities. *The European Journal of Public Health*, *12*, 203–207.

Must, A., Naumova, E. N., Philips, S. M., Blum, M., Dawson-Hughes, B. & Rand, W. M. (2005). Childhood overweight and maturational timing in the development of adult overweight and fatness: The Newton girls study and its follow-up. *Pediatrics*, *116*, 620–627.

Myhill, D. & Brackley, M. (2004). Making connections: Teachers' use of children's prior knowledge in whole class discourse. *British Journal of Educational Studies*, *52*, 263–275.

Myhill, D. & Jones, S. (2006). 'She doesn't shout at no girls': Pupils' perceptions of gender equity in the classroom. *Cambridge Journal of Education*, *36*, 99–113.

NACCCE (National Advisory Committee for Creativity and Culture in Education) (1999). *All our futures: Creativity, culture and education*. London: Department for Education and Employment.

Naglieri, J. A., Rojahn, J. & Matto, H. C. (2007). Hispanic and non-Hispanic children's performance on PASS cognitive processes and achievement. *Intelligence, 35,* 568–579.

Nakamura, K. (2001). Gender and language in Japanese preschool children. *Research on Language & Social Interaction, 34,* 15–43.

Nakashima, D. & Vaddhanaphuti, C. (2006). An education rooted in two worlds: The Karen of northern Thailand. *International Social Science Journal, 58,* 117–120.

Nansel, T. R., Haynie, D. L. & Simons-Morton, B. G. (2003). The association of bullying and victimization with middle school adjustment. *Journal of Applied School Psychology, 19,* 45–61.

National Institute for Health and Clinical Excellence (2008). *Promoting children's social and emotional wellbeing in primary education*. Manchester: NICE.

National Institute for Health and Clinical Excellence (2012). *Social and emotional wellbeing: Early years. Public health Guidance 40.* Manchester: NICE.

National Institute for Child Health and Human Development, Early Child Care Research Network (1999). Child care and mother–child interaction in the first three years of life. *Developmental Psychology, 35,* 1399–1413.

NICHD (National Institute for Child Health and Human Development, Early Child Care Research Network) (2001). *Early child care and children's development prior to school entry.* Symposium presented at the biennial meeting of the Society for Research in Child Development, Minneapolis, MN.

National Literacy Trust (2005). *Why do so many young children lack basic language skills?* A discussion paper. Talk to Your Baby Campaign, NLT: London. www.literacytrust.org.uk/talktoyourbaby/discussionpaper.pdf (accessed 3 June 2008).

National Literacy Trust (2012). *Boys' Reading Commission. The report of the All-Party Parliamentary Literacy Group Commission.* London: NLT.

Nazzi, T. & Gopnik, A. (2000). A shift in children's use of perceptual and causal cues to categorization. *Developmental Science, 3,* 389–396.

Nepomnaschy, P. A., Welch, K. B., McConnell, D. S., Low, B. S., Strassmann, B. I. & England, B. G. (2006). Cortisol levels and very early pregnancy loss in humans. *Proceedings of the National Academy of Sciences of the United States of America, 103,* 3938–3942.

NESS (National Evaluation of Sure Start) (2004). *The impact of Sure Start local programmes on three year olds and their families.* Nottingham: DfES Publications.

Neville, H. J., Bavelier, D., Corina, D., Rauschecker, J., Karni, A., Lalwani, A., Braun, A., Clark, V., Jazzard, P. & Turner, R. (1998). Cerebral organization for language in deaf and hearing subjects: Biological constraints and effects of experience. *Proceedings of the National Academy of Sciences, 95,* 922–929.

Newcomb, A. F. & Bagwell, C. L. (1995). Children's friendship relations: A meta-analytic review. *Psychological Bulletin, 117,* 306–347.

Newcombe, N. S. & Huttenlocher, J. (2003). *Making space: The development of spatial representation and reasoning.* Cambridge, MA: MIT Press.

Newman, A. J., Bavelier, D., Corina, D., Jezzard, P. & Neville, J. (2001). A critical period for right hemisphere recruitment in American Sign Language processing. *Nature Neuroscience, 5,* 76–80.

Newman, H. H., Freeman, F. N. & Holzinger, K. J. (1937). *Twins: A study of heredity and environment.* Chicago, IL: University of Chicago Press.

NHS Information Centre (2010). *Health Survey for England – 2010: Trend Tables.* Available at: www.ic.nhs.uk/pubs/hse10trends

NHS Information Centre, (2012). *Lifestyles statistics on obesity, physical activity and diet: England, 2012.* The Health and Social Care Information Centre, Lifestyles Statistics.

Nickols, S. & Nielsen, R. (2011). 'So many people are struggling': Developing social empathy through a poverty simulation. *Journal of Poverty,* January, *15*(1), 22–42.

Nichols, S. & Stich, S. (2000). A cognitive theory of pretense. *Cognition, 74,* 115–147.

Nigg, J. T. (2006). *What causes ADHD?: Understanding what goes wrong and why.* New York: Guilford Press.

Nind, M. (2001). Enhancing the communication learning environment of an early years unit. Available at www.leeds.ac.uk/educol/documents/00001920.htm

NLT/NAHT (National Literacy Trust and National Association of Head Teachers) (2001). *Early language survey of head teachers,* www.literacytrust.org.uk/talktoyourbaby/survey.html (accessed 31 August 2008).

No Smoking Day (2008). *A guide for midwives* at www.nosmokingday.org (accessed 26 March 2008).

Noland, J. S. & Rodrigues, N. P. (2012). Direct touches to clear barriers: Developmental sensitivity of a new measure of the production of ineffective responses in infancy. *Child Neuropsychology, 18*(5), 506–511.

Nørgård, B., Nørgaard, M., Czeizel, A. E., Puhó, E. & Sørensen, H. T. (2006). Maternal herpes labialis in pregnancy and neural tube defects. *Developmental Medicine & Child Neurology, 48,* 674–676.

Nuclear Energy Institute (2005). *NEI – the Chernobyl accident and its consequences,* www.nei.org/doc.asp?docid=456 (accessed 24 March 2008).

Numerato, D. (2009). The institutionalisation of regional public sport policy in the Czech Republic. *International Journal of Sport Policy and Politics, 1*(1), 13–30.

Nutbrown, C. (2006). *Key concepts in early childhood education and care.* London: Sage.

Nyman, E. S., Loukola, A., Varilo, T., Ekelund, J., Veijola, J., Joukamaa, M., Taanila, A., Pouta, A., Miettunen, J., Freimer, N., Järvelin, M. R. & Peltonen, L. (2009). Impact of the dopamine receptor gene family on temperament traits in a population based birth cohort. *American Journal of Medical Genetics. Part B, Neuropsychiatric Genetics: The*

*Official Publication of the International Society of Psychiatric Genetics, 150*(6), 854–865.

Oakland, T., Alghorani, M. A. & Dong Hun, L. (2007). Temperament-based learning styles of Palestinian and US children. *School Psychology International, 28,* 110–128.

Ochiltree, G. (1994). *Effects of child care on young children: Forty years of research.* Melbourne: Australian Institute of Family Studies.

O'Connor, J., Alfrey, L. & Payne, P. (2012). Beyond games and sports: A socio-ecological approach to physical education. *Sport, Education and Society, 17*(3), 365–380.

O'Connor, T. G. & Croft, C. M. (2001). A twin study of attachment in preschool children. *Child Development, 72,* 1501.

O'Connor, T. G., Rutter, M., Beckett, C., Keaveney, L., Kreppher, J. M. & the English and Romanian Adoptees Study Team (2000). The effects of global severe privation on cognitive competence: Extension and longitudinal follow-up. *Child Development, 7,* 376–390.

O'Dell, N. & Cook, P. (1997). *Stopping hyperactivity – A new solution.* Garden City Park, NY: Avery Publishing Group.

OECD (2010). (Organisation for Economic Co-operation and Development). *PISA 2009 at a glance.* Paris: OECD.

OECD (2011). (Organisation for Economic Co-operation and Development). *Health at a Glance.* Available at: www.oecd.org/dataoecd/6/28/49105858.pdf (accessed 10 November 2012).

Ofsted (Office for Standards in Education) (2005). *Could they do better? The writing of advanced bilingual learners of English at Key Stage 2: HMI survey of good practice.* Her Majesty's Inspector's Report 2452, July 2005. London: Ofsted.

Ofsted (Office for Standards in Education) (2007). *The foundation stage.* London: Ofsted.

Ofsted (2010). *Ofsted Annual report for 2009–10.* Manchester: Ofsted.

Ojala, M. & Talts, L. (2007). Preschool achievement in Finland and Estonia: Cross-cultural comparison between the cities of Helsinki and Tallinn. *Scandinavian Journal of Educational Research, 51,* 205–221.

Ojukwu, J. U., Okebe, J. U., Yahav, D. & Paul, M. (2010). Cochrane review: Oral iron supplementation for preventing or treating anaemia among children in malaria endemic areas. *Evidence-Based Child Health: A Cochrane Review Journal, 5*(2), 967–1183.

Olds, T., Maher, C., Zumin, S., Péneau, S., Lioret, S., Castetbon, K. B., de Wilde, J., Hohepa, M., Maddison, R., Lissner, L., Sjöberg, A., Zimmermann, M., Aeberli, I., Ogden, C., Flegal, K. & Summerbell, C. (2011). Evidence that the prevalence of childhood overweight is plateauing: data from nine countries. *International Journal of Pediatric Obesity, 6*(5–6), 342–360.

Onderdonk, R. L. (2007). Making classrooms bully-free zones: Practical suggestions for educators. *Kappa Delta Pi Record, 43*(4), 182–185.

ONS (2010). *Statistical bulletin: Infant and perinatal mortality in England and Wales by social and biological factors, 2010.* www.ons.gov.uk/ons/ (accessed 13 October 2012).

ONS (2013). The Office for National Statistics. www.ons.gov.uk/ons/publications/re-reference-tables.html?edition=tcm%3A77-241261 (accessed 21 April 2013).

Oortwijn, M., Boekaerts, M. & Vedder, P. (2008). The impact of the teacher's role and pupils' ethnicity and prior knowledge on pupils' performance and motivation to cooperate. *Instructional Science, 36,* 251–268.

Opyene-Eluk, P. & Opolot-Okurut, C. (1995). Gender and school-type differences in mathematics achievement. *International Journal of Mathematical Education in Science & Technology, 26,* 871.

Osei, E. K. & Kotre, C. J. (2001). Equivalent dose to the fetus from occupational exposure of pregnant staff in diagnostic radiology. *British Journal of Radiology (BJR), 74,* 629–637.

Ostad, S. A. & Sorensen, P. M. (2007). Private speech and strategy-use patterns. *Journal of Learning Disabilities, 40,* 2–14.

O'Toole, C. & Fletcher, P. (2012). Profiling vocabulary acquisition in Irish. *Journal Of Child Language,* 1 January, *39*(1), 205–220.

Our Children (2005). PTAs fight the childhood obesity epidemic. *Our Children, 30,* 12–15.

Oyserman, D., Brickman, D. & Rhodes, M. (2007). School success, possible selves, and parent school involvement. *Family Relations, 56*(5), 479–489.

Pace, C., San Martini, P. & Zavattini, G. (2011). The factor structure of the Inventory of Parent and Peer Attachment (IPPA): A survey of Italian adolescents. *Personality And Individual Differences, 51*(2), 83–88.

Pagura, J., Cox, B. J., Sareen, J. & Enns, M. W. (2006). Childhood adversities associated with self-criticism in a nationally representative sample. *Personality & Individual Differences, 41,* 1287–1298.

Paley, V. G. (2004). *A child's work: The importance of fantasy play.* London & Chicago, IL: University of Chicago Press.

Palmer, S. (2004). Boys, girls and . . . brains? *Child Education, 81,* 40–41.

Pantev, C., Oostenveld, R., Engelien, A., Ross, B., Roberts, L. E. & Hoke, M. (1998). Increased auditory cortical representation. *Nature, 392,* 811–813.

Park, G., Lubinski, D. & Benbow, C. P. (2007). Contrasting intellectual patterns for creativity in the arts and sciences: Tracking intellectually precocious youth over 25 years. *Psychological Science, 18,* 948–952.

Parke, R. D. (1981). *Fathering.* London: Fontana.

Parten, M. (1932). Social participation among preschool children. *Journal of Abnormal and Social Psychology, 27,* 243–269.

Pasnak, R., Kidd, J., Gadzichowski, M., Gallington, D. & Saracina, R. (2008). Can emphasising cognitive development improve academic achievement? *Educational Research,* September, *50*(3), 261–276.

Pasquinelli, E. (2012). Neuromyths: Why do they exist and persist? *Mind, Brain & Education.* Jun, *6*(2), 89–96.

Patterson, C. (2008). *Child development.* New York: McGraw-Hill.

Payne, G. (2007). Social divisions, social mobilities and social research: Methodological issues after 40 years. *Sociology*, October, *41*(5), 901–915.

Payne, J. M., France, K. E., Henley, N., D'Antoine, H. A., Bartu, A. E., O'Leary, C. M., Elliott, E. J., Bower, C. & Geelhoed, E. (2011). RE-AIM evaluation of the Alcohol and Pregnancy Project: Educational resources to inform health professionals about prenatal alcohol exposure and fetal alcohol spectrum disorder. *Evaluation & the Health Professions*. Mar, *34*(1), 57–80.

Pearson, B. Z., Fernandez, S. C. & Oller, D. K. (1993). Lexical development in bilingual infants and toddlers: Comparison to monolingual norms. *Language Learning*, *43*, 93–120.

Peck, M. N. & Lundberg, O. (1995). Short stature as an effect of economic and social conditions in childhood. *Social Science and Medicine*, *41*, 733–738.

Pellegrini, A. D. & Smith, P. K. (1998). Physical activity play: The nature and function of a neglected aspect of play. *Child Development*, *69*, 577–598.

Penha-Lopes, V. (2006). 'To cook, sew, to be a man': The socialization for competence and Black men's involvement in housework. *Sex Roles*, *54*, 261–274.

Penn, H. (2005). *Understanding early childhood. Issues and controversies*. Maidenhead: Open University Press.

Penner, A. M. & Paret, M. (2008). Gender differences in mathematics achievement: Exploring the early grades and the extremes. *Social Science Research*, *37*, 239–253.

Pennington, B. F., Moon, J., Edgin, J., Stedron, J. & Nadel, L. (2003). The neuropsychology of Down's syndrome: Evidence for hippocampal dysfunction. *Child Development*, *74*, 75–93.

Perner, J., Leekam, S. R. & Wimmer, H. (1987). Three-year-olds' difficulty with false belief: The case for a conceptual deficit. *British Journal of Developmental Psychology*, *5*, 125–137.

Perner, J., Ruffman, T. & Leekam, S. R. (1994). Theory of mind is contagious: You can catch it from your sibs. *Child Development*, *65*, 1228–1238.

Perovic, S. & Radenovic, L. (2011). Fine-tuning nativism: The 'nurtured nature' and innate cognitive structures. *Phenomenology and the Cognitive Sciences*, September, *10*(3), 399–417.

Peskin, J. (1992). Ruse and representations: On children's ability to conceal information. *Developmental Psychology*, *28*, 84–89.

Petrie, A. (2001). Home education in Europe and the implementation of changes to the law. *International Review of Education*, *47*, 477–500.

Petrill, S. A. & Deater-Deckard, K. (2004). Task orientation, parental warmth and SES account or a significant proportion of the shared environmental variance in general cognitive ability in early childhood: Evidence from a twin study. *Developmental Science*, *7*, 25–32.

Pharoah, P. O. D. (2006). Risk of cerebral palsy in multiple pregnancies. *Clinics in Perinatology*, *33*, 301–313.

Piaget, J. (1932). *The moral judgment of the child*. New York: Macmillan.

Piaget, J. (1951). *Play, dreams and imitation in childhood*. New York: Norton.

Piaget, J. (1952a). *The child's conception of number*. London: Routledge & Kegan Paul.

Piaget, J. (1952b). *The origins of intelligence in children*. New York: International Universities Press.

Piaget, J. (1957). *Construction of reality in the child*. London: Routledge & Kegan Paul.

Piaget, J. (1960). *Psychology of intelligence*. Patterson, NJ: Littlefield, Adams.

Piaget, J. (1962). *Play, dreams, and imitation in childhood*. London: Routledge & Kegan Paul.

Piaget, J. (1967). *Six psychological studies*. New York: Vintage.

Piaget, J. (1969). *The mechanics of perception*. New York: Basic Books.

Piaget, J. & Inhelder, B. (1966). *La psychologie de l'enfant [The psychology of the child]*. Paris: Presses Universitaires de France.

Pickens, J. N. (1994). Perception of auditory–visual distance relations by 5-month-old infants. *Developmental Psychology*, *30*, 537–544.

Pillay, P. (2006). Human resource development and growth: Improving access to and equity in the provision of education and health services in South Africa. *Development Southern Africa*, March, *23*(1), 63–83.

Pinker, S. (1994). *The language instinct: How the mind creates language*. New York: William Morrow.

Plaud, J. (1991). Oil on the troubled waves: John Broadus Watson and the ways of behaviorism. *Current Psychology*, December, *10*(4), 305–310.

Plomin, R. (1990). Familial IQ correlations. *Nature and Nurture: An Introduction to Human Behavioural Genetics* (pp 68–72). Pacific Grove, CA: Brooks/Cole.

Plomin, R. (1995). Genetics and children's experiences in the family. *Journal of Child Psychology and Psychiatry*, *36*, 33–68.

Plomin, R. (2000). Behavioral genetics in the 21st century. *International Journal of Behavioral Development*, *24*, 30–34.

Plomin, R. (2004). Intelligence: Genetics, genes, and genomics. *Journal of Personality and Social Psychology*, *86*, 112–129.

Plomin, R. & Petrill, S. A. (1997). Genetics and intelligence: What's new? *Intelligence*, *24*, 53–78.

Plomin, R., DeFries, J. & Fulker, D. (1988). *Nature and nurture during infancy and early childhood*. Cambridge: Cambridge University Press.

Plunkett, S., Henry, C., Robinson, L., Behnke, A. & Falcon, P. (2007). Adolescent perceptions of parental behaviors, adolescent self-esteem, and adolescent depressed mood. *Journal of Child & Family Studies*, *16*, 760–772.

Poddiakov, N. (2011). Searching, experimenting and the heuristic structure of a preschool child's experience. *International Journal of Early Years Education*, March, *19*(1), 55–63.

Poehlmann, J. (2005). Representations of attachment relationships in children of incarcerated mothers. *Child Development*, *76*, 679–696.

Pollitt, E. (1994). Poverty and child development: Relevance of research in developing countries to the United States. *Child Development*, 65, 283–295.

Pollock, L. (1983). *Forgotten children: Parent–child relations from 1500–1900*. Cambridge: Cambridge University Press.

Pope, A. & Bierman, K. L. (1999). Predicting adolescent peer problems and antisocial activities: The relative roles of aggression and dysregulation. *Developmental Psychology*, 35, 335–346.

Poulou, M. (2005). The prevention of emotional and behavioural difficulties in schools: Teachers' suggestions. *Educational Psychology in Practice*, 21, 37–52.

Povinelli, D. J., Landau, K. R. & Perilloux, H. K. (1996). Self-recognition in young children using delayed versus live feedback: Evidence of a developmental asynchrony. *Child Development*, 67, 1540–1554.

Preece, P. F. W. (1979). Student teacher anxiety and class-control problems on teaching practice: A cross-lagged panel analysis. *British Educational Research Journal*, 5(1), 13–19.

Prentice, A. M. & Moore, S. E. (2005). Early programming of adult diseases in resource poor countries. *Archives of Disease in Childhood*, 90, 429–432.

Pressley, M., Wharton-McDonald, R., Allington, R., Block, C. C., Morrow, L., Tracey, D. *et al.* (2001). A study of effective first-grade literacy instruction. *Scientific Studies of Reading*, 5, 35–58.

Prinzie, P. & Deković, M. (2008). Continuity and change of childhood personality characteristics. *Personality & Individual Differences*, 45, 82–88.

Prokop, P., Kubiatko, M. & Fančovičová, J. (2007). Why do cocks crow? Children's concepts about birds. *Research in Science Education*, 37, 393–405.

Pruitt, A. W., Anyan Jr., W. R., Hill, R. M., Kauffman, R. E., Mofenson, H. C., Singer, H. S., Spielberg, S. P., Ballin, J. C., Catz, C., Farchione, L., Freeman, M. M., Niebyl, J., Smith, D. L., Licata, S. A., Oakley, G., Sawchuck, S., Brewer, E. J. & Leer, J. A. (1983). The transfer of drugs and other chemicals into human breast milk. *Pediatric*. Sep, 72(3), 375.

QCA (Qualifications and Curriculum Authority) (2000). *Standards at Key Stage 2 – English, Mathematics and Science*. London: QCA.

QCA (Qualifications and Curriculum Authority) (2001). *Standards at Key Stage 1 – English and Mathematics*. London: QCA.

Qin, Y., Buddavarapu, K. & Dahia, P. L. M. (2009). Pheochromocytomas: From genetic diversity to new paradigms. *Hormone and Metabolic Research*, September, 41(9), 664–671.

Quar, T. K., Ching, T. Y. C., Mukari, S., Zamratol-Mai, S. & Newall, P. (2012). Parents' Evaluation of Aural/Oral Performance of Children (PEACH) scale in the Malay language: Data for normal-hearing children. *International Journal of Audiology*, April, 51(4), 326–333.

Radke-Yarrow, M., McCann, K., DeMulder, E., Belmont, B., Martinez, P. & Richardson, D. T. (1995). Attachment in the context of high risk conditions. *Development and Psychopathology*, 7, 247–265.

Rafiefard, F., Yun, Z. B. & Örvell, C. (2008). Epidemiologic characteristics and seasonal distribution of human metapneumovirus infections in five epidemic seasons in Stockholm, Sweden, 2002–2006. *Journal of Medical Virology*, 80(9), 1631–1638.

Raine, J. E., Donaldson, M. D. C., Gregory, J. W., Savage, M. O. & Hintz, R. L. (2006). *Practical endocrinology and diabetes in children*. Oxford: Blackwell Publishing.

Ramey, C. T. & Ramey, S. L. (2001). Early educational interventions and intelligence. In E. Zigler & S. Styfco (Eds), *The Head Start debates*. New Haven, CT: Yale University Press.

Rao, S., Yajnik, C. S., Kanade, A., Fall, C. H., Margetts, B. M., Jackson, A. A., Shier, R., Joshi, S., Rege, S., Lubree, H. & Desai, B. (2001). Intake of micro-nutrient-rich foods in rural Indian mothers is associated with the size of their babies at birth: Pune Maternal Nutrition Study. *The Journal of Nutrition*, 131, 1217–1224.

Rathus, A. R. (2004). *Psychology: Concepts and connections*. Belmont, CA: Thomson/Wadsworth.

Rauscher, F. H., Shaw, G. L. & Ky, K. N. (1993). Music and spatial task performance. *Nature*, 365, 611.

Ray, B. D. (2002). *A quick reference worldwide guide to home-schooling: Facts and stats on the benefits of home school, 2002–2003*. Nashville, TN: Broadman & Holman Publishers.

Raymond, C. M., Brown, G. & Weber, D. (2010). The measurement of place attachment: Personal, community, and environmental connections. *Journal of Environmental Psychology*, 30(4), 422–434.

Reinke, W. M., Herman, K. C., Petras, H. & Ialongo, N. S. (2008). Empirically derived subtypes of child academic and behavior problems: Co-occurrence and distal outcomes. *Journal of Abnormal Child Psychology*, 36, 759–770.

Remberk, B., Namysłowska, I. & Rybakowski, F. (2012). Cognitive impairment and formal thought disorders in parents of early-onset schizophrenia patients. *Neuropsychobiology*, June, 65(4), 206–215.

Reynolds, M. R., Keith, T. Z., Ridley, K. P. & Patel, P. G. (2008). Sex differences in latent general and broad cognitive abilities for children and youth: Evidence from higher-order MG-MACS and MIMIC models. *Intelligence*, 36, 236–260.

Reynolds, S., Wilson, C., Austin, J. & Hooper, L. (2012). Effects of psychotherapy for anxiety in children and adolescents: A meta-analytic review. *Clinical Psychology Review*, June, 32(4), 251–262.

Rheingold, H. & Eckerman, C. (1970). The infant separates himself from his mother. *Science*, 168, 78–83.

Rhode, M. (2005). Mirroring, imitation, identification: The sense of self in relation to the mother's internal world. *Journal of Child Psychotherapy*, 31(1), 52–71.

Richards, M. P. M. (1995). The International Year of the Family – family research. *The Psychologist*, 8, 17–20.

Richards, M. P. M. & Wild, L. G. (2003). Exploring parent and child perceptions of interparental conflict. *International Journal of Law, Policy and Family*, 17, 366–384.

Richter, J., Brandstrom, S., Emami, H. & Ghazinour, M. (2007). An Iranian (Farsi) version of the temperament and character inventory: A cross-cultural comparison. *Psychological Reports*, 100, 1218–1228.

Rieffe, C., Ketelaar, L. & Wiefferink, C. H. (2010). Assessing empathy in young children: Construction and validation of an Empathy Questionnaire (EmQue). *Personality and Individual Differences*, 49(5), 362–367.

Rieser, J., Yonas, A. & Wilkner, K. (1976). Radial localization of odors by human neonates. *Child Development*, 47, 856–859.

Riggs, N. R., Jahromi, L. B., Razza, R. P., Dillworth-Bart, J. E. & Mueller, U. (2006). Executive function and the promotion of social–emotional competence. *Journal Of Applied Developmental Psychology*, 27(4), 300–309.

Rikhye, K., Tyrka, A. R., Kelly, M. M., Gagne, G. G., Mello, A. F., Mello, M. F., Price, L. H. & Carpenter, L. L. (2008). Interplay between childhood maltreatment, parental bonding, and gender effects: Impact on quality of life. *Child Abuse & Neglect*, 32, 19–34.

Rindermann, H. (2008). Relevance of education and intelligence at the national level for the economic welfare of people. *Intelligence*, 36, 127–142.

Rittle-Johnson, B. & Siegler, R. S. (1998). The relation between conceptual and procedural knowledge in learning mathematics: A review. In C. Donlan (Ed.), *The development of mathematical skills* (pp 75–110). Hove: Psychology Press.

Rivera, H. H. & Waxman, H. C. (2007). Studying the classroom learning environment of resilient and non-resilient Hispanic children. *Journal of At-risk Issues*, 13, 11–19.

Rivero, L. (2002). Progressive digressions: Home schooling for self-actualization *Roeper Review*, 24(4), 197–202.

Robinson, K. (2001). Mind the gap: The creative conundrum. *Critical Quarterly*, 43, 41–45.

Robson, T. (1999). Topics in computerized visual-stimulus generation. In R. H. S. Carpenter & J. G. Robson (Eds), *Vision research. A practical guide to laboratory methods*, pp 81–105. Oxford: Oxford University Press.

Rodriguez, A. & Bohlin, G. (2005). Are maternal smoking and stress during pregnancy related to ADHD symptoms in children? *Journal of Child Psychology and Psychiatry (formerly Journal of Child Psychology and Psychiatry and Allied Disciplines)*, 46, 246–254.

Rodriguez, C. M. & Richardson, M. J. (2007). Stress and anger as contextual factors and preexisting cognitive schemas: Predicting parental child maltreatment risk. *Child Maltreatment*, 12, 325–337.

Rogers, C. (1961). *On becoming a person: A therapist's view of psychotherapy*. Boston, MA: Houghton-Mifflin.

Rogers, S. & Rose, J. (2007). Ready for Reception? The advantages and disadvantages of single-point entry to school. *Early Years: An International Journal of Research and Development*, March 2007, 27(1), 47–63.

Rogers, S. J. & Ozonoff, S. (2005). Annotation: What do we know about sensory dysfunction in autism? A critical review of the empirical evidence. *Journal of Child Psychology and Psychiatry (formerly Journal of Child Psychology and Psychiatry and Allied Disciplines)*, 46, 1255–1268.

Rogoff, B. (1998). Cognition as a collaborative process. In W. Damon (Gen. Ed.), D. Kuhn & R. S. Siegler (Vol. Eds), *Handbook of child psychology: Vol. 2. Cognition, perception and language* (pp 670–744). New York: Wiley.

Rogoff, B. (2003). *The cultural nature of human development*. Oxford: Oxford University Press.

Rogoff, B., Mistry, J., Goncu, A. & Mosier, C. (1993). Guided participation in cultural activity by toddlers and caregivers. *Monographs of the Society for Research in Child Development*, 58 (8, Serial No. 236).

Rohlfing, K. J., Longo, M. R. & Bertenthal, B. I. (2012). Dynamic pointing triggers shifts of visual attention in young infants. *Developmental Science*, 15(3), 426–435.

Rolfe, S. A. & Crossley, S. A. (1991). The effects of prior experience in early childhood programmes and play setting on social behaviour and play in preschoolers. *Early Child Development and Care*, 72, 23–37.

Romi, S., Lewis, R., Roache, J. & Riley, P. (2011). The impact of teachers' aggressive management techniques on students' attitudes to schoolwork. *Journal of Educational Research*. 104(4), 231–240.

Rosé, C., Wang, Y., Cui, Y., Arguello, J., Stegmann, K., Weinberger, A. & Fischer, F. (2013). Analyzing collaborative learning processes automatically: Exploiting the advances of computational linguistics in computer-supported collaborative learning. *International Journal of Computer-Supported Collaborative Learning*, 2013, Preprints, 1–35.

Rose, J. (2006). *Independent Review of the Teaching of Reading*. London: DES.

Rosenshine, B. & Meister, C. (1994). Reciprocal teaching: A review of research. *Review of Educational Research*, 64, 479–530.

Ross, D. B., Bondy, E., Gallingane, C. & Hambacher, E. (2008). Promoting academic engagement through insistence: Being a warm demander. *Childhood Education*, 84, 142–146.

Roth, T. L. & Sullivan, R. M. (2005). Memory of early maltreatment: Neonatal behavioral and neural correlates of maltreatment within context of classical conditioning. *Biological Psychiatry*, 57, 823–831.

Roth-Hanania, R., Busch-Rossnagel, N. & Higgins-D'Alessandro, A. (2000). Infants' development of self and empathy in early infancy: Implications for atypical development & young children. *An Interdisciplinary Journal of Special Care Practices*, 13, 1–14.

Rothbart, M. K. & Bates, J. E. (1998). Temperament. In N. Eisenberg & W. Damon (Eds), *The handbook of child psychology: Vol. 3. Social, emotional, and personality development* (5th ed., pp 105–176). New York: Wiley.

Rothbart, M. K., Ahadi, S. A. & Evans, D. E. (2000). Temperament and personality: Origins and outcomes. *Journal of Personality and Social Psychology*, 78, 122–135.

Rothbaum, F. & Pott, M. (2000). The development of close relationships in Japan and the United States: Paths of symbiotic harmony and generative tension. *Child Development, 71,* 1121.

Rothermel, P. (2003). Can we classify motives for home education? *Evaluation & Research in Education, 17,* 74–89.

Rowe, J. B. & Siebner, H. R. (2012). The motor system and its disorders *NeuroImage, 61*(2), 464–477.

Rubin, K. H. & Coplan, R. (1992). Peer relationships in childhood. In M. Bornstein & M. Lamb (Eds), *Developmental psychology: An advanced textbook,* 5th ed. (pp 619–700). Hillsdale, NJ: Erlbaum.

Rubin, K. H., Bukowski, W. & Parker, J. G. (1998). Peer interactions, relationships, and groups. In W. Damon (Gen. Ed.) & N. Eisenberg (Vol. Ed.), *Hand-book of child psychology: Vol. 3. Social, emotional, and personality development,* 5th ed. (pp 619–700). New York: Wiley.

Rubin, K. H., Fein, G. G. & Vandenberg, B. (1983). Play. In E. M. Hetherington (Ed.), *Handbook of child psychology: Vol. 4. Socialization, personality, and social development* (pp 693–744). New York: Wiley.

Rueger, S. Y., Katz, R., Risser, H. & Lovejoy, M. C. (2011). Relations between parental affect and parenting behaviors: A meta-analytic review parenting. *Science and Practice, 11*(1), 1–33.

Rush, E. B., Quas, J. A. & Yim, I. S. (2011). Memory narrowing in children and adults. *Applied Cognitive Psychology,* November, *25*(6), 841–849.

Rushton, J. P. (2002). Jensen effects and African/Coloured/Indian/White differences on Raven's Standard Progressive Matrices in South Africa. *Personality & Individual Differences, 33,* 1279.

Russ, S. W. (2011). Changes in children's pretend play over two decades. *Creativity Research Journal,* October, *23*(4), 330–338.

Rutter, M. (1981). *Maternal deprivation reassessed,* 2nd ed. Harmondsworth: Penguin.

Saarni, C. (1999). *The development of emotional competence.* Guilford Series on Social and Emotional Development. New York: Guilford Press.

Saarni, C., Campos, J. J. & Camras, L. (2006a). Emotional development. In W. Damon & R. M. Lerner (Gen. Eds) & N. Eisenberg (Vol. Ed.), *Handbook of child psychology: Vol. 3. Social, emotional, and personality development,* 6th ed. New York: Wiley.

Saarni, C., Mumme, D. L. & Campos, J. J. (2006b). Emotional development: Action, communication, and understanding. In N. Eisenberg (Ed.), *Hand-book of child psychology: Vol. 3. Social, emotional, and personality development,* 6th ed. New York: Wiley.

Sabiston, C. M. & Crocker, P. R. E. (2008). Exploring self-perceptions and social influences as correlates of adolescent leisure-time physical activity. *Journal of Sport & Exercise Psychology, 30,* 3–22.

Sachdeva, S., Singh, P. & Medin, D. (2011). Culture and the quest for universal principles in moral reasoning. *International Journal of Psychology, 46*(3), 161–176.

Saffran, J. R. & Griepentrog, G. J. (2001). Absolute pitch on infant auditory learning: Evidence for developmental reorganization. *Developmental Psychology, 37,* 74–85.

Sáinz, M. & Eccles, J. (2012). Self-concept of computer and math ability: Gender implications across time and within ICT studies. *Journal Of Vocational Behavior, 80*(2), 486–499.

Salmon, A. (2008). Promoting a culture of thinking in the young child. *Early Childhood Education Journal, 35,* 457–461.

Sanz, M. T. & Menendez, J. (2010). Parents' training: Effects of the self-help skills programme with Down's syndrome babies. *Early Child Development and Care,* July, *180*(6), 735–742.

Saran, R. (2007). Cries in the night. *Working Mother, 30,* 102.

Sarver, D. E., Rapport, M. D., Kofler, M. J., Scanlan, S. W., Raiker, J. S., Altro, T. A. & Bolden, J. (2012). Attention problems, phonological short-term memory, and visuospatial short-term memory: Differential effects on near- and long-term scholastic achievement. *Learning and Individual Differences,* February, *22*(1), 8–19.

Savelsbergh, G. J. P. & Van der Kamp, J. (2000). Information in learning to coordinate and control movements: Is there a need for specificity of practise? *International Journal of Sport Psychology, 31,* 476–484.

Scarr, S. & Dunn, J. (1987). *Mother care/other care.* Harmondsworth: Penguin.

Scarr, S. & McCartney, K. (1983). How people make their own environments: A theory of genotype environment effects. *Child Development, 54,* 424–435.

Schaffer, H. R. (2006). *Key concepts in developmental psychology.* London: Sage.

Schaffer, H. R. (1996). *Social development.* Cambridge, MA: Blackwell.

Schaffer, H. R. & Emerson, P. E. (1964). *The development of social attachments in infancy.* Lafayette, IN: Child Development Publications of the Society for Research in Child Development.

Schickedanz, J. A., Schickedanz, D. I., Hansen, K. & Forsyth, P. D. (1993). *Understanding children* (2nd ed). London: Mayfield Publishing Company.

Schmidt, M. E., Rich, M., Rifas-Shiman, S. L., Oken, E. & Taveras, E. M. (2009). Television viewing in infancy and child cognition at 3 years of age in a US cohort. *Pediatrics,* March, *123*(3), 370–375.

Schmidt, R. A. (1975). A schema theory of discrete motor skill learning. *Acta Psychologica, 53,* 61–97.

Schneider, B. H. (2000). *Friends and enemies: Peer relations in childhood.* London: Arnold.

Schnitzer, G., Andries, C. & Lebeer, J. (2007). Usefulness of cognitive intervention programmes for socio-emotional and behaviour problems in children with learning disabilities. *Journal of Research in Special Educational Needs, 7,* 161–171.

Scholtens, S., Diamantopoulou, S., Tillman, C. & Rydell, A. (2012). Effects of symptoms of ADHD, ODD, and cognitive functioning on social acceptance and the positive illusory bias in children. *Journal of Attention Disorders, 16*(8), 685–696.

Schore, A. N. (2005). Developmental affective neuroscience describes mechanisms at the core of dynamic systems theory. *Behavioral and Brain Sciences, 28,* 217–218.

Schellenberg, E. G., Nakata, T., Hunter, P. G. & Tamoto, S. (2007). Exposure to music and cognitive performance: Tests of children and adults. *Psychology of Music, 35*, 5–19.

Schraw, G. (2007). The use of computer-based environments for understanding and improving self-regulation. *Metacognition & Learning, 2*, 169–176.

Schuler, M. E. & Nair, P. (1999). Brief report: Frequency of maternal cocaine use during pregnancy and infant neurobehavioral outcome. *Journal of Pediatric Psychology, 24*, 511–514.

Secco, L., Profit, S. & Letourneau, N. (2006). A self directed behavioural family intervention with telephone consultations improved toddler behaviour and parenting skills. *Evidence-Based Nursing, 9*, 106.

Segall, M. H., Campbell, D. T. & Herskovits, M. J. (1966). *The influence of culture on perception.* New York: Bobbs-Merrill.

Segalowitz, S. J. (1999). Why twin studies really don't tell us much about human heritability. *Behavioral and Brain Sciences,* October, *22*(5), 904–905.

Seghier, M. L., Kherif, F. J. & Goulven Price, Cathy J. (2011). Regional and hemispheric determinants of language laterality: Implications for preoperative fMRI. *Human Brain Mapping,* Vol. 32(10), Oct, 2011, 1602–1614.

Sénéchal, M., Pagan, S., Lever, R. & Ouellette, G. P. (2008). Relations among the frequency of shared reading and 4-year-old children's vocabulary, morphological and syntax comprehension, and narrative skills. *Early Education & Development, 19*, 27–44.

Seo, H., Hähner, A., Gudziol, V., Scheibe, M. & Hummel, T. (2012). Influence of background noise on the performance in the odor sensitivity task: effects of noise type and extraversion. *Experimental Brain Research,* October, *222*(1–2), 89–97.

Serbin, L. A., Poulin-Dubois, D., Colburne, K. A., Sen, M. G. & Eichstedt, J. A. (2001). Gender stereotyping in infancy: Visual preferences for and knowledge of gender-stereotyped toys in the second year. *International Journal of Behavioral Development, 25*, 7–15.

Sesardic, N. (2005). *Making sense of heritability.* Cambridge: Cambridge University Press.

Seymour, B., Kinn, S. & Sutherland, N. (2003). Valuing both critical and creative thinking in clinical practice: Narrowing the research–practice gap? *Journal of Advanced Nursing, 42*, 288–296.

Shachar, R. (2012). Structuring of gender in Israeli society through children's reading and textbooks: Where is mom's apron? *Journal of Research in Childhood Education, 26*(3), 249–263.

Shaffer, A. & Sroufe, L. A. (2005). The developmental and adaptational implications of generational boundary dissolution: Findings from a prospective, longitudinal study. *Journal of Emotional Abuse, 5*, 67–84.

Shaffer, D. R. (1999). *Developmental psychology. Childhood & adolescence,* 5th ed. Pacific Grove, CA: Brooks/Cole.

Sharma, A. & Campbell, J. (2011). A sensitive period for cochlear implantation in deaf children. *Journal of Maternal-Fetal and Neonatal Medicine,* October, *24*(1), Supplement 1, 151–153.

Sharp, C. & Hutchinson, D. (1997). *How do season of birth and length of schooling affect children's attainment at Key Stage 1? A question revisited.* Slough: National Foundation for Educational research.

Sharpe, T. T. (2001). Sex-for-crack-cocaine exchange, poor black women, and pregnancy. *Qualitative Health Research, 11*, 612–630.

Shepherd, S., Depp, C. A., Harris, G., Halpain, M., Palinkas, L. A. & Jeste, D. V. (2012). Perspectives on schizophrenia over the lifespan: A qualitative study. *Schizophrenia Bulletin,* March, *38*(2), 295–303.

Sheridan, M. (1975). *The developmental progress of infants and young children,* 3rd ed. London: HMSO.

Sheridan, M. D. (1997). *From birth to five years. Children's Developmental Progress.* London: Routledge.

Shin, M. (2010). Peeking at the relationship world of infant friends and caregivers. *Journal of Early Childhood Research, 8*(3), 294–302.

Shirley, M. M. (1963). The motor sequence. In D. Wayne (Ed.), *Readings in child psychology.* Englewood Cliffs, NJ: Prentice-Hall.

Shonkoff, J. & Phillips, D. (Eds) (2000). *From neurons to neighbourhoods.* Washington, DC: National Academy Press.

Shulman, S., Kedem, P., Kaplan, K. J., Sever, I. & Braja, M. (1998). Latchkey children: Potential sources of support. *Journal of Community Psychology, 26*(2), 185–197.

Shyers, L. E. (1992). A comparison of social adjustment between home and traditionally schooled students. *Home School Researcher, 8*, 1–8.

Siegler, R. S. (1996). *Emerging minds: The process of change in children's thinking.* New York: Oxford University Press.

Siegler, R. S. (1998). *Children's thinking.* Upper Saddle River, NJ: Prentice-Hall.

Siegler, R. S. & Alibali, M. W. (2005). *Children's thinking.* Upper Saddle River, NJ: Prentice-Hall.

Sifft, J. M. & Khalsa, G. C. K. (1991). The effect of educational kinesiology upon simple response times and choice response times. *Perceptual and Motor Skills, 73*, 1011–1015.

Sigelman, C. K. & Rider, E. A. (2006). *Life-span human development.* Florence: Wadsworth Publishing.

Sigman, A. (2007). *Remotely controlled.* London: Ebury Press.

Sigmundsson, H. (2003). Perceptual deficits in clumsy children: Inter- and intra-modal matching approach – A window into clumsy behavior. *Neural Plasticity, 10*(1), 1–7.

Silverman, W. A. (2002). The schizophrenic career of a 'monster drug'. *Pediatrics, 110*, 404–406.

Singer, L. T., Minnes, S., Short, E., Arendt, R., Farkas, K., Lewis, B., Klein, N., Russ, S., Meeyoung, M. O. & Kirchner, L. H. (2004). Cognitive outcomes of preschool children with prenatal cocaine exposure. *JAMA: Journal of the American Medical Association, 291*(20), 2448–56.

Siraj-Blatchford, I. (2010). Learning in the home and at school: How working class children 'succeed against the odds', *British Educational Research Journal, 36*(3), 463–428.

Siraj-Blatchford, I., Mayo, A., Melhuish, E., Taggart, B., Sammons, P. & Sylva, K. (2011). *Performing against the odds: Developmental trajectories of children in the EPPSE 3–16 study*. Research Report DFE-RR128. London: Institute of Education.

Sirois, S. & Mareschal, D. (2004). An interacting systems model of infant habituation. *Journal of Cognitive Neuroscience, 16*, 1352–1362.

Sjöberg, A., Lissner, L., Albertsson-Wikland, K. & Mårild, S. (2008). Recent anthropometric trends among Swedish school children: Evidence for decreasing prevalence of overweight in girls. *Acta Pediatrica, 97*, 118–123.

Skinner, B. F. (1953). *Science and human behavior*. New York: Macmillan.

Skinner, B. F. (1957). *Verbal behavior*. New York: Appleton-Century-Crofts.

Skinner, B. F. (1966). *Preface. In the behavior of organisms: An experimental analysis* (7th printing). New York: Appleton-Century-Crofts.

Slater, A. & Bremner, G. (2003). *Introduction to developmental psychology*. Oxford: Blackwell.

Slater, L. (2004). *Opening Skinner's box: Great psychological experiments of the twentieth century*. London: Bloomsbury.

Sleiman, P. M., Flory, J. & Imielinski, M. (January 2010). Variants of DENND1B associated with asthma in children. *The New England Journal of Medicine 362*(1), 36–44.

Slobodskaya, H. R. (2007). The associations among the Big Five, behavioural inhibition and behavioural approach systems and child and adolescent adjustment in Russia. *Personality & Individual Differences, 43*, 913–924.

Slovinec, C. H. (2000). Erste Magnetresonanztomographie: In-vivo-Messungen von T2-Relaxationszeiten in der humanen Plazenta und der fetalen Lunge mit Einsatz von Echo-Planar-Sequenzen bei. *The first magnet resonance tomography: In vivo measurements of T2-Relaxation in the human placenta and the foetal lung with the application of echo sequences*. Google Books http://books.google.co.uk/books.

Smagorinsky, P. (2001). Rethinking protocol analysis from a cultural perspective. *Annual Review of Applied Linguistics*, January, *21*(1), 233–245.

Smith, A. & Call, N. (1999). *The Alps approach. Accelerated learning in primary schools*. Stafford: Network Educational Press.

Smith, C. & Fluck, M. (2000). (Re-) Constructing pre-linguistic interpersonal processes to promote language development in young children with deviant or delayed communication skills. *British Journal of Educational Psychology, 70*, 369–389.

Smith, L. (2000). Learning how to learn words: An associative crane. In R. M. Golinkoff *et al.*, (Eds), *Breaking the word learning barrier: What does it take?* New York: Oxford Press.

Smithers, A. & Robinson, P. (2012). *Educating the highly able*. University of Buckingham: Centre for Education and Employment Research.

Snowling, M. (2000). *Dyslexia*. Oxford: Blackwell.

Society for Research in Child Development (2007). *Ethical standards for research with children*. Committee on Ethical Conduct in Child Development research, SRCD.

Sontag, J. (1996). Toward a comprehensive theoretical framework for disability research. *The Journal of Special Education, 30*(3), 319–344.

Sorce, J. F., Emde, R. N., Campos, J. & Klinnert, M. D. (1985). Maternal emotional signaling: Its effect on the visual cliff behavior of one-year olds. *Developmental Psychology, 21*, 195–200.

Søreide, G. E. (2006). Narrative construction of teacher identity: Positioning and negotiation. *Teachers and Teaching: Theory and Practice, 12*, 527–547.

Soussignan, R., Boivin, M., Girard, A., Pérusse, D., Liu, X. & Tremblay, R. E. (2009). Genetic and environmental etiology of emotional and social behaviors in 5-month-old infant twins: Influence of the social context. *Infant Behavior and Development, 32*(1), 1–9.

Sparrow, J. (2007). What's all fuss? *Parent & Child, 15*, 36.

Spaulding, L. S., Mostert, M. P. & Beam, A. P. (2010). Is Brain Gym® an effective educational intervention? *Exceptionality*, Jan–Mar, *18*(1), 18–30.

Spelke, E. S. (1987). The development of intermodal perception. In P. Salapatek & L. Cohen (Eds), *Handbook of infant perception: Vol. 2. From perception to cognition* (pp 233–274). New York: Academic Press.

Spencer, E. J. & Schuele, C. (2012). An examination of fast mapping skills in preschool children from families with low socioeconomic status. *Clinical Linguistics & Phonetics, 26*(10), 845–862.

Spiegler, T. (2003). Home education in Germany: An overview of the contemporary situation. *Evaluation & Research in Education, 17*, 179–190

Spitz, R. A. (1971). The adaptive viewpoint: Its role in autism and child psychiatry. *Journal of Autism and Developmental Disorders, 1*(3), 239–245.

Sroufe, L. A., Egeland, B. & Carlson, E. A. (1999). One social world: The integrated development of parent–child and peer relationships. In W. A. Collins & B. Laursen (Eds), *Minnesota Symposia on child psychology: Vol. 30. Relationships as developmental contexts* (pp 241–261). Mahwah, NJ: Erlbaum.

Sroufe, L. A., Egeland, B., Carlson, E. A. W. A., Collins, W. A. & Hastings, Roger. (2007). The development of the person: The Minnesota study of risk and adaptation from birth to adulthood. A review. *International Journal of Psychoanalytic Self Psychology*, June, *2*(3), 367–379.

Stables, A. (2012). The unnatural nature of nature and nurture: Questioning the romantic heritage. *Studies in Philosophy and Education*, 2012, Preprints, 1–12.

Stamps, J. A. & Groothuis, T. G. G. (2010). Developmental perspectives on personality: Implications for ecological and evolutionary studies of individual differences. *Philosophical Transactions B: Biological Sciences*, December, *365*(1560), 4029–4041.

Standage, M. & Gillison, F. (2007). Students' motivational responses toward school physical education and their relationship to general self-esteem and health-related quality of life. *Psychology of Sport and Exercise, 8*(5), 704–721.

Staroverova, T. (2011). Home education in Russia. *Russian Education & Society*, October, *53*(10), 23–36.

Stasavage, D. (2005). The role of democracy in Uganda's move to universal primary education. *The Journal of Modern African Studies*, *43*, 53–73.

Stattin, H. & Magnusson, D. (1990). *Pubertal maturation in female development*, Vol. 2. Hillsdale, NJ: Erlbaum.

Steer, A. (2005). *Learning behaviour*. Nottingham: Department for Education and Skills.

Steiner, C. (2003). *Emotional intelligence: Intelligence with a heart*. London: Bloomsbury.

Steiner, C. & Perry, P. (1997). *Achieving emotional literacy*. London: Bloomsbury.

Steinhausen, H.-C., Willms, J., Winkler Metzke, C. & Spohr, H.-L. (2003). Behavioural phenotype in foetal alcohol syndrome and foetal alcohol effects. *Developmental Medicine & Child Neurology*, *45*, 179–182.

Stephens, C. (2012). Urban inequities; urban rights: A conceptual analysis and review of impacts on children, and policies to address them. *Journal of Urban Health*, *89*(3), 464–485.

Stephenson, J. (2009). Best practice? Advice provided to teachers about the use of Brain Gym® in Australian schools. *Australian Journal of Education* (ACER Press), Aug, *53*(2), 109–124.

Stephenson, J. & Dowrick, M. (2005). Parents' perspectives on the communication skills of their children with severe disabilities. *Journal of Intellectual & Developmental Disability*, *30*(2), 75–85.

Sternberg, R. J. & Okagaki, L. (1989). Continuity and discontinuity in intellectual development are not a matter of 'either–or'. *Human Development*, *32*, 158–166.

Stifter, C. A., Coulehan, C. M. & Fish, M. (1993). Linking employment to attachment: The mediating effects of maternal separation anxiety and interactive behaviour. *Child Development*, *64*, 1451–1460.

Stiles, J. (2000). Neural plasticity and cognitive development. *Developmental Neuropsychology*, *18*, 237–272.

Stipek, D. J., Recchia, S. & McClintic, S. (1992). Self-evaluation in young children. *Monographs of the Society for Research in Child Development*, *57*, Serial No. 226.

Stomfay-Stitz, A. & Wheeler, E. (2007). Cyberbullying and our middle school girls. *Childhood Education*, *83*, 308.

Strand, S., Deary, I. J. & Smith, P. (2006). Sex differences in cognitive abilities test scores: A UK national picture. *British Journal of Educational Psychology*, *76*, 463–480.

Strang-Karlsson, S., Räikkönen, K., Kajantie, E., Andersson, S., Hovi, P., Heinonen, K., Pesonen, A., Järvenpää, A., Eriksson, J. G. & Paavonen, E. J. (2008). Sleep quality in young adults with very low birth weight – the Helsinki study of very low birth weight adults. *Journal of Pediatric Psychology*, May, *33*(4), 387–395.

Strayer, J. & Roberts, W. (2004). Children's anger, emotional expressiveness, and empathy: Relations with parents' empathy, emotional expressiveness, and parenting practices. *Social Development*, *13*, 229–254.

Striano, T. & Rochat, P. (2000). Emergence of selective social referencing in infancy. *Infancy*, *1*, 253–264.

Strina, A., Cairncross, S., Prado, M. S., Teles, C. A. S. & Barreto, M. L. (2005). Childhood diarrhoea symptoms, management and duration: Observations from a longitudinal community study. *Transactions of the Royal Society of Tropical Medicine and Hygiene*, June, *99*(6), 407–416.

Strong, C. (2008). Cloning and adoption: A reply to Levy and Lotz. *Bioethics*, February, *22*(2), 130–136.

Strother, M. A. (2007). A mind for adventure. *Reclaiming Children & Youth*, *16*, 17–21.

Strunk, J. A. (2008). The effect of school-based health clinics on teenage pregnancy and parenting outcomes: An integrated literature review. *Journal of School Nursing* (Allen Press Publishing Services Inc.), Feb, *24*(1), 13–20.

Stryker, R. (2012). Emotion socialization and attachment in Russian children's homes. *Global Studies of Childhood*, *2*(2), 85–96.

Stuart, S. (2010). Conscious machines: Memory, melody and muscular imagination. *Phenomenology and the Cognitive Sciences*, *9*(1), 37–51.

Stunkard, A. J., Harris, J. R., Pedersen, N. L. & McClearn, G. E. (1990). The body-mass index of twins who have been reared apart. *New England Journal of Medicine*, *322*, 1483–1487.

Sullivan, R. M., Taborsky-Barba, S., Mendoza, R., Itano, A., Leon, M., Cotman, C. W., Payne, T. F. & Loft, I. (1991). Olfactory classical conditioning in neonates. *Pediatrics*, *87*, 511.

Sulston, J. & Ferry, G. (2002). *The common thread – a story of science, politics, ethics and the Human Genome*. London: Bantam Press.

Sumner, E., Connelly, V. & Barnett, A. (2013). Children with dyslexia are slow writers because they pause more often and not because they are slow at handwriting execution. *Reading and Writing*, 2013, Preprints, 1–18.

Sunder, D. & Uddin, L. (2007). A comparative analysis of Bangladeshi and Pakistani educational attainment in London secondary schools. *InterActions: UCLA Journal of Education & Information Studies*, *3*, Article 5.

Sundet, J. M., Borren, I. & Tambs, K. (2008). The Flynn effect is partly caused by changing fertility patterns. *Intelligence*, *36*, 183–191.

Sungur, S. (2007). Modeling the relationships among students' motivational beliefs, metacognitive strategy use, and effort regulation. *Scandinavian Journal of Educational Research*, *51*, 315–326.

Sur, M. & Rubenstein, J. L. R. (2005). Patterning and plasticity of the cerebral cortex. *Science*, *310*, 805–810.

Svensson, A. (2000). Computers in school: Socially isolating or a tool to promote collaboration. *Journal of Educational Computing Research*, *22*, 437–453.

Sylva, K., Melhuish, E., Sammons, P., Siraj-Blatchford, I. & Taggard, B. (2004). *The Effective Provision of Pre-School Education (EPPE) Project: A longitudinal study funded by the DfES 1997–2004. Final report*. Research Brief RBX15-03. London: Department for Education and Skills.

Sylva, K., Melhuish, E., Sammons, P., Siraj-Blatchford, I. & Taggart, B. (2008). *Final Report from the Primary phase: Pre-school, school and family influences on children's development during Key Stage 2 (Age 7–11) EPPE*. Research Report DCSF-RR061. Nottingham: DCSF Publications.

Sylva, K., Melhuish, E., Sammons, P., Siraj-Blatchford, I., Taggart, B. & Elliot, K. (2003). *The Effective Provision of Pre-school Education (EPPE) Project*. Nottingham: DfES Publications.

TDA (2007). *Professional Standards for Teachers: Qualified Teacher Status*. London: TDA.

Tajalli, H. & Opheim, C. (2005). Strategies for closing the gap: Predicting student performance in economically disadvantaged schools. *Educational Research Quarterly, 28*, 44–54.

Tandon, N., Fall, C., Osmond, C., Sachdev, H., Prabhakaran, D., Ramakrishnan, L., Dey Biswas, S., Ramji, S., Khalil, A., Gera, T., Reddy, K., Barker, D., Cooper, C. & Bhargava, S. (2012). Growth from birth to adulthood and peak bone mass and density data from the New Delhi Birth Cohort. *Osteoporosis International, 23*(10), 2447–2459.

Tannenbaum, M. (2008). An analysis of self-concept among Ethiopian immigrant and Israeli-born children and adolescents. *International Journal of Behavioral Development, 32*, 188–198.

Tauber, M. (1979). Parental socialization techniques and sex differences in children's play. *Child Development, 50*, 225–234.

Taylor, A. (2011). Reconceptualizing the 'nature' of childhood. *Childhood*, November, *18*(4), 420–433.

Taylor, J. W. (1986). Self-concept in home-schooling children. *Home School Researcher, 2*, 1–3.

Taylor, M. J., Donner, E. J. & Pang, E. W. (2012). fMRI and MEG in the study of typical and atypical cognitive development. *Neurophysiologie Clinique/Clinical Neurophysiology*, January, *42*(1–2), 19–25.

Taylor, S., Asmundson, G. G. & Wald, J. (2007). Psychopathology of panic disorder. *Psychiatry, 6*(5), 188–192.

Thakkar, R. (2011). A doctor's diary . . . rubella. *Nursery World*. 10/18/2011, *111*(4280), 26–26.

The Good Childhood Report 2012: *A review of our children's well-being*. London: The Children's Society. www.childrens society.org.uk/what-we-do/research/well-being/good-childhood-report-2012 (accessed 1 April 2013).

The NHS Information Centre (2010). Health survey for England – 2010: Trend tables. Available at: www.ic.nhs.uk/pubs/hse10trends

The NHS Information Centre, Lifestyles Statistics (2012). Statistics on obesity, physical activity and diet: England, 2012. The Health and Social Care Information Centre, Lifestyles Statistics.

Thelen, E., Schöner, G., Scheier, C. & Smith, L. B. (2001). The dynamics of embodiment: A dynamic field theory of infant perseverative reaching errors. *Behavioral and Brain Sciences, 24*, 1–86.

Thelen, E. & Smith, L. B. (1994). *A dynamic systems approach to the development of perception and action*. Cambridge, MA: MIT Press.

Thelen, E. & Ulrich, B. D. (1991). Hidden skills: A dynamical systems analysis of treadmill stepping during the first year. *Monographs of the Society for Research in Child Development, 56*, serial 23.

Thiessen, E. D. & Saffran, J. D. (2003). When cues collide: Use of stress and statistical cues to word boundaries by 7- to 9-month-old infants. *Developmental Psychology, 39*, 706–716.

Thomas, A. & Chess, S. (1986). The New York Longitudinal Study: From infancy to early adult life. In R. Plomin & J. Dunn (Eds), *Changes, continuities and challenges*. Hillsdale, NJ: Erlbaum.

Thomas, A. & Chess, S. (1977). *Temperament and development*. New York: Brunner/Mazel.

Thomas, K. T. & Thomas, J. R. (2008). Principles of motor development for elementary school physical education. *Elementary school Journal, 108*, 181–195.

Thompson, D. A. & Christakis, D. A. (2005). The association between television viewing and irregular sleep schedules among children less than 3 years of age. *Pediatrics, 116*, 851–856.

Thorndike, E. (1913). *Educational psychology: The psychology of learning*. New York: Teachers College Press.

Thorndike, E. (1932). *The fundamentals of learning*. New York: Teachers College Press.

Thorngren-Jerneck, K. & Herbst, A. (2006). Perinatal factors associated with cerebral palsy in children born in Sweden. *Obstetrics and Gynecology, 108*, 1499–1505.

Thurstone, L. L. (1934). The vectors of the mind. *Psychological Review, 41*, 1–32.

Tickell, C. (2011). *The early years: Foundations for life, health and learning, an independent report on the early years foundation stage to Her Majesty's Government*. London: DFE.

Tizard, B. & Hodges, J. (1978). The effects of early institutional rearing on the development of eight year old children. *Journal of Child Psychology and Psychiatry, 19*, 99–118.

Todrank, J., Heth, G. & Restrepo, D. (2011). Effects of in utero odorant exposure on neuroanatomical development of the olfactory bulb and odour. *Proceedings B: Biological Sciences, 278*(1714).

Tomasello, M. (2006). Acquiring metalinguistics constructions. In W. Damon & R. M. Lerner (Series Eds) and D. Kuhn & R. Siegler (Vol. Eds), *Handbook of child psychology*, Vol. 2. New York: Wiley.

Tomlinson, C. A. (2005). Grading and differentiation: Paradox or good practice? *Theory into Practice, 44*, 262–269.

Tooley, J. (1998). *Educational research: A critique (Tooley Report)*. London: OfSTED.

Topping, K., Dekhinet, R. & Zeedyk, M. S. (2007). Hindrances for parents in enhancing child language. *Educational Psychology Review*, Sep 2011, *23*(3), 413–455.

Topping, K. J. & Trickey, S. (2007). Collaborative philosophical enquiry for school children: Cognitive effects at 10–12 years. *British Journal of Educational Psychology, 77*, 271–288.

Tosey, P. & Mathison, J. (2003). Neuro-linguistic programming and learning theory: A response. *Curriculum Journal*, *14*, 371–388.

Toso, L., Roberson, R., Abebe, D. & Spong, C. Y. (2007). Neuroprotective peptides prevent some alcohol-induced alteration in gamma-aminobutyric acid A-beta3, which plays a role in cleft lip and palate and learning in fetal alcohol syndrome. *American Journal of Obstetrics and Gynecology*, *196*(3), 259–259.

Tovey, H. (2007). *Playing outdoors: Spaces and places, risk and challenge*. Maidenhead: Open University Press.

Tracey, L., Madden, N. & Slavin, R. (2010). Effects of co-operative learning on the mathematics achievement of years 4 and 5 pupils in Britain: A randomized control trial. *Effective Education*, March, *2*(1), 85–97.

Trehub, S. E., Thorpe, L. A. & Morrongiello, B. A. (1985). Infants' perceptions of melodies: Changes in a single tone. *Infant Behavior and Development*, *8*, 213–223.

Ttofi, M. & Farrington, D. (2012). Bullying prevention programs: the importance of peer intervention, disciplinary methods and age variations. *Journal of Experimental Criminology*, *8*(4), 443–462.

Tudge, J. R. H., Mokrova, I., Hatfield, B. E. & Karnik, R. B. (2009). Uses and misuses of Bronfenbrenner's bioecological theory of human development. *Journal of Family Theory and Review*, December, *1*(4), 198–210.

Tulviste, T. & Koor, M. (2005). 'Hands off the car, it's mine!' and 'The teacher will be angry if we don't play nicely': Gender-related preferences in the use of moral rules and social conventions in pre-schoolers' dyadic play. *Sex Roles*, *53*, 57–66.

Tymms, P., Merrell, C. & Henderson, B. (1997). The first year at school: A quantitative investigation of the attainment and progress of pupils. *Educational Research and Evaluation*, *3*, 101–118.

Uline, C. L. & Johnson, J. F. (Guest Eds) (2005). Closing the achievement gap: What will it take? *Theory Into Practice*, *44*(1).

UNICEF (2012). *The state of the world's children; Children in the urban world 2012*. **www.unicef.org/sowc/** (accessed 14 October 2012).

Uusitalo-Malmivaara, L. & Lehto, J. (2013). Social factors explaining children's subjective happiness and depressive symptoms. *Social Indicators Research* (Preprints), 1–13.

Vachha, B. & Adam, R. (2005). Influence of family environment on language outcomes in children with myelomeningocele. *Child: Care, Health & Development*, *31*, 589–596.

Vaivre-Douret, L., Lalanne, C., Charlemaine, C., Cabrol, D., Keita, G., Sebbane, O., Golse, B. & Falissard, B. (2010). Relationship between growth status at birth and motor and cognitive development in a French sample of gifted children. *Revue Europeenne de Psychologie Appliquee*, *60*(1), 1–9.

Valenza, E., Leo, I., Gava, L. & Simion, F. (2006). Perceptual completion in newborn human infants. *Child Development*, *77*, 1810–1821.

van Balen, L., Dijkstra, L. & Hadders-Algra, M. (2012). Development of postural adjustments during reaching in typically developing infants from 4 to 18 months. *Experimental Brain Research*, *220*(2), 109–119.

Van den Heuvel, H., Tellegen, G. & Koomen, W. (1992). Cultural differences in the use of psychological and social characteristics in children's self understanding. *European Journal of Social Psychology*, *22*, 353–362.

van Ijzendoorn, M. H. & Sagi, A. (1999). Cross-cultural patterns of attachment. In J. Cassidy & P. R. Shaver (Eds), *Handbook of attachment: Theory, research, and clinical applications* (pp 713–734). New York: Guilford.

van Kuyk, J. (2011). Scaffolding – how to increase development? *European Early Childhood Education Research Journal*, March, *19*(1), 133–146.

Van Steensel, R. (2006). Relations between socio-cultural factors, the home literacy environment and children's literacy development in the first years of primary education. *Journal of Research In Reading*, *29*(4), 367–382.

Van Stralen, M. M. *et al.*, (2012). Weight status of European preschool children and associations with family demographics and energy balance-related behaviours: A pooled analysis of six European studies. *Obesity Reviews*, March. Suppl. 1: pp. 29–41. VU University Medical Center, Amsterdam: EMGO Institute for Health and Care Research and Department of Public and Occupational Health.

VanderLaan, D., Gothreau, L., Bartlett, N. & Vasey, P. (2011). Separation anxiety in feminine boys: Pathological or prosocial? *Journal of Gay & Lesbian Mental Health*, January, *15*(1), 30–45.

Varendi, H., Christensson, K., Porter, R. H. & Winberg, J. (1998). Soothing effect of amniotic fluid smell in newborn infants. *Early Human Development*, *51*, 47–55.

Vatne, T. M., Ruland, C. M., Ørnes, K. & Finset, A. (2012). Children's expressions of negative emotions and adults' responses during routine cardiac consultations. *Journal of Pediatric Psychology*, *37*(2), 232–240.

Ventrella, A. R., Semproli, S., Jürimäe, J., Toselli, S., Claessens, A. L., Jürimäe, T. & Brasili, P. (2008). Somatotype in 6–11-year-old Italian and Estonian schoolchildren. *HOMO – Journal of Comparative Human Biology*, *59*(5), 383–396.

Viholainen, H., Ahonen, T., Cantell, M., Lyytinen, P. & Lyytinen, H. (2002). Development of early motor skills and language in children at risk for familial dyslexia. *Developmental Medicine and Child Neurology*, *44*, 761–769.

Viholainen, H., Ahonen, T., Lyytinen, P., Cantell, M., Tolvanen, A. & Lyytinen, H. (2006). Early motor development and later language and reading skills in children at risk of familial dyslexia. *Developmental Medicine & Child Neurology*, *48*(5), 367–373.

Villani, S. (2001). Impact of media on children and adolescents: A 10-year review of the research. *Journal of the American Academy of Child & Adolescent Psychiatry*, *40*, 392–401.

Vinson, J. (2012). Covering national concerns about teenage pregnancy: A visual rhetorical analysis of images of pregnant and mothering women. *Feminist Formations*. Summer, *24*(2), 140–162.

Visscher, C., Elferink-Gemser, M. T. & Lemmink, K. A. P. M. (2006). Interval endurance capacity of talented youth soccer players. *Perceptual & Motor Skills*, 102, 81–86.

Vitkauskas, R. (2007). National identity and musical education: Problems, parallels. *Pedagogy Studies*, 87, 112–118.

Vivier, P., Hauptman, M., Weitzen, S., Bell, S., Quilliam, D. & Logan, J. (2011). The important health impact of where a child lives: Neighborhood characteristics and the burden of lead poisoning. *Maternal and Child Health Journal*, 15(8), 1195–1202.

Vogel, M., Monesson, A. & Scott, L. S. (2012). Building biases in infancy: the influence of race on face and voice emotion matching. *Developmental Science*, 15(3), 359–372.

Vygotsky, L. S. (1962). *Thought and language*. Cambridge, MA: MIT Press.

Vygotsky, L. S. (1978). *Mind in society: The development of higher psychological processes*. Cambridge Massachusetts: Harvard University Press.

Vygotsky, L. S. (1987). Problems of general psychology. *The Collected Works of L. S. Vygotsky*, Vol. 1, trans. Norman Minick. New York: Plenum.

Waddington, C. H. (1962). *New patterns in genetics and development*. New York: Columbia University Press.

Wagmiller Jr, R. L., Kuang, L., Aber, J. L., Lennon, M. C. & Alberti, P. M. (2006). The dynamics of economic disadvantage and children's life chances. *American Sociological Review*, 71, 847–866.

Wagner, K. (2000). Management system design for a learner centered school. *Educational Management Administration and Leadership*, 28, 373–388.

Walker, S. & Plomin, R. (2005). The nature–nurture question: Teachers' perceptions of how genes and the environment influence educationally relevant behaviour. *Educational Psychology*, 25, 509–516.

Walkley, J., Holland, B., Treloar, R. & Probyn-Smith, H. (1993). Fundamental motor skill proficiency of children. *ACHPER National Journal*, Spring, 11–14.

Wallace, W. H. B. & Kelsey, T. W. (2010). Human ovarian reserve from conception to the menopause. PLoS ONE 5(1): e8772. doi:10.1371/journal.pone.0008772

Walters, S., Barr-Anderson, D. J., Wall, M. & Neumark-Sztainer, D. (2009). Does participation in organized sports predict future physical activity for adolescents from diverse economic backgrounds? *Journal of Adolescent Health*, 44(3), 268–274.

Ware, F. (2006). Warm demander pedagogy: Culturally responsive teaching that supports a culture of achievement for African American students. *Urban Education*, 41(4), 427–456.

Warfield, J. J., Kondo-Ikemura, K. & Waters, E. (2011). Measuring infant attachment security in rhesus macaques (Macaca mulatta): Adaptation of the attachment Q-set. *American Journal of Primatology*, 73(2), 109–118.

Warin, J. (2000). The attainment of self-consistency through gender in young children. *Sex Roles*, 42(3–4), 209–231.

Warner, T. D., Dede, D. E., Garvan, C. W. & Conway, T. W. (2002). One size still does not fit all in specific learning disability assessment across ethnic groups. *Journal of Learning Disabilities*, 35, 500–508.

Watamura, S. E., Donzella, B., Alwin, J. & Gunnar, M. R. (2003). Morning to afternoon increases in cortisol concentration for infants and toddlers at child care: Age differences and behavioural correlates. *Child Development*, 74, 1006–1020.

Watamura, S. E., Phillips, D. A., Morrissey, T. W., McCartney, K. & Bub, K. (2011). Double jeopardy: Poorer social emotional outcomes for children in the NICHD SECCYD experiencing home and child care environments that confer risk. *Child Development*, January, 82(1), 48–65.

Waterland, R. A. & Garza, C. (2002). Early postnatal nutrition determines adult pancreatic glucose-responsive insulin secretion and islet gene expression in rats. *The Journal of Nutrition*, 132, 357–364.

Watson, C. (2004). Temporal acuity and the identification of temporal order: Related, but distinct, auditory Abilities. *Seminars In Hearing*, 25(3), 219–227.

Watson, J. B. (1919). *Psychology from the standpoint of a behaviourist*. Philadelphia, PA: Lippincott.

Watson, J. B. (1924/1925). *Behaviorism*. New York: People's Institute Publishing Company.

Watson, J. B. (1928). *Psychological care of infant and child*. New York: W. W. Norton & Co.

Watson, J. B. & Raynor, R. (1920). Conditioned emotional reactions. *Journal of Experimental Psychology*, 3, 1–14.

Wearden, A., Peters, I., Berry, K., Barrowclough, C. & Liversidge, T. (2008). Adult attachment, parenting experiences, and core beliefs about self and others. *Personality & Individual Differences*, 44, 1246–1257.

Weare, K. (2004). *Developing the emotionally literate school*. London: Paul Chapman Publishing.

Wechsler, D. (2003). *Wechsler Intelligence Scale for Children* (4th ed.). Toronto: Psychological Corporation.

Weerman, F. (2011). Diachronic change: Early versus late acquisition. *Bilingualism: Language and Cognition*, March, 14(2), 149–151.

Wehberg, S., Vach, W., Bleses, D., Thomsen, P., Madsen, T. O. & Basbøli, H. (2008). Girls talk about dolls and boys about cars? Analyses of group and individual variation in Danish children's first words. *First Language*, Feb, 28(1), 71–85.

Wei, H. & Chen, J. (2012). The moderating effect of Machiavellianism on the relationships between bullying, peer acceptance, and school adjustment in adolescents. *School Psychology International*, 33(3), 345–363.

Weisbrot, M., Baker, D. & Rosnick, D. (2006). The scorecard on development: 25 years of diminished progress. *International Journal of Health Services*, 36, 211–234.

Weizman, Z. O. & Snow, C. E. (2001). Lexical output as it relates to children's vocabulary acquisition: Effects of sophisticated exposure as a support for meaning. *Developmental Psychology*, 37, 265–279.

Wellman, H. M. (1990). *The child's theory of mind*. Cambridge, MA: MIT Press.

Wells, J., Barlow, J. & Stewart-Brown, S. (2003). A systematic review of universal approaches to mental health promotion in schools. *Health Education*, *103*, 197–220.

Wennborg, H., Bodin, L., Vainio, H. & Axelsson, G. (2001). Solvent use and time to pregnancy among female personnel in biomedical laboratories in Sweden. *Occupational and Environmental Medicine*, *58*, 225–231.

Wentzel, K. R. (2003). Motivating students to behave in socially competent ways. *Theory into Practice*, *42*, 319–326.

Werner, L. A. (2007). Issues in human auditory development. *Journal of Communication Disorders*, *40*, 275–283.

Westermann, G., Ruh, N. & Plunkett, K. (2009). Connectionist approaches to language learning. *Linguistics*, March, *47*(2), 413–452.

Whitam, Frederick L. (1977). Childhood indicators of male homosexuality. *Archives of Sexual Behavior*, March, *6*(2), 89–96.

Whitehurst, G. J. & Valdez-Menchaca, M. C. (1988). What is the role of reinforcement in early language acquisition? *Child Development*, *59*, 430–440.

Whiting, B. B. & Edwards, C. P. (1988). *Children of different worlds: The formation of social behaviour*. Cambridge, MA: Harvard University Press.

Whiting, B. B. & Whiting, J. W. M. (1975). *Children of six cultures: A psycho-cultural analysis*. Cambridge, MA: Harvard University Press.

Wichman, A. L., Rodgers, J. L. & MacCallum, R. M. (2006). A multilevel analysis of birth order effects. *Personality and Social Psychology Bulletin*, *32*, 117–127.

Wijngaards-de Meij, L., Stroebe, M., Schut, H., Stroebe, W., van den Bout, J., van der Heijden, P. G. M. & Dijkstra, I. (2007). Patterns of attachment and parents' adjustment to the death of their child. *Personality & Social Psychology Bulletin*, *33*, 537–548.

Wiley, R., Berman, S., Marsee, M., Taylor, L., Cannon, M. & Weems, C. (2011). Age differences and similarities in identity distress following the Katrina Disaster: Theoretical and applied implications of Erikson's theory. *Journal of Adult Development*, December, *18*(4), 184–191.

Wilgus, G. (2009). Male early childhood teachers negotiate classroom dilemma: Class, family, community and culture in models for moral reasoning. *Journal of Gender Studies*, *18*(3), 215–230.

Wilson, J. G. (1959). *Environment and birth defects* (Environmental Science Series). London: Academic Press.

Wimmer, H. & Perner, J. (1983). Beliefs about beliefs: Representation and constraining function of wrong beliefs in young children's understanding of deception. *Cognition*, *13*, 103–128.

Winkelmann, P. (2000). Brain Gym in a program for teachers and health staff in North Sulawesi, Indonesia. *Brain Gym Journal*, *XV*, Nos 1 & 2.

Wohlwill, J. (1973). *The study of behavioral development*. New York: Academic Press.

Wolff, P. H. (1966). The causes, controls and organization of behavior in the neonate. *Psychological Issues*, *5*(1), Monograph 17. New York: International Universities Press.

Wood, D., Bruner, J. & Ross, G. (1976). The role of tutoring in problem solving. *Journal of Child Psychology and Psychiatry*, *17*, 89–100.

Wood, R. M. & Gustafson, G. E. (2001). Infant crying and adults' anticipated caregiving responses: Acoustic and contextual influences. *Child Development*, *72*, 1287.

Woodard, J. L. & Fine, M. A. (1991). Long-term effects of self-supervised and adult-supervised child care arrangements on personality traits, emotional adjustment, and cognitive development. *Journal of Applied Developmental Psychology*, *12*, 73–85.

Woodhead, M. (1989). School starts at five … or four years old? The rationale for changing admission policies in England and Wales. *Journal of Education Policy*, *4*, 1–21.

Wooldridge, M. B. & Shapka, J. (2012). Playing with technology: Mother–toddler interaction scores lower during play with electronic toys. *Journal of Applied Developmental Psychology*, *33*(5), 211–218.

Woolfolk, A., Hughes, M. W. H. & Walkup, V. (2012). *Psychology in education (2nd Ed.)*. Harlow: Pearson Education.

World Health Organization (2012). *Maternal Mortality Fact Sheet Number 348*. www.who.int/mediacentre/factsheets/fs348/en/ (accessed 13 October 2012).

Wright, B. C. & Mahfoud, J. (2012). A child-centred exploration of the relevance of family and friends to theory of mind development. (Scandinavian) *Journal of Psychology*, *53*(1), 32–40.

Wrynn, A. M. (2011). Beyond the standard measures: Physical education's impact on the dialogue about obesity in the 20th century. *Quest*, May, *63*(2), 161–178.

Wynn, K. (1990). Children's understanding of counting. *Cognition*, *36*, 155–193.

Xia, Y., Tang, L., Yao, L., Wan, B., Yang, X. & Yu, L. (2012). Literature and patent analysis of the cloning and identification of human functional genes in China. *Science China Life Sciences*, March, *55*(3), 268–282.

Yalisove, D. L. (2004). *Introduction to alcohol research: Implications for treatment, prevention, and policy*. London: Pearson/Allyn & Bacon.

Yang, H.-J., Lay, H.-L., Liou, Y.-C., Tsao, W.-Y. & Lin, C.-K. (2007). Development and evaluation of computer-aided music-learning system for the hearing impaired. *Journal of Computer Assisted Learning*, *23*, 466–476.

Yiyuan, X., Farver, J. A. M., Lei, C. C., Zengxiu, Z. & Jiangsu, L. Y. (2007). Moving away or fitting in? *Merrill-Palmer Quarterly*, *53*, 527–556.

Ylonen, M. & Cantell, M. (2009). Kinaesthetic narratives: Interpretations for children's dance movement therapy process. *Body, Movement and Dance in Psychotherapy*, *4*(3), 215–230.

Yongho, K. & Kellogg, D. (2007). Rules out of roles: Differences in play language and their developmental significance. *Applied Linguistics*, *28*, 25–45.

Yoon Phaik, O., Ang, R. P., Fung, D. S. S., Wong, G. & Yiming, C. (2006). The impact of parent–child attachment on aggression, social stress and self-esteem. *School Psychology International*, 27, 552–566.

Young, K. (2008). Toward a model for the study of children's informal Internet use. *Computers in Human Behavior*, 24, 173–184.

Younger, M. & Warrington, M. (2005). *Raising boys' achievement*. Nottingham: DFES Publications.

Yu, C. K. H., Teoh, T. G. & Robinson, S. (2006). Obesity in pregnancy. *BJOG: An International Journal of Obstetrics and Gynaecology*, 113, 1117–1125.

Zafrana, M. & Nikoltsou, K. (2000). Effective learning of writing and reading at preschool age with a multisensory method. *Perceptual & Motor Skills*, 91, 435.

Zhang, J., Hebert, J. R. & Muldoon, M. F. (2005). Dietary fat intake is associated with psychosocial and cognitive functioning of school-aged children in the United States. *Journal of Nutrition*, 135, 1967–1973.

Zile, M. H. (2001). Function of vitamin A in vertebrate embryonic development. *Journal of Nutrition*, 131, 705–708.

Zimmermann, B. J. (2000). Self-efficacy: An essential motive to learn. *Contemporary Educational Psychology*, 25, 82–91.

Zinner, S. H., McGarvey, S. T., Lipsitt, L. P. & Rosner, B. (2002). Neonatal blood pressure and salt taste responsiveness. *Hypertension*, 40, 280–285.

Zohar, A. (2006). Connected knowledge in science and mathematics education. *International Journal of Science Education*, 28, 1579–1599.

# Glossary

**Accelerated learning** A brain-based approach to learning which matches teaching strategies to preferred learning styles: visual, auditory, kinaesthetic.

**Accommodation** Building new schemes when the existing ones appear redundant.

**Achievement motivation** A desire on the part of learners to be successful and to measure themselves against external standards and to feel pleasure in performing well.

**Active interactions** Interactions sought out by individuals that are in keeping with their inherited tendencies.

**Adaptation** Constructing schemes as a result of engaging directly with the environment.

**Affective domains** Aspects of development that are to do with feelings and emotions.

**Affordances** Properties of objects that allow a variety of ways for an individual to interact with them.

**Age of viability** The point when the baby is able to survive outside the womb. The period is between 22 and 26 weeks.

**Allele** A version of the gene pair.

**Altruism** Acting with a selfless concern for others.

**Amnion** The innermost membrane that encloses the embryo.

**Amniotic fluid** Forms inside the amnion to protect the embryo.

**Animistic thinking** Thinking of young children typified by a belief that objects can take on human qualities.

**A-not-B search errors** Mistakes made by 8–12-month-old children. When an object is moved from location A to B, they still look for it in the first location.

**Antecedents** Earlier events and circumstances; what happened, or what was before, to bring about the present situation.

**Anthropometric measures** Measurements used to assess physical growth: including height, and weight measurements.

**Apgar Scale** A scale used to assess a newborn's physical state after birth.

**Aphasia** The loss of ability to understand or express speech, owing to brain damage.

**Assimilation** The absorption of a new idea or experience into a current schema.

**Atopic conditions** Allergic reactions which have strong genetic connections but are triggered by environmental teratogens.

**Attachment** Personal connection that produces a desire for contact and a distress on separation.

**Attachment Q-set** A technique of assessing attachment security of infant – carer used frequently in natural settings.

**Attention** The degree of focus on the task in hand measured in time.

**Autism** A mental condition characterised by self-absorption and a reduced ability to respond to or communicate with the outside world.

**Axioms** Self-evident principles or ones that are accepted as true without proof. For example: any two points can be joined with a straight line.

**Axon** A long thread-like part of a nerve cell, conducting impulses from the cell body.

**Basic emotions** Anger, disgust, fear, happiness, sadness and surprise. These emotions emerge from about 2 months onwards. They are generally believed to have a biological foundation.

**Bayley scales of infant development** Preverbal measure to assess general health and developmental milestones.

**Behaviourist** A learning perspective which considers that everything we do – acting, thinking and feeling – can be regarded as behaviours which are conditioned by our experiences.

**Big Five** The personality traits of extroversion, conscientiousness, agreeableness, neuroticism and openness.

**Bilingual** Fluency in two languages.

**Bilingual education** Educational programmes that teach two languages simultaneously.

**Blastocyst** A hollow ball formed by cells in the first 4 to 10 days after fertilisation.

**Body mass index (BMI)** Body weight (in kilograms) divided by height (in metres) squared.

**Bonding** Becoming emotionally attached.

**Brain Gym** A perceptual-motor programme designed to enhance the experience of whole-brain learning.

**Brazelton Neonatal Behavioural Assessment Scale** A rating used to assess a newborn's reflexes and responsiveness after birth.

**Caesarean section** An operation for delivering a child by cutting through the wall of the mother's abdomen.

**Canalisation** Heredity restrictions on development to a single or few outcomes.

**Categorical speech perception** Phones are perceived as the same within a particular phonemic group.

**Cells** The smallest unit of an organism that is classified as living. They contain an individual's genetic code.

**Centration** Pre-operational thinking that focuses on one aspect of the task only.

**Cephalic** Pertaining to the head.

**Cephalocaudal** Growth that proceeds in sequence from the head to the toes.

**Cerebral cortex** The outer layer of cells covering the brain's cerebrum and which is responsible for higher functioning.

**Cerebrum** The two interconnected hemispheres of the brain.

**Cervix** The neck of the womb.

**Chromosomes** Rod-shaped structures in each cell body that contain DNA, store and send genetic information and are arranged in 23 pairs.

**Classical conditioning** Learning that pairs a response with a stimulus that leads to the stimulus evoking the response.

**Cloning** A procedure for producing multiple copies of genetically identical organisms.

**Code switching** The ability of a bilingual child to switch comprehension and output from one language to the other depending on their audience.

**Cognition** Knowing through the formation, memorisation and recall of ideas.

**Cognitive development** The changes in one's mental abilities that take place over the lifespan.

**Cognitive developmental theory** Emphasises cognition over other aspects of development such as personality.

**Communication** A process by which information is transmitted and received.

**Complex emotions** Embarrassment, shame, guilt, pride and envy. These secondary emotions appear late in the second year.

**Compound variables** Information not only about one particular variable, but about relationships between variables.

**Concept** A general category of ideas, objects, people or experiences whose members share certain properties.

**Concrete operational stage** The third of Piaget's four stages of cognitive development (between 7 to 11 years), this stage is characterised by children's use of logic to solve problems that apply to actual (concrete) objects or events, and not abstract concepts or hypothetical tasks.

**Congenital** Existing from birth.

**CONSPEC mechanism** A brain system that passes on information about face processing to the cortex and directs an infant's gaze to the human face.

**Contractions** The shortening of the uterine muscles during childbirth.

**Control group** A 'parallel' group similar to an experimental group and treated in the same way, except that the experimental treatment is not applied.

**Convergent thinking** Thinking oriented towards the single solution to a problem.

**Co-operative learning** Children work in small groups sharing a common goal in their learning.

**Coregulation** A joint development of the way in which infants and parents make up the rules for how they will behave during shared activities, particularly feeding to start with.

**Corpus callosum** The bundle of fibres that connect both halves of the brain.

**Correlation coefficient** A statistical measure that summarises the strength and direction of the relationship between two variables.

**Cortisol** Known as 'the stress hormone' because stress activates cortisol secretion which can be identified in urine and saliva.

**Critical periods** Periods of time in the development of the brain during which its self-organising capability is at its most potent.

**Cross-cultural studies** Such studies compare children in different cultural contexts.

**Crossing over** The exchange of material between chromosomes from both parents, during the first division of cells, resulting in new combinations of genes.

**Cross-sectional designs** Those where individuals of different ages are studied at the same point in time.

**Cultural-centric** Views, beliefs and practices are restricted to a particular set of cultural values.

**Curricula** A set of courses, and their content, offered in a school or university.

**Decentration** The ability to focus simultaneously on several aspects of an activity.

**Defining attributes** Distinctive features shared by members of a category.

**Dendrites** The part of the neuron that receives signals from other neurons and sends the information to the cell body.

**Dependent variables** Those aspects of the situation which result from researchers manipulating independent variables.

**Deprivation** The effect of a poor or loveless attachment figure.

**Depth perception** The ability to judge distances from, to or between objects.

**Developmentally appropriate practice (DAP)** Ways of working with children that are suited to their stage of development.

**Deviation IQ scores** IQ showing how far performance deviates from average performance of others of the same age.

**Dilation** Widening of the cervix caused by contractions in the uterus.

**Directed reaching** More advanced controlled action that is co-ordinated to specific targets.

**Display rules** Cultural and situational rules that indicate the appropriateness of emotional expression in particular contexts.

**DNA** Deoxyribonucleic acid: molecules of DNA that make up the chromosome.

**Dominant gene** A gene that if present in a gene pair will be expressed as a characteristic, e.g. brown hair.

**Dominant–recessive inheritance** The combination of one powerful allele that affects our characteristics and a recessive allele which, though at odds with its dominant partner, remains dormant.

**Down's Syndrome** A chromosome disorder in the child receiving three rather than the normal two chromosomes. Also known as Trisomy 21.

**Dynamic systems** Movement defined and analysed by using mathematical terms, symbols and values.

**Dyslexia** A brain-based abnormal difficulty with reading and spelling, not explained as a general learning difficulty.

**Dyspraxia** The partial loss of the ability to co-ordinate and perform certain purposeful movements like writing.

**Ecological systems theory** A theory which emphasises the different social contexts or systems – e.g. the family – in which a child develops.

**Ectoderm** One of the three layers of cells in the embryo, which will develop into the nervous system, skin, hair, nails, mammary glands, sweat glands and tooth enamel.

**Ectomorph** A person with a lean and delicate build of body and large skin surface in comparison with weight.

**Efferent organisation** Carrying away from a central part; specifically designating nerves that carry impulses away from a nerve centre.

**Egocentric (1)** In the context of Piagetian accounts of cognitive development, it is the belief that pre-operational thinking is thinking from a child's own perspective only.

**Egocentric (2)** The self is not yet constructed as something separate from others – commonly thought of as a self-centred view of the world.

**Embryo** A human offspring in the first 8 weeks from conception.

**Embryonic period** The second period of prenatal development, 3–8 weeks after conception.

**Emergent literacy** The way in which children construct literary knowledge by means of their everyday experiences.

**Emotional intelligence** An awareness and understanding of one's own emotions and of others' emotions, and being motivated to develop relationships.

**Emotional literacy** The ability to express one's feelings and understand other people's emotions.

**Emotional self-regulation** Strategies used to adjust our emotional state to allow us to achieve our goals.

**Empathy** The attribute of being able to understand different emotions, to take another person's perspective or to respond similarly.

**Empiricists** People who reject sticking to out-of-date beliefs and opinions, preferring instead to rely on observation and experience.

**Enculturation** A process by which people learn about the practices and values of the society in which they live.

**Endoderm** One of the three layers of cells in the embryo, which will develop into the lungs, the lining of the gastrointestinal tract, liver, pancreas and thyroid.

**Epigenesis** The interaction between forces of environment (nurture) and factors of heredity (nature).

**Epoch** A period of history marked by notable events relevant to the issues being discussed.

**Equilibration** Adding to, or demolishing and reconstructing, existing schemes by using assimilation and accommodation.

**Equipotentiality hypothesis** Proposes that areas in the left and right brain have the same potential, among other functions, for language.

**Ethnic identity** An awareness of and a sense of belonging to a particular ethnic group.

**Ethnocentrism** Evaluating other races and cultures using criteria specific to one's own.

**Ethnographic approach** A research method in which a researcher tries to understand a culture or society by living or being within it.

**Ethology** Both the science of animal behaviour and the science of character formation in human behaviour.

**Evocative interactions** Traits in children that cause other people to behave toward them in certain ways.

**Evolutionary developmental psychology** The study of genetic and environmental mechanisms that govern human behaviour.

**Exemplar** A specific example of a given category that is used to classify an item.

**Exosystem** The cultural system outside the family, e.g. church or parents' employment.

**Face perception** Infants seem to prefer the pattern of features of the face and can discriminate between the slightly different patterns of unique faces.

**False-belief task** A test which identifies whether or not a child is able to represent what another person knows, when this is different from what the child knows.

**Family literacy** The term referring to the interrelated literacy practices of parents, children and others at home, and the educational programmes that recognise the family dimension for children's literacy learning.

**Fast mapping** The process through which a child learns and understands a word after hearing it once or twice.

**Feminist perspective** Links feminist theory and child development and includes issues of social justice, gender stereotyping and the use of appropriate language.

**Field experiments** Those research studies carried out in real-world settings, such as in the home or in educational settings.

**Foetal period** The third and final period of prenatal development, taking place 9 weeks after conception and extending until the end of the pregnancy.

**Foetus** An unborn human, more than 8 weeks after conception.

**Fontanelles** Gaps in the skull that allow the head of the baby to pass through the birth canal.

**Formal games** Play that takes the form of any game with a rule structure.

**Formal handling** Stretching and massage activities used by parents in some African and Jamaican communities to promote early walking.

**Fraternal (dizygotic) twins** Children in the same pregnancy who have developed from two separate fertilised ova.

**Frontal lobe** Area of the brain responsible for higher functioning.

**Fundamental movement phase** The third phase of movement development with movements such as throwing, catching, hopping, etc. Occurs between 2 and 7 years.

**Fuzzy trace theory** Proposes a continuum exists in which we encode information from verbatim or literal representations to fuzzy representations.

**Gametes** Specialised sex cells. Each gamete has 23 chromosomes, rather than the usual 23 pairs.

**Gender schema** The mental structures that organise information relevant to gender.

**Generalisability** The extent to which theories developed from the observation of a few cases can be said to be valid for other similar cases.

**Genes** Units of heredity composed of DNA, forming part of the chromosomes that make up the nucleus of the human cell.

**Genetic code** The specific sequence of base chemicals in our DNA that determines our inherited characteristics.

**Genetics** The study of how genes transmit biological traits over generations.

**Genotype** A person's complete collection of genetic instructions for creating and replacing cells.

**Germinal period** The first period of prenatal development, in the first 2 weeks after conception.

**Gestation** The process of being carried in the womb between conception and birth.

**Giftedness** Characterised by an IQ of 130 or above. Individual also shows an exceptional talent in one or more areas.

**Glia** Cells whose function is to support neurons.

**Glycaemic foods** Foods that contain carbohydrates that release glucose into the bloodstream.

**Goodness of fit** A match between child-rearing practice and the individual child's temperament.

**Grammar** The structure of language necessary for constructing unambiguous sentences.

**Growth plates** The area of growing tissue near the ends of the long bones in children and adolescents, also known as epiphyseal plates or physis.

**Guided participation** Children's interactions with adults that bridge children's understanding with that of the adults.

**Habituation** Evidence of learning where a child 'makes a habit' of attending to a new stimulus and stops attending to sensations that become boring.

**Haptic perception** The process of recognising objects through touch.

**Head Start** US programme of the 1960s for disadvantaged preschool children, which had both academic and social directions.

**Heritability** An estimate of the correlation $0 \leq 1$ between a behaviour or condition, and an identified gene.

**Heritability estimates** Calculations of the extent of differences in a trait for a particular group at a given time.

**Heuristics** Methods for learners to solve problems or find out things for themselves.

**Holophrase** A single word used to express a complete thought or sentence.

**Horizontal decalage** A term indicating that children can operate in different stages at the same time, in different kinds of tasks.

**Hormones** Chemicals in specialist cells that pass between other cells.

**Hostile aggression** Aggressive behaviour intended to hurt a person or group deliberately, for example, through name-calling.

**Hot-housing** Intense exposure to stimuli or study in order to stimulate the child's mind.

**Hot-housing programmes** Specific programmes intended to accelerate cognitive development.

**Human development** The pattern of change that all individuals undergo from conception through the span of life.

**Human genome** The sequence that specifies the order of the whole hereditary information encoded in the DNA for all humans.

**Human growth** The gradual but not necessarily steady increase in size of the body.

**Hyperplasmia**  Growth by cell division.

**Hypertrophy**  Growth by cell fattening.

**Hypothalamus**  Part of the limbic system in the brain that, among other functions, is involved in eating and sexual responses.

**Hypothesis**  A supposition which provides a starting point for further investigation.

**Identical (monozygotic) twins**  Children in the same pregnancy who have developed from the same fertilised ovum.

**Imprinting**  The development in a newly born of a pattern of behaviour, showing recognition and trust, usually for its own species.

**In utero**  Within the uterus.

**Independent variables**  Those aspects in the environment that the researcher is able to control.

**Induction**  Disciplining where the effects of bad behaviour on others are communicated to the child.

**Infant-directed speech (IDS)**  A simplified speech style adopted by adults when talking to young children, using slower speech, repetition of words and higher pitch. Also called 'motherese'.

**Information-processing approaches**  These view cognitive development as a series of steps to process information from the environment.

**Innate**  Born with or inborn due to naturally occurring experiences prior to birth or heritable dispositions.

**Instrumental aggression**  Aggression used to achieve an end, for example, taking possession of a toy from someone else.

**Intelligence quotient**  How well one performs on a standardised test of intelligence relative to others of that age.

**Interdisciplinary**  Study or research that draws on more than one branch of learning.

**Intermodal perception**  Using sensory information from more than one sensory modality.

**Internal working model**  Expectations arising from early care experiences about carers which become a model for later close relationships.

**Interpretivist research methods**  Based on a belief that a researcher works from the data to the conclusion and employs qualitative research methods of observation in natural settings and interpretation.

**Invariances**  Those aspects in the environment that are constant.

**Iron-deficiency anaemia**  Nutritional deficiency from inadequate amounts of iron in the diet.

**Jaundice**  A yellowing of the skin or whites of eyes caused by slow proper functioning of the liver.

**Joint-action formats**  Simplified action sequences created by infants and carers that are repeated regularly and to a set pattern, for example, nappy changing or getting ready for bed.

**Kinaesthetic acuity**  The ability to match or detect differences between qualities such as location, distance, weight or speed.

**Kinaesthetic memory**  Memory capacity that allows reproduction of earlier movements.

**Kinaesthetic sense**  The human awareness of posture and movement of parts of the body with respect to each other.

**Language**  A system of sounds, symbols or gestures to communicate with others according to a set of agreed rules.

**Language acquisition support system (LASS)**  A set of strategies used predominantly by parents to foster language.

**Lanugo**  Soft hair covering the whole body of the foetus.

**Lateralisation**  The process in which the brain's two halves become specialised and can carry out specific functions.

**Laws**  Statements describing an unchanging relationship between observations made for all cases in the same context: e.g. the law of gravity (because the apple always falls given the same conditions of temperature and pressure anywhere on the Earth's surface).

**Learned helplessness**  A belief that one can do nothing to affect one's control of one's environment.

**Learning**  The process through which a person's experiences of their environment result in relatively permanent changes to how people feel, think and behave.

**Learning goals**  Targets related to specific skills, knowledge or understanding.

**Locomotion skills**  Motor skills that allow the body to move through space.

**Longitudinal designs**  Those studies involving the same subjects over a considerable period of time.

**M space**  Capacity to retain information. Increases with age and experience.

**Macrosomia**  A newborn with an excessive birth weight.

**Macrosystem**  The larger society in which the family exists.

**Magic window thinking**  Beliefs held by young children that what is seen on television is reality.

**Makaton**  An international communication programme combining speech, hand actions and symbols.

**Manipulation skills**  Motor skills that allow the body to manipulate objects by using hands or feet.

**Maternal deprivation hypothesis**  Bowlby's claim that serious damage would occur to a child's emotional development if the attachment between child and mother was severed in the first years of the child's life.

**Maturation**  The process of following the 'biological developmental plan' contained in our **genes**.

**Maturation theory**  Focuses on the unfolding of genetically determined sequences of development.

**Medulla**  The continuation of the spinal cord within the skull, forming the lowest part of the brainstem.

**Meiosis**  Cell division that forms gametes.

**Mental representation** Way of depicting information internally, either as images or concepts.

**Mesoderm** One of the three layers of cells in the embryo, which will develop into the heart, circulatory system, skeleton, connective tissues, urinogenital system and muscles.

**Mesosystem** The extended family, friends, neighbours and teachers in school.

**Metalinguistic awareness** An ability to know about language and its characteristics as a system.

**Metamemory** Knowing what strategies work best for an individual to memorise information and to retrieve information from memory.

**Microgenetic designs** These designs study changes in development that occur quickly and over short periods of time.

**Microsystem** The child's own close family and friends.

**Mitosis** The process of cell duplication.

**Motor milestones** Early and fundamental motor skills that appear in a relatively consistent sequence but with individual timing variations.

**Multifactorial transmission** The combination of genetics and the environment that produce complex characteristics.

**Multiple attachments** Attachments to more than one person, usually the other parent, grandparents, siblings and care-givers.

**Myelin** A fatty layer that covers neurons.

**Myelination** The process by which the neurons of the central nervous system become covered in an insulating fatty layer (myelin) which allows an increase in speed of the electrical impulses.

**Naming explosion** Marked increase in vocabulary during the second year.

**Nativism** A set of beliefs that favours the idea that much of our behaviour is due to biological pre-programming.

**Natural selection** Physical or behavioural changes leading to a survival advantage are passed on through genes. If no advantage is gained, these are eventually not passed on.

**Naturalistic** Observations of behaviour in natural contexts (e.g. homes, classrooms) rather than structured observations in laboratories.

**Naturalistic observation** Observations made in real-life settings.

**Negative predictor** Where there is an increase in one variable, you can predict a decrease in a second variable.

**Negative reinforcement** Similar to a reward. When something negative is removed from a person's experience as a way to increase the likelihood of a wanted behaviour happening again.

**Neonate** A newborn baby.

**Neo-Piagetian theory** A recent interpretation of Piaget's theory in an information-processing framework.

**Neurons** The nerve cells that send and receive electrical signals to the brain and the nervous system.

**Neutral stimulus** A stimulus that initially produces no specific response other than focusing attention (in the example on this page, focusing on the rat).

**Nexus** A bonded or connected group.

**Niche picking** A term for where individuals choose environments that are compatible with their inherited dispositions.

**Non-verbal communication** The types of communication that do not involve speech, including gestures, facial expressions and posture.

**Normative** A form of assessment where an individual's or group's results are compared with a much larger set of results in a standardised test.

**Nucleus** The centre of the cell body.

**Obesity** More than 20 per cent increase over average body weight, taking into consideration age, sex and body build.

**Observational learning** Where significant learning takes place merely by watching other people model behaviour.

**Obstetric** Relating to childbirth and the branch of medicine and surgery related to midwifery.

**Occipital lobe** Brain area responsible for processing colour, shape and movement.

**Operant conditioning** Learning where the likelihood of behaviour recurring is increased by reinforcement and decreased by punishment.

**Operations** In the context of Piagetian accounts of cognitive development operations are thinking or procedures that obey logical rules.

**Organisation** The ways in which schemes are linked together in a connected network.

**Ossification** The process through which cartilage becomes bone.

**Overextension** Where the word's meaning is given to objects with similar properties.

**Overregularisation** Applying a strict regularity rule to words that change irregularly.

**Ovum** The gamete produced by the female which, if fertilised, forms the new being.

**Paradigm** Philosophical or theoretical framework of any kind resulting from the application of scientific theory – simply a different way of viewing the world.

**Parietal lobe** Brain area that processes touch and taste sensations and provides information about spatial location.

**Passive interactions** Structures and environments provided by parents to suit their child's genetic traits.

**Pathology** The science of bodily disease.

**Patterned speech** Strings of phonemes are combined that resemble true yet unrecognisable speech.

**Pedagogy** The ways or methods of teaching and learning – how something is taught in schools.

**Peer collaboration** Classroom learning technique involving two students working together to achieve a particular goal.

**Peer tutoring** A method of teaching in which an older more experienced child tutors one who is younger and/or less experienced.

**Peers** Others of roughly the same age and developmental level.

**Perception** The processes through which we organise and interpret information from the senses.

**Performance goals** Targets comparing performance of the individual with those in the same class or age group.

**Perinatal** Of or relating to the time immediately before or after birth.

**Perinatal mortality** Still births plus early neonatal deaths (deaths at under 7 days of life).

**Person permanence** Understanding that a person still exists even when no longer in view.

**Personality** Differences in the ways in which people relate to objects or other people around them.

**Phenotype** The observable characteristics of an individual, the way we develop, inherited from parents together with effects of physical and social environments.

**Phonemes** The smallest parts of language that define or change meaning.

**Phones** Speech sounds.

**Phonological loop** A short-term store and retrieval system for sounds and words.

**Phonology** The study of sounds in a language.

**Physique** The bodily structure, development and organisation of an individual.

**Pincer grasp** More advanced grip using opposing index finger and thumb.

**Pituitary gland** A small ductless gland at the base of the brain secreting various hormones essential for growth and other bodily functions.

**Placenta** A flattened circular organ in the uterus of pregnant mammals nourishing and maintaining the foetus through the umbilical cord and expelled after birth.

**Plasticity** The brain is flexible and adaptable.

**Pons** Part of the brainstem that links the medulla and the thalamus (which are the two masses in the forebrain).

**Positive predictor** Where there is an increase in one variable, you can predict an increase in a second variable.

**Positive reinforcement** Anything that increases the likelihood of behaviour being repeated in the same situation.

**Positivist research methods** Based on a belief that the only authentic knowledge is scientific knowledge, and that such knowledge can come only from positive affirmation of theories through strict scientific method.

**Post-partum** Following childbirth.

**Poverty of the stimulus** Suggests that language heard by children is grammatically too simplistic to allow them to develop complex syntax.

**Pragmatics** The conventions of language in different contexts.

**Praxis** Professional practice informed by theory.

**Pre-eclampsia** A complication of pregnancy. Women with pre-eclampsia have high blood pressure, and high levels of protein in their urine. If left untreated, it can develop into eclampsia, the life-threatening occurrence of siezures during pregnancy.

**Preference technique** Method of study requiring a child to show one preference over another that is offered.

**Prenatal development** The progress of maturity of a baby prior to birth.

**Pre-operational stage** The second stage in Piaget's model from age 2 to 7 years. It is characterised by an advancement in mental representation.

**Pre-reaching** Early stage of motor control where the infant has limited control over limbs.

**Primary intersubjectivity** Person-to-person responses between infants and carers through language/sounds, actions, gestures and facial expressions.

**Primitive reflexes** Automatic responses to stimulation, with no conscious thinking and are in no way learned.

**Privation** The term used with reference to the absence of an attachment figure.

**Proactive aggression** The use of force to dominate another.

**Proprioception** The 'internal' sense the body has of position and balance, movement and posture, and which gives us an awareness of where our body is and what it is doing.

**Prosocial behaviour** Intentional, voluntary behaviour intended to benefit another person for which there is no reward expectation.

**Protodeclarative gestures** Gestures intended as statements, to alert someone else's attention to something.

**Proto-imperative gestures** Gestures intended to get another person to do something on the child's behalf.

**Prototype** Best or 'averaged' representative of a category.

**Proximodistal** Development proceeding from the centre of the body outwards in sequence.

**Psychodynamic theory** The explanation of how psychological forces shape human behaviour.

**Psychopathology** The study of mental illness.

**Psychosexual development** The view that behaviour is governed by unconscious as well as conscious processes.

**Qualitative research methods** Analysis that highlights themes or patterns perceived through detailed observation of phenomena.

**Quantitative research methods** Analysis that involves counting observations of occurrence and change, and manipulating the totals using statistical methods.

**Range of reaction** Possibilities for development arising from interaction with one's environment.

**Reactive aggression** Aggression in response to an attack.

**Recessive gene** A gene that by itself in a gene pair will not be expressed as a characteristic, but will be expressed if two recessive genes are present e.g. red hair.

**Reciprocal friendships** Mutually supportive and close friendships with one other peer.

**Reciprocal teaching** Small groups having dialogue on a subject so that the level is beyond an individual's present capability but within ZPD.

**Reflexes** Automatic responses to stimulation. Many fade out in the first year after birth.

**Reflexive movement phase** The stage at which the first movements are evident. Reflexes are spontaneous sub-cortically controlled movements and are the first phase of development.

**Reliability** The measure by which we judge that, if an experiment or observation was carried out at a different time or in a different place, very similar results would be forthcoming.

**Representative sample** A group that resembles the larger population about which data are being collected.

**Research questions** The specific questions of a study for which the research is seeking answers.

**Reversibility** The idea that a mental operation can be reversed by carrying out a second operation opposite to the first.

**Rudimentary movement phase** The second stage in movement development occurring between birth to 2 years.

**Scaffolding** Role played by more knowledgeable others by which children can go beyond their zone of proximal development. Crucial to the idea is progressive withdrawal of support as learner's own competence increases.

**Schema** A set of ideas about the common features of a particular object, being or concept.

**Schemes** Repeatable patterns/organised ways of making sense of an experience. They alter with age.

**Scientific method** The application of scientific principles in an orderly manner, and with the appropriate technique, to find an answer to a question.

**Secondary intersubjectivity** Person-to-person responses between infants and carers through objects and shared events, like a shared book or exchanging toys.

**Self-awareness** The explicit understanding that 'me' exists as a separate individual with private thoughts, and that other people are similarly self-aware.

**Self-efficacy** Believing yourself to be capable of the desired outcome.

**Self-evaluative emotions** The emotions that depend on knowledge of 'self' and of social norms of behaviour.

**Semantics** How words are used in combinations to create different meanings.

**Sensation** The process of detecting a stimulus event via a sensory system.

**Sensitive periods** Brief periods of time when an individual is very responsive to influences in the environment.

**Sensorimotor stage** The first stage in Piaget's model from birth to age 2 in which the child moves from an action-based way of understanding the world to thinking about it using symbols.

**Sensory register** The sensory register hold sounds and images that last no more than about a second.

**Sequential designs** The study of groups of children of different ages over long periods of time.

**Seriation** The ability to order objects quantitatively, e.g. by weight or length.

**Shape constancy** Perception of an object's shape being constant even if movement alters its shape on the observer's retina.

**Siblings** Children having one or more parents in common.

**Size constancy** Perception of an object's size is constant regardless of the distance away from the observer.

**Skeletal age** A way of estimating physical maturity based on the development of the bones in the body.

**Social cognition** Understanding of our own mental state and other people's mental states to gauge feelings and predict behaviours.

**Social cognitive theory** The view that children learn by classical and operant conditioning (features of behaviourism) and by observing others.

**Social comparisons** How individuals define themselves with reference to the skills, interests and values held by others.

**Social constructivism** An approach that draws upon sociology, cross-cultural studies and philosophy.

**Social learning theory** Explains how children learn by watching and imitating others in social situations.

**Social referencing** A reliance upon someone else's emotional reaction to make sense of a new or uncertain situation.

**Social smile** An intentional smile first seen at around 6 weeks.

**Socialisation** The process by which parents can influence their children's attitudes and behaviours to fit those expected within a given society.

**Sociocultural context** The knowledge and cultural tools that a child acquires from other members of the community.

**Sociometric techniques** Tools to measure relationships, status and social acceptance in a group.

**Somatosensory system** A sensory system that detects experiences labelled as touch or pressure, temperature, pain, muscle movement and joint position including posture, movement, visceral (internal) senses and facial expression.

Visceral senses have to do with sensory information from within the body, such as stomach aches.

Somatotyping The classifying of children and adults according to body build.

Specialised movement phase This phase occurs after the basic movement skills are in place. It is sports-specific and tends to be technique-oriented.

Spiral curriculum Any subject can be taught to any child at any stage of development as long as it is developmentally appropriate.

Stability skills Those motor skills that include axial movements and balance.

Stanford–Binet test Early intelligence test for school-aged children.

Strange Situation A series of separation and reunion events that determine the quality of infant – carer attachment.

Structured observation Observations that a researcher records in situations specifically constructed for that purpose. Frequently occurring under laboratory conditions.

Sure Start UK programme in disadvantaged areas aiming to provide better outcomes for children, parents and local communities.

Survival reflexes Reflexes associated with early survival, also called adaptive reflexes.

Synapse The gap between the end of one neuron and the dendrites of another.

Synaptic pruning The process through which the brain rids itself of unused brain cells.

Synaptogenesis The process of proliferation of the connections between neurons in early development.

Synchronised routines Simplified action sequences created by mother and infant together, such as feeding and dressing.

Synchrony Among other uses, describes early interactions which parents and infants engage in by watching and copying and responding to each other.

Synergy The combined effect or action of two or more (areas of development) that exceeds the sum of the individual (area).

Syntactic boot strapping The idea that information is gained about a word from its context in a sentence.

Syntax Specifies how words are combined into sentences.

Systems theory A framework by which one can analyse and/or describe any group that work in concert.

Temperament A matrix of core qualities apparent in infancy that inform a child's future personality.

Temperament hypothesis Proposes that attachment behaviours are strongly linked to temperament.

Temporal lobe Area of the brain that processes characteristics of sound, speech and balance.

Teratogen An environmental factor or agent that can cause harm to the embryo or foetus.

Theory A framework of concepts that assist in organising and explaining observations.

Theory of mind Being able to think of other people's mental states and construct theories about their thinking.

Thromboembolism The formation in a blood vessel of a clot (thrombus) that breaks loose and is carried by the bloodstream to plug another vessel.

Transitive inference problems The ability to seriate objects mentally on a quantitative continuum in order to achieve a solution.

Trauma A physical wound or injury, physical shock following injury or an emotional shock sometimes leading to long-term neurosis.

Triangulate To use more than one research method to further validate the findings of a study.

Trimester A 3-month period of the 9-month pregnancy.

Ulnar grip Early form of grasping where the fingers close against the palm.

Underextensions Refusal to use a word, for example, *animal*, in the belief that every animal has to have the same characteristics.

Uterus Another name for the womb.

Uterine Of or belonging to the womb.

Validity The property we would give to research which uses methods that accurately measure or describe the behaviour we are observing.

Vernix caseosa A cheese-like substance covering the foetus that prevents chaffing.

Vestibular awareness The sense that provides information about balance and stillness.

Visual accommodation The change in shape of the lens in the eye.

Visuo-spatial sketchpad A short-term store and retrieval system for images and movements.

Visual acuity Sharpness of vision.

Wechsler intelligence scales Both preschool and school-age tests of reasoning, mathematical and verbal reasoning and spatial skills.

Womb The organ in which a baby is carried between conception and birth.

Zone of proximal development This is the state of developmental readiness defined as the gap between the actual developmental level and the level of potential development.

Zygote A fertilised egg.

# Index